REFORMING THE COURT

REFORMING THE COURT

TERM LIMITS FOR SUPREME COURT JUSTICES

Edited by

Roger C. Cramton

Paul D. Carrington

CAROLINA ACADEMIC PRESS
Durham, North Carolina

Library of Congress Cataloging-in-Publication Data

Reforming the Court : term limits for supreme court justices / by Roger C.
Cramton & Paul D. Carrington, editors.
    p. cm.
  Includes bibliographical reference and index.
  ISBN 1-59460-213-1 (alk. paper)
  1. United States. Supreme Court--Congresses. 2. Judges--United States--
Congress. I. Cramton, Roger C. II. Carrington, Paul D., 1931- III. Title.

KF8742.A5R43 2006
347.73'26--dc22

                                                              2005031269

CAROLINA ACADEMIC PRESS
700 Kent Street
Durham, North Carolina 27701
Telephone (919) 489-7486
Fax (919) 493-5668
www.cap-press.com

The judicial Power of the United States, shall be vested in one supreme Court, and in such inferior Courts as the Congress may from time to time ordain and establish. The Judges, both of the supreme and inferior Courts, shall hold their Offices during good Behaviour, and shall, at stated Times, receive for their Services a Compensation which shall not be diminished during their Continuance in Office.

The United States Constitution
art. III, § 1 (1789)

CONTENTS

Appendix: The Editors' Initial Proposal

REFORMING THE COURT

Reforming the Supreme Court: An Introduction

*Paul D. Carrington & Roger C. Cramton**

This symposium deals with an important issue concerning the "ascendant branch" of the federal government—the Supreme Court of the United States—that has received remarkably little attention: the lengthening tenure in office of Supreme Court justices. The Framers provided in Article III, section 1 of the Constitution that federal judges would serve "during good Behaviour," in contrast to the relatively short and fixed terms of other federal offices. The phrase was drawn from earlier legislation by Parliament enacted to protect royal judges who had long served at the pleasure of the British crown and its ministers and were subservient to them. The purpose of the Good Behavior Clause was to protect federal judges from control by the President or the Congress. This constitutional provision has served that purpose well with respect to lower federal court judges, but questions of its meaning and continued efficacy with respect to Supreme Court justices have been raised in the past. Those questions should now be seriously considered.

The factual background of the symposium's topic is not in dispute and is elaborated in the leading article by Steven Calabresi and James Lindgren,[1] and discussed in many of the other papers. The undisputed factual predicate is that justices today serve much longer than they did throughout our history. There are three general reasons why this is so.

---

* Paul D. Carrington is Chadwick Professor of Law, Duke University; Roger C. Cramton is Stevens Professor of Law Emeritus, Cornell University Law School.

1. Steven G. Calabresi & James Lindgren, *Term Limits for the Supreme Court: Life Tenure Reconsidered*, pp. 15–98.

First, improved public health and modern medicine have enormously increased the life expectancy of a mature person of an age likely to be considered for appointment to the Supreme Court. Indeed, life expectancy at age fifty, for example, has more than doubled since 1789. Moreover, the life expectancy figures are rising steadily every year and those in a position to receive the best medical care, which includes justices, usually survive beyond the averages. For reasons to be discussed below, few justices in modern times have voluntarily retired from the Court until they became physically or mentally incapacitated. The inevitable conclusion from these undisputed facts is that future appointees to the Court are likely to occupy an office that has become one of the most powerful in the land for twenty-five to forty or more years. A tenure in office of a generation or more was not contemplated by the Framers when, in a desire to protect judicial independence, they adopted the Good Behavior Clause.

The second factor that results in justices continuing in office until they die or become seriously incapacitated is that, unlike their predecessors prior to 1925, the Court now has virtually total control over its workload. Each justice today is entitled to the assistance of a very capable personal staff, including four law clerks. Prior to 1925, justices such as Holmes and Brandeis wrote twenty or more opinions for the Court each year, assisted by only a single secretary or law clerk who provided research and proof-reading assistance. Prior to 1986 the Court rendered full opinions in about one hundred fifty cases a year, an amount that itself was much lower than earlier in the twentieth century. Since then, the Rehnquist Court has reduced the number of full opinions on the merits each year by one-half, to about seventy-five cases a year. Each justice today is responsible for only eight or nine opinions per year. In varying degrees, each justice now delegates much of the initial drafting of opinions to law clerks. These changes in the burdensomeness of the Court's work permit aging justices to continue to serve even as energy declines with advanced age. Although ordinary Americans retire in largest number at age sixty-two and most have retired by age sixty-five, Supreme Court justices continue to work on during their seventies and eighties. It was truly extraordinary that Justice Sandra Day O'Connor stepped down in 2005 at the mere age of seventy-five, and while still fully mobile. But Chief Justice Rehnquist stayed in office thirty-four years until his death at age 80 and Justice Stevens, who is eighty-three and has held office for thirty years, has not retired.

The third and most important factor resulting in the justices' lengthening tenure is a consequence of the enormous increase in the power and saliency of the Court's decision-making. The power of the Court to give new meaning to old language of the Bill of Rights has made the Supreme Court, in a former Solicitor General's language, "the ascendant branch" of the federal government.[2] Each justice occupies an office that is perhaps the second most powerful in the land. And all other powerful federal offices are accountable to the people through fixed terms and periodic elections. Even the rare congressional leader who is regularly reelected exercises the authority of a majority or minority leader for a much shorter period.

Every informed observer, whether of the left, the right or the center, recognizes that the Court is now an institution exercising extraordinary power. It is not surprising that justices relish the exercise of the great power the Court now possesses. The celebrity that now renders sober justices as famous as rock stars, is flattering, enjoyable, stimulating, and provides many opportunities for travel and influence. The justices are honored by prestigious academic and private organizations; and they are invited and paid to travel to events throughout the country and around the world. On today's terms, it is a great job. Who would give it up voluntarily? Well, Justice O'Connor did, but Chief Justice Rehnquist, who was older and suffered from physical ailments for a very long time, remained in office until removed from it by his sudden death.

We believe that the facts stated and our general conclusions are accepted by all twenty-one of the diverse and talented authors who have contributed to this symposium, although they would probably state them in somewhat different language. All agree that the lengthening tenure of Supreme Court justices raises a challenge to life tenure that is worthy of serious inquiry and debate by academics, politicians and the public. This view is also supported by the following scholars, bar leaders, and distinguished judges, who have expressed agreement "in principle" with the specific legislative proposal advanced by the two of us and which was the subject of an academic conference held at Duke in April 2005. Most of the papers in this book arose out of that conference.

> Bruce A. Ackerman, Yale Law School
> Albert W. Alschuler, University of Chicago Law School
> Vickram D. Amar, University of California Hastings College of Law
> Jack M. Balkin, Yale Law School
> Jerome A. Barron, George Washington University Law School
> Kevin M. Clermont, Cornell Law School
> John J. Costonis, Chancellor, Louisiana State University
> John J. Curtin, Jr., Esq., Boston (Former President, American Bar Association)
> Walter E. Dellinger III, Duke University School of Law
> Norman Dorsen, New York University School of Law

---

2. The phrase is that of Seth Waxman, Esq., a recent Solicitor General of the United States, quoted in the National Law Journal C7 (Aug. 6, 2001).

Craig Enoch, Esq., Dallas, Texas (former Justice, Supreme Court of Texas)

Garrett Epps, University of Oregon School of Law

Richard A. Epstein, University of Chicago Law School

James G. Exum, Esq., Greensboro, North Carolina (former Chief Justice of North Carolina)

Richard H. Fallon, Harvard University Law School

John H. Garvey, Boston College Law School

Lino A. Graglia, University of Texas School of Law

Michael Heise, Cornell Law School

Wythe Holt, University of Alabama Law School

R. William Ide III, Esq., Atlanta, Georgia (former President, American Bar Association)

Yale Kamisar, University of Michigan Law School

Larry D. Kramer, Stanford University Law School

Lewis Henry LaRue, Washington & Lee University School of Law

Sanford Levinson, University of Texas School of Law

George Liebmann, Esq., Baltimore, Maryland, Visiting Scholar, Cambridge University

Theodore J. Lowi, Senior Professor of American Institutions, Cornell University

Ira C. Lupu, George Washington University School of Law

Robert MacCrate, Esq., New York City (former President, American Bar Association)

Frank I. Michelman, Harvard University Law School

Thomas D. Morgan, George Washington University Law School

Alan Morrison, Stanford University Law School

Robert R. Nagel, University of Colorado School of Law

Philip D. Oliver, University of Arkansas at Little Rock School of Law

Russell Osgood, President, Grinnell College

William G. Paul, Esq., Oklahoma City, Oklahoma (former President, American Bar Association)

Richard D. Parker, Harvard University Law School

Michael John Perry, Emory University School of Law

H. Jefferson Powell, Professor of Law and Divinity, Duke University School of Law

L. A. (Scot) Powe, Jr., University of Texas School of Law

John Phillip Reid, New York University School of Law

William L. Reynolds, University of Maryland School of Law

Thomas D. Rowe, Jr., Duke University School of Law

Theodore St. Antoine, University of Michigan Law School

Christopher H. Schroeder, Professor of Law and Policy Sciences, Duke University

Peter H. Schuck, Yale Law School

David L. Shapiro, Harvard University Law School

Carol S. Steiker, Harvard University Law School

Nadine Strossen, New York Law School

Peter L. Strauss, Columbia University School of Law

Lawrence H. Tribe, Harvard University Law School

Mark V. Tushnet, Georgetown University Law Center

Jon M. Van Dyke, University of Hawai'i School of Law

Herbert P. Wilkins, Boston College Law School (former Chief Justice of Massachusetts)

Michael D. Zimmerman, Esq., Salt Lake City (former Chief Justice of Utah)

Informed readers will recognize that this list includes persons of almost every imaginable political orientation.

The needed inquiry and debate concern the questions that are the subject of the original papers written for this symposium: (1) what harmful consequences, if any, are caused by the life tenure of Supreme Court justices; (2) are those consequences sufficiently serious that remedial proposals should be considered; and (3) what remedies are most appropriate?

All participants in the symposium agree that current arrangements for Supreme Court justices have resulted in at least two harmful consequences. First, David Garrow's prior work and that of others establish that instances of harm to the Court because an aging justice is mentally or physically compromised occur much more frequently than is generally understood.[3] Second, current arrangements create incentives for strategic behavior by presidents, justices and senators that may not be in the interest of the Court or the public. Presidents have an incentive to choose a less-experienced and less-qualified younger appointee who, if a correct assessment is made of the appointee's future constitutional decision-making, is likely to provide the President an even longer influence on the Court's decisions. Justices often seek to time their retirements so that like-minded presidents will appoint their successors. Experience suggests, for example, that Justice O'Connor, a Reagan appointee, might not have retired when she did had John Kerry been elected President in 2004. And senators, aware of the high stakes inherent in the appointment of a justice who could serve

---

3. *See infra* David J. Garrow, *Protecting and Enhancing the U.S. Supreme Court*, pp. 271–289. *See also* David J. Garrow, *Mental Decrepitude on the U.S. Supreme Court*, 67 U. Chi. L. Rev. 995 (2000).

for a generation or more, may frustrate the president's power of appointment by using procedural tactics to prevent a vote on the appointment.

Other possible consequences are more intangible, uncertain, and value-laden. Longer tenure decreases the rotation in office that naturally occurred before the life expectancy of a mature person doubled or tripled. The randomness of death in office and of some retirement decisions results, as Daniel Meador[4] and Thomas Merrill[5] emphasize, in situations in which vacancies may be bunched. Some presidents harvest four or five appointments (e.g., Taft and Nixon) and others none (e.g., Carter). The lack of regular turnover decreases the political accountability of a branch of the federal government that has become a major policy-making institution. The popular will of an electorate that is guaranteed "a Republican Form of Government" is increasingly governed by a non-accountable gerontocracy. And the lengthened tenure, by increasing the stakes of every appointment, may have contributed to the contentiousness of confirmation. These issues are discussed from various vantage points in the articles in this symposium.

Most of the authors agree with us that these problems are serious and justify prompt consideration of alternative solutions. Daniel Meador, Alan Morrison,[6] and Scot Powe[7] join us in favoring legislative consideration of alternatives, especially term limits. Powe provides a useful discussion of a justice's usual life cycle, including a discussion of the intellectual autopilot that often results once a justice is past his or her prime. He also provides a comparison of length of tenure of congressional leaders with that of justices. Morrison, after agreeing that a system of limited tenure should replace current life tenure, discusses another concern: the powers and manner of appointment of the chief justice. Morrison contends that needed statutory change should include a provision authorizing the president to appoint the chief justice without a separate Senate confirmation proceeding when a vacancy in that office arises, but only from among the sitting justices. Judith Resnik also emphasizes the exceptional role of the chief justice as the chief executive officer of the third branch and advocates a measure of political accountability for the conduct of that role.[8]

---

4. See infra Daniel J. Meador, *Thinking About Age and Supreme Court Tenure*, pp. 115–123.

5. See infra Thomas W. Merrill, *Internal Dynamics of Term Limits for Justices*, pp. 225–248.

6. See infra Alan B. Morrison, *Opting for Change in Supreme Court Selection, and for the Chief Justice, Too*, pp. 203–223.

7. See infra L. A. Powe, Jr., *"Marble Palace, We've Got a Problem—with You,"* pp. 99–113.

8. See infra Judith Resnik, *Democratic Responses to the Breadth of Power of the Chief Justice*, pp. 181–200.

Ward Farnsworth[9] and Arthur Hellman[10] present dissenting views favoring the status quo. While not questioning the factual premises stated above, Farnsworth argues that the voice from the past is a useful element of stability for the republic and often results in a justice moving in a "liberal" (and, from his point of view, desirable) direction. Arthur Hellman argues that staggered eighteen-year terms would make the appointment process even more politically contentious because potential opponents would know when a vacancy would arise and which justice would be leaving. He also contends that regular new appointments would accentuate strategic behavior of justices in making certiorari decisions, i.e., expediting or slowing the consideration of a constitutional issue around the departure of a particular justice. Hellman also argues that term limits for justices would threaten the stability of precedent, which might in turn lead the public to believe that decisions do not rest on "impersonal and reasoned judgments."

Philip Oliver[11] supports the editors' statutory proposal but prefers a constitutional amendment imposing term limits on justices. His proposed amendment would expand the size of the Court through regular appointments by each president and diminish its size with each retirement, resignation or death.

Robert Nagel bases his support for substitution of term limits for the current life tenure system primarily on value-laden issues: the Court has regularly adopted policy positions that damage federalism and especially the effectiveness of state and local governments. This frustration of local action closer to the people frustrates participation in government, forces national homogeneity rather than local and regional variation, and moves decisionmaking from where people live and work to a national level. In doing so, the Court's decisions frustrate and alienate those who disagree with the values forced on them. Moreover, the Court now views every aspect of ordinary life as within its control and advances its homogenizing program through "authoritarian claims on behalf of [its] judicial power."[12] His views are generally shared by Paul Carrington,[13] who holds that Congress has a constitutional duty to impose on the Court constraints that are consistent with the principles of judicial independence and federalism.

---

9. *See infra* Ward Farnsworth, *The Case for Life Tenure*, pp. 251–269.

10. *See infra* Arthur D. Hellman, *Reining in the Supreme Court: Are Term Limits the Answer?*, pp. 291–316.

11. *See infra* Philip D. Oliver, *Increasing the Size of the Court as a Partial but Clearly Constitutional Alternative*, pp. 405–414.

12. *See infra* Robert F. Nagel, *Limiting the Court by Limiting Life Tenure*, pp. 127–136.

13. *See infra* Paul D. Carrington, *Checks and Balances: Congress and the Federal Courts*, pp. 137–179.

Thomas Merrill's paper considers the effect of staggered terms on the norms governing the Court's decisional process, the Court's efficiency in deciding cases, and the ability of justices to form fairly stable voting blocs. Norm change, he concludes, would be somewhat more likely under a term limits regime, efficiency in decisionmaking would be somewhat reduced, and ad hoc rather than stable voting blocs would be more common. Conceding that these predictions are highly speculative, he concludes that, on balance, replacement of life tenure with fixed non-renewable terms would be desirable. Terri Peretti,[14] viewing term limits proposals in the light of political science insights, also explores the various consequences and implications of term limits proposals; she is especially concerned about the uneven distribution of Supreme Court appointments under current arrangements.

The constitutionality of a statutory proposal, such as the one the co-editors have proposed, is considered in a number of papers. Sanford Levinson,[15] affirming the power of Congress on this subject, argues that the Good Behavior Clause should be given a purposive or functional interpretation that reflects the fact that circumstances have changed sine 1789. The problem in his view is that of mobilizing the national constituency that would be necessary to get a valid statute enacted. Roger Cramton[16] emphasizes the broad power given to Congress to regulate the federal courts, including the Supreme Court. Throughout our history Congress by legislation has created and abolished federal courts and has regulated the size and other aspects of the Court. For 121 years the justices were required to "ride circuit," deciding cases on lower federal courts. The only directly relevant judicial decision upheld legislative authority in broad language. Paul Carrington[17] compares the constitutionality of term limits imposed on other members of the federal judiciary, more numerous than the Article III judges, who are in even greater need of judicial independence.

John Harrison[18] and William Van Alstyne,[19] on the other hand, argue that the texts of Articles II and III of the Constitution, and the purposes of those

---

14. *See infra* Terri L. Peretti, *Promoting Equity in the Distribution of Supreme Court Appointments*, pp. 435–453.

15. *See infra* Sanford Levinson, *Life Tenure and the Supreme Court: What Is to Be Done?*, pp. 375–383.

16. *See infra* Roger C. Cramton, *Constitutionality of Reforming the Supreme Court by Statute*, pp. 345–360.

17. *See infra* Carrington, *Checks and Balances*, pp. 137–179.

18. *See infra* John Harrison, *The Power of Congress over the Terms of Justices of the Supreme Court*, pp. 361–373.

19. *See infra* William Van Alstyne, *Constitutional Futility of Statutory Term Limits for Supreme Court Justices*, pp. 385–402.

texts, make the Supreme Court, unlike other federal courts, a unique institution and prevent Congress from manipulating the office of a justice. In their view, substantial participation in the Court's decisionmaking process without a fixed limitation of term is an inherent quality of the office that is immune from legislative change. Richard Epstein's brief discussion of constitutionality takes much the same position.[20]

Another line of argument concerning constitutionality is raised by several papers: if Congress successfully exercised authority to redefine the office of a justice, the temptation of political majorities to tinker with it for political purposes might become a serious problem.[21] The contrary view is that the obvious importance of the structural integrity of the Court will prompt thoughtful and extensive legislative consideration quite unlike momentary and impulsive aberrations like the *Schiavo* incident.[22] Like social security, it would be treated as fundamental legislation to be changed very rarely and only for good reasons.

Cumulative or alternative proposals are advanced in five papers. Richard Epstein argues that a mandatory retirement age of seventy should be coupled with the term limits proposal, each reinforcing and benefiting the other.[23] Alan Morrison and Judith Resnik would include a provision relating to the office of chief justice in any statutory revision.[24] Scot Powe, concerned about the increased delegation to law clerks on the part of justices, suggests that each justice be limited to only one clerk, forcing them to do more of the hard work of drafting opinions, a burden that would produce better decisions and lead justices to think more seriously of retirement as they aged. Paul Carrington proposes substantial revision of the 1925 legislation empowering the Court to control its own docket.[25] And, finally, George Liebmann[26] provides a glimpse at another alternative or cumulative proposal: legislation that restricts the jurisdiction of the Supreme Court.

An appendix provides the Carrington-Cramton proposal for statutory reform of the Court.

---

20. *See infra* Richard A. Epstein, *Mandatory Retirement for Supreme Court Justices,* pp. 415–433.

21. *See infra,* e.g., Harrison pp. 361–373 and Hellman pp. 291–316.

22. The case of Theresa Schiavo is reported by Abby Goodnough, *The Schiavo Case: The Overview: Schiavo Dies, Ending Bitter Case over Feeding Tube,* N.Y. Times A1 (Apr. 1, 2005).

23. *See infra* Epstein pp. 415–433.

24. *See infra* Morrison pp. 203–223.

25. *See infra* Carrington pp 137–179.

26. *See infra* George W. Liebmann, *Restraining the Court by Curbing District Court Jurisdiction and Improving Litigation Procedure,* pp. 455–463.

Altogether, the articles provide a feast of information and ideas relating to an important and little-considered public problem. We hope that readers will be persuaded that the superannuation of Supreme Court justices is a problem that deserves study, debate and reflection on the part of the people and its governors. We believe that the result of such inquiry and discussion will inevitably lead to the conclusion that the time for action has come.

Is the Prolonged Tenure of Justices a Problem Requiring Attention?

TERM LIMITS FOR THE SUPREME COURT: LIFE TENURE RECONSIDERED

Steven G. Calabresi[1] *& James Lindgren*[2]

1. George C. Dix Professor of Constitutional Law, Northwestern University.

I began working on this idea in the summer of 2001 with Jeff Oldham of the Northwestern Law School Class of 2003. Jeff was helping me at the time as a summer research assistant, and this was the project I was working on. I set Jeff to work compiling the data on the increasing tenure of Supreme Court Justices on the Court, the increasing length of time between vacancies on the Court, the older average age upon retirement of Justices, and comparative data about judicial term limits in foreign countries and in the 50 U.S. states. Once I realized the very substantial empirical nature of the project I had launched, I invited my colleague and friend, Jim Lindgren, a trained social scientist, to join us in gathering data and crunching the numbers. Subsequently, Jeff Oldham did substantially more work on the project as part of a third year legal writing paper, which he wrote in several drafts under my direction. Jeff produced the critical first draft of this article with strong direction from me and with considerable help from Jim Lindgren on the empirical data. Jim and I have subsequently done multiple additional drafts. We, of course, invited Jeff to be a co-author on the paper; he had been planning to be a co-author with the two of us until for professional reasons (he has been a court clerk), he decided he had to decline to be listed as a co-author. The bottom line, gentle reader, is that Jeff Oldham made as big a contribution to the execution of this piece as did Professors Calabresi and Lindgren. Although Jeff has not been involved in the later drafts, he has encouraged us to go forward without him.

Beyond thanking Jeff Oldham, we are grateful for the helpful comments of Al Alschuler, Akhil Amar, Charles Fried, Richard Fallon, Philip Hamburger, John Harrison, Gary Lawson, Daniel Lev, Saikrishna Prakash, and David Presser.

2. Benjamin Mazur Research Professor, Northwestern University.

Introduction

In June 2005, at the end of the October 2004 term of the U.S. Supreme Court, its nine members had served together for almost eleven years, longer than any other group of nine justices in the nation's history.[3] The average tenure of a Supreme Court justice from 1789 through 1970 was only 14.9 years, yet, of those justices who have retired since 1970, the average tenure has jumped to 26.1 years. Moreover, before the death of Chief Justice Rehnquist in September 2005 and Justice Sandra Day O'Connor's announcement of her pending resignation in July 2005, five of the nine justices had served on the Court for more than seventeen years and three of these had served more than twenty-three years.[4] The other four justices have already spent between ten and fourteen years on the Court. At the same time, four of the nine members of the Court were seventy years of age or older, and only one of them was under sixty-five, once the traditional retirement age in business.[5] Because of the length of tenure of members of the Rehnquist court, there were no vacancies on the High Court from 1994 to the middle of 2005.[6]

We believe the American constitutional rule granting life tenure to Supreme Court justices is fundamentally flawed, resulting now in justices remaining on the Court for longer periods and to a later age than ever before in American history. This leads to significantly less frequent vacancies on the Court, which reduces the efficacy of the democratic check that the appointment process provides on the Court's membership. The increase in the longevity of justices' tenure means that life tenure now guarantees a much longer tenure on the

---

3. *Note*: All calculations in this Article are current as of October 3, 2005, the first day of the October 2005 Term. For purposes except listing the ages and tenures of the current justices and assessing mental decrepitude, Justice Sandra Day O'Connor is treated as having resigned on that day (we do not think that it would be fair to assert how infrequently resignations occur while excluding from our data analysis a pending resignation).

See Akhil Reed Amar & Steven G. Calabresi, *Term Limits for the High Court*, Washington Post A23 (Aug. 9, 2002). By September 4, 2005 when Justice Rehnquist died, it was about eleven years since a vacancy had arisen on August 3, 1994, a vacancy filled by Stephen Breyer. This was the second longest gap between vacancies in the nation's history; the longest was between June 19, 1811 and March 18, 1823, a gap of eleven years and nine months between the vacancies filled by Gabriel Duvall and Smith Thompson; the third longest was only about six years.

4. For tenure of justices as of October 3, 2005, see Appendix.

5. For the ages of the current justices as of October 3, 2005, see Appendix.

6. For the year of appointment of the current justices, see Appendix.

Court than was the case in 1789 or over most of our constitutional history.[7] Moreover, the combination of less frequent vacancies and longer tenures of office means that when vacancies do arise, there is so much at stake that confirmation battles become much more intense. Finally, as was detailed in a recent article by Professor David Garrow,[8] the advancing age of past Supreme Court justices has at times led to a problem of "mental decrepitude" on the Court, whereby some justices have been physically or mentally unable to fulfill their duties at the final stages of their career.[9] A regime that allows high government officials to exercise great power, totally unchecked, for periods of thirty to forty years is essentially a relic of pre-democratic times: although life tenure for Supreme Court justices may have made sense in the eighteenth-century world of the Framers, it is particularly inappropriate now, given the enormous power that Supreme Court justices have come to wield.[10]

In this essay, therefore, we call for change. First, we analyze the historical data on the tenure of Supreme Court justices and conclude by describing the approach that all other major democratic nations and U.S. states have taken to judicial tenure and by showing that, comparatively, the U.S. Supreme Court's system of life tenure is truly an outlier.[11] A proposed solution is then offered—that lawmakers pass a constitutional amendment instituting a system of staggered, eighteen-year term limits for Supreme Court Justices.[12] The Court's membership would be constitutionally fixed at nine justices, and their terms would be staggered such that a vacancy would occur on the Court every two years at the end of the term in every odd-numbered calendar year. Every one-term president

---

7. *See* Gregg Easterbrook, *Geritol Justice: Is the Supreme Court Senile?*, The New Republic (Aug. 19, 1991) ("When the Constitutional Convention of 1787 conferred on Supreme Court Justices a lifetime tenure almost impossible to revoke, court membership did not mean what it means today.").

8. David J. Garrow, *Mental Decrepitude on the U.S. Supreme Court: The Historical Case for a 28th Amendment*, 67 U. Chi. L. Rev. 995 (2000). *See also* David N. Atkinson, *Leaving the Bench: Supreme Court Justices at the End* (Kansas 1999) (combining a series of articles, written during the 1970s and 1980s, into a book).

9. *See* Garrow, *supra* n. 8 (detailing this observation). *See also* Atkinson, *supra* n. 8.

10. *See* Steven G. Calabresi, *Overrule Casey! Some Originalist and Normative Arguments Against a Strict Rule of Stare Decisis in Constitutional Cases,* Constitutional Commentary (forthcoming 2005); Steven G. Calabresi, *Text, Precedent, and Burke: Some Arguments from Practice Against a Strict Rule of Stare Decisis in Constitutional Cases,* Alabama L. Rev. (forthcoming 2006).

11. *See infra* text accompanying notes 115–132 (one state, Rhode Island, also has life tenure for its Supreme Court).

12. We address the possibility of term limits only for the Supreme Court. Any attempt to institute term limits for lower federal court judges would present enormous administrative complexities that might outweigh any benefit of limited tenures for those judges.

would thus get to appoint two justices, and every two-term president would get to appoint four. This term limits proposal would not be applied to any of the nine currently sitting justices, nor to any of the nominees of the President who is sitting when the constitutional amendment is ratified. We believe Supreme Court term limits ought to be phased in, as was done with the two-term limit for presidents, which did not apply to the incumbent president when it was ratified. If the amendment were ratified before 2009, the term limit should begin to apply during the tenure of whoever is elected President in 2008. Since we are all behind a veil of ignorance as to the partisan identity of the winner in 2008, this seems to be a fair and optimal time for term limits to start.

This proposal builds on the views of a number of distinguished commentators and judges from broadly varying backgrounds who have opposed life tenure for federal judges, including some of the most venerable figures in American history. Thomas Jefferson, for example, denounced life tenure as being wholly inconsistent with our ordered republic. Accordingly, he proposed four- or six-year renewable term limits for federal judges.[13] And Robert Yates, who wrote as Brutus during the ratification period, railed against the provision for life tenure for federal judges and the disastrous degrees of independence from democratic accountability that it would lead to.[14]

Most relevant to our own proposal are the thoughtful suggestions by several modern commentators in favor of imposing eighteen-year term limits. First, in 1986, Professor Philip Oliver carefully considered how best to restructure the tenure of Supreme Court justices.[15] Oliver proposed fixed, staggered terms of eighteen years, and he explained that, among other benefits, such a system would allow for more regular appointments (every two years), would balance the impact that all Presidents can have on the Court's makeup, and would eliminate the possibility of justices' remaining on the Court beyond their vigorous years.[16] Following Professor Oliver, other commentators similarly called for limits to the tenure of Supreme Court justices, or of fed-

---

13. Letter from Thomas Jefferson to William T. Barry (July 2, 1822), in 7 *The Writings of Thomas Jefferson* 256 (H.A. Washington ed., 1859); *Thomas Jefferson, A Biography in His Own Words* (1974); *see also* Charles Cooper, *Federalist Society Symposium: Term Limits for Judges?*, 13 J.L. & Pol. 669, 674–75 (Summer 1997) (discussing Jefferson's criticism of life tenure and his proposals for term limits).

14. Robert Yates, *Brutus No. XV* (1788), *reprinted in The Anti-Federalists* 350, 352 (Cecilia M. Kenyon ed., 1966).

15. Philip D. Oliver, *Systematic Justice: A Proposed Constitutional Amendment to Establish Fixed, Staggered Terms for Members of the United States Supreme Court*, 47 Ohio St. L.J. 799 (1986).

16. *Id.* at 802–16.

eral judges generally, but did not propose terms of eighteen years.[17] After this chapter was written and discussed publicly, but before it was published, students James DiTullio and John Schochet proposed a system of eighteen-year term limits for Supreme Court Justices.[18] Their primary concerns were not that justices are staying too long on the Court but that the current system allows for strategic timing of retirements, encourages the appointment of young nominees to the Court, and fails to distribute appointments evenly across different presidencies.[19] Finally, Professor L. A. Powe, Jr., recently identified life tenure on the Supreme Court as being the stupidest feature of the American Constitution,[20] and he, too, called for eighteen-year term limits on Supreme Court Justices.[21] Of the leading legal scholars to write about Supreme Court term limits to date, only one major figure—Professor Ward Farnsworth, of Boston University—has defended life tenure.[22]

Although many commentators have thus called for term limits on Supreme Court Justices, their proposals have received little attention, perhaps for two

---

17. *See* Laurence H. Silberman, *Federalist Society Symposium: Term Limits for Judges?*, 13 J. L. & Pub. Policy 669, 674–75, 687 (suggesting individuals be selected to sit on the Supreme Court for a term of five years, then sit on the federal courts of appeals for the remainder of their life tenure); Easterbrook *supra* n. 7 (proposing a constitutional amendment to replace life tenure for the justices with ten-year fixed terms with the option for retired justices to serve on lower federal courts); Henry Paul Monaghan, *The Confirmation Process: Law or Politics*, 101 Harv. L. Rev. 1202 (1988) (recommending lawmakers consider both an age limit and a term limit of fifteen to twenty years for justices); Saikrishna B. Prakash, *America's Aristocracy*, 109 Yale L.J. 541, 570–73 (1999) (arguing a notion of life-tenured judges is fundamentally at odds with representative democracy and advocating term limits for all federal judges). Professor Prakash also argues that the President and Senate should have more power to remove justices for improper decisions. *Id.* at 568. We decline to adopt this suggestion because we think it would threaten judicial independence. *See also* John O. McGinnis, *Justice Without Justices*, 16 Const. Comm. 541, 541–43 (1999) (advocating a model similar to that of Judge Silberman: members of the lower federal courts would be assigned to serve on the Supreme Court for short periods of time, like a year, then return to their positions on the lower courts for life); Amar & Calabresi, *supra* n. 3 (expressing support for either formal or informal limits on the justices' tenures).

18. James E. DiTullio & John B. Schochet, Student Authors, *Saving this Honorable Court: A Proposal to Replace Life Tenure on the Supreme Court With Staggered, Nonrenewable Eighteen-Year Terms*, 90 Va. L. Rev. 1093 (2004).

19. *Id.*

20. L. A. Powe, Jr., *Old People and Good Behavior*, in *Constitutional Stupidities, Constitutional Tragedies*, 77–80 (William N. Eskridge, Jr. & Sanford Levinson eds., 1968).

21. *Id.* at 79.

22. Ward Farnsworth, *The Regulation of Turnover on the Supreme Court*, 2005 U. Ill. L. Rev. 407, 408 (2005).

reasons. First, many Americans mistakenly believe that a system of life tenure is necessary to preserve an independent judiciary. Second, these scholars' proposals have received little attention because, even apart from romanticized resistance, a relatively comprehensive case has not yet been made in the literature for the need to reform life tenure. We seek to make that case by showing a strong, non-partisan justification for reconsidering life tenure—that the real-world, practical meaning of life tenure has changed over time and is very different now from what it was in 1789 or even in 1939.

Our proposal is ultimately a Burkean reform because all we would do is to move the justices back toward an average tenure that is similar to what the average tenure of justices has been over the totality of American history. Just as the two-term limit on Presidents restored a tradition of Presidents stepping down after eight years in office, our eighteen-year term limit on Supreme Court justices would push the average tenure of justices back toward the 14.9-year average tenures that prevailed between 1789 and 1970 and away from the astonishing 26.1-year average tenure enjoyed by justices who stepped down between 1971 and 2005. Our proposed amendment would thus merely restore the practice that prevailed between 1789 and 1970 and would guarantee that vacancies on the Court would open up on average every two years, with no eleven-year periods without a vacancy as has happened between 1994 and 2005. This then is a fundamentally conservative call for reform, all the more so because we resist the calls of many commentators for a very short tenure for Supreme Court justices. The eighteen-year nonrenewable term we propose is more than long enough to guarantee judicial independence without producing the pathologies associated with the current system of life tenure.

Our proposal for imposing on Supreme Court Justices a staggered, eighteen-year term limit, with a salary for life and an automatic right to sit on the lower federal courts for life, could theoretically be established in a variety of ways, but the only way we approve of is through passage of a constitutional amendment pursuant to Article V.[23] Accordingly, we outline below our proposal for a constitutional amendment instituting term limits.[24] We then highlight the advantages to passing such an amendment and address potential counter-arguments. Short of amending the Constitution, Professors Paul Carrington and Roger Cramton have recently proposed a system of term limits for Supreme Court Justices instituted by statute. We consider two statutory proposals for instituting Supreme Court term limits, one of our own devising and the other being the

---

23. *See* U.S. Const. art. V.
24. *See infra* text accompanying notes 30–45.

Carrington-Cramton proposal.[25] We consider the arguments in favor of and against the constitutionality of these two proposed statutes, concluding that statutorily imposed term limits on Supreme Court justices are unconstitutional. The statutory proposal presents some close constitutional questions, and one grave danger it poses is that it would be manipulable by future Congresses.[26] For these reasons, we believe that term limits ought to be established by a constitutional amendment and that the proposed statute is unconstitutional.

Finally, we argue that a system of term limits could in theory be achieved more informally through a variety of measures.[27] Specifically, we consider the opportunities that the Senate, the Court, and even individual justices have for informally instituting term limits: the Senate by imposing term limits pledges on nominees in confirmation hearings;[28] the Court through an adjustment of its internal court rules and seniority system; and individual justices by establishing an informal tradition of leaving the Court after a term of years, as Presidents did before passage of the Twenty-Second Amendment.[29]

We are opposed to term limit pledges exacted by the Senate during the confirmation process. We believe this practice would greatly weaken a newly appointed justice in the eyes of his colleagues since that newly appointed justice would be seen as having compromised judicial independence by taking a term limits pledge to win confirmation. We are similarly quite skeptical of the idea that individual justices ought to try to establish a tradition of retiring after eighteen years. Even if one or two justices were to try to set such a good example, we believe that, given current levels of partisanship on the Supreme Court, the other justices on the Court would fail to follow their good exam-

---

25. *See* Amar & Calabresi, *supra* n. 3, *see infra* Paul D. Carrington & Roger C. Cramton, *The Supreme Court Renewal Act: A Return to Basic Principles,* pp. 467–471.

26. *See* McGinnis, *supra* n. 17, at 546 (noting the problem of manipulability if a system of term limits were instituted under a statute).

27. *See* Amar & Calabresi, *supra* n.3.

28. *See infra* text accompanying notes 61–85.

29. *See* David Kyvig, *Explicit and Authentic Acts: Amending the U.S. Constitution, 1776–1995,* 325 (Univ. Press of Kansas, 1996) (stating the two-term tradition of Presidents was "established by George Washington, reinforced by Thomas Jefferson, and observed for one reason or another by the seven other once-reelected chief executives" before President F.D. Roosevelt); Doris Kearns Goodwin, *No Ordinary Time* 106 (1994) ("[E]ver since George Washington refused a third term, no man had even tried to achieve the office of the Presidency more than twice."). *See generally* Bruce G. Peabody & Scott E. Gant, *The Twice and Future President: Constitutional Interstices and the Twenty-Second Amendment,* 83 Minn. L. Rev. 565, 574–75 (1999) (summarizing the literature covering the two-term tradition, though challenging the existence of this tradition).

ple. We thus conclude that the only way to realize a system of Supreme Court term limits is by the passage of a constitutional amendment. We urge lawmakers to consider passing such an amendment before a new wave of resignations occurs. Establishing a system of term limits is an important reform that would correct the problem of a real-world, practical increase in the actual tenure of Supreme Court justices.

The Need for Reform:
The Expansion of Life Tenure, Its Potential Causes, and Its Detrimental Effects

The Expansion of Life Tenure

Life tenure for Supreme Court justices has been a part of our Constitution since 1789, when the Framers created one Supreme Court and provided that its members "shall hold their Offices during good Behaviour."[30] In so providing, the Framers followed the eighteenth-century English practice, spawned in the wake of the Glorious Revolution of 1688, of securing judicial independence through life tenure in office for judges.[31] But since 1789, Americans have seen drastic changes in medicine, technology, politics, and social perceptions of judges and of the law, which have changed the practical meaning of life tenure for justices.

We analyzed how this meaning has changed over time by calculating the age and tenure of office for each justice[32] and by examining the number of years between openings on the Court. This analysis revealed three critical and significant trends: the real-world, practical meaning of life tenure has been

---

30. U.S. Const. art. III, §1.

31. Prior to the Act of Settlement of 1703, English judges served for the term of the sovereign who appointed them. With the sovereign's death, the judges' terms came to an end. Proponents of the Glorious Revolution of 1688 saw life tenure of judges as vital to making them independent of the Crown, a notion borrowed by Americans in 1787.

32. Sources for this data included the Federal Judicial Center, Washington, DC, History of the Federal Judiciary <http://www.fjc.gov/history/home/nsf> (Aug. 4, 2002); Henry J. Abraham, Justices, Presidents, and Senators (Rev. ed., 1999). We counted two terms each for Justices Hughes and Rutledge, who both served as associate justices, resigned their positions for a number of years, and then were reappointed as Chief Justices. In Rutledge's case, his recess appointment was rejected by the Senate and he resigned. The date of swearing in was used as the start of a justice's service on the Court for purposes of computing tenure of office.

**Chart 1.   Length of Tenure on Court by Period
of Leaving the Supreme Court**

103 Terms (101 Justices), 1789 - October 2005

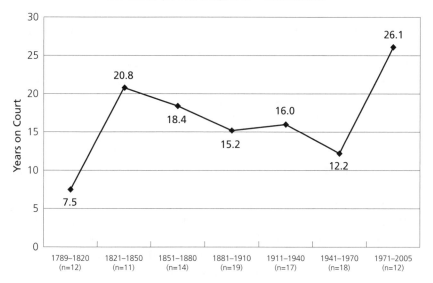

expanding over time, justices have been staying on the Court to more advanced ages than in the past, and, as a result, vacancies have been occurring
less frequently than ever before.

Surprisingly, these trends have not been gradual.

First, as Chart 1 summarizes, the average tenure of a Supreme Court justice has increased considerably since the Court's creation in 1789, with the
most dramatic increase occurring between 1970 and the present. In the first
thirty years of the Supreme Court's history, justices spent an average of just
7.5 years on the Court, which may have been due in large part to the difficult
conditions of circuit riding and a series of very short-lived initial appointments, including a short recess appointment for Chief Justice Rutledge.[33] The
average tenure of justices then increased significantly between 1821 and 1850
to 20.8 years before declining over the next four thirty-year periods (spanning

---

33. *See, e.g.*, Joshua Glick, *On the Road: The Supreme Court and the History of Circuit
Riding*, 24 Cardozo L. Rev. 1753, 1765–67, 1780–81, 1797–98, 1806–07, 1810–11,
1814–15 (2003) (documenting the practice of circuit riding and the burdens it placed on
the justices, and noting the role that some justices' dislike of circuit-riding figured in their
retirement decisions).

from 1851 through 1970) to an average tenure of only 12.2 years. Then, from 1971 to 2000, justices leaving office spent an average of 26.1 years on the Court—an astonishing fourteen-year increase over the prior period, 1941–1970.[34] Justices leaving office between 1971 and 2000 thus spent more than double the amount of time in office, on average, than did justices leaving office between 1941 and 1970. A cumulative average for the period of 1789–1970 puts this dramatic increase, reflected in tenure of post-1970 retirees, in perspective. Compared to the average of 26.1 years in office for justices retiring since 1970, the average justice leaving office between 1789 and 1970 spent only 14.9 years in office. Thus, regardless of the basis for comparison—the average of 12.2 years for justices leaving office during 1941–1970 or the average of 14.9 years for justices leaving office from 1789 through 1970—the increase to an average tenure of 26.1 for justices leaving office since 1970 is astounding.

Not only are justices staying on the Court for longer periods, but they also are leaving office at more advanced ages than ever before. As Chart 2 highlights, the average age at which justices have left office has generally risen over time, but, like the trend in the average tenure of office, it has dramatically increased for those retiring in the past thirty-five years.

In the five thirty-year intervals between 1789 and 1940, the average age upon leaving office rose from 58.3 to 72.2 years of age, but then dropped to about 67.6 years for the 1941–1970 period. Yet in the next period, from 1971 through 2005, justices have left office at an average age of 79.5 years. Justices who have left office since 1970 have thus been, on average, twelve years older when leaving the Court than justices who left office in the preceding thirty-year period, 1941–1970, and more than seven years older than justices in the next-highest period (1911–1940), one that famously included the era of the so-called nine old men. In addition, comparing the average age since 1970 with a cumulative average age of all justices retiring from 1789 through 1970 is no less revealing. The average justice leaving office after 1970 (age 79.5) is eleven years older than the average justice leaving office prior to 1970 (age 68.3). Thus, the average age at which justices have left office has increased remarkably throughout history, and most sharply in the past thirty-five years. Life tenure today means a significantly longer tenure than it meant in 1789.

---

34. Here we treated Justice O'Connor as resigning at the start of the October 2005 term on October 3, 2005, though she continues to serve until her resignation takes effect when her replacement is confirmed.

Chart 2.   Age at Death or Resignation by Period of Leaving the Supreme Court
103 Terms (101 Justices), 1789 - October 2005

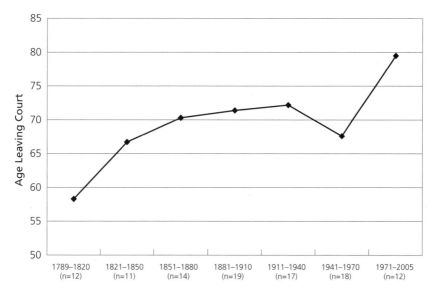

The mean age for both men and women electing to receive Social Security retirement benefits has hovered around 64 since 1970,[35] and the age for receiving full benefits is being increased to age 67 for those born after 1960. While in 2000 47% of Americans of ages 62–64 were still in the labor force, that proportion drops in half for ages 65–69 (24%). Only 13.5% of Americans are still in the labor force at ages 70–74, and only 5.3% are still working at ages 75 and older.[36] This compares to a mean retirement age on the Court since 1971 of 79.5 years. On the current Court, all but the last two justices appointed, Justices John Roberts and Clarence Thomas, are at an age when most Americans have already retired.

Given that justices have been staying on the Court for longer periods and later in life than ever before, it is not surprising that vacancies on the Court have been opening up much less frequently than historically was the case. In-

---

35. William A. Wiatrowski, *Changing Retirement Age: Ups and Downs*, Monthly Labor Review 1, 6 (April 2001).

36. *Id.* at 8.

Chart 3.   Mean Years Since Last Supreme Court Vacancy by Period
1789 - October 2005
Excludes Initial Six Appointments, Treats O'Connor Seat as Vacant on October 3, 2005

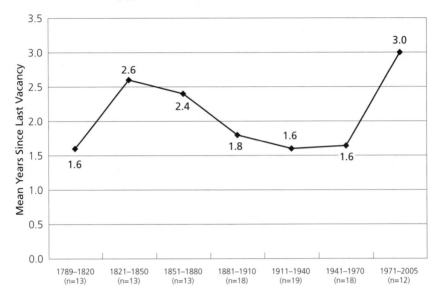

deed, as Chart 3 indicates,[37] the average number of years between vacancies has increased sharply in the past thirty-five years.

These figures are affected, of course, by the varying size of the Supreme Court over time.[38] During most of the first two periods in Chart 3, the Court had fewer than nine members, which means the figures calculated for those periods are higher than they would have been with a larger Court: with fewer

---

37. For purposes of calculating the figures used in Chart 3, the first six appointments to the Court in 1789–1790 were excluded; the count began with the last of the 1790 commissions. In addition, as these data were finalized in September 2005, Justice O'Connor had announced her retirement but was sitting until replaced. She is treated as resigning on Oct. 3, 2005 (which, of course, reduces the mean in the last period).

38. Congress created the Supreme Court in 1789 with only six members, Abraham, *supra* n. 32, at 53–54, and extended it to seven members in 1807, *id.* at 64. In 1837 Congress added two more seats to expand the Court from seven to nine members, *id.* at 76–77, and it added yet another seat in 1863 to bring the Court's membership to ten, *id.* at 89–90. During President Andrew Johnson's tenure, Congress passed bills to eliminate two of these seats, *id.* at 93, but added one more seat in 1870 to bring the Court to nine members, *id.* at 95–96.

justices, open seats can be expected to occur less frequently.[39] In the third period, from 1851 through 1880, the lags between vacancies are more difficult to compare because the size of the Court varied from eight to ten members.[40] Yet, looking at the figures for the first two periods, it is safe to assume that if the Court had been the size it is today, the time between vacancies would tend to be closer to the figures from 1881 through 1970. Indeed, the increase in 1837 from seven to nine members, though primarily a power grab by the Jacksonians, may also have been in small part a reaction to the longer tenure, advanced ages, and longer gaps between retirement after 1811 (as suggested by the data in Charts 1–3). Since 1869 the Court's membership has been fixed at nine justices, which makes a comparison to the last four periods the most meaningful for our purposes. Chart 3 demonstrates that from 1881 through 1970, the average number of years between commissions stayed consistent at about 1.6 to 1.8, but that since 1970 it has nearly doubled to over 3.0 years.

Moreover, the Court went for nearly eleven years—between 1994 and 2005—without a vacancy, the longest period between vacancies since the Court's membership was fixed at nine justices.[41] A period of eleven years that passes without any new vacancies is a period long enough, in the abstract, to deprive a successful, two-term President of the chance to appoint even a single justice.

The cumulative average from 1789 through 1970 further highlights the remarkable increase in time between vacancies that has occurred since 1970: on average, vacancies occurred on the Court every 1.91 years from 1789 to 1970 and then began occurring only every 3.0 years since 1971. After the two 1971 appointments, 3.4 years have elapsed between vacancies. Thus, in the past three decades, vacancies have opened up every 3–3.4 years, which is about double

---

39. In the first period, 1789–1820, the Court had only six members for the first eighteen years of the period and only seven members for the last thirteen years. The second period—1821–1850—contains a period (1821–1837) when the Court had only seven members, and a period (1837–1850) when the Court had nine members.

40. The third period—1851–1880—contains two periods (1851–1863 and 1870–1880), comparable because the Court had nine members, a period (1863 to about 1866) when the Court had ten members, and a period (about 1866 to 1870) when the Court had eight members.

41. The longest period without vacancies in the Court's history was the twelve-year period between the 1811 vacancy that Justice Gabriel Duvall filled and the 1823 vacancy filled by Justice Smith Thompson. If one were to measure by dates of swearing in, then the period would run from the swearing in of Justice Joseph Story in 1812 (to a seat that opened in 1810) and the swearing in of Thompson in 1823. During this period there were only seven seats on the Supreme Court. Abraham, *supra* n. 32, at 68.

those in the most comparable years—from 1881 through 1970—and more than one year longer than the cumulative average from 1789 through 1970.

Strikingly, since the Court was fixed at nine members in 1869, three of the five longest times between vacancies occurred in the last thirty years: between November 12, 1975, and July 3, 1981; between July 3, 1981, and September 26, 1986; and between August 3, 1994, and September 4, 2005. Jimmy Carter was the only President in American history to serve at least one complete term and never make an appointment to the Supreme Court. If George W. Bush had lost his bid for re-election in 2004, he would have been the second. As it is, he is only the third person elected twice to the presidency who has had to wait until his second full term to make his first Supreme Court appointment (the others being Franklin Roosevelt and James Monroe). Of the thirty-four presidential terms since the number of justices was finally fixed at nine in 1869, only four expired without an appointment to the Supreme Court. Among the first twenty-seven terms from 1869 through 1973, only once did a four-year presidential term pass without an appointment (FDR, 1933–1937). By contrast, among the last seven completed terms, three—almost half—were devoid of Supreme Court appointments: Jimmy Carter's term, Bill Clinton's second term, and George W. Bush's first term. There can be no doubt that Supreme Court vacancies are opening up much less often in the post-Warren Court era.

If one takes a lagging average of the last nine appointments to the Court (Chart 4), the mean period between openings was 3.8 years when Chief Justice Rehnquist died, the longest lagging average in Chart 4, and should be about 3.3 years when Justice O'Connor is replaced, the third longest nine-justice average in history. Note that since 1869 when the Court was fixed at nine justices, the average number of years for the last nine vacancies has gone above 2.1 years only twice: in 1937 when the "nine old men" held sway, and continuously since 1986, the entire period of the Rehnquist Court.

These historical trends represent nothing short of a revolution in the practical meaning of the Constitution's grant of life tenure to Supreme Court justices. The Founding Fathers were famously known for their disdain for "unaccountable autocrats out of touch with the typical citizen's concerns—officials who cling to power long after they have sufficient health to perform their duties, officials who cannot be removed from office by democratic agency."[42] The Framers gave Supreme Court justices life tenure in an era when the average American could expect to live to only thirty-five years of age.[43]

---

42. Easterbrook, *supra* n. 7.

43. "Population Explosion Among Older Americans" <http://www.infoplease.com/ipa/ A0780132.html> (Aug. 28, 2002). Although no precise background source is given for this

**Chart 4.   Mean Years Since Last Supreme Court Vacancy
Lagging Average of the Last Nine Vacancies**
1789 - October 2005
Treating O'Connor Seat as Vacant on October 3, 2005

Now justices are appointed at roughly the same average age as was the case in the early years of our history,[44] but they benefit from an average life expectancy of seventy-seven years.[45] Of course, this statement alone significantly overstates the relevant difference because of higher rates on infant mortality two hundred years ago. Thus, a more relevant comparison might be that in 1850 white men who reached the age of forty could expect to live another 27.9 years, compared to such men in 2001 who could expect to live another 37.3 years. This represents an increase of 9.4 years in the life expectancy of a forty-year-

---

commonly cited estimate, it may be based on 1799–1803 data from England and Wales showing a life expectancy of 35.9 years. *See* Indur M. Goklany, *Economic Growth, Technological Change, and Human Well-Being*, in *Property Rights: A Practical Guide to Freedom and Prosperity* 59, Table 2.2 (Terry Anderson & Laura Huggins eds., Hoover Institution, 2003).

44. Chart 5 demonstrates that although the average age of justices upon commission has risen somewhat over the past 150 years, it was only fifty-three years in the most recent period (1971–2000), which is not significantly different from preceding periods.

45. U.S. Census Bureau, "Vital Statistics," Statistical Abstract of the United States 2001, at Table 96 <www.census.gov/prod/2002pubs/01statab/vitstat.pdf> (Sept. 28, 2005).

old between 1850 and 2001. Largely as a result of this 9.4-year increase in life expectancy for forty-year-olds, today the average justice who is appointed to the Court in his early fifties can expect to sit on the Court for nearly three decades, whereas the average justice appointed to the Court in his early fifties in 1789 might have expected to sit on the Court for only two decades. Today's justices enjoy a tenure that is at least fifty percent longer than that of their typical eighteenth- and nineteenth-century predecessors.

Explaining the Trends in Life Tenure

Identifying the trend toward longer tenures is much easier than explaining all its causes. Nevertheless, one cause is the increased average life span of human beings who have lived to reach adulthood in recent times.[46] Presidents have appointed justices of substantially similar ages throughout American history: the average age of justices when appointed or commissioned has been relatively constant—between fifty-two and fifty-seven years since 1811, as Chart 5 illustrates. Indeed, this consistency is shown by the average from the most recent period

---

46. As the historical data indicates, the length of tenure and retirement age of Supreme Court justices has increased fairly suddenly within the past thirty years. One could argue the recency of this change indicates that the historical trends cannot be explained only by increasing life expectancies, which, one might think, have been more gradual. E-mail conversation from Professor Akhil Amar to Professors Vikram Amar and Bill Stuntz, Aug. 9, 2002 (on file with authors). But average life expectancies throughout history may very well explain much of this seemingly sudden increase. When the nation was founded, the average life expectancy was thirty-five years of age. "Population Explosion Among Older Americans" <http://www.infoplease.com/ipa/A0780132.html> (Aug. 28, 2002). See *supra* n. 43. From the founding until 1850, the average life expectancy increased only about three years, to thirty-eight years of age. "Life Expectancy by Age, 1850–1999" <http://www.infoplease.com/ipa/A0005140.html> (Aug. 28, 2002) See *supra* n. 43. Similarly, from 1850 through 1890, the life expectancy increased only about four years of age, to forty-two years. *Id.* Then, in the next forty years—from 1890 through 1930—the life expectancy increased from forty-two years to almost sixty years—an increase of almost twenty years. Importantly, this dramatic increase in life expectancy corresponds to the dramatic increase in the tenure of Supreme Court Justices since 1970: justices retiring after 1970 were born predominantly between 1890 and 1930. Moreover, since 1930, the life expectancy has continued to rise at a fast pace, as it rose another eight years to approximately sixty-eight years of age in 1970. *Id.*; "Population Explosion Among Older Americans" <http://www.infoplease.com/ipa/A0780132.html> (Aug. 28, 2002). Based on these data, the dramatic increase in tenures of Supreme Court justices since 1970 is understandable, given the enormous increase in life expectancy between the years of the most relevant period, from 1890 to 1930.

Chart 5.   Mean Age at Swearing In by Period of Joining Court
111 Terms (109 Justices), 1789 - October 2005

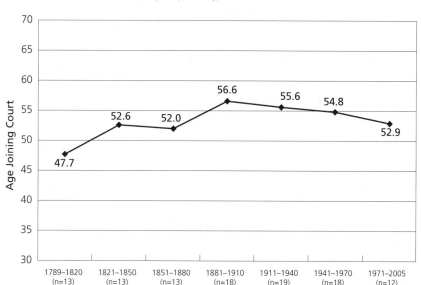

(1971–2005), fifty-three years, matching almost exactly that throughout the Court's history (1789–2005). Yet justices are retiring at much more advanced ages than ever before. Thus, the expansion of life tenure is caused not by Presidents' appointing younger justices, but by their living longer and retiring later.

A second possible cause for longer tenures—the increased politicization of the Court over the last century—may have made political motives a more important factor in justices' retirement decisions, which could have resulted in their deciding to stay on the Court longer for strategic reasons.[47] While it has always been recognized that the Court has had some influence on politics, in the last fifty to eighty years the Court has come to be seen as a more important player than ever before in effectuating political and social change.[48] As a

---

47. *See* Amar & Calabresi, *supra* n.3.

48. For example, in the 1920s and 1930s, the legal realists exposed the subjectivity of judicial decisionmaking and the role of judges' political viewpoints in the creation of law. The Warren Court then displayed a kind of social activism in the 1950s and 1960s that demonstrated how the Court could play an important role in shaping society and influencing politics, as evidenced most dramatically in *Brown v. Board of Education. See*, e.g., Garrow, *supra* n. 8, at 1041 ("[The] previously uncontroversial political status of the United States Supreme Court had been utterly transformed by the burgeoning conflict kicked off

result, the political views of individual justices have become correspondingly more important. To sitting justices contemplating retirement, the political views of a likely replacement (and hence those of the presiding President) may lead to timing their resignations strategically.[49] Such strategic resignations may have led more politically minded justices to stay on the Court longer and later in age, which has expanded the real-world, practical meaning of life tenure.

Politics and strategic factors in justices' retirement decisions may have been enhanced in recent years by frequent splits in party control of the Senate and the executive branch between 1968 and 2002. When one party controls both the Presidency and the Senate, that party should be more likely to name a justice who reflects its views.[50] For this reason, a justice thinking about retirement might feel more comfortable resigning if his or her party controlled both the White House and the Senate. But when different parties are in control, the likelihood of controversial confirmation hearings for any replacement goes up. A justice considering retirement in such a political environment will naturally want to avoid putting the country, and his party, through political controversy and will therefore wish to remain on the Court for longer periods of time. Thus, the political dynamic of the Presidency and the Senate being controlled by different parties could lead to longer tenures on the Court, older justices, and less regular vacancies. And because such split-party control of the Senate and the Presidency has been a mainstay of the last thirty-seven years, it could easily have contributed to the trend of justices staying longer on the Court during that period.

Indeed, strategic, political behavior by a series of justices may help explain part of the increase in justices' terms on the Supreme Court since 1970.[51] For example, Chief Justice Earl Warren purportedly (and unsuccessfully) tried to

---

by the Court's initial...ruling in *Brown*....''). Such developments have made the Court a more political body than it has ever been—certainly one that the public increasingly recognizes as being political. *See generally* William N. Eskridge, Jr., *Some Effects of Identity-Based Social Movements on Constitutional Law in the Twentieth Century*, 100 Mich. L. Rev. 2062 (2002) (noting the Court's increased social activism in the mid-twentieth century and the increasing public recognition of the Court as a means of effecting political change).

49. Amar & Calabresi, *supra* n. 3.

50. Of course, with the increasing politicization of the confirmation process, even this principle is no longer accurate. Indeed, as evidenced by the recent filibusters by Senate Democrats to block a number of lower-court nominations, majority control by a political party in the Senate is no longer necessarily sufficient to guarantee confirmation of a President's nomination of qualified nominees—even at the lower court level.

51. E-mail between Akhil Amar and Bill Stuntz, Aug. 9, 2002 and Aug. 13, 2002 (on file with authors). *See* DiTullio and Schochet, *supra* n. 18, at 1101–06.

time his resignation in order to let a Democratic President name his succes-sor, although in Warren's case this did not involve staying longer in office.[52] Justices Black and Douglas, both very liberal in their jurisprudential outlook, allegedly stayed on the Court as long as possible, in a futile attempt to avoid letting Presidents Nixon or Ford name their successors.[53] Likewise, Justices Marshall and Brennan supposedly stayed on the Court for as long as possible in order to wait out the twelve years of Presidents Reagan and Bush; ultimately, though, they had to retire.[54] Justice White, a Kennedy appointee, was alleged to have considered retirement in 1978 because of his concerns that President Carter would not be re-elected, and he ultimately remained in office long enough to allow fellow Democrat Bill Clinton to name his successor in 1993.[55] And some have speculated that several current justices have remained on the Court for as long as they have in order to avoid letting President Clinton (or President Bush, depending on the justice) name a successor.[56]

Anecdotal evidence aside, the historical data is mixed on whether there is statistically significant evidence that justices engage in strategic decision-mak-ing regarding their retirements.[57] Of the forty-nine justices who have died in office, twenty-nine died during the term of a President of the opposite party than that appointing them. In contrast, of the fifty-four justices who resigned, thirty-five resigned in the term of a President of the same party as the one who appointed them. The odds that a justice will retire when the President belongs to the justice's party or that she will die in office when the President belongs to a different party are significantly greater than the opposite occurrences. The odds of a justice resigning while the President is of the same party are 35:19;

---

52. *See* Oliver, *supra* n. 15, at 805–06 (noting the politicized nature of Chief Justice Warren's departure from the Court) (citing *G. White, Earl Warren: A Public Life* 306–08 (1982); Bernard Schwartz, *Super Chief* 680–83, 720–25 (1983)).

53. *See, e.g.,* Oliver, *supra* n. 15, at 806–07 (noting that Justice Douglas remained on the Court in order to give a Democratic President the ability to name his successor). Bob Woodward and Scott Armstrong's probing investigation of the Court, *The Brethren: Inside the Supreme Court* 161 (1979).

54. *See* Oliver, *supra* n. 15, at 808 (noting the speculation that then-Justices Brennan and Marshall would have been retired but for their desire not to let President Reagan name their successors).

55. Dennis Hutchinson, *The Man Who Once Was Whizzer White* (Free Press, 1998).

56. *See* Amar & Calabresi, *supra* n.3; Akhil Reed Amar & Vikram David Amar, *Should U.S. Supreme Court Justices be Term-Limited?: A Dialogue* <http://writ.corporate.find law.com/amar/20020823.html> (Aug. 23, 2002).

57. Farnsworth, *supra* n. 22, at 41, *citing* Timothy M. Hagel, *Strategic Retirements: A Political Model of Turnover on the United States Supreme Court*, 15 Pol. Behav. 25 (1993).

the odds of a justice dying while the President is of the same party are 20:29. The relative odds for these two outcomes is a statistically significant 2.7:1, thus supporting the hypothesis that justices make strategic retirement decisions, resigning when a President is of the same party, and not resigning (but dying while trying to hold out) when the President is of the opposite party. Although this analysis does not prove that justices have engaged in strategic gaming—and indeed, more sophisticated time-series analyses would be advisable—the data are consistent with that conclusion, which is bolstered by the anecdotal evidence. Engaging in this kind of strategic behavior—delaying retirement in order to allow a particular President to name one's successor—leads directly to longer tenures on the Court, retirements at an older age, and more time passing between vacancies.

A third explanation for the trend toward lengthier tenure is drastic improvement in the social status associated with being a justice and in the social perception of law and of judges more generally. For example, the life of a justice in the Court's early days was marked by time-consuming and physically demanding circuit-riding. Indeed, the arduous lifestyle of justices riding circuit is widely thought to have caused a number of premature resignations. With the lack of a stable working environment and the other numerous difficulties involved in being a Supreme Court justice in those days, it is not surprising that many retired relatively young and after short periods on the Court. Since the working conditions have improved dramatically with the elimination of circuit-riding, and since the prestige of being a Supreme Court justice has increased immensely, more recent justices have understandably wanted to serve longer tenures and have been able to serve later in their lives.

Of course, the impact of circuit-riding on the tenure and retirement age of justices cannot begin to explain the most recent upward trends in tenure since the mid-twentieth century. Circuit riding was abolished at the end of the nineteenth century, and longer life expectancies were already largely a reality by 1950; yet the longevity of Supreme Court justices appears to have surged most dramatically only in the last thirty-five years. This appearance is somewhat misleading for some of the longest serving retirees of the 1971–2005 period were Justices Black and Douglas, both appointed in the late 1930s, so the revolution in Supreme Court tenure lengths was, for them at least, well underway throughout the 1960s. Yet this trend toward greater longevity may suggest that recent enhancements in the general social perception of law and of judges—and of Supreme Court justices, in particular—may have made serving longer on the Court more desirable.

Fourth, increases in the size of the justices' law clerk support staff since the late 1960s have likely enabled justices to serve on the Court much longer.[58] The justices went from having two law clerks each prior to 1970, to four since 1978.[59] This doubling in the size of the law clerk support staff makes the job of serving as a justice on the Court much less demanding and allows for the delegation to law clerks of significant amounts of work. It is striking that the increase in the number of law clerks post-1970 corresponds with the period during which justices have been staying longer on the Court.

Finally, reductions in the workload of the Court—stemming both from Congress's near elimination of the Court's mandatory caseload and from the Court's drastic reduction in the number of certiorari petitions that it grants each year[60]—have probably also made it possible for justices to serve longer. In the last fifteen years, the Court has gone from hearing about 150 cases per year to only about 80. This, too, is a huge change—a staggering reduction of nearly half of the justices' workload. The fact of the matter is that the job of being a Supreme Court justice is much easier today with four law clerks, no mandatory jurisdiction, reduced grants of certiorari, and three months of summer vacation than was the case at other times in American history. These factors, coupled with lengthened life expectancies and the enhanced prestige of being a Supreme Court justice, help explain why justices are staying on the Court now for ever longer periods of time.

Consequences of the Expansion of Life Tenure

These historical trends—later retirement and less frequent vacancies— have three primary consequences for the current state of the judiciary: the Court's separation from democratic accountability, the increased politicization of the confirmation process, and the potential for enhanced mental decrepitude of those remaining too long on the bench.

A Supreme Court Divorced from Democratic Accountability

The Supreme Court is, by design, independent of the political branches of government.[61] Indeed, one of the most admired features of our judiciary is

---

58. E-mail between Bill Stuntz and Akhil Amar, Aug. 9, 2002 and Aug. 13, 2002 (on file with authors).

59. Richard Posner, *The Federal Courts: Challenge and Reform* 139 (1996).

60. To see the shift, *compare* Statistical Recap of Supreme Court's Workload During Last Three Terms, 62 U.S.L.W. 3124 (1993) (83 cases in the 1992–93 Term) *with* 59 U.S.L.W. 3064 (1990) (157 cases in the 1987–88 Term).

61. *See* William H. Rehnquist, *The Supreme Court* 209 (2001) ("The performance of the judicial branch of the United States government for a period of nearly two hundred

that Supreme Court justices (and other federal judges) decide cases without the threat of political recourse or retaliation by other elected officials.[62] The Constitution provides only two methods of democratic accountability for the justices: the appointment process and impeachment. The only democratic control over the Supreme Court beyond the selection and removal of its members is the very remote possibility that Supreme Court decisions be overturned by constitutional amendment.[63]

Supreme Court Justices are selected, first, by nomination by the popularly elected President, then confirmed by the people's representatives in the Senate. Conversely, the people, through their representatives in the House and the Senate, retain the power to remove Supreme Court justices. Other than these explicit mechanisms for controlling justices, the Court is subject to no other formal checks or balances.[64]

Democratic checks on the Court via constitutional amendment are unlikely, and impeachment has been of no use whatsoever for controlling the behavior of Supreme Court Justices. In 216 years of American history, not a single justice has

---

years has shown it to be remarkably independent of the other coordinate branches of that government.").

62. *Id.* at 210 ("We want our federal courts, and particularly the Supreme Court, to be independent of popular opinion when deciding the particular cases or controversies that come before them.").

63. Only four Supreme Court decisions have been overturned by constitutional amendment in 216 years. *Chisholm v. Georgia*, 2 U.S. 419 (1793) was overturned by the Eleventh Amendment. *Dred Scott v. Sandford*, 60 U.S. 393 (1857) was overturned by the Fourteenth Amendment. *Pollack v. Farmer's Loan & Trust Co.*, 158 U.S. 601 (1895) was overturned by the Sixteenth Amendment. And *Oregon v. Mitchell*, 400 U.S. 112 (1970) was overturned by the Twenty-Sixth Amendment.

64. To be sure, Congress or the public have indirect means to impart the public's political values onto the Court. For example, Congress holds the power to restructure judicial salaries, pensions, and other benefits, and it controls in large part the Court's jurisdiction, tools it could in theory use under some circumstances to attempt to influence the Court's decisionmaking, although such tools can hardly be considered effective means of rendering the Court democratically accountable.

Another, more important democratic check on the Supreme Court is public opinion. *See* Eskridge, *supra* n. 48, at 84 ("[P]olitics is the main constraint on an activist Court."). On most issues, public opinion establishes certain norms, or boundaries, the Court could not transgress without risking its ability to command respect in our democratic government. "Any Supreme Court decision...viewed as challenging a national equilibrium in favor of a norm or against a despised group will be subject to likely political discipline." *Id.* Although the Court's reliance on public opinion for its own legitimacy is an important check, it is ineffective as a practical tool for shaping the Court's jurisprudence, other than by setting very broad and permissive boundaries.

ever been successfully impeached and removed from office by the Senate.[65] This is not for lack of justices deserving of impeachment. Surely, at a minimum, those justices who decided the *Dred Scott* case deserved to be impeached and removed.

The appointment process is thus far and away the most direct and important formal source of democratic control on the Supreme Court.[66] Realistically, it is the only check that the other two branches have on the Supreme Court. Indeed, other countries that like the United States provide for political appointments to their respective constitutional courts do so precisely because "the democratic legitimacy of constitutional review rests upon the appointment of judges by elected authorities."[67] Even former Chief Justice William Rehnquist made essentially this point, writing that "the institution has been constructed in such a way that...the public will, in the person of the President of the United States...have something to say about the membership of the Court, and thereby indirectly about its decisions."[68]

For this process to work, turnover on the Court must be relatively frequent and regular. Although turnover occurred regularly from 1789 through 1970, since 1970 justices have stayed on the Court for longer than ever before, and the democratic instillation of public values on the Court through the selection of new judges has been correspondingly irregular. Moreover, as the Virginia Note-writers complain, when vacancies do occur they are sometimes packed together in hot spots, such that a number of years will pass without

---

65. "[I]mpeachment can never be used as a means of keeping judges accountable. Its hurdles are far too high.... Impeachment is a phantom menace." Prakash, *supra* n. 17, at 571, n.141. Of course, the Republicans' attempted impeachment of Federalist Justice Samuel Chase may serve as a counterexample to this general proposition, although that the attempt failed supports the proposition. *See* Raoul Berger, *Impeachment: The Constitutional Problems* 224–30 (1973); Martin H. Redish, *Judicial Discipline, Judicial Independence, and the Constitution: A Textual and Structural Analysis*, 72 S. Cal. L. Rev. 673, 676 (1999).

66. *See* Rehnquist, *supra* n. 61, at 223 ("The Supreme Court is to be independent of the legislative and executive branch of the government, yet by reason of vacancies occurring on that Court, it is to be subjected to indirect infusions of the popular will...."). Particularly if one believes that judges are inherently partisan, as legal realists claim, then monitoring the appointment process appears to be the most important means of controlling the political makeup of the Court. *See* Eskridge, *supra* n. 48, at 36–37.

67. Vicki C. Jackson & Mark Tushnet, *Comparative Constitutional Law* 474 (1999).

68. Chief Justice Rehnquist has noted:

When a vacancy occurs on the Court, it is entirely appropriate that that vacancy be filled by the president, responsible to a national constituency, as advised by the Senate, whose members are responsible to regional constituencies. Thus, public opinion has some say in who shall become judges of the Supreme Court.

Rehnquist, *supra* n. 61, at 210.

any openings and, suddenly, two, three, or even four seats may open up within the space of a few years, followed by another long period without any vacancies.[69] When this happens, the party in power at that particular time has a disproportionate impact on the Supreme Court, which can again prevent the American people from being regularly able to check the Court when it has strayed from following text and original meaning.

We think the problem of hot spots is a serious one that can contribute to the Court being out of step with the American people's understanding for long periods of time. For example, the Court of the "nine old men" was largely a function of the fact that Presidents Taft and Harding made six and four Supreme Court appointments, respectively, while Woodrow Wilson made only three appointments even though he served for longer as president than Taft and Harding combined. Other famous hot spots include Richard Nixon's appointment of four justices in five years as president, followed by Jimmy Carter's inability to appoint even a single justice in four years as president. It is hard to see why some four-year or eight-year presidents should get so many more appointments than others, particularly when the phenomenon may be in part a result of strategic retirement decisions by the justices. Spacing appointments out evenly, so each president gets two in four years, and eliminating the incentive to retire strategically, would in our view do a great deal to promote the public's and the justices' respect for the rule of law.

Of course, Supreme Court justices ought to be independent of at least some political pressures and with fixed eighteen-year nonrenewable terms they would still be quite independent. As Professor Martin Redish has noted, "Absent an independent judiciary free from basic political pressures and influences, individual rights intended to be insulated from majoritarian interferences would be threatened, as would the supremacy of the countermajoritarian Constitution as a whole."[70] The point, however, is that judicial independence is not the only value at stake here. If it were, then there would be no reason not to allow the justices to elect their own successors—as happens in some countries—because such an appointment process would lead to a judiciary that is even more independent of the political process than is the system we have now. The reason we do not allow the justices to pick their successors is precisely because we believe that the judiciary, just like the legislature and the executive, needs to be subject to the system of checks and balances. As a practical matter, the only check on the Supreme Court is the

---

69. *Id.* at 1116–1119. Professor Bill Stuntz, E-mail conversation between Akhil Amar and Bill Stuntz, Aug. 9, 2002 and Aug. 13, 2002 (on file with authors).

70. *Id.* at 683.

appointment process. With justices staying on the Court since 1970 for ten years longer than they have historically, and with vacancies on the Court opening up less than half as often, this key check on the Court has been allowed to atrophy. It is time for us to go back to our practice from 1789 of having independent justices who stay on the Court for closer to fifteen than twenty-six years.

In sum, judicial independence is not an unqualified good. What we really need is a balance between a substantial measure of judicial independence, combined with some degree of a democratic check on the Court. To get back to the right balance, we need to amend the Constitution to provide for fixed, staggered eighteen-year terms for Supreme Court justices. There should be no hot spots of vacancies and no eleven-year or even four-year droughts. There should also be no incentive to retire strategically and no ability of one political movement to lock the Court up for thirty years, as Republicans did at the start of the twentieth century and as Democrats did after the New Deal. A Supreme Court completely divorced from democratic accountability is an affront to the system of checks and balances. Accordingly, we should return to the practice that prevailed in this country from 1789 to 1970—when Supreme Court vacancies opened up on average once every two years and when justices stayed on the Court for closer to fifteen years than to twenty-six years.

Increased Politicization of the Confirmation Process

A second cost incurred by less frequent vacancies and by justices serving for ever longer periods of time is that the process for confirming all federal judges can become so political and contentious as to grind the process itself to a halt.[71] Under the current system, the irregular occurrence of vacancies on the Supreme Court means that when one does arise, the stakes are enormous, for neither the President nor the Senate can know when the next vacancy might arise. Moreover, a successful nominee has the potential to remain on the Court for a very long (and uncertain) period of time. So much is at stake in appointing a new justice that the President and the Senate (especially when controlled by the party opposite the President) inevitably get drawn into a political fight that hurts the Court both directly and indirectly—directly, since it is deprived of one of its nine members, and indirectly, since rancorous confirmation battles lower the prestige of the Court.

---

71. The Virginia Note writers also make this point. *See* Note, *Saving This Honorable Court*, supra n. 18, at 1139–1144.

Of course, a breakdown in the confirmation process is nothing new. Political battles between the President and the Senate over Supreme Court confirmations have occurred throughout history.[72] However, in the last twenty years, with the lack of vacancies and the lengthening duration of the justices' terms, the fighting between the political branches over the confirmation of Supreme Court justices has reached new lows. The 1987 confirmation hearings of Judge Robert H. Bork and the 1991 confirmation hearings of Justice Clarence Thomas were among the most bitterly fought Supreme Court confirmations in all of American history. Moreover, the high profile confirmation fights over Bork and Thomas created a powerful (and undesirable) reason for Presidents to find candidates without paper trails.[73] Thus, the increased politicization of the confirmation process for Supreme Court justices in recent years has undermined the ability of the President to fulfill his constitutional duty to appoint the best new justices to the Court and even the ability of the Supreme Court itself to function effectively.

Indeed, fighting over federal judicial appointments in general has been so intense that it almost caused the confirmation process for lower federal court of appeals judges to break down completely. Many of the current President Bush's court of appeals nominees could hardly get hearings from the Democrat-controlled Senate Judiciary Committee between 2001 and 2003, and more recently Bush's nominees have faced filibusters and other obstructionist tactics by the Democratic minority in the Republican-controlled Senate. Between 1995 and 2001, President Bill Clinton met similar resistance to his lower federal court judicial nominees from the Republican-controlled Senate, which refused to grant hearings to such qualified judicial nominees as the current Harvard Law School Dean, Elena Kagan. Although it is debatable whether Supreme Court confirmations have ever before been so politicized,[74] there is no question that the fighting over court of appeals seats in the last decade has reached a new low. The irregular occurrence of vacancies on the Supreme

---

72. Indeed, as Professor Monaghan notes, in the first 105 years of our history, approximately one-fourth of all nominees to the Supreme Court were rejected by the Senate. Monaghan, *supra* n. 17, at 1202 (noting the contentiousness throughout history of Senate confirmation of Supreme Court candidates, and the intensely political nature of these confirmation battles).

73. *See* Amar & Amar, *supra* n. 56 (noting the tendency towards stealth candidates because of the heightened politicization of the appointment process).

74. Indeed, Professor Monaghan seems to argue that the Senate plays a smaller role in Supreme Court confirmations than it has historically. *See* Monaghan, *supra* n. 17, at 1202–03.

Court and the lengthening terms of that Court's justices have led to infirmities in the confirmation process that could be avoided with a shorter, fixed, and staggered tenure.

A Rise in "Mental Decrepitude"[75] on the Court

The problem of justices suffering mental or physical health problems while serving on the Court, though occurring throughout American history, has arisen more frequently in recent years. This serious and persistent problem has been recognized by many as one that threatens the legitimacy of the Court.[76] The illnesses have on occasion been so severe as to deprive justices of the ability to handle their duties competently without substantial help and influence from their law clerks and other staff. Professor David Garrow, who recently provided a comprehensive account of the historical evidence pertaining to the cases of mental decrepitude on the Court, notes that "the history of the Court is replete with repeated instances of justices casting decisive votes or otherwise participating actively in the Court's work when their colleagues and/or families had serious doubts about their mental capacities."[77] In fact, the recurring problem of mentally incapacitated justices has from time to time led to efforts by the American Bar Association, Congressional members, and even executive branch officials to institute a mandatory retirement age for Supreme Court justices or for all federal judges.[78]

Although mental decrepitude of justices has been a problem on and off for 200 years, David Garrow reports that "a thorough survey of Supreme Court historiography reveals that mental decrepitude has been an even more frequent problem on the twentieth-century Court than it was during the nineteenth."[79] Before the twentieth century, the Court was plagued by only five justices whose

---

75. This is the term used by Professor David Garrow. *See* Garrow, *supra* n. 8.

76. *See* Amar & Calabresi, *supra* n. 3; Easterbrook, *supra* n. 7; McGinnis, *supra* n. 17, at 543; Monaghan, *supra* n. 17, at 1211–12; Oliver, *supra* n. 15, at 813–16.

77. *Id.* at 995.

78. *See id.* at 1018–26 (detailing the movement for mandatory retirement age proposals during the New Deal, led by executive officials and members of Congress); *id.* at 1028–43 (detailing the movement in the 1940s and 1950s among Congressional members and the American Bar Association for a constitutional amendment imposing a mandatory retirement age on federal judges); *id.* at 1056–65 (detailing the movement in the 1970s and 1980s by the American Bar Association and Congressional leaders for a constitutional amendment or a statute imposing a mandatory retirement age limit on federal judges, but perhaps excluding Supreme Court Justices).

79. Garrow, *supra* n. 8, at 995.

mental abilities were diminished; in the twentieth century, at least twelve justices served longer than they should have.[80] Of the justices retiring in the 182 years from 1789 through 1970, twelve were decrepit; of the justices retiring in the thirty-five years since 1970, five were allegedly suffering from mental or serious physical decrepitude making them unfit to serve.[81] Thus, on average, a decrepit justice retired every fifteen years before 1970; since 1970, a decrepit justice has retired every seven years. Viewed by the years of their retirements,[82] more mentally decrepit justices have retired from the Court in the 1971–2000 period than at any other thirty-year period in American history. Of the six justices with the longest tenures on the Court, four (67%) were mentally decrepit (Justices Field, Black, Brennan, and Douglas). Of the twenty-seven jus-

---

80. *Id.* at 1084–85. Professor Garrow notes that perhaps two more justices from the pre-twentieth century might have suffered from mental decrepitude: Justices Rutledge and Cushing. *Id.* However, in Justice Rutledge's second appointment he never was confirmed to serve on the Court and served only several months as a recess appointee. As Professor Garrow admits, there was not enough evidence of mental decrepitude regarding Justice Cushing to conclusively count him in the tally. *Id.* at 998–1001.

81. As Professor Garrow details, the following justices, who all retired prior to 1970, were at some point evidently suffering from mental or physical decrepitude that affected their ability to perform their duties: Justice Henry Baldwin, Justice Robert C. Grier, Justice Nathan Clifford, Justice Ward Hunt, Justice Stephen J. Field, Justice Melville Fuller, Justice Joseph McKenna, Chief Justice William H. Taft, Justice Oliver Wendell Holmes, Justice Frank Murphy, Justice Sherman Minton, and Justice Charles E. Whittaker. *Id.* at 1001–51. The following justices, who all retired after 1970, were recorded by Professor Garrow as having been affected by mental or serious physical decrepitude while serving in office: Justice Hugo L. Black, Justice William O. Douglas, Justice Lewis F. Powell, Justice William J. Brennan, and Justice Thurgood Marshall. *Id.* at 1051–80.

82. Using the same thirty-year periods from above: Between 1789 and 1820, no retiring Justices were decrepit (except perhaps for Justices Rutledge and Cushing, who, as we detail *supra* n. 80, we do not count among the decrepit justices). Between 1821 and 1850, only one Justice, Henry Baldwin (1844), retired after having served on the Court while stricken by mental decrepitude. Between 1851 and 1880, only one justice, Robert C. Grier (1870), served on the Court despite being mentally incapacitated and physically ill. Between 1881 and 1910, four Justices, Nathan Clifford (1881), Ward Hunt (1882), Stephen J. Field (1897), and Melville Fuller (1910), served on the Court while being either mentally or physically disabled. Between 1911 and 1940, three justices, Joseph McKenna (1925), Chief Justice William H. Taft (1930), and Oliver Wendell Holmes (1932), all were stricken by mental incapacity during part of their tenures on the Court. Between 1941 and 1970, three justices, Frank Murphy (1949), Sherman Minton (1956), and Charles E. Whittaker (1962), remained on the Court for some period of time despite being mentally and/or physically incapacitated. *Id.* at 1001–51. Yet in the period from 1971–2000, five justices were recorded by Professor Garrow as having been affected by mental or physical decrepitude while serving in office. *Id.* at 1051–80.

tices with the longest tenures on the Court, ten (37%) were similarly mentally incompetent to serve by the time they died or retired. Of the twenty-three justices who served longer than eighteen years and who retired since 1897, fully eight (35%) were mentally or seriously physically decrepit. Perhaps most stark is that nearly half the last eleven justices to leave office (45%) were mentally decrepit and half of the last six justices to leave office were mentally decrepit in their last years on the Court.

For those commentators who pretend the current system does not need reform — "If it ain't broke, don't fix it"[83] — it is time to recognize that the system is definitely broken. Whether one uses as the relevant rate of decrepitude 35% (of those leaving office after serving more than eighteen years since 1897), 45% (of the last eleven justices leaving office), or 50% (of the last six justices leaving the bench), the rate is unreasonably high. Mental decrepitude, a rare problem in the past, now strikes from a third to a half of justices before they are willing to retire.

The most common responses to the problem of mental decrepitude on the Court, as detailed by Professor Garrow, have been proposals for a constitutional amendment or a statute imposing a mandatory retirement age upon Supreme Court Justices.[84] But a mandatory retirement age for justices and

---

83. See Monaghan, *supra* n. 17, at 1212.

84. Such proposals have been supported by major movements three times. First, instead of FDR's court-packing scheme during the New Deal, several executive branch officials pushed for the creation of a compulsory retirement age measure, and several Senators even proposed a constitutional amendment imposing mandatory retirement at age seventy for all federal judges. Garrow, *supra* n. 8, at 1019–20, 1024–26. However, the likely delays of passing a constitutional amendment, and thus the lack of short-term impact of such a proposal, led FDR to disregard this idea and push instead for his court-packing statute that could have more immediate effect. *Id.* at 1020–21.

Second, another campaign for a constitutional amendment imposing mandatory retirement for Supreme Court justices at age seventy-five occurred in the late 1940s and early 1950s, initiated by author Edwin A. Falk. This campaign was supported and led primarily by the American Bar Association, and several members of Congress introduced the idea as a formally proposed amendment. *Id.* at 1028–43. Importantly, this proposal received strong support by former Justice Owen J. Roberts, *id.* at 1040, and in the course of holding hearings, the Senate Judiciary Committee even concluded that "continued active service by Justices over the age of 75 tends to weaken public respect for the Supreme Court." Composition and Jurisdiction of the Supreme Court, S. Rep. No. 1091, 83rd Cong., 2d Sess. 10, at 5 (Mar.24, 1954), reproduced in Garrow, supra n. 8, at 1037. However, this second wave of support for a mandatory retirement age eventually collapsed after a series of Warren Court rulings shifted the focus of public attention to other matters. Garrow, supra n. 8, at 1042–43. Third, in the mid- to late-1970s, there was yet a third reform ef-

judges would be unfair in that it would blindly discriminate against judicial service on the basis of age in a harsh way, one that does not take into account the actual mental condition of a given individual.[85] A term limit on the tenure of Supreme Court justices, such as that we propose, would achieve nearly all the goals intended by a mandatory retirement age in a more uniform and respectful manner, without discriminating against a member of the Court based solely on age.

The Rarity of Life Tenure in the World's Constitutional Courts

The United States is alone "among the constitutional courts of western democracies…that [have] had judicial review since at least the early 1980s,"[86] and it is alone among all but one of its own states in providing its justices with life tenure. The American system of life tenure for Supreme Court justices has been rejected by all other major democratic nations in setting up their highest constitutional courts.[87] Even the nation upon whose legal system the U.S.

---

fort to set a mandatory retirement age for federal judges, perhaps arising as a reaction to the decrepit state of Justice William O. Douglas. *Id.* at 1056–57. This campaign was led by several members of Congress, most notably Senator Sam Nunn, and contemplated mandatory age retirements through statute, as well as by constitutional amendment. *Id.* at 1059–61. Ultimately, legislators rejected the application of a mandatory retirement age on Supreme Court justices, and instead passed a statute that merely created a mechanism for the Judicial Conference to recommend to Congress that it impeach lower federal court judges who were deemed to be mentally incompetent. *Id.* at 1062–65.

Apart from these more concerted movements, there have been a number of other significant informal proposals for mandatory retirement age requirements. For example, Chief Justice William H. Taft wrote a book in 1913, *see* William Howard Taft, *Popular Government: Its Essence, Its Permanence and Its Perils* 159 (Yale 1913), that proposed mandatory judicial retirement at age seventy. Ironically, Taft later served until he was seventy-two and, according to his biographer, beyond the point at which he was mentally healthy. Garrow, *supra* n. 8, at 1016–17 Likewise, Charles Fairman, in 1938, argued for a mandatory retirement age in order to prevent disabled justices from continuing in office. Charles Fairman, *The Retirement of Federal Judges*, 51 Harv. L. Rev. 397, 433 (1938). Indeed, Professor Garrow himself recommends a mandatory retirement age requirement. Garrow, *supra* n. 8, at 1086–87.

85. *See Saving This Honorable Court, supra* n. 18, at 1133–1137.

86. Jackson & Tushnet, *supra* n. 67 at 489.

87. By "constitutional courts," we mean to compare the U.S. Supreme Court to the most similar courts of other nations, which are the highest courts in other countries that pass on the constitutionality of laws passed by other government bodies. *See generally* Jackson & Tushnet, *supra* n. 67, at 488–542 (discussing the structure, composition, appointment

legal system is based—England—has eliminated the guarantee of life tenure for its judges. Every major democratic nation, without exception,[88] instead provides for some sort of limited tenure of office for its constitutional court judges.[89] Members of the constitutional courts in France,[90] Italy,[91] Spain,[92] Portugal,[93] Germany,[94] and Russia[95] serve fixed, limited terms of between six and

---

and jurisdiction of various constitutional courts around the world). In many countries, "constitutional courts" are specialized courts that are not necessarily the highest courts in that country, since in those countries not all courts can conduct constitutional review. *See id.* at 460–61. Yet these courts represent the most apt comparison to the U.S. Supreme Court, since these constitutional courts perform the same fundamental role as the U.S. Supreme Court in its constitutional review aspects. *Id.* at 462.

88. There is one country that has the potential to be considered an exception, though we do not consider it to be, and the leading comparative constitutional law textbook agrees. *See* Jackson & Tushnet, *supra* n. 67, at 540. In Russia, there is the Russian Constitutional Court and the Russian Supreme Court. The Russian Constitution does not explicitly create one "highest" court in Russia, and proponents of both the Russian Constitutional Court and the Russian Supreme Court claim their respective court as the "highest" court. *See* Gennady M. Danilenko & William Burnham, *Law and Legal System of the Russian Federation* 57–58 (2000). While the Russian Supreme Court grants life tenure to its members, judges on the Russian Constitutional Court serve twelve-year, nonrenewable terms of office. Since our focus is on the major constitutional courts around the world, we count the Russian Constitutional Court, which is arguably the highest court in Russia designed to pass on the constitutionality of government actions. *See* Jackson & Tushnet, *supra* n. 67, at 540 (referring to the Russian Constitutional Court, which is limited by a twelve-year nonrenewable term, as the relevant court to comparatively analyze). Thus, in our view, the most relevant court to compare, the Russian Constitutional Court, fits within the overall global trend of limited tenure. To the extent that one views the Russian Supreme Court as the appropriate point of comparison, however, it would be the one exception to our general rule. *See generally* Danilenko & Burnham, *supra*, at 62–63 (discussing the distinction between the Russian Constitutional and Supreme Courts, and the various roles and characteristics of each).

89. Jackson & Tushnet, *supra* n. 67, at 489.

90. Judges on the French Constitutional Council serve nine-year, nonrenewable terms. Fr. Const. art. 56; John Bell, *French Constitutional Law* 34 (1992).

91. Members of the Italian Constitutional Court serve nine-year terms, which are not immediately renewable. Jackson & Tushnet, *supra* n. 67, at 490–91.

92. Members of the Spanish Constitutional Tribunal serve nine-year, renewable terms. *Id.*

93. Members of the Portuguese Constitutional Court serve six-year terms. *Id.*

94. Members of the Federal Constitutional Court of Germany serve twelve-year, nonrenewable terms. Jackson & Tushnet, *supra* n. 67, at 490–91; David P. Currie, *The Constitution of the Federal Republic of Germany* 27 (1994).

95. Judges on the Russian Constitutional Court serve twelve-year nonrenewable terms. However, as noted previously, it is not clear that the Russian Constitutional Court is the

twelve years. Moreover, judges on Germany's constitutional court also face a mandatory retirement age of sixty-eight, in addition to the twelve-year, non-renewable term.[96] Likewise, members of the Russian Constitutional Court face a mandatory retirement age of seventy, in addition to the fixed term of twelve years.[97] Through term limits, many countries provide for regular, relatively frequent rotation in the membership of their constitutional courts.

Instead of fixed term limits, many other countries limit the tenure of their constitutional court justices and judges by imposing a mandatory retirement age. For example, the highest courts in such western common law democracies as Canada,[98] Australia,[99] and England[100] enjoy tenures limited by a mandatory retirement age of sixty-five, seventy, or seventy-five, respectively. In addition, other major countries, such as India[101] and Japan[102] have instituted a mandatory retirement age in order to limit the tenure of members of their respective constitutional courts. Like Germany and Russia, South Africa adds a compulsory retirement age onto a fixed term of office,[103] further limiting the tenure of its highest constitutional court judges, though not to the exacting degree that fixed term limits would achieve.

Thus, every other single major democratic nation we know of—all of which drafted their respective constitutions or otherwise established their supreme constitutional courts after 1789—has chosen not to follow the American model of guaranteeing life tenure to justices equivalent to those on our highest court. In light of the strong worldwide trend against having lifetime tenure for members of the highest courts, the U.S. Supreme Court system of life tenure is truly an anomaly.

---

single "highest" court in Russia, and members of the other possible supreme tribunal enjoy life tenure. *See* Jackson & Tushnet, *supra* n. 67 at 540.

96. Jackson & Tushnet, *supra* n. 67, at 490–91; Currie, *supra* n.94, at 27.

97. Jackson & Tushnet, *supra* n. 67, at 540.

98. Members of the Canadian Supreme Court face a mandatory retirement age of 75. Jackson & Tushnet, *supra* n. 67, at 490–91.

99. Members of the Australian High Court face a mandatory retirement age of 70. *Id.*

100. Members of the English House of Lords' Lords of Appeal in Ordinary face a mandatory retirement age of 75. Judicial Pensions and Retirement Act, 1993, c.8, part II, §26(4) & (5) (Eng.); *see also* Henry J. Abraham, *The Judicial Process* 280–82 (7th ed. 1998).

101. Members of the constitutional court of India face a mandatory retirement age of 65. Jackson & Tushnet, *supra* n. 67, at 489.

102. Judges on the Japanese Supreme Court face a mandatory retirement age of 70. Kenneth L. Port, *Comparative Law: Law and the Legal Process in Japan* 65–67 (1996).

103. Members of the Constitutional Court of South Africa serve nonrenewable twelve-year terms and also are compelled to retire by age 70. Jackson & Tushnet, *supra* n. 67, at 489.

Not only is lifetime tenure a rarity for judges worldwide, but, within the United States, nearly all states considering the question since 1789 have decided against giving life tenure to the members of their courts of last resort. Of the fifty U.S. states, only one—Rhode Island—provides for a system of life tenure for its Supreme Court Justices,[104] and even in Rhode Island, Supreme Court justices can be recalled by a majority vote of the State Legislature. Every one of the remaining states provides for an explicit limit on the tenure of its highest court members, in varying forms.[105] Justices on the high courts in Massachusetts and New Hampshire face a mandatory retirement age of seventy.[106] North Carolina's justices, who must be re-elected every eight years, must nonetheless retire at seventy-two.[107] The other forty-six states all provide for limited terms of office for the justices of their highest courts, with the terms ranging from six to fourteen years.[108] Moreover, all states with an intermediate appellate court have opted against providing life tenure for the members of that court as well.[109] The nearly unanimous consensus against life tenure for state judges, both on the highest courts and on intermediate appellate courts, is telling, and it provides further evidence of the undesirability of maintaining a system of lifetime tenure in the present day.

---

104. The Council of State Governments, 37 *The Book of the States* 309, table 5.1 (Keon S. Chi et al. eds., 2005).

105. *See id.* at 309–10. New Jersey does provide for tenure following an initial seven-year term limit, however. *See id.*

106. *Id.* at 309.

107. *Id.*; N.C.G.S. §7A-4.20 ("No justice or judge of the General Court of Justice may continue in office beyond the last day of the month in which he attains his seventy-second birthday, but justices and judges so retired may be recalled for periods of temporary service as provided in Subchapters II and III of this chapter.").

108. The Council of State Governments, 33 *The Book of the States* 309–10, table 5.1 (Keon S. Chi et al. eds., 2005). States with six-year terms for the justices of their highest courts are Alabama, Arizona, Florida, Georgia, Idaho, Kansas, Minnesota, Nebraska ("[m]ore than three years for first election and every six years thereafter"), Nevada, Ohio, Oklahoma, Oregon, Texas, Vermont, and Washington. Maine and New Jersey provide for seven-year terms. Arkansas, Connecticut, Iowa, Kentucky, Michigan, Mississippi, Montana, New Mexico, North Carolina, South Dakota, Tennessee, and Wyoming all provide for eight-year terms. States with ten-year terms are Alaska, Colorado, Hawaii, Illinois, Indiana ("[i]nitial two years; retention ten years"), Louisiana, Maryland, North Dakota, Pennsylvania, South Carolina, Utah ("[i]nitial three years; retention ten years"), and Wisconsin. California, Delaware, Missouri, Virginia, and West Virginia provide for twelve-year terms. New York provides for fourteen-year terms for members of its highest court. *Id.*

109. *Id.* at 133–34.

This comparative analysis—both outside the United States and within it—bolsters the case against life tenure and raises this question: Given the trend in all other jurisdictions as well as the pathologies associated with life tenure, if the Philadelphia Convention were reconvened today, would the Framers still opt for life tenure?

Term Limits for the Supreme Court

Historically, the most powerful case for life tenure for Supreme Court Justices was made by Alexander Hamilton in the Federalist, Number 78. But Hamilton's argument has not stood the test of time. As Professor Prakash notes: "Some of [Alexander Hamilton's] empirical claims or predictions [in Federalist 78 defending life tenure] no longer ring true…[and o]ther assertions never held water and contradicted the Constitution's first principles."[110]

First, the Supreme Court is far more powerful today than Hamilton could ever have imagined in the 1780s, so it is far less in need of protection from the President and Congress than Hamilton expected.[111] Second, life tenure is no longer justified, as Hamilton claimed in Federalist 78, by the need to encourage the best candidates to aspire to be justices. Today, other incentives lure the best candidates to want to be Supreme Court justices.[112] Third, Hamilton's desire to insulate the Supreme Court from public opinion, more generally, has been turned on its head, since, as we believe, the post-1970 Supreme Court is, if anything, too insulated from public opinion, because justices stay on the Court for an average of twenty-six years and because vacancies open up only once every three years or so. The Supreme Court should be made more responsive to the popular understanding of the Constitution's meaning, not less so.[113] Fourth, contrary to Hamilton's argument that life tenure is necessary for us to attract justices who will follow the Constitution, life tenure does not cause the justices to follow the text and origi-

---

110. Prakash, *supra* n. 17, at 574–75. Professor Monaghan also suggests that the defense for life tenure once made by Hamilton is no longer "fully persuasive," and argues that both a term limit and an age limit should be placed upon Supreme Court justices' tenure in order to account for the fact that individuals are now able to serve on the Court for "four decades." Monaghan, *supra* n. 17, at 1211–12.

111. Prakash, *supra* n. 17, at 575–76.

112. *Id.* at 577.

113. *Id.* at 578.

nal meaning of the Constitution. In fact, as Prakash argues, life-tenured justices are less likely to be textualists and originalists, not more so.[114] Long tenures on the Supreme Court can, and do, seem to corrupt the justices and to cause them to become policymakers, instead of followers of the law. Thus, Alexander Hamilton's defense of life tenure in Federalist 78 rings hollow today.[115]

All these arguments against life tenure for Supreme Court justices support our belief that the United States should adopt a system of term limits for its justices. The section below lays out constitutional, statutory, and other informal ways of imposing an eighteen-year term limit on Supreme Court justices.

Imposing Term Limits through Constitutional Amendment

We start with a proposed amendment to the United States Constitution. Article III, section 1 of the Constitution says that "the Judges, both of the supreme and inferior Courts, shall hold their Offices during good Behaviour...."[116] It is well established that the Good Behavior Clause guarantees life tenure to all federal judges. As a result, all the advocates of Supreme Court term limits to date, except for Professors Carrington and Cramton,[117] have conceded that life tenure can only be limited by means of a constitutional amendment.[118] We agree, and we take up the merits of such an amendment below.

---

114. Prakash, *supra* n. 17, at 578–80. This is a point also made by Professor McGinnis, who proposes short (six month or one year) periods of office for Supreme Court justices because of the corrupting influence that long periods of time can have on justices' fidelity to the text of the Constitution. *See* McGinnis, *supra* n. 17, at 541–43.

115. *See* Prakash, *supra* n. 17, at 581 ("Life tenure, by completely insulating judges from accountability, ignores these fundamental truths of self-government. If people could be trusted with life tenure, we would not need government, let alone the courts. The very fact that we need government suggests that we cannot tolerate life tenure.").

116. U.S. Const. art. III, § 1.

117. *See infra* Carrington & Cramton, *The Supreme Court Renewal Act*, pp. 467–471.

118. *See* Silberman, *supra* n. 17, at 687; Oliver, *supra* n. 15, at 800 n.9; Easterbrook, *supra* n. 7; Prakash, *supra* n. 17, at 567. *But see* McGinnis, *supra* n. 17, at 545–46 (noting the possibility of instituting "Supreme Court riding," his version of a term limits proposal, through statute); Amar & Calabresi, *supra* n. 3 (noting the possibility of a statutory term limits proposal).

The Term Limits Proposal

We propose that, in accordance with the Article V amendment process,[119] Congress and the states should pass a constitutional amendment imposing an eighteen-year, staggered term limit on the tenure of Supreme Court justices.[120] Under our proposal, each justice would serve for eighteen years, and the terms would be established so that a vacancy on the Court would occur every two years beginning at the beginning of the summer recess in every odd-numbered year.[121] These terms would be structured so the turnover of justices would occur during the first and third year of a President's four-year term.[122] This would diminish the possibility of a Supreme Court appointment's being held up by Senate confirmation so as to deprive the President of the ability to nominate either of his two justices.[123] The terms would also be set up so an outgoing justice would complete his tenure on the last day of the Supreme Court's term and the new justice could be confirmed in time to begin serving his term in October, before the beginning of the Supreme Court's next term.[124] The

---

119. *See* U.S. Const. art. V.

120. As we noted in the Introduction, and as we discuss below, this portion of our term limits proposal closely follows the proposal made by Professor Philip Oliver, *supra* n. 15.

121. This configuration assumes that the size of the Court remains stable at nine members. In the event that the size of the Court were to be altered, then the terms would need to be changed to reflect it. One possibility is to include in the constitutional amendment a provision that would fix the size of the Court at nine. *See* Oliver, *supra* n. 15, at 822–24. However, as Professor Oliver notes, the power to change the size of the Supreme Court, though not used since 1870, represents an important check that Congress has over the Court. *Id.* at 823–34.

122. For example, if this amendment were currently in effect, President Bush would have been entitled to appoint a new justice in the summer of 2001 and in the summer of 2003.

123. *See* Oliver, *supra* n. 15, at 824–25. Indeed, as Oliver points out, having Supreme Court appointments fall in Presidential election years would be a problem, as history shows that the Senate has oftentimes been willing to stall on nominations in order to deprive the sitting President of the Supreme Court nomination and to permit the next President to make the selection. *See generally* Abraham, *supra* n. 32 (summarizing the history of Supreme Court nominations and noting that Senate confirmations have sometimes been stalled in order to deprive an outgoing President of the ability to nominate an individual to the Court).

124. Oliver, *supra* n. 15, at 824. Of course, as this may have the unwanted effect of constitutionalizing the current structuring of the Court's term, this aspect of our proposal could be left out of the express proposal and instead be worked out through practice or by statute.

aim of such term limits would be to guarantee that, while accommodating the Court's schedule, every elected President would make two appointments to the Supreme Court. The justices' terms would be nonrenewable: no justice could be re-appointed to a second term.[125] This would help guarantee the independence of the justices by removing any incentive for them to curry favor with politicians in order to win a second term on the High Court. Retired justices would be permitted to sit, if they wanted to, on the lower federal courts.

Two problems concerning implementation of our proposal merit special discussion: (1) its application to the current justices or to the sitting President and its phase-in period, and (2) the treatment of vacancies that arise midterm due to the death or early resignation of a justice.

First, we propose that any term limit would be prospective only and that it would take effect only upon the election in 2008 of a new President. Although a constitutional amendment abolishing life tenure and retroactively replacing it with a system of term limits would by definition be permissible both as to the current President and as to the current nine justices, such a retroactive application of a Term Limits Amendment would be both unfair and unnecessary. Given that the current justices were appointed to the Court on the assumption that they would have life tenure, it would be unfair to them, as well as to the appointing parties (both the President and the Senate), to alter the arrangement struck in the appointment. Moreover, given the controversy that a retroactive amendment might generate, and given that a gradual phase-in of a system of term limits is feasible, it is unnecessary and unwise to apply the term limits to the current justices.[126]

---

125. *See* Oliver, *supra* n. 15, at 801. Professor Oliver, however, has a provision by which a successor justice, if he is appointed to a term of less than two years and the appointing President will still be President when the next vacancy becomes available, will automatically be reappointed to serve a full term. *Id.* We do not include such a provision in our proposal because it permits justices to serve longer than eighteen years, although we recognize that it has some appeal and are not entirely opposed to it.

126. Professor Oliver advocates making his term limits proposal applicable to current justices, saying that the amendment needed to take immediate effect in order to alleviate the problems that life tenure creates. *See* Oliver, *supra* n. 15, at 825–26. However, given the likelihood that several openings on the Court could occur in the next few years, it is probable that our amendment, even if made applicable to current justices, would not advance the effect of the proposal. In other words, it is unlikely that delaying the application of our term limits proposal would have any appreciable impact on the benefits of the proposal.

Similar concerns apply to the sitting President and lead to the conclusion that any term limits proposal should apply only to new appointments made by the next-elected President after ratification. Most obviously, applying any term limits system to any sitting President might raise important fairness concerns, especially a president elected after substantial controversy over which presidential candidate would get to appoint life-tenured justices to the Supreme Court. Instead, like the precedent set when the two-term limit on Presidents was adopted, the current incumbent justices and President should be exempt from this proposed change. Thus, we propose that our term limits system (if passed immediately) become effective following the next general election, in 2009 if a term limits proposal were passed today. Such a phase-in of Supreme Court term limits is the only fair way to accomplish this important constitutional change.

Instituting our proposal without immediately applying it to the current justices or the sitting President would not be difficult. For example, suppose the amendment were ratified immediately.[127] When the first new vacancy occurs after a new president takes office, the new justice would be put into the eighteen-year slot that, if an odd year, started that year. If the vacancy arose in an even year, the justice would be put into the slot that started the following year, and she would also serve the additional year until that slot began. So if the first vacancy occurred in 2009, the first transitional justice would be appointed to an eighteen-year term starting in 2009. If the first vacancy arose in 2010, then the newly appointed justice would be appointed to the slot beginning in 2011, plus the period between appointment in 2010 and the beginning of the slot in 2011. If the next vacancy occurred in 2015, then the slot starting that year would be filled. If the next slot were already filled with a transitional justice, then the justice would be appointed to the next open slot, plus the time until that slot began. Thus, during the phase-in period, some justices would be appointed to the Court for eighteen years, while others would be appointed to somewhat longer terms. Of course, those who replaced these transitional justices would serve only eighteen years. If an associate justice were elevated to be chief justice, she would remain in her eighteen-year slot, and leave the Court after serving a total of eighteen years.

Another special problem that might arise under our system of term limits is the early death or resignation of a justice. Indeed, the fact that we propose

---

127. As we stated above, however, we do not propose immediate application of the amendment. Rather, we argue that the proposed amendment should apply only after an interceding Presidential election occurs. But here we suppose immediate application for purposes of illustrating the amendment's phase-in procedure.

an eighteen-year term, which is longer than the fifteen-year average tenure of Supreme Court justices throughout history,[128] would seem to make the occurrence of early deaths or resignations likely. To handle this situation, we propose that if a justice dies or resigns prior to the expiration of her term, an interim justice would be appointed through the regular confirmation process (Presidential nomination and Senate confirmation) to fill the remainder of the deceased or retired justice's term. For example, if a justice were to leave the Court following her tenth year of service, the sitting President at the time of death or resignation would be entitled to appoint a replacement justice who, subject to confirmation by the Senate, could then serve only the remaining eight years of the departing justice's eighteen-year term. She would then be constitutionally ineligible for reappointment to the Court. This method of naming successor justices to complete only the original eighteen-year term of the predecessor justice would enable mid-term turnover without sacrificing the benefits of staggered term limits—namely, regularizing the updating of the membership of the Supreme Court.[129] This would also eliminate the current incentive of justices to time their retirements strategically, since retiring early would not result in one's successor being able to serve longer than the eighteen-year term to which one was appointed initially.[130]

---

128. *See supra* Chart 1.

129. Professor Oliver raises the possible objection that, if the early retirement of a justice were to leave a short period on the Court, the best-qualified candidates may be uninterested in the position of succeeding the justice for a brief period. Oliver, *supra* n. 15, at 827. However, we agree with Oliver that "when one considers the prestige of the United States Supreme Court in the American legal community, the argument sinks of its own weight," since plenty of tremendously qualified individuals "would form a very long line for the privilege of serving for a week, not to speak of a year or two." *Id.* Moreover, since our proposal would provide for automatic designation of even a successor justice to a federal circuit court, there would be additional incentives for the best-qualified candidates to take a Supreme Court position for even a short period of time.

130. Professor Oliver, who advocates a similar replacement provision, also raises a very interesting possibility: if a justice retires mid-term during the tenure of a President of the opposing party, it might be appropriate for the congressional members of the justice's party, rather than the President, to name a successor. For example, assume that a particular justice was appointed by a Republican President. Since the winning party in a Presidential (and Senatorial) election is entitled to appoint justices, then that justice basically would be on the Court as a Republican representative. Now suppose that the justice resigned or died after nine years, and his resignation or death occurred while a Democrat was President. At that time, the public would have voted for a Democrat as the person deserving of appointing two Supreme Court members. Should the unexpectedly vacant seat be controlled by Republicans, since the original justice's appointment was the result of a Republican-

This proposed system of appointing an interim justice to serve only a limited portion of the term finds support both in the high courts of other nations and in many other government positions in this country. For example, the judges of the French Constitutional Council serve a nonrenewable term of nine years.[131] When a vacancy occurs prior to the expiration of a member's term, a new member is then nominated for the Council for the remainder of the deceased member's term.[132] Likewise, Vice-Presidents of the United States,

leaning public, or should the seat be controlled by the Democratic President that the public more recently elected?

Although it is a close question, we advocate using the normal (and constitutionally provided) appointment method of allowing the sitting President to appoint a successor, regardless of who had appointed the predecessor justice. First, we agree with Professor Oliver that devising the alternative scheme would require at least some recognition of political parties in the Constitution, which is an extremely controversial proposition. Second, we believe that if any popular mandate should be adhered to, it is that of the President inhabiting the White House at the time of an unexpected resignation or death. In short, voters will be aware of the possibility of more than two vacancies when they elect a President, and it can hardly be maintained that a public that elects one President to name two Supreme Court justices would have changed their minds if they knew that the President would get more than two vacancies. Third, although we favor staggered terms on the Supreme Court, we do not want to encourage justices or the public to think of particular seats as belonging to one party or the other. We would prefer to encourage Americans to view the Court as an impartial arbiter of the law and for this reason we do not like Professor Oliver's proposal. As a result, we think that when a justice leaves the Court prior to completing her term, the sitting President ought to nominate, and the Senate ought to confirm, a successor justice to finish the unexpired portion of the term.

131. Bell, *supra* n. 90, at 34.

132. *Id.* It is true, as Bell notes, that in France the replacement "is then usually nominated for a nine-year term in his own right," after fulfilling the remainder of the deceased member's term. *Id.* at 34 n. 57. Thus, a replacement judge could potentially serve on the Council for longer than nine years. A similar provision permits a Vice-President who becomes President for less than two years to still serve two full terms as an elected President.

Such a system could also be incorporated into our proposal. For example, a provision could be made that if a justice died with less than one-third of his term remaining, any replacement justice could be made eligible to be nominated and confirmed for a full eighteen-year term following his completion of the remainder of the deceased member's term. However, this generally creates problems of judicial independence, since the replacement justice would (like in a retention election) feel compelled to act in certain ways in order to receive the re-appointment following his completion of the first term. For this reason, we do not make this provision part of our proposal, though we note that it is a possibility that deserves consideration.

An especially interesting and unique situation could arise if a justice retired with less than two years in his term, and his retirement occurred during the first year of a President's term. Thus, the successor justice would be serving out less than two years and the Presi-

when acting for longer than two years as replacements for deceased Presidents, lose their eligibility to run as an elected President for one term.[133] More generally, Vice Presidents, Senators, and Representatives in this country who succeed a deceased or a resigned predecessor always fill out only the unfinished portion of their predecessor's term before they must be re-elected. Such a provisional replacement system is a sensible way of preserving the consistency of the staggered term limits proposal, as evidenced by substantial precedent in the United States and abroad.

Our term limits proposal resurrects the views of Thomas Jefferson[134] and our American Brutus, Robert Yates,[135] who long ago advocated limits on the tenure of Supreme Court justices and predicted calamity as a result of the life-tenured judges who, in Yates's words, "will generally soon feel themselves independent of heaven itself."[136] Moreover, our specific proposal is a combination of the suggestions and plans advocated by Judge Laurence Silberman[137] and Professor Oliver[138] and draws heavily on the plans put forth by others like Gregg Easterbrook[139] and Professors John McGinnis,[140] Saikrishna Prakash,[141] and Henry Monaghan.

Of all the prior commentaries advocating Supreme Court term limits, the one we are most persuaded by is the term limits proposal first made by Pro-

---

dent appointing him would have another appointment to the Court following the successor Justice's two-year service. Under Professor Oliver's proposal, which does not incorporate automatic designation to a federal court of appeals, he worries about the "serious danger of a lack of independence [that] would arise where the Justice, after completing his stint on the Court, hoped to obtain appointment to another position from the same President who named him to the Court." Oliver, *supra* n. 15, at 828. To account for this situation, Oliver advocates a provision whereby the successor justice that would be able to serve less than two years of an unexpired term would automatically be reappointed to the Supreme Court for a full eighteen-year term. Oliver, *supra* n. 15, at 828. We do not support such a provision, since we do not want to permit any tenures of longer than eighteen years, and since, under our proposal where re-appointment to a lower federal court would be automatic, the problem of a lack of judicial independence would not arise.

133. *See* U.S. Const. amend. XXII.

134. *See* Jefferson, *supra* n. 13, at 256. Jefferson even went so far as to propose the institution of a four- or six-year term limit that would be renewable. *Id.*

135. *See* Yates, Brutus No. XV, *supra* n. 14.

136. *See id.* at 352.

137. *See* Silberman, *supra* n. 17.

138. *See* Oliver, *supra* n. 15.

139. *See* Easterbrook, *supra* n. 7.

140. *See* McGinnis, *supra* n. 17.

141. *See* Prakash, *supra* n. 17.

fessor Oliver in 1986.[142] Oliver begins by stating that "the primary features of the proposal are that Justices should serve for staggered eighteen-year terms, and that if a Justice did not serve his full term, a successor would be appointed only to fill out the remainder of the term. Reappointment would be barred in all cases."[143] Although our justification for abolishing life tenure and replacing it with term limits is different from Oliver's, and although our complete proposal has important differences from Oliver's plan, we explicitly endorse his proposal.[144] Our final proposal is therefore an amalgamation of the views of Professors Oliver, McGinnis, Prakash, the students DiTullio and Schochet, Gregg Easterbrook, and Judge Silberman and benefits from all the proposals that have gone before it.[145]

Advantages of the Proposal

Our term limits proposal responds directly to the jump in the average tenure of Supreme Court Justices from an average of 12.2 years during 1941–1970, and 14.9 years during 1789–1970, to an average tenure of 26.1

---

142. *See* Oliver, *supra* n. 15.

143. *Id.* at 800.

144. Like Professor Oliver, several other commentators have advocated comparable term limits that are reflected in our plan. For example, Gregg Easterbrook's ten-year term limit proposal is structured similar to ours, though we disagree with his provision for reappointment of justices to additional terms and we advocate a longer term than ten years. Easterbrook, *supra* n. 7. Similarly, our proposal mirrors Professor McGinnis's "Supreme Court riding" proposal, except that we propose a significantly longer term than his suggested six months to one year. McGinnis, *supra* n. 17, at 541. Professor Monaghan also proposed term limits, as well as age limits, and suggested both a mandatory retirement age requirement and fixed terms of fifteen to twenty years. Monaghan, *supra* n. 17, at 1211–12. While we do not support a mandatory age retirement, as we discuss further below, we agree with Monaghan's call for term limits and propose a scheme that is similar to his suggestions. The Virginia Note-writers endorse an eighteen-year term limit proposal that is similar to our plan, though their phase-in proposal results in extremely short initial terms. *See* Note, *Saving This Honorable Court*, *supra* n. 18. Finally, Professor Prakash advocated instituting fixed term limits of three, four, or more years in order to "bring the judiciary much closer to the people" and "usher in a populist constitutional law." Prakash, *supra* n. 17, at 568. Prakash went even further and also proposed either a stronger removal power or a reappointment option, *id.* at 571–72, which we do not advance here because we believe that both provisions would risk undermining the independence of the judiciary. Yet we embrace the spirit of Prakash's proposal, and, like the proposals of the other commentators, we endorse his specific call for fixed terms for Supreme Court justices.

145. Indeed, the diversity of political and jurisprudential viewpoints of the various commentators we follow demonstrates the non-partisan nature of our proposal.

years during 1971–2005.[146] It also responds to the fact that, since 1970, justices have retired or died at an average of 79.5 years old, while the average for the almost two-hundred-year period before that was 68.5 years.[147] Finally, because of these other two trends, our proposal responds to the fact that vacancies on the Court have occurred much less regularly since 1970 than over the whole of American history. Although between 1789 and 1970, a vacancy on the Court occurred, on average, every 1.9 years, in the last thirty-five years a vacancy has occurred only every 3.0 years.[148]

Our proposal should reverse all these trends. First, our term limits proposal would set eighteen years as the fixed term rather than the norm since 1970 of 26.1 years.[149] Since the average tenure of all justices throughout history is 16.2 years,[150] our proposal would guarantee justices a term longer than the historical average from 1789 to 2005, yet shorter than the current post-1970 trend of alarmingly long terms. Our proposed term limit is considerably more moderate than the proposals of commentators like Judge Silberman,[151] Gregg Easterbrook,[152] Professors Prakash,[153] and Professor McGinnis,[154] who all propose much shorter term limits than we do.

Second, our proposed fixed term of only eighteen years would lead in practice to a younger average retirement age for justices than the current age of 79.5 years. For example, assuming Presidents continued to appoint new justices who are on average between fifty and fifty-five years old,[155] those justices would complete their terms at an average age of sixty-eight to seventy-three years. Thus, while our proposed amendment does not absolutely guarantee that the average retirement age of justices would decline, since it does not set a mandatory retirement age and since it does not set a maximum appointment age, it does increase the likelihood that justices will no longer serve into their late seventies. Moreover, our proposal makes it significantly more likely that the average retirement age will not go even higher than its current level, 79.5 years of age,[156] and very likely that the average retirement age will decline.

---

146. *See supra* text accompanying notes 30–45; Chart 1.
147. *See supra* Chart 2.
148. *See supra* Charts 3–4.
149. *See* Chart 1.
150. *See supra* text accompanying Chart 1.
151. *See* Silberman, *supra* n. 17, at 687 (proposing five-year term limit).
152. *See* Easterbrook, *supra* n. 7 (proposing ten-year term limit).
153. *See* Prakash, *supra* n. 17, at 568 (proposing a term limit of three to four years).
154. *See* McGinnis, *supra* n. 17, at 541 (proposing a term limit of six months to a year).
155. *See* Chart 4.
156. *See* Chart 2.

Third, and perhaps most important, our proposal would respond to the problem of hot spots and the increasingly irregular timing of vacancies by guaranteeing that a vacancy on the Court will occur like clockwork once every two years.[157] As Chart 3 reveals, and as we argued above, the number of years between vacancies has historically been about two years, but has risen dramatically in the last thirty years.[158] By fixing terms of eighteen years, and staggering them, a vacancy would occur at least once every two years.[159] This would have two important effects: First, it would guarantee that every elected President would be able to appoint two individuals to the Court in a four-year presidential term.[160] Second, it would reduce the stakes and eliminate the uncertainty that now exists about when vacancies will occur, which has had bad consequences for the confirmation process of justices and for democracy itself.

Our proposal would not only correct all the current problems posed by life tenure for justices, but it would make the Supreme Court more democratically accountable and legitimate by providing for regular updating of the Court's membership through the appointment process. Each time the public elects a President, that President could make two nominations to the Supreme Court,[161] leading to a more direct link between the will of the people and the tenor of the Court.[162] Our proposed term limit "would ensure that high courts that have become too conservative or too liberal can be turned over on a reasonable basis in keeping with the people's will (as reflected by the party they put in the White House)."[163] While this would not make the Court accountable to popular sentiment in any direct sense, which would endanger judicial independence, it would reinforce the one formal check on the Court's understanding of the Constitution that actually works.

At this point, it is logical to ask whether the popular understanding of the Constitution's meaning ought to guide the Supreme Court's understanding

---

157. See Note, *Saving This Honorable Court, supra* n. 18, at 1116–1119.

158. See Chart 3; *supra* text accompanying notes 30–45.

159. See *supra* text accompanying notes 119–145.

160. As we noted above, *see supra* notes 121–122 and accompanying text, the vacancies would arise in the first and third years of a President's four-year term.

161. See Oliver, *supra* n. 15, at 809–12.

162. See *id.* at 810 ("As voters have historically changed the occupants of the White House, they have, indirectly but inexorably, changed the makeup of that Court.").

163. Easterbrook, *supra* n. 7. Easterbrook also notes that a proposal like ours would permit a more pluralistic representation of society on the Court: "Supreme Court term limits would also help make the Court a pluralistic institution whose composition reflects American society, since regular succession of seats would provide many more opportunities to appoint women and members of minority groups." *Id.*

more directly. We believe that it should: the general public is more likely than are nine life-tenured lawyers to interpret the Constitution in a way that is faithful to its text and history, which is how constitutional decision-making ought to proceed.[164] The general public has a great reverence for the constitutional text and for our history, and much of the public intuitively understands that radical departures from text and history are illegitimate. The lawyer class in this country, on the other hand, is still imbued with a legal realist or postmodernist cynicism about the constraints imposed by the constitutional text. For this reason, we believe that enhancing popular control over the Court's constitutional interpretations will actually lead to better decisions than are produced by the current system.

Further, regularizing the occurrence of Supreme Court vacancies would equalize the impact of each President on the composition of the Court and would eliminate occasional hot spots of multiple vacancies. Under our current system of life tenure, the irregular occurrence of vacancies means that some Presidents have a hugely disproportionate impact on the Court, while others are unlucky and are unable to make even a single appointment.[165] The variability of appointments under our current system of life tenure thus leads to an inequitable allocation of vacancies among presidents. By requiring that a vacancy occur once every two years, and by guaranteeing that each President thus be able to make at least two appointments to the Court, our proposal would equalize the impact each President has on the Court.[166] And "ensuring that every chief executive would have regular influence on the makeup of the Court...would not only restore some of the check-and-balance pressure the Founders intended for all government branches but also inject more public interest into presidential campaigns."[167]

Because of this democracy-enhancing goal of term limits for the Supreme Court, our proposal should not be viewed as merely another tired application of the once popular term-limits movement. Term limits for elected officials

---

164. *See generally,* Robert H. Bork, *The Tempting of America: The Political Seduction of the Law* (1990) (setting forth and defending the theory of originalism in constitutional interpretation); Randy Barnett, *An Originalism for Nonoriginalists,* 45 Loy. L. Rev. 611 (1999); Calabresi, *The Tradition of the Written Constitution, supra* n. 10; Calabresi, *Overrule Casey!, supra* n. 10. One of us, James Lindgren, believes that one should begin with a careful analysis of the original meaning of a text, but is less certain of what interpretive principles should guide further analysis.

165. *See id.* at 809–12.

166. *See* Easterbrook, *supra* n. 7 (noting that staggered term limits like those we are proposing "would afford the president a fairly steady...Supreme Court appointment...").

167. *Id.*

(like presidents, congressmen, or governors) restrict the ability of one candidate to seek office in a regularly scheduled election, which is arguably undemocratic because it limits the choices for the voting public. Term limits for unelected officials like Supreme Court justices, on the other hand, provide for regular and more frequent appointments. Regularizing the timing of appointments to the Court thus has a dramatic democracy-enhancing effect, since it permits the people, through their elected representatives in the Senate and through the President, to update the membership of the Court more frequently and predictably to keep it in line with popular understandings of constitutional meaning. For this reason, a limit on the tenure of Supreme Court justices, unlike other forms of term limits, would actually provide for a Supreme Court that is more, rather than less, democratically accountable.

By making vacancies a regular occurrence, and by limiting the stakes of each confirmation to an eighteen-year term rather than the thirty-year period that has recently prevailed for some justices, our proposal should reduce the intensity of partisan warfare in the confirmation process. Under the current system of life tenure, the uncertainty over when the next vacancy on the Supreme Court might arise, as well as the possibility that any given nominee could serve up to four decades on the Court,[168] means the political pressures on the President and Senate in filling any Supreme Court vacancy are tremendous.[169] Our proposed amendment, by eliminating nearly all of the uncertainty over the timing of vacancies and by reducing the stakes associated with each appointment,[170] promises to reduce the intensity of the political fights over confirmation.[171]

Some may argue that our proposed amendment would actually increase the politics surrounding confirmations—that because there is so much at stake

---

168. If Justice Thomas serves to the same age as did Justice Marshall, he will have served on the Court for forty years. *Id.*

169. *See supra* text accompanying notes 71–74.

170. Given that an eighteen-year term is long and therefore some justices will likely leave the Court prior to the completion of their terms, there is still some uncertainty. Yet this uncertainty is of a completely different nature than the uncertainty that plagues the confirmation process under the system of life tenure. In the case of an early retirement, the only effect is that a democratically elected President gets a third appointment to the Court, and this extra choice is limited by the fact that the successor justice would serve only the remainder of the original justice's term. Increasing the number of appointments for such a limited time should not raise the political stakes of any given nomination because it would not affect any subsequent vacancies.

171. *See* Easterbrook, *supra* n. 7 (stating that a term limit for Supreme Court justices "would end the ridiculous Borkstyle snippet battles that push the Senate and the White House both to their lowest common denominators").

in appointing Supreme Court justices (or even lower federal appellate judges), our systematizing of the process would only make the already political event occur more often. This, some might argue, would cumulatively increase the political nature of confirmations and, by letting parties plan on when the next vacancy might occur, our proposal would make the politics of confirmations begin even before the vacancy occurs.[172] We disagree. The regularization of vacancies on the Court and the more frequent appointments to the Court would make each appointment less important politically and should have a net effect of reducing the politicization of the process.

From the current appointment battles we have direct evidence that the stakes do matter. President George W. Bush's federal district court nominees were seldom opposed, while many of his circuit court of appeals nominees were filibustered or not acted on. And when John Roberts was confirmed for the U.S. Court of Appeals, his confirmation on the Senate floor was by acclamation, whereas when he was nominated to be chief justice, many Senate Democrats opposed him. To those academics who would argue that lowering the stakes of a Supreme Court appointment would not lower the acrimony, we have ample evidence tending to support the opposite conclusion. By creating a predictable schedule of frequent appointments, our proposed amendment should reduce the intensity of the politics associated with confirmations at the Supreme Court level.

Our proposal's institution of a fixed term would also reduce the incentive presidents currently have to appoint the youngest possible candidate they can get away with.[173] If presidents know in advance that their Supreme Court nominees can serve only eighteen years, there will no longer be any reason for them to avoid nominating a healthy sixty- or sixty-five-year-old to the High Court. In so doing, our amendment will enlarge and improve the pool of potential nominees. Since nominating a forty-five-year-old will not lock up a Supreme Court seat for the next thirty-five years, and since Presidents will know the seat they are filling will open up again in eighteen years, Presidents will have much less of an incentive

---

172. Similarly, one might argue that by setting term limits, interests groups and the Senate will know better what issues would be presented to that justice during his tenure, and therefore they will more vigorously follow and become active in Senate confirmations, which would additionally increase the politicization of the process. *See* Kyle Still, *Kyle Still Free Press* <http://kylestill.blogspot.com/2002_08_01_kylestill_archive.html> (Aug. 9, 2002). Yet we are proposing an eighteen-year term, which is a significantly long period of time, and therefore this argument becomes irrelevant.

173. *See* Note, *Saving This Honorable Court, supra* n. 18, at 1110–1116. *See also* Oliver, *supra* n. 15, at 802–04.

than they do now to discriminate against older candidates. By reducing the impact of age as a factor in making nominations, our proposed amendment could lead to the appointment of more experienced justices to the Supreme Court.

To be sure, a relatively long fixed term means that Presidents will probably still tend to select younger individuals rather than seventy- or seventy-five-year-olds. In fact, for Presidents considering new vacancies, our proposal may have no impact on the current trend of appointing individuals in their fifties.[174] Yet our amendment will still have a critical impact on age as a factor in selecting Supreme Court justices, for several reasons.

First, the amendment will eliminate the incentive Presidents currently have to find candidates who are even younger than the average appointment age of fifty to fifty-five.[175] Second, under our proposed system, a President will, within the constraints of finding a candidate young enough to be likely to complete an eighteen-year term,[176] consider experience and talent as being more important, since a few more years of possible service on the Court would be irrelevant. Third, since the length of our proposed term could result in some instances of early resignations or deaths, Presidents could be appoint older, more experienced candidates to finish only that term, who might not otherwise be considered for full eighteen-year terms but who might well turn out to be the best possible choices for a shorter replacement term of, say, three or four years.[177] Therefore, although our proposal would not eliminate the practice of Presidents considering the age of potential nominees in selecting justices—indeed, we would not desire such an outcome—it would, at the margins, play a very positive role in reducing the central importance that age has played in recent years.

---

174. *See* Chart 4.

175. *See* Oliver, *supra* n. 15, at 804 ("Because the proposed amendment would reduce any preference for very young candidates, it would be more likely that the appointment would be made on the basis of the relative qualifications of the potential appointees."). Admittedly, the fact that our proposal incorporates automatic designation to a lower federal court for life may negate this advantage, since Presidents will still be appointing persons for a lifetime judicial position. However, we believe that the incentives for nominating youthful candidates, at the expense perhaps of experience, is a more common practice—or at least a larger problem—in Supreme Court nominations than it is for lower federal court judges.

176. *See id.* ("If a President wished for his appointee to exercise continuing influence for as long as possible, a President would prefer to appoint as Justice someone young enough that it would be reasonable to expect that good health and sufficient vigor for a demanding job would continue for eighteen years.").

177. Oliver, *supra* n. 15, at 804, 814 n. 79.

Fourth and finally, our proposal, though not directly responsive to the problem of mental decrepitude on the Court, would significantly further the goal of preventing mentally or physically decrepit justices from serving on the Court. Limiting the length of service of any justice to only eighteen years would reduce greatly the likelihood of a justice continuing service on the Court despite incapacity.[178] Of the eighteen instances of mental decrepitude on the Supreme Court discussed by Professor David Garrow,[179] nine—fifty percent—involved justices who had been on the Court for more than eighteen years, and most of the most serious instances of decrepitude involved justices serving for even longer.[180] Strikingly, not one of these nine instances of

---

178. *See* Easterbrook, *supra* n. 7 ("A term limit would also put a halt to the spectacle of Justices being carried from the Court chambers on stretches moments before they expire, and end the psychological and political pressure on Justices to hang on long after their mental acuity falters."); Oliver, *supra* n. 15, at 813 ("By assuring that Justices would serve no more than eighteen years, the proposed amendment would tend to assure a relatively vigorous Court, and tend to protect the Court from an infirm Justice who refused to retire.").

179. The eighteen mentally decrepit justices discussed by Garrow include: 1) John Rutledge, who ought never to have been nominated; 2) William Cushing who served twenty-one years, became decrepit after seven, and could not retire for lack of a pension; 3) Henry Baldwin, who ought never to have been nominated; 4) Robert Grier, who served for twenty-four years and became mentally decrepit after twenty-one years; 5) Nathan Clifford, who served for twenty-three years and had mental problems after nineteen years; 6) Stephen Field, who served for thirty-five years and suffered mental decline after twenty-seven years; 7) Joseph McKenna, who served for twenty-seven years and suffered mental decline after twenty-three years; 8) William Howard Taft, who suffered only a slight mental decline and who then retired; 9) Oliver Wendell Holmes, who served thirty years and showed signs of decrepitude after twenty-six years; 10) Frank Murphy, who served nine years and should have stepped down one year earlier than he did; 11) Sherman Minton, who served seven years and was feeble at the end; 12) Charles Whittaker, who served five years, had mental problems from the start, and ought never to have been nominated; 13) Hugo Black, who served thirty-four years and suffered mental decline after thirty years; 14) William O. Douglas, who served thirty-six years and was decrepit after thirty-five years; 15) William Rehnquist, who had a drug addiction after ten years; 16) Lewis Powell, who served for sixteen years, which was two years too long; 17) William J. Brennan, who served for thirty-four years and fell asleep once on the bench in his final year; and 18) Thurgood Marshall, who served for twenty-four years and was decrepit after twenty years. *See* Garrow, *supra* n. 8.

180. For example, Garrow claims that the following nine Justices who served more than eighteen years all became mentally decrepit sometime after their eighteenth year in office: Robert Grier (decrepit after twenty-one years); Nathan Clifford (decrepit after nineteen years); Stephen Field (decrepit after twenty-seven years); Joseph McKenna (decrepit after twenty-three years); Oliver Wendell Holmes (decrepit after twenty-six years); Hugo Black

mental decrepitude would have occurred, had our constitutional amendment been in place.

Admittedly, even given an eighteen-year term,[181] some justices could still become mentally or physically decrepit during their tenure and continue to serve on the Court. Nonetheless, an eighteen-year term would still be an improvement over the status quo, for one thing because term limits would "end the psychological and political pressure on Justices to hang on long after their mental acuity falters."[182] Whereas life tenure would allow (and perhaps even persuade) a disabled justice to continue serving on the Court until his death, an eighteen-year tenure would affirmatively cap the justice's career. This would ameliorate dilemmas with an unsound justice "because forced retirement at the end of a stated term of office, rather than at death, would cause the situation to arise less often."[183] Moreover, Presidents would likely formulate some informal maximum ages for their appointees; those maximum ages would necessarily impose a mandatory retirement age eighteen years older than the age at nomination.[184] Thus, if a President were to choose nominees no older than sixty when nominated, those justices, once appointed, could retire no older than at seventy-eight.

Several scholars have instead proposed mandatory retirement ages for the justices as a way of reducing mental decrepitude on the Supreme Court.[185] A mandatory retirement age is unacceptable, either as a substitute or as a complement to an eighteen-year term. First, a mandatory retirement age is unfair, for it blindly discriminates against individuals based on age and cannot account for the capability of a seventy-year-old continuing in office, while a

---

(decrepit after thirty years); William O. Douglas (decrepit after thirty-five years); William J. Brennan (decrepit after thirty-three years); and Thurgood Marshall (decrepit after twenty years according to Garrow, although we would say sooner than that). *Id.*

181. For example, term limit of six months to one year, such as that proposed by Professor McGinnis, *supra* n. 17, at 541, would more effectively eliminate the problem of mental decrepitude. *See id.* at 543 (noting that his "Supreme Court riding" would have "curtailed the effects of senility and the excessive delegation of power to young and energetic law clerks by reducing the temptation to cling to the bench into very old age").

182. Easterbrook, *supra* n. 7.

183. Oliver, *supra* n. 15, at 815.

184. *See id.* at 813–14.

185. For example, Professor Garrow, Garrow *supra* n. 9, at 1086–87 and Professor Monaghan, Monaghan, *supra* n. 17, at 1211–12, have both proposed the enactment of a mandatory retirement age and commonly, these proposals call for mandatory retirement of judges at the ages of sixty-five, seventy, or seventy-five. Moreover, as we have seen, many foreign countries impose mandatory retirement ages as limits on the tenure of the members of their highest constitutional courts. Thus, instituting a mandatory retirement age does stand as an alternative, or a complement, to our own proposal.

sixty-year-old might be best advised to retire.[186] A term limit would more fairly permit individualized and informal determinations of capacity.[187]

Second, it is a mistake in general to write numbers into the Constitution because they can become obsolete with the passage of time.[188] The requirements that presidents be at least thirty-five years old and that the right to jury trial be preserved in all suits at common law in which more than twenty dollars is at stake are classic examples of this. It seems quite possible that in fifty or one hundred years a mandatory retirement age of seventy or even seventy-five might seem absurdly young if people were routinely living to be over 100. It would be a bad idea to insert a mandatory retirement age for justices into constitutional law.

An eighteen-year term offers several other benefits, including bringing the tenure of the members of our highest court into conformity with the practice of the rest of the world and of forty-nine of our fifty states.[189] Assuming an

---

186. There are two other arguments against mandatory retirement ages. First, we do not believe that a mandatory retirement age requirement, as compared to a fixed term limit, would accomplish any greater deterrent to mentally or physically decrepit justices continuing in office. For example, admittedly it is possible under a system of fixed terms that a justice could become senile or physically unable to perform his duties within the first eight years of his term. Yet at the same time, under a system with mandatory retirement ages, there is also a chance of a sixty-year-old justice becoming mentally or physically decrepit notwithstanding a mandatory retirement age of sixty-five or seventy. Thus, while a mandatory retirement age can perhaps be tied more closely than a term limit to what scientific experience teaches is an age at which the average individual becomes incapacitated, the imprecise nature of such calculations severely limits the value of a mandatory retirement age.

Second, our proposed amendment would indirectly produce the benefits of a mandatory retirement age because, as noted above, it would enable Presidents and Senators to plan in order to avoid the problem of mental decrepitude. Importantly, allowing individualized determinations of the likelihood of any particular nominee experiencing mental decrepitude is fairer and more effective than a blanket rule against all persons over a particular age continuing in office.

187. Similarly, we oppose the notion of allowing individualized determinations by a political body as to the competence of a given justice. Professor Prakash suggests something similar to this, arguing for a stronger removal power that would enable the President or the Senate to remove judges and justices based on senility or even a disagreement with substantive decisions. Prakash, *supra* n. 17, at 571–72. Even if such a removal power were limited to determinations of senility and physical capacity, we would disagree with such a provision because of the manipulability and politicization of the Supreme Court that it might cause.

188. Guido Calabresi, *A Common Law for the Age of Statutes* (1982).

189. *See generally supra* text accompanying notes 86–109 (comparatively analyzing the tenures of judges on the highest constitutional courts of major Western democracies and of U.S. states, evincing the conclusion that the U.S. provision for life tenure for its justices is a true outlier).

eighteen-year term were coupled with permitting retired justices to sit on the lower federal courts following their Supreme Court service, the lower federal courts would be enriched with the justices' experiences and knowledge,[190] tracking the current system whereby retired senior district or circuit court judges can sit on the lower federal courts.

Finally and of critical importance, our proposal would eliminate the current practice of justices strategically timing their resignations, a practice that embroils justices in unseemly political calculations that undermine judicial independence and that cause the public to view the Court as a more nakedly political institution than it ought to be.[191] This concern with strategically timed resignations was the principal focus of the recent Virginia student Note advocating an eighteen-year term limit for justices.[192] We noted above that there is substantial evidence that justices throughout American history have timed their resignations for political reasons, including what is often a delay in retirement in order to avoid allowing a sitting President of the opposite party to name a successor.[193] Our eighteen-year fixed term limit, however, would make it impossible for a justice to time his resignation strategically.[194] Of course, a justice could still leave the Court prior to the completion of her term for political reasons, but under our proposal the retiring justice's successor would be appointed only to complete the remainder of a fixed eighteen-year term. Therefore, an early strategic retirement decision would be of no avail for it would not permit a President to lock up a Supreme Court seat for another eighteen years[195] As a result, under our proposal the justices would lose the power they now have to keep a Supreme Court seat in the hands of their own political party by retiring strategically. This would promote the rule of law, and the public's respect for the Court, by precluding nakedly political decision-making by justices with respect to retirement.

---

190. Easterbrook, *supra* n. 7; Amar & Amar, *supra* n. 56. Our proposed amendment, by providing that a judge sit on the Court for eighteen years and then become eligible for service on the lower federal courts, would closely track the current system whereby retired Justices, or other senior district or circuit judges, currently can sit on the lower federal courts.

191. *See* Amar & Calabresi, *supra* n. 3; Oliver, *supra* n. 15, at 805–09. *See also* Note, *Saving This Honorable Court*, *supra* n. 18, at 1101–1110 (stating authors' concern with strategically timed resignations).

192. Note, *Saving This Honorable Court*, *supra* n. 18.

193. *See supra* n. 50 and accompanying text.

194. *See* Oliver, *supra* n. 15, at 808.

195. *Id.* at 809.

Objections to the Proposal

Moving to a system of Supreme Court term limits would significantly enhance the overall legitimacy and functioning of the Court and of our constitutional democracy. Yet our proposal is not uncontroversial.[196] To date, by far the best case against Supreme Court term limits has been made by Professor Ward Farnsworth of Boston University, and we highly recommend his article to anyone interested in this subject.[197]

First, many will argue that our proposed amendment would impair judicial independence, a value our Constitution protects and upon which our legal system is based. Along with the Compensation Clause,[198] the argument goes, the guarantee of life tenure[199] was intended to protect the independence of the judiciary.[200] As Alexander Hamilton argued, life tenure secures the freedom of a judge from the political branches, as well as from public opinion, ensuring that judges can objectively interpret the law without risk of political reprisal.[201] This benefit of life tenure is still recognized as critical: Professor Marty Redish argues, "Article III's provision of life tenure is quite obviously intended to insulate federal judges from undue external political pressures on their decisionmaking, which would undermine and possibly preclude effective performance of the federal judiciary's function in our system."[202] Impinging upon life tenure, it is argued, would weaken this insulation, jeopardizing judicial independence.

We would not favor this proposed constitutional amendment if we thought it would undermine judicial independence in any serious way. As others have argued, moving from life tenure to a lengthy fixed term—a term longer than

---

196. We surely have not addressed all of the arguments that could be waged against our proposal. Yet by dispelling (or at least considering) some of the most important objections, we hope to strengthen the case for our term limits proposal and therefore put the onus on proponents of life tenure to formulate a strong case for that system, which we believe has not yet been done.

197. Farnsworth, *supra* n. 22. *See also infra*, Ward Farnsworth, *The Case for Life Tenure*, pp. 251–269.

198. U.S. Const. art. III, § 1 ("The Judges, both of the supreme and inferior Courts,... shall, at stated Times, receive for their Services, a Compensation, which shall not be diminished during their Continuance in Office.").

199. U.S. Const. art. III, § 1 ("The Judges, both of the supreme and inferior Courts, shall hold their Offices during good Behavior...").

200. *See* Alexander Hamilton, Federalist No. 78 (1788); *see also supra* n. 110.

201. *Id.*

202. *See* Redish, *supra* n. 65, at 685.

the average tenure of justices who have served on the Court between 1789 and 2005—means that no independence will be lost relative to the other branches or to the public generally.[203] Professor Monaghan states:

> But even assuming that such complete judicial independence is desirable, eliminating life tenure need not materially undermine it. Presumably, what relieves judges of the incentive to please is not the prospect of indefinite service, but the awareness that their continuation in office does not depend on securing the continuing approval of the political branches. Independence, therefore, could be achieved by mandating fixed, nonrenewable terms of service.[204]

As this quote shows, the key to securing judicial independence is to guarantee that a justice's tenure is not subject to the political decisions of the other branches or of the public. Life tenure has made judges independent of the political branches, and we believe that this independence would be secured by our lengthy eighteen-year nonrenewable term limit with a salary set for life.[205] Our eighteen-year term limits proposal would preserve judicial independence because it does not allow for reappointment, because it guarantees the justices a longer tenure on average than they have historically had between 1789 and 2005, because it guarantees justices their salary for life, and because the justices would be secure from new means of their removal by the political branches. As a result, except for the minimal and positive effect that more regular appointments would make the Supreme Court more responsive to the public and the political branches' understanding of the Constitution's meaning, there is no plausible argument that judicial independence would be endangered by our proposal.

Professor Ward Farnsworth offers a pragmatic defense of life tenure and suggests that that an advantage of our current constitutional structure is that its resulting judicial independence contributes to a faster and a slower form of lawmaking, the first accomplished by Congress through the ordinary legislative process and the second accomplished by the Supreme Court.[206] That the Supreme Court represents the political forces that prevailed ten or fifteen years ago and that it may take decades for a political movement to gain control over

---

203. *See* McGinnis, *supra* n. 17, at 543; Monaghan, *supra* n. 17, at 1211; Oliver, *supra* n. 15, at 816–21.

204. Monaghan, *supra* n. 17, at 1211.

205. The importance of eighteen-year terms being nonrenewable and long is discussed in Note, *Saving This Honorable Court, supra* n. 18, at 1127–1131.

206. Farnsworth, *supra* n. 22, at 411–21.

the Supreme Court's slower law-making process appeals to this scholar, whose argument is fundamentally conservative. In essence, Farnsworth thinks it is a good thing that progressives had to struggle from 1901 to 1937 to gain a majority on the Supreme Court and that conservatives had to struggle from 1968 to 1991 to get five solidly Republican justices who even then refused to overrule *Roe v. Wade*.[207] Farnsworth sees the Court as a major anchor to windward that slows down social movements for change, and he argues that to some extent judicial independence is desirable because a slowed down law-making process is desirable as a matter of good public policy.[208]

Farnsworth's argument is a powerful one, and we are sympathetic to his claim that it is desirable for the Court to slow down the forces of change in our democracy. Indeed, for these very reasons we favor the cumbersome law-making system crafted by the Framers with separation of powers, checks and balances, and federalism instead of a national, parliamentary British-style regime where change can happen very suddenly. The question, however, is just how much conservatism one wants in one's lawmaking processes. Arguably, with separation of powers, checks and balances, federalism, and the Senate filibuster, we do not also need a Supreme Court whose fundamental direction can be reversed only by a sustained twenty-five or thirty year campaign. Different conservatives will answer this question in different ways, and those who are most averse to legal change may join Professor Farnsworth in praising life tenure. A Supreme Court with eighteen-year term limits will still be an anchor to windward in the American polity: it just will not be as much of an anchor as has become the case in the last thirty-five years.

A second big objection that could be raised against our proposal is that it could lead to "Supreme Court capture." If a particular party were to prevail in five consecutive Presidential elections, then, assuming that the President nominates and the Senate confirms individuals of the President's party,[209] that party would have "captured" the entire Supreme Court for itself, a result that life tenure is designed to protect against. And, as Ward Farnsworth points out, even the appointment of four justices by a two-term President could be enough to tip the ideological balance on the Court from Republicans to De-

---

207. 410 U.S. 113 (1973).

208. Farnsworth, *supra* n. 22, at 419–21.

209. Admittedly, this entire discussion is simplistic in that it assumes that if a Democrat wins the Presidency, then the selected justice will properly be thought of as a Democrat, or a liberal, during his tenure on the Court. This assumption has proven to be very wrong in reality.

mocrats or vice versa.[210] Accordingly, Professor Charles Fried has suggested to us that our proposal could cause the Supreme Court to become like the National Labor Relations Board, which is always captured by labor under Democratic Administrations and by management under Republican rule.[211] Farnsworth adds that because a "two-term President may reflect a single national mood...there may be value in a court that cannot be remade by one such gust."[212]

As a practical matter, however, Supreme Court capture would be extremely difficult to accomplish. First, members of either political party represent a diversity of viewpoints on judicial philosophy. For example, both Presidents and justices range from extreme to moderate in their viewpoints, and sometimes moderates cannot be thought of as Democrats or Republicans as we label them.[213] The seven Republican appointees on the current Supreme Court certainly do not vote as a block any more than Democrat Byron White voted in lock-step with Democrat Thurgood Marshall. Indeed, the most left-wing and most right-wing members of the current Court (Justices Stevens and Thomas[214]) were both appointed by Republicans. That some of our most liberal justices were appointed by surprised Republican Presidents[215] and some of our more conservative justices were appointed by surprised Democrats[216] makes Supreme Court capture an unlikely result, regardless of the tenure term.

Second, giving a two-term president four seats on the Court should not bother traditionalists like Farnsworth. From the time that the Court was fixed at nine justices in 1869 until 1980, every president who served two full terms except Wilson was able to appoint at least four justices: Presidents Grant

---

210. Farnsworth, *supra* n. 22, at 416, 435.

211. Conversation between Professor Steven Calabresi and Professor Charles Fried, Fall of 2003.

212. Farnsworth, *supra* n. 22, at 416.

213. Clearly, Justices Kennedy and O'Connor serve as two examples on the current Court of this fact, and before them, Justices Powell and White.

214. *See* Lee Epstein & Jeffrey A. Segal, *Advice and Consent: The Politics of Judicial Appointments* 131 (2005).

215. The classic example is Chief Justice Earl Warren, whose liberal activism that changed the Court forever shockingly resulted from the appointment by conservative President Dwight Eisenhower, who later remarked that appointing Warren to the Court was among his biggest mistakes as President. *See* Abraham, *supra* n. 32, at 192–97.

216. Perhaps the best example from recent history, though not as extreme as Eisenhower's appointment of Warren, *see id.*, is the fact that Democratic President John F. Kennedy appointed Justice Byron White, who ended up being far more conservative (particularly on civil liberty and criminal procedure issues) than Kennedy suspected. *See id.* at 210–11.

(four), Cleveland (four), Franklin Roosevelt (eight, with five in his first two terms alone), and Eisenhower (five). Indeed, five presidents who served less than two full terms got at least four appointments: Harrison (four), Taft (five), Harding (four), Truman (four), and Nixon (four). Wilson got three appointments, as did Hoover and Teddy Roosevelt (as well as Ronald Reagan after the temporal meaning of life tenure had changed). If our term limit proposal had been in force from 1869 through 1980, it would have enabled Wilson to get his fourth slot, but its primary effect on capture would have been to *reduce* the number of presidents who got to choose four or five justices though they served as president less than two full terms.

Third, with the gradual change that staggered terms would encourage, we should expect less violent lurches to the left or to the right of the kind that we have experienced since the 1930s. Any capture that did occur would tend to be mild and temporary. For example, the longest that one party has held the White House in the last sixty years is the Republicans in 1981–1993. Some people worried about our proposal imagine a court with four Reagan appointees and two by George H.W. Bush. But remember that such a Court should have had two Carter appointees as well, and if the elder President Bush's first appointment remained Justice Souter, he might well have replaced Justice Rehnquist when he would have stepped down in 1989. Even at the height of Republican influence in the brief window between 1991 and 1993, the Court might plausibly have had Justices Stevens, Souter, and two Carter appointees on the left, Justices O'Connor and Kennedy in the middle, Justices Scalia and Thomas on the right, and another Reagan appointee in the middle or on the right. In short, instead of Justices Blackmun and White, we should have had two Carter appointees and instead of Rehnquist, we might have had a Reagan appointee like O'Connor, Kennedy, or Scalia. In short, at the height of possible Republican capture, the likeliest of many possible 1991–1993 Courts might well have been to the left of the one that we in fact had in 1993. And the probable stability of the Court under our proposal is also suggested by considering the likely effect of adding four Clinton appointees starting in 1993. The Clinton justices might not have shifted the Court much to the left because the first three should have been replacing Stevens and the two Carter appointees, and the last would have replaced O'Connor. The point of this counter-factual scenario is not to pretend that we know what the world would have been like (we don't), but simply to suggest that the sudden swings that can be imagined in capture scenarios would have been unlikely to have occurred in our last period of maximum capture by one party.

In addition to these practical difficulties of Supreme Court capture, the political check of Senate confirmation can and often does prevent a party from capturing the Court. While it is not uncommon for one of the two major political parties to prevail in consecutive presidential elections,[217] since the election of President Nixon nearly forty years ago, it has been relatively rare for a President and the Senate to be controlled by the same party for more than two to four years.[218] The Senate, when controlled by the party opposite the President, can use its constitutional role in confirming justices to ensure that a President will appoint moderate individuals.[219] For example, during the twenty years of Democratic rule when Presidents Franklin D. Roosevelt and Harry S. Truman were in office, of the twelve appointments they made, one seat went to an Independent (Frankfurter) and two seats went to Republicans (Stone and Burton).[220] Moreover, even some of the Democrats that FDR and Truman appointed were quite conservative, such as Justices Reed and Vinson.[221] Thus, even in an era in which one party ruled the White House for twenty years and the Senate for sixteen of those years, that political party was not able to pack the Court completely with justices sharing its views, in large part because of the political checks of public opinion and Senate confirmation. A Senate controlled by the party opposite to that of a President will tend to mitigate the influence of a presidency long controlled by one party and will make Supreme Court capture much less likely.

Moreover, even to the extent that our system permits a party to "capture" the Supreme Court, the current system of life tenure permits precisely the same result. For example, during the twenty years of Democratic rule between 1933 and 1953, Presidents Franklin Roosevelt and Harry Truman were able to appoint a total of twelve justices[222]—a perfect opportunity to capture the Supreme Court and one realized as to economic issues but not as to civil liberties. Additional examples abound: from 1829–1841, two Democratic Presidents—Jackson and Van Buren—appointed eight justices;[223] from 1861–1885, four Republican Presidents—Lincoln, Grant, Hayes, and

---

217. Indeed, it appears that political parties have tended to win 2–4 consecutive elections at a time. See id., at 377–81 (listing the Presidents throughout history).

218. See David Roper, Party Control of U.S. Government, <http://arts.bev.net/roperl-david/politics/PartyControl.htm> (visited September 29, 2005).

219. U.S. Const. art. II, §2 ("[The President] shall nominate, and *by and with the Advice and Consent of the Senate*, shall appoint…Judges of the supreme Court….") (emphasis added).

220. See Abraham, *supra* n. 32, at 380.

221. See id.

222. See id.

223. See id. at 378.

Arthur—appointed fourteen justices;[224] from 1897–1913, three Republican Presidents—McKinley, Theodore Roosevelt, and Taft—appointed ten justices;[225] and, most recently, from 1969–1993, four Republican Presidents—Nixon, Ford, Reagan, and the first President Bush—were able to appoint eleven justices.[226] As a result, although our proposed term limit might make it slightly more likely that opportunities to capture the Court would arise, since our proposal leads to vacancies at reliable two-year intervals, the fact is that, even under the current system of life tenure, Supreme Court capture is always a real possibility.[227] The primary effect of our proposal on capture should be to make it less intense and less persistent. Thus, we do not believe our proposal would make Supreme Court capture a substantially more serious problem than is presently the case. This is so in part because our proposal has the Burkean feature that it simply restores the practice of justices serving for less than twenty years which prevailed between 1789 and 1970—a practice we have departed from only recently.

Nevertheless, one overriding goal of our proposal is to make the Supreme Court somewhat more reflective of the popular understanding of the Constitution than is presently the case.[228] If a party manages to "capture" the popular will for consecutive elections with its vision of constitutional law, then that party will best represent the popular understanding of the Constitution's text and original meaning; it is arguably proper that the Supreme Court reflect that understanding. By tying the makeup of the Court more closely to Presidential elections, we will allow the people to select (albeit indirectly) the kind of justices they want on the Court, given the prevailing public understanding of the Constitution's text and original meaning. If the public becomes dissatisfied with the Court, then an eighteen-year term would permit the public to elect a new President who could initiate change on the Court with the next two appointments. Thus, our proposal causes the Supreme Court's judicial

---

224. *See id.* at 378–79.

225. *See id.* at 379.

226. *See id.* at 381.

227. Significantly, this list of historical examples shows that even when parties win consecutive elections, and the result is that that party gets to make many appointments to the Court, it still cannot lead to a captured Court. For example, although Presidents Nixon through Bush appointed eleven justices, the result is still only a moderately conservative Court. Thus, this historical evidence strengthens the earlier points about the importance of Senate confirmation and the fact that appointing a like-minded justice is not as easy as it might appear.

228. *See supra* text accompanying notes 61–71 and 146–195.

philosophy and understanding of constitutional meaning to more truly reflect that of the public's judicial philosophy and understanding of constitutional meaning than is currently the case. We emphatically believe this would be both a good thing and a return to the practice that prevailed for most of American history.

A third objection that might be raised against our proposed constitutional amendment is that imposing a limit on the tenure of Supreme Court justices would force them to become too activist. Justice Kennedy, responding to a Judiciary Committee questionnaire during his confirmation process, wrote: "life tenure is in part a constitutional mandate to the federal judiciary to proceed with caution, to avoid reaching issues not necessary to the resolution of the suit at hand, and to defer to the political process."[229] Eliminating life tenure, one might argue, would endanger the virtue of patience that life tenure affords a Supreme Court justice. Individuals with a limited opportunity to affect the law as Supreme Court justices might overreach in important cases and actively seek out opportunities to change doctrine. Alternatively, justices in their final years in office might face a final period incentive to go out with a splash, knowing that in a short time they might no longer have to work with and live with their current Supreme Court colleagues.

Any proposal leading to such judicial activism would undermine one of the chief advantages of an independent (and life-tenured) Supreme Court. Indeed, some of the more radical term limits proposals would more predictably lead to such problems. For example, under a term ranging from one to five years proposed by Judge Silberman[230] and Professors McGinnis[231] and Prakash,[232] justices would likely feel pressure to accomplish a great deal in a very short amount of time.[233] Under an eighteen-year term limit, however, no such activism should re-

---

229. Quoted in Nadine Cohodas, *Kennedy Finds Bork an Easy Act to Follow*, 45 Cong. Qtrly. 2989, Weekly Report (1987).

230. *See* Silberman, *supra* n. 17, at 687 (proposing a five-year term limit).

231. *See* McGinnis, *supra* n. 17, at 541 (proposing a term limit of six months to one year).

232. *See* Prakash, *supra* n. 17, at 568 (proposing a term limit of three to four years).

233. In the term limits proposals made by Silberman and McGinnis, where the justices would be designated to lower federal courts following their service on the Court, there might be less reason to worry about such judicial activism resulting from short terms. *See* McGinnis, *supra* n. 17, at 543–44. Yet, contrary to McGinnis's reassurances that "new Justices have typically behaved for their first few years much as they did as lower court judges," *id.* at 544, the fact that the proposed terms are so short makes it inevitable that there is a larger risk of judicial activism than if a term were longer, such as our eighteen-year term. Those who believe that very short terms on the Court and the promise of either be-

sult, for such a period is sufficiently long that any individual justice ought not to feel hurried in making his impact on the law. Under our proposed term, justices would have the luxury to, in Justice Kennedy's words, "proceed with caution" and "defer to the political process."[234]

Moreover, it is hard to believe that final-period problems would be more severe under our proposal than under the current system, in which old, life-tenured justices know that retirement is just around the bend. Surely, on the current Court, Justice O'Connor knew and Justice Stevens knows that they are in the final period of their tenure on the Court. Yet no one suggests their behavior reflects a final-period problem just as Chief Justice Rehnquist's behavior did not change during his last year on the Court when he knew he faced a final-period problem, though his presence at the Court was limited by his illness. We do not see why such a final-period problem would be any more likely under our system of fixed eighteen-year terms. Except for those justices who die suddenly and youthfully, like Justice Robert Jackson, the current system of life tenure poses just as much risk of final-period problems for each justice as would our proposed system of eighteen-year term limits.

A fourth objection that could be made against our term limits proposal is its potential to erode the prestige of the Court by producing constant turnover. A system of staggered term limits, however, would in no way erode the prestige associated with the job of being a Supreme Court justice. Significantly, each justice's term would still be eighteen years long, which is ample time for justices to become known individually and to acquire prestige. Nor would the justices suffer a loss of prestige from a less weighty task: the immense powers and responsibilities of the Court's members would remain unchanged from what they are now. At most, the public's esteem and respect might be shifted from individual justices and onto the Supreme Court as an institution—a very positive development.

A fifth objection that might be raised against our proposal is that by making the Court more obviously responsive to public opinion, our amendment would cause the public to think of the Court as being even more of a policymaking body and even less a body restrained by law than is presently the case. Our proposal could thus be faulted on the ground that it would undermine the textual and historical constraints that ought to bind the Court by making everyone

---

coming a lower court judge following that short period or being subject to congressional removal would cause justices to act in a more restrained manner and with a greater sense of duty to the Constitution will object that we have not gone far enough in limiting the tenure of justices because it would preserve the current incentive structure for justices to act on their own personal motives instead of out of their sense of duty to the Constitution.

234. *See supra* n. 227 and accompanying text.

think of the Court more as being an indirectly elected, political body. As Ward Farnsworth says, our eighteen-year term proposal "may cause the justices to think of themselves as political office-holders in a more traditional way than they now do."[235] This is a very substantial objection, and it is one that gives us pause. Happily, we think there are a number of responses that can be made to this point.

First, our amendment would end the current distasteful process whereby justices strategically time their departures depending on which party controls the White House and the Senate when they retire. This process causes informed elites to view the justices as being very political creatures, and it surely breeds cynicism about whether the justices are currently applying the law or are making it up. We think getting rid of the strategic timing of retirements would do a lot to encourage both the public and the justices themselves to think of the Court as being an ongoing legal institution. Justices might be restrained in what they do by the knowledge that justices appointed by the opposing political party could soon regain a majority on the Court and overrule any activist decisions that a current majority might have the votes to impose.

Second, we think the American public is now more committed than are lawyerly elites to the notion that constitutional cases should be decided based on text and history. We thus think that augmenting public control over the Court will lead to more decisions grounded in text and history than are arrived at by life tenured lawyers schooled in legal realism or post-modernism. The American public has a more old-fashioned belief in law as a constraining force than do lawyerly elites. It is for this very reason that we consider it so desirable to empower the American public relative to those lawyerly elites.

Professor Farnsworth challenges this idea and, citing Richard Posner, he argues that "the popular demand for originalism is weak."[236] We disagree. We think the public has consistently voted since 1968 for presidential candidates who have promised to appoint Supreme Court justices who would interpret the law rather than making it up. Even the Democrats who have won since 1968, Jimmy Carter and Bill Clinton, were from the moderate wings of the Democratic party, and the two Democrats appointed to the Court since 1968 are well to the right of Earl Warren or William Brennan. We think the public, while it is not very well informed about what outcomes originalism leads to,

---

235. Farnsworth, *supra* n. 22, at 438.

236. Farnsworth, *supra* n. 22, at 431, citing Richard Posner, *Overcoming Law* 254–55 (1995).

is still more originalist than are members of the elite lawyer class that under a system of life tenure dominates the Supreme Court, which is why Supreme Court opinions claim to follow text and precedent rather than claiming to follow Rawls, Nozick, Dworkin, Ackerman, or Tribe. The public may be induced, as it was in the Bork confirmation, into opposing an occasional originalist nominee. (Even then, it should be noted that in the Thomas confirmation fight public opinion supported Thomas's appointment). Overall, however, we think the public is more supportive of text and history in constitutional interpretation than are elite realist or post-modernist lawyers. We thus disagree with Farnsworth and Posner that popular support for originalism is weak.

Finally, we note again that the system our amendment would create of vacancies opening up on the Supreme Court once every two years is merely a return to the system that prevailed between 1789 and 1970. Ours, then, is a conservative reform—a restoration if you will of the traditional American status quo. What is revolutionary is for the nine-member Court to go for eleven years without a single vacancy opening up on the Supreme Court and for the justices to stay on that Court for twenty-six years on average instead of for fifteen years. Our amendment, like the amendment restoring the two-term limit on Presidents, is a return to the way things used to be.

A sixth objection that might be raised to our proposal is that it could lead to strategic behavior by senators who would know that additional vacancies on the Court were going to open up in two and four years. Imagine, hypothetically, that the Court has five Republican and four Democratic leaning justices and that one of the Republicans is scheduled to step down in the third year of the presidency of an unpopular Republican President. Imagine too that the next two seats to come open are held by Democrats and so, even if Democrats were to win the next presidential election and get to fill those two seats, the Court would remain 5 to 4 Republican. Under these circumstances, a Democratically controlled Senate might refuse to confirm *any* Republican nominee put forward in the third year of an unpopular Republican President's term. This would hold the crucial fifth swing seat open until after the next presidential election allowing Democrats to gain control of the Court.

In response to this concern, it might be noted first that a similar incentive exists now for Senators to hold seats open and for this reason it is widely assumed that any Supreme Court seat that opens up in a presidential election year will be unfillable because of filibuster threats. Our proposed amendment then does not make it any more likely than is currently the case that Senators would block a President from filling a Supreme Court seat in the third year of his term. Second, under the hypothetical constructed above, where Democrats control the Senate and are clearly going to recapture the White

House in two years, it may be arguably appropriate that the Supreme Court seat in question go to a Democrat or at least to a Democrat who is also acceptable to the unpopular incumbent Republican President. We believe that in these situations public opinion will force the President and the Senate to arrive at a reasonable compromise, just as public opinion forced Senate Democrats in 1988 to accept President Reagan's nomination of "moderate" Justice Anthony Kennedy, his third nominee for that seat, rather than waiting for the 1988 presidential elections and hoping to claim the seat outright for themselves.

Undoubtedly, there are additional objections to our proposal that we have failed to address. But those who would object should remember that our amendment merely restores American practice with respect to Supreme Court vacancies to what it was between 1789 and 1970.[237] Quite simply, until now, the system of life tenure has been retained mostly by inertia; the affirmative defenses of life tenure, and the objections to term limits for Supreme Court Justices, have not been thoroughly made. Our hope is that making a strong case for abolishing life tenure and replacing it with eighteen-year term limits will put the burden on the proponents of life tenure to make a reasoned case for preserving the current system.[238]

Imposing Term Limits by Statute

In light of the great difficulty of passing an amendment, some have asked whether Supreme Court term limits could be created instead by statute. Here we consider two statutory proposals—one of our own devising and one by Professors Paul Carrington and Roger Cramton. Because we conclude both are unconstitutional, instituting a staggered, eighteen-year term limit through a constitutional amendment seems to us to be the only way in which such a limit can be implemented.

---

237. There are a number of arguments that we have not taken up in this subsection, but which we have addressed in other sections of the paper. For example, to the objection that our proposal might be unfair to current justices, we have stated that our proposal would be prospective only. See supra text accompanying notes 119–145. Also, to the argument that our proposal might not be feasible, see Easterbrook, supra n. 7, we argue below that we recognize the difficulty in passing a constitutional amendment and therefore consider alternative ways of imposing term limits. See infra text accompanying notes 239–282. At the same time, by making our proposal relatively modest, we believe we have presented a term limits amendment that can garner widespread support, thereby making even a constitutional amendment more likely.

238. See Monaghan, supra n. 17, at 1212 (first raising such a call, over ten years ago).

Two Statutory Term Limits Proposals

The Calabresi-Lindgren statutory proposal would essentially provide for the same kind of term limits as would be accomplished by constitutional amendment. The statute would be carefully tailored, however, in the ultimately vain hope of avoiding constitutional problems.[239] Our statute would provide, first, that the President would appoint an individual to a vacancy on one of the lower federal courts,[240] where, as Article III, section 1 dictates, that person must enjoy life tenure.[241] Then, by a separate act of presidential nomination and senatorial confirmation, that life-tenured lower federal court judge would be "designated"[242] to serve on the Supreme Court for a term dictated by statute to last for eighteen years.[243] At the end of the eighteen years, the statutory designation of the lower federal court judge to sit on the Supreme Court would expire, ending the justice's tenure on the Supreme Court, and returning the justice to the federal circuit court or district court bench for life.[244] Thus, the individual would always enjoy life tenure (subject to impeachment) as a member of the federal judiciary, but he or she would serve on the Supreme Court for only eighteen years. In constitutional terms, the judge would at all times

---

239. For purposes of illustrating how our statute would work, we assume that the Senate would confirm the President's nomination.

240. We suggest that Supreme Court nominees who are not already on the lower federal courts would be appointed to a federal circuit court, since this would make the later re-designation simpler.

241. *See* U.S. Const. art. III, § 1. Of course, if the President were appointing to the Court an individual who was already a federal judge, then this first step might be unnecessary.

242. By "designate," we do not mean to suggest that this would involve a different process than the typical appointment process. *See* U.S. Const. art. II, § 2 (giving the President the power to appoint Supreme Court justices, subject to Senate confirmation). The President would nominate, and "by and with the Advice and Consent of the Senate," would appoint the judge as a justice. *See id.* We use the term "designate" merely because it helps to conceptualize the process in the same way that circuit-riding and sitting-by-designation work.

243. Although the process would technically involve two confirmations processes — one for the individual to become a life-tenured federal judge, and another for the individual to become a Justice — we believe that an informal arrangement can easily be struck between Presidents and Senates to hold one hearing for both purposes.

244. The statute would thus operate like the current provision for the position of chief judge on each individual circuit. According to circuit rules or customs, a particular judge on that circuit is named to become chief judge. Following her years of service as chief judge, she is no longer chief judge, but rather is simply a judge once again, as she was before becoming a chief judge.

"hold [his] Office[] during good Behaviour" on "the supreme and inferior Courts."[245] As Professor Vik Amar writes, "the Justices would be federal judges with life tenure—but not all of that tenure would be served on the Court."[246]

This statutory proposal strongly resembles two judicial practices our country has permitted, one of which still exists. The first is the early practice of circuit-riding, under which justices would sit by statutory designation on the lower federal courts in addition to fulfilling duties as Supreme Court justices.[247] In effect, an individual was implicitly appointed by the President and served simultaneously as both an inferior federal judge and as a Supreme Court justice.[248] Even though the Constitution arguably contemplates that these two positions would be separate,[249] this practice is a historical antecedent to the Calabresi-Lindgren statutory proposal, under which individuals would serve on both courts as if the positions were interchangeable. "[O]ur early traditions suggest that the inferior courts and the Supreme Court did not have to possess completely separate personnel."[250]

Second, we currently allow active lower federal court judges, as well as retired justices and senior lower court judges, to sit by designation on other lower federal courts. This "sitting-by-designation" system takes several forms, in each of which the judge or justice is designated to a lower court by its chief judge. Active circuit court judges and district court judges can be designated to serve on a lower federal court;[251] active or retired Supreme Court justices likewise may sit on circuit courts or district courts.[252] Senior circuit court judges are authorized to sit on panels of sister circuits and on district courts by order of the chief judge of that court.[253] Moreover, senior district court judges are permitted to sit on circuit court panels anywhere in the country by order of the chief judge

---

245. U.S. Const. art. III, § 1.

246. Amar & Amar, *supra* n. 56.

247. *See generally,* Glick, *supra* n. 33.

248. To be sure, there were not two separate appointments. Rather, the practice was simply established that Supreme Court justices also served on lower federal courts. We do not claim otherwise, but our point here is to demonstrate that under circuit-riding, the effect of the practice was to have a judge simultaneously serving two positions—both inferior judge and Supreme Court justice.

249. *See, e.g.,* U.S. Const. art. III, § 1 ("The judicial power of the United States, shall be vested in one *supreme* Court, and in such *inferior* Courts as the Congress may from time to time ordain and establish.") (emphasis added).

250. McGinnis, *supra* n. 17, at 545.

251. *See* 28 U.S.C. §§ 291(b), 292(a) (2003).

252. *See id.* §§ 294(a), 294(c).

253. *See id.* § 294(c).

of the circuit court in question.[254] In all of these arrangements, the statutory power to "designate" a judge to sit temporarily on a court to which he was not commissioned belongs to the chief judge of the respective circuit or district.[255]

Importantly, as with circuit-riding, this practice of sitting by designation basically permits a justice to serve on an inferior court and decide cases, even though he is never actually commissioned or appointed to that court, and it similarly permits active and senior judges of circuit and district courts to serve on other circuits and on the district courts without an additional commission or appointment. This statutory system of sitting-by-designation even authorizes federal district court judges to sit on the circuit court level by designation, despite their not having been appointed to that higher appellate court. This custom of sitting-by-designation, in its different forms, therefore serves as an additional instance of Congress's treating the Supreme Court and the various inferior courts interchangeably, apparently without undermining the Constitution.[256] The Calabresi-Lindgren proposal for Supreme Court statutory term limits thus draws on these rich historical precedents for authority. Under this proposal, lower federal court judges would "ride" temporarily for eighteen years on the Supreme Court, in exactly inverse fashion to the way Supreme Court justices originally rode on the circuit courts. Moreover, the act of designating a lower court judge to ride on the Supreme Court for eighteen years would be by a separate act of presidential nomination and senatorial confirmation instead of by the order of a chief judge or justice. If circuit riding was constitutional, as the First Congress thought, and, as the Supreme Court held in *Stuart v. Laird*, then Supreme Court riding for an eighteen-year period of designation ought to be constitutional as well.

Under the statutory proposal put forward by Professors Paul Carrington and Roger Cramton, the Court's membership would be constitutionally fixed at nine justices; one new justice would be appointed in each two-year session of

---

254. *See id.*

255. *See id.* §§ 291(b), 292(a), 294(a), 294(c).

256. We do not address at length, in this Article, the serious possibility that the arrangements for sitting-by-designation and circuit-riding are unconstitutional as a matter of the original meaning of the Constitution because they violate the Appointments Clause. Both practices are well established in our constitutional system, and although circuit-riding is no longer used, the reasons for its termination were practical, not constitutional. *See generally*, Glick, *supra* n. 33. Specifically, the physical and practical difficulties in riding circuit and its detrimental impact on the ability to attract the best qualified candidates to the Court, coupled by the geographic expansion in the United States, caused Congress to create separate inferior courts that do not require Supreme Court justices to sit by designation. *See id.*

Congress. At any given time, the Supreme Court would consist of the nine most junior commissioned justices. Other, more senior justices would be eligible to sit by designation on the lower federal courts. Those senior justices could also be called back to the Court if one of the nine junior justices were recused or during any period when the Senate failed to fill a vacancy on the Court during a session of Congress.

As with our statutory proposal, the Carrington-Cramton version is bolstered by the constitutional tradition of circuit riding whereby membership on different Article III courts could be exercised by someone commissioned to sit only on the Supreme Court. The main difference between the Carrington-Cramton proposal and circuit riding is that, under the former, justices would spend their first eighteen years on the Supreme Court and any other time beyond that sitting by designation on the lower federal courts. With circuit riding, justices simultaneously spent part of each year either sitting on the Supreme Court or riding circuit.

The objection that the Appointments Clause contemplates a separate office of Supreme Court justice might also be made to the Carrington-Cramton proposal, which envisions something less than life tenure as an active duty Supreme Court justice for officers commissioned to the Supreme Court. Given that the Appointments Clause seems to contemplate a separate office of judge of the Supreme Court, it is hard to see how that office could be filled for only eighteen years and not for life. Furthermore, the Carrington-Cramton proposal contemplates dual service of Supreme Court justices on the Supreme Court and on the lower federal courts with the first eighteen years being on the Supreme Court and any remaining time being on the lower federal courts. In this respect, the Carrington-Cramton proposal contemplates commissioned Supreme Court justices as having duties on both the Supreme and inferior federal courts, which is arguably inconsistent with the constitutional requirement that there be a separate and distinct office of Supreme Court judge.

Under the U.S. Supreme Court's Appointments Clause caselaw, it is permissible for Congress to annex new duties to an existing office so long as those duties are germane to the duties of the existing office. In *Weiss v. United States*,[257] the Court considered the question of whether military judges could be picked from the ranks of commissioned officers of the armed services without those military judges being separately nominated by the president and confirmed by the senate to their positions as military judges. The Court

---

257. 510 U.S. 163, 173–76 (1994).

rightly concluded that it had been settled by history and practice that the duty of serving as a military judge and meting out military discipline was germane to the ordinary and accepted duties of all commissioned military officers. Therefore, the Court concluded it was constitutional for Congress to allow judge advocates general to appoint commissioned officers to be military judges even without a separate act of presidential nomination and senatorial confirmation.

Applying the *Weiss* germaneness analysis to the Calabresi-Lindgren statutory proposal, the issue raised would be whether it is germane to the duties of a lower federal court judge to take time out from serving on their lower federal court for eighteen years to be a Supreme Court justice. Quite simply, this seems preposterous. An eighteen-year total sabbatical from one's regular duties as a lower federal court judge is hardly germane to those duties in the way that occasionally sitting by designation on other lower courts might be. The same criticism applies to the Carrington-Cramton proposal as well. Under their proposal, after eighteen years Supreme Court justices will do little work on the Supreme Court except rulemaking and (for the most recently retired justice) occasionally filling in for recused justices. Their duties would consist almost entirely of sitting on the lower federal courts. Such lower federal court service—done to the exclusion of Supreme Court work—hardly seems to us to be germane to the job of being a Supreme Court Justice. Thus, both the Calabresi-Lindgren and the Carrington-Cramton statutory proposals for instituting an eighteen-year term limit flunk the Appointments Clause test of *Weiss v. United States*. Both statutes unconstitutionally attach nongermane duties to an office rendering that officer the holder of two offices rather than one, thus violating the Appointments Clause.

Defenders of the two statutes might respond, as previously noted,[258] that the statutes in question would require an act of Presidential nomination and Senatorial confirmation before a judge could come to sit by designation or otherwise on the Supreme Court. In this way, the statutory proposals would preserve the President's power to appoint any judges or justices to the federal judiciary and to the Supreme Court. In fact, by preserving the President's appointment power even for designations, the Calabresi-Lindgren statutory proposal could be argued to be *more* constitutional than the prevailing sitting-by-designation systems, whereby the chief judges of the various circuits and districts are authorized to designate active and senior judges and justices to sit on other circuit or district

---

258. *See supra* notes 240–246 and accompanying text, and particularly *supra* n. 242.

courts.[259] Thus, the two statutory proposals could be argued to pose no more of a threat to the President's appointment power than was posed by the ancient practice of justices commissioned to sit on the Supreme Court being required as well to ride circuit and sit as circuit judges—a post to which they had not been commissioned.

It is a close question, but we believe that the best and most plausible reading of the Appointments Clause is that it does contemplate a separately commissioned office of Justice of the Supreme Court. We thus do not believe that someone who has been confirmed to a lower federal court judgeship can be authorized to sit-by-designation on the Supreme Court for eighteen years, since the duty of serving for eighteen years on the Supreme Court would not be germane to the job of being a lower federal court judge. If this were to happen, there would be no separately commissioned offices of being a Supreme Court justice and being a lower court judge. This seems to us to be contrary to the situation the Appointments Clause presumes will prevail. Arguably, circuit riding, which involved appending some limited lower court duties to the job of being a Supreme Court justice, still respected the mandate of the Appointments Clause that there be a separate office of Supreme Court justice. Moreover, spending most of each year as a Supreme Court justice and only a few months circuit riding arguably meant that some germane lower court duties had been attached to the job of being a Supreme Court justice. Under a system of lower court judges riding on the Supreme Court, there would be no separate office of Supreme Court justice and the lower court judge would be taking an eighteen-year complete sabbatical from his lower federal court judgeship. This can hardly be described as the addition of a germane additional duty. We are thus in the end unpersuaded that the circuit-riding precedent permits a practice of lower court judges sitting by designation on the Supreme Court.

Moreover, we are not completely persuaded, *Stuart v. Laird* notwithstanding, that circuit riding was itself constitutional as a matter of pure originalism. The question depended on whether the justices' lower court duties were so extensive that they were not germane to the job of being a Supreme Court justice. While we think that some limited lower court duties like riding circuit for a month or two might be germane to the job of being a Supreme Court justice, the very onerous lower court duties imposed on Supreme Court justices during our early constitutional history were arguably not germane and were a threat to judicial independence.[260] It is not even clear that the ancient

---

259. *See supra* n. 255.

260. *See* Steven G. Calabresi & David Presser, *A Proposal to Reinstitute Circuit Riding*, Minn. L. Rev. (forthcoming 2006).

practice of chief judges designating judges commissioned on other courts to sit on their courts does not raise an Appointments Clause issue, although here, at least, the duties of occasionally sitting on courts other than the one a judge has been commissioned to are germane. In any event, the constitutionality of judges sitting by designation is certainly established as a matter of practice.

On the other hand, many of the original Supreme Court justices apparently thought circuit riding was unconstitutional because they had been appointed and commissioned to sit on the Supreme Court and not on the circuit courts. It has been suggested by Professor Bruce Ackerman that the Federalist Justices decided *Stuart v. Laird* the way they did, more out of fear of the Jeffersonians who were then clearly in power, than because they agreed that circuit riding was constitutional.[261] *Stuart v. Laird* upholds circuit riding by saying it was established as a matter of precedent by the First Congress when that Congress provided for circuit riding in the Judiciary Act of 1789. This is not the same thing as saying that as an original matter circuit riding was constitutionally permissible. If extensive and onerous circuit-riding duties are constitutionally dubious as an original matter, then perhaps *Stuart v. Laird* ought not to be extended to allow a new practice of lower federal court judges riding on the Supreme Court—a practice that unlike circuit riding would fly in the face of 215 years of contrary practice. Nor should we extrapolate from the dubious circuit-riding precedent the notion that one can be assigned to spend one's first eighteen years as a Supreme Court justice sitting on the Supreme Court and any subsequent years sitting on the lower federal courts, as Carrington and Cramton would do. The circuit-riding precedent suggests that Supreme Court justices can in the same year have duties on both the Supreme and inferior federal courts. It does not necessarily suggest further that one can carve up a justice's total term and allocate the first eighteen years of it to Supreme Court business and the remainder to lower federal court cases. What Carrington and Cramton propose is an extension beyond circuit riding. If one thinks extensive and onerous circuit riding duties were constitutionally dubious as an original matter, as we do, one ought not to extend this dubious precedent to the new situation Carrington and Cramton contemplate.

At the end of the day, we think that originalists ought to find both the Calabresi-Lindgren and the Carrington-Cramton statutory proposals to be constitutionally problematic as violating the Appointments and Commission Clauses, which presume that the office of Supreme Court justice is a separate and distinct office to which nongermane duties cannot be attached. Burkean

---

261. Bruce Ackerman, *The Failure of the Founding Fathers: Jefferson, Marshall, and the Rise of Presidential Democracy* 163–198 (2005).

constitutional law traditionalists ought to conclude that the precedent of circuit riding cannot be extended to allow Supreme Court riding because of 215 years of contrary practice wherein we have always assumed that the offices of Supreme Court justice and lower court judge were separate and distinct offices. We conclude therefore that the best reading of the Appointments Clause is that it contemplates a separate office of Supreme Court justice to which individuals must be appointed for life and not merely for eighteen years.

This reading of the Appointments Clause is in our view bolstered by the Clause in Article I that provides that there shall be a chief justice of the United States who shall preside over Senate impeachment trials of the President. That clause clearly contemplates a separate office of chief justice, much as the Appointments Clause contemplates a separate office of justices of the Supreme Court. Put together, we think the most plausible reading of these two clauses—and clearly the reading most in accord with 215 years of actual practice—is that the office of Supreme Court justice is a separately commissioned office.

More importantly, the two statutory proposals could be challenged under the provision granting life tenure to members of the federal judiciary. Article III, section 1 of the Constitution provides that "The Judges, both of the supreme and inferior Courts, shall hold their Offices during good Behavior...."[262] This language might be read in two ways. First, the more natural reading: because of the phrase "both of" and because of the placement of "their," the provision might require that "Judges" of the Supreme Court must have life tenure, as must "Judges" of the inferior courts. This reading would dictate that the Supreme Court and the inferior courts are to be distinct entities, and therefore that life tenure must be guaranteed to members of both courts.[263] It would follow that limiting the tenure of "Judges" of the "supreme Court," under both statutory proposals violates this provision even though it would grant life tenure to the former justice as a judge of the "inferior" court.

This is not the only plausible way to interpret this provision for life tenure. It can easily be read to require simply that "Judges" at all levels ("both of the supreme and inferior Courts") must enjoy life tenure,[264] a proposition that does not at all mandate that life tenure on the Supreme Court and life tenure on the inferior courts be mutually exclusive. Under this interpretation, limit-

---

262. U.S. Const. art. III, § 1.

263. *See* McGinnis, *supra* n. 17, at 545 (noting that this interpretation is probably the more natural reading).

264. U.S. Const. art. III, § 1.

ing an individual's tenure on the Supreme Court would pass constitutional muster so long as that individual otherwise enjoyed life tenure on the federal bench (i.e., on the "supreme and inferior Courts.") The statutory term limits proposals, which would limit the tenure of Supreme Court justices while guaranteeing life tenure as a federal judge, would thus be constitutionally valid.

The text of Article III, section 1 (unlike that of the Appointments Clause) is ambiguous on whether it specifies a Supreme Court distinct from inferior courts.[265] It could be read to mean that life tenure must be guaranteed to Supreme Court justices, as well as to lower federal judges, in distinct capacities. Or it could as easily be read to support the interpretation Carrington and Cramton would defend: that judges at all levels ("both of the supreme and inferior Courts") must enjoy life tenure. Under this latter reading, the text poses no special requirement that judges have life tenure on that particular court. In fact, had the Framers intended to ensure that all persons appointed to the Supreme Court have life tenure to that Court, and that all persons appointed to the inferior courts should have life tenure to those particular courts, they easily could have done so. They might have provided, "The Judges, both of the supreme and inferior Courts, shall hold their respective Offices during good behavior." Such a clarification would have shown conclusively that the first reading is correct. Yet the constitutional text as it stands is ambiguous between these two interpretations; it plausibly supports the Carrington-Cramton reading that life tenure is guaranteed to members of the federal judiciary in general.[266]

The response to this point, however, is that the Appointments Clause and the Clause providing for the chief justice to preside at Senate impeachment trials of the President seem most plausibly to us to suggest that the office of being a Supreme Court justice is a separate and distinct office to which nongermane lower federal court duties cannot be attached. Admittedly, this is a somewhat formalistic reading of these two clauses in conjunction with the good behavior clause, but separation of powers rules often are somewhat formulistic. Absent the Appointments Clause and the Chief Justice Presiding Clause, we might agree with Carrington and Cramton that the Good Behavior Clause standing alone is ambiguous, although even then we would argue that for 215 years we have acted as though the office of Supreme Court justice was a separate office to which nongermane lower federal court duties cannot be attached. Reading all of these clauses together, however, and knowing what the practice has been

---

265. *See* McGinnis, *supra* n. 17, at 545 ("The most natural reading may require (and the Framers certainly expected) judges to be appointed to a distinct Supreme Court, but the language is ambiguous.").

266. *See* Amar & Calabresi, *supra* n. 3.

for 215 years, we are not persuaded that the Carrington-Cramton reading of the Good Behavior Clause is a permissible one. For that reason, we think both our statutory term limits proposal and the Carrington-Cramton statutory proposal are doomed.

Carrington and Cramton might nonetheless argue that their reading of the Good Behavior Clause is consistent with the purpose behind the life tenure provision—to preserve judicial independence—by ensuring judges do not depend on the political branches for their tenure of office. To achieve this purpose, it is not at all necessary that life tenure be guaranteed for any particular court.[267] Rather, judges need only be guaranteed that they may stay on the federal bench for life and that they will not face retaliation for their decisions by Congress, the President, or the public. Both statutory proposals would satisfy this purpose and would guarantee that judges have life tenure and that their terms on the Supreme Court are fixed by time.

The Appointments Clause and the Chief Justice Presiding Clause, however, both seem to contemplate a separate office of Supreme Court justice—a problem unaddressed by this functionalist argument. The Carrington-Cramton proposal runs afoul of these two clauses, no matter what functional justifications might underlie it. Under a textualist approach to constitutional interpretation, the purposes underlying a constitutional provision cannot be allowed to trump the plain meaning of the constitutional text.

Carrington and Cramton might also argue that their interpretation of the Good Behavior Clause providing for life tenure is supported by historical practice. And the practices of circuit-riding and sitting-by-designation are important historical antecedents to both statutory term limits proposals.[268]

> [T]he early Supreme Court Justices who rode circuit sat as members of inferior courts and thus our early traditions suggest that the inferior courts and the Supreme Court did not have to possess completely

---

267. Of course, one could easily argue that life tenure in appointment to a particular court is important, since Congress could otherwise punish judges for their decisions by demoting them to a lower court. We completely agree with this argument, which is why we believe that a fixed term is the only justifiable limit on the tenure of justices (as opposed to retention elections, stronger removal powers, or renewable term limits). *See infra* notes 283–299.

268. Indeed, the Calabresi-Lindgren statutory term limits proposal would be even better because it preserves the President's nomination power and the Senate's confirmation power, whereas the other practices permit(ed) sitting-by-designation with the approval of only the chief judge of the circuit courts.

separate personnel. Even today, retired Justices sometimes sit by designation on courts to which they were never appointed, as do many district and circuit judges.[269]

Indeed, historical practice demonstrates that the first interpretation—that life tenure on the "inferior and supreme Courts" must be treated as mutually exclusive—did *not* carry the day in 1789 when the Judiciary Act was passed by the First Congress. Rather, the established practices of circuit-riding and sitting by designation could be said to support the interpretation Carrington and Cramton defend—that life tenure must be preserved for members of the federal judiciary generally, without any distinction between the two courts. And this has been the prevailing view.[270] Given the textual ambiguity of the Good Behavior Clause and the fact that the purpose of life tenure is satisfied by the statutory term limits proposals as effectively as by the current system of life tenure, this historical support should be an important factor for consideration.

The problem with this historical argument is, again, that it assumes as a given that extensive and onerous circuit riding duties were constitutional, a point we are not convinced is correct, and, second, it assumes that if circuit riding is constitutional its mirror image—Supreme Court riding—must be constitutional as well. Alternatively, in the case of the Carrington-Cramton proposal, the historical argument presumes that, just because Congress could ask justices to sit in the same year on both the Supreme and inferior federal courts, it could therefore carve up a justice's total tenure and allocate the first eighteen years of it solely to Supreme Court business and any time beyond eighteen years to lower court business.

All of this, however, seems to us to fly in the face of the Appointments Clause's and the Chief Justice Presiding Clause's presumption that the office of Supreme Court justice is a separate and distinct office to which nongermane lower federal court duties may not be attached. We think this presumption has been sanctioned by 215 years of unbroken practice, which is why most people's first instinct is that statutorily imposed term limits on Supreme Court justices are unconstitutional. In this case, we think most people's first instinct is also the conclusion that one ought to reach. The argument that the Good Behavior Clause does not contemplate separate offices for Supreme and Inferior Court federal judges is too clever by half.

---

269. McGinnis, *supra* n. 17, at 545.
270. *See id.*

The Desirability of Imposing Term Limits by Statute

Even if the two statutory proposals could pass constitutional muster, which we believe they cannot, there would still remain the question whether it is desirable to institute a system of Supreme Court term limits by statute. The primary advantage of reforming life tenure through a statute, as opposed to a constitutional amendment, is that passing a statute is far easier than amending the Constitution. To pass an amendment, two-thirds of both Houses of Congress, or two-thirds of the states, would first have to propose the amendment.[271] Then, three-fourths of the states would have to ratify it.[272] Throughout history, excluding the Bill of Rights, only seventeen provisions have successfully made it through this process.[273] Moreover, many of the amendments that made it through the Article V process were the product of incredibly strong historical forces, as was the case with the Reconstruction Amendments,[274] or they were the result of historical incidents that exposed fundamental flaws in the original Constitution.[275]

There is, however, a key problem in the whole concept of establishing term limits through a statute, which is that term limits established by statute rather than by constitutional amendment are subject to greater manipulation by future Congresses:

> If statutory Supreme Court riding had been adopted and had proved superior to our current system in curbing the Supreme Court's nationalizing tendencies, interest groups that generally benefit from eviscerating the restraints of federalism would have tried to amend the statute. Moreover, the President and a Congress of one party might have been tempted to create the position of Supreme Court Justice instead of Supreme Court rider to give more power to their prospective appointees.[276]

---

271. *See* U.S. Const. art. V.

272. *See id.*

273. *See* U.S. Const. amend. XI-XXVII. This includes, of course, the two amendments on prohibition that cancel out. *See* U.S. Const. amend. XVIII, amend. XXI (repealing the Eighteenth Amendment).

274. *See* U.S. Const. amend. XIII (ratified in 1865), amend. XIV (ratified in 1868), amend. XV (ratified in 1870).

275. *See*, e.g., U.S. Const. amend. XXV (providing for Presidential succession, the need for which was revealed after the assassination of President Kennedy). The Reconstruction Amendments would also fit in this category.

276. McGinnis, *supra* n. 17, at 546.

Thus, adopting a statutory term limits proposal runs the risk, as Ward Farnsworth points out, that interest groups, Congress, or the President might attempt to tamper with the statutory scheme of term limits in the future in order to achieve political gain.[277] For example, if one party were to gain control over both the Presidency and Congress, they might manipulate the statute to permit their appointees to serve for longer than eighteen years or even for life, a result that would be particularly pernicious if the other party had abided by the statutory term limits during preceding years when they were in power.[278] This risk of manipulation through the political process, which would not exist for a term limits constitutional amendment, greatly undermines the desirability of any effort to reform life tenure by statute. Of even greater concern is that, if Congress were to establish a precedent of being able to change the tenure of justices and other federal judges by statute, Congress might become even more daring and later experiment with other independence-threatening forms of limits, perhaps even in substantive ways. For example, as Professor Redish suggests, interpreting the constitutional provision as Carrington and Cramton have suggested might permit Congress to pass a statute that allows it to demote a single justice to the lower federal courts whenever it chooses.[279] By sanctioning statutory alterations in the justices' tenure, the argument continues, Congress could be empowered to undermine judicial independence in a disastrous way.

Carrington and Cramton might respond to this objection by claiming that there would be immense political pressures on Congress and the President (including the possible political check of the President on Congress, or vice versa) to make the theoretical possibility of abuse one that is unlikely to occur in practice. Moreover, Carrington and Cramton might contend that the statutory analysis conducted above revealed that the Court should find a term limits proposal to be constitutional only if it preserves the core of judicial independence from political pressure, which is a fundamental requirement of Article III.[280] Indeed, using the structural constitutional analysis of judicial in-

---

277. Farnsworth, *supra* n. 22, at 432–34.

278. For example, suppose that Democrats are in control of both the executive and legislative branches, and, after passing the statute, they abide by it for three appointments. Their appointments are therefore bound by the eighteen-year term limit. Then, suppose that Republicans gained control of both the executive and legislative branches, repealed the statute in order to re-institute life tenure, and then appointed several members to the Court for life. This outcome demonstrates the dangers that this manipulability problem presents.

279. Conversation between Jeff Oldham and Professor Martin Redish, Oct. 16, 2002.

280. *See supra* notes 267–269 and accompanying text.

dependence that Professor Redish advocates, a term limits statute that enabled Congress to demote justices for political reasons would violate more fundamental constitutional principles of independence than the Article III salary or tenure provisions.[281] Carrington and Cramton might claim that their specific proposal protects the Court from political pressure at the same time as it modestly limits justices' tenure. If Congress were to venture beyond this proposal and attempt to provide substantive limits on justices' tenure, then the Court would be justified in striking down those efforts.

We think the manipulability of statutory term limits by future Congresses makes this a very dangerous constitutional road to go down. We are not persuaded that, once Congress has tampered with the life tenure of Supreme Court justices by instituting eighteen-year terms, it might not be tempted to tamper with that independence further to manipulate the outcomes of particular cases. The tenure of justices of the Supreme Court is not a matter that should be settled by Congress as a matter of good public policy: it is something that ought to be constitutionally fixed. Thus, even if the statutory term limits proposals were constitutional, which they are not, we believe it would be a bad idea as a matter of policy for Congress to start tinkering by statute with the tenure of Supreme Court justices for the first time in American history.

The Carrington-Cramton statutory proposal suffers from an additional and very serious defect because it provides that if Congress does not fill a vacancy during a two year session of Congress, a senior justice who would otherwise be unable to sit as an active Supreme Court justice, would again become an active member of the Court. Imagine a situation where the justice in his eighteenth year about to be bumped into retirement is a Democrat. Now imagine that a Republican President were to try to fill the statutory vacancy with a Republican but that President had to persuade a Democratic Senate to go along. The President would want to fill the vacancy right away to remove the Democratic justice. The Democratic Senate, however, would want to wait until the very end of the session to fill the vacancy to keep the Democratic justice present and voting on the Supreme Court for a longer time. The Democratic Senate might even refuse to fill the vacancy at all, thus keeping the eighteen-year Democratic justice on active Supreme Court duty beyond his supposed eighteen-year term. This is a statutory scheme that is rife with possibilities for abuse. For this reason alone, we would reject any such statute out of hand.[282]

---

281. See Redish, supra n. 65, at 677.

282. The Carrington-Cramton proposal has been revised to remove this defect and adopt fixed terms much like our own proposal.

Imposing Term Limits through Informal Practice

Aside from constitutional amendments or statutory term limits proposals, a variety of informal options are available to lawmakers, and to the justices themselves, for reforming the system of life tenure. In this section we focus on ways in which the Senate, the Court, or individual justices might move a technically life-tenured Court toward a de facto system of term limits, leading eventually to a more formal system of term limits.[283]

Senate-Imposed Limits through Term Limit Pledges

The Senate has an important constitutional role to play in the appointment process, and it could use this role to push us toward a system of term limits for the Supreme Court by "insist[ing] that all future court nominees publicly agree to term limits, or risk nonconfirmation. Though such agreements would be legally unenforceable, justices could feel honor-bound to keep their word."[284]

Like the recent movement toward term limits pledges for federal legislators[285] that has developed since *U.S. Term Limits, Inc. v. Thornton*,[286] in which the Court struck down state legislative attempts to set term limits on federal legislators, Senators could require each nominee to agree to resign after eighteen years, or after some other suitable term. Of course, such an agreement would be unenforceable, and there is no guarantee that a justice would feel compelled to follow the pledge. Indeed, having made a term limits pledge has not deterred some legislators from continuing to run for Congress beyond their allotted terms. The most common justification for such actions has been, in short, that if "the people" want the legislator to continue in office, then the term limits pledge has been drowned out by the voice of democracy.[287] This justification for not abiding by the term limits pledge would not aid justices, of course, since their continuance in office would not be a direct result of "the will of the peo-

---

283. This section expounds upon Amar & Calabresi, *supra* n. 3.

284. *Id.*

285. Jonathan L. Entin, *Insubstantial Questions and Federal Jurisdiction: A Footnote to the Term-Limits Debate*, 2 Nev. L.J. 608 (2002).

286. 514 U.S. 779 (1995).

287. Former Congressman J.C. Watts is an example of one who ran for re-election in 2000 despite a 1994 pledge to serve no more than three terms. See Republican Term Limits Debate and Poll <http://www.youdebate.com/DEBATES/term_limits_rep.HTM> (visited September 29, 2005). Watts was re-elected in 2000, but decided not to run for a fifth term.

ple." But a justice's failure to resign after the promised term could generate a public backlash leading eventually to a constitutional amendment establishing term limits.

This kind of term limits pledge "would not raise judicial independence or due process problems" that accompany the kinds of "promises" that nominated justices are sometimes asked to make in Senate confirmations, like pledges to rule certain ways on particular issues.[288] Unlike such substantive promises, term limits pledges are merely "a promise to resign on a fixed date,…comport[ing] with judicial integrity."[289]

Notwithstanding these considerations we do not favor term limit pledges.[290] Any justice who arrives on the Court having pledged to step down after a term of years will likely be viewed by the other members of the Supreme Court as having compromised a key bulwark of judicial independence. He would look so eager to serve on the Court that he was willing to undercut a standard practice of the Court, thereby increasing pressures on future nominees. If a justice thinks it proper to step down after eighteen years, he may do so; what he probably should not do is seem to offer a promise to step down to gain a place on the Court. We think the other justices would so disapprove of a new justice having taken a term limits pledge that it could compromise that justice's ability to function in his job. Voluntary term limits pledges might be observed by some justices and not by others, which would make a mockery of the whole idea of eighteen-year limited and staggered terms. For both of these reasons, we would encourage any Supreme Court nominee who was importuned to take a term limits pledge to decline to do so on judicial independence grounds.

Court-Imposed Limits through Internal Court Rules

The Supreme Court itself could play a role in deterring justices from serving as long as possible on the Court and in moving us toward a system of de facto term limits. The Court holds powerful tools for moving us toward such a system, such as its internal court rules, or, more subtly, its ability to modify the seniority system: just as the House of Representatives adopted internal term limits in 1994 for some committee chairs. As Professors Akhil Amar and Calabresi observed, "perhaps the justices themselves might collectively codify retirement guidelines in court rules modifying the seniority system or creat-

---

288. Amar & Amar, *supra* n. 56.

289. Amar & Calabresi, *supra* n. 3, at A23.

290. Professor Calabresi was persuaded by Professor Lindgren that it was a bad idea for him to endorse term limits pledges in confirmation hearings in his 2002 op-ed piece with Professor Akhil Amar.

ing an ethical norm of retirement at certain milestones."[291] The Court could thus adopt a retirement rule requiring justices to step down after eighteen years of service on the Court. Though such internal rules would not be legally enforceable, the pressure on a justice from his fellow justices and from the institution could be a valuable method of limiting tenure. Moreover, the Court's imposing such limits on itself would be a highly desirable way of bringing about term limits for its justices.

Another way for the Court itself to decrease the incentives for justices to remain on the bench is to modify its seniority system.[292] Currently, the most senior justice in the majority decides which justice will write the majority opinion.[293] Thus the chief justice assigns the opinion whenever he finds himself in the majority; if the chief justice dissents, then the next most senior justice assigns the majority opinion.[294] Rewarding the most senior justices with priority in deciding which opinions to write creates enormous incentives for justices to remain on the Court for long periods and into a later age.[295] By eliminating this seniority system, or modifying it in some regard, the Court can itself eliminate these incentives.[296]

To be sure, appointing more senior justices to assign decisions is logical; abolishing the seniority system might seem too drastic. Alternatively, through its various political checks on the Court, Congress could play a positive role in persuading the Court to develop a system of term limits through its internal court rules. For example, "Congress could...restructure judicial salaries, pensions, office space and other perks to give future justices incentives" to step down after a set number of years.[297] Giving a huge pension to any Supreme Court justice who retired after his eighteenth year of service might well accomplish a de facto term limit. Or Congress could reduce the number of law clerks allowed each justice, which, by increasing the justice's personal responsibilities, might reduce the ability—or willingness—of a justice to continue serving as late in age as they currently do.[298] Likewise, by statutorily increasing the mandatory jurisdiction of the Court or otherwise adding to the

---

291. Amar & Calabresi, *supra* n. 3.

292. *See id.*

293. *See, e.g.,* J. Clark Kelso & Charles D. Kelso, *Statutory Interpretation: Four Theories in Disarray,* 53 S.M.U. L. Rev. 81, 120 n. 55 (2000).

294. *See id.*

295. *See* Amar & Calabresi, *supra* n. 3.

296. *See id.*

297. *Id.*

298. Professor Bill Stuntz, E-mail conversation between Professors Akhil Amar and Bill Stuntz, Aug. 9, 2002 (on file with authors).

Court's workload, Congress can reduce the incentives for justices to remain on the Court as long as they currently do.

Of course, a political war between Congress and the Court over these incentives is undesirable; Congress must be cautious and deliberative in using these mechanisms as a way of encouraging the Court to move voluntarily toward a system of term limits. But these measures may be effective ways for Congress to encourage the justices to move toward informal term limits. And, short of amending the Constitution, Court-imposed term limits on justices, with or without congressional prodding, might be the most desirable method of reforming life tenure.

Justice-Imposed Limits through Tradition

In theory, at least, Supreme Court justices themselves could individually lead the way toward a reform of life tenure, even without a formal Court-ordered arrangement. Conceivably, a group of justices could try to start a tradition of retiring from the Court after a certain number of years, or at a set age, in the hopes that institutional pressure could develop that would bear on all future justices. Some federal courts of appeals, like the Second Circuit, do have an established norm that all judges on the court take senior status on the first day they are legally eligible to do so. Eventually, one might hope such a practice might lead to a custom of justices resigning from the Court after a fixed number of years, or perhaps even at a certain age.[299] After enough iterations of custom, such a practice might even be formalized by passage of a constitutional amendment much as the two-term tradition for Presidents was eventually formalized by constitutional amendment.

But this solution has its difficulties. Is it realistic or even desirable for one or two justices to try to start a tradition of retiring from the Supreme Court after a set number of years? Probably not. Such justices would face a major collective-action problem in trying to persuade their long-serving colleagues to follow their good example. Given the level of partisan hostility on the Supreme Court at the moment, and given the extent to which most recent justices seem to have tried to practice strategic retirement, we believe urging a justice to retire after a set term without regard to strategic considerations would be like unilateral disarmament during the Cold War. There is quite simply very little reason to hope that, if one justice were to retire early, any other justice currently on the Court would follow such a good example. In this respect, the Supreme Court is fundamentally different from the presidency be-

---

299. *See* Amar & Calabresi, *supra* n. 3.

cause one President like George Washington or Thomas Jefferson could set a tradition for all succeeding Presidents, whereas one of nine justices essentially cannot. We therefore do not urge any of the current justices to retire early but hope instead for a Supreme Court term limits amendment that will prospectively usher in such an era of term limits after 2009.

Conclusion

We join in Professor Prakash's view that "life tenure is a long-lived constitutional aberration that we should belatedly repudiate."[300] Although defenders of life tenure have long been able to say, "[i]f it ain't broke, don't fix it,"[301] this essay has shown that the current system of life tenure for justices is deeply flawed. The effects are subtle and not readily visible to the American public, but the dangers are real and the threat is severe. Life tenure deserves serious reconsideration; indeed, it should be abolished. Inertia should no longer justify its continuation.

In place of life tenure, we join several other commentators in advocating a system of staggered, nonrenewable term limits of eighteen years, after which justices would be able, if they wanted, to sit on the lower federal courts. We believe this system must be achieved through a constitutional amendment; it cannot be done, as Professors Carrington and Cramton propose, by statute. We do not favor a system whereby Supreme Court nominees are forced to take term limits pledges in their confirmation hearings but would favor other informal methods of encouraging justices to step down after eighteen years, such as offering a pension at that time or modifying the Court's internal seniority rule so no justice who stayed longer than eighteen years would have the power by virtue of his seniority to assign an opinion. We do not think it realistic to hope that the justices would follow George Washington's example and relinquish power voluntarily because we doubt any other justice could trust her colleagues to follow her example.

Moving to a system of eighteen-year, staggered terms for Supreme Court justices is fundamentally a conservative idea that would restore the norms in this country that prevailed on the Court between 1789 and 1970. During that period, vacancies occurred about once every two years, and justices served an average of 14.9 years on the Court. Only since 1970, after the Warren Court Revolution, have Supreme Court vacancies begun to occur more than three

---

300. Prakash, *supra* n. 17, at 581.
301. Monaghan, *supra* n. 17, at 1212.

years apart. Only since 1970 have justices been leaving the bench after serving an average of 26.1 years. We recommend a Burkean, revolution, whereby the country recommits itself by constitutional amendment to the tenure practices that held for Supreme Court justices for most of our history. The United States Supreme Court ought not to become a gerontocracy like the leadership cadre of the Chinese Communist Party. It is high time that we imposed a reasonable system of term limits on the justices of the U.S. Supreme Court.

APPENDIX

Table 1.
Justices of the U.S. Supreme Court
Beginning of October 2005 Term

	Age	Year Appointed	Year on Court
Justice John Paul Stevens	85.5	1975	29.8
Justice Sandra Day O'Connor	75.5	1981	24.0
Justice Antonin Scalia	69.6	1986	19.0
Justice Anthony M. Kennedy	69.2	1988	17.6
Justice David H. Souter	66.0	1990	15.0
Justice Clarence Thomas	57.3	1991	14.0
Justice Ruth Bader Ginsburg	72.6	1993	12.2
Justice Stephen G. Breyer	67.1	1994	11.2
Chief Justice John G. Roberts	50.7	2005	0.0
Mean	68.2	1989	15.9
Median	69.2	1990	15.0

"Marble Palace, We've Got a Problem—with You"

L. A. Powe, Jr.[*]

From all indications a very good job has gotten even better. Ever since circuit riding was abolished, an appointment to the Supreme Court has been a great prize. And now, if the length of time justices have been savoring that prize is any measure, it has become even more desirable. Up to thirty years ago, on average, justices left the Court a little before their seventieth birthdays after holding the job for fifteen years. The tenure of the second John Marshall Harlan fit these averages almost perfectly. Recently, however, justices have been staying longer—lots longer. Over these past three decades, on average, the justices have exited at nearly eighty years old, having put in a quarter-century on the Court. In terms of average longevity, the current Court ranks right on top with the Marshall Court of 1834,[1] with an average tenure of nineteen years.

What this has meant for recent Presidents is a very skewed pattern of appointments to the Court, particularly in the last decade and a half. Bill Clinton became the first two-term president since James Monroe not to get at least three appointments to the Court. George W. Bush, so far, is faring well enough, although the vacancies he will now fill did not occur until his second term. One does not need to linger in a statistics course to agree that a period of three and a half decades of Supreme Court retirements does not produce a statistically significant sample, particularly with the anomalies of the years 1996–2004. One might claim, with reason, that this period should be thrown out of the mix—or at least placed into a category by itself. With Whitewater

---

[*] Anne Green Regents Chair, The University of Texas. I would like to thank Tom Krattenmaker, Sandy Levinson, and H.W. Perry for comments on earlier drafts.

1. Just before William Johnson and Marshall died and Gabriel Duvall resigned.

99

first and Monica Lewinsky next, Clinton's second term was plagued by scandal (real or imagined). The Court's own participation in the election of George W. Bush would have made his first-term selection of new justices (who would in turn decide the 2004 presidential election) problematical. That participation could have caused justices who might otherwise have retired earlier to delay their retirement until the taint of *Bush v. Gore*[2] was diluted by a new presidential election, decided by more than five voters. Nevertheless, even if good reasons underlie the lack of vacancies over the past decade, the problem of justices' enjoying a very lengthy stay at the fair does seem more entrenched than the happenstance of two iffy presidents facing a Senate capable of creating havoc and bloodying the sitting justices in the process.

Living Longer with Better Working Conditions

To some extent longevity at the Court reflects the increased lifespans of contemporary Americans, which in turn reflects the advances made in medicine during the past several decades. Even more, perhaps, it may reflect the extraordinary medical care that is available for the most affluent or powerful Americans. William J. Brennan recovered from throat cancer in 1978, a stroke the next year, and prostate cancer two years before he retired.[3] Lewis F. Powell experienced heavy bleeding following routine surgery yet served three more years. Cancer caused Harry A. Blackmun to have a radical prostatectomy in 1978, and it reappeared ten years later when he entered the Mayo Clinic for a hernia operation.[4] He continued on the Court, nevertheless, for another six years. Perhaps a Charles Whittaker, forced off the Court by deep depression in 1962 at age sixty-one,[5] might today find the right chemicals to extend a lackluster presence for at least another decade.

Still, medicine alone seems unable to explain justices' staying at the job longer and longer. Even without a Twenty-second Amendment, a six-term president is inconceivable; and while some members of the House or the Senate last upward of eighty, most do not. It is something about the Court. Most notably, that something is the lack of any forced retirement mechanism—one

---

2. 530 U.S. 98 (2000).

3. David N. Atkinson, *Leaving the Bench: Supreme Court Justices at the End* 154–55 (1999).

4. *Id.* at 161.

5. *Id.* at 128–30.

of the many unfortunate oversights of the Framers. In the twentieth century, no other country has made this error in drafting a constitution. Democracies have either a mandatory retirement age or term limits.[6] America is the odd country out.[7] For those who believe looking outside our borders is constitutional heresy, what the rest of the world does is confirmed by the fifty states. With the arguable exception of Rhode Island,[8] none has life tenure for judges.[9]

Our federal government is the only sovereign run by elected legislators who stay on the job only so long as they win elections, while justices, once confirmed, last as long as they exhibit "good behavior." Thurgood Marshall used to quip that he "was appointed to a life term and [he] intend[ed] to serve it,"[10] and he struggled on through the Reagan presidency, "looking like an old, sick man," with glaucoma that made reading difficult and hearing aids in both ears, not to mention a propensity to nap during oral arguments.[11]

We all note how presidents visibly age on the job. Justices do not seem to age so quickly. How has this come about? For an answer, we must go back almost two decades.

It is easy to recall the soft-ball question to Robert Bork at his confirmation hearings: "Why do you want to be a Supreme Court justice?" Bork answered: "Because it would be an intellectual feast."[12] Since he never was known for his sense of humor, his answer had to be taken seriously. He would feast on the rights of Americans.

It is far harder to recall the same question being asked a year earlier to William Rehnquist. He responded, "as you know[,] Earl Warren and Warren Burger worked the Brethren to death. My priority is to half the important workload of the Court without cutting staff." He then added with a smile "and I can do it without unionizing the Brethren." Rehnquist was known for a sense of humor and was perceived as adding a little levity into the proceedings, so, if he indeed made these remarks, no one took him seriously[13]—until he did just what he said he would.

---

6. *See supra* Steven Calabresi & James Lindgren, *Term Limits for the Supreme Court*, pp. 44–48.

7. *Id.*

8. Rhode Island has life tenure, but an easy removal process.

9. *See supra* Calabresi & Lindgren, pp. 44–48.

10. Atkinson, *supra* n. 3, at 158.

11. Juan Williams, *Thurgood Marshall: American Revolutionary* 379 (1998).

12. Hearings on the Nomination of Robert H. Bork before the Senate Judiciary Committee, 100th Cong., 1st Sess. Part I, at 854 (1987).

13. For those inclined to take the foregoing seriously, I made it up.

That's the remarkable thing. The Court now hears argument and decides between seventy-five and eighty cases a year, down from the 140 of the previous eras. And staffing has not diminished—far from it. Although justices in the Warren era would decide their 140 cases with the aid of only two law clerks, the current justices can have up to four (as seven of them do). Since every law clerk wants to play grown-up, the opinion-writing (at least at the early drafts) is turned over to these ever-eager and ambitious youths.

These working conditions are great. Thus for years John Paul Stevens has lived in Florida and commuted at 500 miles-per-hour, six miles above the old southern circuit to Washington only as necessary for oral argument[14] or Conference, the sole tasks that cannot be delegated to his clerks. He is not likely to be the last to do this—although the capitol and its party circuit have their attractions as A-list justices can attest.

Peaks and Valleys

The wonder is not why the justices last so long but why they retire at all (and the answer there seems to be that they are, like Marshall, "old and coming apart" when they finally do decide to retire).[15] Thus the four retirements in the last decade and a half were Brennan at eighty-four, to die seven years later; Marshall at eighty-two, to die at eighty-four; White, a veritable baby at seventy-five, and living to eighty-two; and Blackmun at eighty-five, the fourth oldest in Court history, dying within five years.[16] It is thus conceivable that White could have lasted past eighty, as well, and that Blackmun and Brennan could have, like Holmes, stayed on until ninety. With the possible exception of White (who seemingly had been bored for two decades), none was near the top of his game.

Many retire when they are nowhere near their top. Despite urgings from Chief Justice Warren and from his own wife, Hugo Black clung to his seat, memory slipping, trying unsuccessfully to surpass Stephen J. Field's longevity record (as had the first John Marshall Harlan). William O. Douglas in fact did surpass Field's record, but he had been bored with the Court's work for years

---

14. Apparently he cuts his arrival time so close that if his flight is canceled he cannot make oral argument. At least that is what happened on February 22, 2005. New York Times A14 (Feb. 23, 2005).

15. Howard Ball, *A Defiant Life: Thurgood Marshall and the Persistence of Racism in America* 379 (1998).

16. Justice Sandra Day O'Connor, who announced her retirement at age seventy-five, may now be added to this list. Chief Justice Rehnquist died in office at eighty.

(although he could be given a modest pass for not voluntarily yielding his seat easily to Nixon and Gerald Ford, since they had directly attacked judicial independence by attempting to impeach him for being too liberal[17]). By the late 1980s Marshall would occasionally need to be told how Brennan had voted so he could know how he should vote.[18] Blackmun had started fantasizing that the Constitution was in jeopardy because of his mortality.[19] Two of Powell's clerks during the 1985 Term believed he should step down, and others close to Powell thought his doing so in 1985 was already a year too late.[20] He stayed through the 1986 Term.

So one consequence of life tenure is that people stay too long. Another is that older people, like the rest of us (and dogs), do not learn (or care to learn) new tricks after awhile. Yet another consequence is that fewer opportunities arise for new vacancies. Perhaps one-third to one-half fewer Americans will sit on the twenty-first century Court than sat on the previous Courts. The country will never know what it has lost in that process.

In some sense, that Black, Blackmun, Brennan, Douglas, Marshall, and Powell were decidedly past their peaks is typical. As in sports, with the possible exception of Harlan, no one goes out on top.[21] For most justices, as for most professional athletes, there is a natural cycle: a couple of years to break in, a few more to peak, then a number of years enjoying that performance, then the inevitable decline of age. How long each period lasts and whether certain justices may prove exceptions to the averages, is debatable, but the hard fact of a curve exists. With the exception of Hugo Black's attacks on balancing in *Barenblatt*[22] and *Anastaplo*,[23] the outstanding justices of the twentieth century had staked out every major position they were going to take by the eighteenth anniversary of taking their seats.[24] And, for the typical justice, leav-

---

17. James E. DiTullio & John B. Schochet, *Saving This Honorable Court*, 90 Vir. L. Rev. 1093 (2004) lead with Douglas's attempt to outlast Ford and clearly side with the need for Douglas to have retired. They elide the impeachment by referring to Ford as Douglas's "old nemesis." *Id.* at 1094.

18. David Garrow, *Mental Decrepitude on the U.S. Supreme Court*, 67 U. Chi. L. Rev. 995, 1072 (2000).

19. Webster v. Reproductive Health Services, 492 U.S. 490, 538 (1989); Planned Parenthood v. Casey, 505 U.S. 833, 943 (1992).

20. John Jeffries, *Justice Lewis F. Powell, Jr.* 538–40 (1994).

21. Okay, Jim Brown and Barry Sanders did.

22. Barenblatt v. United States, 360 U.S. 109 (1959).

23. In re Anastaplo, 366 U.S. 82 (1961).

24. L. A. Powe, Jr., *Go Geezers Go*, 25 Law & Social Inquiry 1227, 1235–37 (2000). Douglas is an exception with Poe v. Ullman, 367 U.S. 497, 509 (1961) (dissent), Griswold

ing the Court after eighteen years would be leaving it at the peak. The country may get splendid performance out of aging justices, but it does not get new performance. The advantage of a set term limit on justices (and I favor eighteen years) is that it will virtually always mean the nation will have gotten the best out of its justices and that they will be leaving before the inevitable decline sets in. By introducing new members to the Court, new ideas and new approaches to problems become more likely. Or perhaps it may introduce challenges to the older approaches that will improve them.

Nevertheless, a set term brings with it two disadvantages: One is that the nation will lose some years of justices at the top of their learning curve—continuing to operate near their peaks. The other is, as Ward Farnsworth ably argues,[25] that we do not want too rapid a change in constitutional law, and introducing new justices regularly may promote such instability.

These downsides must be balanced against the upsides: having a Court with no one being too old or too long past prime, eliminating the incentives from retirement and appointment politics, and avoiding a Court that is too out of touch with the political consensus of the nation. Furthermore, rotation in office is a plus and is both implicit in republican theory and explicit in various constitutions, dating from the Articles of Confederation. Rotation in office brings in new people with (hopefully) new (and, even more hopefully, better) ideas. It also seems more democratic to spread power around than to leave it in the hands of a lucky few. Indeed, that is the premise of the Twenty-second Amendment, as well as that of various provisions in state constitutions limiting executive terms.

Putting the Justices Back into Politics

Who the President is matters. John F. Kennedy entreated Felix Frankfurter to leave, but Frankfurter, identifying the President with his infamous father, Joseph P. Kennedy, refused, only to yield his seat because of strokes[26] after *Baker v. Carr*.[27] In 1968, Earl Warren was coasting along at age seventy-seven.

---

v. Connecticut, 381 U.S. 479 (1965), and the equal protection revolution from Douglas v. California, 372 U.S. 353 (1963) through Levy v. Louisiana, 391 U.S. 68 (1968). But if there had been an eighteen-year term limit, a man of Douglas's age—forty—would never have been appointed.

25. Ward Farnsworth, *The Regulation of Turnover on the Supreme Court*, U. Ill. L. Rev. (2005).

26. Lucas A. Powe, Jr., *The Warren Court and American Politics* 205, 211 (2000).

27. 369 U.S. 186 (1962).

Then Lyndon B. Johnson announced that he would not seek the Democratic nomination, and Robert Kennedy, who Warren thought would be the next president, was assassinated. With Richard Nixon now having a seeming lock on the White House, Warren realized he was unlikely to survive a two-term Nixon presidency and suddenly retired so LBJ could pick his successor.[28]

Thurgood Marshall candidly announced (and Brennan fully agreed) that he wished to outlast the outrage—Ronald Reagan—whom the American people had misguidedly placed in the White House: "For all those people who wish very dearly for me to give up and quit and what-have-you, I hope you will pardon me for saying it, but, don't worry, I'm going to outlive those bastards."[29] Both he and Brennan then tried unsuccessfully to outlast Reagan's successor. They were hardly the first justices to have had this idea, and they have not been the last.

Roger Taney probably should have given James Buchanan, the Pennsylvania doughface, an opportunity to make an appointment when Taney was in his early 80s. He must have been stunned by the 1860 election that brought Lincoln to the White House; he then stayed on the Court until he died at age eighty-eight. His goal during his last three years was to block as much of the Northern war effort as possible so the South could successfully dismember the country.[30] Seventy years later, the oldest Court to that time afforded President Franklin Roosevelt not a single vacancy during his first term—the first time a President serving a full term was unable to make a single appointment. Four of the oldest justices—Willis Van Devanter, James McReynolds, George Sutherland, and Pierce Butler—had been invalidating every New Deal measure they could reach. They hoped for an electoral vindication in 1936 that never came; its absence ultimately forced their retirements. Life tenure should insulate the Court (to some extent) from partisan politics; perversely, however, it seems increasingly to encourage political calculation about when best to retire and present the seat to the President and party of the justice's choice. Apart from whether they would have chosen this system in the first place, justices seem forced to engage in purely political calculation about retirement.

Political calculation affects appointments as well as retirements. Politicians are fully aware of justices' staying longer on the bench and of Presidents' as-

---

28. Powe, *supra* n. 24, at 465, 474. (Warren's plan was thwarted by a Republican filibuster. *Id.*).

29. Ball, *supra* n. 15, at 379.

30. Writing to former president, Franklin Pierce, June 12, 1861, Taney expressed his hopes for peaceful separation of the North and South. Carl B. Swisher, *The Taney Period* 850 (1974).

sociated hopes of imposing their values on future generations.[31] One way for a current majority to take advantage of this situation is to appoint younger justices who will stay on the bench longer. Again, the data pool is too small to support any certainty that this is happening. Nevertheless: Although Lewis Powell initially thought himself too old at sixty-three, Ruth Bader Ginsburg was sixty; Robert Bork, a year younger when nominated. Stevens and Stephen G. Breyer were both fifty-five. Sandra Day O'Conner, Antonin Scalia, Anthony Kennedy, and David Souter were all in their early fifties. William Rehnquist was forty-seven. But the two who stand out and who illustrate one extreme of this trend are Clarence Thomas at forty-three and Douglas Ginzburg at forty-one.

Even if Presidents have not bought into the youth movement in practice, the incentives are to appoint younger justices and so extend the views of those who nominate and confirm them, long after those actors have passed from the scene. But these incentives are doubly perverse. There can be no democratic justification for decisionmaking by unelected officials a quarter-century down the road (from appointment). Furthermore, younger nominees may lack life's seasoning. Experience in life matters (another argument against the current practice of appointing only those who have first gone to try-out camp on a federal court of appeals). Even if it had no other advantages, an eighteen-year term would likely push the age of appointment into the mid- and upper-fifties, thereby offering the likelihood that the nominee had somewhat more life experience.[32]

If Seventy-Five Is Good for a Justice, Is It Good for a Majority Leader?

It is striking to compare the ages of the Court's justices at appointment with those of the leadership in the House and Senate. Some of the latter attained their leadership positions in their sixties—Carl Albert, Tip O'Neill, Tom Foley (as Speaker), and Nancy Polosi in the House; Mike Mansfield, Hugh Scott, Bob Dole, and Harry Reid in the Senate. Most, however, were in their fifties—

---

31. DiTullio & Schochet, *supra* n. 17, at 1111 n.74 (noting continuing Democratic criticism of Clinton for appointing the sixty-year-old Ruth Bader Ginsburg, no matter how qualified she was).

32. It is also likely that this would mean the overwhelming majority of justices would live out their terms. Because any vacancy during a term would be filled only until the end of that term, it should preclude political calculation about early retirement.

Gerald R. Ford, John Rhodes, Bob Michel, Jim Wright, Dick Armey, Newt Gingrich, Dennis Hastert, and Tom Delay in the House; Robert Byrd, Howard Baker, George Mitchell, Trent Lott and Bill Frist in the Senate. Only a couple were in their forties: Richard Gephardt and Tom Daschele. In the House only Tip O'Neill lasted until age seventy-four; Tom Foley was second at age sixty-six; most were gone by their late fifties or early sixties. Senators did better: Mansfield, Scott, Byrd, and Dole stayed in leadership positions into their seventies; Baker and Mitchell were out at sixty-two; Daschele and Lott left their posts (albeit involuntarily) a few years younger.

So although the age of ascension to important positions is very similar in the elected and judicial branches, the difference in longevity and therefore the age at ceding power is huge. Only Scott, who left his minority leadership position at an age seventy-seven, approached the average retirement age of justices. No one in a leadership position of the elected branches has approached the twenty-five years of service that is average for Supreme Court Justices. Tip O'Neill leads with sixteen years as majority leader, then speaker — but that is not even two-thirds the Court average. Even an eighteen-year term for a newly appointed justice would exceed the length of time in a leadership position of any of the elected branches, often substantially so.

To the best of my knowledge, no one has attempted to justify why justices should hold onto their jobs at ages that significantly exceed those of other leaders with comparable responsibilities. Life experiences do matter, but life in the Marble Palace (where a tough decision is often whether to summer in Tuscany or Salzburg) is both isolated and rarefied. We apparently do not need septuagenarians to lead in the legislature. Why, then, do we need them for appropriate constitutional interpretation? Indeed, why would anyone create a system in which so much influence would be vested in individuals in their late seventies?

Countermajoritarian Difficulties and Hollow Hopes: *Merryman*,[33] a Case in Point

As justices' careers move on, they become farther removed from the political consensus that brought them to the Court. Hugo Black and William O. Douglas were enthusiastic New Dealers who outlasted the Great Society. Brennan and Marshall were post-war liberals who would have been shocked to hear

---

33. Ex parte Merryman, 17 F. Cas. 144 (1861).

that the era of big government had been declared over. Roger Taney was appointed at the height of the slaveocracy's power, indeed, at a time at which slavery appeared uncontroversial; twenty-five years later, though, he was delivering the oath of office to Abraham Lincoln. Should we want justices, perhaps a majority of those sitting, eventually to be so far removed from the politics that brought them such good fortune?

The end of Roger Taney's tenure on the bench was remarkable. He was from a key border state; his sympathies, like the consensus that had sent him to the Court, were wholly southern; and he had to know that many people blamed him (and *Dred Scott*[34]) for precipitating the Civil War. He wanted a peaceful separation for the South, and he was willing to help this happen.

In April 1861, Marylanders sympathetic to the Confederacy hoped to create conditions whereby they could quickly capture Washington D.C. and with it achieve independence for the South relatively peacefully. To this end, men like John Merryman, a prominent farmer, state legislator, officer in the state militia, and ardent secessionist, were destroying bridges and railroad track to prevent reinforcement of the city by rail. Lincoln had declared martial law in Maryland, and at two o'clock in the morning, Merryman was arrested, taken to Fort McHenry, and charged with treason. Merryman petitioned for a writ of habeas corpus from Taney in his capacity as chief justice. Taney responded with an opinion for delivery to Lincoln, the strongest part of which accused Lincoln of exercising a power that even George III had neither exercised nor claimed. When the mayor of Baltimore congratulated him on preserving the integrity of the writ, Taney responded: "I am an old man, a very old man, but perhaps I was preserved for this occasion."[35] Taney's opinion was applauded by Democrats in the North, loved by secessionists, and ignored by Lincoln.

Let us remove Taney's support for the South from *Merryman* and treat the case on its merits. None doubt habeas corpus can be suspended in time of war; the issue in *Merryman* is by whom. The proper answer has to be the President, acting with the consent of Congress. But Congress was not sitting when Merryman and others sabotaged rail passage to Washington. Lincoln was faced with a choice of acting or doing nothing. It is possible that the suspension of habeas corpus was both unconstitutional[36] *and* the right thing to do (just as forcing the South to ratify the Fourteenth Amendment as a price of readmission to the union could not be squared with Article V, but seemed like a good

---

34. [Dred] Scott v. Sandford, 60 U.S. 393 (1857).

35. Quoted in Carl Swisher, *The Taney Period* 848 (1974).

36. The placement of the Suspension Clause is in Article I, and, as Taney's example of George III suggests, we do not want a dictator.

idea then and seems so now.)[37] From a constitutional viewpoint, perhaps *Merryman* is the best of all worlds. Taney protected the right to habeas corpus, and Lincoln ignored the writ. When Congress got around to considering Lincoln's actions, it approved them retroactively.[38]

Apart from Taney's motivations for behaving as he did, this is a perfect example of the judiciary's behaving as many claim it should. The Court is protecting individual liberties against an oppressive government. Yet in this *Merryman* was unique. During none of the nation's other crises—the Sedition Act crisis, World War I, World War II, the Cold War, or the immediate instigation of the war on terror—have courts been willing to check the government while the crisis appeared critical. Everyone tried under the Sedition Act was convicted, two Republican papers folded, and several others suspended publication while their editors were in jail.[39] Only Learned Hand tried to stand up (in a limited way) to an expansive interpretation of the Espionage Act, and he was quickly reversed.[40] Oliver Wendell Holmes and his colleagues affirmed Eugene Debs's conviction.[41] Two decades later, the New Deal justices validated the Japanese Relocation.[42] *Dennis* sent leaders of the Communist Party to jail.[43] In 2002 both the Defense Department and the Department of Justice had their way. No Roger Taney was holding the government to the full sweep of the Constitution, even though the national crisis of 1861 exceeded (on the particulars of each piece of litigation) all the others. To the extent that protecting civil liberties at all costs is seen as attractive, *Merryman* stands out with a big plus, but it also stands alone.

When Taney took his seat, both the Democrats and the Whigs—parties created to debate economic issues—accepted the consensus that the South was to prevail on all issues involving slavery. After the Mexican War, the Kansas-Nebraska Act, Bleeding Kansas, and *Dred Scott*, that mid-1830s consensus was hotly contested, and slavery was not only put back on the table, it was the only issue that mattered. Although the mid-1830s consensus retained close to one hundred percent sway in the South, it had lost majority support in the North.

---

37. Bruce Ackerman, *We the People: Transformations* vol. 2 (1998).

38. On August 6, 1861 it approved of "all the acts, proclamations, and orders of the President...respecting the army and navy of the United States." 12 Stat. 326. In 1863 Congress passed legislation that specifically authorized presidential suspension of habeas. 13 Stat. 1863.

39. Geoffrey R. Stone, *Perilous Times* 48, 63 (2004).

40. Masses Publishing Co. v. Patten, 224 F. 535 (S.D.N.Y. 1971), *rev'd* 246 Fed. 24 (2d Cir. 1917).

41. Debs v. United States, 249 U.S. (1919).

42. Korematsu v. United States, 323 U.S. 214 (1944).

43. Dennis v. United States, 341 U.S. 494 (1951).

In *Merryman* Taney was enforcing the consensus he knew and understood. Given the northerners' reaction to *Dred Scott*[44] and Lincoln's subsequent election, he had to know the consensus had broken down. But that was someone else's problem; he would do right in *Merryman*. His behavior indicates one possible judicial response to a new political consensus: rejecting it. In this respect, Taney was in the identical position as Van Devanter, McReynolds, Sutherland, and Butler during Franklin Roosevelt's first term, all of whom stood for older constitutional values against a new political majority. With hindsight, it is possible to say who was right and who was wrong, but there is no a priori way of knowing whether the new will prove superior to the old.[45]

Justices and the Political Consensus: Do They Care? Does It Matter?

If justices are going to continue to stay on the Court longer, then we are sure to have more situations in which they are out of step with solutions offered by a newer political consensus. This point offers a back-door entrance into two debates between law professors and political scientists. Do justices follow the political consensus, and do the decisions of the Court matter all that much?

At least since Robert Dahl's seminal 1957 article, *Decision-Making in a Democracy: The Supreme Court as National Policy-Maker*,[46] political scientists have believed the courts will follow the lead of the political branches. Dahl rhetorically asks, how it could be otherwise? How could justices appointed under one political consensus turn on that consensus? Law professors, by contrast, have assumed some autonomy for law as well as the socialization of professional norms and therefore have tended to downplay political influences on the Court. Naturally, there is quite a bit to be said for both positions, and it is a pretty rare scholar who, regardless of his position on the issue, does not acknowledge some force to the other side's position.

If one wishes a Court at some remove from current politics, then an aging Court is one means of achieving it. Justices with twenty-five-plus years on

---

44. In the South, *Dred Scott* was not even mildly controversial, but the opposite holding might have provoked secession under Buchanan.

45. An alternative, nicely illustrated by Black and Douglas in the 1960s, is that issues wholly (or nearly) irrelevant at the time of nomination will achieve great importance on the Court's docket. In the 1960s, a fifth of the Court's docket involved criminal law and procedure, issues far removed from the New Deal vision.

46. 6 J. Pub. L. 279 (1957).

the Court are a long way from the time of appointment and may not even be fully current on the nuances of politics. That, of course, has plusses and minuses, and may mean the justices will miss signals about the limits of judicial freedom.

If one wishes a Court more in tune with current politics, then a less experienced one will be the way to go. This is an issue on which reasonable minds could differ and is thus fully appropriate for democratic decision-making. Yet right now this choice is being made for the country by the justices themselves.

Whatever law professors have thought, historically the Court has not traveled too far from the reigning political consensus.[47] To be sure, there are a few significant counter-examples. The aging Marshall Court was way out of touch with the Jacksonian consensus when it decided *Cherokee Cases*.[48] Later, in the late nineteenth and early twentieth centuries, opinions invalidating the income tax[49] and various pieces of labor legislation[50] probably reflected older views of appropriateness. And, of course, the Court's behavior in the two years following the New Deal's mid-term landslide in 1934 is the most stunning example of a Court that was out of touch with a new political consensus.[51]

More typically, from the Marshall Court's retreat on circuit riding and abolition of courts in *Stuart v. Laird*[52] to the Rehnquist Court's dismantling of the Democrats' feel-good legislation after the Republican takeover in 1994,[53] the Court has either yielded to the political consensus or has been part of it. Even *Dred Scott* can be understood, against a background of national institutions either splitting or dying because of debates over slavery, as the Court's attempt to side with and protect the last major surviving institution—the Democratic Party. A decade and a half later, as northern support for Reconstruction waned, the Court gutted judicial enforcement of the Fourteenth Amendment in *Slaughter House Cases*[54] and subsequently Congressional enforcement was

---

47. L. A. Powe, Jr., *The Court and Elections in The United States Supreme Court* (Christopher Tomlins ed., 2005).

48. Cherokee Nation v. Georgia, 30 U.S. (5 Pet.) 1 (1831); Worchester v. Georgia, 31 U.S. (6 Pet.) 515 (1831).

49. Pollock v. Farmers Loan & Trust, 157 U.S. 459 (1895).

50. E.g., Hammer v. Dagenhart, 247 U.S. 251 (1918); Coppage v. Kansas, 236 U.S. 1 (1915).

51. L. A. Powe, Jr., *The Politics of Judicial Review*, 38 Wake Forest L. Rev. 697, 716 n. 154 (2003).

52. 5 U.S. (1 Cranch) 299 (1803).

53. E.g., United States v. Lopez, (1995) (invalidating the Gun Free School Zone Act).

54. 83 U.S. 36 (1873).

gutted as well in the *Civil Rights Cases*.[55] From there it was a small step to *Plessy v. Ferguson*.[56]

From these examples, it seems clear that holding to an outmoded political consensus is not necessarily a bad thing. But there is no a priori way to know that. So the question becomes: Would we rather ex ante have a group of older people clinging to the consensus of the past or a group of middle-aged (and slightly older) people supporting the political consensus that reigns. It is a decision that should be debated and decided by the elected branches.

The other debate, about the importance of the Court's decisions, was sparked by Gerald Rosenberg, who claimed in *The Hollow Hope* that Supreme Court decisions are not all that important and that normal politics plus economic incentives are the dominant determinants of how successful a decision will be.[57] Law professors (and special interest groups) think much more highly of judicial power (perhaps in part because some of them understand they cannot achieve their objectives through the democratic process). The battles over judicial nominations during the past decade attest fully to the political success of law professors in the debate. But to the extent that Rosenberg's thesis is accurate, it may not matter who is on the Court or how long they choose to stay; if Rosenberg is wrong, then one must at least consider why decisionmaking by people possibly quite distanced from a political consensus makes sense and is appropriate.

Conclusion

Previously, we have had justices who stayed too long after their faculties had faded. We have also had justices, epitomized by Taney and both Marshalls, who lasted on the Court far beyond the political consensus that sent them there. Changes in working conditions and medicine have more recently made staying too long an increasingly common option for every single justice and thus perhaps a constant fact. Compounding the problem is Legal Realism 101—the lessons of the nomination of Robert Bork.[58] Everyone believes that

---

55. 109 U.S. 3 (1883).

56. 163 U.S. 537 (1896).

57. Gerald N. Rosenberg, *The Hollow Hope* (1991).

58. "The Bork hearings…had given the entire nation a basic and too easily understood lesson in Legal Realism 101. The Constitution protected a right to abortion. No Article V changes to the Constitution were possible. If Bork were confirmed, then the Constitution would change and not protect a right to abortion. Therefore, we are (at least in part) a government of men and not of law." Powe, *supra* n. 51, at 725.

so much is at stake in a nomination that they wish to get full value for any vacancy. This puts sitting justices into the political calculation as they make the decision to linger on, hoping for a better President. It also creates perverse incentives to name younger justices, which, in turn, could exacerbate the problem of justices outliving the consensus responsible for their appointments

Like so much else, it is a balance. I have called life tenure the stupidest provision of the 1787 Constitution that has any impact today.[59] It is not, however, the Framers' fault. They could not foresee a society in which wealthy and powerful individuals could routinely live and function acceptably into their eighties.[60] That society is upon us, and we should not leave it to Supreme Court justices to make the decision when to exit (and upon whom to bestow political patronage) all by themselves.

---

59. L. A. Powe, Jr., *Old People and Good Behavior*, 12 Const. Comm. 195 (1995).

60. At a time that the Burger Court was sporting a majority of justices born during the Roosevelt Administration—Teddy's—Lash LaRue wrote an op-ed piece advocating term limits for justices. *Fifteen Years is Enough*, Washington Post D7 (Oct. 7, 1984).

Thinking about Age and Supreme Court Tenure

*Daniel J. Meador**

Supreme Court justices, like all judges appointed pursuant to Article III of the United States Constitution, are assured tenure "during good behavior," realistically referred to as an appointment for life. Short of death, an appointment can be terminated only by action of the justice, through retirement or resignation, or by action of Congress through impeachment. No justice has ever been removed by impeachment, and that procedure is unlikely ever to be employed successfully. As a practical matter, only death or a voluntary act of the justice can terminate service on the Court. This means that the length of tenure among the justices varies widely and unpredictably, often extending to well over twenty years and sometimes to more than thirty.

That situation has given rise to concerns about the consequences of the advanced ages that can be and have been attained by justices and the timing and spacing of appointments. Those concerns in turn have produced proposals that would eliminate life tenure on the Court. Those ideas deserve serious consideration in light of experience over the last two centuries and of the circumstances existing today. This paper addresses only one aspect of the subject—problems associated with advanced ages of justices holding life tenure.

One of the most important and dramatic changes in American life is the lengthened life expectancy and life spans of our citizens. Life expectancy now stands at just over seventy-seven years, about twice what it was in the nation's founding period. It is anticipated that the figure will continue to increase at the rate of about three months every year. The impact of this change on the tenure of Supreme Court justices can be seen by comparing the life spans of

---

* James Monroe Professor of Law Emeritus, University of Virginia.

the earliest justices with those of justices in the second half of the twentieth century.

The founding generation of presidents—Washington, Adams, Jefferson, Madison, and Monroe—appointed a total of nineteen members of the Supreme Court. One died in his forties, two died in their fifties, ten in their sixties, three in their seventies, two in their eighties, and one at ninety-two. In other words, of the nineteen, thirteen did not reach their seventieth birthdays, and three of those did not even live to be sixty. The average age at death was 67.8 years.[1]

It may reasonably be assumed that life spans of that sort were typical of that time and were familiar to the men who wrote and ratified the Constitution. That picture of longevity is the backdrop against which they provided for tenure on the Court "during good behavior."

Leaping forward to the middle of the twentieth century, the five post-World War II presidents—Truman, Eisenhower, Kennedy, Johnson, and Nixon—appointed a total of seventeen members of the Court. Of those, sixteen are deceased. One died before seventy, seven died in their seventies, five in their eighties, and three died at ninety or older. The average age at death was seventy-nine, more than eleven years longer than that of the earliest justices.

The October Term, 1954 is illustrative of that period. I pick that term because it is exactly fifty years ago, and all nine of its justices are deceased. Also, I happened to be there as a law clerk for Justice Hugo Black. No member of the Court that year died before the age of seventy-two. Four died in their seventies, four in their eighties, and one at ninety-six. The average age at death was 81.1 years, about fourteen years longer than that of the founding justices. Two-thirds of that early group died at an age before any one of the 1954 justices died. Five of the 1954 justices—over half—lived beyond eighty, whereas only three of the nineteen early justices made it past that age, less than one-sixth.

The most recent term of the Court from which there is now no living justice was the October Term, 1970. Of the nine justices then on the Court, only two died before the age of eighty (at seventy and seventy-two). Five died in their eighties, two in their nineties. The average age at death was 82.7, about fifteen years longer than the average for the early nineteenth century justices.

Experience in the twentieth century has shown that the lengthened life spans among life-tenured Supreme Court justices have also meant lengthened service on the Court. Among the nineteen earliest justices, the average length of service was 15.6 years. Among the justices in the 1954 Term, the average

---

1. Information about the justices' ages and service on the Court in this and succeeding paragraphs comes from David G. Savage, *Guide to the U.S. Supreme Court* vol. 2, 1186–89 (4th ed., 2004).

service was 20.1 years. Among the justices in the 1970 term, only two served less than twenty-two years (sixteen and seventeen years). Four served more than thirty years. The average length of service was 26.3 years, more than ten years longer than the average of the early nineteenth century justices. Lengthened tenure and life span are dramatically illustrated by our having to go back thirty-five years to the 1970 Term before reaching a term from which there is no justice still living.

The main reason that a lengthened life results in lengthened service is the reluctance of the justices to retire. Such reluctance was understandable in earlier years because of inadequate provision for pensions or retired pay. But that is no longer a problem, as a retired justice continues to receive the same pay as an active member of the Court. Nevertheless, aversion to leaving the bench continues. Within the Court there appears to be a culture of non-retirement. It is as though each justice takes it as a personal challenge to stay as long as possible. Motivations cited for this reluctance to leave include a sense of indispensability, fear of loss of status, unwillingness to give up power, fascination with the work, hope of setting a record for length of service, and objection to having the seat filled by the incumbent president. In short, every incentive works toward hanging on until forced to give up by physical or mental debilitation.

The combination of longer life and reluctance to retire means that "good behavior" has stretched out in time to a point well beyond what could have been contemplated by the founders who wrote that provision into the Constitution in 1787. It is fair to wonder whether they would have provided for lifetime appointments if life spans and other circumstances had been then as they are today. The tenure system they established need not and should not be viewed as sacrosanct merely because it has existed from the beginning. One is reminded of Jefferson's proposition that the earth belongs to the living. A democratic society is always free to re-examine the institutional arrangements by which it is governed. In that spirit I suggest that circumstances today call for a discontinuance of lifetime tenure on the Supreme Court.

Several factors, combined with lengthened life spans and reluctance to retire, contribute to this conclusion. The most basic and important is the diminished capacity, either mental or physical or both, that inevitably comes with advancing age. This is a sensitive subject to discuss, but in a matter of public concern as important as the Supreme Court it needs to be faced frankly. The degree to which such capacity is diminished varies, of course, from one individual to another. But in structuring institutions and laws we necessarily deal with generalities and probabilities. As Holmes said, any line appears arbitrary when compared with that which lies immediately on either side of it, but that does not rule out the drawing of lines. Of course, we do not know in advance in an individual case what the timing, progression or degree of decrepitude will be. For some it may become evident by age seventy-five or younger, while in others it may not appear until well after eighty. Nevertheless, we know that it has occurred and no doubt will occur among Supreme Court justices as well as among the population at large.

Advancing age would not be a problem for the Supreme Court if the justices took retirement in line with the general American pattern. According to statistics drawn from government sources, the average retirement age for American men and women is approximately sixty-two; it has been getting younger over the last decade.[2] The average age of the last six Supreme Court justices to retire (Blackmun, White, Marshall, Brennan, Powell, Burger), at the time of retirement, was eighty-one years, nearly twenty years beyond the average for their fellow citizens. (Rare exceptions to this typical pattern include Potter Stewart, who retired in good health at sixty-six, and Sandra Day O'Connor who announced her retirement, pending the appointment of her successor, July 1, 2005 while still in good health at the age of seventy-five.) The tendency to remain in office until forced out by health problems makes it likely that mental slippage will have begun, sometimes progressing to a serious stage, as with Justices William O. Douglas and Thurgood Marshall, the most dramatic cases in the late twentieth century.[3] But a problem of this sort has occurred in every generation throughout the Court's history.

When this does occur it adversely affects public respect for the Court. Confidence in this important institution of governance is bound to be lessened by awareness that one or more of this small group of decision makers is impaired and not fully functional. The American people are entitled to have nine justices in full possession of their faculties. We know from long experience that lifetime tenure almost guarantees that at times this will not be the situation. This is made even more likely in the future by two aspects of working conditions in the Court today that are different from those of a few decades ago.

One of those conditions is the Court's reduced workload. Over the last two decades there has been a substantial decrease in the number of cases the Court annually hears and decides on the merits. The changed picture is vividly

---

2. Murray Gendell, *Retirement Age Declines Again in 1990s*, Monthly Labor Review 12–21 (Oct. 2001).

3. *See* Daniel N. Atkinson, *Leaving the Bench — Supreme Court Justices at the End* 146–49, 156–60 (1999); David J. Garrow, *Mental Decrepitude on the U.S. Supreme Court — The Historical Case for a 28th Amendment*, 67 U. Chi. L. Rev. 995, 1052–56, 1072–80 (2000). These two sources provide information about the numerous cases of decrepitude that have occurred throughout the Supreme Court's history.

painted by Phillip Lacovara in *The American Lawyer*.[4] As pointed out there, during most of the 1970s and 1980s the Court functioned at a level illustrated by the 1976 Term. The Court then heard oral argument in 176 cases and issued 154 signed opinions, 22 per curiams, and 207 summary dispositions on the merits (on appeals as a matter of right, since abolished). After the 1980s the number of dispositions on the merits began steadily to decline. In the 1992 Term there were 107 cases decided after oral argument. The number dropped to ninety-two in the 1997 Term. Then it dropped to well below ninety per term; now it is less than eighty. Lacovara says the Court today is deciding barely twenty percent of the cases it once decided. All of this is by choice of the justices, who have near total control over their docket.

While oral arguments and decisions on the merits have substantially decreased, the amount of help provided the justices has doubled. Each justice now has four law clerks, up from two. With Justice Black in the 1954 Term, my one co-clerk and I prepared a memorandum on each of the certiorari petitions filed that year. Now that work is performed for eight justices in a "cert pool," relieving most of the clerks in those chambers of that work. As to opinions, Justice Black himself wrote the original draft of the opinion of the Court, in cases assigned to him, and of any concurring and dissenting opinions. His clerks came into the opinion-writing process only as editors and suggestors after he had prepared his draft. Today, in many chambers, it is common practice for clerks to prepare initial drafts of opinions, with the justices doing the editing, a reversal of roles. The increased number of clerks, mostly relieved of certiorari petition work, means that clerks have much more time than they did a generation ago for opinion drafting, freeing the justices of that onerous task.

The combination of lightened opinion drafting and more help makes it possible for a member of the Court to carry on into a more advanced age than would have been likely with a heavier workload and less help. Indeed, with a complement of able clerks, a justice can function in effect on automatic-pilot, actually doing no opinion writing and little real decision making, all masked from public view. This seems to have been the situation with Justices Douglas and Marshall toward the end of their time on the Court. This is surely a spectacle that cannot be justified on any ground. But with lifetime tenure and an ever-lengthening life span this could become an increasing reality. With life expectancy predicted to increase three months every

---

4. Philip Lacovara, *The Incredible Shrinking Court—If Their Productivity Were Measured by Private Sector Standards, the Supremes Might Receive Pink Slips*, American Lawyer 53 (Dec. 2003).

year, in four years the current expectancy of seventy-seven years will be seventy-eight. In twelve years it will be eighty. It is not unimaginable that Strom Thurmond, if he had been on the Supreme Court, could have continued functioning through four law clerks until his one hundredth birthday, as he did in the Senate.[5] Advances in medical science make it ever more likely that one can continue to function minimally even though in substantial mental decline.

It is worth noting that in other democratic nations of the western world devoted to the rule of law, judicial tenure for life does not exist. For example, on the Austrian Constitutional Court judges hold office until the age of seventy. On the Italian Constitutional Court the judges serve terms of nine years; on the Federal Constitutional Court in Germany the terms are twelve years. In England, legal ancestor of the United States, all judges must retire at seventy; until recently the retirement age was seventy-five. Under a bill recently passed by Parliament, a Supreme Court for the United Kingdom will be established, replacing the House of Lords as the court of last resort, with judges appointed for twelve-year terms. If there were value in tenure for life, one would think that at least one other nation would be attracted to the idea. But so far as I am aware, none has been. Nor have forty-nine states in the American Union.

Apart from the problem of mental or physical impairment, there is something a bit unseemly about decisions affecting the lives and fortunes of American citizens being made by persons nearly all of whose contemporaries, if not deceased, are disengaged from the active workforce. As mentioned above, the average age of retirement for Americans is approximately sixty-two. Between the ages of seventy-five and seventy-nine, only seven percent of men and three percent of women in the United States are actively employed.[6] The symbolism is not good, even if no justice is in fact impaired. If the earth belongs to the living, there is something to be said for having governmental decision makers more closely connected in age to the bulk of the active population governed by their decisions. Detachment from society is a constant threat for the justices in the seclusion of the marble palace. In those elegant surroundings, with an abundance of help and deferential treatment, the real world can seem far away. That sense of detachment is likely to increase as time passes in that

5. *See* John F. Harris, *Where Age and Power Go Together—Washington Accepts Elderly Leaders*, The Washington Post A8 (March 29, 2005), reporting that Senator Thurmond served for many years as chairman of the Armed Services Committee, "in ways that committee aides said showed only minimal awareness of the business at hand, reading prepared opening statements while staff members hovered anxiously nearby."

6. Murray Gendell, *supra* n. 2, at p. 17.

environment and the justices grow older and ever more distant from the employed generations and from the political forces that put them on the Court.

Continuity and stability in the membership of a court of last resort are, of course, highly desirable, but so is a gradual infusion of new blood. An appropriate balance needs to be maintained by the rate of turn-over among the judges. The extended life spans and reluctance to retire have reduced turn-over on the Supreme Court from what it was before the late twentieth century. As pointed out above, justices in the 1970 Term served an average of twenty-six years. The current Court, prior to the August 2005 vacancies, served together without change for eleven years. This is a rate of turn-over that, I submit, is too slow, carrying the Court too far away from the country's active generations. Desirable continuity and stability, as well as judicial independence, can still be maintained with replacements more often than every quarter-century.

All of the various proposals that would eliminate life tenure would increase the rate of turn-over. One such proposal is to establish a mandatory retirement age of seventy-five. If that requirement had been in effect over the past forty years it would have required eleven justices, from Warren forward, to leave the Court earlier than they did, moderately increasing turn-over and slightly reallocating appointments among presidents. The result would have been as follows:

> Warren would have retired in 1966, three years earlier than he did, allowing Johnson instead of Nixon to replace him.
>
> Black would have retired in 1961, 10 years earlier than he did, allowing Kennedy instead of Nixon to replace him.
>
> Douglas would have retired in 1973, two years before he did.
>
> Brennan would have retired in 1981, nine years before he did, allowing Reagan instead of Bush to replace him.
>
> Burger would have retired in 1982, four years before he did.
>
> Powell would have retired in 1982, five years before he did.
>
> Marshall would have retired in 1983, eight years before he did, allowing Reagan instead of Bush to replace him.
>
> Blackmun would have retired in 1983, 11 years before he did, likewise allowing Reagan instead of Bush to replace him.
>
> White would have retired in 1992, one year before he did, allowing Bush instead of Clinton to replace him.
>
> Stevens would have retired in 1995, 10 years ago, and Rehnquist in 1999, six years ago.

Altogether the retirements of those eleven justices under mandatory retirement at age seventy-five would have opened up a total of sixty-nine years of service on the court for new appointees.

While the considerations discussed above are sufficient to convince me that appointments to the Supreme Court for life are no longer desirable, the uneven allocation of appointments among presidents is cited as an additional reason for terms other than life. The number and timing of appointments to the Court a president makes depend on unpredictable and unregulated events beyond his control or the control of anyone other than a justice. A president makes an appointment only when a justice dies or decides to retire or resign. The result throughout the twentieth century is shown in the following list, giving the terms served by each president and the number of Court appointments each made.

President	Number of Terms	Number of Appointments
T. Roosevelt	1+	3
Taft	1	6
Wilson	2	3
Harding	1-	4
Coolidge	1+	1
Hoover	1	3
F. Roosevelt	3+	8
Truman	1+	4
Eisenhower	2	5
Kennedy	1-	2
Johnson	1+	2
Nixon	1+	4
Ford	1-	1
Carter	1	0
Reagan	2	3
G. H. W. Bush	1	2
Clinton	2	2
G. W. Bush	1st term	0

As is apparent, the range is large and idiosyncratic. Taft in one term appointed almost as many justices as Franklin Roosevelt did in three terms. Each appointed a majority of the Court. In two terms Clinton appointed only one third as many as Taft did in one term. In less than one full term Harding appointed four, while Carter in one full term appointed none. If Franklin Roosevelt and George W. Bush had been defeated for reelection they would have joined Carter in serving one full term without making any appointment. The result of this pattern is that presidents through their appointments exert influence on the Court in greatly varying degrees, ranging from substantial, as with Taft, Franklin Roosevelt, Eisenhower, Harding, Truman, and Nixon, to little or none, as with Coolidge, Ford, and Carter.

A mandatory retirement age would do nothing to even out appointments among presidents. Accomplishing that would require some variety of staggered terms of years for the justices. Either age limits or fixed terms would, of course, eliminate life tenure. Analyzing the relative merits of such proposals is beyond the scope of this paper. The point being made here is that, by one or another of the proposed changes, an appointment to the Supreme Court should no longer guarantee lifetime case-deciding service on the Court. Termination of active service in deciding cases on the merits should not be left to death or solely to a justice's choice.

Prolonged Tenure of Justices As Part of a Larger Problem

LIMITING THE COURT BY LIMITING LIFE TENURE

*Robert F. Nagel**

I

It is possible to support the idea of eliminating life tenure for Supreme Court justices and yet to sympathize with those who are perplexed or even dismayed by this proposed reform. Forget for a moment the many specific operational issues that arise from this general idea—whether, for example, it would be better to utilize some version of a fixed term or to set a mandatory retirement age or to provide attractive retirement incentives. Forget also the constitutional question whether reform can be achieved through legislation or only through amendment. And even put aside higher political considerations such as whether abandoning life tenure would be consistent with Burkean prudence. Consider, instead, a simpler question: What is it about the Court's record that would cause any serious observer to devote attention and energy to proposals aimed at limiting life tenure?

A naïve outsider might guess that the willingness to re-think life tenure probably arises from evidence about the physical or intellectual incapacity of older justices. And, indeed, some contributors to this volume have studied the performance of aging justices and do hold that concern.[1] However, since I believe (for reasons that will emerge in the next section) that the most serious

---

* Ira C. Rothgerber, Jr. Professor of Constitutional Law at the University of Colorado School of Law.

1. *E.g.*, David J. Garrow, *Mental Decrepitude on the U.S. Supreme Court: The Historical Case a 28th Amendment*, 67 U. Chi. L. Rev. 995 (2000); and *see supra* Steven G. Calabresi & James Lindgren, "Term Limits for the Supreme Court: Life Tenure Reconsidered," pp. 15–98.

damage arising from the Court's performance is traceable to the work of justices who are physically and intellectually vigorous, this is not my reason for supporting limits on life tenure. Moreover, I doubt that it is the chief concern of many of those who are proposing the reforms under consideration here.

The papers collected here put forward a range of less obvious answers to the question. It is said, for example, that life tenure allows justices to time their retirements based on political calculations.[2] This is no doubt true. But, while somewhat unseemly from some perspectives, timed retirement decisions are not obviously different from any number of strategic decisions that justices routinely make in an effort to prolong and maximize their influence. Indeed, virtually every aspect of the job—from voting to hear particular cases to deciding them on the merits, from constructing major doctrines to dropping suggestive footnotes—can be understood in part as exercises in influencing the future development of constitutional law.[3] It would only seem natural that a person who sincerely believes the jurisprudential views expressed during the nomination and confirmation process should, once placed on the Court, hope to be replaced by someone with similar views. In any event, even on the assumption that timed retirements are different from and more regrettable than other efforts at prolonged influence, it is not clear why they are suddenly such a serious problem as to warrant changing the long-standing practice of life tenure.

It is also said that limiting life tenure would reduce stress on the confirmation process.[4] The thought is that since justices would serve a shorter period, the political stakes in any particular nomination would be reduced. What some call "stress," of course, others call "robust review."[5] While I myself agree with those who think that some recent tactics have crossed the line to wretched excess, it seems highly doubtful that term limitations would significantly affect the tone or content of senatorial review. Everyone knows that nominations are controversial essentially because justices now routinely resolve highly controversial and important public issues.[6] They do so virtually every term.

---

2. Even Ward Farnsworth describes strategic retirement as "bothersome." *See infra* Ward Farnsworth, *The Case for Life Tenure*, pp. 251–269. *See also supra* Calabresi & Lindgren, pp. 15–98.

3. For a depiction of such tactics as statesmanship, *see* Owen Fiss, *Dombrowski*, 86 Yale L. J. 1103 (1977).

4. *See supra* Calabresi & Lindgren, pp. 15–98.

5. *See*, e.g., Michael Comiskey, *Seeking Justices: The Judging of Supreme Court Nominees* (2004).

6. For a blunt acknowledgment in the popular press, *see* David Brooks, *Roe's Birth, and Death*, N.Y. Times A23 (April 21, 2005).

No matter how life tenure is limited, therefore, justices will still have an opportunity to resolve momentous questions; the stakes in any particular nomination will, one would think, therefore remain high enough to trigger highly contentious, sometimes ugly, hearings.

Other proponents of limiting life tenure argue that prolonged service on the high court undermines conventional legal skills.[7] The problem is thought to be that Supreme Court opinions have become sloppy and unmoored from the relevant legal authorities; indeed, the workman-like job of jurist has been transformed into the more elevated role of statesman or moral oracle. This, needless to say, is a serious set of concerns, and addressing them effectively would not only help to depoliticize the confirmation process but would also have much larger political and social consequences. Nevertheless, even assuming that longevity on the Court is a cause of these problems, it is unlikely to be a major cause. After all, many judges of the state courts and of the lower federal courts use methodologies fundamentally like those employed by the justices of the Supreme Court[8] and appear to suffer from similar delusions of grandeur. Apparently, then, the decline of the lawyers' craft and the elevation of the role of judge are a result of background intellectual and political trends. These presumably include developments in legal philosophy, shifts in legal education, the iconic status of certain landmark decisions (such as *Brown v. Board of Education*) and diffuse cultural factors. In light of all these possible causes, a focus on limiting life tenure—at least at first glance—seems at best narrow and at worst futile. More fundamentally, it is doubtful that legal conventionalism is related to judicial humility or restraint.[9] It is at least possible, for example, that common law techniques actually promote hubris[10] and that strict textualism might require the justices to intervene pervasively and massively in economic and social policy.[11]

---

7. Saikrishna B. Prakash, *America's Aristocracy*, 109 Yale L. J. 541 (1999); John O. McGinnis, *Justice Without Justices*, 16 Const. Comm. 541 (1999).

8. *See* Hans Linde, *Are State Constitutions Common Law?*, 34 Arizona L. Rev. 215 (1992).

9. However, for a good example of the fairly common argument that there is such a relationship, *see* Lino A. Graglia, *Our Constitution Faces Death By "Due Process,"* Wall Street Journal A12 (May 24, 2005).

10. *See* Robert F. Nagel, *Judicial Power and American Character: Censoring Ourselves in an Anxious Age* 129–32 (1994); Robert F. Nagel, *Common Law and Common Sense*, First Things 42, 44 (February, 2004).

11. Consider, for example, the potential implications of a systematic implementation of Justice Thomas' interpretation of "commerce among the states." *See* United States v. Lopez, 514 U.S. 549, 584 (Thomas, J., concurring) (1995).

Finally, some critics of life tenure think that the present system prevents appropriate political responsiveness.[12] Because turnover on the Court is slow and irregular, the Court, it is said, tends not to respond soon enough or fully enough to political dissatisfactions and aspirations. One version of this criticism rather surprisingly suggests that better political responsiveness would produce better legal craft because the public values conventional legal methodologies more than do the elites who exercise influence over the judiciary now.[13] Other versions are primarily concerned that case outcomes are excessively at variance with popular sentiments—a position sometimes derided as being merely substantive or partisan. As to the empirical claim that the public would push for legalistic values, my own position is that the confirmation process has been too dominated by doctrinal and jurisprudential considerations and that this emphasis is unfortunate precisely because it gives excessive influence to elites.[14] The "partisan" critique, however, seems to me to contain the seed of a serious explanation for the wisdom of limiting life tenure; however, for reasons that require separate development this critique should be recast in broader cultural terms.

II

Given that most constitutional doctrines openly call on the justices to assess the importance of public purposes (illegitimate, important, compelling, and so on) and to determine how such purposes might best be achieved, it is certainly plausible to think that the justices should be responsive to political preferences. At the very least, the public has some relevant opinions about such quintessentially legislative matters. The only real question (if everyone were not so inured to the practice of modern constitutional law) is why anyone would think that the justices' opinions are especially relevant. Of course, this democratic objection to judicial autonomy becomes more intense when combined with substantive disagreement with the outcomes of the Court's decisions. But the democratic objection does not for this reason become nothing but the ideological objection, and no amount of cynicism or realism can make the two the same.

Since most observers profess attachment to democratic values and all are intensely unhappy with some of the Court's outcomes, the curious fact is that

---

12. See supra Calabresi & Lindgren, pp. 15–98.

13. See infra Farnsworth, pp. 251–269.

14. See Robert F. Nagel, Advice, Consent, and Influence, 84 Northwestern U. L. Rev. 858 (1990).

the democratic objection, while commonly voiced, has not had more traction intellectually or politically. (Why, for example, was life tenure not limited years ago?) One major component of an explanation for American tolerance for judicial power and autonomy is the well documented fact that the justices' decisions are seldom far out of line with the preferences of national majorities as measured by polls or by working majorities in Congress.[15] They sometimes are, as in the case of flag desecration and partial birth abortion. But usually the Court's decisions are not counter-majoritarian in this sense. It seems to many, then, that there is no burning need for better political responsiveness through more frequent and more regular turnover because those aging, insulated justices somehow manage to be reasonably sensitive to majoritarian preferences.

The democratic objection to judicial isolation, therefore, must either remain a largely abstract concern or it must be re-conceptualized in broader political and cultural terms. A first step towards a re-conceptualization is to resist the widespread undervaluation of federalism[16] and consider the fact that the substantive outcomes imposed by the Court do frequently conflict with officially registered preferences of majorities within state and local governments. On some issues, including not only high profile issues like abortion but also low visibility issues such as vagrancy laws and the regulation of anonymous campaign literature, the Court's decisions conflict with preferences authoritatively expressed in most of the states.[17] On many others those decisions conflict with majoritarian preferences expressed in a significant number of states. Whatever its immediate benefits, judicial interference with local democracy inevitably does serious damage even if that interference reflects the values of national majorities.[18] It undermines and frustrates local political action that requires effort and sacrifice. It forces homogeneity on regions and populations that still exhibit significant diversity in morality, religion, economics, and politics. And it moves effective decisionmaking away from where peo-

---

15. *See, e.g.,* Comiskey, *supra* n. 5, at 177; L. A. Powe, Jr. *Are "The People" Missing in Action (and Should Anyone Care)?*, 83 Texas L. Rev. 856, 886–89 (2005).

16. Many decry the impoverishment of political life at the local level, but few are concerned about the weakening of state institutions. For a discussion of this combination of views and an argument that political activity at the state level helps maintain political life in local communities, *see* Robert F. Nagel, *States and Localities: A Comment on Nisbet's Communitarianism*, 34 Publius 125 (2004).

17. Stenberg v. Carhart, 530 U.S. 914 (2000); Chicago v. Morales, 527 U.S. 41 (1999); McIntyre v. Ohio Elections Commission 514 U.S. 334, 371 (Scalia, J., dissenting) (1995).

18. I attempted to elaborate on this claim in *The Implosion of American Federalism*, 85–179 (2001).

ple live and work so that politics comes to be unsatisfying—less personal, more staged, and largely beyond control.

A second step towards a fuller understanding of the democratic objection is to recognize that, whether one agrees or disagrees with the outcomes imposed by the Court, those outcomes very frequently relate to issues, like the limits of sexual freedom and respect for human life, that are central to individuals and society. Thus, in those instances where the Court has departed from the preferences of national majorities (as occasional as those departures may be), it has sometimes done so in circumstances that can provoke anger and even despair. And in the more common instances where the Court interferes with local majorities, the Court's program often interferes with locally expressed preferences precisely where their intensity is highest. The result, of course, goes beyond frustration and passivity to a deeper fury and alienation. To say that the Court's program has not generally offended national majorities, then, is far from saying that it is justified or without dangerous consequences.

A third step is to acknowledge that the Court's program is now normal and pervasive. Despite the fact that most justifications for judicial review entail some degree of exceptionality,[19] over the past several decades there is virtually no aspect of ordinary life that has not been the subject of one judicial foray or another. This familiarization naturally induces increased reliance on courts and corresponding political enervation. But it also creates a kind of background anxiety and insecurity because no aspect of public policy is immune from potentially far-reaching judicial intervention—not ordinary decision-making in public schools, not the content of holiday celebrations, not even the nature of marriage. Institutions, laws, and customary arrangements are all made precarious, subject to the possibility of sweeping changes initiated by obscure activists using intellectual tactics understood only by lawyers and judges.

Finally, it is important to consider the degree to which the Court's program is increasingly characterized by authoritarian claims on behalf of judicial power.[20] These claims not only discourage participation by the other branches and levels of government in constitutional decisionmaking—which, I repeat,

---

19. I mean, for example, well known arguments that the Court should vigorously protect discrete and insular minorities, or society's most fundamental values, or preferred rights like free speech. Even general textualist justifications of the sort found in *Marbury v. Madison* presume that subjects not covered by the text are outside judicial oversight.

20. For one interesting account of this growing authoritarianism, *see* Larry D. Kramer, *Forward: We the Court*, 115 Harv. L. Rev. 4 (2001).

is decisionmaking on virtually all significant political and moral issues—but also stigmatize dissenters as irresponsible and dangerous outsiders. The predictable result is to aggravate an already ugly climate of fear and hatred.

In short, the democratic objection to justices' insulation from political influence is not, or should not, be premised on national majoritarianism as an overriding value. It should focus instead on the effects of the Court's behavior on the quality of political life at every level. The damage done by that record is not confined to jurisprudential or majoritarian values. In my view, the damage is ultimately cultural. Over the past sixty years, the Court's use of its power, whatever good it has accomplished on discrete issues, has heightened social conflict, drained political self-confidence, undermined healthy local political participation, and impoverished the scope and significance of public decisionmaking. This aspect of the Court's record, while certainly more diffuse than the substantive outcomes of its cases, is destructive and should be of concern even to those who share the political preferences promoted by the Court. But, once again, even if it is of concern, what about this record justifies attention to the issue of life tenure?

III

It may be that the Court's record does not often depart from majoritarian preferences as measured by national opinion polls and congressional action, but it does appear to have departed from those preferences as measured by presidential elections. Since at least 1970 there has been a sustained effort by both Republican and Democratic presidents to appoint justices who will reduce the role of the Supreme Court in resolving controversial social and political problems. This campaign was originally traceable to political dissatisfaction with Warren Court decisions on such matters as school integration and police practices, but it eventually became an expression of dissatisfaction with decades of Burger and Rehnquist Court decisions on abortion, flag burning, and a host of other social issues. Although national majorities did not disapprove of all or even most of these decisions, many of them represented a deep and continuing insult to core constituencies of the Republican Party, whose presidents have made most of the appointments to the Court since 1970. Moreover, some of the decisions, notably the intervention in the Florida presidential election of 2000 but also the abortion and flag desecration decisions, represented acute insults to important components of the Democratic Party. In short, for decades there has been a widespread, if deeply ambivalent, sense that the Court needs to be constrained. However, this sense, while producing some effective responses on particular issues, has not been potent enough to induce the use of the strongest available political checks on judicial authority.[21] Jurisdiction stripping bills are periodically introduced but are always voted down, as are proposed constitutional amendments aimed at reversing even profoundly unpopular decisions of the Court. In recent decades, the main check, other than the occasional enactment of recalcitrant statutes, has been the nomination to the Court of individuals who profess themselves to be opposed to judicial lawmaking or activism and who appear to be politically and jurisprudentially moderate. That is, political dissatisfaction has been sufficiently widespread and effective to induce rhetorical and stylistic concessions, but at the operational level the justices remain adamant about continuing the overall practice of modern judicial review.

The inexorable march of judicial control and authority is the result of a complex interplay between the Court and an ultimately compliant culture.[22] The sources of that compliance are, of course, complex. One source, no doubt, is the Court's ability to reflect (or at least not unduly offend) the preferences of national political majorities, which find their expression mainly in the confirmation process.[23] Another, in my view, is cultural depletion—that is, the very sense of enervation, self-doubt, and anxiety that the Court has

---

21. For detail on political opposition to the Court, *see* L. A. Powe, Jr., *supra* n. 15 at 864–84. Powe thinks much of this opposition is regrettable and that its time has passed. *Id.* at 894.

22. One such factor is the high respect Americans have for rule-of-law values. This holds even for those who have great cause to disapprove of many substantive outcomes. *See, e.g.,* Theodore B. Olson, *Lay Off Our Judiciary*, Wall Street Journal A16 (April 21, 2005). I attempted a broader survey of these factors in *The Implosion of American Federalism, supra* n. 18. For a complacent view of the American attitude toward judicial authority, *see* Larry Alexander & Lawrence B. Solum, Book Review *Popular? Constitutionalism?*, 118 Harv. L. Rev. 1594, 1638 (2005).

23. *See generally* Comiskey, *supra* n. 5, *passim.* However, I, at least, am using the word "majorities" in a specific and somewhat artificial way. It is by no means clear that the moderation (as observers like Comiskey would term it) induced by the confirmation process is an indicator of national majoritarian preferences in any quantitative sense because the Senate itself is notoriously and intentionally unrepresentative by that measure. The President's choice of nominees may well be a better (but still highly imperfect) indicator of majoritarian preferences. Nevertheless, the Senate does register political preferences in the way that the Constitution calls upon such preferences to be registered. These are "majoritarian" in the same loose but authoritative sense that the results of state legislative processes are majoritarian within their jurisdictions—or as the decision of a president to nominate to the bench someone who reflects the beliefs of the base of his Party. All these decisions reflect majority preferences to the extent and in the way that the Constitution permits.

helped to create. But ultimately the sources of our continuing acceptance of pervasive judicial oversight must, I think, be sought in certain abiding aspects of the American character: our pragmatism, which tends to favor results over process; our optimism, which can sometimes take the form of impatient perfectionism; and, perversely, our underlying fear of disintegration, which seeks security in imposed solutions. The justices' behavior can be expected to change only when these larger forces are either harnessed or influenced. Proposals to limit life tenure, as narrow as they are in comparison to the scope of the problem, have some potential for operating effectively on the cultural causes of judicial excess.

Because the justices, like many other participants in the political system, have come to see American politics as often feckless and sometimes dangerously chaotic, they tend to see political resistance to the exercise of judicial power as illegitimate and even anarchic. This is especially true when political initiatives directly challenge the Court's interpretive function. Unfortunately, the Court often reacts with re-doubled efforts to displace representative institutions. One advantage of proposals to limit life tenure is that they could communicate dissatisfaction without challenging any specific doctrines or results and might, therefore, be perceived by the justices and the public as representing constructive criticism.

The corresponding disadvantage, however, is that the proposals are so separate from interpretive criticism that they might easily be understood as being calls for better legal craftsmanship or more vigor and thus as implicit endorsements of the Court's pre-eminent role. Even a broader message about the need for better political responsiveness could be heard as an endorsement of frequent (but politically sensitive!) interventions in public policy. Such risks can be reduced if the proposed reforms are presented as partial and initial responses to the broad cultural damage that the Court has done. The idea of limiting life tenure, that is, could be defended in a way that helps the public and even the justices begin to consider the real political and cultural harms caused by the Supreme Court's behavior over many decades. It could be presented so as to challenge entrenched assumptions about how judicial decisionmaking is a pragmatic way to achieve progress and to ward off conflict and chaos.

It might well be that emphasis on the cultural damage done by the Court would be seen as an irresponsible attack on an essential institution and thus as further evidence of the need for reliance on an insulated judiciary. This emphasis, however, carries less risk of a defensive reaction than do many reform proposals. Even a severe critique of the kind proposed would not necessarily challenge specific case outcomes or constitutional doctrines or interpretive methodologies. The critique of the Court's insulation could be less that the justices have been insufficiently responsive in specific substantive areas and more that they have been insufficiently responsive to a widely shared sense that the overall pattern of their interventions has been damaging. The political message that the justices have ignored is that a healthy political culture requires a more restrained judicial role.

An important part of this critique, it must be admitted, would have to include a forthright discussion of the Court's destructive impact on state and local governments. Some of the justices themselves might be attentive to this aspect of the critique, but it is not an argument that would especially appeal to either the pragmatic or perfectionist instincts of many Americans. Still, there remains enough of a tradition of localized government that it might be fruitful to engage in an unapologetic inquiry into the social costs of the potent de-legitimization of state and local institutions brought on by the civil rights revolution.[24]

The historical and cultural reasons for American attachment to the Court's power are so large as to dwarf any particular reform proposal. Indeed, they are so large that for decades they have blocked any effective efforts to change the overall pattern of judicial behavior; the result is a kind of political taboo against challenging the Court. Our dependence is so great that concrete steps aimed at restraining judicial power have become politically almost unthinkable. Perhaps the most significant advantage of the proposal to limit life tenure is that there is a commonsensical and unthreatening appeal to the notion that the prerogative of exercising great power should not go on endlessly into old age. It is remotely possible, therefore, that this is one reform aimed at the Court that could overcome the taboo. If the public discovers that the sky does not fall when the Court is challenged in this small way, perhaps the ingrained habit of excessive deference will begin to fall away and other constructive challenges might become possible.

In short, limiting life tenure is a slight and indirect solution to a truly massive problem, but precisely for that reason it might be a useful step. If even this first step is not possible, we will be faced with yet another sign of the extent to which the Court's role, while highly destructive to important social and political values, is impervious to challenge.

---

24. *See* Robert F. Nagel, *supra* n. 16 (discussing potential implications of Theda Skocpol's arresting book, *Diminished Democracy: From Membership to Management in American Civic Life* (2003).

Checks and Balances: Congress and the Federal Courts

Paul D. Carrington[*]

The problem of superannuated justices is fully stated by Steven Calabresi and James Lindgren[1] and others in this symposium. Robert Nagel has stated additional reasons for Congress to address that problem as part of a larger one.[2] My reasons like his go beyond concern for the disabilities of aging or the politics of the appointment process. The Court needs to be less exalted as an icon. It ought to be seen as a part of a larger institution, the federal judiciary, a vast enterprise afflicted with normal human failings, which should be as accountable to the other branches of government as those branches are to it. Congress has long neglected its duty implicit in the constitutional doctrine of separation of powers to constrain the tendency of the Court, the academy and the legal profession to inflate the Court's status and power. The term "life tenure" is a significant source of a sense of royal status having not only the adverse cultural effects noted by Nagel, but also doleful effects on the administration and enforcement of law in the other federal courts for which the Court and Congress share responsibility. Fixing the superannuation problem will not fix everything, but it would be

---

[*] Professor of Law, Duke University. Special thanks to Roger Cramton, Richard Epstein, Peter Fish, George Liebmann, Judith Resnik, and Steve Yeazell for thoughtful responses to an early draft of this paper. Kristin Seeger helped with the documentation.

1. *See supra* Steven G. Calabresi & James Lindgren, *Term Limits for the Supreme Court: Life Tenure Reconsidered*, pp. 15–98.

2. *See supra* Robert F. Nagel, *A Comment on Limiting Life Tenure*, pp. 127–136. In the same vein is Robert F. Bauer, *A Court Too Supreme for Our Good*, Washington Post (Aug. 7, 2005).

a benign step in the right direction. I will conclude by suggesting numerous related reforms that might help more, all of which have been proposed to Congress in times past. Perhaps legislation addressing the superannuation problem would make it more likely that other needed reforms might be achieved in the future, by Congress or by a judiciary more aware of its own frailties.

The Constitution in Congress

The arguments made by numerous authors[3] that statutory term limits of any kind would violate Article III of the Constitution are framed as if addressed to the Court and its celebrants. But the forum to consider those arguments is Congress.[4] I commend to Congress the contrary views on constitutionality expressed in this symposium by Roger Cramton,[5] Scot Powe,[6] and Sanford Levinson.[7] As they contend, the purpose of Article III is to assure the independence of the federal judiciary by securing judges from reward or intimidation. The constitutional objections to term limits legislation rest on restrictive readings of the terms "good behavior" and "one Supreme Court" that cannot be justified by reference to any substantial public harms that might result from a more generous reading that allows Congress to do its job. Justices have long interpreted the text of the Constitution loosely, a practice that may indeed have been indispensable in keeping the Republic more or less on track for two and a quarter centuries. It would be ironic if an uncharitable reading of that text led Congress in an action of self-restraint to forego enactment of reasonable constraints on justices who are seldom constrained by mere texts intimating a principle they deem improvident.

---

3. *See supra* Calabresi & Lindgen, pp. 15–98; *see infra* Ward Farnsworth, *The Case for Life Tenure*, pp. 251–269; *see infra* John Harrison, *The Power of Congress over The Terms of Judges of the Supreme Court* pp. 361–373; *see infra* William Van Alstyne, *Constitutional Futility of Statutory Term Limits for Supreme Court Justices*, pp. 385–402.

4. David P. Currie is providing a history of Congressional attention to the Constitution. *See* his *The Constitution in Congress: Democrats and Whigs 1829–1861* (2005); *The Constitution in Congress: the Jeffersonians, 1801–1829 (2001); The Constitution in Congress: The Federalist Period 1789–1801* (1999). It is fair to say that Congress has been willing and able to read the Constitution for itself.

5. *See infra* Roger C. Cramton, *Constitutionality of Reforming the Supreme Court by Statute*, pp. 345–360.

6. *See supra* L. A. Powe, Jr., *"Marble Palace, We've Got A Problem—with You"*, pp. 99–113.

7. *See infra* Sanford Levinson, *Life Tenure and the Supreme Court: What is to Be Done?*, pp. 375–383.

If Congressional legislation imposing term limits on justices were enacted and were then held unconstitutional by the Court, it would be time to think about a constitutional amendment. At such a time an amendment might be a realistic possibility. Until then, academic objections to the constitutionality of such legislation should be recognized as arguments for the status quo.

The Supreme Court As the One Among Many

Perhaps in part because my professional preoccupation for the last half a century has been not with the Supreme Court but with other federal courts, I view the "one Supreme Court" as the center of a network of subordinate institutions that should be and are constitutionally accountable to representatives of the people they serve. The "lower" courts shape themselves to the highest Court and also influence the Court in ways making them inseparable. When the whole enterprise has overreached itself, as it has, that is a problem that Congress has a constitutional duty to address.[8] The Court, afflicted with its quasi-royal sense of itself, has led the federal courts at all levels to forsake the modest role of deciding the cases and controversies that the Constitution commissions them to decide in order to concentrate on the more exalted and gratifying work of making law on subjects of their own choosing.

Although political scientists and others occupied with opinion sampling may question my premise,[9] I share with others (at least some of whom are federal judges) a sense that there is in the land a growing hostility to the federal judiciary and to the government of which it is a part. Why should this be? One possible reason is that foretold by Montesquieu, that a republic's status as The Great Power results in an infection of arrogance causing its citizens to be more resentful of the leaders who govern them.[10] Perhaps he was right; there is surely evidence of an infection of arrogance in many American institutions. Resentment also seems to be associated with despair over the nation's moral

---

8. See infra Farnsworth, pp. 251–269; see infra Harrison, pp. 361–373; see infra Philip D. Oliver, *Increasing the Size of the Court as a Partial but Clearly Constitutional Alternative*, pp. 405–414; see infra Van Alstyne, pp. 385–402.

9. See infra Stephen B. Burbank, *An Interdisciplinary Perspective on the Tenure of Supreme Court Justices*, pp. 317–342; but see Martha Neil, *Half of U.S. Sees Judicial Activism Crisis*, ABA J., eReport, (September 30, 2005).

10. Charles Secondat de Montesquieu, *The Spirit of Laws*, Book VIII, Chap. 4 (Thomas Nugent trans., London: Nourse, 1750).

state,[11] and with a retreat from the optimism of The Enlightenment on which our national ideology rests.[12] Whatever the causes, those who retain progressive hopes, and see law as a possible instrument of their achievement, as I do, would do well, I perceive, to concede that fellow citizens protesting the moral and political leadership of an unaccountable judiciary placed on a pedestal of immortality may have a point. Prudence calls for an offer of compromise and that is in my mind what our term limits proposals are about.

The Founders' Surprise

Those who wrote Article III did not see the federal judiciary, even the Supreme Court, as the superlegislators they have become. The judges who were known to the Founders were employed merely to decide contested cases. In the common law tradition familiar to eighteenth century lawyers, the judges entertaining appeals heard legal arguments and then expressed their decisions separately and orally, leaving it to a reporter and his readers to derive if possible any legal principles that might have been expressed in their diverse and unrehearsed utterances, a system depicted by Tennyson as "a lawless science," a "codeless myriad of precedent," and a mere "wilderness of single instances."[13] Judges made law, but unselfconsciously as they tried to apply it. So long as they made law only in that modest way, they were indeed, as Alexander Hamilton assured us, "the least dangerous branch."[14] One might fear or resent their power over litigants, but they were not viewed as effective makers of public policy.

That changed in 1801 with the appointment of John Marshall as Chief Justice. Marshall's first decision came in the form of a written opinion of the

---

11. I take this to be the subtext of Thomas Frank, *What's the Matter with Kansas? How Conservatives Won the Heart of America* (2004).

12. Louis Dupre, *The Enlightenment and the Intellectual Foundations of Modern Culture* 153–54 (2004); Jonathan Hill, *Faith in the Age of Reason: The Enlightenment from Galileo to Kant* 7 (2004).

13. Alfred Lord Tennyson, "Aylmer's Field," lines 435–439, in *The Poetic and Dramatic Works of Alfred Lord Tennyson* 241, 246 (1898).

14. The Federalist Papers 78: "the judiciary is beyond comparison the weakest of the three departments of power." And see Alexander M. Bickel, *The Least Dangerous Branch: The Supreme Court at the Bar of Politics* (1962). Montesquieu put it most strongly: "Of the three powers above mentioned, the judiciary is next to nothing." *Supra* n. 10, Book XI, Chap. 6.

Court signed by all seven Justices.[15] Writing such an opinion is a deliberate legislative act quite different from any envisioned by those who created the Court. The importance of the device in elevating the judicial power was confirmed by its immediate adoption by state courts, and, before long, by courts of other nations, not least including England.[16] Combined with the unquestioned constitutional power to invalidate legislation, the opinions of the Court soon became *the* source of constitutional law, making the justices authors and sometime revisors of a constitution that is an extended elaboration of the text written in 1787 and seldom amended by the almost impossible process set forth in its Article V. This transformation of the Court was recognized and decried by Jeffersonians as an illegitimate seizure of legislative powers.[17]

And in 1805, the Jeffersonian leaders of the Senate wisely forswore use of its impeachment power as a means of correcting Justice Samuel Chase's misguided Federalist politics.[18] But the resulting practice of legislative restraint liberated those writing the subtextual constitutional law from any direct personal accountability for the political decisions they had become empowered to make. It became metaphorically appropriate, even if not literally correct, to speak of justices as officers enjoying "life tenure," a phrase previously reserved for royalty.

In a constitutional scheme of "checks and balances", what were the checks to prevent justices from gradually rewriting the Constitution to accord to their preferences? This is an obvious question having no obvious answer. And the Founders' miscalculation in leaving that question open was soon recognized. In the first half of the nineteenth century, all American state constitutions were revised to assure some form of rotation in high judicial offices and/or to provide other means of correcting bad law made by state judges in the opinions of their courts.[19] Frederick Grimké, a justice of the Ohio Supreme Court ex-

---

15. The first appearance of the opinion of the court came in Talbot v. Seeman, 1 Cranch 1 (1801).

16. *See* Paul D. Carrington, *Butterfly Effects: The Political Consequences of Law Teaching*, 41 Duke L. J. 741, 753–754 (1992).

17. E.g., John Taylor, *Construction Construed and Constitutions Vindicated* (1820).

18. *See* William H. Rehnquist, *Grand Inquests: The Historic Impeachments of Samuel Chase and President Andrew Johnson* 22–27 (1992).

19. A Federalist legislature in New Hampshire in 1813 expelled all the Democratic judges from the state courts. Edwin D. Sandborn, *History of New Hampshire from Its First Discovery to the Year 1830* 260–61 (1875). The Democratic legislature elected in Kentucky in 1824 fired all members of their highest court (who were Whigs) and replaced them, as punishment for decisions having unwelcome impact on tenants and debtors. Arndt H. Stickles, *The Critical Court Struggle in Kentucky*, 1819–1829 (1929). For a review of issues and literature in later times, see Paul D. Carrington, *Judicial Independence and Democra-*

plained the view generally prevailing in antebellum times.[20] He expressed what would later be designated as Legal Realism—the observation that high court judges are making political decisions—and he concluded that "[i]f then the judges are appointed for life, they may have the ability to act upon society, both inwardly and outwardly, to a greater degree than the other departments." And, he added, "if it is not wise to confer a permanent tenure of office upon the executive and legislative, it should not be conferred upon the judiciary; and the more so, because the legislative functions which the last perform is a fact entirely hidden from the great majority of the community."[21]

Living with the Mistake:
The Federal Courts in the Nineteenth Century

Although few of his contemporaries expressed disagreement with Grimké, nothing was done by Congress in his time to limit the terms of justices sitting on the Supreme Court of the United States. There were reasons that this was so.

One was that the Supreme Court was an organ of a weak national government and was generally held in limited regard. When the Court proclaimed the rights of the Cherokee to remain in Georgia,[22] President Jackson simply defied it.[23] When it unconstitutionally declared itself to be the premier authority on the nation's private law governing contracts and property,[24] a decision said to result from the superannuation and arrogance of Justice Story,[25] the state supreme courts ignored it. When a minor war arose between political factions in Rhode Island, the Court timidly feared to decide which was le-

---

tic Accountability, 61-1 L. & Contemp. Probs. 79 (1998) (Paul D. Carrington & D. Price Marshall, eds).

20. Frederick Grimké, *Considerations upon the Nature and Tendency of Free Institutions* (H.W. Derby & Co., Cincinnati 1848), republished by Harvard University Press in 1968.

21. *Id.* 355.

22. Worcester v. Georgia, 31 U.S. 515, (Pet.) 560–63 (1832). *See generally* Jill Norgren, *The Cherokee Case: The Confrontation of Law and Politics* (1996).

23. For an account, see Edward A, Miles, *After John Marshall's Decision: Worcester v. Georgia and the Nullification Crisis*, 39 J. S. Hist. 589 (1973).

24. Swift v. Tyson, 41 U.S. 1 (16 Pet.) (1842).

25. John Chipman Gray, *The Nature and Sources of Law* 253 (1909). The unconstitutionality of the decision was declared by the Court in Erie R. R. v. Tompkins, 304 U. S. 64 (1938).

gitimate.[26] When it declared that Americans of African ancestry had no rights,[27] the nation led by President Lincoln initiated a war to overrule it. When it seemed that the Court might impede the war effort, Lincoln appointed a tenth justice to assure that it would not be able to marshal the votes to do so.[28] When the chief justice issued a writ of habeas corpus to free a citizen who was organizing resistance to the military draft,[29] Lincoln ordered the Army to defy the writ. When it seemed that the Court might invalidate Reconstruction legislation, Congress foreclosed its jurisdiction.[30] And when the Court later invalidated the federal income tax,[31] it was in due course reversed by constitutional amendment.[32] No contested policy of substantial national concern that was announced by the Court in the nineteenth century was effectively maintained.

It may also have been pertinent that nineteenth century federal judges were more frequently selected for their political prominence.[33] Virtually all justices were then veterans of the political campaign trail because only such persons were visible to the Presidents who nominated them or the Congressmen who confirmed them. Most were therefore able to maintain social and political ties to the legislators working elsewhere in the Capitol, and with those in the regions from which they came. And they were therefore less likely to see themselves or to be seen by others as persons of exceptional power and status. Nor was their high status entirely dependent on that of the office they held.

And to the extent that the Court successfully exercised significant political power in the nineteenth century, its decisions generally involved enforcement of the federal Constitution against allegedly miscreant state legislatures. In that way, the Court played a significant role in the advent of America's Gilded Age

---

26. Luther v. Borden, 48 U.S. 1 (7 How.) (1849).

27. Scott v. Sandford, 60 U.S. 393 (19 How.) (1857). The decision in that case was at the time encouraged by the President and leading Senators. On its effects, see Martin Siegel, *The Taney Court, 1837–1864* 66–68 (1987); Don E. Fehrenbacher, *The "Dred Scott" Case: Its Significance in American Law and Politics* 307–313 (1978).

28. On Lincoln's appointment of Stephen Field, see Paul Kens, *Justice Stephen Field: Shaping Liberty from The Gold Rush to The Gilded Age* 95–96 (1997).

29. Ex parte Milligan, 71 U.S. 2 (4 Wall.) (1866).

30. Ex parte McCardle, 74 U.S. 506 (6 Wall. 318) (1868).

31. Pollock v. Farmers Loan & Trust Co., 158 U. S. 429, 601 (1895).

32. *See* Robert Stanley, *Dimensions of Law in the Service of Order: Origins of the Federal Income Tax* 1861–1913 at 225–229 (1993).

33. *See*, e.g., Maeva Marcus, *Allen Chair Symposium 2004 Federal Judicial Selection: Symposium Article Federal Judicial Selection: The First Decade*, 39 U. Rich. L. Rev. 797 (2005).

by invalidating state laws enacted to protect workers or regulate business.[34] But Congress and the President did not much mind these transgressions, for it was only state governments that were directly disadvantaged. And Christopher Tiedemann, a leading constitutional scholar of the era could reassure the nation that it need not worry: "the Congress has power to increase the number of the Supreme Court judges, and thus, with the aid of the President, to change the composition and tendencies of the Court. If at any time the Supreme Court should too persistently withstand any popular demand in a case in which the people will not submit to the judicial negative, by an increase in the number of judges…the popular will may be realized."[35]

Finally, it was the fact in the nineteenth century that substantial turnover occurred naturally. Many died while in office, some at advanced ages, but some at ages not so advanced. And some retired without pay. One cause of such resignations was the requirement imposed on the justices by Congress that they "ride circuit" in order to remain in contact with the people whom they governed.[36] An aim of the requirement was to assure that the justices would write opinions of the court that expressed "the common thoughts of men."[37] Circuit-riding required annual trips, often of considerable length, and in horse-drawn vehicles or dangerous steamboats.

The Judiciary Act of 1891:
Creation of Courts of Appeals

The relatively humble status of the Court began to change in 1891 when Congress created the Circuit Courts of Appeals to review most judgments of

---

34. Howard Gillman, *The Constitution Besieged: The Rise and Demise of Lochner Era Police Powers Jurisprudence* (1993);William J. Novak, *The People's Welfare and Regulation in Nineteenth Century America* (1996); Own Fiss, *Troubled Beginnings of the Modern State,* 1888–1910 (1993).

35. Christopher G. Tiedeman, *The Unwritten Constitution of the United States* 162 (1890).

36. An elaborate history of the practice is provided by Joshua Glick, *On the Road: The Supreme Court and the History of Circuit Riding,* 24 Cardozo L. Rev. 1753 (2003).

37. The phrase was provided by Thomas Cooley, a Chief Justice of Michigan and the premier constitutionalist of the late nineteenth century. On receiving an honorary degree from Harvard, he cautioned that: "the strength of law lies in its commonplace character, and it becomes feeble and untrustworthy when it expresses something different from the common thoughts of men." *A Record of Commemoration, November 5 to November 9, 1886, On the Two Hundred Fiftieth Anniversary of Harvard College* 95 (1886).

federal trial courts.[38] The purpose of the new law as proclaimed by its principal champion in the House of Representatives was to achieve "the overthrow and destruction of the kingly power" of the federal trial judges by subjecting them to closer appellate review than the one Supreme Court had provided.[39] Prior to the Act, appeals had seldom been allowed in criminal cases (which were then few in number) or in civil cases involving lesser amounts (of which there were many). In those matters, the trial court had the last and only say. The Court after 1891 continued to hear some direct appeals from lower federal courts as well as from highest state courts, and entertained appeals from the intermediate appellate courts. But the Justices were relieved of the odious duty of riding circuit.[40]

The national economy emerging in the last decades of the nineteenth century brought with it the idea of human capitalism and admiration for all forms of expertise. Professional training became more highly valued in all fields of professional work,[41] not least including law, and became a major source of status in the middle class.[42] The judiciary accordingly began to present themselves more as men of academic learning and less as men of proven political judgment. The Court, and lower federal courts as well, would by the late twentieth century be all but divested of judges with experience as legislators or as candidates for any public office.[43] They became more the instruments of a professional elite.

And the notion that the law, even the Constitution, is a mystery requiring professional training to comprehend became increasingly fashionable. Contrary to early nineteenth century practice in many states, bar organizations appeared; they proclaimed and sometimes even sought to enforce standards of professional conduct for lawyers.[44] The American Bar Association arose in 1878 as a voluntary association of elite lawyers with a broad agenda of law re-

---

38. The story of the enactment is told by Felix Frankfurter & James M. Landis, *The Business of the Supreme Court* 86–102 (1928).

39. 21 Cong Rec. 3403 (1890).

40. It was essentially a "dead letter" by the time the statute was passed. Frankfurter & Landis, *supra* n. 38 at 87.

41. Magali Larsen, *The Rise of Professionalism* (1977).

42. Burton Bledstein, *The Culture of Professionalism: The Middle Class in the Development of Higher Education* 80–92 (1976).

43. Sandra Day O'Connor was the one member of the Court over the last quarter century who had any experience as a legislator; she served briefly in the Arizona senate. Her experience is recounted in Sandra Day O'Connor, *The Majesty of the Law: Reflections of A Supreme Court Justice* 106–107 (2003).

44. *Professions and Professional Ideologies in America* (Gerald L. Geison ed., 1983); *The New High Priests: Lawyers in Post-Civil War America* (Gerard W. Gawalt ed., 1984).

forms.[45] And university law schools materialized.[46] Along with these developments came a growing sense on the part of the public and of Congress that judges were experts who should be trusted to do their work on their own terms, much as lawyers, doctors, engineers and public schoolteachers were then trusted to do their jobs as well as possible for the benefit of those they served with scant accounting for any mistakes they might make.

To maintain their own professional standards and validate that growing trust, each justice came to need the help of a legal secretary or law clerk. And they came generally to prefer young assistants certified by their law teachers to be individuals of uncommon intellect and energy. This practice became the source of a stable relationship between the justices and the law professors at the schools from which the law clerks were drawn, but weakened ties among the justices.[47]

Progressive Judicial Law Reform

Then came the Progressive reform politics of 1900–1915, a development rooted in part in growing confidence in professional expertise as a confirmation of the Enlightenment notion that social problems can be solved by well-trained professionals. Roscoe Pound in 1906 famously expounded his "causes for popular dissatisfaction with the law" as including mindless technicalities that wise lawyers could eliminate.[48] One Progressive campaign was an effort to improve the judiciary by means of "merit selection."[49] But it was also Progressive to assure the accountability of the judiciary for decisions laden with political consequences by means of constitutional referenda, recall elections and the like.[50] And the professional training and status of judges were not deemed sufficient to justify conferring on them royal "life tenure" and the

---

45. An account is Edson Sunderland, *History of the American Bar Association and Its Work* (1953).

46. Robert Bocking Stevens, *Law School: Legal Education in America from the 1850s to the 1980s* (1983).

47. Bradley J. Best, *Law Clerks, Support Personnel, and the Decline of Consensual Norms on the United States Supreme Court 1935–1995* (2002).

48. 29 A. B. A. Rep. 503.

49. Proposed by Albert Kales in 1914, it was first adopted in Missouri in 1940. Maura Ann Schoshinski, *Towards an Independent, Fair and Competent Judiciary: An Argument for Improving Judicial Elections,* 7 Geo. J. Legal Ethics 839 (1994).

50. For a contemporaneous expression of the Progressive view, see Gilbert E. Roe, *Our Judicial Oligarchy* (1912).

power to make almost irreversible political decisions. These ideas did not, however, find their way into the federal government.[51]

William Howard Taft

President Taft played an enormous role in the history of the Court and in the transformation of the entire federal judiciary. He had been a federal judge and a law school dean in Cincinnati.[52] While campaigning for the presidency in Pocatello, Taft uttered words foretelling his future role. "I love judges and I love courts," he told the voters. "They are my ideals. They typify on earth what we shall meet hereafter in heaven under a just God."[53] During his four years as President, Taft had occasion to appoint no fewer than six members of the Supreme Court in whom he presumably detected a measure of divinity. After losing the presidency in 1912, he moved to Yale and wrote about constitutional law, chiefly as it serves to constrain his successors in the White House.[54]

In 1921, President Harding appointed Taft chief justice to preside over the Court on which many of Taft's own appointees sat.[55] He became a powerful voice for a vision of the federal judiciary as a super-professional elite. In this role, he overwhelmed the opposition of Justice Louis D. Brandeis, whose views were generally those reflected in this essay.

The Judiciary Act of 1922: Creating The Judicial Conference

Among Chief Justice Taft's first acts was to forsake the practice of abstaining from any effort to influence legislation in Congress, a practice established

---

51. Pound did express a vision of the role of federal as well as state appellate courts, see Paul D. Carrington, *The Unknown Court*, in Restructuring Justice (Arthur Hellman ed., 1990).

52. 1 Henry F. Pringle, *The Life and Times of William Howard Taft* (1939). On his appointment to the federal bench, see p. 95–96. On his time as dean, see 125.

53. Jeffrey B. Morris, *What Heaven Must Be Like: William Howard Taft as Chief Justice, 1921–30*, 1983 Sup. Ct. Hist. Soc. Y. B. 80, 82 (1983). While President, Taft published an article on judicial administration, *The Delays of the Law*, 18 Yale L. J. 28 (1908).

54. E.g., William Howard Taft, *Our Chief Magistrate and His Powers* (1916).

55. *See* William Howard Taft, *Possible and Needed Reforms in Administration of Justice in Federal Courts*, 8 A. B. A. J. 601 (1922). Justice Frankfurter, no admirer of Taft's politics, later noted, "there was no aspect of judicial reform which did not receive from him a ready

by John Marshall and followed by all of Taft's predecessors. Taft lobbied and soon secured enactment of the Judiciary Act of 1922[56] establishing the institution now known as the Judicial Conference of the United States. The Conference is a low-visibility council composed of chief judges of the federal circuits who acquire their status as chiefs on the basis of their seniority in service on their courts, and of other federal judges selected by their colleagues in the circuits or regions that they represent. The Conference is chaired by the chief justice. It was initially organized to study the needs of the courts and to report them to Congress. By steps, the Conference acquired additional roles and was accorded increasing deference by Congress, with the result that the federal judiciary became substantially self-governing.

In 1934, at the behest of the American Bar Association, Congress enacted the Rules Enabling Act[57] commissioning the Supreme Court to propose rules of civil procedure for use in all federal trial courts, rules designated to become law if Congress did not timely override the proposals. This was not a radical idea, but a Progressive one having antecedents in the longstanding practice of the federal courts in "suits in Equity."[58] Yet it was an exceptional delegation by Congress of explicitly legislative power to judges, power they had not previously exercised. The Court turned to a special committee of fourteen eminent lawyers and scholars. The Federal Rules of Civil Procedure were published by the Court on the committee's recommendation notwithstanding a dissent by Justice Brandeis,[59] and were allowed by Congress to become law in 1938. The new rules were not seen as beneficial to any identifiable group of litigants but as an effective method of resolving disputed facts in accordance with the applicable law, and perhaps as a reflection of the Progressive goals proclaimed by Roscoe Pound and others. They were deemed a great success by lawyers

---

response." *Chief Justices I Have Known,* 39 Va. L. Rev. 883, 898 (1953). On Taft's leadership in the Court, see generally Robert Post, *Judicial Management and Judicial Disinterest: The Achievements and Perils of Chief Justice William Howard Taft,* 1998 J. Sup. Ct. Hist 50; Robert Post, *The Supreme Court Opinion as Institutional Practice: Dissent, Legal Scholarship and Decisionmaking in the Taft Court,* 85 Minn. L. Rev. 1267 (2001);.and Kenneth W. Starr, *William Howard Taft: The Chief Justice as Judicial Architect,* 60 U. Cin. L. Rev. 963 (1992). See generally Peter Graham Fish, *The Politics of Federal Judicial Administration* (Princeton 1973).

56. Act of September 14, 1922, 42 Stat. 837.

57. Act of June 19, 1934, 48 Stat. 1064. On its origins, see Stephen B. Burbank, *The Rules Enabling Act of 1934,* 130 U. Pa. L. Rev. 1015 (1982).

58. On the relation to practice in Equity, see Stephen N. Subrin, *How Equity Conquered Common Law: The Federal Rules of Civil Procedure in Historical Perspective,* 135 U. Pa. L. Rev. 909 (1967).

59. Edward Purcell, *Brandeis and the Progressive Constitution: Erie, the Judicial Power, and the Politics of the Federal Courts in the Twentieth Century* 135 (2000).

and trial judges, and were copied or emulated for use in the courts of most states.[60] Less noticed was the degree to which the new rules enhanced the discretion and power of the individual trial judge.[61]

In time, the committee that had advised the Court by drafting civil rules was replaced by one reporting to the Judicial Conference that in turn reports to the Court.[62] The new committee consisted mainly of federal judges counseled by a few lawyers and professors. Whether this change was provident may be questioned. But the Conference and its committees were then later empowered to recommend criminal rules, rules of evidence, bankruptcy rules and rules of appellate procedure.[63] The Supreme Court has approved almost all the recommendations of the Conference and its advisory committees, and Congress has allowed almost all of them to become law.[64] While issues abide,[65] most would concede that rulemaking by the Conference has

---

60. Arthur T. Vanderbilt, *Improving the Administration of Justice: Two Decades of Development*, 26 Cin. L. Rev. 155 (1957); Geoffrey Hazard, *Undemocratic Legislation*, 87 Yale L. J. 1284, 1287 (1978).

61. Stephen Yeazell, *The Misunderstood Consequences of Civil Process*, 1994 Wis. L. Rev. 631.

62. Act of July 11, 1958, 72 Stat. 356.

63. Amendments to 28 U.S.C. §2071 were made by the Judicial Improvements and Access to Justice Act in 1988 (Pub. L. No. 100-702, Title IV, §403(a)(1)); 28 U.S.C. §2072 was added by Judicial Improvements and Access to Justice Act in 1988 (Pub. L. No. 100-702, Title IV, §403(a)(1)), but was then amended by the Judicial Improvements Act of 1990 (Pub. L. No. 101-650, Title III, §§315, 321); 28 U.S.C. §2073 was added by the Judicial Improvements and Access to Justice Act (Pub. L. No. 100-702, Title IV, §401(a)), and was then amended by the Bankruptcy Reform Act on Oct. 22, 1994 (Pub. L. No. 103-394, Title I, §104(e)); 28 U.S.C. §2074 was added by the Judicial Improvements and Access to Justice Act of 1988 (Pub. L. No. 100-702, Title IV, §401(a)); 28 U.S.C. §2075 was added on Oct. 3, 1964 (Pub. L. No. 88-623, §1, 78 Stat. 1001), and amended on November 6, 1978 (Pub. L. No. 95-598, Title II, §247, 92 Stat. 2672). It was further amended by the Bankruptcy Reform Act of 1994 (Pub. L. No. 103-394, Title I, §104(f)); 28 U.S.C. §2076 was repealed in 1988 by Title IV of the Judicial Improvements and Access to Justice Act (Pub. L. No. 100-702). The subject is now governed by 28 U.S.C. §§2072-2074; 28 U.S.C. §2071 was added by the Federal Courts Improvement Act of 1982 (Pub. L. No. 97-164, Title II, §208(a)), and was amended by the Judicial Improvements and Access to Justice Act in 1988 (Pub. L. No. 100-702, Title IV, §401(b)). It was further amended by the Judicial Improvements Act of 1990 (Pub. L. No. 101-650, Title IV, §406).

64. For example, there was much controversy over the Federal Rules of Evidence when first promulgated; they were amended and, as amended, enacted by Congress but subject to revision by the procedure established pursuant to the 1934 scheme. The story is told by Raymond F. Miller, *Comment: Creating Evidentiary Privileges : An Argument for the Judicial Approach*, 31 Conn. L. Rev. 771, 771–777 (1999).

65. For a current effort of a Congressman to amend Civil Rule 11, see <http://lamar-smith.house.gov/ news.asp?FormMode=Detail&ID=644>. On the recent history of the rule,

been on balance a benign enterprise. The committees have been careful to limit judicial rulemaking to procedural matters having no consciously substantive purpose, but the distinction between procedure and substance is not free of difficulty.

Notwithstanding President Taft's assessment of judges as angels of a sort, they do in their rulemaking manifest a tendency to confirm the "public choice theory" fashioned by academic economists to explain the tendency of lawmakers to take special care of their own interests as professionals.[66] This is not to say that the federal judges are not committed to public service. I can attest from decades of contact with scores of them, that they aspire to nothing but to do justice and maintain fidelity to law. But when they come together on committees, those objectives tend to become conflated with the power and status of the judiciary. It should surprise no one to hear that mortal judges are afflicted with very normal human failings, not unlike those manifested by other professionals, whether public or private.

In 1939, the Conference was supplied with its own support staff by the creation of the Administrative Office of the United States Courts.[67] It served to displace an arm of the Department of Justice that had been performing that role. One of its purposes was to enable the Conference to deal more directly with Congress in the pursuit of its legislative aims.[68] The reform tended to relieve the Executive Branch of responsibility for issues of judicial administration.

On the advice of the Judicial Conference, Congress fashioned a generous retirement system for federal judges.[69] This was done in part in response to awareness of a growing number of superannuated trial judges whose lives were prolonged by twentieth century improvements in public health and whose impatience and arbitrary conduct at trials engendered the mistrust of lawyers

---

see Paul D. Carrington, & Andrew Wasson, *A Reflection on Rulemaking: The Rule 11 Experience*, 37 Loyola L. Rev.563 (2004).

66. For an account of the theory, see Daniel A. Farber & Philip P. Frickey, *Law and Public Choice: A Critical Introduction* (1991); on its application to the judiciary, see Jonathan R. Macey, *Judicial Preferences, Public Choice and the Rules of Procedure*, 23 J. Leg. Stud. 627 (1994); Charles G. Geyh, *Paradise Lost, Paradise Found: Redefining the Judiciary's Role in Congress*, 71 N.Y.U. L. Rev. 1165 (1996).

67. Act of August 7, 1939, 53 Stat. 1223.

68. Peter Graham Fish, *Crises, Politics, and Federal Judicial Reform: The Administrative Office Act of 1939*, 32 J. Pol. 599 (1970).

69. 28 U.S.C. §371 is based on title 28, U.S.C., 1940 ed., §§375 and 375a (Mar. 3, 1911, ch. 231, §260, 36 Stat. 1161; Feb. 25, 1919, ch. 29, §6, 40 Stat. 1157; Mar. 1, 1929, ch. 419, 45 Stat. 1422; Mar. 1, 1937, ch. 21 §§1, 2, 50 Stat. 24; Feb 11, 1938, ch. 25, §1, 52 Stat. 28; May 11, 1944, ch. 192, §1, 58 Stat. 218).

and litigants. Because the retirement plan allows them to retire at full pay, and because service on the lower federal courts is less gratifying than the exercise of the powers of a Justice, judges sitting on those courts retire after an appropriate period of service.[70] Congress thus purchased an end to "life tenure" for district judges and circuit judges.

Justices are afforded the same incentives to retire in a timely way as are the other Article III judges, but they do not choose to subside even though they could draw full pay without working. Judith Resnik suggests that the benefits paid could be made to decline as judges overstay terms to be prescribed by Congress.[71] Possibly Justices might be required to take their retirement after, say, eighteen years of service, or else forfeit the right to receive benefits thereafter.

The Judicial Conference also persuaded Congress to add to the Conference's broad legislative responsibility as procedural rulemaker, responsibilities for managing through its regional councils judicial misconduct resulting from physical or emotional disabilities.[72] While only Congress with its impeachment power can remove a justice or any judge appointed by the President, a system of discipline was established within the Judicial Conference regime. Its councils cannot remove any judge from office but it can terminate his or her authority to sit on cases. This power is exercised with utmost, and perhaps excessive, caution or timidity, but it provides a humane method of dealing with emotional difficulties sometimes manifested by judges in their exercise of "kingly power." On occasion, judges disciplined by other judges have contested the constitutionality of this arrangement as constituting an exercise of power reserved by the Constitution to Congress as a part of its impeachment power, but without success.[73] By conferring this power on the Conference, Congress with the approval of the Court approved the idea that the "life tenure" of federal judges as prescribed in Article III could be forcibly constrained in appropriate circumstances without need to deploy the impeachment process.

And also on the advice of the Conference, Congress in 1968 greatly enlarged the authority of lower federal courts to select and appoint additional judges

---

70. Albert Yoon, *The End of the Rainbow: Understanding Turnover among Federal Judges*, __Am L. & Econ. Rev. ___, ___(forthcoming 2005).

71. *See* Judith Resnik, *So Long*, Legal Affairs 20 (July/August 2005).

72. *Judicial Councils Reform and Judicial Conduct and Disability Act of 1980*, 48 Fed. Reg. 30843, 28 U.S.C. §272.

73. Chandler v. Judicial Council of the Tenth Circuit, 398 U.S. 74 (1970), *see infra* discussion in Cramton pp. 345–360.

who serve limited terms.[74] By stages, the titles, roles, and compensations of magistrate judges and bankruptcy judges have been elevated.[75] They are paid slightly less than the district judges appointed by the President, but they are authorized by Congress to exercise most of their courts' powers.[76]

The creation of these subordinate judgeships is in part a reflection of the Judicial Conference's concerns for the number of Article III judges. As the number of district and circuit judges increased in the twentieth century to handle increasing caseloads, some judges became concerned over the dilution of their status. Federal judges might come to be seen as ordinary mortals and it might be harder to recruit the best and brightest. A policy disfavoring new judgeships came to influence judicial rulemaking and administrative practices.[77] In framing this policy, no account was taken of the relationship between the number of Article III judges and the number of lawyers over whom they preside or the populations they serve, nor of the comparison to other legal systems that employ proportionately many more judges, nor of the increasing number of individual substantive rights conferred on a growing population thereby increasing a demand for services in ever shorter supply. No matter what the need, there can only be so many federal judges!

In sum, the Judicial Conference has come to bear some likeness to a labor union, one whose members are employed by an inattentive management that is Congress. Or perhaps it is more a corporate culture led by executives enjoying utmost rewards in the form of political power but unnoticed by its shareholders who bear the consequences of those executive compensations. This development was only indirectly the result of Chief Justice Taft's initiative in 1922, but it reflected his zeal for the power and status of judges. And Taft had other ideas as well.

---

74. Act of Oct. 17, 1968, Pub. L. 90-578, Title I, § 101, 82 Stat. 1108 [enacting 28 U. S. C. § 631 et seq.]. There were antecedent practices of a similar sort, especially in the administration of the bankruptcy laws.

75. The title "Magistrate Judge" was conferred on magistrates in 1990. The Judicial Improvements Act of 1990, Pub. L. No. 101-650, § 321, 104 Stat. 5089 (1990). *See generally* Linda Silberman, *Judicial Adjuncts Revisited: The Proliferation of Ad Hoc Procedure*, 137 U. Pa. L. Rev. 2131 (1989).

76. The constitutional objections were dismissed. United States v. Raddatz, 447 U.S. 667 (1980); Northern Pipeline Constr. Co. v. Marathon Pipe Line Co. 458 U. S. 50 (1982).

77. Judith Resnik, *Trial as Error, Jurisdiction as Injury: Transforming the Meaning of Article III*, 113 Harv. L. Rev. 924, 984–986 (2000).

The Judiciary Act of 1925:
The Certiorari Power

Taft's 1922 Act was followed by the Judiciary Act of 1925, a law known at the time as "the judges bill."[78] It was responsive to a heavy caseload and backlog in the Court. It authorized the Supreme Court to refuse to hear many of the cases brought to it, leaving unreviewed the merits of many cases decided by the federal courts of appeals or by highest state courts. By stages, this discretion was extended to all cases. And so with trivial exceptions, the Court now decides only those cases it chooses to decide, and indeed only those issues raised in those cases that it deems worthy of its attention,[79] no matter how critical other issues might be to the disposition of a case at hand.

When Congress approved the 1925 Act, the Court was hearing about 330 cases a year, and deciding others without need of hearing. Congress was assured that the number would not be substantially reduced and that the Court would separately confer on each denial of certiorari.[80] In fact, the Court has now reduced its workload to about seventy-five cases a year and declines to consider the other thousands in which its review is sought.[81] The seventy-five are presumably the most important, or at least present the most important issues, but it is not always clear that this is so.[82] The Court's own rule purporting to set standards for selecting cases is "hopelessly indeterminate and unilluminating."[83] Justices seldom explain their reasons for declining to re-

---

78. Act of February 13, 1925, 43 Stat. 936; on the legislative history, *see* Frankfurter & Landis, *supra* n. 38 at 225–294 and Edward Hartnett, *Questioning Certiorari: Some Reflections Seventy-Five Years After the Judges' Bill*, 100 Colum. L. Rev. 1643, 1649–1704 (2000). Hartnett also records later revisions expanding the power. Opposition was expressed by Senator Thomas J. Walsh (D.-Mont.). *See* his *The Overburdened Supreme Court*, 1922 Va. Bar Assn Rep. 216.

79. *See* 28 U. S. C. §§ 1251 et seq.

80. The then Solicitor General, James M. Beck, testifying on behalf of the legislation at Taft's request, "estimated that the number of cases of public gravity that the Court could decide on the merits was between four hundred and five hundred [per year]. Hartnett, *supra* n. 78 at 1646.

81. 2003 Annual Report of the Administrative Office of the United States Courts. A review of the 2003 year is available at <http://www.supremecourtus.gov/publicinfo/yearend/2004year-endreport.pdf> at p. 9.

82. *See* Rules of the Supreme Court of the United States, Rules 10–16.

83. Samuel Estreicher & John Sexton, *A Managerial Theory of the Supreme Court's Responsibilities: An Empirical Study*, 59 N.Y.U. L. Rev. 681, 790 (1994).

view a case. That those reasons are of a diverse political nature and some-times centered on the interests of the federal judiciary, is not to be doubted.[84] This power to select the cases it decides is transformative. With rare excep-tion, the Court only agrees to hear cases that present the justices with op-portunities to legislate on questions they deem worthy of their attention. In-deed, Chief Justice Rehnquist urged the Court to retain jurisdiction over moot cases if they present interesting and important legal issues; the Court should not, in his view, be deprived of an opportunity to legislate merely be-cause the parties have settled their case and are no longer available to argue it.[85]

It is quite plausible that the power of the Court over its agenda gave it the courage to extend the federal Constitution to matters that had previously been regarded as matters of state law. It was a very short time after passage of the 1925 Act that the Court re-interpreted the Fourteenth Amendment so that al-most all the protections of the Bill of Rights applied to the states and thus em-powered itself to review a vast array of state court decisions.[86] As Edward Hart-nett observes, it is difficult to imagine the Court publishing such an opinion making new constitutional law if it meant that all persons convicted of crime by state courts would become entitled to invoke Supreme Court jurisdiction as a matter of federal right. Concentrating on its legislative role, the Court leaves to lower courts narrow concerns about whether specific cases were rightly decided on the facts and the law. In the mode thus established, the Court does still decide cases, but only incidentally to its lawmaking. In this respect, it has turned on its head the judicial role envisioned by the Founders.

An indirect consequence of this arrangement is the nullification of the ar-gument made by Chief Justice Marshall in his celebrated opinion in *Marbury v. Madison*[87] justifying the Court's role in reviewing the constitutionality of legislation. He explained that role as necessitated by its duty to decide the cases brought to it for decision—it could neither refuse to decide nor could it dis-obey the Constitution. But the Court no longer has any such duty to decide a case. And it seldom finds it necessary to decide whether in a specific case the lower courts have actually and correctly applied the controlling law.

---

84. For accounts, see Richard L. Pacelle Jr., *The Transformation of the Supreme Court's Agenda: From the New Deal to the Reagan Administration* (1991); H. W. Perry Jr., *Deciding to Decide: Agenda Setting in the United States Supreme Court* (1991); Doris Marie Provine, *Case Selection in the United States Supreme Court* (1980).

85. Honig v. Doe, 484 U. S. 205, 329–330 (1988).

86. Gitlow v. New York, 268 U. S. 652, 666 (1925).

87. 5 U.S. (1 Cranch) 137, 177–178 (1803).

While the workload of the justices was thus steadily declining after 1925, they were being supplied with more and more help. To help decide seventy-five cases a year, and write eight or so opinions of the Court proclaiming the law to be applied in the future by other lesser courts, each justice is supplied with very bright and energetic law clerks. Their number has been by stages increased from one per justice to four.[88] This help is employed in different ways by different justices. But it has enabled some to go on automatic pilot, delegating much of their work to assistants.[89] And a similar development has occurred in the lower federal courts, where, along with the addition of magistrate judges and bankruptcy judges has come a substantial increase in the staff of law clerks and staff attorneys. There, too, the delegation of power and responsibility is much greater than it was in the time when Louis Brandeis could boast of the Court: "We do our own work."[90]

Just as the Supreme Court focuses its energy on only a few of the matters on which its attention is requested, a similar concentration of effort has occurred in the lower federal courts. A half century ago, as the authors of the Judiciary Act of 1891 envisioned, every litigant in a federal appellate court was assured of the right to an oral hearing at which the three "life-tenured" judges responsible for the decision would appear in person and engage in discourse with counsel to appraise critically the judgment of the court under review.[91] And in due course, the judges hearing the case would publish a decision justifying their action and incidentally giving evidence of their personal attention to the parties' contentions. Those amenities have vanished in many cases.

It ought to be conceded that one reason for this abandonment of appellate procedure has been the duty imposed on federal courts to entertain many appeals presenting no serious issues. These include many routine appeals in criminal cases, or from denials of petitions by prisoners seeking belatedly to challenge their convictions whether in state or federal court, or civil claims of prisoners seeking to gain some improvement in the conditions of their incarceration. The abrupt procedure of the courts of appeals in such cases resembles that of the Supreme Court.

---

88. L. A. Powe, Jr., *Go Geezers Go: Leaving the Bench,* 25 Law and Social Inquiry 1227 (2000).

89. David J. Garrow, *Mental Decrepitude on the U. S. Supreme Court: The Historical Case for a 28th Amendment,* 67 U. Chi. L. Rev. 995 (2000).

90. Bernard Schwartz, *Decision* 48 (1996).

91. The decline of the institution of oral argument was marked by Charles Haworth, *Screening and Summary Procedures in the United States Courts of Appeals,* 1973 Wash. U. L. Q. 257.

But similar change is also seen in the handling of many other cases in which lawyers have appealed from questionable fact findings or procedural rulings and are making arguments that speak to important rights and interests of the parties but that have little resonance in other cases. Such cases present the circuit judges and their law clerks no opportunity to expound the national law. Instead of providing hearings and decisions in such humdrum cases, circuit judges are prone, like justices, to concentrate their efforts on making "the law of the circuit." Time and energy are invested in writing learned opinions justifying a new legal principle. Those resources are also invested in en banc proceedings and in deciding when such proceedings ought to be deemed necessary to assure that all the judges in a circuit are making the same federal law.[92] Oral arguments are often unavailable. Only opinions of the legislative sort are generally published. Less interesting cases are often left to law clerks or staff attorneys whose memoranda are simply endorsed by the circuit judges. Circuit judges have proposed that they be given discretion, similar to that conferred on the Supreme Court, to decline to hear on the merits those appeals deemed by them to be unworthy of close attention by important judges responsible for articulating the law of the circuit.[93] The argument made for that reform is that it would make the law conform to reality.

But it bears notice that the law of the circuit, in contrast to the law made by the Supreme Court, receives virtually no academic attention and only very occasional study by appellate advocates. The reason is that the law of the circuit is necessarily tentative, depending as it does on the absence of any later relevant utterance by the Supreme Court or by Congress or, indeed, the Executive Branch. And it is in some measure illusory: the empirical data suggest that even other judges sitting on the same circuit court of appeals, do not take the law of the circuit very seriously.[94] But like justices, circuit judges and their young law clerks are attracted to the making of authoritative utterances presuming to command the acceptance of their readers. If their readers are few,

---

92. On the frailties of the "law of the circuit," see Paul D. Carrington, *The Obsolescence of the United States Court of Appeals*, 15 J. Law & Politics 515 (1999).

93. E.g., Robert M. Parker & Ron Chapman, *Accepting Reality: The Time for Accepting Discretionary Review in the Courts of Appeals Has Arrived*, 50 S.M.U. L. Rev. 573 (1997); Public Hearing Before the Comm. on Structural Alternatives for the Federal Courts of Appeal, Apr. 24, 1998 (statement of Diarmuid F. O'Scannlain, U.S. Circuit Judge for the Ninth Circuit. *But see* Richard S. Arnold, *The Future of the Federal Courts*, 60 Mo. L. Rev. 540 (1995).

94. Mitu Gulati & C. M. A. McCauliff, *On Not Making Law*, 61-3 L. & Contemp. Probs. 157 (1998).

well the same can be said for academic publications. In this sense, the Federal Reporter containing the published opinions of the courts of appeals can be regarded as just a special sort of academic law review. Meanwhile, many litigants seeking the attention of United States circuit judges are receiving very little of it.

A similar transformation has occurred in the federal district courts. Trials at which adversaries present evidence have become rare events in federal courts.[95] Instead the district judges and their staffs engage in "managerial judging,"[96] a process by which they seek to facilitate settlements and avoid the necessity of making decisions that might burden the court of appeals with the need to review their judgments; or, if a decision must be made, to render it in the form of a summary judgment, ruling one party's proffered evidence to be legally insufficient and hence unworthy of being heard,[97] a procedure that spares the trial judge the need to see and hear witnesses and enables him or her to elaborate the controlling law. And it eliminates the exposure of the judge to contact with actual litigants or jurors. That tendency to employ summary judgment was much encouraged by a trilogy of Supreme Court opinions published in 1986 that enlarged the application of the governing rule without modifying its text.[98] The tendency was further encouraged by a second trilogy of cases empowering judges, again without modifying the Federal Rule of Evidence governing such rulings, to exclude proffered expert testimony that they deemed to be inadequately based in science, a discipline of which few judges are masters. And rendered such rulings subject to review in the courts of appeals only for "abuse of discretion."[99] So empowered, district judges are able to make pretrial

---

95. *See generally* Marc Galanter, *The Vanishing Trial: An Examination of Trials and Related Matters in Federal and State Courts,* 1 J. Empirical Leg. Studies 459 (2004).

96. Arthur R. Miller, *The Pretrial Rush to Judgment: Are the "Litigation Explosion," "Liability Crisis," and Efficiency Clichés Eroding Our Day in Court and Jury Trial Commitments,* 78 N.Y.U. L. Rev. 982 (2003);.Judith Resnik, *Migrating, Morphing, and Vanishing: The Empirical and Normative Puzzles of Declining Trial Rates in Courts,* 1 J. Empirical Leg. Studies 783 (2004); Stephen C. Yeazell, *Getting What We Asked For, Getting What We Paid For, and Not Liking What We Got: The Vanishing Trial,* 1 J. Empirical Leg. Studies 943 (2004).

97. Fed. R. Civ. P. 56. Stephen B. Burbank, *Vanishing Trials and Summary Judgment in Federal Civil Cases: Drifting Toward Bethlehem or Gomorrah?,* 1 J. Empirical Leg. Studies 597 (2004).

98. The cases and reactions to them are recounted in Paul D. Carrington, *Exorcising the Bogy of Non-Transsubstantive Rules and Making Rules to Dispose of Manifestly Unfounded Assertions,* 137 U. Pa. L. Rev. 2067 (1989).

99. The cases are briefly reviewed in Paul D. Carrington & Traci Jones, *Reluctant Experts,* 59-4 L. & Contemp. Probs. 101 (1997).

dispositions of most of the cases on their docket. Why, Judge Patrick Higgin-botham has asked, do we still call them trial judges?[100]

His question might be extended—why do we call any of them judges or justices when they spend most of their time legislating? That would be unduly harsh. Federal judges and justices do still decide cases. But it does appear that the preoccupation of the justices with the few cases most suited to their attentions as lawmakers has trickled down to lower federal courts that are also increasingly selective in how they choose to invest their efforts. Implicit in the change is a disregard for the tasks of resolving issues of fact and hearing the claims and concerns of mere individual litigants.[101]

Meanwhile, as the justices' staffs have enlarged and their docket has fallen, the Supreme Court's calendar has steadily shrunk. The justices take leave for a month in the winter and two months in the summer. During those times, they travel, write books,[102] and engage in other diversions. At all times of the year, and wherever they go, they are feted. When one considers the life style of the justices, it is little wonder that they are disinclined to subside from their high office. The extent to which a similar improvement in life style has occurred for other federal judges is less visible.

Taft's Courthouse Architecture

Yet another source of judicial grandeur was provided by Chief Justice Taft's third legislative initiative, which was to seek and secure Congressional appropriation for the Supreme Court's building. It is easily the most elegant structure in Washington and reflects Taft's sense of the divinity of justices. It is a magnificent Greek temple. Justice Brandeis protested that it made his colleagues into "the nine beetles of the Temple of Karnak" and would cause them to have an inflated vision of themselves.[103] Does working as a celebrity in such

---

100. *So Why Do We Call Them Trial Courts*, 55 S.M.U. L. Rev. 1405 (2002).

101. There may also be a growing problem of lower court judges seeking promotions to higher courts; Guido Calabresi suggests that this development is a threat to judicial independence. *The Current Subtle—and Not So Subtle—Rejection of an Independent Judiciary*, 4 U. Pa. J. Const. L. 637 (2002).

102. E.g. Chief Justice Rehnquist's books are *The Supreme Court: How It Was, How It Is* (1987); *How Grand Inquests: The Impeachments of Justice Samuel Case and President Andrew Johnson* (1992); *All the Laws But One: Civil Liberties in Wartime* (1998); *The Supreme Court* (2001); *Centennial Crisis: The Disputed Election of 1876* (2004).

103. Pnina Lahav, *History in Journalism and Journalism in History: Anthony Lewis and the Watergate Crisis*, 29 J. S. Ct. Hist. 163 (2004).

an environment for decades affect the state of mind of justices? Infuse them with notions of grandeur and indispensability? Informed observers of the Court report that numerous justices serving on the Court in the twentieth century have undergone personal transformations while on the Court that have resulted in policy decisions in many of their most important cases quite different from those anticipated by those responsible for their appointments. It is on this point that concern for superannuation is most closely linked to the concern over hubris and excess that is the subject of this essay. Elementary common sense tells us that a person working for decades on end in such an environment is almost doomed to lose any modesty or sense of proportion he or she might still have retained at the time of confirmation.

Judith Resnik has expressed similar concerns about the wave of more recent federal courthouses in which subordinate federal judges sit and work. Many of them are designed around some of the institutional reforms crafted by the Judicial Conference involving staff enlargements and the diminished likelihood of trial.[104] Their work environment, too, does tend to shape their sense of what it is they are expected to do.

The Norris-LaGuardia Act of 1932

A belated piece of Progressive legislation was enacted by Congress in 1932 on the eve of the coming of the New Deal. The law enacted was a signal example of a wise if belated Congressional response to overreaching by the federal judiciary. As noted, the Supreme Court began in the nineteenth century to invalidate state laws enacted to protect industrial workers. Contemporaneous with that Gilded Age development was the emergence of the strike-breaking injunction issued by lower federal courts. Congress did not by legislation authorize this practice. One legal theory justifying the practice that Circuit Judge Taft had been among the first to advance was that the courts had implied authority to prevent interference with interstate commerce. The import of Taft's opinion explaining his injunction against a rail strike was "that no interference with interstate commerce is ever justifiable."[105] Such an injunction was very effective in breaking strikes, in part because it was a quick response to a walkout, forcing workers back into their plants. So the strike was very likely to be broken at once even if it might later be concluded that a perma-

---

104. *Supra* n.77 at 1031–1036.
105. Felix Frankfurter & Nathan Greene, *The Labor Injunction* 6–7 (1930).

nent injunction would be inappropriate. The Supreme Court was seldom involved in these matters, but it did in 1895 affirm the conviction of union leader Eugene Debs for his failure to get his members back to work, thereby defying a federal court order, notwithstanding the fact that the injunction lacked the sanction of any federal law.[106] By one count, federal judges imposed over 4,300 injunctions on unions between 1880 and 1930.[107]

In 1932, after the death of Chief Justice Taft and his replacement by the Progressive Chief Justice Charles Evans Hughes, the American Federation of Labor at last secured legislative relief from this longstanding practice of federal courts. The Act simply withdrew federal jurisdiction in cases in which employers sought injunctive relief.[108]

Court-Packing

In 1937, not long after the Court moved into its temple, there came the Court-packing incident.[109] There was reason for the Roosevelt administration to fear that the Court might invalidate much of its legislative program. To prevent that, the President proposed to increase the size of the Court by six justices. This was precisely the remedy prescribed by Professor Tiedemann, the constitutionalist of the Gilded Age, and the remedy employed on a modest scale by President Lincoln. The proposal was widely supported by the law professors of the day. Thurman Arnold suggested that the Court should modify its invocation from "God save the Government of the United States and this Honorable Court" to "God save the United States or this Court," because God could not possibly do both and should be given his choice.[110] The organized bar was, however, most vocal in its opposition to the presidential scheme, confirming a connection in the minds of bar leaders between the reverence for the principle of judicial independence and the profession's self-respect. The profession is in a sense a fraternity of which the judicial fraternity is a subset, and in that instance the American Bar Association marshaled a lot of public

---

106. In re Debs, 158 U.S. 564 (1895); United States v. Debs, 64 Fed. 724 (1894).

107. Willam E. Forbath, *Law and the Shaping of the American Labor Movement* 192–98 (1991).

108. 47 Stat. 70, 29 U. S. C. §70.

109. William E. Leuchtenburg, The Supreme Court Reborn: The Constitutional Revolution in The Age of Roosevelt 132–79 (1995); Barry Cushman, *Rethinking the New Deal Court: The Structure of a Constitutional Revolution*, 11–26, 30–32 (1998).

110. *Letter to Mrs. C. P. Arnold, October 23, 1936* in *Voltaire and the Cowboy: The Letters of Thurman Arnold* 234 (Gene Gressley ed., 1977).

support for its brothers. That daunting force is likely one reason Congress has neglected its duty to govern the federal courts, for there is no rival part of its political constituency with as important a stake in issues of judicial administration as that of the professional fraternity.

The threat of the Court-packing plan appears to have enabled the Progressive Chief Justice, Charles Evans Hughes, to restrain his judicial brethren so that no enduring harm was done by the Court to the New Deal.[111] But the President did not withdraw his proposal, and it was in due course defeated in Congress. The event was in time taken as a signal victory of the Court and the legal profession over the Executive Branch.

The Civil Rights Movement

The Court's sense of its grandeur was further enhanced by its experience with civil rights. The Court had earlier declined to enforce the Fifteenth Amendment guarantee of an equal right to vote[112] and it was very slow to enforce the Fourteenth Amendment for the benefit of those whom it was ratified to protect. But its 1954 decision in *Brown v. Board of Education*[113] was a great moment in American law. It inspired a generation of young lawyers to think of constitutional law as a great instrument for social reform. While many billboards called for the impeachment of Chief Justice Earl Warren, those calls were widely rejected.[114] But they did lead to the confrontation in Little Rock in 1956 when President Eisenhower, on the advice of Attorney General Brownell, sent in the 101st Airborne Division to secure the place of nine African American students in Central High School.[115] Judges of lower rank were at times in physical danger; an airborne division was not required for their protection, but there was cause to celebrate their heroism.[116]

A consequence of the invasion of Little Rock was that justices began to think of themselves as commanding a great military force. In the Little Rock case, they were moved to declare that mere state officials were not entitled to

---

111. *But see* Barry Cushman, *Rethinking the New Deal Court: The Structure of a Constitutional Revolution* 11–26, 30–32(1998).

112. *Cf.* Giles v. Harris, 189 U. S. 475 (1903) (per Holmes. J.).

113. Brown v. Bd. of Educ., 347 U. S. 495 (1954).

114. The story is best told by Richard Kluger, *Simple Justice* (1976).

115. Herbert Brownell & John Burke, *Advising Ike: The Memoirs of Herbert Brownell* 365–384 (1993). On the President's reluctance, see Stephen Ambrose, *Eisenhower* 409 (1984).

116. *See* Jack Bass, *Unlikely Heroes* (1983).

read the Constitution for themselves to justify their protests, but were bound to accept whatever meaning of the constitutional text that they, the justices, might determine and that a failure of state officials to do so would be a violation of their oaths of office.[117] The Court thus implied that state officials should be removed from office merely for their disagreement with the Court. The language of the opinion had equal application to the President, members of Congress and other federal government officials, who were thus cautioned against reading the Constitution for themselves. Indeed, as Philip Kurland asked,[118] if an opinion of the Court is so immutable, how could the Court defy its own dictum in *Plessy v. Ferguson*?[119]

That the Court played an important role in the civil rights struggles that continued for two decades is not to be doubted. But neither should it be forgotten that many others played important roles in the cause.[120] While its decisions evoked rage, they also commanded vast popular support created by the efforts of many others over a much longer period of time. And the decisive role was played not by the Court but by Congress in enacting the Civil Rights Act of 1964 that enabled the Department of Justice to play a leading role in bringing force to bear where it was needed. The courts' legal opinions changed few minds.[121]

Judicial Decrees to Change Society

By 1961, the Court, with self-confidence enlarged by the consequences of the several judiciary acts, its semi-divine surroundings, and its then recent history in achieving social change, was prepared to take on numerous other assignments. Under the intellectual and political leadership of Justice William Brennan, it took on the job of making America more humane by proclaiming new constitutional rights. Such rights were not to be found in the explicit

---

117. Cooper v. Aaron, 358 U.S. 1, 18 (1958). *And see* Justice Frankfurter concurring, at 24.

118. Philip Kurland, *Toward A Political Supreme Court,* 37 U. Chi. L. Rev. 19, 31 (1969).

119. 163 U. S. 537 (1896).

120. E.g., David J. Garrow, *Bearing the Cross: Martin Luther King Jr. and the Southern Christian Leadership Conference* (1986).

121. Gerald N. Rosenberg, *The Hollow Hope: Can Courts Bring About Social Change?* (U. Chicago Press 1991); Michael J. Klarman, *From Jim Crow to Civil Rights: The Supreme Court and the Struggle for Racial Equality* (2004); *and see Black, White and Brown: The Landmark School Desegregation Case in Retrospect* (Clare Cushman & Melvin I. Urofsky eds., 2004).

text of the Constitution, but in principles of natural law said to be implied in the text, discerned by judges, and then elaborated in their opinions of the court. Sanford Levinson observed that many lawyers and legal scholars came increasingly during this time to think of the constitutional text in the way that the Catholic Church has traditionally thought of scripture, as a text truly understood only by those professionally invested in its interpretation.[122] Mere literates were told to keep their thoughts to themselves. This form of religiosity was also perhaps traceable to the English common law tradition that Lord Coke explained to King James, defining the law as a subject accessible only to initiates and quite beyond the understanding of a mere royal.[123] Chief Justice Taft expressed the thought thusly: "The people at the polls, no more than kings upon the throne are fit to pass upon questions involving the judicial interpretation of the law."[124] And so a statue of Lord Coke stands in his Greek temple.

As noted, *The Federalist 78* defined the political role of the Court as one of slowing the process of legislation by providing a cautionary restraint on representative government. Ward Farnsworth invokes this notion as a justification for maintaining the extended terms of senior justices better to link the future to the past.[125] Justice Robert Jackson regretted that linkage, noting that it is usually "the check of a preceding generation on the present one," and "nearly always the check of a rejected regime on the one in being."[126]

But in the decades since 1960, it has been the Court more often than Congress that has been out in front with its political agenda. With the encouragement of many lawyers and academics, it has become a primary source of major legislative change. It seemed at times that the Court was more effective than the Kennedy or Johnson administrations in the pursuit of similar political aims, despite the fact that the Court led by Justice Brennan was in form merely reacting to disputes brought to its attention by litigants.

On the other hand, it seems that few if any of the reforms effected through the application of constitutional law by the federal courts have worked as well as was hoped, or as they seemed to promise to those who approved them. And they are the devil to change. The Court did, with the help of Congress and the

---

122. Sanford Levinson, *Constitutional Faith* 9–53 (1988).

123. A lively account of their encounter is Catherine Bowen, *The Lion and the Throne* 304–316 (1957).

124. Quoted by Gerald Gunther, *Learned Hand: The Man and the Judge* 213 (1994).

125. Ward Farnsworth, *The Regulation of Turnover on the Supreme Court*, 2005 U. Ill. L. Rev. 407.

126. Robert H. Jackson, *The Struggle for Judicial Supremacy* 315 (1941).

Department of Justice, put an end to *de jure* segregation (no small achievement), but, alas, racial and ethnic isolation in public schools resulting from residential isolation and the departure of advantaged children from the public schools has resulted in much re-segregation that it seems fruitless to prohibit.[127]

In the 1960s, the Court became increasingly receptive to petitions by persons convicted of crime and by prisoners. Over the years Court decisions established a large and complex regime of constitutional criminal procedure. Numerous new procedural requirements on criminal prosecutions were intended to protect defendants from investigative and prosecutorial abuse and to prevent the conviction of the innocent. The Court also embarked the lower federal courts on the mission of correcting the worst abuses of prisoners in state prisons.

It seems certain that there is less police brutality, and fewer convictions of the innocent, and less gruesome treatment of prisoners than there would have been had the Court remained as politically docile as it had been in its first century. Perhaps in this respect the justices have at least partially redeemed the promise uttered on the face of their temple: "Equal Justice Under Law." There are, however, now two million persons serving sentences in American prisons (more perhaps than in all the rest of the world) and their sentences — negotiated by prosecutors and defense counsel among alternatives presented by ever more severe criminal codes — seem to result in ever longer prison terms. The rise of plea bargaining has now led to efforts of the Department of Justice and some legislators to try to intimidate with possible impeachment federal judges whose sentences are deemed short and thus a restraint on the bargaining power of prosecutors. Those efforts are a genuine threat to the judicial independence Article III is intended to protect, giving rise to concern properly expressed by the American Bar Association[128] and other professional organizations.

The Court chose to review capital cases and seemed for a time to have abolished capital punishment by imposing procedural requirements that had not been met by state courts in reaching capital sentences. But this evoked bitter responses in many states.[129] New procedures were devised to meet the new re-

---

127. E.g. Gerald N. Rosenberg, *The Hollow Hope: Can Courts Bring About Social Change?* (1991); Michael J. Klarman, *From Jim Crow to Civil Rights: The Supreme Court and the Struggle for Racial Equality* (2004); Richard Kluger, *Simple Justice* (2d ed., 2004). And see *Black, White and Brown: The Landmark School Desegregation Case in Retrospect* (Clare Cushman & Melvin I. Urofsky eds., 2004).

128. The American Bar Association formed a committee on the issue called "The ABA Standing Committee on Judicial Independence." The website for this organization, with links to various publications, is http:// www.abanet.org/judind/home.html>.

129. The story is well told in Lee Epstein & Joseph F. Kobylka, *The Supreme Court and Legal Change: Abortion and the Death Penalty* 34–136 (1992).

quirements, and capital punishment may even have become more frequent as a result of the reforms that separated consideration of guilt from consideration of punishment.[130] It is, however, still a topic in litigation in the Supreme Court. The institution of capital punishment remains deeply rooted in the culture of many states.[131]

The Court also chose to review an array of cases presenting arguments for the application of the First Amendment by petitioners seeking to override state or local laws or practices as unlawful inhibitions of freedom of speech or religion.[132] Many arguments for individual rights prevailed in the Court, but engendered resentment by those identifying themselves as a "moral majority." In the school prayer cases, the Court may simply have mandated a revival of nineteenth century practices in most states, practices that strictly protected religious dissidents from forced conformity. But it was on softer ground less sustained by tradition when it suppressed laws against pornography.

And it was on very soft ground indeed when it invoked the First Amendment along with the Equal Protection Clause to restructure the American political system. "One man, one vote," sounded nice, but created worse problems than it solved by disconnecting representatives from the geographical units with which their constituents identified and commissioning diverse partisan officials to adjust district boundaries not only to equalize their populations, but to fit their own partisan aims.[133] The Court then went on to constitutionalize the right of those with wealth to use their money to dominate political discourse in ways facilitated by the advent of television and the spot commercial.[134] "Money is speech?" And then to strip "public figures" such as

---

130. Carol S. Steiker & Jordan M. Steiker, *Sober Second Thoughts: Reflections on Two Decades of Constitutional Regulation of Capital Punishment,* 109 Harv. L. Rev. 355 (1995).

131. *See generally, The Killing State: Capital Punishment in Law, Politics, and Culture* (Austin Sarat ed., New York 1999), *and especially* Franklin E, Zimring, *The Executioner's Dissonant Song: On Capital Punishment and American Legal Values, id.* at 137.

132. *See* Richard H. Hasen, *The Supreme Court and Election Law: Judging Equality from* Baker v. Carr *to* Bush v. Gore (2004).

133. Reynolds v. Sims, 377 U.S. 533 (1964) was the case holding that a state constitution providing an upper house in the legislature seating representatives from each county was trumped by the Equal Protection Clause of the Fourteenth Amendment. On the current state of the issue, see Daniel Ortiz, *Got Theory?,* 153 U. Pa. L. Rev. 459 (2004); Heather K. Gerken, *Lost in the Political Thicket: The Court, Election Law, and the Doctrinal Interregnum,* 153 U. Pa. L. Rev. 503 (2004); Samuel Issacharoff & Pamela S. Karlan, *Where to Draw the Line: Judicial Review of Political Gerrymanders,* 153 U. Pa. L. Rev. 541 (2004).

134. Buckley v. Valeo, 424 U.S. 1 (1976) was the premier decision revisited in McConnell v. Federal Election Commission, 540 U.S. 93 (2003); *see generally* Richard H. Pildes, *The Constitutionalization of Democratic Politics,* 118 Harv. L. Rev. 28 (2004).

candidates of effective protection against defamatory advertising,[135] even in some circumstances anonymous defamation.[136] These law reforms were wrought by justices, seeking to act—I do not doubt—entirely in the public interest, but as (now Judge) Michael McConnell concluded:

> The landscape of American politics today is not an encouraging sight. All too many Americans have come to the conclusion that elections do not matter. Incumbency retention levels rival the most undemocratic regimes of the world. Partisanship and attack politics are the name of the game. Racial appeals abound. It is fair to say that the responsibility for a great deal of the political problem is to be laid at the feet of the Supreme Court's well-meaning reforms from the early 1960s.[137]

It was a fitting confirmation of that reality when a majority of the Court in 2000 decided the presidential election by usurping the roles of the electoral college and the House of Representatives, notwithstanding the text of the Constitution plainly written to exclude the justices from any role in the selection of the President who selects their colleagues.[138] It could not be viewed as incidental that the five prevailing justices picked the presidential candidate more likely to select future justices who would share their views and help make more law meeting with the approval of the five.

Then the Court, having restructured the schools, the prisons, and most other public institutions brought to its attention, commenced to try to tell the people not only how to govern themselves but what to believe about grave moral issues of religious import to many citizens. To decide the constitutionality of the Texas law prohibiting abortions, the Court consulted medical experts for help in codifying principles of medical law it discerned beneath the text of the Constitution.[139] With its opinion legislating in detail the woman's right to choose, the Court not only presumed to leave few choices to be made by elected representatives, but it treated the religious faith of many citizens as undeserving of notice. At the time of the decision, there was a clearly dis-

---

135. New York Times Co. v. Sullivan; 376 U.S. 254 (1964).

136. *Cf.* McIntyre v. Ohio Elections Comm'n, 514 U.S. 334 (1995).

137. Michael McConnell, *Law and the Political Process,* 24 Harv. J. L. & Pub. Policy 103, 117 (2000).

138. For contemporaneous comment by the present author, see *The Right to Self Government after Bush v. Gore,* <http://www.law.duke.edu/pub/selfgov> (with H. Jefferson Powell, December 29, 2001).

139. Roe v. Wade, 410 U. S. 113 (1973).

cernible movement among state legislatures to enlarge the freedom of a woman to make the choice for herself. Some states were even appropriating money to fund free abortions in the hope that this would diminish the need for welfare funds.

But then came the Right to Life Movement.[140] It seems clear that the movement gained much energy from the reaction of adherents of religious faiths to the Court's utterances. These were people who received the Court's opinion on abortion rights as an evil manifestation of Godlessness and an insult to their religious faith. The intensity of their reaction seems not to have been diminished by the Court's later reconsideration of the issue in an opinion that observed its prior decision was supported by "the thoughtful part of the nation."[141] At least partly as a consequence of the Court's political misjudgment in making elaborate law repudiating their faith, and the great difficulty to be encountered in any effort to overrule it by constitutional amendment, religious fundamentalists have become a major force in our national, state, and local politics. And it may now be harder for a woman to get an abortion in some communities than it was before the Court declared her right to do so.

And the reaction is directed at the selection and confirmation of justices and other federal judges, thereby diminishing public interest and awareness of the politics of foreign relations and the national economy that are vital issues exclusively of concern to the federal government and its elected officers. It is reasonable to believe that the Court's decision on the right to abortion controlled the outcome of presidential elections in 1980 and 1988 and has had a political impact even larger than those data might suggest.[142]

The Court was more cautious in telling people what to believe about homosexuality.[143] Attitudes and values bearing on that subject have changed across the land over the last three decades or so, although more in some areas than others. But the Court's more recent decision to take on the issue to the extent of invalidating criminal laws prohibiting homosexual acts[144] did serve further to excite the hostility of religious fundamentalists. It helped provide

---

140. To be sure, there was at the time of the decision religiously-based opposition to the liberalization of state laws on abortion. For an account, see Mark Kozlowski, *The Myth of the Imperial Judiciary: Why the Right is Wrong about the Courts* 151–164 (2003).

141. Planned Parenthood v. Casey, 505 U. S. 833, 864 (1992).

142. *See generally* William G. Ross, *The Role of Judicial Issues in Presidential Campaigns*, 42 Santa Clara L. Rev. 391 (2002).

143. For a salute to their caution see Paul D. Carrington, *A Senate of Five*, 23 Geo. L. Rev. 859 (1989).

144. Lawrence v. Texas, 539 U. S. 558 (2003).

the occasion for placing on the ballot in twenty-five states referenda asking voters to express a view on the meaning of the word "marriage."[145] Because that device brought to the polls many citizens who would otherwise not have voted, it very likely determined the outcome of the presidential election of 2004. Whatever the word "marriage" may ultimately be allowed to mean, there remains an apparent tendency of the American public to become increasingly tolerant of sexual activities that previous generations proscribed. But it is unlikely that the pace of change on such issues will be significantly accelerated by any words uttered in the form of an opinion of the Court. People may observe laws with which they disagree, but few will change their views about sexual behavior on the advice of judges and lawyers. They may listen to those whom they choose, but seldom to those who seek to impose their opinions on moral questions even when they invoke constitutional law embodied in judicial precedents.

In delving into such matters, the Court has quite possibly caused poor Chief Justice Taft to roll in his grave in distress at the substance of what he wrought. For myself, I have no problems with the individual rights the Court has sought to create; if we were senators together in the same state legislature, I would vote with William Brennan on those issues almost every time. But the Court has thus contributed to a dangerous sense of alienation of many citizens sharing traditional moral and religious views on pornography, abortion, capital punishment, and gay rights that they are powerless to express by ordinary democratic political discourse, perhaps especially not given the ugly political system that the Court has crafted to the despair of Judge McConnell and this author.[146]

Judicial Legislation to Accommodate Judges

The Court's ascendance over Congress and state legislatures is not restricted to its interpretations of the Constitution. As Frederick Grimké long ago explained, bicameral legislatures, including Congress, often have difficulty in agreeing on legislative texts that resolve even the most obvious conflicts certain to arise in their enforcement. And they are inevitably slow to correct oversights or misunderstandings manifested years after their enactments. These realities often leave much room for elaboration in opinions of courts that may be transformative.

---

145. Kavan Peterson, *50-State Rundown on Gay Marriage Laws*, Stateline.org <http://www.nationalcoalition. org/legal/50staterundown.html> (July 8, 2004, last visited July 28 2005). Twenty-five states proposed constitutional amendments.

146. *Supra* n. 137.

But acts of Congress did not become frequent subjects of judicial interpretation until the advent of a troubled national economy inspired federal legislation. And it was not until the New Deal that Congress presented the Court with a vast array of laws requiring judicial elaboration and illumination. Often thereafter the Court would resort to committee reports and even speeches of legislators to establish the intent and meaning of federal laws.[147] But it became apparent that such material was frequently available on all sides of a question; it has been said that judges reading legislative history are standing on a balcony and looking into a crowd in search of a friendly face.

As the Court and the lower federal courts became more heavily engaged in the elevated and gratifying task of writing opinions interpreting statutes, they also sometimes again manifested the tendency observed by public choice theorists.[148] Their decisions, although written with utmost integrity, tended to express policies favoring the interests of judges in their collective status and power. Sometimes judge-made policies even defeated the policies expressed in Congressional legislation. And sometimes Congress took no notice.

I offer three examples. The first pertains to the size of juries in civil cases in the federal courts. By the year 1300, it was settled that a common law jury seated twelve citizens. That was a good number—sufficient to distribute responsibility for verdicts across a segment of the public but small enough to provide jurors with a sense of personal responsibility. Many changes were effected in the conduct of jury trials over six or seven centuries, but the number twelve did not change. When the Seventh Amendment provided that the right to trial by jury "in suits at common law" "shall be preserved," that was taken to mean that a citizen contesting a case in a federal court had a right to demand that issues of fact be decided by twelve citizens drawn from the community. Indeed, if anyone questioned the number twelve as implicit in the text of the Amendment, there seems to be no record of the debate.

And in 1968 Congress enacted legislation governing the selection of the jurors to assure that the twelve would fairly reflect the racial and ethnic composition of the district from which it was selected.[149] The Congressional assumption of the number twelve was embodied in the rules limiting the number of objections a party could make to the seating of individual jurors. That number is three. That number allows a party to exclude from a jury individuals

---

147. The development of the techniques of using legislative history is recounted in William N. Eskridge, Philip P. Frickey & Elizabeth Garrett, *Legislation: Statutes and the Creation of Public Policy* at 733–832 (2d ed., 1995).

148. On "public choice", see *supra* n. 66.

149. 28 U. S. C. A. §§1861–1871.

whom that party mistrusts for whatever reason. But it is not large enough to allow a party often to be able to influence materially the race, class, or ethnicity of the twelve who will decide his case. The same assumption of the number twelve was explicit in Rule 48 of the Federal Rules of Civil Procedure authorizing a verdict by a number less that twelve but with consent of the parties.[150]

Soon after the statute was enacted, some federal judges decided that trials would be easier to conduct if juries were reduced by half. A district judge in Montana simply announced a local rule that in his court juries would be six. Never mind seven centuries of tradition, or the assumptions implicit in the text of the Seventh Amendment and the law enacted by Congress, or explicit in the text of the Federal Rules of Civil Procedure. And the Supreme Court upheld the local rule, allowing it to spread to most other district courts.[151] Justice Thurgood Marshall in dissent accurately assessed the decision as "not some minor tinkering with the role of the civil jury, but with its wholesale abolition and replacement with a different institution which functions differently, produces different results, and was wholly unknown to the Framers of the Seventh Amendment."[152]

Justice Marshall's assessment was soon confirmed by experience. Smaller juries are much more likely to be exotic in their demographic composition, in part because of random effect and in part because lawyers have much greater influence over the selection. Smaller juries are much more likely to be dominated by a single strong-minded juror. For these reasons, the verdicts of smaller juries are materially harder to predict. This is likely to be one reason that civil trials are vanishing from federal courts—prudent parties are risk averse. Very few kind words have been uttered in defense of the six-person jury by lawyers or scholars, but Congress has left the matter to the Judicial Conference. In 1995, the Judicial Conference Committee on the Civil Rules proposed a rule amendment returning the jury to twelve.[153] Although supported by a careful review of the data demonstrating the improvidence of the change, the proposal was summarily rejected by the Judicial Conference. Congress has never considered the proper size of a jury.

A second example of free-wheeling self-dealing by the Supreme Court is its 1991 holding that a federal district judge has "inherent power" to impose the

---

150. Fed. R. Civ. P. 48.

151. Colegrove v. Battin, 413 U.S. 149, 174 (1973); for a review of comments on the opinion, see Paul D. Carrington, *The Civil Jury at 199: Reflections on a Forthcoming Bicentennial*, 1990 U. Chi. L. F. 1, 33.

152. *Colegrove* at 166–167. *See also* Carrington *supra* n. 150.

153. In 1991 Federal Rule 48 was amended to state a court "shall seat a jury of not fewer than six and not more than twelve." *See* Amendments to Federal Rules of Civil Procedure, 134 F.R.D. 525, 545 (1991).

costs borne by an adversary on a litigant whose lawyer was said to act "in bad faith."[154] What made this decision remarkable was the existence of a federal law imposing consequences on "vexatious litigants"[155] and of an elaborate provision in the Federal Rules of Civil Procedure authorizing judges to impose cost sanctions on lawyers who are guilty of presenting groundless claims or defenses resulting in costs to an adversary.[156] Neither the statute nor the rule of court authorized the judge to do what he did in the case before the Court. Well, never mind the legal texts; if it seems right, the judge should do it even without explicit authority in the law. Again, Congress has taken no notice but has left the matter entirely to the judges.

My third and most consequential example is the violence done by the Supreme Court to the Federal Arbitration Act of 1925.[157] The Act was written to apply to contracts between businessmen engaged in interstate transactions and validates clauses providing for private arbitration of future disputes between the parties.[158] If businessmen so agree, their contract rights can be fairly determined by an arbitrator because, indeed, their contract rights are whatever the arbitrator decides that they are.

In the American tradition, arbitrators are not bound by the law but can do whatever seems to them right and fair.[159] They may choose to hear a witness or not, or to insist on seeing documentary evidence or not. They have no duty to explain their awards, and the awards can be set aside only if the arbitrator engages in fraud or corruption, or possibly if he should engage in "manifest disregard of the law." But if parties to contracts choose to define the rights they create by their agreement as those to be fashioned by an arbitrator, who can complain?

For half a century, the Supreme Court and lower federal courts interpreted the 1925 Act in keeping with its purpose.[160] They did not permit the use of arbitration clauses to prevent citizens from enforcing their statutory rights in

---

154. Chambers v. Nasco, 501 U. S. 32 (1991). Abuse of process is, of course, a common law tort but the claim does not arise until a judgment favorable to the victim has been entered and a separate suit filed.

155. 28 U. S. C. §1927.

156. Fed. R. Civ. P. 11.

157. 43 Stat. 883, now codified as 9 U. S.C. §1 et seq.

158. Ian R. MacNeil, *American Arbitration Law: Reformation, Nationalization, Internationalization* 15–133 (1992).

159. Ian R. MacNeil, Richard E. Speidel & Thomas J. Syipanowich, *Federal Arbitration Law: Agreements, Awards and Remedies under the Federal Arbitration Act* §16.3.2.2 (1999).

160. For comment on Supreme Court interpretations of the Act, see Paul D. Carrington & Paul Haagen, *Contract and Jurisdiction*, 1996 Sup. Ct. Rev. 331 (1997); Paul D. Car-

law courts. Until the Supreme Court began to change its mind in the 1970s. This was a time when the federal courts were concerned about rising caseloads and the prospect of a sizeable increase in the number of federal district judges. And alternative methods of dispute resolution were coming into fashion as a means perhaps of making civil litigation more civil. It was obvious that a more robust arbitration law would get a lot of troublesome cases presenting mere issues of fact off federal dockets and reduce the need for more judges. Suddenly the Supreme Court reversed itself and declared that arbitration is just another and less costly way to enforce a legal right. And if a party agreed to arbitrate a future dispute, even in a contract of adhesion, it should not matter if his claim was not based on the contract containing the arbitration agreement but on a federal statute enacted to protect the party against whom the arbitration clause is invoked. Nor even state legislation.[161] In other words, no state can assure its citizens of access to its courts to enforce rights it has established for their protection from overbearing conduct by persons or corporations who are in a position to draw them into an arbitration agreement.

In explaining how this happened, the Court has sometimes expressed the unfounded assumption that arbitrators will enforce legal rights and will forego their historic empowerment to do justice as they see fit. In what Alan Rau has described as a quixotic footnote,[162] the Court suggested that arbitral awards in statutory cases might be subject to judicial review for errors of law. The Court's reassurance that arbitrators enforce legal rights even if they are not seen to do so has been revealed for the illusion that it was, and is, by recent holdings of lower federal courts that parties may not agree that an arbitral award rendered pursuant to their contract shall be subject to judicial review for a mere error of law.[163] To allow parties to create jurisdiction to review awards would be an unwelcome increase in the demand for judicial services. The Court has not been willing seriously to address the issue.

Law made in this free spirit by the Supreme Court now seriously impairs the enforcement of many public laws enacted by legislatures with the expectation that they would be invoked by private parties. Many state courts have

---

rington, *Self-Deregulation: The "National Policy" of the Supreme Court*, 3 Nevada L. Rev. 259 (2002).

161. Southland Corp. v. Keating, 465 U.S. 1, 21 (1984).

162. The Culture of American Arbitration and the Lessons of ADR, 40 Tex. Intl. L.J. 449, 526 (2005).

163. E.g., Kyocera Corp. v. Prudential-Bache Trade Services Inc. 341 F 3d 987 (9th cir en banc 2003); *see* Margaret Moses, *Can Parties Tell Courts What to Do? Expanded Judicial Review of Arbitral Awards*, 52 U. Kan. L. Rev. 429 (2004).

been resistant to this radical judicial legislation,[164] and many cases and disputes over the matter continue to rage. Much of the legislation enacted by Congress and by state legislatures to protect consumers and other vulnerable persons may now be entrusted to enforcement in private forums that may or may not be bound by the law. That has been the fate of federal antitrust law, the laws protecting investors, and even the minimum wage law. Yes, even a worker seeking his right to receive the Congressionally-prescribed minimum wage may be required to ask an arbitrator not bound by the law to give it to him.[165] Yet Congress has barely noticed.

With one exception. In 2002, I was retained by the National Association of Automobile Dealers to explain to Congress why dealers should be exempt from the enforcement of arbitration clauses in contracts they make with manufacturers. Congress had long ago enacted the Automobile Dealers' Day in Court Act to protect dealers from overbearing conduct by manufacturers; it assured them of the right to a trial by jury on the question of whether a manufacturer had dealt with them "in good faith."[166] Similar legislation was enacted in nearly all states. When cases were brought under those laws, the manufacturers usually won, but the laws had a benign effect on the way the manufacturers treated their dealers. The dealers recognized that their claims of right under state or federal laws would be substantially weakened if they were forced to present them to an arbitrator who would not be bound by the law, who would not be obliged fully to investigate factual disputes, whose jurisdiction depended on the franchise agreement, and who might be more considerate of the interests of the manufacturer who would be far more likely to have another occasion for employing them. Congress was persuaded by their concerns and a law was enacted to provide that automobile dealers are no longer forced to arbitrate future disputes with automobile manufacturers.[167]

How did this happen? While small in comparison with manufacturers, automobile dealers are sizeable firms and important to the communities in which

---

164. E.g., Harold Allen's Mobile Home Factory Outlet, Inc. v. Butler, 825 S.2d 779 (Ala. 2002). Cash in a Flash Advance of Ark., L. L. C. v. Spencer, 348 Ark. 459, 74 S.W.3d 600 (Ark. 2002); Abramson v. Juniper Networks Inc., 9 Cal. Rptr. 3d 422 (Cal App. 2004); Flyer Printing Co. v. Hill 805 S.2d 829 (Fla. App. 2001); Cheek v. United Healthcare of the Mid-Atlantic Inc. 378 Md. 139 (Md. Ct. App. 2003); State v. Stancil, 559 S.E.2d 789 (N.C. 2002); State ex rel. Dunlap v. Berger. 211 W. Va. 549, 567 S.E.2d 265 (2002). Cf. Armendariz v. Foundation Health Psychcare Services, Inc., 24 Cal. 4th 83, 6 P.3d 669 (2000).

165. E.g. Carter v. Countrywide Credit Industries, 362 F.3d 294 (5th Cir. 2004).

166. 70 Stat. 1125, 15 U.S.C. §§1221 et seq.

167. Act of November 2, 2002, Pub. L. No. 107-273, 116 Stat. 1758, 11,028 (to be codified at 15 U.S.C. 1226).

they are located. They have political clout, and Congress heard their cries for help. But we said nothing to Congress to imply that those who buy automobiles should not be bound by their arbitration agreements with their dealers. Other franchisees selling other goods and claiming rights under state or federal laws enacted for their protection may be able to enforce those laws only in an arbitral forum that is free to do whatever it thinks just. And consumers, workers, patients, investors, borrowers, and diverse others who may think they are in some way protected by state or federal statutes may also find that they are forced to seek enforcement of their rights in tribunals having no accountability for their fidelity to the law. Farmers who grow chickens for processing firms are now seeking in Congress legislative relief similar to that accorded the automobile dealers. What are their chances?

The conclusion I draw from these examples is that the Supreme Court sometimes unwarily takes leave of statutory texts in order to shape the law to the tastes and convenience of the judiciary of which it is a part. As the renovation of arbitration law attests, Justices are so far removed from the concerns of citizens having limited means and capacities that they can be blind to the consequences of the law they make. And Congress and the Department of Justice may take no notice, whether the result is a serious impairment of the enforcement of federal laws or a gratuitous trespass on the sovereignty of a state, or merely a misguided deprivation of ancient civil rights.

On those occasions, rare in the last century, when Congress has been moved to enact laws bearing on judicial administration, it has been moved to do so by a political interest group with a specific substantive agenda, such as "tort reform" or the suppression of securities fraud claims.[168] It is fair to say that its ventures into procedural reform have seldom been effective in advancing the interests they were intended to advance, and have often served to elevate the costs imposed on all sorts of litigants. Indeed, it seems at times that Congress has also lost its bearing in distinguishing its role from that of the courts and may be less interested in enacting wise legislation than in deciding contested cases in accordance with its own lights. Its recent effort to overrule the Florida courts' decision that Ms. Schiavo should be allowed to die is a spectacular recent example.[169] One hesitates to ask such a Congress to think about matters of constitutional importance. And is it not possible that

---

168. The Private Securities Litigation Act of 1995.

169. The unusual matter of Theresa Schiavo is recorded in Abby Goodnough, *The Schiavo Case: The Overview: Schiavo Dies, Ending Bitter Case over Feeding Tube*, N.Y. Times A1 (Apr. 1, 2005).

such antics by Congressmen are in some measure a result of the dreadful reforms imposed by the Court on our election laws?

Suggestions for Legislation

Whatever Congress's own troubles, its attention to issues of judicial administration is overdue. Amending the Constitution is no answer to the need to re-establish the duty of Congress to govern the judiciary. The suggestion has recently been heard in Congress that the federal judiciary needs an inspector general to alert Congress of their occasional failings.[170] Perhaps that is a useful idea. But such an officer would lack the influence or resources to address any of the issues presented in this essay. What then can be done? Structural changes are not only very difficult to achieve because of the resistance of the organized legal profession and the incomprehension of the public but also carry risks of unforeseen adverse secondary consequences. There are, however, proposals worthy of serious consideration by the judiciary committees of Congress. Their mere discussion might have a benign transformative effect by causing justices and judges such as those sitting on committees of the Judicial Conference to be more conscious of their human tendencies to be too much preoccupied with their own status and power. I suggest eight examples of questions to which Congress might usefully attend.

The first, of course, is the problem of superannuation and the possible enactment of a law imposing term limits on the Justices. Or as Roger Cramton and I have proposed, one providing biennial appointments, with reduced duties for those most senior in service.[171] That would be a modest change posing no threat of seriously unwelcome secondary effects. It is one that most people who are not lawyers can readily understand and appreciate. Reasonable minds can differ about the details of the scheme, but any flaws in the scheme would be subject to change if need be. And by addressing the problem directly, Congress will have signaled that it is alive to its responsibility to check and balance the Court.

This proposal should be elevated above all others because it is politically viable. One need not be a political sophisticate, or know, or even care very much about law and courts to recognize the blatant improvidence of allowing persons afflicted with normal human failings to conduct their business in

---

170. Maurice Possley, *Lawmaker Prods Court, Raises Brows*, The Chicago Tribune (July 10, 2005) <http://www.november.org/Blakely/RaisedBrows7-10-05.html>.

171. Our proposal is in the Appendix to this symposium at p. 467.

a temple for decade after decade. Reasonable term limits for justices is a reform likely to be opposed in Congress by lawyer-romantics, but not by many others who seriously consider the problem.

The other issues Congress should consider are more complex. A second item on its agenda might be to give consideration to the question of how the cases going to the highest national court should be selected. It would do much to correct the false grandeur of the Court if the judges selecting the cases to be decided were not precisely the ones making the decisions on the merits. For example, I would favor a law combining the term limits proposal presented in the Appendix with a change in the certiorari jurisdiction. The senior justices, in addition to sitting on rulemaking committees and lower courts, might participate in certiorari decisions or might even be given exclusive authority to rule on certiorari petitions. If need be, they might be aided by circuit judges selected by seniority and serving short terms as acting justices on the certiorari panel. Or the Court could be gradually enlarged to a number of justices sufficient to achieve that result. Those selecting the cases would then not be the justices who would decide them. And Congress could consider specifying a number of cases that the senior panel would be expected to certify to the junior panel for decision. This would re-establish the role of the deciding justices as judges who decide cases that is their job to decide, and not lawmakers who choose what laws to proclaim.

Third, repeatedly over the last forty years, proposals have been advanced for the establishment of an additional national court that would provide oversight of the courts of appeals, resolving conflicts in their decisions, and enabling them to concentrate on their intended role of providing visibility to litigants and close oversight for the district courts. Alternative schemes have proposed a unification of the courts of appeals to provide rotating panels with specific substantive agendas and nationwide jurisdiction. For example, the Federal Circuit devoted to intellectual property law might be replicated, but with modifications to prevent narrow specialization by the judges.[172] Although such ideas have been advanced by distinguished committees,[173] including one

---

172. On the origins of that institution, see *The United States Court of Appeals for the Federal Circuit—A History 1982–1990* (Marion T. Bennett ed., 1991).

173. I directed a study by the American Bar Foundation that was advised by ABA Presidents Bernard Segal and Leon Jaworski, by Circuit Judges Carl McGowan and Thurgood Marshall, and by other eminent persons. *Accommodating the Workload of the United States Courts of Appeals* (1968). A committee appointed by Chief Justice Burger, led by Paul Freund and Alex Bickel, two icons of the time came to similar conclusions; *The Report of the Study Group on the Caseload of the Supreme Court*, 57 F. R. D. 573 (1972). Next came the *Commission on Revision of the Federal Court Appeals System, Structure and Internal Procedures: Recommendations for Change*, 67 F. R. D. 195 (1975); that commission was chaired

led by Senator Roman Hruska and one led by Justice Byron White, none of these schemes have received serious attention in Congress. If a second national court were established to oversee the courts of appeals, and also as proposed the justices selecting cases for decision were separated from those deciding the cases, those justices selecting the cases could be empowered with the alternative of sending appropriate cases raising issues of federal statutory law to the new court. This would be a role for which experienced senior justices would be especially well suited.

Fourth, consideration might also be given to re-establishing the rights of litigants to have their appeals from district court decisions heard in person. Given the availability of inexpensive videoconferencing, there is no good reason why a panel of judges deciding an appeal from the judgment of a federal court should not be required as a form of appellate due process at least to appear on their computer screens to engage in dialogue with counsel. Why should they not be expected to provide at least an oral response to arguments as in the traditional common law proceeding?[174] The rediscovery of the oral opinion on the law rendered by individual judges might result in major economies in the work of the intermediate courts, and serve to give litigants direct, observable evidence that the judges themselves decided their cases.

Fifth, Congress might reconsider the needs of the Supreme Court and courts of appeals for staff support. Scot Powe has suggested that a reduction of law clerks in the chambers of justices from four to two or even one might providentially encourage earlier retirements. A similar reduction in staff for the courts of appeals might serve to reduce the preoccupation of the circuit judges with their writing of the law of the circuit. For all appellate judges, a reduction of staff might be expected to increase the likelihood that the judges would learn less from, and react less to, their staffs and would be more attentive to the legal briefs and arguments of colleagues and counsel. And consideration might be given to elevating all magistrate judges and bankruptcy judges to full rank; they could then enter judgments and be made directly accountable to the courts of appeals.

---

by Senator Roman Hruska (R. Neb.). Then came the 1995 *Report of the Long Range Planning Committee of the Judicial Conference of the United States*, chaired by Hon. Edward Becker, Chief Judge of the Third Circuit, and reported at http//www.uscourts.gov.lrp. CVRPGTOC.com. and finally the 1998 *Report of the Commission on Structural Alternatives for the Federal Courts of Appeals* chaired by Justice. Byron R. White. Every one of these reports has advised Congress to make major structural changes.

174. For my speculation on other uses of technology to transform civil procedure, see Paul D. Carrington, *Virtual Civil Litigation: A Visit to John Bunyan's Celestial City*, 98 Colum. L. Rev. 501 (1998).

Sixth, related consideration might be given to repealing the authority of the courts of appeals to sit en banc. This would also serve to refocus the work of circuit judges on deciding cases in the common law tradition on their factual and legal merits and diminish the attraction of making law in the form of opinions of the court. Given the illusory and tentative nature of the law of the circuit, the loss could not be expected to have grave consequences. This reform would fit neatly with the creation of a second national court. Also, if en banc decisions were eliminated, the number of circuit judges could be increased more readily to supply the judicial manpower needed to provide the appellate due process of oral hearings and explained decisions.

Seventh, similar consideration might be given to the reestablishment of the trial as a means of resolving disputes. Congress should think seriously about whether civil juries should number twelve. Relevant matters not raised in the previous discussion might include expanding the availability and use of video-conferences in trial and in pretrial discovery of evidence or the possible use of more court-appointed expert witnesses to serve as consultants to the trial courts on technical factual issues, of the sort familiar in the courts of virtually all other nations, in lieu of the adversary expert witnesses who are seen in American courts, who occupy much time and attention and magnify costs.

Eighth, Congress should surely consider whether parties invoking statutory rights, even those conferred by state legislatures, can or should be required to test their claims and defenses in private arbitral forums that are not bound by the law. If need really must be, consideration might be given to adopting the system employed in California state courts that enables private parties to "rent a judge" whom they choose,[175] but whose judgment is subject to possible review in the state appellate court for its adherence to the rules of procedure and its fidelity to the law.

Conclusion

All eight of these reforms could be enacted without threat to the rightly cherished independence of the judiciary. If all were done at once, an approach I do not recommend, there would still be no offense to the legitimate aims of Article III, a text written by men who did not foresee the self-aggrandizement of John Marshall, much less that of William Howard Taft. And there are surely many other ideas afloat that are worthy of consideration as means of redi-

---

175. California Rules of Court, Rule 244.

recting the attention of the institutions of the federal judiciary to the work we hire our judges to do. That is to resolve our disputes in a manner that commands our respect and acceptance because it is apparent to all that eminent independent judges have paid close attention to our evidence and our arguments and have decided our cases on the law, as best that can be discerned from the sometimes fuzzy utterances of Congress or the generalities of the Constitution. Serious consideration short of enactment of these reforms might alone serve to correct some of the flaws they aim to redress. Our federal courts, including the Supreme Court, might regain a sense of their own mortality and fallibility and appreciate the wisdom of deference to the law, to other branches and levels of government, and to the people they serve, a deference that sadly declined through much of the twentieth century.

DEMOCRATIC RESPONSES TO THE BREADTH OF POWER OF THE CHIEF JUSTICE

*Judith Resnik**

Some Agreed Upon Facts and Premises

Several relevant facts are not much in dispute. The first is that while Article III of the United States Constitution provides that the "judicial Power of the United States" shall vest in courts with judges holding "their Offices during good Behaviour," and specifies that such judges' salaries cannot be diminished, the Constitution does not define the phrase "during good Behaviour." Second, since the country's founding, Article III judges have not by statute had either a defined term of office or an age for which retirement is mandatory.

Third, in practice, because Article III judges make their own decisions about when to vacate a seat to permit a new appointment, various kinds of problems have emerged. When choosing the timing of retirement, justices and judges may engage in opportunistic behavior—either to make optimal use of

* Arthur Liman Professor of Law, Yale Law School. This article builds on several others, including *So Long*, Legal Affairs 20 (July/August 2005); *Judicial Selection and Democratic Theory: Demand, Supply and Life Tenure*, 26 Cardozo L. Rev. 579 (2005); *"Uncle Sam Modernizes his Justice System": Inventing the District Courts of the Twentieth Century*, 90 Geo. L.J. 607 (2002), *Trial as Error, Jurisdiction as Injury: Transforming the Meaning of Article III*, 113 Harv. L. Rev. 924 (2000). My thanks to Joseph Blocher, Lane Dilg, Marin Levy, Laura Smolowe, and Steven Wu for research help on this essay, to Gene Coakley for all his efforts to locate relevant materials, and to Denny Curtis, Vicki Jackson, Theodore Ruger, Albert Yoon, and Paul Carrington for helpful comments.

federal pension opportunities, to enhance further economic rewards by going "on the market" to find better paid employment, to protect their own leisure time, to respond to personal needs, or to maximize the power of a particular party by creating a vacancy to fill. Some studies of turnover on the lower courts suggest politically-motivated behavior, although more recent work concludes that the vesting of pension rights is a key variable.[1] Yet others, such as David Garrow writing in this symposium, worry that justices serve even as their health and abilities begin to falter.

Fourth, as is also exemplified by several chapters in this volume, many commentators share a reading of the recent data: that today's Article III judges have an unusually long term of service, when compared to jurists in other systems and to their predecessors. Looking at how other democracies protect judicial independence, one finds that the United States has become anomalous. Many democracies provide for judges to retire, including those on their high courts, at a fixed age; others specify that high court jurists serve for a fixed period of time.[2] Both Australia and Israel require retirement at age seventy.[3] In Canada, the age of mandatory retirement is seventy-five.[4] The constitutional

---

1. *See* Deborah Barrow & Gary Zuk, *An Institutional Analysis of Turnover in Lower Federal Courts, 1900–1987*, 52 J. Pol. 457–76 (1990). *But see* Albert Yoon, *The End of the Rainbow: Understanding Turnover Among Federal Judges* (manuscript, spring 2004, cited with permission) (arguing that the study did not sufficiently control for the role played by the availability of pensions and, with different and more data, concluding that pensions play a pivotal role in determining when lower court judges shift from "active" to "senior" status).

2. *See generally* Lee Epstein, Jack C. Knight, Jr., & Olga Shvetsova, *Comparing Judicial Selection Systems*, 10 Wm. & Mary Bill of Rts. J. 7, 23 (2001) (surveying twenty-seven European countries and finding compulsory term limits and/or mandatory retirement in most).

3. Until 1977, when the Australian Constitution was amended by a referendum, judges were appointed for life; judges appointed after the date of that amendment serve until seventy. *See* Austl. Const. ch. III, §72 ("The appointment of a Justice of the High Court shall be for a term expiring upon his attaining the age of seventy years, and a person shall not be appointed as a Justice of the High Court if he has obtained that age.") (also providing that judges of "other courts created by the Parliament," that is, the federal courts, must also retire at that age). Israel's basic law has a similar requirement. *See* Israel, Basic Law: The Judicature, Courts Law [Consolidated Version], 5744–1984, Sections 1–24 <http://www.oefre.unibe.ch/law/icl/is03000_html> (providing for the term to end at the age of seventy, upon removal through specified means including that a person's health makes continuation of service impossible).

4. Supreme Court Act, R.S.C. ch. S-26 §9(2) (1985) (Can.) ("A judge shall cease to hold office on attaining the age of seventy-five years.").

courts of Germany and France rely on another system: fixed terms of twelve and nine years respectively.[5]

Further, as I have detailed elsewhere, during the first twenty years of the life of the United States, justices on the Supreme Court averaged fourteen years in service.[6] Lower court judges averaged sixteen years in office, but just under half (twenty-two out of forty-seven) served fewer than ten years.[7] Looking forward some decades to the period between 1833 and 1853, once again the average length of service on the lower courts was fourteen years, while nine Supreme Court justices who terminated their service during that interval worked for longer—twenty years on average.[8]

Moving centuries forward to the period from 1983 to 2003 and having to deal with a larger group of people coming and going, the average term for the six Supreme Court justices whose service ended during that time period grew larger. On average, the six justices whose service terminated each served on the Court for about twenty-four years. Chief Justice Rehnquist served on the Court yet longer—for some thirty-three years. For the lower courts (again on average based on 530 judges, and with some judgments about how to calculate the relevant intervals), Article III judges served about twenty-four years,[9] about ten years longer than those in the prior century.

5. Article 4, Law of the Federal Constitutional Court of Germany (as amended 1998); France Const. tit. VII, art. 56 (adopted 1958).

6. *See*, e.g., Judith Resnik, *Judicial Selection and Democratic Theory: Demand, Supply, and Life-Tenure* 26 Cardozo L. Rev. 597 (2005).

7. *See id.*, Appendix, Methodological Note on Estimating the Lengths of Service, 1800s/2000s, at 648–58. As noted above, a total of forty-seven judges were counted in the data on the first time period. For Supreme Court justices, a total of sixteen judges. The average length of service is skewed upward by a few judges, who served for unusually long periods of time—including Henry Potter who spent fifty-seven years on the federal bench and William Cranch who served for fifty-five years. As is further detailed in that Appendix, for the earlier time period, one can begin with judges who start their service at 1789. For the later interval, Stephen Wu and I worked back from 2003, looking only at the length of service of those judges who had retired in that year or during the twenty prior years.

8. Resnik, *Judicial Selection and Democracy*, *supra* n. 6 at 618.

9. These data are summarized in Chart 4, *Estimated Lengths of Service: Contrasting Snapshots, 1800s/2000s*, id. at 618. That information comes from government databases that provide information on judges and their length of service. *See* Members of the Supreme Court of the United States <http://www.supremecourtus.gov/about/members.pdf>; Federal Judges Biographical database <http://wwwfjc.gov/newweb/jnetweb/nsf/his>. These estimates are drawn from those sources and informed by those made by Albert Yoon, *Love's Labor Lost? Judicial Tenure Among Lower Federal Court Judges: 1945–2000*, 91 Cal. L.

Many factors account for the growing length of service of members of the federal judiciary. More people are appointed as judges, some at earlier ages, and life spans have lengthened. Further, a trend has emerged in which judges serving at a lower court are promoted to a higher court—making for a career ladder in judging that helps to produce more years in office. And being a federal judge may correlate with longevity and even be good for one's health.

Moreover, an important economic variable—the way that the pension system works—has emerged. Under current federal statutes, when Article III judges or justices retire by taking "senior status," they create vacancies for the courts on which they serve.[10] But they need not *resign* in order to *retire*. Rather, they can continue to sit as judges. Indeed, Congress has created incentives for judges to continue to work as long as they can. Upon reaching the age of sixty-five and if having served for the requisite number of years,[11] judges are eligible for retirement. During "the remainder" of their life-time, those judges "receive an annuity equal to the salary" that they received at the time of taking senior status. Benchmarking the salary to the last year worked may inspire some judges, ever-hopeful that Congress will respond to the many requests for pay raises, to delay "going senior" to get a higher yearly annuity. In addition, to continue to receive that salary, the chief justice or judge of a particular court must certify that the individual has "carried in the preceding calendar year...a caseload which is equal to or greater than the...work" that an "average" active judge would have done over three months.[12] While judges could therefore do much less while maintaining their eligibility for the annuity, many are keenly aware of the workload of their colleagues and generously shoulder a larger proportion of the work than they are obliged to undertake.[13]

Several of the analytic premises that helped to generate these contemporary facts are also not contested. Widespread agreement exists that some form of structural protection for judicial independence is wise and that judges should have terms of office longer than sitting Presidents or Senators. Current

---

Rev. 1029 (2003). As detailed in the methodological note accompanying that article, choices exist about how to analyze the information.

10. 28 U.S.C. §371 (d).

11. If seeking to take senior status at age sixty-five, one has to have had fifteen years of service, whereas if one seeks to take senior status at age seventy, ten years of service is required. *See* 28 U.S.C. §371 (c).

12. 28 U.S.C. §371(a); (b); (e)(1)(A),(B). Other subsections detail the way in which the requirement can be met through administrative work or other special government duties.

13. Yoon, *Understanding Turnover, supra* n. 1.

as well as historical examples make plain that the drafters of the United States Constitution were right to worry about the independence of judges and to craft mechanisms for insulation. Indeed, whether the United States has done enough is a matter of debate. For example, the American Bar Association and some judges have repeatedly complained (and sometimes brought lawsuits), arguing that federal judicial salaries are too low and that the failure to raise salaries to meet increases in cost of living is unlawful, punitive, and/or unwise.[14] Similar concerns have been raised about judicial budgets, both state and federal.[15] Moreover, hundreds of persons—called magistrate, bankruptcy and administrative law judges—hold federal adjudicatory power but are not, under current doctrine, sheltered by the protections of Article III.[16]

In retrospect then, Article III is both too little and too much, missing some important judicial actors and also creating means for individual judges to have a kind of power for a duration that raises concerns, in democratic circles, about the degree to which so much power can be exercised by so few government officials for so long. Some commentators in this volume seek to revisit the text to amend the Constitution. Joining others, I think that statutory interventions are an appropriate and useful route. As I will detail below, during the twentieth century, the Supreme Court was notably open to inventive readings of the strictures of Article III—thereby licensing the devolution of federal judicial power to hundreds of non-life-tenured judicial officers, bank-

---

14. *See* American Bar Association and the Federal Bar Association, *Federal Judicial Pay Erosion: A Report on the Need for Reform* (2001); Williams v. United States, 535 U.S. 911 (2002) (Breyer, J., joined by Justices Scalia and Kennedy, dissenting) (arguing in a class action filed by judges that federal legislation that prevented automatic adjustments to increase pay for judges in relationship to the cost of living violated Article III's non-diminution clause).

In contrast, the Canadian Supreme Court has concluded that the setting of compensation must occur through methods less dependent on the will of a sitting parliament. *See* Reference on Remuneration of Judges of the Provincial Court, 1997 Carswell Nat 3038 (1997); *see also* G. Gregg Webb & Keith E. Whittington, *Judicial Independence, the Power of the Purse, and Inherent Judicial Powers*, 88 Judicature 12 (2004) (describing an expanding doctrine of judicial inherent power to require financing for its processes and describing a 2002 Kansas Supreme Court order requiring an increase in fees to provide funds).

15. *See* Hearings Before the Subcommittee on Commerce, Justice, State, the Judiciary and Related Agencies of the Committee on Appropriations of the U.S. House of Representatives, 108 Cong. (2004) (Statement of Hon. John G. Heyburn, II, Chair, Committee on the Budget of the Judicial Conference of the United States (raising concern about the "crisis" facing the federal courts and about the levels of appropriations planned).

16. *See also* Judith Resnik, *Judicial Independence and Article III—Too Little and Too Much*, 72 S. Cal. L. Rev. 657 (1999).

ruptcy, magistrate, and administrative law judges.[17] Further, Congress has already created both pensions and term limits for the chief judges of the lower courts, thus paving the way for revisiting the kind of pension system provided and for thinking of a new option for the chief justiceship: term limits. Before addressing the kind of statutes that I suggest be drafted and their constitutional plausibility, I need to explain why the particular powers of the chief justice of the United States should be in focus when discussing "reforming the Supreme Court."

The Multiple Sources of Power of the Chief Justice

Although the long length of service on the federal bench has drawn a good deal of attention (generating this volume, inter alia), the recent confirmation of John Roberts to serve as the chief justice of the United States provides the infrequent opportunity to think specifically about that post. The new chief justice is only the seventeenth person to hold the position in the life of the nation. In part because of the very few who have had this job, its status has a special importance. As was explained in the 1980s, when hearings were held on the nomination of William Rehnquist to that position, the chief justice is the "symbol of the Court."[18]

As the senior jurist of nine rendering decisions on America's highest court, the chief justice presides at the Court's sessions and has the ability to affect its agendas, influence case load selection, and (when in the majority) to assign

---

17. Details and analyses are provided by many. *See* Judith Resnik, *"Uncle Sam Modernizes his Justice System:" Inventing the District Courts of the Twentieth Century*, 90 Geo. L. J. 607, 637–43 (2002); Richard H. Fallon, *Of Legislative Courts, Administrative Agencies, and Article III*, 101 Harv. L. Rev. 915 (1988); Paul Bator, *The Constitution as Architecture: Legislative and Administrative Courts Under Article III*, 65 Ind. L. Rev. 233 (1990).

18. *See* Hearings before the Committee on the Judiciary on the Nomination of Justice William Hubbs Rehnquist to be Chief Justice of the United States, 12 *The Supreme Court of the United States: Hearing and Reports on Successful and Unsuccessful Nominations* at 312 (eds. Roy M. Mersky & J. Myron Jacobstein, 1989) (Opening Statement of Chairman Strom Thurmond). At that time, Senator Kennedy offered a parallel comment, that the chief justice "symbolizes the rule of law in our society; he speaks for the aspirations and beliefs of America as a Nation." *See* Hearings before the Committee on the Judiciary on the Nomination of Justice William Hubbs Rehnquist to be Chief Justice of the United States, 12A *The Supreme Court of the United States: Hearing and Reports on Successful and Unsuccessful Nominations* at 1549 (statement of Senator Kennedy).

opinions. Further, aided by special staff, the chief justice is the senior official in charge of the Supreme Court itself. That institution is supported by a budget of about sixty million dollars and employs more than three hundred people. The Court also promulgates special rules of practice for the Supreme Court bar and determines how the public can see its proceedings (currently, without the help of televised proceedings). Many of the aspects of the chief justiceship become plain through the words of Associate Justice Ruth Bader Ginsburg, who in her statement mourning the death of William Rehnquist, called him the "fairest, most efficient boss" whom she had ever had.[19]

But the chief justice is more than the boss of and an icon of the Supreme Court. Chief Justice Roberts is the chief justice not only of the Supreme Court but of the United States.[20] As is revealed in other chapters of this book, however, even law professors are less familiar with the many roles of the chief. The "Chief" is the spokesperson for the entire federal judiciary, is the chair of the Judicial Conference of the United States (which, as detailed below, has evolved into a major policymaking body that opines regularly to Congress about the desirability of enacting various kinds of legislation), is the person charged with appointing judges to certain specialized courts, is the person who authorizes certain judges to "sit by designation" on other courts, and is the person given a host of other, more minor, functions such as service on many boards.

Neither the chief justice's special role on the Supreme Court nor the chief justice's tasks as the chief executive officer of the federal judiciary are constitutionally mandated obligations. Rather, the part of the Constitution devoted to establishing the judicial branch—Article III—makes no mention of a chief justice at all.[21] The one reference that can be found is in the Constitution's dis-

---

19. The Honorable Ruth Bader Ginsburg's comments can be found in *Statements from the Supreme Court Regarding the Death of Chief Justice William H. Rehnquist* <http:///www.supremecourtus.gov/publicinfo/press/pr_09-04-05.html> (Sept. 4, 2005).

20. *See* Judith Resnik & Theodore Ruger, *One Robe, Two Hats*, N.Y. Times 4, 13 (Week in Review) (July 17, 2005). Many scholars have examined these issues. *See*, e.g., Theodore W. Ruger, *The Judicial Appointment Power of the Chief Justice*, 7 U. Pa. J. Const. L. 341 (2004); Robert J. Steamer, *Chief Justice: Leadership and the Supreme Court* (1986); Peter Graham Fish, *The Politics of Federal Judicial Administration* (1973).

21. U.S. Const., Art. III. Although the constitutional text is sparse on this subject, many federal statutes advert to the position of the chief justice. *See*, e.g., 28 U.S.C. § 1 (describing the Supreme Court as comprised of eight associate justices and a "Chief Justice of the United States"). That usage began in the First Judiciary Act. *See* Act of Sept. 24, 1789, § 1 (describing the Supreme Court as consisting of "a chief justice and five associate justices").

cussion of presidential impeachments—vesting sole power for trying impeachments in the Senate and specifying that "the Chief Justice shall preside" when a president is tried.[22] The tasks and parameters of the role of chief justice—including the very question of whether to commit such broad authority to one person—stem not from the Constitution but from dozens of statutes enacted in an ad hoc fashion over many decades, as well as from customs and from the decisions and ambitions of those who have held the office of the chief justice.[23] The current scope of this position is itself a tribute to the impressive leadership of Chief Justice Rehnquist.

A brief historical overview makes plain how much the chief justiceship has changed. At the turn of the twentieth century, about one hundred life-tenured federal judges were dispersed across the nation. Dealing with a total of some 30,000 cases in a year, these judges were mostly left to their own devices, with few shared practices and little means of communicating with each other except through the publication of opinions. This situation prompted Chief Justice William Howard Taft to complain in 1922 that each judge had "to paddle his own canoe."[24]

In contrast today, some 2000 life-tenured and non-life tenured judges (aided by about 30,000 in staff) work in more than seven hundred and fifty courthouse facilities around the United States that deal annually with about 350,000 filings at the trial level, more than a million and a half bankruptcy petitions, and 60,000 appeals.[25] No longer solo actors, judges are linked to-

---

22. U.S. Const., Art. I, cl. 6. The Constitution also does not use either the terms "Chief Justice of the Supreme Court" or "Chief Justice of the United States." The later title, now in use, can be found by the second half of the nineteenth century. *See* Hon. William A. Richardson, *Chief Justice of the United States, or Chief Justice of the Supreme Court of the United States?* (a brief essay by the then Chief Justice of the Court of Claims and reprinted from the N.E. Historical and Genealogical Register, July 1895). Richardson reported that in 1888, Chief Justice Fuller was nominated and commissioned as the "Chief Justice of the United States." The usage also appears in The Judiciary Act of 1869, ch.22, 16 Stat. 44, Apr. 10, 1869. Its opening provision states that "the Supreme Court of the United States shall hereafter consist of the Chief Justice of the United States and eight associate justices...."

23. As Justice Ginsburg noted, *supra* n. 19, "William H. Rehnquist used to great effect the tools Congress and tradition entrusted to him," in his role as the leader of the United States judiciary and of the Supreme Court.

24. William Howard Taft, *The Possible and Needed Reforms in the Administration of Justice in Federal Courts*, 8 A.B.A. J. 601, 602 (1922).

25. *See* Administrative Office of the U.S. Courts, *The Federal Court System in the United States: An Introduction to Judges and Judicial Administration in Other Countries* 42 (2d ed. 2001); Administrative Office of the U.S. Courts, *Judicial Business of the United States Courts 2004*, Caseload Highlights at 10 (2004).

gether through the Administrative Office (AO) of the United States Courts, created in 1939, and they are supported with educational programs and research provided by the Federal Judicial Center (FJC), chartered in 1967.[26] Their central headquarters is in one of Washington's major new buildings, named after Justice Thurgood Marshall and located across from Union Station. The day-to-day management of the entire judicial enterprise and its $5.4 billion budget falls to the director of the AO.[27]

But it is the chief justice of the United States who has the power to appoint and to remove the director of the AO,[28] and it is the chief justice who serves as the permanent chair of the Board of the Federal Judicial Center,[29] who presides at the meetings of the Judicial Conference, who (upon consultation with others) selects the 250 people who sit on the twenty-four committees of the Judicial Conference, and who gives annual addresses to the nation about the administration of justice. This charter to the chief justice began to take shape through congressional responsiveness to the concerns of Chief Justice Taft. In 1922, Congress created the forerunner of what is now called the Judicial Conference of the United States,[30] the policymaking body of the federal judiciary.

Because it may be hard to grasp the import of the role played by the administrative apparatus of the federal court system, a bit more detail about its evolution is in order. Initially a group of eight senior circuit judges were asked to "advise" the Chief Justice about the "needs of his circuit and as to any matters in respect of which the administration of justice in the courts of the

---

26. *See* Act of Dec. 20, 1967, Pub. L. No. 90-219, ch. 42, §620, 81 Stat. 664 (1967); Russell R. Wheeler, *Empirical Research and the Politics of Judicial Administration: Creating the Federal Judicial Center*, 51 L. & Contemp. Probs. 31 (1988), and *"Baby Judges School" Jump Starts Learning Process*, 37 The Third Branch: Newsletter of the Federal Courts 1 (Aug. 2005).

27. *See* 28 U.S.C. §601.

28. *See* 28 U.S.C. §601 (stating that the AO is to be "supervised by a Director and a Deputy Director appointed and subject to removal by the Chief Justice of the United States, after consulting with the Judicial Conference.").

29. *See* 28 U.S.C. §621 (providing that the Chief Justice "shall be the permanent Chairman of the Board").

30. *See* Act of Sept. 14, 1922, Ch. 306, §2, 42 Stat. 837, 836 (creating a Conference of Senior Circuit Judges "to advise [the chief justice] as to the needs of [each] circuit...and the administration of justice"). In 1937, the Act was amended to include participation by the chief judge of the United States Court of Appeals for the District of Columbia, and in 1948, the Conference of Senior Circuit Judges was renamed the Judicial Conference of the United States. *See* Act of June 25, 1948, ch. 646, 62 Stat. 902, now codified at 28 U.S.C. §331 (2000).

United States may be improved."[31] From my reading of the transcripts (stored in the National Archives) of the yearly meetings during the early years, I learned that the Conference discussion consisted of oral reports from the senior circuit judges. They described how the individual judges with whom they worked were (or were not) managing to stay abreast of the work, as well as whether to request more judgeships. Topics ranged from better salaries, facilities, and supplies to concerns about rules of procedure, sentencing laws, and the need to provide indigent defenders with lawyers.[32]

By mid-century, the Judicial Conference took on its current form, with district court judges included.[33] Today, with the chief justice presiding, the Conference has twenty-seven members. By statute, each circuit sends the chief judge of its appellate court, as does the Court of International Trade, and each circuit elects a district judge for a term.[34] Over the decades and influenced by the various chief justices, the Conference has enlarged its own agenda. While it often used to decline to comment on matters related to pending legislation by noting that certain issues were "legislative policy" and therefore inappropriate for judicial input, the Conference now takes positions regularly on an array of proposals. Beginning during the tenure of Chief Justice Earl Warren and then expanding significantly under Warren Burger and William Rehnquist, the Conference has become an important force.

As may be familiar to those who work on the Hill but less obvious to the American public, the judiciary functions in many respects like an administrative agency, seeking to equip itself with the resources needed to provide the service—adjudication—that the Constitution and Congress require. Further, during the last half century, the federal courts have also become an educational institution teaching judges about how to do their job, a research center on the administration of justice, and an agenda-setting organization—articulating future goals and plans. In addition to an Executive Committee, the Conference's committees cover topics that range from technology to criminal justice. The Conference opines on legislation from security and court construction to proposed new civil and criminal jurisdiction for the federal courts.

The chief justice is the presiding officer of this entire apparatus and has the ability, through a host of discretionary judgments, to shape the institutional

---

31. Act of Sept, 14, 1922, §2, *supra* n. 30.

32. Judith Resnik, *Trial as Error, Jurisdiction as Injury: Transforming the Meaning of Article III*, 113 Harv. L. Rev. 924 (2000).

33. District judges became a part of the Conference in 1957. *See* Act of Aug. 28, 1957, Pub. L. No. 85-202, 71 Stat. 476 (codified at 28 U.S.C. §331 (2000)).

34. *See* 28 U.S.C. §331.

decisions of "the federal courts." For example, in 1991, under Chief Justice Rehnquist, the judiciary created its own Office of Judicial Impact Assessment to undertake the difficult task of anticipating the effects of proposed legislation.[35] In 1995, after convening a special committee on Long Range Planning, the Conference issued a *Long Range Plan for the Federal Courts*, a first-ever monograph making ninety-three recommendations about the relationships among state, federal, and administrative adjudication and about the civil and criminal dockets of the federal courts.[36] The *Long Range Plan's* recommendations included asking Congress to have a presumption against enacting any new rights for civil litigants, if those actions were to be enforced in federal court, as well as a presumption against prosecuting more crimes in federal courts.[37]

Further, under the leadership of the chief justice, the Judicial Conference may decide to offer its views on pending legislation even though, if the legislation is enacted, judges may be required to preside on cases calling the legality of a particular provision into question. For example, in the early 1990s, when an initial version of the Violence Against Women Act (VAWA) was introduced, the Judicial Conference created an Ad Hoc Committee on Gender-Based Violence. Appointed by the Chief Justice, the Committee studied the proposed statute, which included a provision for a new civil rights remedy to be made available in federal court to victims of gender-motivated violence. The judiciary's Ad Hoc Committee recommended opposition—which became official federal judicial policy as reported by the Chief Justice in the early 1990s.[38]

After the proposed legislation was modified (in part in response to the concerns raised by judges) and its scope narrowed, the Conference took no posi-

---

35. That process proved complex and controversial in light of the challenges of estimating effects of not-yet enacted laws and of assessing how to count the costs and benefits afforded by enhancing access to the courts. *See generally* Conference on Assessing the Effects of Legislation on the Workload of the Courts: Papers and Proceedings (A. Fletcher Mangum ed., 1995).

36. Judicial Conference of the United States, Long Range Plan for the Federal Courts (Dec. 1995), *reprinted in* 166 F.R.D. 49 (1995). The Conference formally adopted the ninety-three recommendations but did not specifically approve the commentary of the drafting committee.

37. *See id.* at 83 (Recommendation 1); *id.* at 88 (Recommendation 6); *id.* at 84 (Recommendation 2).

38. *See* William H. Rehnquist, *Chief Justice Issues 1992 Year-End Report*, 24 Third Branch 1, Jan. 1993 (objecting that the proposed private right of action was too "sweeping").

tion on the propriety of enacting the civil rights remedy but supported other aspects of the legislation including educational efforts.[39] In 1994, at the behest of some forty state attorneys general and many others, Congress passed the Violence Against Women Act, including its provision of federal jurisdiction (supplemental to that available in state courts) giving civil remedies to victims of gender-motivated violence. Thereafter, and again exercising his discretionary authority, the Chief Justice continued his criticism of VAWA. In 1998, the Chief Justice commented in a speech before the American Law Institute that the legislation raised grave problems of federalism. He cited VAWA (as well as other recent statutes) as inappropriate expansions of federal jurisdiction. In his view, "traditional principles of federalism that have guided this country throughout its existence" should have relegated these issues to state court.[40] In 2000, the Chief Justice wrote the majority opinion that ruled, five to four, that Congress lacked the power under the Commerce Clause to confer that form of jurisdiction on the federal courts.[41]

In addition to guiding the Judicial Conference, which adopts formal policy through voting, the chief justice has an independent platform from which to speak. William Howard Taft and his successors went regularly to the American Bar Association and to the American Law Institute to give major addresses on their views of the judiciary's needs and priorities. That tradition continues.

In the 1980s, Warren Burger initiated another practice—providing annual "state of the judiciary" speeches that are released to the nation. Chief Justice Rehnquist followed suit, beginning each new year by setting out agendas and themes. In that capacity, Chief Justice Rehnquist regularly spoke about the values of judicial independence. Upon occasion, he criticized the Congress or the Executive for engaging in behavior that, he believed, suggested that the coordinate branches of government did not sufficiently appreciate the centrality of an independent judiciary to a thriving democracy.

Yet another aspect of the powers of the chief justice is important: the person holding that position has the authority to select individual judges to serve

---

39. *See* Administrative Office of the U.S. Courts, Report of the Proceedings of the Judicial Conference of the United States 28 (1993).

40. *See* William H. Rehnquist, *Remarks at Monday Afternoon Session*, in Am. Law Inst., 75th Annual Meeting: Remarks and Addresses, May 11–14, 1998 at 13, 17–18 (1998) (also citing bills on juvenile crime, the Anti-Car Theft Act of 1992, the Freedom of Access to Clinic Entrances Act of 1994, and the Child Support Recovery Act of 1992).

41. *See* United States v. Morrison, 529 U.S. 598 (2000).

on specific courts. Rather than using a system of random assignment (for example, staffing a court by assigning sitting judges whose names are drawn by lot), Congress has endowed the chief justice with the power to pick individual judges to sit on specialized tribunals.

Specifically, the chief justice appoints the seven judges on the Judicial Panel on Multidistrict Litigation[42] (with authority to decide whether to consolidate cases pending around the country and to centralize pretrial decisionmaking in a judge selected by that panel). The chief justice also selects the eleven judges who sit for seven-year terms on the Foreign Intelligence Surveillance Act Court (FISA) which, since 1978, has approved of more than 10,000 government requests for surveillance warrants.[43] The chief justice also has the power to select the five judges who constitute the Alien Terrorist Removal Court, chartered in 1996 to respond when the Department of Justice filed cases seeking to deport legal aliens suspected of aiding terrorists.[44] As a result of these various statutes, according to Professor Theodore Ruger, Chief Justice Rehnquist made "over fifty such special court appointments, filling more federal judicial seats than did every individual United States President before Ulysses S. Grant."[45]

In sum, the chief justice is not only the symbolic leader of the federal judiciary. That person also has a number of specific powers and a good deal of practical authority. The chief justice is the most powerful individual in the entire federal judicial apparatus. Time and again, chief justices have proven to be the judiciary's most effective lobbyists, the judiciary's most visible spokespersons, and the nation's most important judicial leaders.

Democratic Constitutional Responses

The repertoire of powers of the chief justice is stunning. The role entails authority significantly different from that of jurists on courts. Judges on appellate courts work collectively; they must persuade others of the correctness of their views in order to prevail. Both constitutional and common law tradi-

---

42. *See* 28 U.S.C. § 1407(d).

43. *See* 18 U.S.C. § 1803(a),(b),(d) (2004) and Ruger, *The Judicial Appointment Power of the Chief Justice, supra* n. 20, at 365–68.

44. *See* The Antiterrorism and Effective Death Penalty Act of 1996, P.L. 104-132, Apr. 24, 1996, 110 Stat. 1214, codified at various parts of Titles 8, 18, 28, 42.

45. Ruger, *The Judicial Appointment Power of the Chief Justice, supra* n. 20, at 343 (footnote omitted).

tions mandate openness in courts. Most decisions are explained in reasoning available to public scrutiny and then revisited as new cases arise. In contrast, the administrative powers of the chief justice are neither officially shared nor constrained by obligations of accounting.

Further, these many grants of power contrast sharply with the authority of other executive officials. Presidents have term limits. Heads of independent agencies generally do as well. Currently, however, the chief justice has lifetime consolidated authority over the administration of both the Supreme Court and the lower federal courts and does not have legal obligations to share that power with other jurists nor to explain the decisions made.

A ready rationale supports long terms of authority for judges, who need insulation from political retribution when ruling on cases that result in judgments likely to be opposed by interests both public and private. But no parallel need exists for insulating the administrative authority of the chief justice to the same extent. Whether turning for models to high level cabinet positions, agency heads, or corporate executives, limited terms are the norm. Indeed, managerial theorists argue that turnover is reinvigorating, helping actors within institutions to revisit and to revitalize their practices.

At the level of policy, then, structural interventions, to enable more people to take on the role of chief justice, have appeal. Several options exist. One approach is age limits, with a mandate that a person holding the office who becomes sixty-five, or seventy or seventy-five, must leave that position. The concern, however, is that such a rule would enable gaming, via appointments of unusually young people to the position. Another option is for the chief justiceship to rotate from one justice to another on a five- or seven-year term—long enough to gain expertise but not so long as to have too much power reside in one person. The rotation could occur by seniority, by a mixture of age and seniority (such as in the lower courts, discussed below) or by election by other justices (such as on some state courts).

Congress could also create economic incentives for a person to resign the position voluntarily. As Professor Albert Yoon has detailed,[46] the current federal judicial pension system prompts some judges to take "senior status" but to continue to serve. Congress could, in contrast, provide significantly better pension benefits to chief justices who serve for no longer than a set period (say seven years). Economic models could assist in fashioning an optimal intervention, just as they have encouraged some universities to offer packages of

---

46. *See* Yoon, *Understanding Turnover, supra* n. 1 (finding that the availability of pension rights is a key variable in a lower court judge's decision to take senior status).

benefits and salary that have prompted tenured professors to take early retirement. Were special pension rights to vest only if a person served a fixed
period, then those for whom money mattered would likely resign to create a
vacancy. But the structural impact of such a reform could depend upon an individual's economic resources, with those of great means not as readily affected by a monetary reward for early retirement.

Another model already exists within the federal system—one that relies
on a system that mixes seniority with term limits for the term of service of
chief judges of the lower federal courts. In 1956, a committee of the Judicial
Conference of the United States began a study on the chief judges of the lower
courts. A survey revealed that, on average, chief judges of the circuits were
about seventy-two years old, and on average about sixty-four at the district
court level; the average length of service about eight and a half years. The
Conference concluded that while many judges of older years did "excellent
work," the "toll of years has a tendency to diminish celerity, promptitude, and
effectiveness."[47] The Conference proposed that Congress enact legislation to
"relieve chief judges of the circuit and district courts from their administrative duties upon reaching the age of 75, so that they may devote their entire
time to the lawwork of the courts and not to the administrative details."[48] The
proposal was argued to be constitutional—for a "distinction is made between
the judge in his judicial capacity and in his administrative capacity,"[49] and
that what was being limited were the administrative tasks. With support from
the President, the Department of Justice, and the Judiciary, the provision became law.

In the 1970s, in a report from the Commission on the Revision of the Federal Court Appellate System: Structure and Internal Procedures (nicknamed
the Hruska Commission in honor of its chair, Roman Hruska), problems were
noted with a straight seniority system—that no account was taken of the abilities of an individual for administration.[50] Rejecting election by one's peers as
politicizing the decision, the Hruska Commission recommended that a chief
judge serve a maximum of seven years and only one term. The results of these
proposals can be found in the statutes that provide for chief judges of both
trial and appellate courts to be those persons "senior in commission" who are

---

47. Courts, Chief Judges, Relinquishment of Office at Age 70, S. Rep. No. 85-1780 at
3 (1958).

48. *Id.* at 1–2.

49. *Id.* at 3.

50. Commission on the Revision of the Federal Court Appellate System: Structure and
Internal Procedures: Recommendations for Change, 67 F.R.D. 195, 274–275 (1975).

sixty-four or under, have served for one year or more as a judge, and have not previously been the chief judge; such persons then have a seven-year term.[51]

The next question is that of legality. I do not believe that the sparse text of the Constitution—referring only to the chief justice in the context of the role of presiding at the impeachment trial of a President—supports a grant of unending power to the chief justice for all the many tasks that have now become part of the repertoire of that role. Rather, the chief justiceship as we have come to know it is not a creature of the Constitution but of Congress. The legislature is the body that endowed that office with the presiding role at the Judicial Conference and with the power to assign sitting judges to special courts, and it is the legislature that located the power to promulgate rules of practice and procedure with the Court. Thus, the legislature can—and should—revisit these grants of power, both by rewriting specific statutes (for example to provide that judges of specialized courts like the Foreign Intelligence Surveillance Act Court are chosen through mechanisms such as random selection from various circuits rather than by the chief justice) and by crafting a new regime of term limits and pension incentives that reduce the length of service.

Let me pause for a moment to expand on the legal argument that Congress could intervene—by addressing the likely objections. I have already noted that I do not believe a strong argument resides in the constitutional text, especially if a statute fixing term limits provided for an automatic extension were the chief justice's term to end during an ongoing impeachment trial of a president. The better argument against a term limit for the chief justice would couple the idea that serving "during good Behaviour" means life tenure with the practice that has emerged for confirming chief justices. The President nominates a chief justice, and the Senate holds a separate confirmation hearing, even when the individual is elevated to the position from within the Court (as was the case with Chief Justice Rehnquist). The claim would be that this custom is not optional but constitutionally compelled. That position might be bolstered by an argument made from the "Appointments Clause," with its mandate to the President to appoint "Judges of the supreme court,"[52] while the appointment of "inferior Officers" may be organized by Congress. Further, while I have noted the absence of a challenge to the statutory term limits for the lower court chief judges, the rejoinder would be that those roles are not mentioned at all in the Constitution. Finally, the view could be that any current chief justice has been vested with that role, making it unalterable.

---

51. 28 U.S.C. §45 (chief judges, circuit courts); 28 U.S.C. §136 (chief judges, district courts).

52. U.S. Const., Art. I, §2, cl. 2.

The responses are straight-forward. The first is that so long as the person who has had a chief justiceship continues in office as an Article III jurist, the obligation to ensure service during good behavior has been fulfilled. A subsidiary argument—joining others in this volume claiming that term limits are constitutionally permissible for all of the justices—is that the relevant constitutional texts are sufficiently capacious, permitting statutory interventions. As noted, the Constitution does not directly address the question of what "good Behaviour" means. The academic inquiry tends to be sparked by events. For example, when debating the lawfulness of efforts to oust Justice William O. Douglas, Professor Raoul Berger traced the phrase "holding their offices during good Behaviour" to the Act of Settlement of 1701 (which protected the independence of English judges by granting them tenure "as long as they conduct[ed] themselves well, and provided for termination" only through a formal request by the Crown of the two Houses of Parliament) as well as to earlier English traditions.[53] Professor Berger argued that Congress had the power to define a breach of good behavior to include more than a "high crime and misdemeanor,"[54] while others disagreed.

A similar debate about the flexibility of Article III took place in the late 1970s, when members of Congress considered how to impose sanctions short of impeachment on Article III judges and how to facilitate the retirement or removal of judges too disabled to work.[55] A statute, the Judicial Conduct and Disability Act of 1980, followed thereafter and has survived a few challenges to its constitutionality.[56] Further, the congressional enactment of statutes providing for term limits for the chief judges of the trial and appellate courts have generated little debate.

Moreover, "constitutionality" depends in part on the interpretative stance of the person undertaking the analysis, and the doctrinal developments of Ar-

---

53. Raoul Berger, *Impeachment of Judges and "Good Behavior" Tenure*, 79 Yale L.J. 1475 (1970).

54. *Id.* at 1530. *See also* Burke Shartel, *Federal Judges—Appointment, Supervision, and Removal—Some Possibilities Under the Constitution*, 28 Mich. L. Rev. 870 (1930); Note, *Removal of Federal Judges: A Proposed Plan*, 31 Ill. L. Rev. 631 (1937).

55. *See* S. Rep. No. 96-362 (1980). *See generally* Stephen B. Burbank, *Procedural Rulemaking Under the Judicial Councils Reform and Judicial Conduct and Disability Act of 1980*, 131 U. Pa. L. Rev. 283 (1982); Richard L. Marcus, *Who Should Discipline Federal Judges, and How?*, 149 F.R.D. 375 (1993).

56. *See* Judicial Councils Reform and Judicial Conduct and Disability Act of 1980, Pub. L. No. 96-458, 94 Stat. 2034 (codified as amended in various sections of 28 U.S.C., including § 372). A challenge, claiming the act was unconstitutional, was rejected in Hastings v. Judicial Conference of the United States, 770 F.2d 1093 (D.C. Cir. 1995), *cert. denied*, 477 U.S. 904 (1986).

ticle III have not been notable as instances in which forms of originalism or textualism have had much sway. Rather, a majority of the Court has repeatedly and decidedly been functionalist, as jurists read Article III to permit devolution of judicial power through statutory grants of power to magistrate and bankruptcy judges sitting inside Article III but lacking life tenure.[57] Through such reinterpretation, much of the "judicial Power of the United States" (words of the Constitution that could be read to limit Congress to creating courts staffed only by life-tenured judges) has been delegated to non-life-tenured jurists in Article III courts and in agencies.[58]

Thus, if the person who served in the position of the chief justice did so for seven years (to parallel the length of service described in the statutes addressing the chief judges of the district and appellate courts), retained the status of a federal judge or justice but not the chief justiceship, that person's tenure is well protected. Further, Congress should be sure that the term provided is not so short as to run afoul of concerns about undue interference,[59] as well as to be sure that reappointment to the position—by either the president or the Congress—is unavailable. Such a statute would protect the values of judicial independence while also cabining the administrative authority of the chief justice.

Turning to the Appointment Clause issue, a textual response is that while the president is instructed to nominate "Judges" of the Supreme Court, no mention is made of a chief justice. Thus the custom of separate nominations and hearings is just that—a practice, not a constitutional mandate. To protect against other constitutional concerns, Congress could enact a statute with prospective application, such that a current chief justice would not lose that seat. Moreover, given that the chief justice has a higher salary than other justices, Congress would need to keep the salary at the same level even after the post is relinquished to avoid arguments that the constitutional mandate against diminution of salaries would be breached. (Alternatively, Congress could abolish salary distinctions, again prospectively.)

---

57. See, e.g., United States v. Raddatz, 447 U.S. 667 (1980); N. Pipeline Constr. Co. v. Marathon Pipe Line Co., 458 U.S. 50 (1982); Commodities Futures Trading Comm'n v. Schor, 478 U.S. 833 (1986).

58. I map the doctrinal revision as well as the boundaries remaining in Resnik, *Inventing the District Courts, supra* n. 17, at 625–648.

59. See, e.g., Starrs v. Ruxton, 2000 J.C. 208 (H.J.C. 1999) (relying on Article 6 of the European Convention on Human Rights and Fundamental Freedoms to conclude that too short a term of office and a term dependent upon the prosecution for reappointment is a violation). Some Canadian cases address a comparable concern. *See* Reference re. Territorial Court Act (N.W.T.) S.6(2) (1997), 152 D.L.R. (4th) 132 (N.W.T. Sup. Ct.).

I should add that the source of change need not come only from Congress. The chief justice could decide to depart from many of the practices that I have described by, for example, asking other judges or justices to take on various tasks or by going to Congress to seek revision of some of the statutory charters that run to that office. The chief justice could also voluntarily step down from that position, thereby opening the slot for another sitting justice.

Democratic Principles and Limited Terms

In many parts of the world, debate is underway about how to select judges; both Canada and Great Britain are examples of old countries making new rules about their processes. In those discussions, it has become plain that as principles of democracies themselves evolve, methods for selection of judges that were once perceived to be legitimate have to be revisited. Over recent decades in the United States and elsewhere, judicial selection processes have begun to intersect with an emergent theme in democracy theory—that all kinds of people are entitled to participate as political equals and that access to judgeships ought to be more fairly distributed across groups of aspirants. In eras when only men had juridical authority and in countries in which only whites had legal standing, judges were drawn exclusively from those pools.

In the contemporary world, where democratic commitments oblige equal access to power by persons of all colors whatever their identities, the composition of a judiciary—if all-white or all-male or all-upper class—becomes a problem of equality and legitimacy.[60] Given the history of exclusion, diversity has recently become a dimension of contemporary selection concerns, worldwide. For example, by statute, Canada has a set-aside to ensure that its highest court includes three justices from Quebec and hence has experts on the civil law, as well as some justices likely to be francophones.[61] Conventions have also developed in Canada that assume some geographical diversity, with more justices coming from the provinces with the highest populations than from other provinces.[62] Similarly, the Treaty of Rome that created the International Criminal Court calls for countries nominating judges to "take into account"

---

60. Jane Mansbridge, *The Descriptive Political Representation of Gender: An Anti-Essentialist Argument*, in *Has Liberalism Failed Women?: Assuring Equal Representation in Europe and the United States* 19–38 (Jytte Klausen & Charles S. Maier eds., 2001).

61. *See* Supreme Court Act, R.S.C. 1985, S-19, s. 6 (Can.).

62. The expectation is that three of the Supreme Court judges come from the Province of Ontario, with one coming from the Western and Northern Provinces and the other from

that among the judges serving should be individuals expert in either criminal law or relevant bodies of international law, that those selected provide "representation of the principal legal systems of the world," "equitable geographical representation," and "a fair representation of female and male judges."[63] Moving inside the United States, the Constitution of Alaska requires that a Judicial Council solicit and screen applicants and that consideration be given to "area representation."[64]

Parallel concerns require revisiting the question of the length of service of judges. Not only would shorter terms enable a more diverse set of individuals to serve but renewed sensitivity to longstanding democratic premises about the concentration of power in individuals requires cabining the length of service of jurists. Built into adjudication is the capacity for revision through the case law method. As the composition of judiciaries changes, the wisdom of a particular rule of law can be tested, in that new members of high courts may not adhere to its premises. But that very capacity to generate change depends on limiting the length of service of individual, and potentially too-powerful, justices. The chief justice is one such position that demands special attention, but as is demonstrated throughout this volume, the problem of serving too long spans the entire Article III system.

---

the Maritimes. *See* About the Supreme Court of Canada <http://www.scc.csc.ga.ca/About-Court/judges/curjudges>.

63. *See* Art. 36, §8(a) of the Rome Statute of the International Criminal Court, July 17, 1998, U.N. Doc. A/CONF. 183/9 (entered into force July 1 2002). The Treaty requires that the Court consist of at least eighteen judges, (*see* Art. 36(1)) with no two being "nationals of the same State." *Id.* at Art. 36 (7). Article 36(3) calls on state parties to nominate persons either with "established competence in criminal law and procedure" or with "established competence in relevant areas of international law such as humanitarian law and the law of human rights." Nominees are then put onto two lists, representing criminal law and international law (a nominee can be listed on both). Art. 36(5). Then, the "Assembly of State Parties" makes selections through secret ballots. Art. 36 (6). In addition to calling on state parties to take into account the need for "fair representation of female and male judges," the Treaty also calls for taking into account the need for judges with "legal expertise on...violence against women or children." But no enforcement mechanism is specified. *See generally* Cate Steins, *Gender Issues*, in *The International Criminal Court: The Making of the Rome Statute* 357–390 (Roy S. Lee ed., 1999).

64. Alaska Const., Art. 4, §§5, 8.

MAKING A SYSTEM OF TERM LIMITS WORK

Opting for Change in Supreme Court Selection, and for the Chief Justice, Too

*Alan B. Morrison**

I agree with Paul Carrington and Roger Cramton, the editors of this symposium, and the authors of the statutory proposal to alter the timing of the appointment of Supreme Court Justices,[1] that it would be advisable to provide for a rotation system for the justices so that, in general, they would serve for eighteen years and then become senior justices. As it is now, justices are serving an average of more than twenty-five years and are retiring only when they are well into their eighties. Both of those numbers seem likely to increase, given what modern medicine can do, especially for those who have the kind of medical plans that are provided for the Supreme Court. The eighteen years that Carrington and Cramton envision, with a new justice being appointed every two years, would seem to restore the prior balance between having a sufficient time on the Court to assure independence and gain experience and providing terms of active service that are not excessive.

Moreover, after eighteen years, a justice would not be forced into retirement, but would be available to sit in the lower courts and, more significantly, to do something that has never been done before: fill in when a justice in the regular rotation is unable to sit. Every term, justices recuse themselves, as re-

* The author is a Senior Lecturer at Stanford Law School and has had an extensive practice before the Supreme Court.

1. *See infra* Paul D. Carrington & Roger C. Cramton, *The Supreme Court Renewal Act: A Return to Basic Principles*, pp. 467–471.

quired by 28 U.S.C. §455, when they own stock in a company with a case before the Court, or when they have a relative who has a direct connection with the case, often as counsel (or a partner of a counsel) for a party, or—as is sometimes the case with Justice Stephen Breyer whose brother is a district judge in the Northern District of California—a connection to the judge who heard the case below. Less commonly, a justice may have had a direct involvement in a case through Government service or in some non-judicial role. The availability of an experienced substitute justice, generally one who has just finished her eighteen years, will eliminate the one justification sometimes offered by justices who choose not to recuse themselves in cases in which it is it is alleged that the justice's "impartiality might reasonably be questioned."[2]

Others have written at length about why they support the Carrington-Cramton proposal, and there is no need for me to repeat their reasons at length. I do have a few thoughts that summarize the basis for my support and that may not have been included in the other submissions. They are set forth below. Then, I deal briefly with the question of whether to proceed by a constitutional amendment, which I oppose, including whether the statutory route is likely to be held unconstitutional (I think not). Finally, I explain why it would be advisable to change the method of choosing the chief justice, and I propose that the President be entitled to designate a sitting justice, with a moderate amount of experience on the Court, to become chief justice, and to serve until his or her regular rotation concluded after eighteen years, with no separate confirmation required.

Why I Support Carrington-Cramton

At the conference at Duke in the Spring of 2005 and in the various papers submitted on this topic, many of which are collected here, no one rationale clearly emerges as the most compelling reason to support Carrington-Cramton. My own preference is that it will produce an orderly succession for justices, instead of the randomness of the current process, under which some Presidents appoint many justices, while others who serve comparable periods,

---

2. 28 U.S.C. §445(a). The author was the attorney for the party that unsuccessfully sought the recusal of Justice Scalia in *Cheney v. United States District Court for the District of Columbia*, 124 S. Ct. 1391 (2004). In his opinion denying the motion, Justice Scalia made specific reference to the possibility of a 4–4 tie, if he did not sit, as a reason to resist recusal. *Id.* at 1394.

appoint one or none.[3] But, randomness does not quite capture the current situation since that term implies a lottery-like process. In fact, as others have argued, most sitting justices have a substantial degree of control over when their replacement will be chosen, suggesting that a phrase like "quirky irregularity" would better describe the timing of Supreme Court vacancies. By contrast, the regularization of the process would make filling openings on the Supreme Court more like the predictable timing for elections for Congress and the President, unlike parliamentary systems under which an election, like a Supreme Court vacancy, can occur at any time, often on very short notice, based on a unilateral decision by the incumbent officeholder. Whether one thinks that justices actually engage in "strategic retirements," as some suggest, there is surely an appearance of that practice, which is not good for the Court or the appointment process.

Regularity is probably a virtue in and of itself for our system of government, but not a crucial one, if there are negatives attached to it. But here, regularity has other pluses. Although the fit is less than perfect, Carrington-Cramton seems likely to reduce the chances that justices will remain active beyond the time when they are physically or mentally capable of doing their jobs properly, or become out of touch with the rest of the country because they have been in their positions of semi-isolation for too long. Nor are there serious negatives to an eighteen-year limit, followed by senior status with full pay continued for life. Under those circumstances, there is no real likelihood that the change would produce any significant loss of judicial independence, which is the core value underlying Article III's protections for federal judges.

---

3. For example, Franklin Roosevelt filled nine vacancies in the twelve years he served as President; for ease of comparison with his successors I translated that into a percentage figure (.750), which I also include for Presidents since Roosevelt: Harry Truman, 4 for 7.75 (.516); Dwight Eisenhower, 5 for 8 (.625); John Kennedy, 2 for 2.75 (.727); Lyndon Johnson, 2 for 5.25 (.381); Richard Nixon, 4 for 5.5 (.727); Gerald Ford, 1 for 2.5 (.400); Jimmy Carter, 0 for 4 (.000); Ronald Regan, 4 for 8 (.500); George H. W. Bush, 2 for 4 (.500); William Clinton, 2 for 8 (.250); and the first term of George W. Bush, 0 for 4 (.000). The Roosevelt and Regan figures include a vacancy created when an associate justice was made chief justice; arguably, their figures should be reduced to 8 for 12 (.667) and 3 for 8 (.375) because they named only 8 and 3 new justices. In addition, Lyndon Johnson had a vacancy when Chief Justice Earl Warren decided to retire, but was unable to fill it when his effort to name Associate Justice Abe Fortas to fill that position was thwarted in the Senate. Had he filled that vacancy, his percentage would have gone to .581, whereas Richard Nixon's would have fallen to .545. Since President Bush has filled one vacancy and has another to fill, his numbers are likely to continue to go up through the end of 2005.

To me, the key question is, what would this change do to the already acrimonious confirmation process, from the perspective of the President, the Senate, and the electorate? The answer is, there is no answer. Under one theory, the stakes in the race for President (and Senate) will be further elevated, because each President will have a guaranteed two seats to fill on the Court. The President will claim that he has a mandate and nominate an extreme candidate. Under that scenario, the Senate, especially when it is of a different party, will see its role as the only check in the process and fight the President with greater ferocity. And this thinking will make Presidential elections even more bitter, knowing that the next two Supreme Court appointees are at stake, especially since the identities of those who will be rotated off will be known with certainty.

On the other hand, it is also possible that, if Supreme Court nominations became a more regular feature of our political landscape, the stakes would be seen as lower, in part because the other party would know that it would get its chance when it captured the White House. Under that theory, Presidents might be less aggressive, fearing what would happen when their party is not in the White House, and the Senate might be less inclined to do battle. If this system reduced the importance of Supreme Court appointments for presidential and senatorial elections, the electorate might be persuaded to focus on issues that will not come up regularly, unlike Supreme Court nominations.

The difficulty is that we are unlikely to find additional information to help us answer this question. As the other papers show, there is ample data on the nominating process, none of which is very helpful on this issue. What we need is a crystal ball, one that is programmed with multiple variables and includes the impact of random and unforeseeable events. Nor would it be helpful to see what happens in those states that appoint their Supreme Courts for terms of years or until a certain age, because the United States Supreme Court is so much more powerful, and the process by which the justices are chosen is so different, that such comparisons will show us almost nothing.

We are, in short, in almost no better position than were the Framers when they drafted Article III and struggled to predict the consequences of their choices. To be sure, we have over two centuries of experience, but none of it is likely to shed light on this issue. This leaves us with little choice but to make our best educated guess and admit that guessing is what we are doing. I am by nature an optimist and so perhaps that is why I think that the change may reduce the acrimony, in part because it is hard to see how the situation could get much worse. Perhaps the change in the process will lead to a change in attitudes, and I for one am willing to take the chance that increased rancor over Supreme Court appointments would not be a byproduct of Carrington-Cramton.

Along with acknowledging this indeterminacy problem we should recognize that, whatever is done or not done, the Supreme Court and the Republic will survive. The Court is not in crisis, and it will do quite nicely with the change or without it. However, for those who disagree and seek radical solutions because they view the current Court as inflicting serious damage on their vision of democracy in America, adoption of Carrington-Cramton will not assuage them. Indeed, even if they saw shorter terms for Supreme Court justices as a good idea, they might oppose this proposal because they would see it as too little change and would fear that it might derail more significant proposals to curtail the power of the Court. There is an old saying that "things are generally neither as good nor as bad as they seem," and this situation seems to fit nicely into that adage.

The Constitutional Questions

I support the statutory remedy, but oppose a constitutional amendment that would achieve the same result. I have three reasons. First, I am not sure that the Carrington-Cramton solution is correct, and if we amend the Constitution to enshrine it there, it will be almost impossible to change. The Line Item Veto was passed as a statute, and later declared unconstitutional, but by that time, many of its supporters did not like what President Clinton had done with his new powers and were happy that he could no longer exercise them. One also wonders how the supporters of the Balanced Budget Constitutional Amendment would react now if it had passed, instead of narrowly failing in the Senate to get the required two-thirds vote. Moreover, in general, I would support an amendment to the Constitution only as a last resort, when other methods have been tried and found wanting, not as a first option.[4]

Second, if an amendment is made to the tenure for Supreme Court justices in Article III, it will be almost impossible to keep off the table the issue of tenure for other federal judges since the same rules apply to all Article III judges. There are many distinctions between the justices and all other federal judges, but it may be very hard to keep from sweeping in all other judges if a term of eighteen years is applied to the justices. In theory, that problem could arise in a statutory amendment context, but the provisions governing the Supreme Court are found in a different part of Title 28 than are those for other Article III judges.

---

4. *See* Great and Extraordinary Occasions, The Constitution Project 7 (1999) (Guideline 3).

My third reason is the most significant for me: no change in the method of Supreme Court selection is worth the risk of opening up Article III to review and re-consideration, particularly these days when the federal courts have become major targets for those who are unhappy with the results of cases coming from our judicial system. Once the amendment of Article III were placed on the table, nothing in it would be safe from change, almost all of it likely to be in a direction that would weaken the vital concept of judicial independence. The current problem is nowhere near severe enough to warrant running such a risk.

One reason to amend the Constitution would be if the statutory solution were obviously unconstitutional. Congress could not change the age at which a person becomes eligible to run for Congress or the Presidency, nor could it decide that foreign-born citizens, who had lived virtually all their lives in the United States, should be allowed to be President. The Constitution is much too clear on those points, and members of Congress take an oath of office in which they swear to uphold the Constitution, and not pass off that responsibility to the judiciary. Carrington-Cramton would not apply to any justice appointed under the current system, and so problems of retroactivity, however defined, would not be a barrier to this statute. As I explain below, while not free from doubt, I believe that this statute has a reasonable basis in the Constitution. Moreover, there are a variety of procedural and perhaps political reasons why it is unlikely that the Court would ever decide such a challenge on its merits.[5]

Article III does not use the term "life tenure," nor any phrase other than "good behavior" that would require that justices be permitted to sit as regular members of the Court for as long as they choose. Those who believe that a statute would not be upheld point to general provisions in Article III that suggest that the position of Supreme Court justice is inseparable from the duties of that office. From that language they conclude that a justice who is no longer regularly sitting on the Court is no longer holding the office, something Article III precludes. Some also observe that the impeachment clause, which directs that the chief justice preside in the Senate, implies that the chief justice at least holds a separate office. None of those arguments seems to contain the kind of clear textual commitment that would make Carrington-Cramton unconstitutional, even for the literalists. And if one views

---

5. I assume for these purposes that, even though the justices would have a direct interest in the adjudication of this issue, they would sit under the "Rule of Necessity," just as they sat in *United States v. Will,* 449 U.S. 200, 213–17 (1980), when their pay increases were at issue.

the protections of Article III as aimed primarily at protecting judicial independence, nothing in this proposal would have any but the most insignificant impacts on the ability of Supreme Court justices to do their jobs without fear of retribution from the political branches. In short, none of the claims of unconstitutionality that I have seen are sufficiently strong to persuade me that a statute embodying Carrington-Cramton would not have a reasonable possibility of being upheld. At the very least, their proposal is not so plainly contrary to law that Congress should decline to pass it on that basis.[6]

There is also a substantial likelihood that the Court will never be asked to decide the constitutional question, or if it is asked, it will find procedural reasons to avoid it. First, there is a high likelihood that the Court would find that, until a justice has been rotated off the Court after eighteen years, the issue is not ripe for decision. Second, even then, it is not clear who would have standing, besides that justice, and he or she may be very reluctant to "sue to keep the job" having accepted the position with the eighteen-year condition as part of the bargain. It is not that the acceptance would have constituted a waiver of the right to object, but rather that it would be seen as quite unseemly for a justice to bring such a claim and ask those with whom he has sat for between two and sixteen years, to bring him back on the bench. It is always possible that a litigant will object to having the newest (replacement) justice sit on a case, but it is not clear that a litigant would have standing to complain, based on the ground that no one has the right to have one justice rather than another sit in a particular case, so long as all of them have been properly appointed to that office in accordance with Article III.

To be sure, the doctrines of standing and ripeness contain a great deal of flexibility, so that the Court could decide to reach the question if it wanted to do so. But that assumes that the justices would be anxious to decide the case, presumably striking down the law, which would have the effect of extending their own terms beyond the eighteen years they expected when they were ap-

---

6. When the statute becomes reasonably set, it will be essential that a detailed memorandum be prepared to defend its constitutionality. It may be too soon to do that now since the constitutional question may be significantly affected by the details of how the proposal is carried out. In the line item veto situation, the proponents never prepared such a document, perhaps because they lacked confidence in the statute's constitutionality. Whether a legal analysis of some of the line item veto proposals might have produced a more defensible bill is a matter that will remain unknown. But the preparation of such a memorandum in this case will show that at least the supporters do not fear a constitutional challenge.

pointed. It would seem that political pressures, especially after eighteen years or more under this system, would generate very great incentives for the justices to let the law stand, and not be seen as acting to extend their own terms of office.

Thus, while the constitutional issues deserve serious attention, they do not seem to be a sufficient barrier to derail the statutory option.

Designating, Not Appointing, The Chief Justice

Designation Not a Separate Appointment.

I began to think about the chief justice in the context of this proposal when I noticed what appeared to be a drafting error in an early version of Carrington-Cramton. When the chief justice reached his eighteenth year, it appeared that the President could fill that vacancy with a sitting justice, who would then start his or her eighteen years running again. I also noticed that there was no general prohibition on re-appointments, so that the President might be able to re-appoint the chief, or for that matter any sitting justice, as long as the Senate would go along. When I pointed this out to the sponsors, they agreed that such maneuvers were inconsistent with their intent, although their proposal does not yet specifically prohibit re-appointments that would extend a justice's active service beyond eighteen years.

That problem could be fixed relatively easily by not permitting "tacking" beyond eighteen years, no matter how many appointments a justice had. But as I thought more about the problem, the notion that a person already on the Court should have to go through another Senate confirmation to be elevated to chief justice did not make much sense. This in turn caused me to think about whether it was desirable, as a general policy matter, for the chief justice to be appointed directly to that position, as has happened for all but four of the nation's seventeen chief justices, or whether the Court and the country would be better off if the chief justice came from among the sitting justices. I concluded that the current system was less than optimal and that Congress should amend Title 28 so that, when a vacancy in the position of chief justice occurs, the President would designate a sitting justice to become chief justice to serve until his or her eighteen years of active service were concluded, with no Senate confirmation required.[7]

---

7. Currently, the chief justice receives $8,700 a year beyond the annual pay of $194,200 of associate justices. *See* note, set out under 5 U.S.C.A. § 5. I am indifferent to whether that

As is as true as for the basic Carrington-Cramton proposal, there is no crisis in the way that the chief justice is currently selected, nor can I identify specific problems caused by having the chief appointed directly to that position. Chief Justice William Rehnquist had served for over fourteen years when he was elevated, whereas his two immediate predecessors, Earl Warren and Warren Burger, had been, respectively, Governor of California and a judge on the court of appeals for the D.C. circuit, before their selections. However one evaluates their roles as chief justice, in contrast to their voting and opinion-writing records as members of the Court, it would be hard to make a case that prior service on the Court was a key factor in their success, or even lack of it.

One of the main reasons that I support the idea of designating a chief justice is that it would reduce the number of confirmation battles, especially those involving sitting justices. I nonetheless recognize that the Court and the country survived the Rehnquist elevation and would survive similar future efforts as well, whether they succeed, as was the case with Rehnquist, or fail, as was true for Abe Fortas, whom President Lyndon Johnson attempted to make Chief Justice when Earl Warren decided to retire in 1968. Put more pragmatically, changing the method of selecting the chief justice is worthy of adoption, but the fight that it would generate as a stand-alone proposal, including the charge that it was politically motivated or aimed at a particular chief justice, would not be worth the gains. However, as part of the Carrington-Cramton package, it is highly desirable.

Elevating a sitting member of a court to be the chief judge of that court is hardly a radical idea. The chief judges of the federal courts of appeals and district courts attain their positions without any additional approval by the Senate, or, in fact, by the President, since their elevations are based on seniority, circumscribed by certain age limits.[8] In addition, although originally the chairs of most multi-member federal regulatory commissions were appointed by the President, with Senate confirmation required, the President may now designate the chair from among the sitting members.[9]

---

practice should continue, but if it does, the increment could not be eliminated after the chief justice became a senior justice without violating the prohibition in Article III against diminishing the pay of any federal judge "during their Continuance in Office."

8. The judge may not become chief if he or she is sixty-five at the time of the elevation, and must step down on reaching age seventy, or after serving seven years, whichever is earlier. 28 U.S.C. §45(a).

9. This was accomplished for the Securities and Exchange Commission and the Federal Trade Commission by Presidential Reorganizations Plans Nos. 8 & 10 of 1950, pursuant to the Reorganization Act of 1949, 5 U.S.C. §901, the relevant provisions of which can be

There is also the Appointments Clause to consider. Article I, section 2, clause 2, provides in pertinent part, that the President "shall appoint Ambassadors, other public Ministers and Counsels, Judges of the supreme court, and all other Officers of the United States, whose Appointments are not herein otherwise provided for, and which shall be established by law: but the Congress may by Law vest the Appointment of such inferior Officers, as they think proper, in the President alone, in the Courts of Law, or in the Heads of Departments." There is no question that the person who would become the chief justice would have satisfied both parts of the advice and consent provisions when he or she was appointed as a justice. The issue would be whether the position of chief justice is a sufficiently separate office that the Constitution requires a separate nomination and confirmation even where Congress has specifically provided otherwise.[10]

Weiss v. United States[11] provides very strong authority that no separate appointment is required. In *Weiss* a member of the Armed Forces was convicted of a crime and objected that his appeal was heard by a court whose members were all commissioned officers, but who had not been separately appointed to that court, under either method permitted by the Appointments Clause. The Court unanimously held that, since all commissioned officers were appointed by the President, with the advice and consent of the Senate, they satisfied the first part of the Appointments Clause. The Court then ruled that the office of judge of a court of military review was not a separate office from that of a commissioned officer, because military officers had always had judicial responsibilities among their duties. The judges whose appointments were challenged in *Weiss* were all lawyers, but the logic of the Court's rationale, which was specifically argued to the Court by counsel for Weiss as a reason not to adopt that position,[12] is that any military officer, including one whose primary work was in the infantry and who had never been to law school, could also serve as an appellate judge reviewing court martial convictions. If the position of a military appeals court judge is not a separate office from that of any

---

found in notes following 15 U.S.C.A. §78d and 15 U.S.C.A. §41, respectively. Those plans also provide evidence of the power of the chair in comparison to that of the other members.

10. The current statute treats them differently by providing that the Supreme Court "shall consist of a Chief Justice of the United States and eight associate justices…" 28 U.S.C. §1.

11. 510 U.S. 163 (1994).

12. Reply Brief for Petitioner at 3–9. The author was counsel of record for petitioner Weiss, whose Appointments Clause arguments were rejected by the Court.

military officer, it is difficult to imagine how the position of chief justice is sufficiently different from that of associate justice that the Appointments Clause requires a separate nomination and confirmation process for it. To be sure, the Constitution does provide, in the impeachment clause, that the chief justice shall preside at trials in the Senate, but that designation, for that limited purpose, appears to be more a gap-filling or administrative matter than to reflect any choice by the Framers that a chief justice must always be subject to a separate appointment, even where Congress concludes to the contrary. Thus, the current practice under which the chief justice must be separately confirmed for that position is a permissible, but not mandatory method of handling the selection process.[13]

Rationales for a Designation System

Moving to a system under which a President who chose to designate a sitting justice as chief justice (even if not required to do so) would have one clear benefit: it would eliminate one confirmation battle. Given the current role of the Supreme Court in our society, it is highly unlikely that any associate justice who was elevated to the position of chief justice would not have a lengthy confirmation hearing and probably an extensive debate on the Senate floor. The process would likely focus on the opinions (and perhaps even the votes) of the nominee as an associate justice, and there would be requests to explain in greater detail opinions written by the nominee. Those kinds of inquiries seem highly inappropriate, but almost inevitable.

In the case of Chief Justice Rehnquist, much of the attention during the 1986 hearings was on voter intimidation that had allegedly occurred when he was a lawyer in Arizona and that had been the subject of questions when he

---

13. It is unclear who, if anyone, would have standing to challenge the absence of a separate appointment for the chief justice. As noted above, it is not at all certain that anyone would be able to challenge the basic Carrington-Cramton proposal, and the situation with respect to the chief justice is even more problematic since, as discussed below, most of his separate powers as chief justice are administrative. The remaining powers are part of the decisionmaking process in cases before the Court, which are subsumed in the ultimate voting, which is done by the Court, all of whose members have been duly appointed under Article I, section 2, clause 2. That no one might have standing would not, of course, be a proper basis to support a plainly unconstitutional law, but even those who support a constitutional amendment do not claim that Carrington-Cramton is clearly unconstitutional, let alone that allowing the President to assign the duties of chief justice to an already confirmed associate justice would clearly violate Article III or any other provision of the Constitution.

was nominated as an associate justice. Although there is no res judicata rule applicable to that situation, going over the same grounds that had proven insufficient to deny him a position on the Court fifteen years earlier is at least troublesome. Some would justify that kind of inquiry on the ground that the reputation of the chief justice is of greater significance than that of one of the other eight justices, but that seems a stretch at best. Moreover, if the Senate were to reject a nominee largely because it disagreed with his or her opinions as a sitting justice, that would send a dubious message to the Court and the President. And, while it might be legitimately informative if the Senate could learn whether a person being elevated had the requisite skills to lead the Court and manage its business, as well as to take on the other duties of the chief justice discussed below, it is hard to imagine how the Senate would be able to gather meaningful information on the topic sufficient to second-guess the President—who presumably would have considered those factors in his decisionmaking—and reject the nominee for that reason alone.[14]

There are two related reasons why it is inadvisable for the Senate to sit in judgment when a sitting justice is elevated to chief justice. First, in such a situation, there will have to be a second confirmation process because someone will be nominated to fill the associate's seat made vacant when he or she is made chief justice. Either that will mean two battles or that one of the nominees will undergo less than full scrutiny. Because the chief, whoever he or she may be, has only one vote, the Senate might reasonably conclude that a fight over the move from associate to chief is not worth the effort. If that were to be the prevailing view (and it has much to commend it), then one has to ask whether it makes sense to require everyone to gear up for a foregone conclusion. On the other hand, and this is what appears to have happened in 1986 when then-judge Antonin Scalia was named to fill the vacancy created when William Rehnquist became Chief, he sailed through, with little opposition, perhaps because the Senate was exhausted from the Rehnquist fight and did not have the will to do it again. But there can be little doubt that the Scalia appointment has had a far greater impact on the Court than the Rehnquist el-

---

14. Abe Fortas' nomination as chief was not defeated, but was subjected to a filibuster. It seems clear that some Senators did not like his record on the Court and others had questions about his relations with Lyndon Johnson and perhaps others. But the fact that there was a presidential election in a few months, in which the Republicans believed that they had a good chance of winning, was probably the main factor in keeping Fortas from becoming Chief Justice. Given the timing of appointments under Carrington-Cramton, that situation would not arise again, unless the Senate were able to filibuster a nominee for more than a year.

evation, quite the opposite of what the expenditure of effort by the Senate, and by those who opposed the Rehnquist elevation, would suggest would be the relative importance of the two events.[15]

The second reason to be concerned about a confirmation process for an elevation of a sitting justice is what almost happened during the 2004–05 Term of the Court. In late October 2004 the chief justice announced he had thyroid cancer, and there was widespread speculation that he would have to step down, creating an immediate vacancy. One of the President's options would have been to promote a sitting justice. If he had decided to do that, the confirmation process would have occurred during a term of the Court, with the chief justice-to-be having to take large amounts of time away from the business of the Court, which would already be short one-ninth of its members. In the current political climate, and especially if the President chose either Justice Scalia or Justice Thomas, both of whom he singled out for praise during his races for President, the confirmation process might have dragged on for a long time and become extremely contentious. If the President were given the power to designate the chief justice from among the sitting justices, that unseemly and very disruptive process would be avoided. Fortunately, Chief Justice Rehnquist's health allowed him to work from home and then to return to the Court, but there is no assurance that next time the Court and the country will be so fortunate.

As it turned out, Chief Justice Rehnquist decided not to resign even after the Court wrapped up its work in June, but his health deteriorated in late August, and he died just before the hearings were to begin on the nomination of Judge John Roberts to succeed Justice Sandra Day O'Connor, who had announced her retired. The President could have chosen to elevate a sitting jus-

---

15. This is not to suggest that, if the Senate had only the nomination of Justice Scalia before it, the outcome would have been different, although perhaps he would not have achieved a 98–0 endorsement. Scalia was then serving on the D.C. Circuit, and his generally conservative views were known. But his caseload on the court of appeals was such that the subjects on which his outspoken opinions have become most well-known on the High Court did not come before him there, and to the extent that they did, he was bound by what the Supreme Court had held, and he did not choose to voice any of his disagreements with existing precedent. Nor could he be fairly accused of holding back on his opinions or of changing his views when he went on the Court. His writings were largely in the area of administrative law, and his opinions at the Office of Legal Counsel at the Justice Department are fully in line with the views that he has expressed on the Court. It is only his style of writing for the Court, which can be characterized as colorful, if not acerbic at times, in which a difference between what he wrote on the court of appeals and what he now does, becomes quite apparent.

tice at that point, but instead nominated Judge Roberts as chief, thereby avoiding an extra set of confirmation proceedings.[16]

The principal effect of a statutory change from a separate appointment to a Presidential designation would be to eliminate a role for the Senate in the process. That change would be significant either in the case of frequent elevations, which there have not been, or if the Senate exercised its power in a meaningful manner appropriate to the level of importance of the elevation from associate to chief justice. I have serious doubts that the Senate has an appropriate role to play when the President elevates a sitting justice. Furthermore, as I now argue, the elevation is not of such great significance that the Senate's role is worth the effort of a separate confirmation process.

The Chief Is Different, But Not Very

In its single most important aspect, being chief justice has no significance because the chief, like all other justices, has one and only one vote. There are ways in which the chief exercises more power than his colleagues, but in the most important aspect of the job, he is only the first among equals. This is not to say that the chief justice has no powers. He does, and they are not without some significance, but not enough to warrant a separate confirmation for a sitting justice.

When he is in the majority, the chief decides who will write the opinion for the Court, including assigning the case to himself. No one disputes that the power of assignment can be very significant, at least in some cases, but it should be noted that Chief Justice Rehnquist was not in the majority in most of the Court's most controversial and important cases in the last few years. He

---

16. It is hard enough for any new justice to acclimate to that position, but becoming chief justice, with the added responsibilities of that office, will make these transitions even more difficult. The problems were compounded for Justice Roberts because the first case was argued almost immediately after he was confirmed, leaving him very little time to read the briefs and study the record in some very complex matters. In addition, the September conference, which reviews a three months backlog of cert petitions, took place without his participation, but left some difficult choices to be made once he took office. On top of all this, Roberts had been a judge for only two years, although he had substantial experience with the Supreme Court, first as a law clerk (twenty-four years before his elevation to the bench) and then as a frequent advocate. Finally, Chief Justice Roberts at age fifty will be the youngest justice, by seven years compared to Justice Thomas, and by from fifteen to thirty-five years for the remaining members of the Court. Given the perceived advantages to the President of appointing younger justices, this situation is likely to repeat itself, although there is unlikely to be a new chief justice for several decades.

dissented in the same-sex sodomy case,[17] the affirmative action cases,[18] the 2003 campaign finance cases,[19] the mental retardation[20] and juvenile death penalty[21] cases, and the constitutionality of the sentencing guidelines.[22] And he has never been in the majority in any of the abortion cases to come before the Court. On the other hand, on issues of federalism and state's rights, his vision of the Constitution, which he enunciated in dissent when he was an associate justice, has become the prevailing view in recent years, and he has able to assign those opinions to himself or others. Other examples on both sides could be provided, but the point is only that the power to assign opinions in the cases that matter most is significantly circumscribed because it applies only if the chief justice votes with the majority. Moreover, given the long-standing practice of assigning approximately equal numbers of majority opinions to all of the justices (although not equal numbers of important opinions), there are further practical limits on the assignment power.

Compare the office of the chief justice with the head of a regulatory body like the Federal Trade Commission or the Securities and Exchange Commission. The chairs of those agencies have far more powers within their domains than does the chief justice. In most multi-member bodies, the top staff is hired by the chair, with the implicit or sometimes explicit consent of the remaining members.[23] Once hired, staff works largely for the Chair, particularly in terms of setting priorities, such as what investigations to undertake or what rules to put through the lengthy rulemaking process. Overall, the policy direction of the agency is set by the chair, and he or she is generally the principal spokesperson for it. The chief justice, by contrast, has a much smaller and less significant staff over which he has control and those staff members have few significant policy making aspects to their jobs. The justices hire their own law clerks, and most but not all, of the remainder of the senior Court staff serve for long periods of time, some for most of their careers. The principal policies that the Court makes are through its decisions, on which all members have an equal vote. Perhaps the most discretionary aspect of the Supreme Court's operations is its control over what cases to decide. It takes only four votes to grant review and the chief's assent need not be among them.

---

17. Lawrence v. Texas, 539 U.S. 558 (2003).
18. Grutter v. Bollinger, 539 U.S. 306 (2003).
19. McConnell v. Federal Election Comm., 540 U.S. 93 (2003).
20. Atkins v. Virginia, 536 U.S. 304 (2002).
21. Roper v. Simmons, 125 S. Ct. 1183 (2005).
22. United States v. Booker, 125 S. Ct. 738 (2005).
23. *See* Reorganization Plans *supra* n. 9.

That said, the chief justice does have significant influence on the certiorari process. It is he who, by tradition, circulates what is known as the "discuss list," which constitutes those cases that he deems worthy of further discussion at the Court's conference at which it decides which cases to hear. Other justices can add to the list, but going first creates the agenda. Similarly, the chief is by tradition the first one to speak when the justices meet to decide the outcomes of the cases that they have heard during oral argument, which sets the tone for further debate. It is also the chief who approves the recommendations of the clerk of the Court on which cases will be heard on which days, in which order, and he also makes preliminary rulings on matters such as requests for additional time for oral argument. As those who have witnessed oral argument when Chief Justice Rehnquist was presiding know, he was a strict task master on time and cut off lawyers in mid-sentence when their thirty minutes expired, in contrast to Justice John Paul Stevens, who acted as chief when Rehnquist was unable to attend court sessions, and who was willing to give some additional time to a lawyer trying to finish his point. No one would suggest that these powers are inconsequential, but neither are they substantial enough that, on their own, they would justify a full-blown confirmation process for a person who is already a justice and to whom these additional duties would be assigned.

There are two small sets of public data that at least hint at, although do not prove, that the chief justice has other fairly significant powers as well. The first relates to the number of cases each term on which the Court hears oral argument and writes a full opinion. In a general way, that number is one measure of the amount of law that the Court makes, although not all new law is equally significant. Thus, resolving a statutory conflict under the tax code does not have the same impact as upholding affirmative action at public universities. Nonetheless, the number of constitutional decisions can be seen at least as a rough measure of the relative activism of the Court, and the number of reversals is a general statement of how much it is willing to leave to the lower federal courts and the highest courts of the states. Its willingness to resolve issues of statutory interpretation matters to litigants and lawyers in terms of eliminating uncertainty and perhaps regional disparities, and to Congress to which these conflicts may be referred if the Court declines to end them.[24]

---

24. The number of cases heard also matters to lawyers who specialize in Supreme Court cases or who write amicus briefs, since fewer cases mean less business for them and more competition for a smaller number of argued cases. The Office of the Solicitor General is particularly affected by a reduction in cases granted since it has a very large share of the docket in almost every term.

During the tenure of William Rehnquist as chief justice there was a reduction of over forty-three percent in the number of cases argued as compared to the prior period when he was an associate justice.[25] In the eleven full terms in which he served as an associate justice, the Court averaged more than 136 full opinions per term, including an average of 147 in the last four years of the Burger tenure. In the first seven years of the Rehnquist era, the number dropped to 125 per term, with the most significant change between the 1989 and 1990 terms when the number went from 131 to 119. The drop in the next eleven terms was even more dramatic, down to 77.6 decisions per year, not counting the 2004 term in which the figure was almost the same.

The numbers do not "prove" anything, but it is hard to believe that this is all a coincidence. If there are four votes to grant a writ, the case will be heard, but the fact is that, for whatever reason or combination of reasons, the Court has gone on a crash diet, and it has kept off the extra cases. The Chief Justice never said that he was trying to reduce the number of cases heard, but neither did he deny it. The change has real significance for the country, and it is a reasonable inference that, for better or for worse, much of the credit (or blame) should go to the chief justice.

Second, *Bush v. Gore*[26] is a case in which it is arguable that the power of the chief justice influenced its outcome very significantly, although this conclusion is based on inferences from undisputed facts about the case, not on inside information. The Chief's substantive rationale for siding with candidate Bush did not command a majority of the Court in the decisive second case, but a review of the chronology of the two cases suggests that it was the strong guiding hand of the Chief Justice that made it possible for the Court to hear two separate cases and decide them both within twenty-one days.[27]

The Florida Supreme Court issued its first decision, purportedly based on state law grounds only, on Tuesday November 21, 2000. A cert petition was filed on behalf of candidate Bush the next day, and on Friday, the day after Thanksgiving, the Court granted review on a day on which no conference was scheduled. Petitioner's brief was ordered filed the following Tuesday, respondents' brief on Thursday, with oral argument set for Friday. The next Monday the Court reversed the decision below and directed the Florida courts to act consistently with the Court's unanimous, but unsigned, opinion. Round one was thus concluded in less than two weeks from the time of the Florida court ruling.

---

25. Data obtained from the annual statistics published by the Harvard Law Review.

26. 531 U.S. 98 (2000).

27. All dates are from the official U.S. Reports and the petitions and briefs filed in the two cases.

Round two was even speedier, in part because of approaching statutory deadlines that arguably imposed real barriers to further proceedings. Four days after the Supreme Court reversed the Florida Supreme Court, the latter court issued another opinion, also adverse to candidate Bush. The very next day (Saturday December 9th) the Court granted the petition and required all briefs to be filed on Sunday, in time for a Monday morning argument. Less than thirty-six hours later, around ten p.m. eastern time on Tuesday, December 12th, the Court issued its decision, sealing the election for candidate Bush.

I recognize that lawyers for candidate Bush, the clerk's office at the Supreme Court, and the procedures in place for dealing with emergency matters (principally stays of execution in death penalty cases) played a role in assuring that the cases were able to be heard in time to make a difference. But suppose that the chief justice had been of a different political party, or had been less on top of the matter, or more willing to allow his fellow justices time to reflect on whether to hear the first case; for example, not granting the petition until Monday and scheduling oral argument the following week. Even if the same first opinion had been issued just a week later, the effect on what happened in Florida might have been very different, and there might never have been a second case, or at least not one that was argued on the same grounds and with the same record as the actual second one was. Given the Thanksgiving holiday and the novel legal issues presented, not to mention the enormous political effect of intervening at all, no one could have reasonably criticized the Court (or the chief justice) if a little more time had elapsed before acting on the first petition or scheduling oral argument. On those matters, the chief justice is the obvious person to take the lead and sometimes, as in *Bush v. Gore*, it makes a great deal of difference in the outcome who the chief is, even though he has only one vote.

Suppose that, instead of a chief justice who had been on the Court for almost twenty-nine years and been chief for fourteen when *Bush v. Gore* came to the Court, there had been a new chief justice, who had been appointed directly to that position in 1999. That could easily happen under Carrington-Cramton or any other system in which such a direct appointment may be made. Would a relatively new chief justice have been willing to take the lead and able to muster the support of the Court to act in a timely fashion? It is impossible to know, but it surely would have been harder for someone new to the Court and new to relationships with the other justices. Merits aside, my own view is that the Court had an obligation to decide in a timely fashion whether to take the case and, if it did, to issue a decision as soon as possible. We have come to expect so much of the Supreme Court when it comes to deciding difficult legal questions, such as those involved in *Bush v. Gore*, that the

Court had an obligation to resolve the issues there, although not necessarily in the way that it did. A new chief justice would have made that task more difficult, which is one of the reasons that supports my proposal to permit the President to choose from among only those justices with at least a few years experience on the Court.

Another case in which Chief Justice Rehnquist apparently played a constructive role in helping to resolve difficult scheduling matters is *McConnell v. FEC*.[28] In March 2002, sixteen cases were filed, challenging the constitutionality of the recently-enacted Bipartisan Campaign Reform Act, known as BCRA. Massive discovery was undertaken, and multiple and lengthy briefs and replies were filed prior to oral argument being held before a special three-judge district court in December 2002. Although the statute required expedition, there was no decision until early May, when the court issued a series of opinions totaling almost 743 printed pages in the federal reporter.[29]

Under BCRA, the appeals went directly to the Supreme Court, and almost everyone appealed something and defended something else. Motions were made asking the Court to set an expedited briefing and argument schedule, to grant additional pages for briefing, and to decide in what order the briefs (and any reply briefs) should be filed. As one of many counsel in the cases, I think it is fair to say that no one was completely satisfied with every aspect of these very prompt rulings, but the results seemed tolerable and workable for all.

The Court came back early and heard four hours of argument in early September, for which the justices were extraordinarily well prepared given the size of the briefs they had to digest, the complexity of the statutory scheme and constitutional issues, and the large number of issues and sub-issues that had to be resolved. The ruling came down in early December, with the Chief Justice in dissent on the most important issues, in time for the 2004 elections and with a result that did not leave the parties in doubt. Again, much of the credit for the fair and effective movement of the cases in the Court belongs to the Chief Justice, and it is doubtful that a newly appointed chief could have done nearly as well on these partially, although not entirely, administrative matters. Of course, the cases would have been decided in due course, whoever was chief, but the general agreement among the participants that the handling was fair and efficient is also an important part of our system of justice, as is a belief by litigants that they have been accorded due process of law.

---

28. 540 U.S. 93 (2003). I say apparently because it is known that the Chief Justice was involved in these matters, and these orders bear evidence of his very pragmatic approach.

29. 251 F. Supp. 2d 176–919 (D. D.C. 2003).

Finally, there are a significant number of duties assigned to the chief justice, mainly by Congress, which do not involve decisions in cases, but are generally related to the state of the federal judiciary, although some, such as service on the Board of Regents of the Smithsonian, seem quite peripheral.[30] More than twenty years ago, my co-author Scott Stenhouse and I published an essay about them,[31] in which we questioned the advisability on a number of grounds for giving many of those assignments to a sitting justice, let alone giving all of them to the chief justice. I stand behind those views, but for these purposes the relevance of those duties is that they are extensive and that most of them deal with the federal judicial system in one way or other. Therefore, both because it takes most justices some period of time before they become accustomed to the work of the Court, and because persons appointed directly to the Court may have relatively little familiarity with the federal courts, it is a decided advantage for a person who must carry out these additional duties of the chief justice to have been on the Court for some years before taking them on.

The Specifics of a Chief Justice Proposal

Beyond the symbolism, being chief justice is different from being an associate justice in a number of ways, but not in the single most important respect: voting on cases. The differences that exist suggest both that it matters who is chief justice (and hence the position should not be filled by seniority alone, or by rotation every two or four years, or by drawing straws), but that they are not important enough to warrant having a separate confirmation battle when an associate is elevated to chief. Those differences tend to be in matters more on the administrative, than the strictly legal, side of the Court's work. This suggests that a person with more experience on the Court would, all other things being equal, do a better job than one who has been made chief from outside the Court.[32]

These observations lead me to make the following proposal, which should be considered as a package, not in its separate parts, and in conjunction with

---

30. 20 U.S.C. §42.

31. Alan B. Morrison & Scott Stenhouse, *The Chief Justice of the United States: More Than Just the Highest Ranking Judge*, 1 Constitutional Commentary 57 (1984). There have been changes in these duties since then, mainly additions. For these purposes there is no need to list them all to appreciate the breadth of the chief justice's not-adjudicative responsibilities.

32. Judith Resnik argues persuasively for the importance of the non-judicial powers and responsibilities of the chief justice. *See supra* Judith Resnik, *Democratic Responses to the Breadth of Power of the Chief Justice* pp. 181–200.

Carrington-Cramton. The President should be empowered by statute to designate a sitting justice to serve as chief justice, with no further Senate confirmation. In order to assure both that the person serving as chief justice had substantial prior High Court experience and would serve a substantial, but not excessive period in that position before rotating off at the end of eighteen years of active Supreme Court service, the President would be required to choose from among those justices (probably four in number) with at least five years on the Court and fewer than eleven. As a result, a chief would serve somewhere between six and twelve years in that position, long enough to have an impact, but not so long as to become entrenched. These numbers are, in any event, merely suggestive of what seems an appropriate balancing between assuring some Court experience, and not unduly limiting the President's choice of chief justice.[33]

There is a tradeoff: in exchange for freeing the President of a confirmation battle for his chief justice, the President must accept a limitation on his choices to a group of sitting, experienced justices, with some, but not too much, time on the Court. The President may choose any person he believes can be confirmed for the position of associate justice, and perhaps make that person the chief later on, but no longer could a President make a Supreme Court novice the chief justice. Whether a nomination of that kind made sense in earlier days, it no longer seems wise today. Thus, if Congress enacts the Carrington-Cramton proposal, it should include in that statute the necessary changes to allow the President to designate an associate justice to become the chief justice of the United States.

---

33. In most situations, a President would have an associate justice appointed by a President from his or her party from which to choose, but that might not always be the case. That might be a reason to expand the window of designation slightly on one or both ends, with no great harm done to the basic concept.

Internal Dynamics of
Term Limits for Justices

Thomas W. Merrill[*]

What would be the effect on the Supreme Court if the tenure of justices were changed from indefinite lifetime appointment—the current system—to a system of staggered terms of eighteen years? Other contributors to this book have discussed the impact of such a change on the composition of the Court and the confirmation process. I will offer a perspective that has not been given equal prominence: the effect of staggered term limits on the internal dynamics of the Court.

The system of life tenure, at least as it has operated in recent decades, tends to produce a pattern in which the membership of the Court remains stable for a significant period of time, punctuated by irregular bursts of turnover. The Rehnquist Court, for example, saw a turnover of six justices during the first eight years of its existence, followed by no turnover for the next eleven years, with two vacancies suddenly arising in the summer of 2005. The Burger Court experienced a similar, if less dramatic, pattern. It is not clear why life tenure should produce such a pattern, and recent experience may be a fluke. But whatever the cause of irregular turnover, staggered term limits would clearly bring it to an end. The Court would experience very consistent and predictable turnover, with one justice departing and her replacement arriving every two years, like clockwork. The question I will address is how this shift in the pattern of turnover would affect the internal dynamics of the Court.

Neither legal scholars nor political scientists have paid much attention to the possible significance of the rate of change in membership on multi-member courts in analyzing judicial behavior. So I am operating here in largely un-

---

[*] Charles Keller Beekman Professor, Columbia Law School.

charted territory.[1] Nevertheless, I will argue that appellate courts whose membership is stable will behave in ways perceptibly different from courts experiencing membership change. First, I will sketch in broad brush fashion the relevant differences between stable courts and courts experiencing turnover, and will offer some general speculations about how a system of staggered term limits would stack up relative to either a stable court or a changing court. Then, I will take up the differences between stable courts and changing courts in greater detail, and provide further assessment of how a Court subject to staggered term limits would behave.

Stable Courts, Changing Courts, Staggered Courts

The differences between stable courts and changing courts can be traced to three behavioral phenomena that characterize collegial courts to one degree or another: socialization, knowledge, and cooperation. I will briefly consider each in turn.

Socialization. The Court, like other institutions, is governed to a significant degree by norms. Some examples of important Supreme Court rules that are the product of norms rather than positive law include: the rule that it takes four votes to hear a case, the rule that opinions are assigned by the senior justice in the majority, and the rule that deliberations take place in secret.[2] These norm-based rules are passed down from justice to justice as they join the Court. As Caldiera and Zorn observe: "[S]ocialization to the behavior of the justices is learned from other justices upon taking office. Normally, a single justice joins the Court on which sit eight veterans of the institution. Thus, we expect norms...to be propagated from one generation of justices to the next... imbuing them with long-memory characteristics."[3]

---

1. For my own tentative efforts to consider this phenomenon, upon which the present essay builds, see Thomas W. Merrill, *The Making of the Second Rehnquist Court: A Preliminary Analysis*, 47 St. Louis U. L. J. 569, 639–51 (2003). Another work that briefly alludes to this factor is Thomas G. Walker et al., *On the Mysterious Demise of Consensual Norms in the United States Supreme Court*, 50 J. Politics 361, 373–74 (1998) (discussing the possible role of "youth and inexperience" on the Court).

2. *See* Lee Epstein & Jack Knight, *The Choices Justices Make* 118–35 (1998); Gregory A Caldeira & Christopher J.W. Zorn, *Of Time and Consensual Norms in the Supreme Court*, 42 Am. J. Pol. Sci. 874 (1998).

3. Caldeira & Zorn, *supra* n. 2 at 880.

The fact that the Court is a norm-governed institution and that its norms are learned through a process of socialization suggests one difference between a stable Court and a Court experiencing membership change. A stable Court will consist of well-socialized justices—as socialized as they are ever likely to get. Such a Court will tend to be conservative in an institutional sense, adhering to established tenets of collective behavior, unless perhaps impelled to change by some powerful outside force.[4] A Court experiencing significant turnover, in contrast, will include some justices who are not yet fully socialized into the pathways of the institution. This may produce conditions that allow shifts in norms to take place, particularly if the newer justices include a "norm entrepreneur" who succeeds in persuading other newcomers to adopt norms different than those that have governed in the past.

Knowledge. Being a justice is a tremendously complicated job. Thousands of legal issues are presented for decision, enmeshed in cases with dozens of different procedural complexities. Moreover, if we think of the job in strategic actor terms, as political scientists often do these days,[5] the complexities multiply many times over. The objective for each justice from this perspective is to attempt to forge alliances with at least four other justices in order to produce binding precedents. This entails having knowledge about the likely preferences of the eight other justices, spread over all the legal issues presented with all their procedural complexities. No human being, however observant and knowledgeable, could ever obtain complete mastery of the informational demands such a job presents. The best we can hope for is reasonable proficiency.

How long does it take a new justice to develop a reasonably proficient degree of knowledge about the legal issues that arise, the conventions for handling different procedural complexities, and the preferences of the other justices? No doubt the answer varies for each justice. But there is reason to believe that for the ordinary mortal the learning curve is steep for the first few years.[6]

---

4. Roosevelt's threat to impose his Court-packing plan would be an example. I suppose a movement to adopt staggered term limits for justices might be another example of an outside force or threat. This suggests that my analysis should ideally include the possibility of internal norm-change in response to the very proposal I seek to analyze, but I will ignore the complications here of such reflexivity.

5. *See,* e.g., Lawrence Baum, *The Puzzle of Judicial Behavior* 89–124 (1997); Epstein & Knight, *supra* n. 2; Forest Maltzman, et al., *Crafting Law on the Supreme Court: The Collegial Game* (2000). The original inspiration for this perspective is Walter F. Murphy, *Elements of Judicial Strategy* (1964).

6. For evidence on this point, *see* Sandra L. Wood et al., *"Acclimation Effects" for Supreme Court Justices: A Cross-Validation, 1888–1940,* 42 Am. J. Pol. Sci. 690 (1998); Timothy M. Hagle, *"Freshmen Effects" for Supreme Court Justices,* 37 Am. J. Pol Sci. 1142 (1993).

Justice White was fond of quoting Justice Douglas to the effect that "it takes five years to go around the track once."[7] Although the remark conceivably refers to socialization, it is my sense that it does not take five years for a typical new justice to assimilate the internal norms of the Court. The point of the remark, rather, seems to be that it typically takes five years for a new justice to acquire enough knowledge to operate as a fully engaged participant in the decisional processes of the Court.

If this is correct, then it suggests another difference between a stable Court and a Court experiencing turnover. A stable Court will be composed of experienced justices, relatively speaking, and hence will consist of justices who have significant collective knowledge pertinent to performing the collegial tasks at hand. A Court experiencing turnover, in contrast, will include a number of newcomers who are still finding their way, and hence are not yet operating at full effectiveness.

Cooperation. The norms of the Court prohibit explicit contracts among the justices over the results and contents of opinions in particular cases, and prohibit logrolling between cases. Nevertheless, there is little doubt that pairs or groups of justices form bonds of cooperation among themselves over significant periods of time. Examples include the "Four Horsemen" who opposed much of the legislative program of the New Deal, Justices Brennan and Marshall who worked together seeking to preserve the legacy of the Warren Court, or the "Federalism Five" of the Rehnquist Court who have done much to remake the law of federal-state relations.

Game theorists have suggested that the interactions of the justices take the form of an indefinitely repeated game, in which patterns of cooperation tend to emerge.[8] Cooperation from this perspective is dependent on norms and knowledge. But it also requires, in addition, reciprocal behavior—justices rewarding cooperation by other justices and punishing defection by other justices. In an environment without hierarchical controls or external sanctions, these kinds of reciprocal responses are necessary to cement bonds of cooperation among justices, who are otherwise entirely free to respond as they wish to any particular case. These patterns of cooperation take time to develop. Justices have to sit through a significant number of cases together before they can accurately perceive whether accommodation on their part

---

7. See Dennis J. Hutchinson, *The Man Who Once Was Whizzer White* 349 (1998).

8. For two notable efforts at such an application of the theory, *see* Eric Rasmussen, *Judicial Legitimacy as a Repeated Game*, 10 J. L. Econ. & Org. 63 (1994); Erin O'Hara, *Social Constraint or Implicit Collusion: Toward a Game Theoretic Analysis of Stare Decisis*, 24 Seton Hall L. Rev. 736 (1993).

will reliably result in a favorable response from another, or whether any gesture of accommodation on their part will be ignored or taken for granted by another.

Here again, we can see that a stable Court should differ from a Court in flux. On a stable Court, each of the justices will have had dozens of opportunities to experiment with gestures of accommodation toward other justices, and to perceive whether these gestures result in some type of favorable reciprocity. This prolonged interaction may lead to the emergence of distinct blocks of justices, which remain relatively stable over time. On a Court experiencing significant turnover, in contrast, some of the justices will be strangers to the networks of reciprocity that have emerged among the more senior justices. The newcomers will be perceived as "wild cards" by the veterans. To the extent their votes are critical to outcomes, they will be regarded warily by more experienced justices, which will result in greater tentativeness in relying upon them to write opinions or form a majority in closely contested cases.

When we put these three distinguishing behavioral traits together—socialization, knowledge, and cooperation—we can predict that a stable Court will differ from a Court in flux in three significant ways. A stable Court will be (1) unlikely to change its internal norms; (2) tend to operate relatively efficiently in producing new precedents; and (3) tend to form relatively stable voting blocks. A Court subject to turnover will have the opposite tendencies, namely, it will (1) be more receptive to internal norm change; (2) relatively inefficient in producing new precedents; and (3) more prone to ad hoc voting alliances rather than stable voting blocks. I will spell out the reasoning for these conclusions, and provide some supporting evidence, in subsequent sections of this essay.

But first, let us consider how the introduction of a system of staggered term limits would likely affect the Court along these behavioral dimensions. A Court governed by life tenure will tend to oscillate, at least to some degree, between the behavioral traits associated with a stable Court and a Court in flux. A Court subject to staggered term limits would not oscillate between these poles, but would behave more consistently over time. Would such a Court consistently behave more like a stable Court, or more like a Court in flux? The answer may depend on the relative influence of three factors: the length of the term, the staggering feature, and the existence of a fixed service-termination date for each justice.

Consider first the behavioral effects of the length of the term. For a nine-member Court, one could devise systems of staggered term limits of nine years, eighteen years, or twenty-seven years. A system of twenty-seven-year terms would produce a mean level of experience of 13.5 years and would operate at all times with seven justices with at least five years experience.[9] Clearly it would share the characteristics of a stable Court along both the socialization and knowledge dimensions. The Carrington-Cramton proposal for a system of eighteen-year terms would result in a Court with a median of nine years experience. This is significantly less than the median years of experience in recent decades under the system of life tenure, but not too different from the historical median.[10] Moreover, there would always be six justices with at least five years experience. Again, the eighteen-year term would probably produce a Court more like a stable Court, at least on the socialization and knowledge dimensions. A nine-year term would produce a Court with relatively little collective experience, and would operate at all times with only four justices with at least five years experience. Such a Court would fall closer to the mode of behavior of a Court in flux along the socialization and knowledge dimensions.

The second and arguably even more important factor is the regularity of staggered appointment for a fixed term. This would eliminate any bunching of appointments. Instead, it would establish a system of appointment "titration," in which one new justice drops into the Court and another leaves at evenly spaced intervals. This would have at least two effects relevant to the behavioral traits that distinguish stable and changing Courts. On the one hand, it would isolate each new member of the Court in the face of eight veteran justices, thereby reinforcing the process of socializing new justices into the existing norms of the Court. On the other hand, by regularly removing an established player from the judicial "game," and injecting a new player, it might continually disrupt the process of forging bonds of cooperation among the justices. This is especially true if voting blocks tend to consist of five or fewer justices, in which case changing the identity of one justice would nearly always have the potential for upsetting existing patterns of cooperation.

The last relevant feature is the fixed service-termination date for each justice. This could result in a final period phenomenon, whereby other justices cease to cooperate with the most senior justice during his or her final term of service, since the retiring justice will no longer be around to reciprocate in future terms. This feature is thus also relevant to the cooperation variable, and further suggests that term limits would to some degree push the Court in the direction of a Court in flux.

When we combine the effects of term length, staggering of terms, and the fixed service-termination date, we can see that the net effect of staggered term

---

9. I ignore the complexities that would be created by early retirement or death.

10. *See supra* Steven G. Calabresi & James Lindgren, *Term Limits for the Supreme Court: Life Tenure Reconsidered*, pp. 23–24 for figures.

limits on internal dynamics is difficult to determine when measured against a system of life tenure. On some dimensions, namely socialization and knowledge, a system of staggered term limits would (at least for longer terms) likely mimic the behavior of a stable Court. But on the cooperation dimension, arguably, a system of staggered term limits would mimic the behavior of a Court in flux. Critically, however, a staggered-term Court would exhibit this peculiar package of traits *all the time,* not only during periods of membership stability that alternate with periods of turnover. In order to assess the desirably of changing the internal dynamics of the Court in this fashion, we need to give closer consideration to how patterns of turnover influence norm change, efficiency and cooperation, and to whether the behavioral traits associated with stability or flux, as the case may be, are desirable.

Receptivity to Change in Institutional Norms

As we have seen, one difference between a stable Court and a Court in flux concerns the degree to which the justices have been socialized into the norms of the Court. This, in turn, is relevant to the Court's receptivity to change in these institutional norms. Change in norms requires new ideas and a willingness to modify established patterns of behavior. New justices are much more likely to have new ideas and to be receptive to trying out other people's new ideas than are veteran justices. Change is probably most likely to occur with the appointment of a new chief justice. But turnover among other justices will be important as well, since consensual norms are supported by all members of the Court.[11] Thus, we would expect norm change to be most likely to occur upon the appointment of a new chief justice closely associated in time with the appointment of several other new justices. In contrast, when all nine justices have sat together on the Court for many years, we would expect to see little in the way of norm change.

We can see some confirmation of this hypothesis in the history of the Burger Court. The Burger Court, like the Rehnquist Court, started off with a burst of turnover (Burger, 1969; Blackmun, 1970; Powell, 1972; Rehnquist, 1972; Stevens, 1975) and then settled down to a period of stability (six years

---

11. *See* Walker, *supra* n. 1 at 373 (noting the possibility that the sudden rise in the percentage of cases with dissenting and concurring opinions in the Stone Court may have been due in part to the high percentage of young and inexperienced justices, and observing that "[h]igh levels of inexperience may also provide conditions conducive to a breakdown in decision-making norms").

with no turnover from 1975 to 1981). The early years of the Burger Court were a period of significant change for the Court in terms of its internal practices. The time allotted to oral argument was cut in half (thereby doubling the Court's capacity to hear merits cases); the number of law clerks per justice was doubled from two to four (thereby doubling the capacity to write merits opinions); the certiorari pool was established (permitting the justices to spend more time on merits cases rather than case selection); even the shape of the bench was changed to permit better interaction among justices at oral argument.[12] Perhaps as a consequence of these changes, the number of cases heard per term increased significantly, from around 120 to 150. In the later years of the Burger Court, there were no institutional changes of equivalent magnitude. A plausible explanation for this pattern is that during the early years of the Burger Court, new blood (including a new chief justice) brought with it new ideas about how to discharge the Court's business, and a receptiveness to adopt these new ideas, which was missing during the later period of stability.

Additional confirmation of the hypothesis about the importance of turnover in producing norm change is provided by the remarkable contraction in the size of the Court's docket that occurred during the early years of the Rehnquist Court. The docket began to shrink shortly after the ascension of William Rehnquist to the chief justiceship and the appointment of Antonin Scalia as associate justice in October 1986, fell fairly steadily for several years, paused at around one hundred fifteen cases per year in the early 1990s, and then plunged to a new level at around seventy-five to eighty-five argued cases per year after the retirement of Justice White in 1993. Ever since the docket reached this new equilibrium, it has remained essentially at the same level.

A variety of explanations have been advanced for this remarkable change in the collective behavior of the Court.[13] Explanations grounded in external

---

12. *See* David O'Brien, *Storm Center: The Supreme Court in American Politics* 166 (1986) (noting that the number of law clerks was two per justice throughout the Warren Court and increased to three and then four after 1970); Bernard Schwartz, *The Ascent of Pragmatism* 4 (1990) (describing changes in the shape of the bench); David M. O'Brien, *Join-3 Votes, the Rule of Four, the Cert. Pool, and the Supreme Court's Shrinking Plenary Docket*, 13 J. Law & Pol. 779, 790, (1997) (tracing origins of certiorari pool to a suggestion made by newly appointed Justice Powell, which was then endorsed by Chief Justice Burger).

13. For overviews of possible explanations and the evidence for and against each, *see* Margaret Meriwether Cordray & Richard Cordray, *The Supreme Court's Plenary Docket*, 58 Wash & Lee L. Rev. 737 (2001); Arthur D. Hellman, *The Shrunken Docket of the Rehnquist Court*, 1996 Sup. Ct. Rev. 403. For longer term trends in the number of opinions issued by the Court per year, *see* Robert Post, *The Supreme Court Opinion as Institutional Practice: Dissent, Legal Scholarship, and Decisionmaking in the Taft Court*, 85 Minn. L. Rev. 1267,

variables, such as a decline in lower court activism or increased ideological harmony within the ranks of the federal courts, do not appear to fit the evidence. If these factors were the primary cause, one would not expect to see such a precipitous drop followed by a leveling off. Instead, toward the end of the second Clinton Administration, as the courts of appeals began to include increasing numbers of Democratic appointees, but the Supreme Court remained dominated by Republicans, one could expect to see an upturn in the docket as the ideological harmony started to wear off. But there was no upturn.[14]

Nor does another popular explanation—the growing number of justices participating in the certiorari pool—fit the data. The "cert pool," as it is usually called, started out in the early years of the Burger Court with five chambers participating (the four Nixon appointees to the Court plus Justice White) and four not participating (Justices Douglas, Brennan, Stewart, Marshall). When Justice O'Connor was named to the Court in 1981, she joined the pool, increasing the participation to six chambers. Then, when Justices Brennan and Marshall retired in 1990 and 1991, their successors (Justices Souter and Thomas) also joined the pool, bringing the participation up to eight chambers. After 1991, only Justice Stevens remained outside the pool. Justices Gins-

---

1280 (2001). Before the Judiciary Act of 1925, the Court typically rendered over 200 opinions per year. This fell to a level of about 100 per year during the Vinson Court, increased to about 120 cases per year during the Warren Court, and then jumped back up to 150 per year during the Burger Court. This history suggests that the long-term trend is in the direction of fewer opinions per year (200 per year prior to 1925 to 80 per year today) but that significant variations exist from one natural Court to another (e.g., 150 per year under Burger to 80 per year under Rehnquist). See also Cordray & Cordray, *supra* at 745–750 (describing how personnel change in the early years of the Vinson Court led to a drop in the size of the docket from 150 cases per year to about 100 cases per year).

14. *See* Cordray & Cordray, *id.* at 772. The one external factor that appears to have some explanatory force is a reduction in requests for review by the Solicitor General in civil cases starting in the mid-1980s, which apparently tracks a reduction in the number of losses experienced by the federal government in such cases in the lower courts. *Id.* at 763–771. Cordray & Cordray show that the decline in government requests in the civil area appears to be partly a function of fewer civil suits involving the government, and partly a function of higher government success rates in the lower courts in civil cases. *Id.* at 768–770. But this factor accounts for at most only about one-third of the magnitude of the change. *Id.* at 764. Cordray & Cordray estimate that the decline in civil petitions by the Solicitor General is responsible for a reduction in about fifteen cases per year, and a decline in petitions support by amicus briefs filed by the Solicitor General for about ten cases per year. This would account for about twenty-five cases out of a total decline in the size of the docket of about seventy-five cases per year.

burg and Breyer also joined the pool, but their participation merely kept the level of participating chambers at eight. The pattern of growth of the cert pool does not fit the pattern in the decline in the caseload either. There was no decline in the docket when the pool expanded from five to six (in 1981), the recent decline began in 1987, well before the further expansions to seven and then eight justices in the cert pool took place, and the decline resumed with the resignation of Justice White, after the size of the pool had been fixed at eight.[15]

The best explanation for the change in the size of the docket appears to be that a new norm about what kinds of cases qualify for Supreme Court review began to develop with the onset of the Rehnquist Court in 1986, which norm then spread and became entrenched as other new justices came on board during a period of rapid turnover. This explanation is supported by the findings of several scholars who have examined the available data, each of whom has concluded that the most plausible explanation for the shrinkage in the docket is that the justices "have been applying a different—and more rigorous—standard in deciding whether to hear cases."[16]

In short, the behavior of both the Burger Court and the Rehnquist Court suggests that a high rate of turnover among justices is associated with change in institutional norms, and a low rate of turnover is associated with stasis in institutional norms. A system of staggered term limits would produce a level of norm socialization equal to or perhaps even greater than that associated with a stable Court. Given the staggering feature, new justices would be titrated onto the Court one at a time, and would remain isolated in their junior status for two years (under the eighteen-year version). This should be long enough to assure their socialization to the existing norms of the Court before the next new justice arrived. More importantly, the staggering feature would eliminate bunching of appointments, which seems to be a precondition of norm change under most conditions. As a result, the imposition of staggered term limits—at least for eighteen-year terms or longer—could produce a state of more-or-less permanent norm entrenchment on the Court.

Whether a state of norm entrenchment would be a good thing or a bad thing depends on whether the Court is amenable to reform through other forces, such as legislation, and on how badly one thinks the Court is in need of reform. If one thinks the Court's current practices are sound, and should be preserved in perpetuity, then staggered term limits would seem to be the

---

15. *See id.* at 792–93.

16. Hellman, *supra* n. 13 at 425. *Accord,* Cordray & Cordray, *supra* n. 13; O'Brien, *Join-3 Votes, supra* n. 12.

way to protect the status quo against change. However, if one thinks the Court's current practices are in need of significant reform, and that reform by Congress is unlikely, then life tenure may be preferred. Life tenure will produce little or no change during periods of stability, but at least leaves the door open to internal reform during periods of bunched turnover.

An illustration of how staggered term limits might affect reform is provided by the question whether the Court should allow oral arguments to be televised. Congress could mandate such a reform. But Congress might be reluctant to dictate to the Court about such a matter, and if it did, it is conceivable the Court would declare the requirement unconstitutional as a violation of separation of powers. Thus, televising arguments is most likely to occur if the justices conclude such a reform is warranted, and decide to impose it on themselves. Yet such a change is unlikely to occur without the appointment of a group of new justices who are receptive to such a change. From the perspective of someone who wants to see televised arguments, therefore, the current system of life tenure should be preferred to staggered term limits, since only life tenure is likely to produce the periods of bunched turnover that create the conditions for internal change.

This is not to say that internal reform will always be wise or well-considered. The Court's record on internal reform through norm change over the last forty years—most notably the sudden increase in the size of the docket in the early 1970s followed by an equally sudden decline in the size of the docket in the late 1980s—is not very impressive. If this erratic behavior is what internal reform means, then one is tempted to say that it is not worth preserving. Still, it is troubling to think that staggered term limits might have the effect of insulating the Court from any type of significant internal reform. To the extent we conclude that bunched turnover in personnel is a necessary condition of internal reform of the Court, this is a strike in favor of the system of life tenure.

Decisional Efficiency

Another difference between a Court with stable membership and a Court experiencing turnover is the amount of information each justice has about the legal issues that come before the Court, the conventions concerning the treatment of these issues given their procedural posture, and the preferences of the other justices with regard to these matters.

If we assume that each justice would like to see his or her jurisprudential views adopted in opinions that command a majority of the Court, then information about the views of the other justices is especially critical. No justice will ever have perfect information about the preferences of the other justices. Each must act on a subjective estimate of the likely position each of the other justices will take on each issue in each case that appears before the Court as a candidate for decision. But these subjective estimates are continually being updated with each case the Court decides as it sits together. The longer a given Court sits together, the more accurate become the estimates that each justice will make regarding the other justices.[17]

As an illustration, consider the situation of the justices in trying to determine the views of Justice David Souter when he was first appointed to the Court. The other justices were presumably anxious to develop a sense of Souter's views on controversial questions such as whether the Court should overrule *Roe v. Wade*. Each of the other justices started with some information about Souter—he is a white Protestant from New England, he is a bachelor, he previously served as a criminal prosecutor, he was appointed to the Court by the first President Bush, and so forth—and on the basis of these fragmentary bits of information would develop a preliminary estimate of the probability that Souter would vote to overrule *Roe*. The other justices would then observe Souter as he set to work deciding cases with them. If a case arose presenting a substantive due process question, for example, they would observe closely to see whether he was comfortable invoking this doctrine (on which *Roe* is based). In effect, they would revise their initial probability estimate by factoring in Souter's behavior in the substantive due process case. Then suppose another case arises, presenting a question of how much weight to give to stare decisis in constitutional law. The justices would revise their estimate again, based on Souter's views on whether to overrule a constitutional precedent. The process would proceed in this fashion, with each justice presumably developing a more accurate estimate of probability of Souter's decisive vote on overruling *Roe* as the decisional process unfolded.

The point of all this is that the accuracy of the estimates of positions of each of the other justices will differ significantly on a Court with stable membership relative to a Court experiencing turnover. When the Court's mem-

---

17. The process by which a Court of nine justices continually updates probability estimates of the preferences of other justices can be described in Bayesian terms. For a general introduction, see Richard D. Friedman, *Assessing Evidence*, 94 Mich. L. Rev. 1810 (1996). Each justice is continually reassessing the probability that the other justices will take a particular position with respect to particular issues. The process involves continuously updating initial probability estimates as new information comes in. The more opportunities there are to recalibrate the initial estimates, the more accurate the final estimate of probability becomes.

bership is stable, each additional year in which the nine justices sit together represents an increase in their collective information about the probable behavior of the others. Probability estimates continually improve in their predictive accuracy, although presumably at a diminishing rate. For a Court experiencing turnover, in contrast, each new appointment means that the other justices must start from scratch in developing estimates of probabilities for each new justice's position on a host of issues. Insofar as the behavior of the new justice is critical in close cases, the other justices must make crude guesses about his or her likely behavior, rendering their estimate of the overall outcome uncertain.

What this means, in practical terms, is that the justices on a changing Court will make more "mistakes" about the positions of other justices than the justices on a Court with stable membership. The senior justices on a Court in flux will be operating with inaccurate estimates of the positions of the junior justices, and the junior justices may be operating with somewhat inaccurate estimates of the positions of the senior justices (assuming that one gains information from personal interaction that goes beyond what can be learned by studying prior opinions). The mistakes created by this incomplete information will take many forms: justices will vote to grant certiorari predicting a particular outcome on the merits and the outcome will be different; the chief justice or the senior associate justice will assign opinions assuming a certain mode of analysis and the analysis will be different; justices will draft proposed opinions for the Court assuming at least four supporting votes and there will be fewer than four supporting votes. In a word, a Court in flux will perform less "efficiently" in generating new law than will a Court with stable membership.

These conjectures find support in the patterns of plurality decisions generated by the Court—the issuance of decisions in which no single opinion represents the views of a majority of the justices hearing the case. Plurality opinions can be seen as potential majority opinions that fail to materialize because of a lack of complete information about the preferences of at least four other justices. Given the high premium placed on securing five votes for a single opinion in support of judgment,[18] we can assume that immediately after conference on a case, at which point the preliminary vote on the judgment is known but no opinion has yet been drafted, the justices voting in the majority would nearly always like to see at least five votes for a single rationale. If

---

18. One of the unwritten norms of the Court is that a rationale for a judgment—an opinion—will be regarded as a binding precedent only if supported by a majority of participating justices. *See* Saul Levmore, *Ruling Majorities and Reasoning Pluralities*, 3 Theoretical Inquiries in Law 87 (2002).

the justices voting in the majority fail to achieve this result, then the reason in most cases is because someone miscalculated the views of one or more of the others in the majority. One would never expect the Court to eliminate all plurality opinions, since novel issues have a way of popping up, as to which there will inevitably be uncertainty about the positions of the justices. Also, some justices' views may change over time, creating another source of uncertainty. Nevertheless, all else being equal, a Court with stable membership should be more efficient at turning alliances of five votes for a judgment into five votes for a single opinion of the Court.

The recent history of the Court seems to confirm this hypothesis. If we look back to 1946, the Court terms that produce especially high rates of plurality decisions (five percent or more) tend to come during or just after periods of high turnover or the appointment of a new chief justice.[19] Conversely, periods characterized by low rates of plurality opinions tend to coincide with periods of stability in the Court's membership. The Rehnquist Court is particularly striking in this regard. The first six years of the Rehnquist Court, which experienced significant turnover, averaged nearly four percent plurality decisions per year; in a similar six-year period after its membership stabilized, the Court averaged only two percent plurality decisions per year.[20] A plausible explanation would be that as the membership of the Court stabilized, and the justices came to have more and better information about each other's preferences, the number of mistakes declined, and the Court's efficiency in producing precedents increased.

How would a system of staggered term limits affect the Court's decisional efficiency? Decisional efficiency seems to be largely a function of the collective knowledge of the Court. Collective knowledge, in turn, is presumably positively related to average length of service, with the important caveat that as justices get older and begin to decline in their intellectual capacities, long service may be associated with some reduction in decisional efficiency. A sys-

---

19. The years with more than five percent plurality decisions include 1948 (shortly after a new chief justice and one associate justice); 1950 (after two consecutive years of new associate justices); 1953 (new chief justice); 1971 (shortly after new chief justice and new associate justice); 1975 (new associate justice); 1988 (shortly after a new chief justice and two new associate justices); and 1995 (after three consecutive years of new associate justices). Three years do not fit this pattern: 1950, 1977, and 1979. The data are taken from *The Supreme Court Compendium* 226–27 (Table 3–5) (Lee Epstein et al., 3d ed. 2002). They undoubtedly undercount the number of plurality decisions, since "per curium" decisions are omitted.

20. *Id.* (data for years 1991–96).

tem of staggered eighteen-year term limits would reduce tenure of service from an average of 26.1 years to one of eighteen years,[21] and to this extent would reduce the overall level of knowledge of the Court. The staggering feature, however, would eliminate the bunching of significant numbers of inexperienced justices during periods of high turnover. This would eliminate any compounding effects of multiple inexperienced justices. Moreover, the fixed service-termination feature would presumably eliminate most problems of decrepitude, which would also tend to enhance overall decisional efficiency. On balance, it would seem that a staggered term limit Court with terms of at least eighteen years would tend to behave at a fairly high level of efficiency—and of course would do so on a consistent basis.

Is decisional efficiency a good thing? Ordinarily one would think that efficiency must be good, since any asset is always more valuable to society if it can be deployed more efficiently. But we are speaking here of efficiency in a specialized sense. One possible and very narrow meaning of decisional efficiency is that it refers to the rate at which a court transforms decisional opportunities into precedents. The *rate* of precedent formation may matter to the judges that sit on the court, but it is not clear that it is of great concern from a societal perspective. A court like the U.S. Supreme Court that has complete discretion over its docket can always increase the number of precedents it creates simply by granting and deciding more cases. Deciding one hundred twenty cases per year at ninety percent efficiency (producing one hundred eight precedents) would likely be more valuable to society than deciding eighty cases per year at ninety-eight percent efficiency (yielding only seventy-eight precedents).

Other, broader, definitions of decisional efficiency are conceivable. For example, one might posit that an efficient Court will produce precedents that are sound, in the sense that they faithfully account for all relevant legal authorities. But it is not clear that this kind of efficiency is an unalloyed good thing from a societal perspective either. When law is made in the common-law mode, sometimes there are benefits when the court produces decisional mutations. Most mutations are likely to prove unworkable or will operate as discordant elements in the larger doctrinal framework, and must eventually be discarded as mistakes.[22] But some may turn out to be innovations with enduring value. The *Chevron* doctrine in administrative law, for example, which

---

21. *See supra* Calabresi & Lindgren, pp. 23–24.

22. *See* Lingle v. Chevron U.S.A. Inc., 125 S. Ct. 2074 (2005) (decision by the Court repudiating language introduced in an opinion eighteen years earlier).

originated from a short-handed Court in an opinion rushed through at the end of the Term, eventually became a cornerstone of modern understanding of court-agency relations.[23]

I do not want to push these notions too far. *Ceteris paribus*, decisional efficiency is a good thing, and thus it is probably a plus for staggered term limits that they would tend to produce a relatively efficient Court. It would not be as efficient as the Rehnquist Court in its latter days of extreme stability, but it would probably be more efficient than a life-tenured Court overall, when we average together the periods of stability with the periods of flux.

The Formation of Blocks

It is likely that a Court with stable membership differs from a Court in flux in ways more profound than simply operating more efficiently in producing new precedents. A Court that sits together for a long period of time is more likely to coalesce into blocks of justices, and those blocks may grow in strength over time.[24] This at least would seem to be a plausible prediction suggested by game-theory. That literature indicates that participants in infinitely-repeated games are more likely to adopt cooperative strategies than are participants in single-play games or games with fixed termination points.[25] This literature further indicates that games of uncertain length will resemble infinitely-repeated games.[26] Finally, the literature suggests that in such an indefinitely-repeated game, strategies with higher collective payoffs for multiple players will tend over time to dominate strategies with lower collective payoffs.[27]

If Supreme Court decisionmaking can be modeled as a repeated game, it is obviously an extraordinarily complex one. Nevertheless, we can think of the Court as being engaged in a collegial game of uncertain length, the object of which is to produce precedents that advance the justices' individual policy

---

23. *See* Thomas W. Merrill, *The Story of Chevron: the Making of an Accidental Landmark*, in *Administrative Law Stories* (Foundation Press forthcoming).

24. One political scientist has argued that "cliques" would be a more accurate term, but this usage has not caught on. *See* Sidney S. Ulmer, *Toward a Theory of Sub-Group Formation in the United States Supreme Court*," 27 J. Politics 133 (1965).

25. *See generally* Robert Axelrod, *The Evolution of Cooperation* (1984); Michael Taylor, *The Possibilities of Cooperation: Studies in Rationality and Social Change* (1987).

26. *See* Douglas G. Baird et al., *Game Theory and the Law* 167 (1994).

27. *See* Randal C. Picker, *Simple Games in a Complex World: A Generative Approach to the Adoption of Norms*, 64 U. Chi. L. Rev. 1225 (1997).

preferences. Moreover, it is plausible to think that, over time, such a game will tend to produce blocks of justices who share similar preferences over a range of issues, and who discover that they can do more to advance those preferences by cooperating with other members of the block, rather than simply approaching each case on an ad hoc basis.[28] More specifically, one would predict that voting blocks of justices would form that have the capability of joining in the formation of majority opinions on a frequent basis; that the cooperation among the justices within these blocks would persist across cases; and that if the payoffs from this cooperation were high enough, the range of cases over which the coalition cooperated would very likely expand as the "game" progressed.

The possibility of cooperation among justices implies strategic behavior that goes beyond the strategic exercise of individual discretionary choices by justices, such as whether to vote to grant certiorari in a particular case or whom to assign the task of writing an opinion for the majority. Rather, it implies that justices will suppress their sincere views about outcomes of cases and about the rationales used to support outcomes in an effort to accommodate the preferences of other justices. These accommodative gestures will occur, the model suggests, to elicit or reward similar accommodative gestures by other justices on other issues or in other cases. As bonds of accommodative reciprocity begin to take hold, a block of justices that engages in this kind of reciprocating behavior will grow in strength, and will gradually begin to expand its reach into new issues and areas of law.

The exact mechanism by which an extraordinarily complex, nine-player game of uncertain duration would generate block behavior is unclear, and such an outcome is by no means guaranteed. The players may eventually learn of the benefits of forming blocks by trial and error, or they may stumble upon strategies like tit-for-tat (in which players respond to cooperation by rewarding the cooperator, and respond to defection by punishing the defector) which may conduce toward stable cooperation.[29] The relevant point for present purposes is that whatever the precise mechanism by which blocks come into existence, if the game is sufficiently complex and has multiple players, it presumably takes time to develop a cooperating block. A Court in flux is unlikely to achieve such a state, because the introduction of new players disrupts the expectations and strategies of the other players, requiring in effect that the game start over. A Court with stable membership, in contrast, may be able to

---

28. *See* Maltzman et al., *supra* n. 5 at 73, 101.

29. *See id.* at 73 ("Because justices are engaged in long-term interactions with their colleagues, we expect tit-for-tat relationships to develop.").

sustain enough rounds of play so that cooperation becomes the dominant and stable strategy within a block of justices.

The post-1994 Rehnquist Court provides an illustration of how such block behavior can emerge over time on a Court of great stability. The Court, during the period before Justice O'Connor's retirement and Chief Justice Rehnquist's death in August 2005, had congealed into two blocks of justices. One block consisted of Chief Justice Rehnquist, Justice Scalia and Justice Thomas, joined often by Justices O'Connor and Kennedy. The other block consisted of Justices Stevens, Souter, Ginsburg, and Breyer, joined occasionally by Justices O'Connor and/or Kennedy. The Rehnquist block during this period remade much of the law of constitutional federalism, including the scope of federal power under the Commerce Clause and section 5 of the Fourteenth Amendment, Tenth Amendment limitations on federal power, and state sovereign immunity from private lawsuits reflected in the Eleventh Amendment.[30] It also acted as a block in rendering significant decisions on religious accommodations, voting rights, associational rights, post-conviction relief, and, of course, the 2000 election.[31] This block reflected all the elements predicted from the game-theoretic perspective, namely, that a block formed, was persistent, and seemed to grow in strength over time, both in terms of the range of issues covered, and the degree of controversy associated with the rulings it was willing to support.

For reasons that are unclear, this majority block begun to unravel in recent years, with the second or Stevens block emerging as the more successful coalition, capturing victory in many of the high-profile decisions.[32] This shift is in no way inconsistent with the game-theoretic model, since it is clear that both blocks were competing for the votes of Justices O'Connor and Kennedy throughout this time period. Perhaps the Stevens block ultimately got the upper hand because it had four core members rather than three, making it easier to form majority coalitions. Or perhaps the Stevens block simply got better over time in figuring out how to offer reciprocal benefits to the swing

---

30. See Merrill, supra n. 1, for details.

31. See, e.g., Zelman v. Simmons-Harris, 536 U.S. 639 (2002) (upholding school vouchers); Boys Scouts of America v. Dale, 530 U.S. 640 (2000) (invalidating state effort to require scouts to admit openly gay leaders); Bush v. Gore, 531 U.S. 98 (2000) (ending challenge of Vice President Gore to election of George W. Bush); Shaw v. Reno, 509 U.S. 630 (1993) (vacating electoral districting plan where race was likely the predominating factor in determining the configuration of districts).

32. See, e.g., Grutter v. Bollinger, 539 U.S. 892 (2003); Lawrence v. Texas, 539 U.S. 558 (2003); Tennessee v. Lane, 541 U.S. 509 (2004); Gonzales v. Raich, 125 S. Ct. 2195 (2005); Kelo v. City of New London, 125 S. Ct. 2655 (2005).

justices. In any event, once Justices O'Connor and/or Kennedy began to break ranks with the Rehnquist block and join the Stevens block in several critical cases, the logic of reciprocal cooperation would lead one to expect the new majority block to become relatively more powerful, and to become entrenched and expand thereafter. Something like that may have started to happen. The 2005 vacancies, however, will unquestionably bring forth new patterns of alignment among the justices.

How would a system of staggered term limits affect the propensity of the Court to coalesce into blocks? Insofar as socialization and knowledge about the preferences of other justices are both necessary for the formation and maintenance of blocks, then staggered term limits should satisfy these pre-conditions reasonably well, for the reasons previously discussed. But on the critical cooperation variable, it is doubtful that staggered term limits (except perhaps a twenty-seven-year version) would create long enough overlapping terms of service to allow majority block formation to occur. Certainly if the Court is relatively evenly divided between two core blocks of less than full majority strength, as has been the case throughout the Rehnquist Court, any majority voting block that emerges will be very fragile, and must count on every member remaining loyal to the majority block if it to maintain its dominance.[33] Any system of appointment that removed one member from the Court every two years and injected a new member would likely be very destabilizing to such majority blocks. Each such change would threaten to subtract from the strength of one block and add to another. Moreover, each new justice, regardless of his or her jurisprudential views, would have no established bonds of reciprocity with any other justice, and hence would fit into the existing blocks in ways that are completely unpredictable. The staggering feature would thus systematically frustrate majority block formation.

The fixed service-termination date established by term limits compounds the difficulties of majority block formation. Game theorists have shown that when a long-running game has a fixed termination point, the players have an

---

33. One intriguing question is whether stable nine-member collegial courts are naturally prone to fragment into rival coalitions. In the history of the U.S. Supreme Court, the other extreme example of a stable Court is the Marshall Court, which did not fragment into rival coalitions but rather remained united throughout most of its tenure. The Marshall Court, however, was composed of seven rather than nine justices, and the seven lived and worked together in a boarding house while they were in session. See Jean Edward Smith, *John Marshall: Definer of a Nation* 286–87 (1996). Consequently, the collegial interaction on the Marshall Court did not exactly replicate the conditions that prevailed on the Rehnquist Court.

incentive to defect rather than cooperate in the final period.[34] What is worse, the players' awareness of such a final period may undermine cooperation in earlier rounds of the game as well: if players assume there will be no cooperation in the final period, this may induce them to stop cooperating in the second-to-last period, which may lead them to stop cooperating in the period before that, and so forth.[35] This would suggest that fixing a pre-established final period for every justice might systematically undermine the level of cooperation among justices.

The most recently completed term of the Court may provide an illustration of the final-period problem. For most of the term, it was widely assumed that Chief Justice Rehnquist would retire at the end, meaning that the other justices may have thought they were in a final period relationship with the chief (as it turned out they were). And indeed, for whatever reasons, Chief Justice Rehnquist was unable to secure a majority for his biggest opinion-writing assignment of the term,[36] and ended up on the dissenting end of an unusually high percentage of controversial decisions throughout the term.[37] As previously discussed, the blocks did not dissolve, but the swing justices tended to defect to the Stevens block.

Admittedly, this analysis of cooperation on a staggered-term Court is disputable. Combining a relatively lengthy term of eighteen years with consistent spacing of turnover might translate into long enough overlapping terms of service to allow "rolling blocks" of justices to form and perpetuate themselves. Although the blocks would be disrupted every two years with a new arrival and the departure of a veteran, all other justices with intermediate degrees of service would continue to interact as before, and this might be enough to generate a type of block behavior. My own sense is that this is unlikely, but only actual experience with staggered term limits would refute this possibility.

If staggered term limits would tend to frustrate block voting, then from a normative perspective this feature should count in its favor. As other contributors to this volume have stressed, it is important in a democracy that the preferences of the justices, insofar as they act as lawmakers, mirror the pref-

---

34. *See,* e.g., Baird et al., *supra* n. 26 at 167.

35. *See* Linda Cohen & Matthew Spitzer, *Term Limits,* 80 Geo. L. J. 477, 498–99 (1992) (advancing this argument in the context of legislative term limits).

36. Van Orden v. Perry, 125 S. Ct. 2854 (2005) (upholding the display of the Ten Commandments on a tablet placed on the lawn of the Texas State Capitol Building).

37. *See,* e.g., Gonzales v. Raich, 125 S. Ct. 2195 (2005); Kelo v. New London, 125 S. Ct. 2655 (2005); Granholm v. Heald, 125 S. Ct. 1885 (2005); McCreary County v. ACLU, 125 S. Ct. 2722 (2005); Roper v. Simmons, 125 S. Ct. 1183 (2005).

erences of the electorate. The principal mechanism for assuring such congruence is having justices nominated by the president and confirmed by the Senate, both of which offices are elective. This selection process should produce justices who embody a range of preferences, but over time the range should more-or-less reflect the range of preferences within the electorate. Since the justices will embody a range of preferences, it is also important how these preferences are aggregated in producing precedents. As a rule, the outcome that will most closely conform to the preferences of the electorate is the one that reflects the preferences of the median member of the multi-member decisionmaking body.[38] Which pattern of behavior by such a multi-member body is most likely to generate decisions that reflect the preferences of the median lawmaker/judge: a system of ad hoc alliances, or a system of majority block voting?

It seems fairly obvious that a system of ad hoc alliances is more likely to produce results that correspond to the views of the median lawmaker/judge and hence to correspond more faithfully to the view of the median voter. Assume the ideological preferences of the justices fall into three clusters composed of three justices each—the Left Group, the Median Group, and the Right Group (see figure 1). The ideal set of outcomes, in terms of mirroring the preferences of the public, would be for precedents to reflect the views of the Median Group. If decisions are reached by ad hoc alliances, then precedents will be formed by alliances between the Median Group and either the Right Group or the Left Group. If each case is decided ad hoc, i.e., without logrolling, then on average the precedents will tend to cluster around the views of the Median Group. Indeed, the Median Group will tend to play the Right Group and the Left Group off each other, with the result being outcomes fairly close to those preferred by the Median Group.

In contrast, assume instead that two of the groups join forces to form a majority block. This will require that the Median Group form a more-or-less stable coalition with either the Right Group or the Left Group. A Right Group-Median Group majority block would be sustained by reciprocal accommodations confined to members of these two groups, with the result that precedents would tend to reflect views intermediate between the Right Group and the Median Group. A Left Group-Median Group coalition would be sustained by reciprocal accommodations confined to members of these groups, shifting the out-

---

38. "As a rule" means that potential complications like multi-peaked preferences or different intensities of preference are ignored. *See*, e.g., Dennis C. Mueller, *Public Choice II* 65–66 (1989).

Figure 1.

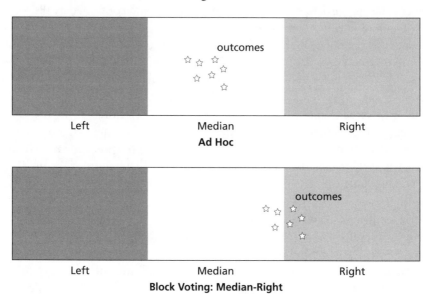

comes to those intermediate between the Left Group and the Right Group. Either way, the Court's precedents would tend to deviate from the median toward either the right or the left—to a further degree than would be the case under a system of ad hoc alliances where the Right Group and Left Group competed for the votes of the Median Group in every case.

If one favors the jurisprudential views of the Right Group, and if the majority block is composed of the Right Group and the Median Group—as was true during most of the years of the Rehnquist Court after 1994—then this would suggest a partisan reason to favor block voting. But of course, such outcomes cannot be guaranteed to last, as the Rehnquist Court has also demonstrated.

As a matter of ideal constitutional design, majority block voting is hard to defend. Insofar as staggered term limits would tend to undermine majority block voting and promote ad hoc alliances, on a more or less continuous basis, this provides a powerful reason to support such a reform. Indeed, the deleterious effect of staggered term limits on majority block voting would seem to be the most important consequence of this proposal in terms of the internal dynamics of the Court.

Conclusion

Adopting a system of staggered term limits would undoubtedly have other consequences on the internal dynamics of the Court. It would be extremely important to know, for example, what impact such a change would have on the Court's fidelity to precedent. Precedent-following or stare decisis is a very complex norm that can be seen as entailing a type of cooperative behavior.[39] But it involves cooperation not just with the present complement of justices, but also with justices of past and future generations. Thus, even if staggered term limits would weaken the proclivity toward cooperation among sitting justices, and hence would reduce the tendency toward block voting, it is not clear that it would weaken the bonds of cooperation that justices feel toward the Court as an institution. To be sure, there is evidence suggesting that Courts undergoing personnel change are more likely to overrule precedents than are stable Courts.[40] This gives rise to concern about the possible effects of an institutional change that would weaken the bonds of cooperation among justices, and, on this dimension at least, make the Court behave more like a Court in flux. But the penchant of Courts in flux to overrule precedents may be due simply to changes in collective preferences brought on by personnel change, rather than any weakening in the general fidelity justices have toward precedent. Consequently, although it would be very important to know how staggered term limits would affect the Court's attitude toward stare decisis, it is impossible (for me at least) to predict what that effect would be.

What can be predicted with confidence is that a staggered-term Court would eliminate oscillations between the behavioral traits characteristic of a stable Court and those associated with a Court undergoing personnel change. It can also be predicted, although with less confidence, that a staggered-term Court would socialize new justices to the norms of the Court almost as effectively as a stable Court, with the result that a staggered-term Court would be highly resistant to institutional change. As a normative matter, I believe this would probably be undesirable. It can further be predicted, again with less than complete confidence, that a staggered term Court would have a high level of collective knowledge—although not as high as the level of knowledge on a stable Court—and hence it would exhibit a generally high level of decisional efficiency. As a normative matter, I believe on balance that this would probably be desirable. Finally, it can be predicted—although here with the lowest

---

39. *See supra* n. 8.

40. Christopher P. Banks, *The Supreme Court and Precedent: An Analysis of Natural Courts and Reversal Trends*, 75 Judicature 262 (1992).

level of confidence—that a staggered term Court would be less prone to co-operative behavior than a stable Court, and consequently would be less likely to coalesce into majority voting blocks. As a normative matter, I believe this would be highly desirable.

Netting out the effects on internal dynamics, taking into account confidence levels and the different directions of desirability, leaves me with little faith that one can say a Court subject to staggered term limits would be clearly better or worse than a life-tenured Court. If the three effects I have discussed were the only ones that mattered, then I would be inclined to say that on balance the reform would be salutary, primarily because of the effect on majority block voting. But my confidence in my predictions is not high, especially with respect to the key variable, cooperation. And there would undoubtedly be other effects, such as on the Court's attitude toward precedent, which I am unable to foresee with any clarity. If one tends to be naturally cautious about far-reaching institutional transformations, as I am, then the uncertainties about the impact on internal dynamics provide a reason to be cautious about this proposed reform.

This is not to say that I believe the effort to raise the possibility of staggered term limits is misguided. The Supreme Court is hardly a perfect institution, and there is far too little serious discussion about how it might be reformed. Two examples that I have briefly mentioned—the Court's contraction of the size of its case load, and its delegation of case selection to a single pool of law clerks—are institutional changes of far-reaching significance. These changes were adopted with no input from the public and no public justification by the Court. The changes may have been congenial to the Court, by freeing up more time for justices to hone their rhetoric in cases of great political import. But it is not clear that they have well served the legal system of which the Court is a critical part. We need more rather than less discussion of the proper institutional design of the Court, and the debate over staggered term limits opens a window into the Court that should encourage that discussion to expand in the future.

ARGUMENTS THAT PROLONGED TENURE IS NOT A PROBLEM

THE CASE FOR LIFE TENURE

*Ward Farnsworth**

Introduction

My purpose in this essay is to offer a defense of life tenure for Supreme Court justices, and in the process to offer some new ways of thinking about the current function of life tenure and its implications. I argue that while there are some solid arguments for replacing life tenure with fixed terms, there likewise are strong arguments for leaving it in place; many of the benefits claimed for fixed terms are illusory or likely would be offset by new problems they would cause. I also discuss the case for age limits and find it somewhat stronger than the case for fixed terms.

Faster and Slower Law: A Pragmatic Account of the Function of Life Tenure

Americans live under two types of law, fast-moving and slow. The faster law is made by Congress, state legislators, and other actors subject to replacement every few years through normal political channels. The slower law mostly is made by a committee of officials called justices. (Subordinate officials known as judges make contributions as well, but my focus will be on the Supreme Court.) The fast and slow labels arise from several features of legislation and adjudication; a key feature of the Court that causes it to move slowly, and my focus here, involves turnover. Since the justices keep their jobs

---

* Professor of Law and Nancy Barton Scholar, Boston University. For more extended discussion of the arguments presented here, and fuller citations to the literature, see Farnsworth, *The Regulation of Turnover on the Supreme Court*, 2005 U. Ill. L. Rev. 407.

for a long time, it takes a long time to replace them if the public does not like what they do.

The special value of the Court as a slow lawmaker is based on distrust of short-term or even medium-term majoritarian judgments relative to long-term ones. Putting issues on a slower track helps protect them from swifter currents of opinion more likely to produce bad law, perhaps because the swift currents are more likely to have disproportionate force of the kind discussed by public choice theorists or because they represent views that seem appealing for a while but whose deficiencies become clear with time. A constitutional document may not serve much of a slowing function if the act of interpreting it is made too politically responsive. When people want things done they will find lawyers who think the Constitution allows their preferred results and fit them with robes. The slowing function arises when the authority to declare the trumping law is assigned to an institution whose members are replaced infrequently, and still more when the replacements are made through a means that provides some insulation from the public will. Rare but steady turnover on a constitutional court thus may be a superior mechanism to constitution-plus-amendment if the goal is to test the durability of an idea before adding it to a slow-moving corpus of law.

The question is whether these mechanisms of braking and entrenchment have value. Sometimes the difficulty of remaking the Court makes it harder to overthrow good and bad legal conventions alike. The attractiveness of the package depends on one's satisfaction with current legal conditions and fear of the alternatives. The Court is set up to reflect a strong sense of satisfaction with the outlines of the slower law and a corresponding interest in decelerating changes in them. Speeding up the rate of change would create winners and losers, but it is hard to be sure who they would be, and in the meantime most Americans enjoy a combination of expansive liberties and social stability that makes them understandably risk-averse. If they interested themselves in the debate over the Court's role they would find Robert Bork on the right and Mark Tushnet on the left, both dismayed by the Supreme Court's frustration of their projects; possibly our hypothetical onlookers would say that any institution capable of providing so much discouragement to both men must be doing something right.

These points can be made more concrete. A main consequence of the most common proposals for fixed terms—the proposals to have justices serve for eighteen years apiece—is that they would guarantee every two-term president at least four appointments to the Court: the ability to create a near-majority, which easily could become a majority with the addition of an interim appointment or the presence on the Court of a like-minded justice appointed some years before. This can happen already, but it usually does not. The question is whether we should ensure that it always does. A two-term president may reflect a single national mood, and I contend there is value in a Court that cannot be remade by one such gust. And as the lengths of the proposed terms get shorter, the risks become greater that a burst of political sentiment will take the slower law along with it as well as the faster—or rather that the slower law would not be much slower after all.

The likely consequences of the changes just sketched are a matter of fair debate. The important point, though, is that when advocates of term limits claim the Court has become too distant from the public, they are taking a position on how much to trust conclusions majorities reach over shorter and longer periods of time. The idea that the justices should be replaced more often needs a defense on these terms, and has not yet received it.

Senses of Accountability

Many critics of life tenure believe it has made the Supreme Court insufficiently accountable. But what do they mean? A first kind of accountability involves outcomes of specific cases. The Court might make decisions the public hates; the sooner the justices are forced to retire, the sooner they can be replaced with nominees the president thinks will reverse the disliked decisions. This often is what people have in mind when they speak of holding the Court accountable. They want *Roe v. Wade* reversed or want to prevent its reversal. But there are good reasons to avoid tampering with the Court's turnover mechanisms to make particular decisions easier to change. First, one of the valuable things courts do is make unpopular decisions that stick—decisions protecting the rights of minorities or preserving structural features of the Constitution that frustrate the majority's will but have long-run benefits. The public naturally may feel outrage when decisions of that sort are made, yet might rather endure the outrage than make it easier to convert it into reversal. At present we put a large share of trust in a body we know will let us down often instead of taking chances on a more responsive system that would allow good and bad outrage alike to carry the day and let us down in other ways. Forcing the reversal of a disliked decision by replacing the justices who made it is kept a possibility only in the very long run.

A different but related kind of accountability involves more amorphous preferences. Presidents, senators, and interested members of the public take an interest in what *sorts* of decisions the justice will make; they do not know quite what questions will arise but are anxious that they not be disappointed by the Court's answers to them. So they settle for (or object to) the appointment of types to the Court—a conservative or liberal type, a hawk or a dove. The types refer to clusters of values and preferences that a holder of them is expected to bring to bear when confronted with whatever problems arise later. Thus in the twelve years leading up to 1992 the country elected Republican presidents friendly toward notions of states' rights and skeptical of the value of a large federal government. Those presidents made five appointments to the Court. In 1995 their appointees began issuing decisions limiting congressional power and enhancing the power of the states in various ways. The decisions in these cases often owed nothing to conservative judicial philosophy, and in their details they probably were not foreseen by those involved in the appointment of the justices who made them. The decisions nevertheless were congenial to conservatives as matters of policy and can be heard as echoes of the elections that indirectly produced those justices' appointments. Those federalism cases illustrate how the Court often is responsive to the public will in a general and delayed fashion. One might object that the responsiveness should be greater, but it seems unlikely that a shortage of this type of accountability is what troubles the critics of life tenure, for many of them are originalists who decry the Court's tendency to reflect the recent political past.

Perhaps what critics of life tenure mean when they worry about accountability is that it should be easier for the public to rein in the Court when it makes bad decisions as matter of method rather than outcome. The trouble with trying to make the Court more accountable to the public as a matter of method, however, is that there is no evidence the public understands these issues or is interested in them. Nor is there much evidence that presidents are interested when they pick their nominees. There are no known cases where a president nominated a justice because he liked the nominee's theory of interpretation despite thinking he would produce disagreeable results. Meanwhile the opposite pattern is common: a president picks someone expected to produce pleasing results even though the nominee's views about interpretation, if any, are hard to discern. These practices sometimes create the illusion that theories of interpretation make an important difference: originalists fantasize that their theory is making headway on the Court when it is just the felt desirability of the outcomes produced by originalism that is making headway; when those outcomes lose their appeal, originalism loses appeal or adapts to produce other outcomes. There is no evidence to support the notion that anyone involved in the selection process is interested in interpretive theory *per se*.

Now of course one could argue that all this is unfortunate: we need a new commitment to appointing justices for their ideas about interpretation in some purer sense, not the results they would produce. The crucial point for our purposes, though, is that whether the current tendencies are good or bad, adjusting the length of the justices' terms would not be likely to change them. Indeed, life tenure and the long terms it creates is the regime most consistent with a vision of the justices as impersonal appliers of interpretive theories. Fixed terms would give us more often what we already get; they would cause the public's appetites to be satisfied more regularly, but there is no reason to think they would change the content of the appetites or the relationship between the appetites and judicial behavior.

Politicization

The meaning and causes of politicization. It often is said that the process of confirming justices has become too politicized. The hard part is figuring out what this claim means. Sometimes nominations provoke bitter combat—but only sometimes: the two most recent ones, those of Ginsburg and Breyer, did not give rise to any savagery; nor did the recent hearings on the confirmation of John Roberts. It is true, of course, that some other recent nominations have been hotly contested and that fear of such contests helped produce the tamer nominations just mentioned. This is the heart of the matter: the proceedings turn ugly when presidents put forth nominees believed to have strong, evident ideologies. The most conspicuous example is Robert Bork. Bork's difficulty, however, was not that he would be serving for life rather than for eighteen years; he was sixty years old, so he probably would not have stayed on the Court for much more than eighteen years anyway. The trouble was that he held controversial views. One can complain about the result if one thinks Bork would have made a good justice, but it is hard to see why his defeat represents a failure of the nomination process if one believes (as opponents of life tenure generally do) that nominations provide an important chance for the public to have something to say about how the Court makes its decisions.

Let us look harder at why some nominations produce bitter debate. The stakes are high when a president puts forward a nominee likely to try to change the slower law in a way that much of the country does not want. It becomes worthwhile for those who do not like the nominee to inflict costs on him, on their opponents, and on themselves to prevent him from being confirmed. If one wants to lower the heat associated with nominations, one can pick nominees who seem moderate and will not provoke aggressive efforts to derail them. Or one can be more unyielding and stand the heat. As an example of the latter approach we cannot do better than the advice once offered by Steven Calabresi: "a conservative President must at all costs keep nominating one pro-

Rule of Law Justice or judge after another."[1] Very well, but no one who urges such a strategy should be heard to complain when its opponents resist with the same ferocity. The resulting process will be a negotiation, and negotiations of such a high-stakes character usually are not enjoyed by the participants and do not put them in an attractive light. Things are said that one regrets; relationships are injured and reputations soiled; the impression that the process has become undignified and unpleasant—politicized—naturally takes hold. The unpleasantness becomes especially likely when either or both sides are committed to playing hardball, as Calabresi evidently is—an insistence on having one's way, as he says it, "at all costs."[2] Nor can it be surprising if the strategy is reciprocated by one's opponents in the bottom half of the inning.

Of course it is possible that this account complements rather than contradicts the case for limited terms; it may be that life tenure inflames the perceptions that lead to the hard results and that fixed terms would put both sides into a more giving humor. Yet it is hard to see why. There would be no evident reason for the advice we just saw Calabresi offer to change if the justices served for eighteen years, nor any reason to think the best reply to such tactics would be different. There has been no shortage of polarizing debate over controversial recent nominees to other positions where they are expected to serve for no more than a few years.

Meanwhile there is reason to worry that fixed terms would make the unappealing features of the confirmation process worse. By attaching nominating chances to presidencies they would create more natural cycles of revenge. The effect *could* work the other way: knowing that more nominations will be coming soon, everyone would show restraint; knowledge that the other player will have chances for revenge can help deter bad behavior. But games of this kind can go badly if distrust runs high and the best play for each side depends on error-prone judgments about the good faith of the other. Each comes to think the other misbehaved first and needs a lesson. We see this pattern now in nominations to the courts of appeals, and perhaps one reason we have not seen cycles quite like it in Supreme Court nominations, despite the occasional rancorous case, is that they do not arise frequently and predictably enough to provoke this structured sort of turn-taking.

A related objection to fixed terms is that they would facilitate the work of interest groups trying to influence the composition of the Court. If justices served terms of eighteen years, one no longer would speak of the *possibility*

---

1. Steven G. Calabresi, *Advice to the Next Conservative President of the United States*, 24 Harv. J. L. & Pub. Policy 369, 376–378 (2001).

2. *Id.*

that the winner of a presidential election might make appointments to the Court. Every winner would be guaranteed two of them. The stakes for the Court in every campaign thus would be higher than they currently are; interest groups would see larger expected returns from pressuring candidates to make promises about how they would use their two nominations if elected, from condemning candidates who fail to do so or who say the wrong things, from putting pressure on those who say the right things to keep their promises, and so forth. As the expected returns on political pressure rise, so will investments in creating it. Fixed terms also would make it easier to coordinate pressures farther in advance. Today vacancies on the Court arise unpredictably. Suddenly a retirement is announced; there is an outburst of political jostling; usually a nominee is named a few weeks later and confirmed within a month or two. But with fixed terms everyone would know far ahead of time when the next vacancy would arrive and what seat would be involved. Campaigns to have it filled would begin far in advance, just as a new political campaign begins as soon as the prior one ends. Of course many groups already try to build reserves of pressure in advance of retirements on the chance that they might pay off, but their labors often end up a waste of time when nobody retires. Fixed terms would eliminate that risk. Depriving pressure groups of a fixed target, as life tenure does, makes it a little harder for them to organize their efforts and concentrate their energies too pointedly.

A note on pressure to appoint the young. It sometimes has been suggested that life tenure creates too strong an incentive for presidents to choose young nominees. Although the complaint has intuitive appeal at first, its logic and empirical basis need a closer look. The average age of appointment over the past thirty years is the same as it had been during the previous one hundred eighty years: about fifty-three years old. The only recent justices who were younger than fifty when appointed were Rehnquist, who was forty-six, and Thomas, who was forty-three. Thomas's appointment might have been expected to provoke retaliatory nominations of young justices next time a Democrat got the chance. It did not happen. The next was made by President Clinton; it was Ruth Ginsburg, who was sixty. Clinton's next appointment was Stephen Breyer, who was almost fifty-six.

Why have we not had a race to the bottom? One reason is that presidents make decisions in the shadow of the confirmation process; repeated efforts to appoint forty-three-year-olds to the Supreme Court are likely to be met with public hostility because most people of that age have not accomplished enough to inspire confidence in their judgment. But probably the more important reason why presidents do not usually appoint the youngest plausible candidates they can find is that they lack incentives to do so. An actual goal of many presidents—perhaps most of them—is to maximize their political fortunes. Those fortunes will depend largely on the influence a president is perceived to have on the fortunes of his constituencies; the insights of public choice theory have their application to the selection of judges as well as to the creation of legislation. Both the president and the constituencies he worries about satisfying may have limited time horizons, applying a discount rate that makes the present value of possible changes on the Court twenty-five years away too small to matter.

It might seem to follow from these arguments that presidents *should* race to the bottom, picking the youngest plausible nominees they can find. But then it equally follows that the president's opponents in the Senate should resist those attempts. The real implication simply is that we should see more attention to the matter. Whether nominees ought to be young or old, and thus have expected terms of twenty years or forty, is a matter of fair debate, but there is no case for treating a question of such consequence as a side issue. It has more practical importance than most of the differences between nominees commonly discussed in the debates over them.

The Distribution of
Appointments among Presidents

Uneven allocation and its consequences. Probably the best argument for fixed terms is the one pressed hardest by Professor Oliver: they would spread nominations to the Court evenly among presidents.[3] The argument is impressive but not, I think, as decisive as it might seem at first. First, there are countervailing influences that help smooth out misallocations of chances to the two parties. It usually is hard to predict how someone will behave on the Court; there is noise in the process that prevents appointments from being very accurate registers of political consensus. But the more important point is that the Senate helps compensate for the lumpy way in which nominations are distributed to presidents. The Republican presidents who appointed John Stevens and David Souter wanted to avoid trouble in the Senate and so deliberately chose nominees who carried more ideological risk

---

3. Philip D. Oliver, *Systematic Justice: A Proposed Constitutional Amendment to Establish Fixed, Staggered Terms for Members of the United States Supreme Court*, 47 Ohio St. L.J. 799 (1986).

than the alternatives. The risks paid out badly for conservatives; but another way to view the results is that pressure from the Senate helped prevent flukes in the timing of justices' retirements from causing a comparable shift in the balance of ideologies on the Court. Nobody in the Senate needed to have been thinking this way at the time. They served a useful purpose just by providing friction against the president's preferences; in this way the Senate works as a hedge against the vicissitudes of election cycles and retirements from the Court. To make the practical point explicit, the idea that the Senate should not second-guess Supreme Court nominations on ideological grounds is not compatible with life tenure. Deference of that sort magnifies the effects of the uneven distribution of nominating chances between presidents.

The marginal contribution of fixed terms to political equity. Another question is how helpful fixed terms really would be in giving the Court a better political pedigree. This part of the argument for fixed terms supposes that the distribution of Supreme Court nominations ought to correspond in an intelligent way to the distribution of political will in the society at large. The premise makes enough sense, but promising two appointments to every president hardly would assure any such correspondence. Presidential elections are themselves lumpy, winner-take-all events. There is no guarantee that a political minority representing x percent of the population will carry x percent of elections. They may win none, and a large minority that repeatedly fails to win any presidential elections may not see its views represented at all on the Court. Meanwhile the narrow winner of a presidential election gets no fewer nominating chances than a winner by a landslide.

These sorts of anomalies are common features of our political system; there are various ways that fifty-one percent of some set of voters can wind up with one hundred percent of the power. But there also are mechanisms in place to check and dilute those effects. If one wants ideological control over the Court tied in a satisfying way to the ideological composition of the polity, using checks is a sounder strategy than trying to make sure every president gets the same number of appointments. The obvious check would be to shift more power in the nominating process to an institution that reflects a wider range of inputs: the Senate. We have seen that a strong role for the Senate helps mitigate the effects of the arbitrary assignment of nominations to presidents. Now we can also see that it helps tie the Court's membership to a source of political authority more satisfying than the presidency even if every president were to get two appointments. The Senate has great shortcomings as a representative institution, of course, but at least both parties always are represented there at the same time and so create possibilities for debate and compromise missing if the choice is given to the president alone. Giving two appointments to every president will make only a small contribution to political equity if the Senate has a weak role; and if the Senate's role is strong, the distribution of appointments to presidents becomes less important in any event.

If a strong role for the Senate is salutary in this way, notice that it is likely to be reduced by giving the justices fixed terms. The two appointments given to a president would likely be claimed by as his own to spend as he sees fit. He earned them. No doubt many in the Senate and elsewhere would resist this way of thinking, but the case for deference to the president's choices undoubtedly would be strengthened relative to where it currently stands; for at present the Senate justly can resist a president's aggressive nominations on the ground that the chance to make them was delivered to him by luck. By weakening this argument fixed terms would enlarge the president's powers and worsen the distortions created by putting nominations into a single person's hands.

Costs of fixed terms: enlarging the power of two-term presidents; dynamic effects. Another likely drawback of precisely allocating appointments to presidents would be the dynamic consequences: they might increase the justices' sense of obligation to carry out the wishes of whoever appointed them. We find a danger here parallel to the one concerning the Senate. If everyone knows that two seats on the Court are a spoil the president won fair and square, those seats may be regarded as his to fill in a stronger sense than we currently see; so his nominees may feel more pressure to carry out the president's agenda. They will know they owe their membership on the Court to a decision by the leader of a political party about how to spend his turn and that turns are given to the other party in regular fashion, not distributed by luck. They will be Republican appointees or Democratic appointees in a more explicit sense than they now are. Some may therefore view their own roles in a manner a little more political and a little less law-like.

There are other reasons to think fixed terms would increase the political character of the justices' work. Fixed terms resemble the arrangements in the legislative and executive branches of the government and so may cause justices to think of themselves as political office-holders in a more traditional way than they now do. Moreover, some of the proposals for fixed terms are pitched expressly as efforts to make the Court more responsive to popular will. New justices will be familiar with the rationale of such a plan if it is enacted; they will understand that they are serving fixed, limited terms precisely in order to keep the Court accountable to current political values. The implication is that the justices are supposed to give effect to those values and to popular sentiment when they make their decisions—but this is just how we do not want them thinking about their jobs. Maybe it will be possible to drown out those messages by saying the opposite to nominees during their confirmation hearings, but maybe not. In this sense switching to fixed terms is worse than would have been their adoption in the first instance.

Other Dynamic Effects: Limited Terms and Humility

Professors McGinnis and Prakash, along with Judge Silberman, want limited terms for the sake of other dynamic effects they hope they will produce.[4] Their theory is that once judges become justices they gradually stop thinking of their job as being to decide cases; they style themselves more as statesmen and soon cannot resist declaring their policy preferences as constitutional law. The first point to grasp in reply is that most of the hubris in Supreme Court opinions probably is attributable mostly to sources other than life tenure. It may be true, as McGinnis suggests, that leaving justices on the Court for a long time increases their incentive to make rulings that enlarge the Court's power because they know they will be around to enjoy it. Yet if this were quite how it worked one might expect young justices to be the most aggressive and older ones to become more deferential as they have less prospect of using any powers they accumulate for themselves. No such pattern appears to exist. A more plausible conjecture—also unsubstantiated, though McGinnis claims it as his impression—is that as some justices spend years at the Court they start to enjoy a sense that the world revolves around their decisions and then make rulings that perpetuate the feeling. A more generous reading of the emboldening phenomenon, if it exists, is that only after handling several years' worth of cases does a justice develop a strong sense of an area and feel comfortable suggesting something different; it takes a long time for justices to understand their role in the country's system of liberty. At any rate, an empirical case has yet to be made for the claim that the justices lose their humility as years go by.

Meanwhile there are reasons more conventional than life tenure why the Court's work differs from that produced by other courts. First, circuit judges write humbler opinions because they are bound by the Supreme Court's case

---

4. John O. McGinnis, *Justice Without Justices*, 16 Const. Comm. 541 (1999); Saikrishna B. Prakash, *America's Aristocracy*, 109 Yale L.J. 541 (1999); Laurence H. Silberman, *Federalist Society Symposium: Term Limits for Judges?*, 13 Harv. J.L. & Pub. Policy 669, 683–87 (Summer 1997).

law in a way that the justices are not. Second, the Supreme Court's docket does not resemble the docket of a court of appeals, which in most situations must decide every case brought to it. Many appellate cases are easy in the sense that judges with different ideologies quickly agree on how they should be resolved. The Supreme Court hears about one percent of the cases in which review is sought, and they tend to involve questions to which the legal materials furnish no conclusive answer (that is *why* they are taken for review; they provoked disagreement below). So it should not be surprising that Supreme Court opinions are less likely than ordinary appellate opinions to confine themselves humbly to the legal materials involved; and none of this would change if the justices served shorter terms.

The Question of Age Limits

Mental decrepitude. Life tenure creates a risk that justices will stay on the job after their powers of judgment have deserted them. Professor Garrow's fine study of decrepitude[5] found eleven such cases during the twentieth century and five since 1970; he makes convincing claims that some justices have stayed on the Court despite slipping below any reasonable threshold of competence one might propose for them. Garrow makes a good prima facie case for age limits, but there are some arguments against them as well. The first is that the problem of decrepitude is less serious than it sounds. Garrow believes that justices have become mentally decrepit eleven times since 1900, and in no case did the problem last more than a year or two. Thus of the nine hundred man-years of service provided by Supreme Court justices since the start of the twentieth century, perhaps ten or twenty of those years—between one and two percent of them—were tainted by serious mental deterioration.

When decrepitude did occur it was mitigated in two ways. Its impact was diluted by the presence of the eight other justices; while a decrepit justice may serve as a swing vote, he generally cannot do anything significant unless four of his colleagues go along with him. Second, the onset of mental infirmity causes the justice's responsibilities to devolve to his law clerks, who generally can keep a chambers running without a drop-off in quality remotely commensurate with the justice's drop-off in functionality. This may sound appalling, and of course there are good reasons not to want it to occur. But as a practical matter the devolution can help control—it undoubtedly *has* helped

---

5. David J. Garrow, *Mental Decrepitude on the U.S. Supreme Court: The Historical Case for a 28th Amendment*, 67 U. Chi. L. Rev. 995 (2000).

control—the consequences of decrepitude until the justice leaves the Court. Thurgood Marshall may have stayed on the Court for a period of time when he was not fully engaged in the work of his chambers. Yet it is difficult to detect a difference between the opinions bearing his name from this period and the ones that issued from his chambers ten or twenty years earlier. The implications of this seamlessness may be troubling in their own right, but that is a question for another day. The point for now is that we should pause before trading away the advantages of life tenure to address a problem that sounds bad but seems to have been, as a practical matter, relatively minor.

Another difficulty in departing from life tenure involves the question of outplacement. Most members of the Supreme Court are content to make the job of justice the last one they hold—so long as they can hold it for as long as they like. But any regime other than life tenure will push some justices out of office while they still are lucid and thus create a risk that they will use their time at the Court to angle for attractive situations afterwards. It need not be a question of bad faith; the greater hazard is a subtle bias reminding its holder that letting down one's friends now can have disappointing professional consequences later. The problem is especially important for proposals to give the justices fixed terms (as opposed to an age limit), since the result often may be to produce ex-justices still in the prime of their careers.

Some critics of life tenure believe the outplacement problem can be solved by making service on the Supreme Court a temporary form of work followed by life service on a court of appeals. But the critics err in taking for granted that a justice would accept such a designation. Life tenure is an offer, not a sentence, and perhaps not all justices would want to become circuit judges afterwards any more than former presidents want to become vice-presidents. Those who did become appellate judges would find that they were served a duller diet of cases than they were accustomed to seeing, that they were more constrained in what they could say about them, and that the world was less interested in their pronouncements. Some might be comfortable with this; others might seek more intriguing opportunities elsewhere. Apart from the remunerative lure of affiliation with firms, there would be the chance to pursue interesting positions in public service—cabinet posts, ambassadorships, and so on, the prospects for which would depend on the justice's ability to stay well-liked by the party in power. (The advocates of these proposals also overlook another nagging implication of them: a justice would be limited to eighteen years partly out of fear of mental decrepitude, but then would be assigned to a court of appeals—as if mental decrepitude there were not a concern.)

The average justice may be affected by none of these possibilities, succumbing neither to dementia nor to the temptations of career planning regardless of whether any new proposals were enacted. Both risks would exist at the margin, like most of the others discussed in this essay. Whatever the severity of the risks, however, there are stronger objections to limited terms than to age limits. A justice at the end of an eighteen-year term may still be in his sixties and thus have significant professional prospects—better prospects, at any rate, than would tempt a justice who knows he will be forced out at seventy-five. At the same time, another justice appointed later in life to an eighteen-year term may well serve *past* age seventy-five, making limited terms also less reliable than age limits as measures to reduce the risk of decrepitude.

Strategic retirement. A most bothersome feature of life tenure is that the justices—or at least those who retire before death, which includes most of them—decide for themselves when to leave the Court and thus determine who will choose their replacements. Everyone suspects that some justices have taken advantage of this by trying to retire when they can be replaced by a president of their preferred party. Most of the suspicions are founded in conjecture, but in some cases the worries seem supported by fairly reliable reporting, and Chief Justice Rehnquist said publicly that justices have a "slight preference" for leaving under a president of their own party. Here as in the case of mental decrepitude, however, it is not clear that the problem of strategic retirement is very serious in fact. There is convincing statistical evidence that it occurs, but how often is hard to say. The plausible window of retirement for a justice tends to be short enough to make such decisions hard to carry out. Some have supposed that William Douglas, Thurgood Marshall and William Brennan tried to hold out in hopes of being replaced by a Democrat; if so, they failed. Meanwhile other justices seem to enjoy their positions enough to make strategic retirement a low priority. They leave no sooner than they must. The net result during the twentieth century was that a seat on the Court rarely stayed in the hands of the same party more than twice in a row.

It seems likely in any event that most problems of strategic retirement can be met with age limits without need for fixed terms. Notice that there are two kinds of strategic retirement: justices who hang on longer than they otherwise would while waiting for a friendly president to take office, and justices who step down earlier than they otherwise would to make sure the current president names their replacements. But against the latter possibility there is a natural check. Justices do not want to leave their jobs too early; they like their positions, and the cost to them of giving up their power and prestige while they still are vigorous helps offset the benefit of knowing their replacements will share their ideologies. Thus the problem of strategic retirement more often appears to take the other form: justices waiting rather than rushing to retire. In the case of the justice who waits there is not much check on temptation; the costs to him are not very high if he decides to hang on in hopes that a like-minded president will arrive to rescue his seat. If an elderly justice goes this route he can delegate most of his work to his law clerks while continuing to enjoy the pleasures of his rank. This analysis suggests that an age limit of seventy-five probably would cure most justices of the temptation to retire strategically. It would force them out while the benefits they derive from their jobs are great enough to discourage them from leaving voluntarily any sooner.

An age limit would relieve the problem of strategic retirement in another way as well. There currently is no default assumption about when justices should leave the Court; they are expected to retire when they feel like retiring, which could be at sixty-five, seventy-five, or eighty-five. But of course the justices often may be unsure whether they quite feel like leaving. With the decision about when to leave unguided by any external criteria, it no doubt is hard for them *not* to think about who their replacement will be when considering whether to stay or go. Resistance would be easier if there were an objective benchmark suggesting the right time to leave. An age limit of seventy-five or eighty would provide such a marker—a focal point. The natural thing would be for justices to serve until seventy-five if they can; for a justice in good health to voluntarily step aside at seventy-three under a friendly president would look bad, and the fear of tainting one's legacy by that hint of corruption would discourage strategic behavior. The legal academy can help enforce the norm by heaping opprobrium on whoever defies it.

Constitutional vs. Statutory Avenues of Reform

The idea that justices generally serve on the Court until they die, choose to retire, or are impeached has always been understood as a constitutional rule. Professors Carrington and Cramton want to change that.[6] They hope to replace life tenure with fixed terms *by statute*; and one consequence of doing this would be to establish that Congress has a general ability to tinker with the lengths of the justices' terms so long as the justices continue to serve for life in some capacity on the federal courts. Calabresi and Lindgren, in their ear-

---

6. *See supra* Paul D. Carrington, *Checks and Balances: Congress and the Federal Courts*, pp. 137–179; *see infra* Roger C. Cramton, *Constitutionality of Reforming the Supreme Court by Statute*, pp. 345–360; *see infra* Paul D. Carrington & Roger C. Cramton, *The Supreme Court Renewal Act: A Return to Basic Principles*, pp. 467–471.

lier analysis, have concluded on formalist grounds that this would be unconstitutional.[7] I agree with them, but want to add a few more pragmatic notes about why.

Many of the consequences of life tenure are invisible; they are things we *have not* seen. Here is an example: even in moments of the Court's greatest unpopularity, nobody has called for Congress to jigger the justices' terms; nobody has called for this because everyone has thought that it obviously would be unconstitutional. A court-packing plan was discussed during the Roosevelt administration, but not a plan for reducing the justices' terms to, say, a few years apiece of service followed by assignment to a court of appeals or to an inactive role on the Supreme Court. Such a plan would refresh the voting membership of the Court very quickly. Before anyone dismisses it as too ridiculous to contemplate, I point out that similar suggestions have been openly made already by John McGinnis, Sai Prakash, and Laurence Silberman.[8] Nor have we had attempts by Congress to isolate individual justices and say that *this* one's service at the Court shall end, say, right now, with immediate reassignment to some other federal court.

It seems to me that all the moves just described become constitutional once one admits the logic of the Carrington-Cramton proposal. Life tenure is the only safeguard in Article III (besides the provision about pay) to prevent the kinds of retaliation I have described; if its meaning is diluted, there is no other provision to fall back on to avoid abuses. It is true that the scenarios I have sketched raise far deeper policy concerns than the eighteen-year terms now being proposed, but I do not see how one can map those different policy concerns onto any hook in the Constitution. The language to be interpreted here is quite brief: it is a reference to "good Behaviour." Once that term is defined as Carrington and Cramton suggest, then any subdistinctions, such as the idea that one can not single out individual justices, or can not make the terms as short as one or two years, have to be invented out of nowhere.

The saving distinction most often mentioned in reply to this argument is that perhaps changes to the meaning of life tenure are constitutional so long as they are prospective—so long, in other words, as they always apply only to justices still to come, and never to justices already sitting on the Court. I do not find the distinction as reassuring as others do even if it were tenable as a practical matter, since it would imply that Congress could limit future justices' terms to very brief rotations on the Supreme Court (followed by a return to a lower

---

7. *See supra* Steven G. Calabresi & James Lindgren, *Term Limits for the Supreme Court: Life Tenure Reconsidered*, pp. 15–98.

8. *Supra* n. 4.

federal court). But in any event there is a deeper problem with the distinction between prospective and retrospective efforts to redefine life tenure: it is, again, that the distinction is made up for the sake of convenience. There is no such distinction in Article III. It is offered by the proponents of fixed terms simply because it sounds sensible to them and they hope it will save their proposal from devastating objections. And yet it does not even do that; for as John Harrison suggests in his contribution to this book, even a limitation to prospective changes would allow abuses.[9] A bad-humored Congress could define life tenure as meaning "tenure on the Supreme Court for life," then confirm its favorite nominees, and then rewrite the rule on a prospective basis so that future justices (who the Congressional majority expects not to like so well) serve shorter terms. Is all this *likely* to occur? Of course not; but rules about the separation of powers generally are not written, and should not be written, for times of ordinary temper. When it is time to decide whether those boundaries have been breached, public passions tend to be running high and the dangers of self-serving interpretation are high as well. We should want everything as clear, and as capable of objective determination, as it can be made.

Finally, one might suggest that tinkering with the lengths of the justices' terms is just one of many ways that Congress can tamper with the Supreme Court within the bounds of Article III. Congress can change the number of justices; it presumably could move the Court to some less attractive location; shortening the justices' terms is just another such mechanism, no more worrisome than the others. I have some sympathy with this argument, but would note the strong custom disfavoring the use of any of these tools. Assigning the justices eighteen-year terms by statute would be like moving the Supreme Court to New York City: it would be a relatively small change, but by setting a precedent it would open up the possibility of further changes of the same sort in the future—such as moving the Court to Buffalo or giving the justices much shorter terms. I consider it a good thing that Congress does not generally feel comfortable passing legislation to bring the Court more into line; I would not welcome inroads against that custom.

Conclusion

Most claims about the consequences of life tenure and fixed terms are speculative. Terms of eighteen years would cause more frequent turnover than we

---

9. See *infra* John Harrison, *The Power of Congress over the Terms of Justices of the Supreme Court*, pp. 361–373.

now see; this may or may not have perceptible effects on the Court's output. Fixed terms might decrease the intensity of the politics that characterize the confirmation process, or might make matters worse. They would even out the chances for presidents to make nominations, a good thing, but they might cause justices to feel more responsibility to the parties who chose them. They would reduce the risks of strategic retirement and mental decrepitude, but then so would age limits. And at the same time it is not clear that either problem is great as a practical matter. These all are empirical questions, and the discussion here has shown that there are two plausible sides to most of them. The resulting uncertainties make it hard to conclude that any of these approaches is likely to produce noticeably better results than the others. Talk of the urgency of fixed terms, or the urgency of avoiding them, probably is misplaced. Other countries give fixed terms to the judges on their highest courts and seem to get along well enough; we also have gotten along well enough without them. Indeed, two out of the last four nominees to the Supreme Court at this writing (Ginsburg and Miers) were sixty years old at the time of their nominations, making it unlikely that either would serve much more than eighteen years anyway; recall that Sandra Day O'Connor recently resigned at the age of seventy-five. Other recent nominees have started younger than sixty or served until older than seventy-five, of course, but there are benefits as well as costs to slowing down the rate of turnover on the Court. It is a question of whether we value the tendencies in the law and in the political process that longer (and varying) tenure creates.

Dramatic measures are worthwhile to address problems that are clear and serious. The benefits of an age limit are fairly clear and there are few costs on the other side. It is true that age limits would make it easy to predict the day of departure for most justices many years in advance, thus facilitating the coordination of political pressures on the process. And an age limit probably would increase the temptation to appoint young justices. But these costs may be worth incurring to discourage the risks of strategic retirement and mental decrepitude. Age limits also preserve some flexibility in fashioning the expected lengths of the justices' terms while avoiding some of the drawbacks of fixed terms—the explicit assignment of appointments to presidents and other features that might increase the justices' sense that their duties are political. The case for age limits deserves serious consideration.

In closing, note that there are some arguments for life tenure I have not considered here—viz., that justices who serve for long periods of years come to be more protective of liberties over time, perhaps because they see at length how vulnerable the citizenry is to the legislative and executive branches. I regard those arguments as strong, but whether they appeal to the reader naturally will depend on whether the reader shares this preference for a protective Supreme Court—an ideological position. As this essay has shown, however, there are powerful arguments for retaining life tenure even if that position is not shared.

Protecting and Enhancing the U.S. Supreme Court

*David J. Garrow**

What most troubles the present-day U.S. Supreme Court? What harms the quality of its judicial performance and damages its public reputation? Many assert that the infrequency of regular turnover in the Court's membership in and of itself has a seriously detrimental impact on the Court. They cite the absence of any judicial vacancies between 1994 and 2005, and additionally assert that since 1970, justices have remained on the Court far longer than was the norm at any earlier time in American history.

But the increased duration of judicial service, per se, has occasioned almost no public criticism at all in recent years. Whatever one may think of the jurisprudential contributions of John Paul Stevens, Justice Stevens has not been the target of any critical commentary asserting that he has overstayed his welcome even as his judicial service has moved past the thirty-year mark. Seventy years ago the argument was common that the "Nine Old Men" of the Supreme Court were largely and increasingly out of touch with the social and political trends of the 1930s,[1] but no such assault whatsoever has been mounted over this past decade of unusual judicial stability, and none appears to be in the offing. Some might have been tempted to argue that the Rehnquist Court's so-called "federalism revolution" reflected a fundamentally "back to the past" denial of the rapidly increasing interconnectedness of modern life, but the Court's recent suspension of that pursuit most decisively blunts any such suggestion.[2] Indeed, any fair-minded overview of the Rehnquist Court's record

---

* Senior Research Fellow, Homerton College, University of Cambridge, CB2 2PH.

1. *See*, e.g., Drew Pearson and Robert S. Allen, *The Nine Old Men* (Doubleday 1936).

2. *See* Nevada Department of Human Resources v. Hibbs, 538 U.S. 721 (2003), Tennessee v. Lane, 124 S. Ct. 1978 (2004), and Gonzales v. Raich, 2005 WL 1321358 (2005).

would readily acknowledge that on any measure of up-to-date social-consciousness, many of the Court's most notable decisions have been criticized—including sometimes from within—for being too much in accord with popular present-day sentiments, rather than too little.[3]

At the same time that the average duration of service on the Court has grown considerably over the past three decades, the number of cases annually argued and decided has plummeted by fully half, from a mid-1970s norm of approximately one hundred fifty such cases per term to an early twenty-first century average of about seventy-five. In addition, the creation and growth of the "cert pool," whereby each petition for certiorari is summarized and evaluated for eight Justices—all save John Paul Stevens—by one single clerk has further dramatically lessened the Court's cumulative work load.

But a third notable development has been the doubling in the number of young law clerks—from two to four—available to each Justice since 1970. That increase—to three clerks apiece in 1970, and then to four in 1976 (although Chief Justice Rehnquist alone continued to appoint only three)—has occasioned relatively little scholarly comment, yet it has dramatically increased the Court's work force at the same time as the work load itself has been shrinking.

All three of these changes—longer service, fewer cases, more clerks—are arguably *less* important, however, than a far more damaging and dangerous development which at times does indeed seriously threaten the Court, namely justices who are not doing their own work. This problem is of course not by any means entirely a post-1970 occurrence, and it manifests itself in two distinct but sometime related fashions—justices who are too decrepit to remain fully involved in cases pending decision, and justices who delegate substantive initiative for their votes and opinions to their clerks in the absence of any mental or medical disability.

Both of these two failings were manifest on the Court well prior to 1970. The history of mentally decrepit justices reaches from John Rutledge in the final years of the eighteenth century[4] through Robert C. Grier[5] and Stephen J. Field[6] in the latter part of the nineteenth to Joseph McKenna[7] and Charles

---

3. *See,* e.g., Romer v. Evans, 517 U.S. 620 (1996), Grutter v. Bollinger, 539 U.S. 306 (2003), Lawrence v. Texas, 539 U.S. 558 (2003), and Roper v. Simmons, 2005 WL 464890 (2005).

4. *See* David J. Garrow, *Mental Decrepitude on the U.S. Supreme Court: The Historical Case for a 28th Amendment,* 67 U. Chi. L. Rev. 995, 998–1000 (2000).

5. *Id.* at 1003–05.

6. *Id.* at 1008–11.

7. *Id.* at 1012–16.

E. Whittaker[8] in the twentieth. On the other hand, Chief Justice Fred M. Vinson was in no way decrepit during his service from 1946 to 1953, but the historical record makes clear that Vinson handed off to his law clerks the major portion of his work on Court opinions that were issued in his name.[9] Justice Frank Murphy, who likewise allowed almost all of the work on his opinions to be carried out by his clerks,[10] certainly suffered from a seriously debilitating medical condition—drug addiction—during a significant portion of his Supreme Court career.[11]

The post-1970 era, however, has featured two especially stark examples of judicial failure: the publicly visible mental disability of Justice William O. Douglas in 1975 following a serious stroke,[12] and the far less dramatic scandal of Justice Harry A. Blackmun increasingly allowing his law clerks to hold greater and greater sway over his opinions during the 1980s and early 1990s.[13] In addition, at least three other justices since 1970—Hugo Black,[14] Lewis Powell,[15] Thurgood Marshall[16]—have suffered mental decrepitude that seriously impaired their ability to do their jobs, and Justice Marshall was handing off most of his work on opinions to his law clerks even well prior to when his ability to understand the cases before the Court began to fail.[17]

---

8. *Id.* at 1045–50.

9. *See* Philip B. Kurland, *Book Review*, 22 U. Chi. L. Rev. 297, 299 (1954), and Dennis J. Hutchinson, *The Man Who Once Was Whizzer White: A Portrait of Justice Byron R. White* 206 (1998).

10. *See* Sidney Fine, *Frank Murphy: The Washington Years* 162 (1984) ("Murphy expected his clerks to play a major part in the writing of his opinion[s].... Frequently, the clerks wrote the opinion[s] with very little if any guidance from the justice, and Murphy then revised the draft or perhaps accepted it without change"). *See also* David J. Garrow, *"The Lowest Form of Animal Life"?: Supreme Court Clerks and Supreme Court History*, 84 Cornell L. Rev. 855, 865 n. 72 (1999) (collecting additional sources).

11. *See* Garrow, *supra* n. 4 at 1027–28.

12. *See id.* at 1052–56.

13. *See* David J. Garrow, *The Brains Behind Blackmun*, Legal Affairs 26–34 (May–June 2005). *See also* Linda Greenhouse, *Becoming Justice Blackmun* 148–49, 176–79 (2005), Jeffrey Rosen, *A Pivotal Justice Less Than Supremely Confident*, N.Y. Times E43, (May 6, 2005) (reviewing Greenhouse), and David J. Garrow, *The Accidental Jurist*, The New Republic 36–41, (June 27, 2005 (reviewing Greenhouse).

14. *See* Garrow *supra* n. 4 at 1050–52.

15. *Id.* at 1069–70.

16. *Id.* at 1072–80.

17. *See* John C. Jeffries, Jr., *Justice Lewis F. Powell, Jr.* 260, 615 (1994); and Garrow, *supra* n. 4 at 1072.

Even the most charitable review of Supreme Court history readily reveals that Justices unable or otherwise disinclined to exercise full initiative over the obligations of their job have been a serious and recurring institutional problem. But that problem also has been, and remains, one that draws visible attention only when an undeniable disability such as Justice Douglas's forces the issue onto the public agenda. In contrast, the amount and intensity of expressly *ideological* criticism and debate directed at the Court is nowadays at an all-time historical high, far exceeding what transpired during the 1937 Roosevelt "Court-packing" controversy or any of the several bouts of "Impeach Earl Warren" bombast that occurred between the mid 1950s and the late 1960s.

The Court has become the most popular piñata in the increasingly angry, partisan, and ideologically-driven warfare that presently consumes U.S. politics at the very same time that the Court itself repeatedly has demonstrated both mainstream moderation in its decisionmaking and a decided aversion to unnecessarily provoking cultural warriors. Fans of Justice Antonin Scalia, like the Justice himself, will cavil at the assertion that rulings like *Planned Parenthood v. Casey*,[18] the *VMI* case,[19] *Romer*, *Grutter*, and *Lawrence* reflect political moderation, just as millions of liberals remain convinced that *Bush v. Gore*[20] was anything but unprovocative.

Yet as the Court's all-but-embarrassing "duck" in the 2004 *Newdow* pledge of allegiance case[21] dramatically highlighted, the Rehnquist Court was quite eager to practice self-abnegation when doing so served to avoid stepping into the cultural or political crosshairs during the run-up to a hotly-contested national election. Commentators such as Jeffrey Rosen can rightly assert that the Court, particularly in many of its pre-2003 federalism cases, repeatedly betrayed an attitude of "judicial imperialism,"[22] but there is no denying that in most of its high-visibility rulings, the Court consistently has sought to minimize the extent of political controversy generated by its decisions.

One important but little-acknowledged reason for why today's Supreme Court has become such a popular political whipping-boy is because of the degree to which those who ought to be most energetically defending the Court's

---

18. 505 U.S. 833 (1992).

19. U.S. v. Virginia, 518 U.S. 515 (1996).

20. 531 U.S. 98 (2000).

21. Elk Grove Unified School District v. Newdow, 542 U.S. 1 (2004).

22. *See,* e.g., Jeffrey Rosen, *Getting Over Our Depression*, N.Y. Times Book Review 16 (March 11, 2001); *See also* Rosen, *Pride and Prejudice*, The New Republic 16, (July 10–17, 2000); Rosen, *The End of Deference*, The New Republic 39 (November 6, 2000); and Rosen, *Sister Act*, The New Republic 14 (June 16, 2003).

exercise of its judicial review power have increasingly acquiesced in or expressly endorsed assertions that the muscular exercise of judicial power should be reined in. This disappointing phenomenon is in part an understandable but misguided reaction to the conservative judicial activism manifested in the pre-2003 Rehnquist Court federalism cases, as well as in *Bush v. Gore*, and it unfortunately has found significant encouragement, and supposed justification, in ill-informed analyses that seek to disparage the social utility of landmark judicial decisions including even *Brown v. Board of Education*.[23] This sad misuse of history has produced a certain attitude of "c'est la vie" among liberal constitutionalists who are now forsaking the progressive vision of *Carolene Products*[24] and musing publicly about whether the Court's power of judicial review is truly desirable.[25]

This attenuation or indeed abandonment of support for the Court from what still should be its most resolute defenders has left the Court more exposed to emotive, partisan controversy than at any time in the past century, including 1937. These defections, compounded by the seemingly partisan division exhibited in *Bush v. Gore*, have placed the Court in the midst of a political maelstrom that its justices are absolutely helpless to extract it from.

From the long-term vantage point of a historian, then, what the present-day Court most needs is a surcease in the external warfare that threatens to force more and more partisan politicization upon it, along with whatever reforms might best insure that present and future justices alike are carrying out their judicial responsibilities to a standard that Justices Douglas, Marshall, and Blackmun all at times failed to meet. But into this mix we now have interjected the claims that (a) the justices, their work-habits aside, are staying too long, that (b) they are insufficiently responsive to current political and social

---

23. 347 U.S. 483 (1954). *See* Gerald Rosenberg, *The Hollow Hope: Can Courts Bring About Social Change?* (1991); Michael J. Klarman, *Brown, Racial Change, and the Civil Rights Movement*, 80 Va. L. Rev. 7 (1994); and Klarman, *From Jim Crow to Civil Rights: The Supreme Court and the Struggle for Racial Equality* (2004). *But see* David J. Garrow, *Hopelessly Hollow History: Revisionist Devaluing of Brown v. Board of Education*, 80 Va. L. Rev. 151 (1994) (critiquing the Rosenberg and Klarman claims), and Garrow, *"Happy" Birthday, Brown v. Board of Education? Brown's Fiftieth Anniversary and the New Critics of Supreme Court Muscularity*, 90 Va. L. Rev. 693, 722–29 (2004) (critically reviewing *From Jim Crow to Civil Rights*).

24. U.S. v. Carolene Products Co., 304 U.S. 144, 153 n. 4 (1938).

25. *See, e.g.,* Mark Tushnet, *Taking the Constitution Away From the Courts* (1999). *See also* Richard A. Posner, *Appeal and Consent*, The New Republic 36 (August 16, 1999) (reviewing Tushnet). *But see* Erwin Chemerinsky, *Losing Faith? America Without Judicial Review?*, 98 Michigan L. Rev. 1416 (2000) (critically reviewing Tushnet).

trends, that (c) when they do retire, they increasingly are manipulating the timing of their departures for partisan advantage, and (d) that newly-named justices are increasingly too young.

These contentions are mustered together in an attempt to advance an argument that non-renewable eighteen-year terms for each justice, occurring in a once-every-two-years rotation, are precisely the structural reform that the Supreme Court most needs.[26] Advocacy of term-limits for the justices is not wholly new. Calls for ten-year terms reach back almost two decades,[27] as does at least one recommendation for a fourteen-year term.[28] Indeed, there is nothing entirely new even in a proposal for eighteen-year terms, as Professor Oliver advanced just such a suggestion in 1986[29] and additional endorsements followed in the late 1990s and early 2000s.[30]

In 2004 two University of Virginia Law School students authored the most extensive proposal for eighteen-year terms since Professor Oliver's.[31] Like Oliver, they readily acknowledged that "[e]nding life tenure would require a constitutional amendment,"[32] but they attempted to buttress their case by insisting that so-called "strategic retirements"—departures of a justice from the bench timed to allow a politically-sympathetic president to nominate another like-minded successor—have been "practically universal since 1968"[33] and represent "a problem in need of an immediate solution."[34]

---

26. *See infra* Paul D. Carrington & Roger C. Cramton, *The Supreme Court Renewal Act: A Return to Basic Principles*, pp. 467–471.

27. *See* Doug Bandow, *End Life Tenure for Judges*, N.Y. Times 27 (September 6, 1986); Gregg Easterbrook, *Geritol Justice*, The New Republic 17 (August 19–26, 1991).

28. *See* Sanford Levinson, *Letter to the Editor*, N.Y. Times A26 (October 15, 1986).

29. *See* Philip D. Oliver, *Systematic Justice: A Proposed Constitutional Amendment to Establish Fixed, Staggered Terms for Members of the United States Supreme Court*, 47 Ohio State L. J. 799 (1986).

30. *See* John Gruhl, *The Impact of Term Limits for Supreme Court Justices*, 81 Judicature 66 (1997); L. A. Powe, Jr., *Go Geezers Go: Leaving the Bench*, 25 Law and Social Inquiry 1227, 1235 (2000); Akhil Reed Amar & Steven G. Calabresi, *Term Limits for the High Court*, Washington Post A23 (August 9, 2002); Amar & Vikram David Amar, *Should U.S. Supreme Court Justices Be Term Limited?*, Findlaw, August 23, 2002, available at <http://writ.news. findlaw.com/amar/20020823.html>.

31. James E. DiTullio & John B. Schochet, *Saving This Honorable Court: A Proposal to Replace Life Tenure on the Supreme Court With Staggered, Nonrenewable Eighteen-Year Terms*, 90 Va. L. Rev. 1093 (2004).

32. *Id.* at 1097.

33. *Id.* at 1101.

34. *Id.* at 1110.

Serious questions of interpretive accuracy mar that contention. Granted that Chief Justice Warren and Justices Douglas, Brennan, and Marshall all appear to have adopted such a strategy, it is indisputable that all four of them *failed* in the attempt, with the choices of their successors going to Republican Presidents Richard M. Nixon, Gerald R. Ford and George H. W. Bush. Justices Hugo L. Black and John M. Harlan both retired on the very verge of death, and no evidence suggests that the timing of Justice Potter Stewart's surprise retirement in 1981 was at all ideologically motivated.[35] Chief Justice Warren E. Burger's 1986 departure may well have been informed by such calculations, but Justice Lewis F. Powell, Jr.'s 1987 one clearly was not.[36] Justices Byron R. White and particularly Harry A. Blackmun may well have found it attractive to retire during a Democratic presidency, but few observers would categorize White as a liberal, and Blackmun originally had been a Republican nominee.

Most of DiTullio and Schochet's contentions about "strategic retirements" fare very poorly indeed when compared to the far less result-oriented analysis presented by Professor Saul Brenner, well-known as a careful student of Supreme Court history.[37] As Brenner persuasively demonstrates, sitting justices since 1937 have time and again delayed and postponed their retirements rather than step down at ideologically advantageous earlier opportunities.[38]

The Virginia authors further assert that "youth has been elevated from one factor among many to one of the most important considerations" in the selection of nominees,[39] but that contention too suffers badly when compared with the conclusions reached by other scholars. As Professor Ward Farnsworth has reported, "The average age of appointment over the past thirty years is the same as it had been during the previous 180 years: about fifty-three years old."[40] Selective examination allows one to highlight how unusually young Justice Clarence Thomas was at the time of his nomination, but no one can seriously contend that the two subsequent nominees, Ruth Bader Ginsburg and Stephen G. Breyer, were selected with youthfulness in mind. New Chief Jus-

---

35. *See* Garrow *supra* n. 4 at 1066.

36. *See* Jeffries *supra* n. 17 at 538–44. *See also* Garrow *supra* n. 4 at 1069–70.

37. *See*, e.g. Saul Brenner, *The Memos of Supreme Court Law Clerk William Rehnquist: Conservative Tracts, or Mirrors of His Justice's Mind?*, 76 Judicature 77 (1992).

38. Saul Brenner, *The Myth That Justices Strategically Retire*, 36 Social Science Journal 431 (1999). *See also* Ward Farnsworth, *The Regulation of Turnover on the Supreme Court*, U. Ill. L. Rev. 407, 447–450.

39. DiTullio & Schochet, *supra* n. 31 at 1113.

40. Farnsworth, *supra* n. 38 at 429.

tice John G. Roberts, Jr., joined the Court at age fifty, but given Roberts's professional resume, his relative youth occasioned only modest comment.

The Virginia students' call for the imposition of non-renewable eighteen-year terms has now been adopted and expanded by Professors Paul D. Carrington and Roger C. Cramton in their proposal for a "Supreme Court Renewal Act." Carrington and Cramton declare that they want to increase "the accountability of the Court to the political process"[41] because of how the Court "has come to exercise powers over the lives of citizens that in important respects exceed those of the other branches of the federal government and even more those of the states."[42]

That statement gives more than a gentle hint of the political sentiments that appear to underlie the Carrington-Cramton proposal, and an article written by Professor Carrington six years earlier further illuminates those underpinnings.[43] Explaining that he wanted to "dispel undue reverence for the Court,"[44] Carrington asserted that "a constitutional amendment to correct excessive judicial independence is long overdue."[45] While remarking that imposing a "maximum age of seventy" on the justices "is justified,"[46] Carrington called term limits a "sound" idea and endorsed either a fifteen or eighteen-year term.[47]

Carrington and Cramton have tried to argue that their present proposal for non-renewable eighteen-year terms can be implemented by statute rather than requiring the adoption of a constitutional amendment. However, the overwhelming consensus of the critical commentary that has appeared since they first stepped forward, even from those who otherwise support the substance of their plan, undeniably indicates that only a change in the Constitution itself could properly convert Justices of the Supreme Court into simply lesser Article III federal judges.[48]

With all due respect to Carrington and Cramton, however, by far the best and most extensive argument on behalf of a constitutional amendment mandating non-renewable eighteen-year terms is that now advanced elsewhere in

---

41. *See infra* Carrington & Cramton, pp. 467–471 [March 5, 2005 ms. p. 2].

42. *Id.*

43. Paul D. Carrington, *Restoring Vitality to State and Local Politics By Correcting the Excessive Independence of the Supreme Court*, 50 Ala. L. Rev. 397 (1999).

44. *Id.* at 419.

45. *Id.* at 397.

46. *Id.* at 457.

47. *Id.* at 454, 456.

48. *See*, e.g., Steven G. Calabresi & James Lindgren, *Supreme Gerontocracy*, Wall Street Journal A12 (April 8, 2005).

this volume by Professors Calabresi and Lindgren.[49] Just like Carrington and Cramton, however, Calabresi and Lindgren clearly show their political stripes, stating that "the modern Supreme Court ought to be made more democratic and responsive to the popular understanding of the Constitution's meaning."[50] Eighteen-year terms, they write, "would make the Supreme Court a more democratically accountable institution,"[51] since life tenure "makes it too hard for democratic majorities to bring the Supreme Court into line with their understandings of constitutional meaning."[52]

Calabresi and Lindgren's argument certainly qualifies as an example of "popular constitutionalism," perhaps the legal academy's most overrated fad in recent memory, but Calabresi and Lindgren's version of popular constitutionalism is one that even such a self-professed textualist as Justice Scalia could enthusiastically embrace. Invoking the specter of "the lawyer class in this country"[53] in words that directly hearken to Justice Scalia's own emotionally fervent warnings,[54] Calabresi and Lindgren proclaim that "we believe the general public is more likely than are nine life tenured lawyers to interpret the Constitution in a way that is faithful to its text and history."[55]

While from one perspective that declaration may appear to be a remarkable and perhaps unprecedented example of lawyerly humility, Calabresi and Lindgren's agenda is of course ideologically political, not professionally reformist. "The American public is now more committed than are lawyerly elites

---

49. *See supra* Steven G. Calabresi & James Lindgren, *Term Limits for the Supreme Court: Life Tenure Reconsidered*, pp. 15–98. Calabresi and Lindgren reiterate, as they previously warned in their *Wall Street Journal* op-ed, *supra* n. 48, that "statutorily imposed term limits on Supreme Court justices are unconstitutional" and that "the only way to realize a system of Supreme Court term limits is by passage of a constitutional amendment." Calabresi & Lindgren, *Term Limits*, *supra* pp. 15–98. All quotations to the Calabresi & Lindgren essay are to their manuscript pages, from which I understand some deletions and alterations have been made for publication in this book.

50. *Id.* at [ms. pp. 45–46]. Notwithstanding that admission, Calabresi and Lindgren nonetheless profess that "[o]ur term limits proposal is emphatically not a partisan idea." *Id.* at [ms. p. 77].

51. *Id.* at [ms. p. 57].

52. *Id.* at [ms. p. 70].

53. *Id.* at [ms. p. 57].

54. *See*, e.g., Romer v. Evans, 517 U.S. 620, 652 (1996) (Scalia, J., dissenting) ("the lawyer class from which the Court's Members are drawn"), *id.* at 636 (Scalia, J., dissenting) ("the elite class from which the Members of this institution are selected"), Lawrence v. Texas, 539 U.S. 558, 602 (2003) (Scalia, J., dissenting) (a Supreme Court "which is the product of a law-profession culture").

55. *See supra* Calabresi & Lindgren, pp. 15–98 [ms. p. 57].

to the notion that constitutional cases should be decided based on text and history,"[56] they claim, and thus "augmenting public control over the Court will lead to more decisions grounded in text and history than are arrived at by life-tenured lawyers."[57] In other words, "enhancing popular control over the Court's constitutional interpretations will actually lead to better decisions than are produced by the current system."[58]

"Better" is a highly revealing word, and reflects Calabresi and Lindgren's hope that non-renewable eighteen-year terms will produce decidedly different, more traditionalist, or in other words more politically conservative rulings than a Court composed of life-tenured Justices would issue. With that acknowledgement, or confession, the game is up: the "better" Supreme Court that Calabresi and Lindgren seek, like Carrington and Cramton, is not one where "better" would mean nine fully competent justices always exercising complete authorial initiative over the opinions issuing in their names, but one that would be dramatically more conservative in its judicial behavior.

Not to be unnecessarily impolite about it, but it thus becomes all too undeniably clear that the present initiative for Supreme Court term-limits is in its essence an ideologically-motivated "Trojan Horse" masquerading as a non-partisan modernization reform. Furthermore, Calabresi and Lindgren's design would, if adopted, intensely heighten the partisan politics that already threaten to swamp the Court's commitment to the rule of law. "The popular understanding of the Constitution's meaning will clearly be best represented," they frankly assert, by a political party that wins consecutive national elections, and they conclude that "it is only proper than this dominant party be able to make the Supreme Court reflect its values" by having the power to nominate no fewer than four new Justices.[59]

---

56. *Id.* at [ms. p 79]. They also passingly but tellingly volunteer that sometimes "[t]he public may be fooled, as it was in the Bork nomination." *Id.* In fact, a far more powerful argument can be made that Judge Bork's unsuccessful confirmation hearings revealed all too clearly to a wide swath of the American people just how deeply unpalatable the constricted reading of the Bill of Rights offered by "textualists" and "originalists" actually is. *See*, e.g., David J. Garrow, *Liberty and Sexuality: The Right to Privacy and the Making of Roe v. Wade* 669–71 (rev. ed. 1998) (detailing how unpopular Judge Bork's 1987 testimony criticizing the constitutional right to privacy was).

57. *See supra* Calabresi & Lindgren, pp. 15–98 [ms. p. 79].

58. *Id.* at [ms. p. 57].

59. *Id.* at [ms. p. 74]. Calabresi and Lindgren also revealingly note that Calabresi, but not Lindgren, "would support a constitutional amendment that authorized a two-thirds majority of both houses of Congress to override judicial decisions." *Id.* at [ms. p. 77]. What more could Tom DeLay dream of?

This starkly partisan belief that seats on the U.S. Supreme Court should rightly be "political spoils" that belong to whoever wins the White House is a startlingly consistent theme among term-limits advocates. The Virginia students complained that a random distribution of Supreme Court vacancies across differing presidencies constitutes "unfairness to the voters who elect a given president to a given term."[60] Any such "unfairness," however, could occur only if voters believed and expected that nominations to no fewer than two Supreme Court seats should be part and parcel of each presidential election victory in much the same way as are nominees to executive branch Cabinet posts.

Calabresi and Lindgren manifest a desire identical to that of the Virginia authors, one of "equalizing the impact that each President has on the composition of the Court."[61] At the same time, however, they insist that "we do not want to encourage Justices or the public to think of particular seats as belonging to one party or the other,"[62] and they readily admit that "bitter confirmation battles politicize and generally degrade the prestige of the Court."[63] Their prescription, of course, calls for Supreme Court confirmations to occur at least every other summer, in odd-numbered years,[64] and they concede that "[h]aving such an intense political event" occur so often and so predictably "would cumulatively increase the political nature of confirmations."[65]

The two Northwestern professors nonetheless maintain that the increased frequency of Supreme Court confirmations "will make each and every appointment less important politically," thereby "reducing the politicization of the process" in the long run.[66] That claim, frankly, amounts to nothing more than a wishfully hopeful assertion, and one that is persuasively countered by Professor Farnsworth's argument that "fixed terms would make the unappealing features of the confirmation process worse," not better.[67] As he emphasizes, "with fixed terms everyone would know far ahead of time when the next vacancy will arrive and what seat will be involved."[68] Furthermore, Farnsworth persuasively observes that "fixed terms would increase the political character of the Justices'

---

60. DiTullio & Schochet, *supra* n. 31 at 1117.
61. *See supra* Calabresi & Lindgren, *Term Limits,* pp. 15–98 [ms. p. 57].
62. *Id.* at [ms. p. 51].
63. *Id.* at [ms. p. 30].
64. *Id.* at [ms. p. 4].
65. *Id.* at [ms. p. 59].
66. *Id.*
67. Farnsworth, *supra* n. 38 at 433.
68. *Id.* at 434.

work,"[69] for nominees would be presumptively viewed as partisan representatives of the president who selected them. "They will be Republican appointees or Democratic appointees in a more explicit sense than they are now."[70]

In addition, Farnsworth presciently highlights another serious but little-discussed side-effect that the presidential-spoils justification for term-limited justices would bring about. By amending the Constitution to guarantee each four-year president at least two Supreme Court nominees, "the case for deference to the president's choices undoubtedly would be strengthened relative to where it currently stands" with respect to the behavior of U.S. Senators.[71]

Of course the entire debate over implementing a non-renewable eighteen-year limited term for Justices is made largely academic by one simple and painfully obvious fact: the extreme difficulty of winning the adoption of *any* amendment to the U.S. Constitution, never mind as lengthy and highly-complicated a one as this initiative necessarily would require. The exceptionally long odds on prevailing suggest that no appreciable forward motion is likely to be realized absent the sort of highly-visible judicial crisis that Justice Douglas's 1975 disability last represented. Professors Carrington and Cramton's efforts notwithstanding, no public outcry over the length of justices' service has arisen even in the wake of Chief Justice Rehnquist's serious bout with thyroid cancer.

Looked at in a comparative, long-term perspective, the prospects of so complicated an amendment as the implementation of term limits would entail are very poor indeed, no matter how much academic cheerleading its conservative proponents can muster. Even a far simpler proposed amendment, which would have imposed a mandatory retirement age of seventy-five for Supreme Court justices, failed to win congressional approval in the early 1950s notwithstanding the hearty and energetic support of the extremely influential leadership of the American Bar Association.[72] The ABA's degree of influence within Congress at that time far outstripped anything that nowadays can be brought to bear on behalf of a term-limits constitutional amendment, and even the advent of extensive new historical analyses detailing how a mandatory-retirement age of seventy-five could have saved the Court from a long list of historical embarrassments has done little indeed to spark any resurgence of widespread interest in a constitutional amendment imposing such an age-limit.[73]

---

69. *Id.* at 438.

70. *Id.* at 437.

71. *Id.*

72. *See* Garrow, *supra* n. 4 at 1028–43.

73. *But see* Tony Mauro, *Geriatric Justices*, Legal Times 51, April 2, 2001; and John Dean, *When Supreme Court Justices Refuse to Retire* <http://writ.findlaw.com/dean/20010720.html> (July 20, 2001).

Calabresi and Lindgren acknowledge that "the problem of mental decrepitude on the Court is a serious one" and indeed is "worsening,"[74] but they nonetheless "oppose a mandatory retirement age" since it would "blindly discriminate[]...on the basis of age."[75] Termination of active service at age seventy-five would of course explicitly "discriminate" against aging justices in precisely the same way that existing U.S. law, without any hint of controversy whatsoever, presently terminates the active service of federal firefighters at age fifty-five,[76] of air traffic controllers at age fifty-six,[77] and of all federal law enforcement officers at age fifty-seven.[78] In addition, in a gesture that some but certainly not all current justices would endorse, Calabresi and Lindgren admit that Australia, Canada, England, Germany, India, Japan, and Russia all presently impose mandatory judicial retirement at ages ranging from sixty-five to seventy-five.[79]

It is difficult to resist the supposition that if proponents of an eighteen-year term-limit for justices were truly interested *only* in enhancing and ensuring the justices' ability to do their work, rather than in altering control of the Court so as to generate ideologically "better" decisions,[80] they would be far less dismissive of a constitutional amendment mandating retirement at age seventy-five. Indeed, there is no denying that each of the two most extensive recent scholarly inquiries into the manner and condition in which justices leave the Supreme Court independently concluded that approval of a constitutional amendment imposing retirement at age seventy-five would be highly desirable.

My own article on that topic is well known,[81] but Professor Artemus Ward's 2003 book, *Deciding to Leave: The Politics of Retirement from the United States Supreme Court*,[82] has to date unfortunately received far less attention from

---

74. *See supra* Calabresi & Lindgren, *Term Limits*, pp. 15–98 [ms. p. 38].

75. *Id.*

76. *See* 5 U.S.C. 8335(b) and 5 U.S.C. 8425(b).

77. *See* 5 U.S.C. 8335(a) and 5 U.S.C. 8425(a).

78. *See* 5 U.S.C. 8335(b)-(d) and 5 U.S.C. 8425(b)-(d). Case-by-case individual exemption is possible up to age 60. *Id. See also* U.S. Department of Justice Human Resources Order DOJ 1200.1 (B.5) (January 28, 2000).

79. *See supra* Calabresi & Lindgren, *Term Limits*, pp. 15–98 [ms. pp. 40, 43].

80. *See id.* [ms. p. 57].

81. *See* Garrow, *supra* n. 4; *See also*, e.g., Sanford Levinson, *Testimony Before the Committee on the Judiciary of the U.S. Senate* <http://judiciary.senate.gov/testimony.cfm?id=1022&wit_id=2919> (January 27, 2004) (calling that analysis "a remarkable article"); *see infra* Arthur D. Hellman, *Reining in the Supreme Court: Are Term Limits the Answer?*, at p. 293 (terming it "persuasive").

82. Artemus Ward, *Deciding to Leave: The Politics of Retirement from the United States Supreme Court* (2003).

legal academics than it should have.[83] Proponents of term-limits could draw some sustenance from Ward's work, for he strongly identifies "strategic retirements" as a problem that has grown over time: "generous retirement benefits coupled with a decreasing workload have reduced the departure process to partisan maneuvering."[84]

But Ward's extensive research leads him to conclude that "[c]ompulsory retirement at a set age such as seventy or seventy-five would not only solve the problem of partisan departures, but it would also go a long way toward protecting the intellectual health of the Court from mentally failing justices."[85] Thus he recommends that "a constitutional amendment for mandatory retirement at age seventy-five" would "go...the furthest" toward "combating partisanship and mental decrepitude" while "preserving judicial independence."[86]

Ward acknowledges that "[f]or an amendment to be seriously considered and then pass, it would likely take the prolonged public incapacities of one or more of the justices to prompt it."[87] That hurdle will confront any proposed amendment, but a compulsory retirement measure would carry with it none of the seriously weighty ideological baggage that already is indelibly attached to the eighteen-year term-limit movement. It is important to recognize that a mandatory age amendment is not a "magic bullet." Some justices who indisputably lost the ability to perform adequately were well under age seventy at the time.[88] But Professor Farnsworth likewise recommends that "[t]he case for age limits deserves serious consideration,"[89] and he correctly rules out another alternative that some Supreme Court commentators have informally suggested. "Justices could not be subjected to annual mental examinations to assess their competence without discomfort and humiliation."[90]

Yet neither an annual mental examination, nor mandatory retirement at age seventy or seventy-five, could avert Blackmun-style devolutions where a justice adequately capable of performing the job nonetheless chooses to give away to law clerks not only the actual writing of opinions but significant in-

---

83. *But see* Tony Mauro, *Courtside*, Legal Times 10 (June 2, 2003).

84. Ward, *supra* n. 82 at 12.

85. *Id.* at 229.

86. *Id.* at 248, 24.

87. *Id.* at 230.

88. *See* Garrow, *supra* n. 4 at 1085. *See also* Lee Epstein et al., *Comparing Judicial Selection Systems*, 10 William and Mary Bill of Rights Journal 7, 26 (2001) (same), and Michael J. Mazza, *A New Look at an Old Debate: Life Tenure and the Article III Judge*, 39 Gonzaga L. Rev. 131, 149 (2003) (same).

89. Farnsworth, *supra* n. 38 at 453.

90. *Id.* at 445.

dependent influence over their substantive content.[91] Several years ago Professor Powe was perhaps the first to suggest a reform of a different order, one that would encourage decrepit justices to retire: "[i]n funding the Court, Congress should authorize only enough funds for each justice to have two law clerks," rather than today's complement of four apiece.[92]

Professor Powe's recommendation to halve the number of law clerks is one that not only could hasten the departure of decrepit justices but also could prevent the occurrence of Blackmun-style situations. To maximize both effects, however, Professor Powe's suggestion should be taken one step further: only one *single* law clerk should be available to each justice.[93]

In recent years a wide variety of commentators have complained about the excessive influence of law clerks on the Court's work.[94] In truth, however, dependable accounts of clerks exercising undeniably substantive influence on the Court's rulings reach back at least to Louis Lusky's confession to Alpheus T. Mason that Lusky, as Justice Harlan Fiske Stone's law clerk in October Term 1937, was almost wholly responsible for the inclusion of the famous "footnote four" in *United States v. Carolene Products Co.*[95]

Not as well known, but perhaps more surprising, was Laurence H. Tribe's subsequent account of how his October Term 1967 clerkship with Justice Potter Stewart allowed him to author one of Stewart's best-known opinions:

> One of the exciting things about the clerkship was that he [Justice Stewart] would let his law clerks, if he liked their style, write drafts and very often the drafts would become the opinion. A number of opinions I worked on that term are really almost exactly as I drafted them; cases like Katz v. United States [389 U.S. 347 (1967)] dealing

---

91. See Garrow, *The Brains Behind Blackmun, supra* n. 13, and Garrow, *The Accidental Jurist, supra* n. 13.

92. Powe, *supra* n. 30 at 1238. Chief Justice Rehnquist continued to appoint only three law clerks per Term.

93. *See* David J. Garrow, *When Court Clerks Rule*, Los Angeles Times M5 (May 29, 2005) (recommending "no more than two law clerks or, better yet, just one" per justice each Term).

94. *See*, e.g., Edward Lazarus, *Closed Chambers: The First Eyewitness Account of the Epic Struggles Inside the Supreme Court* 6 (1998) ("a Court where Justices yield great and excessive power to immature, ideologically driven clerks" who "manipulate their bosses"); John O. McGinnis, *Justice Without Justices*, 16 Constitutional Commentary 541, 543 (1999) (criticizing "the excessive delegation of power to young and energetic law clerks").

95. 304 U.S. 144, 153 n.4 (1938); Alpheus T. Mason, *Harlan Fiske Stone: Pillar of the Law* 513 (1956) (quoting Lusky). *See also* Louis Lusky, *By What Right?: A Commentary on the Supreme Court's Power to Revise the Constitution* 108–12 (1975).

with the fact that electronic eavesdropping is a form of search even though there's no physical trespass. I wrote some of the key phrases thinking that this is what Stewart would want to say, and it turned out to be exactly what he wanted. '[T]he Fourth Amendment protects people, not places' [389 U.S. at 351] is a line from my draft in Katz.[96]

Justice Stewart's papers are not yet available for scholarly review, so it is presently unclear as to whether Tribe's experience was exceptional, or whether Stewart in time will be revealed to have been an earlier example of Blackmun-like judicial abdication. But Blackmun's regrettable relinquishment, and the possibility that previous or subsequent justices whose papers are unavailable behaved similarly, underscores most poignantly how the dangers of judicial nonperformance that threaten the Court are *not* limited simply to the onset of decrepitude that some justices experience as they get older.

While a constitutionally-imposed retirement age would greatly shrink but not wholly eliminate the threat of mental decrepitude to the Court, a reduction in the number of clerks to just one per justice would return the Court to the level of assistance that prevailed from the late nineteenth century until 1946. At that time, the Court was deciding more than one hundred sixty cases each year; nowadays, with four times as many law clerks, it decides approximately seventy-five cases each year. Imposition of compulsory retirement, like term limits, would require a constitutional amendment; a reduction in the number of law clerks, as Professor Powe initially noted, would require only a modest statutory enactment.

Why not, then, have an extensive scholarly conversation about a significant reform that *can* be easily achievable, as opposed to debates about admittedly imperfect constitutional amendments whose prospects for enactment range from unimaginable to unlikely? One possible answer is that professors at elite law schools, who are well represented in the world of Supreme Court commentary, often are either themselves former clerks deeply attached to a once-formative experience, and/or mentors to students whose clerkship prospects are an important but little-acknowledged source of prestige and connections for their sponsoring professors. It may sound like faculty-lounge humor, but it is far from entirely laughable to suggest that those with the most to lose in a major cutback of Supreme Court clerkships are constitutional law teachers at the nation's top five to ten law schools.

No doubt most if not all current justices would also oppose a three-fourths reduction in the number of their law clerks. But the justices might well be even

---

96. Andrea Sachs, *Laurence Tribe*, Constitution 24, 28 (Spring–Summer 1991) (quoting Tribe).

more loath to enter into any public discussion, even with the usually deferential members of the House Appropriations subcommittee before whom two
of the justices appear once each year at the annual hearing on the Court's
budget, that would focus upon how a more than fifty-percent reduction in the
justices' work load has been accompanied by a 400% increase in their professional staff assistance. In short, should Congress become convinced that it
would be better for the American people, and for the Supreme Court itself, to
seek to insure that each of the nine justices is personally carrying out the responsibilities of his or her office, such a change could be implemented with
considerable alacrity.

The story of Justice Blackmun's judicial self-abnegation has now been
widely acknowledged as revealing a most serious problem indeed.[97] Were each
justice to enjoy the assistance of only one single law clerk, the opportunities
for surrendering much of the substance of a justice's work to young aides-de-
camp would be greatly reduced. Just as with compulsory retirement, however,
such a reform would not necessarily be a "magic bullet," for the historical
record is sadly clear about how Justice Frank Murphy gave up even more of
his job to one sole clerk—Eugene Gressman—than did Harry Blackmun to
three or four.[98]

But can anyone truly doubt or question that the presence of just *nine* clerks
at the Court would minimize as greatly as could any imaginable reform *both*
a decrepit justice's ability to remain on the Court *and* able justices' temptations to "give away essential pieces of their job"?[99] With the Court for well over
a decade now annually hearing argument in and deciding roughly eighty cases
per Term, any competent jurist should be able to handle the resulting workload with just a sole clerk. Authorship of roughly nine majority opinions per
justice over the course of a nine-month Term is a far from onerous burden,
and a like number of concurrences and dissents are similarly easily manage-
able. Indeed, as Stuart Taylor recently observed, not only have at least three
justices—the late Chief Justice Rehnquist and Justices O'Connor and

---

97. *See*, e.g., Rosen, *supra* n. 13; Stuart Taylor, Jr., *Term Limits for Supreme Court Justices Would Reduce a Host of Ills*, Legal Times 44 (June 27, 2005); and *see infra* Hellman, p.
294.

98. *See* Kurland, *supra* n. 9 at 299; Fine, *supra* n. 10 at 162, 483; J. Woodford Howard,
Mr. Justice Murphy: A Political Biography 458–59 (1968); Hutchinson, *supra* n. 9 at 206;
David M. O'Brien, *Storm Center: The Supreme Court in American Politics* 159–60 (4th ed.
1996).

99. Alex Kozinski, *The Real Issues of Judicial Ethics*, 32 Hofstra L. Rev. 1095, 1100
(2004).

Thomas—invested significant time in writing memoirs or works of history in addition to their judicial opinions, some of the justices also undertake a remarkable number of discretionary speaking trips each year. As Taylor highlighted, Justice O'Connor reported "twenty-eight trips in 2004 alone" for which her travel expenses were reimbursed.[100] That works out to more than two a month, and it starkly illuminates how serving as a Justice on the United States Supreme Court has become a highly cosseted part-time job for those who choose to handle their responsibilities in a less than thoroughly painstaking manner.

Every conservative originalist should experience hardly a moment's hesitation before endorsing a statutory reform that would powerfully encourage justices to do their own work rather than fob off their official tasks in favor of pursuing off-the-bench diversions. Likewise, progressive liberals who have complained loudly over what they see as the emergence and ongoing growth of a powerfully interwoven network of intensely conservative judicial clerks, former clerks, and sponsoring jurists should eagerly support a reform that would dramatically reduce the role young clerks play inside the U.S. Supreme Court.

However, as noted earlier, one powerfully self-interested group stands in the way of congressional consideration of a three-fourths reduction in the number of clerks: legal academia. Could it be that law professors actually prefer to debate and discuss proposals which have no chance of enactment whatsoever, and ergo represent a purely "ivory tower" enterprise, rather than wrestle with a tangible, real-world possibility whose significant advantages are obvious to all but would negatively impact top law schools and some of their top students? Perhaps it would be just normal human selfishness for the professoriate to try to avoid confronting or embracing an easily-achievable reform whose enactment would significantly protect and enhance the Court, and its justices' reputations, but such a failure would represent a serious disservice to the Court and to future justices.

One danger in proposing any significant institutional reform is that pre-existing enemies of that institution may choose to endorse it for purely spiteful reasons. So as much as a return to a Court with nine clerks for nine justices deserves congressional attention and sponsorship, Representative Tom DeLay and Senator John Cornyn are of course not this reform's ideal proponents. But perhaps at least some voices within legal academia will put aside complicated proposals for constitutional amendments that have no imaginable chance of enactment, and which in all great likelihood would significantly harm the

---

100. Taylor, *supra* n. 97.

Supreme Court, and instead focus upon and champion a statutorily simple reform which if implemented would go a very long way indeed toward protecting and enhancing the integrity of the Court and the reputation of its justices.

Reining in
the Supreme Court:
Are Term Limits the Answer?

Arthur D. Hellman[*]

When the Supreme Court concluded its 2000–2001 Term—the term that will be remembered for the late-night ruling that cut short the Florida presidential vote count—Professor Walter Dellinger called attention to a striking pattern in the Court's decisions. The Court, he said, "assumes that it is more qualified than Congress to resolve electoral votes, more entitled than the President's agencies to fill gaps in federal law, and better equipped than the professional golf association to determine the rules of golf."[1]

Four years later, at the conclusion of the 2004–2005 Term, Professor Dellinger might have identified a similar pattern—but based on an entirely different set of examples. The Court, he might have said, assumes that it is more qualified than Congress and the sentencing commission to determine sentencing policies,[2] more entitled than state legislatures to decide when be-

---

[*] Sally Ann Semenko Endowed Chair and Professor of Law, University of Pittsburgh School of Law. The author thanks David Stras for comments on an earlier version and Richard Alec Hall for research assistance.

1. *See* Charles Lane, *Laying Down the Law, Justices Ruled With Confidence; From Bush v. Gore Onward, Activism Marked Past Term*, Wash. Post A06 (July 1, 2001) (available on NEXIS) (quoting Professor Dellinger). In addition to Bush v. Gore, 531 U.S. 98 (2000), Professor Dellinger was presumably referring to FDA v. Brown & Williamson Tobacco Co., 529 U.S. 120 (2000) (rejecting FDA's assertion of statutory authority to regulate tobacco products); and PGA Tour, Inc., v. Martin, 532 U.S. 661 (2001) (holding that use of a golf cart is not a modification that would "fundamentally alter the nature" of golf tours sponsored by PGA).

2. *See* Booker v. United States, 125 S. Ct. 738 (2005).

liefs about morality should be embodied in criminal prohibitions,[3] and better equipped than citizen-jurors to apply "evolving standards of decency."[4]

The Court that handed down these more recent decisions was the same Court that Professor Dellinger was describing in July 2001. In fact, prior to the resignation of Justice O'Connor and death of Chief Justice Rehnquist in mid-2005, the same justices had served together for eleven years. Not since the early nineteenth century has a single group of justices remained together for so long.

This was also a Court that increasingly called to mind the "nine old men" who became notorious for striking down the economic legislation enacted by Congress as part of President Franklin D. Roosevelt's New Deal. Of course the Court of 1994–2005 included two women, but one of those women, Justice O'Connor, was seventy-five when she announced her retirement; the other, Justice Ginsburg, was seventy-two at the close of the 2004 Term. Two of the male justices were considerably older than either of the women: Justice Stevens (eighty-five) and Chief Justice Rehnquist (just short of eighty-one at the time of his death). Two justices (Justice Scalia and Justice Kennedy) will soon turn seventy. Only Justice Thomas is under the age of sixty-five—the age at which most Americans have retired from active employment.[5]

In sum, the Court that sat during the first half-decade of the twenty-first century was an entrenched, elderly Court—and also a Court that could be characterized as self-assured to the point of arrogance. Is there a connection between that self-assurance (or arrogance) and the fact that the justices have stayed on so long? And even if the two phenomena are unrelated, has the time come to move away from life tenure for Supreme Court justices and replace it with something else—age limits, perhaps, or terms of specified length?

Those questions are addressed in the essays that make up this book—essays based on presentations at a conference on "Reforming the Supreme Court?" held at Duke Law School in April 2005. Two major proposals for eliminating life tenure were offered at the conference. Professors Steven G. Calabresi and James Lindgren advocated "a system of staggered, nonrenewable

---

3. *See* Lawrence v. Texas, 539 U.S. 558 (2003).

4. *See* Roper v. Simmons, 125 S. Ct. 1183 (2005).

5. In fact, only eighteen percent of men and ten percent of women remain in the civilian labor force over the age of sixty-five. *See* U.S. Census Bureau, *The Older Population in the United States: March 2002* <http://www.census.gov/prod/2003pubs/p20-546.pdf> (last visited June 15, 2005).

term limits of eighteen years," designed so that each President would have the opportunity to fill two vacancies, one in each Congress of the presidential term.[6] A second proposal, by Professors Paul Carrington and Roger Cramton, was similar in its approach.

In this essay, I shall analyze the likely consequences of adopting a system of eighteen-year terms along the lines proposed by Calabresi-Lindgren and by Carrington-Cramton. First, however, I shall briefly address the question: are the proponents persuasive in arguing that "the American constitutional rule granting life tenure to Supreme Court justices is fundamentally flawed?"[7]

Life Tenure and Its Discontents

Two sets of arguments are advanced against the current system of life tenure for Supreme Court justices. One involves the age of the justices; the other focuses on the length of time that the justices remain on the Court and the resulting infrequency of vacancies.

Age and Mental Decrepitude

The first set of arguments is neatly summed up in the title of Professor David Garrow's "Mental Decrepitude on the U.S. Supreme Court."[8] Professor Garrow marshals evidence in support of the proposition that "mental decrepitude among aging justices is a persistently recurring problem that merits serious attention."[9] While some of his examples are less convincing than others, his overall conclusion is persuasive. Indeed, we can count ourselves fortunate that, in recent decades, the justices who most plainly stayed too long on the Court did not often cast deciding votes in important cases. If Justice Lewis F. Powell had reached the same state of decline in his last years as Justices William O. Douglas and Thurgood Marshall did in theirs, a cloud would hang over much of the constitutional jurisprudence of the late Burger and early Rehnquist Courts.

---

6. *See supra* Steven G. Calabresi & James Lindgren, *Term Limits for the Supreme Court: Life Tenure Reconsidered* pp. 15–98. All quotations to the Calabresi & Lindgren essay are to their manuscript pages, from which I understand some deletions and alterations have been made for publication in this book.

7. *See supra* Calabresi & Lindgren, pp. 15–98 [ms. p. 2).

8. David J. Garrow, *Mental Decrepitude on the U.S. Supreme Court: The Historical Case for a 28th Amendment*, 67 U. Chi. L. Rev. 995 (2000).

9. *Id.* at 995.

Others have discussed the conditions under which the justices carry out their work today, and they explain persuasively why those conditions reinforce the view that the lack of a mandatory retirement age (or other cutoff) is something we should worry about.[10] I will add only one point.

The "hot bench" of today, with the justices firing questions at the lawyers, is a relatively recent development. If other members of the Court were to follow Justice Thomas's example and simply listen during the oral arguments, outsiders would have a very hard time finding out whether a justice was starting to slide into mental decrepitude. Indeed, even if a justice was active in posing questions, we would have to review the transcript to determine whether the justice was genuinely engaged or perhaps simply asking isolated questions supplied by a law clerk. And given the protectiveness of justices' staff and families, we have no guarantee that insiders would take action to accelerate the retirement of a justice who could no longer do the job.

This last concern has been reinforced by the controversy generated by Professor Garrow's recent article on the role of Justice Blackmun's law clerks. Professor Garrow, after studying the voluminous collection of internal memoranda and other files that Justice Blackmun deposited with the Library of Congress, concluded that Blackmun "increasingly ceded far too much of his judicial authority to his [law] clerks."[11] When the article was published, several Blackmun clerks disputed Garrow's conclusion, insisting that it was based on "half the evidence."[12] I think Garrow's analysis withstands the challenges that have been levied against it, but even if others take a different view, the episode underscores the point that law clerks are extremely protective of their justices. That fact, together with the rule of confidentiality that binds all Court staff, means that unless a justice's decrepitude becomes evident at oral argument sessions, outsiders are not likely to become aware that a justice has reached the point where he or she should step down.

Lengthy Tenures and Democratic Accountability

The second set of arguments against life tenure is based on the notion — stated very broadly — that the Supreme Court should follow the election re-

---

10. *See supra* Calabresi & Lindgren, pp. 15–98 [ms. p. 24–25] and many of the other authors contributing to this Symposium.

11. David J. Garrow, *The Brains Behind Blackmun*, Legal Affairs (May–June 2005).

12. *Readers Respond: Justice Blackmun*, Legal Affairs <http://www.legalaffairs.org/issues/May-June-2005/feature_response_mayjun05.msp> (last visited, June 15, 2005).

turns.[13] At least at a very general level, I accept the premise.[14] As Chief Justice Rehnquist explained, in a passage quoted with approval by Professors Calabresi and Lindgren, "the institution [of the Supreme Court] has been constructed in such a way that…the public will, in the person of the President of the United States…have something to say about the membership of the Court, and thereby indirectly about its decisions."[15] But I can not take the next step and endorse the proposition that each President should have the same number of appointments to the Court. The argument fails to take account of the numerous other circumstances that affect the relationship between the direction of public opinion in the country and the direction of the Court's decisions.

Consider the situation today. The Republican Party has won seven out of the last ten presidential elections. The Republicans have controlled the House of Representatives without interruption since the Gingrich takeover in 1994; they have controlled the Senate for five of the last six Congresses. There are now twenty-eight states with Republican governors, compared with only eighteen in 1992. Overall, it is fair to say that the nation has moved in a conservative direction. Moreover, Republican Presidents have appointed seven of the nine sitting justices. Thus, if the premises of the Calabresi-Lindgren plan are correct, the Supreme Court too should have moved in a conservative direction. But it has not. On the issues that have the capacity to stir the electorate, the Court's decisions over the past decade are far closer to the mainstream of the Democratic Party than they are to the positions generally held by Republicans. Abortion is the most prominent, but others include homosexual rights, racial preferences, and acknowledgments of religion in public schools.[16]

To be sure, the Court's decisions limiting Congressional power under the Commerce Clause and section 5 of the Fourteenth Amendment are probably

---

13. This phrase, of course, was first popularized by humorist Finley Peter Dunne, reporting the observations of the fictional "Mr. Dooley." Ironically, the controversy that prompted the remark is totally forgotten today except by constitutional historians.

14. Of course, the premise should not be carried too far. As developed later in this essay, the Court's legitimacy would be impaired if its decisional law constantly shifted direction as a result of changes in the membership of the Court.

15. William H. Rehnquist, *The Supreme Court* 209–10 (2001), quoted in Calabresi & Lindgren, *supra* pp. 15–98 [ms. p. 27].

16. "On every issue of interest to the Left—abortion, affirmative action, the death penalty, homosexual rights, campaign finance law—the supposedly conservative Rehnquist Court has done as progressives desire." Michael S. Greve, *How to Think about Constitutional Change, Part I: The Progressive Vision*, Federalist Outlook AEI Online <http://www.aei.org/publications/filter.all,pubID.22622/pub_detail.asp> (last visited June 17, 2005).

more congenial to Republicans than to Democrats. But from the standpoint of democratic accountability these rulings are largely irrelevant because they barely impinge on popular consciousness. Michael S. Greve of the American Enterprise Institute has aptly contrasted the impact of the two sets of cases:

> The Rehnquist Court's federalism "revolution"—the principal target of liberal wrath—consists of margin-nibbling decisions that no ordinary American has heard of, and recent (and, probably, forthcoming) decisions strongly signal an abandonment. At the same time, the supposedly conservative Court has cranked out an amazing array of newfangled rights, especially on sexual mores.[17]

The proponents of the eighteen-year term plan might respond to this line of argument by pointing out that, under the present system, President Carter might well have gotten four appointments (as President Nixon did in his first term); President Clinton might have been able to fill five vacancies during his two terms (as President Eisenhower did). Under either of these scenarios, the Court presumably would have moved even further away from the currents of public opinion. (To be sure, one or more of President Carter's appointees might have stepped down by the time President Clinton made his appointments.) The eighteen-year term plan would not have allowed these outcomes.

I acknowledge that the eighteen-year term plan would preclude extreme scenarios such as those I have hypothesized. But the more important point is that when we look at the Court's actual decisions during this period, we do not find anything like the imbalance we would expect from the fact that one Democratic President (Carter) did not get any appointments, and another (Clinton) got only two rather than four. Somehow, other aspects of the process have compensated for "the random nature of [the] vacancies"[18] over the last forty years. And when we consider that the proponents rest their arguments almost entirely on "the increase in justices' terms on the Supreme Court since 1970,"[19] the paucity of support from the justices' behavior during that period is quite telling.

This brings me to a broader point. One section of the Calabresi-Lindgren article has the title "A Supreme Court divorced from democratic accountabil-

---

17. Michael S. Greve, *Liberals in Exile; Beware Their Grand Plan to Impose a Radical, European-style Constitution on America*, Legal Times, May 2, 2005, LEXIS, News Library, Legal Times File. Note that Greve correctly anticipated the decision in Gonzales v. Raich, 125 S. Ct. 2195 (2005) (holding that Congress has power under the Commerce Clause to "prohibit the local cultivation and use of marijuana in compliance with California law").

18. *See supra* Calabresi & Lindgren, pp. 15–98 [ms. p. 57].

19. *Id.* [ms. p. 22].

ity." It just happened that at the same time that I was reading a draft of the article, two other sets of statements about courts and democratic accountability crossed my desk.

The first was this: "The Congress of the United States for many, many years has shirked its responsibility to hold the judiciary accountable. No longer.... We will look at an arrogant, out of control, unaccountable judiciary." The second statement was this:

> The point, finally, is this: to control the Supreme Court, we must first lay claim to the Constitution ourselves. That means publicly repudiating Justices who say that they, not we, possess ultimate authority to say what the Constitution means.... The Constitution leaves room for countless political responses to an overly assertive Court: Justices can be impeached, the Court's budget can be slashed, the President can ignore its mandates, Congress can strip it of jurisdiction or shrink its size or pack it with new members or give it burdensome new responsibilities or revise its procedures. The means are available, and they have been used to great effect when necessary....

The first set of statements received wide publicity in the media in early 2005; the speaker was House Majority Leader Tom Delay.[20] The second statement is from the book "The People Themselves" by Stanford Law Dean Larry Kramer.[21]

Tom Delay and Larry Kramer are probably as far apart politically as any two public figures in America today. If they are both saying that the judiciary has gotten out of control and should be brought to heel, we may have a problem of democratic accountability that goes far beyond justices who stay too long on the bench, and which will not be cured by limiting Supreme Court tenure.

To pursue this point would take me far beyond the topic of this book. Yet it is difficult to separate the concerns raised by the system of lifetime tenure from broader issues centering on the current Court's willingness to override the results of democratic processes. I shall return to these broader issues at the conclusion of this essay.

---

20. *See Fox Special Report With Brit Hume* (Fox News television broadcast, Apr. 1, 2005), LEXIS, Nexis Library, Fox News File; *U.S. Representative Tom Delay (R-TX) Delivers Remarks on the Death of Terri Schiavo*, FDCH Political Transcripts (Mar. 31, 2005), LEXIS, Nexis Library, FDCH Political Transcripts File.

21. Larry H. Kramer, *The People Themselves: Popular Constitutionalism and Judicial Review* 247, 249 (2004).

The Plan for Staggered Eighteen-Year Terms

I turn now to the proposals for staggered eighteen-year terms arranged so that there would be two appointments in each presidential term, with one in each Congress. The proposals differ in details, but in this essay I shall ignore the differences and focus on the basic concept. I see three areas of concern, which I shall discuss in the order in which they would come up in the usual course of events. First, there is the effect on the appointment and confirmation process. Next, there is the effect on the selection of cases and the handling of the cases that the Court does take. Finally, there is the effect on the Court's treatment of its own precedents.

The Appointment and Confirmation Process

I believe that the eighteen-year term plan would significantly increase the politicization of the appointment process even beyond what it is today. Proponents of the plan strongly dispute this assertion; I will explain why I think it is correct.

To begin, it is helpful to recall the 2004 campaign. The possibility of a Supreme Court vacancy was on the horizon, and some people saw it as a major issue. But most did not. Indeed, when the National Election Pool carried out its exit poll survey to determine "which one issue mattered most in determining how [the survey participant] voted for president," the list of issues did not even include "appointments to the Supreme Court."[22]

One reason the issue did not loom large in most people's minds is that the prospect of a vacancy was diffused. Certainly there was widespread speculation that Chief Justice Rehnquist would step down. But Justice Stevens was another possibility, and so was Justice O'Connor. I even saw some speculation about Justice Ginsburg.[23]

Let us put Justice Ginsburg aside and consider only the most senior justices—the three who in 2004 were viewed as most likely to retire during the presidential term beginning in 2005. The effect of a Rehnquist vacancy would be very different from the effect of a Stevens vacancy, and an O'Connor va-

---

22. National Election Pool, *National Exit Poll Questionnaire* <http://www.exit-poll.net/election-night/Nat_Final.pdf> (last visited May 26, 2005).

23. *See,* e.g., Charlie Savage, *Win May Bring Power to Appoint 4 Justices*, Boston Globe A3 (July 7, 2004), (listing Justice Ginsburg as one of four Justices who might retire during presidential term beginning in 2005; noting that Justice Ginsburg "has battled cancer since 1999").

cancy would be different from either. With so many possibilities in play, there was a real limit to the ability of interest groups to rouse their followers to put the issue front and center.

Now suppose we knew that under a system of staggered eighteen-year terms, Justice O'Connor's tenure would be coming to an end in the 2005–06 biennium. Every pressure group would have focused on that vacancy, not only in the presidential election but in every state with a contested senatorial election. For many people, the election would have been a referendum to select the O'Connor successor. That cannot be healthy, even if you think the Court should be more accountable to democratic majorities than it is today.

It is true that we cannot assume that a "swing" justice like Justice O'Connor will be stepping down in the immediate aftermath of every presidential election. But a system that guarantees each President two opportunities to fill a vacancy presents numerous other possibilities for drawing the Court more deeply into the swirl of politics. Consider, for example, how the two major party candidates would deal with the upcoming appointments in speeches, debates, and interviews. Perhaps they would confine themselves to describing the kind of individuals they planned to select. But some candidates might go further and announce a "short list" of the names from among whom they would select a nominee for the first vacancy of their presidency.[24] The election would then become, to some degree, a referendum on whether one of those individuals should be appointed.

If, like Brigham Young University political science professor Richard Davis, you believe that Supreme Court justices should be selected through a process that incorporates popular elections, you will probably applaud this outcome.[25] But those who have observed judicial elections in the states would probably say that this carries democratic accountability further than is desirable.[26]

---

24. The candidates could not promise to appoint any particular individuals. *See* 18 USC § 599 (prohibiting candidates from "directly or indirectly" promising to appoint any person to a public position "for the purpose of procuring support in his candidacy"). However, they could give strong hints. Thus, in the 2000 presidential campaign, Gov. George W. Bush, without making a formal commitment, made clear his intention to appoint Colin Powell as Secretary of State.

25. *See* Richard Davis, *Electing Justice: Fixing the Supreme Court Nomination Process* (2005); Michael McGough, *Intellectual Capital: Confirmation Conversion?* Pittsburgh Post-Gazette (Mar. 14, 2005) (noting that under one of the proposals floated by Davis, "the president would nominate a set number of candidates, perhaps three, for the general election ballot").

26. *See* Republican Party of Minnesota v. White, 536 U.S. 765, 788–92 (2002) (O'-Connor, J., concurring) (outlining concerns about popular election of judges in the states).

Not surprisingly, Professors Calabresi and Lindgren view the comparison very differently. One of the key points of their argument is the proposition that the infrequency of Supreme Court vacancies under the current system is partly responsible for the increased politicization of the confirmation process for all federal judges. They write:

> Under the current system, vacancies on the Supreme Court arise very irregularly, which means that when one does arise, the President and Senate both act without knowing when the next vacancy might be. Moreover, a successful nominee has the potential to remain on the Court for a very long (and uncertain) period of time. As a result, the political pressures on the President and the Senate are overwhelming. There is simply so much at stake in appointing a new Justice that the President and the Senate (when controlled by the party opposite the President) inevitably become engaged in a bitter political contest that harms the Court both directly and indirectly.[27]

But if infrequency of vacancies is the culprit, why are there so many "bitter political contest[s]" over nominations to the federal courts of appeals? Vacancies on the courts of appeals are anything but infrequent. At the start of President George W. Bush's first term, there were twenty-six open seats on the twelve regional courts of appeals. Over the next two years, nine of those vacancies were filled, while fifteen new seats opened up. By the start of President Bush's second term, eight additional positions had become vacant. Nevertheless, the Democrats mounted vigorous offensives against more than a dozen of President Bush's nominees and succeeded in driving at least three from the field.[28]

The Democrats have pursued this course even though they must be aware that if their party prevails in the presidential election of 2008, there will be no shortage of appellate vacancies for their standard-bearer to fill. If we assume that judges appointed by Democratic Presidents will not be inclined to retire during the presidency of George W. Bush, we can expect that there will be at least thirty-two court of appeals positions to be filled during the presidential term that begins in 2009.[29]

---

27. *See supra* Calabresi & Lindgren, pp. 15–98 [ms. p. 30].

28. Miguel Estrada withdrew as a nominee to the District of Columbia Circuit; Carolyn Kuhl declined to be renominated to the Ninth Circuit; and Charles Pickering chose to retire after his recess appointment to the Fifth Circuit expired.

29. This figure includes twenty-two Democrat-appointed judges who will be eligible to retire during George W. Bush's term and ten who will become eligible during the first three

Moreover, it can hardly be said that "[there is] so much at stake in appointing" judges to the intermediate appellate courts. For example, consider the controversy over Carolyn Kuhl, who was nominated for a seat on the Ninth Circuit Court of Appeals in June 2001, but who fell victim to a Democratic filibuster. That was one position on a court of twenty-eight authorized judgeships (not to mention the twenty or so senior judges who regularly hear cases). The court in question was (and, at this writing, remains) a court heavily dominated by Democratic appointees: in June 2001, eighteen of the twenty-five active judges had been appointed by Democratic Presidents.[30] Not coincidentally, this was also a court that has been notorious for its "liberal" decisions, particularly on issues of criminal procedure and First Amendment rights. How much power would Judge Kuhl have had to move the court in a conservative direction? Even if her views were "outside the mainstream," how much could she have done to impose those views on the citizens of the Ninth Circuit? But the modest stakes for Judge Kuhl's and other court of appeals nominations have not stopped the participants from engaging in fierce combat in a take-no-prisoners mode.

Every now and then, one of these participants will acknowledge how little is really at stake. Senate Democrats and their allies spent four years trying to keep Texas Supreme Court Justice Priscilla Owen from being appointed to the Fifth Circuit Court of Appeals. One of the most vocal members of the opposition was an organization called Texans for Public Justice (TPJ).[31] In May 2005, after a group of Senators negotiated a compromise that averted a showdown over the use of the filibuster, Justice Owen was confirmed to the federal bench. A spokesman for TPJ said:

> We were against her on the principle that judges with such an activist, pro-business background as Owen do not deserve lifetime appointments. Having said that, her confirmation likely won't have much of an impact on the 5th Circuit, which is one of the most conservative circuits in the United States today.[32]

With the confirmation of Justice Owen, one vacancy still remains unfilled on the Fifth Circuit. Do not be surprised if TPJ and the other organizations

---

years of the presidential term beginning in 2009. (The assumption is that vacancies occurring during the last year of a presidential term are not likely to be filled in that year.)

30. As of June 2005, sixteen of the twenty-four active judges are Democratic appointees.

31. For a list of letters and press releases, see <http://www.tpj.org/page_view.jsp?pageid=333> (visited June 12, 2005).

32. Michelle Mittelstadt, *Divided Senate confirms Owen*, Dallas Morning News (May 25, 2005) (quoting Craig McDonald).

that opposed the Owen nomination launch a new campaign to defeat the new nominee—even though the appointment "likely won't have much of an impact" on the court.

My own view is that the "judicial confirmation wars," with their extreme rhetoric and unwillingness to compromise, are driven in very large part by the agendas of advocacy groups for whom the nominees are trophies—trophies of power and influence. How this came to be is a long and complex story, but I do not think it is coincidental that the escalation of hostilities has occurred at about the same time that the McCain-Feingold campaign finance law went into effect. That law severely restricts the ability of political parties and candidates to raise and spend money to win national elections. But campaigns do require money, and if the parties cannot provide enough of it, the advocacy groups are happy to help out—at a price. The price, of course, is support for the group's program. And it happens that judicial nominations are uniquely well-suited for measuring a legislator's fealty to a group's agenda. When issues of policy come before Congress, the legislation can be nuanced, and votes on the floor or in committee can be ambiguous. But with judicial nominations, there is no room for uncertainty or equivocation. Groups can draw a line in the sand; a Senator is with them or against them.[33]

Efforts are under way in Congress to further revise the campaign finance laws, but even if these bear fruit, it is highly unlikely that any new legislation will diminish the influence of advocacy groups in the judicial confirmation process. To be sure, the groups are not all-powerful. Members of the Senate have their own interests and agendas, and every now and then they will find a compromise that averts all-out war. But these truces are likely to be temporary. And for the reasons given, it is unrealistic to think that the intensity of the conflicts would moderate if vacancies on the Supreme Court opened up every two years rather than at unpredictable (and generally longer) intervals.

Calabresi and Lindgren further argue that "by making vacancies a regular occurrence, and by limiting the stakes of each confirmation to an eighteen-year rather than a forty-year term, [their] proposal would greatly reduce the

---

33. As one Republican lobbyist said of the battle over judicial nominations, "there's no incentive for a politician to be reasonable, there's no political force to be moderate. For the [Democrats], environment and abortion groups don't become important by letting people get confirmed. And on our side, it doesn't help them if the president nominates moderate judges." T.R. Goldman, *Fail Safe: Defusing the Nuclear Option*, Legal Times 14, 16 (May 23, 2005) (quoting former Senate aide Stewart Verdery).

intensity of partisan warfare in the confirmation process."[34] This assumes that Senators and other participants in the confirmation process would see a dramatic difference between eighteen-year terms and forty-years terms for Supreme Court justices. I disagree. British Prime Minister Harold Wilson famously observed that "a week is a long time in politics." Although Wilson was speaking rhetorically, judicial nomination battles in this country confirm the basic thrust of his comment.

Recall, for example, the controversy over President George W. Bush's nomination of District Judge Charles Pickering to the Fifth Circuit Court of Appeals. Pickering was just shy of his sixty-fourth birthday when he was nominated in 2001. He would have been eligible for retirement in 2004. Nevertheless, his nomination aroused intense opposition and ultimately a filibuster. (The President gave him a recess appointment, but he resigned rather than run the confirmation gauntlet again for a lifetime position on the court of appeals.) If the prospect of as little as three years of service by one judge on an intermediate appellate court of seventeen judges was enough to trigger a filibuster, what reason is there for thinking that a term of "only" eighteen years for a Supreme Court justice would be regarded with equanimity by those who view the nominee as anathema?

Any discussion of this subject necessarily entails some speculation, but for the reasons I have given, I believe that the eighteen-year staggered term plan would lead to a permanent war over Supreme Court appointments, akin to the "permanent campaign" and indeed perhaps part of it. Perhaps court of appeals nominations would go through more easily, but that would be because the energies now devoted to the confirmation process at the intermediate appellate level would shift to the Supreme Court.

Selection (and De-Selection) of Cases

The second area where I think the eighteen-year-term proposal would have pernicious consequences involves the management of the Court's docket. One of the premises of the proposal is that justices are tempted to engage in—and do engage in—"strategic, political behavior" in deciding when to retire from the Court.[35] But anyone who accepts that premise should be equally concerned about the kinds of strategic behavior the justices would be tempted to engage in if the eighteen-year term limit proposal were adopted. I shall discuss two

---

34. *See supra* Calabresi & Lindgren, pp. 15–98 [ms. p. 60].
35. *Id.* at [ms. p. 22].

overlapping aspects of the Court's work: the selection of cases for plenary consideration and the treatment of threshold issues in the cases that the Court agrees to hear.

Today, in selecting cases, the justices consider not only whether a certiorari petition presents an important question, but also whether the case is an appropriate "vehicle" for resolving the issue. "Vehicle" problems can be of many kinds. The facts may be complicated or disputed, or the "record may be cloudy."[36] The important issue may be entangled with other questions of lesser magnitude. The judgment brought for review may rest on alternate grounds, one of which is clearly not "certworthy." The issue that deserves review may not have been clearly raised in the court below. The attorneys may have done "a poor job of advocacy."[37] Indeed, the quality of the petition or the brief in opposition may itself suggest that the Court should await a better "vehicle." Any of these circumstances may lead the Court to deny certiorari notwithstanding the presence of an issue that plainly requires Supreme Court resolution.[38]

In shaping the docket, the justices also act upon the belief that it is often wise to allow issues to "percolate" rather than to resolve them prematurely. Two decades ago, then-Justice Rehnquist, writing for a unanimous Court, emphasized "the benefit [the Supreme Court] receives from permitting several courts of appeals to explore a difficult question before this Court grants certiorari."[39] Justice Rehnquist cited an earlier decision, also unanimous, in which the Court explained how percolation had worked in the particular case:

> This litigation exemplifies the wisdom of allowing difficult issues to mature through full consideration by the courts of appeals. By eliminating the many subsidiary, but still troubling, arguments raised by industry, these courts have vastly simplified our task, as well as having underscored the reasonableness of the agency view.[40]

Other examples can be found, not only on statutory issues, but also on issues of constitutional interpretation.[41]

---

36. Maryland v. Baltimore Radio Show, Inc., 338 U.S. 912, 918 (1950) (opinion of Frankfurter, J.).

37. Colorado Springs Amusements, Ltd. v. Rizzo, 428 U.S. 913, 918 (1976) (Brennan, J., dissenting from denial of certiorari).

38. *See* Arthur D. Hellman, *Never the Same River Twice: The Empirics and Epistemology of Intercircuit Conflicts*, 63 U. Pitt. L. Rev. 81, 104–05 (2001).

39. United States v. Mendoza, 464 U.S. 154, 160 (1984).

40. E.I. duPont de Nemours & Co. v. Train, 430 U.S. 112, 135 n. 26 (1977).

41. For further discussion of percolation, see Arthur D. Hellman, *Preserving the Essential Role of the Supreme Court: A Comment on Justice Rehnquist's Proposal*, 14 Fla. St. U.

Concerns about finding the right vehicle and allowing percolation to take its course are not simply matters of docket management. If the Court chooses the wrong case, or steps in too soon, it may decide the question on the basis of a distorted or incomplete view of the legal and practical setting. That in turn tends to produce decisions that are at best inconclusive and at worst fatally skewed by their idiosyncratic facts or substandard advocacy or other problems.

But if a justice knows to a virtual certainty that this will be his or her last opportunity to confront the issue, the temptation to overlook the "vehicle" infirmities will be very strong. A vote to grant certiorari would be easy enough to rationalize: a cloudy record might simply require writing a different kind of opinion; poor advocacy by the parties could be compensated for by amicus briefs or extra efforts on the part of law clerks. So too with issues that have not received "full consideration by the courts of appeals;" amicus briefs (or academic commentaries) could be seen as taking up the slack.

I have similar concerns about the justices' willingness to overlook issues relating to justiciability. Standing, mootness, and ripeness are malleable doctrines at best. Bending them a little more in order to be able to decide an important issue before a justice was required to leave the Court would not place a great strain on the justice's conscience.

Here, too, the consequences extend well beyond docket management. The various justiciability doctrines apply in the lower courts as well as in the Supreme Court. Thus, the effect of any "bending" would be felt not only in the quality of the Supreme Court's decisions, but also in the substance of the law that other courts have to apply.

Calabresi and Lindgren argue that we do not have to worry about "final period problems," because we do not see justices at the end of their careers rushing to resolve issues under the current system. They write:

> Surely, Justices Rehnquist, Stevens, and O'Connor on the current Court know that they are in the final period of their life tenure on the Supreme Court. Yet no one suggests that these Justices are behaving in a way that suggests the existence of a final period problem. We do not see why such a final period problem would be any more likely under our system of fixed eighteen-year terms.[42]

L. Rev. 15, 22–23 (1986); Arthur D. Hellman, *The Proposed Intercircuit Tribunal: Do We Need It? Will It Work?* 11 Hastings Const. L.Q. 375, 404–06 (1984).

42. *See supra* Calabresi & Lindgren, pp. 15–98 [ms. p. 76].

This response is not persuasive. To begin with, the concerns I have expressed do not rest solely on a justice's awareness of his or her own impending departure from the Court. Under the eighteen-year term plan, each justice will also know how long his ideological allies (and adversaries) will be staying. That would provide a powerful incentive to decide controversial issues while a sympathetic majority is on the Court—or to defer them until a hostile majority is gone.

We should also keep in mind that it is not only the justices whose behavior would be affected. Today, major issues are often shepherded through the lower courts by organizations like the American Civil Liberties Union and the Institute for Justice. We can expect that under a system of eighteen-year fixed terms, these organizations would calibrate the pace of litigation based on their knowledge of when particular justices will or will not be on the Court.

Even under the current system, institutional litigants occasionally accelerate or retard the progress of litigation in order to assure that a particular issue will—or will not—reach the Supreme Court at a particular moment. The best-known example is the decision by Planned Parenthood of Pennsylvania to file its petition for certiorari in the 1991 Pennsylvania abortion case as soon as possible, rather than waiting until the end of the ninety-day window. The organization "spent barely two weeks drafting [its] petition," because it wanted to give the Court the opportunity to overrule *Roe v. Wade* before the 1992 presidential election and thus to make the election "a referendum on the right to abortion."[43] A few years later, supporters of racial preferences paid a white plaintiff $433,500 to assure that the Supreme Court would not decide an "affirmative action" case that the Court had already accepted for review and scheduled for argument.[44]

This kind of behavior is rare today, largely because groups like Planned Parenthood and the Black Leadership Forum generally have no reason to think that a delay of a few months or a year in the Supreme Court's consideration of an issue would mean that the issue will be decided by a different group of justices. Under the Calabresi-Lindgren and Cramton-Carrington plans, however, that prospect would loom large in the litigation tactics for many such organizations.

---

43. Linda Greenhouse, *Becoming Justice Blackmun: Harry Blackmun's Supreme Court Journey* 200–01 (2005).

44. *See* Douglas Lederman, *Settlement Prevents Supreme Court From Hearing Key Affirmative-Action Case*, Chronicle of Higher Education A48 (Dec. 5, 1997) (available on NEXIS).

More fundamentally, the "final period" for the elderly justices on the Court today is not at all equivalent to the situation that would be created by a regime of fixed eighteen-year terms. It is one thing to know that you will be leaving the Court "soon"—but at a time that is within your control (as long as you remain alive and in possession of your faculties). It is quite another to know that your term will expire next year or the year after that, and that no decision you make will allow you to remain on the Court beyond that point.

A dramatic example is close at hand. Chief Justice Rehnquist was diagnosed with a serious case of thyroid cancer early in the Court's 2004–2005 Term. He was then eighty years old. He underwent radiation treatment and chemotherapy, and he wore a tracheotomy tube in his throat. He missed four of the Court's seven argument sessions before returning to the bench in March. Many observers (including myself) believed that he was certain to retire at the end of the term. But in mid-May, Stuart Taylor, Jr., a respected commentator, offered a different view: "Rehnquist appears remarkably robust, mentally sharp, and chipper in private, according to friends. And he has always seemed to carry his opinion-writing and administrative workloads effortlessly. So maybe Rehnquist will surprise a lot of people and stay on for another term or two."[45]

We will never know how long the chief justice might have stayed.[46] In early September his condition deteriorated rapidly, and he died over Labor Day weekend. But this outcome does not diminish the force of the point I am making. When a prominent and widely cited commentator like Stuart Taylor believes that a seriously ill justice might "stay on for another term or two," it is reasonable to assume that the other members of the Court also consider that to be a viable possibility.[47] The justice himself would weigh his medical condi-

---

45. Stuart Taylor Jr., *The Rehnquist Court*, Nat'l J. 1 (May 21, 2005), LEXIS, News Library, National Journal File. Another respected commentator wrote in a similar vein in a Web analysis posted on June 9, 2005. *See* Lyle Denniston, *Commentary: The Rehnquist Riddle*, The Supreme Court Nomination Blog, <http://www.sctnomination.com/blog/> (June 9, 2005).

46. In mid-July 2005 the chief justice issued a public announcement "to put to rest the speculation and unfounded rumors of my imminent retirement." He stated: "I will continue to perform my duties as chief justice as long as my health permits." Linda Greenhouse, *Despite Rumors, Rehnquist Has No Plans to Retire Now*, N.Y. Times A-10 (July 15, 2005).

47. In fact, the justices "indicated that they were as surprised as the rest of the country to learn late Saturday night that the chief justice had died." One member of the Court added that the chief justice "had an amazing few months," and that his decision at the end of the term not to retire had not seemed unreasonable. Linda Greenhouse, *News Was Surprising To Colleagues on Court*, N.Y. Times A-1 (Sept. 5, 2005) (available on NEXIS).

tion against the poisonous atmosphere in Washington that might make it impossible to confirm a successor. But it is highly unlikely—especially when we consider the reluctance of most people to confront their own mortality—that the justice would be engaging in final-period stratagems. The situation would be quite different if the nation had adopted a regime of fixed eighteen-year terms.

Perhaps it is wrong to assume that justices of the United States Supreme Court ever engage in strategic behavior to achieve policy or ideological goals. But if you believe that such behavior is within the bounds of possibility—as supporters of the eighteen-year term plan do—then the "final period" problem is very real. Moreover, the phenomenon may manifest itself in ways other than those I have discussed (for example, in encouraging justices to decide some cases on a broad rather than a narrow basis). It thus provides a strong reason for opposing any plan for fixed terms for members of the Court.

Stability of Precedent

The final area of concern involves the stability of Supreme Court precedent. I believe that a system of staggered eighteen-year terms would destabilize the law to some degree by weakening the norm that puts pressure on justices to adhere to decisions that they would not endorse if the particular issue were coming to the Court for the first time.

At the outset, I must acknowledge that even today, stare decisis does not seem to carry enormous weight with the Court. Thus, Justice Kennedy, who has sometimes spoken so eloquently about "the rule of law," is quite willing to overturn a recent precedent when his inner voice tells him that the Constitution means something different today from what it did fifteen years ago.[48] But I think stare decisis would get even less respect on a Court whose membership was changing

---

48. Justice Kennedy has elaborated on his reverence for "the rule of law" in at least two major speeches: an address at the American Bar Association Annual Meeting in San Francisco on Aug. 9, 2003; and a speech to the Hong Kong High Court on Feb. 5, 1999. In the latter, he emphasized that "the law transcends the judge" and that "the check on the judge... is the law itself." Consistent with that approach, he joined Justice Scalia's opinion in Stanford v. Kentucky, 492 U.S. 361, 377–78 (1989), "emphatically reject[ing]" the suggestion that the Court should apply its "'own informed judgment' regarding the desirability of permitting the death penalty for crimes by 16- and 17-year-olds." However, in 2005, he wrote the opinion of the Court in Roper v. Simmons, 125 S. Ct. 1183 (2005), repudiating Stanford and relying on the majority justices' "own judgment...on the question of the acceptability of the death penalty under the Eighth Amendment." *Id.* at 1191.

every two years, particularly when one purpose of the new system is to allow the incumbent President to put his—and his party's—stamp on the Court.

Today, it is generally accepted that a change in the composition of the Court is not an acceptable reason for overruling a precedent.[49] In part, this is because one of the "[v]ery weighty considerations" that underlie the practice of stare decisis is "the necessity of maintaining public faith in the judiciary as a source of *impersonal* and reasoned judgments."[50] But under a system of staggered eighteen-year terms, the law—or at least the law announced by the Supreme Court—would become somewhat less "impersonal." Each new justice would come to the Court as the appointee of a President who was entitled by law to make that appointment—and under a system that was explicitly designed to make the Supreme Court "more responsive to the public and the political branches' understanding of the Constitution's meaning."[51]

It would not be unreasonable for a justice to take that purpose into account when confronted by a case in which recent precedent appears to require one result, while the justice's own analysis of the Constitution points to the opposite outcome. As the Court has often said, adherence to precedent "is not an inexorable command," especially in constitutional cases.[52] The altered understanding of the Court's role that would underlie the new regime would make it easier for a justice to reject a precedent handed down by a differently composed Court a few years earlier.

It is instructive to consider the experience of the National Labor Relations Board (NLRB). The NLRB is composed of five members who are appointed by the President for staggered terms of five years. Over the last four decades, the course of adjudication by the board has been marked by frequent reversals of precedent as majority control has shifted from appointees of one Pres-

---

49. *See*, e.g., Florida Dept. of Health and Rehabilitative Services v. Florida Nursing Home Assn., 450 U.S. 147, 153 (1981) (Stevens, J., concurring). In Payne v. Tennessee, 501 U.S. 808 (1991), Justice Marshall, in dissent, accused the majority of overruling a recent precedent based on nothing more than a change in "this Court's own personnel." *Id.* at 850 (dissenting opinion). Justice Marshall said that the Court acknowledged that it was doing this, but nothing in the Court's opinion alludes to the change in membership. On the contrary, the Court was careful to give reasons that did not depend on a shift in personnel. *See id.* at 827–30 (majority opinion). However, Justice Marshall was correct in saying that one member of the new majority had previously endorsed the legitimacy of overruling based on a change in membership. *See* South Carolina v. Gathers, 490 U.S. 805, 824 (1989) (Scalia, J., dissenting).

50. Moragne v. States Marine Lines, Inc., 398 U.S. 375, 403 (1970) (emphasis added).

51. *See supra* Calabresi & Lindgren, pp. 15–98 [ms. p. 67].

52. Payne v. Tennessee, 501 U.S. 801, 828 (1991).

ident to appointees of a new President of the opposite party.[53] The "Kennedy Board" overruled decisions of the "Eisenhower Board;" the "Nixon Board" overruled the "Kennedy Board;" and so to the present, with the George W. Bush Board overturning decisions of the Clinton Board.[54] The current chairman of the NLRB, Robert J. Battista, recently presented a candid and illuminating account of this process:

> [Changes in the law] can come about because of social and economic developments, or because of differing perceptions of what is right and just....
>
> With respect to the differing perceptions, it must be recognized that Congress established an agency whose Members would serve relatively short and staggered terms. Obviously, the Board majority would reflect, to some degree, the governing philosophy of the appointing President. Purists may gnash their teeth at this, but it was part of the congressional design.
>
> This is not to say that Congress intended that one party would blindly overrule the precedents of the other party. [All] holdings must be within the fundamental principles set out in the Act, and all changes must be explained. The Board is an administrative agency, charged with not only an interpretative, but a policy-making role. It is not an Article III court and thus the doctrine of stare decisis does not strictly apply. However, all responsible Members recognize the value of having stability, predictability, and certainty in the law. But, if a Member honestly believes that a prior precedent no longer makes sense, and that a change would be within the fundamental principles described above, he/she can vote to change the law. To be sure, the values of stare decisis counsel against an onslaught of changes. But

---

53. *See* Arthur D. Hellman, *Getting It Right: Panel Error and the En Banc Process in the Ninth Circuit Court of Appeals*, 34 U.C. Davis L. Rev. 425, 466 n. 150 (2000).

54. *See*, e.g., Charles J. Morris, *The Case for Unitary Enforcement of Federal Labor Law—Concerning a Specialized Article III Court and the Reorganization of Existing Agencies*, 26 Sw. L.J. 471, 477 (1972) (noting "tendency for certain Board policies to make pendulum-type swings which reflect shifts in national political administrations); Samuel Estreicher, *Policy Oscillation at the Labor Board; A Plea for Rulemaking*, 37 Admin. L. J. 163, 163–66 n. 1 (1985) (listing 37 decisions by "Reagan Board" overruling precedents); Michael D. Goldhaber, *Is NLRB in a Pro-Labor Mood?*, Nat'l L.J., Oct. 9, 2000, at B1 (noting that Board, controlled by Democrats, issued twenty-two decisions overruling precedent in two-year period); Special Report, 176 LRR 330, 333 (2005) (reporting observation by NLRB member that Board "has reversed precedent in about eight or nine cases" since Republican appointees became a majority).

prudently exercised, change is proper and indeed was envisioned by Congress.[55]

There is some ambivalence in this description, but the overall thrust is clear. Although Chairman Battista acknowledges that the Board "is not an Article III court and thus [that] the doctrine of stare decisis does not strictly apply," he also emphasizes "the value of having stability, predictability, and certainty in the law." Nevertheless, he points out that the "the structure set up by Congress" invariably and properly leads to "changes in the law" when a newly constituted majority votes in accordance with "the philosophic views of the President" who appointed the members.

I am not suggesting that a system of eighteen-year staggered terms for Supreme Court justices, with the Court's membership changing every two years, would lead to overruling on the scale seen in the NLRB. The Supreme Court *is* an Article III Court, and the doctrine of stare decisis *does* apply. But I do believe that a dynamic similar to the one described by Chairman Battista would come into play. Justices could well take the position that it was "part of the [new constitutional] design" that members of the Court "would reflect, to some degree, the governing philosophy of" the President who appointed them. And if a justice "honestly believe[d] that a prior precedent [did not correctly interpret the Constitution]," he or she could properly vote for a different interpretation. This thread of reasoning might seem especially attractive if the new interpretation reflected not only the justice's own view of constitutional doctrine, but also the "governing philosophy" of the appointing President.

There is no way of knowing how often the justices—individually or in numbers sufficient to constitute a majority—would act upon this line of thinking.[56] But what matters is not only the actual incidence of overruling, but also the willingness of the Court to reconsider its precedents. The stability of the law can be impaired even if the actual incidence of overruling is not

---

55. Robert J. Battista, *The NLRB at 70: Its Past and Its Future*, 58th NYU Annual Conference on Labor, <http://www.nlrb.gov/nlrb/press/releases/chairman_052005_nyu_speech.pdf> (May 20, 2005).

56. It is surely not necessary to expound at length on why the frequent overruling of precedent would be undesirable. Judge John R. Roberts, at his confirmation hearing after he was nominated as Chief Justice of the United States, summed up the point succinctly: "Adherence to precedent promotes evenhandedness, promotes fairness, promotes stability and predictability. And those are very important values in a legal system." Second Day of Hearings on the Nomination of Judge Roberts, <http://www.nytimes.com/2005/09/13/politics/politicsspecial1/13text-roberts.html?pagewanted=print> (visited Sept. 18, 2005).

great. And for the reasons given, I believe that greater instability would be one of the consequences of implementing the Calabresi-Lindgren plan.

Conclusion

Like the other contributors to this book, I have engaged in a great deal of speculation. Thus, I must acknowledge that the consequences of the staggered-term plan may not be as harmful as I have suggested. But the risks are real, and I believe they are substantial.

This leads to a more general point that warrants emphasis. In the preceding analysis I have tried to anticipate the likely behavior of justices, members of Congress, advocacy groups, and institutional litigants (among others) if the proposed new system were to be implemented. But the Supreme Court interacts with so many legal and political actors that no one can confidently predict all of the consequences of change. Moreover, each response is likely to trigger others.

I agree with Professor Farnsworth that those who propose amending the Constitution to replace life tenure for Supreme Court justices with a system of fixed staggered terms bear the burden of showing that the new arrangement would *clearly* create net benefits.[57] When the consequences of that new arrangement will be determined by the reactions and counter-reactions of so many different actors, there is simply no way that the proponents can meet that burden.

Other Possible Measures

Calabresi and Lindgren insist that their plan for staggered eighteen-year terms for Supreme Court justices "is fundamentally a conservative, Burkean idea that would restore the norms in this country that prevailed between 1789 and 1970 as to the tenure of Supreme Court justices."[58] This characterization is not persuasive. There is a vast difference between an eighteen-year *tenure* that comes to an end because the justice dies or chooses to retire and an eighteen-year *term* that is commanded by law. There is a vast difference between an average interval of two years between vacancies and a statute (or constitutional provision) that creates a vacancy for a particular seat at a particular moment.

---

57. *See supra* Ward Farnsworth, *The Case for Life Tenure*, pp. 251–269.
58. *See supra* Calabresi & Lindgren, pp. 15–98 [ms. p. 101].

The more important question, however, is not whether the eighteen-year term proposal would restore the norms of earlier eras but whether it represents good policy for the future. From that perspective, one could argue that some form of term limits would serve a purpose today that would have been largely unnecessary before the Warren Court era. During the nineteenth century and the first half of the twentieth century, there were historical moments when the Supreme Court played a central role in the political life of the nation, but these moments were intermittent. Today, the Court's influence is pervasive. And if justices are lingering on the bench longer than they should, or if lengthy tenures result in a Court too far removed from democratic accountability, the consequences are far more severe.

For the reasons given above, I believe that the proposed system of eighteen-year staggered terms would create more problems than it would solve. I turn now to other possible measures for dealing with concerns about justices' mental decrepitude and for restoring greater democratic accountability.

Averting Mental Decrepitude

Although it is true that mental decrepitude is not necessarily a consequence of advanced age, the correlation is sufficiently great that the most direct way of avoiding mental decrepitude on the Court would be to amend the Constitution to require justices to step down at a specified age. Professor Farnsworth has cogently summarized the arguments for and against this approach. He concludes that "[t]he case for age limits deserves serious consideration."[59]

Professor Farnsworth's analysis is persuasive, but I doubt that even this modest reform is politically feasible. Any attempt to enact a compulsory retirement provision for Supreme Court justices would almost certainly be met with cries of "invidious discrimination" from some quarters of the civil rights community. Indeed, Calabresi and Lindgren themselves decry "mandatory retirement age requirements generally because they blindly discriminate against individuals based on age."[60] Given the difficulty of gaining approval for a constitutional amendment, this is probably a fatal obstacle apart from everything else.

The prospect that one or more justices will remain on the bench establishing the law of the nation for some period after they are no longer mentally

---

59. *See supra* Farnsworth, p. 268.

60. *See supra* Calabresi & Lindgren, pp. 15–98 [ms. p. 63]. I disagree with Calabresi and Lindgren on this point. If mental decrepitude in members of the Court is as serious a threat as they believe it to be, a measure that "blindly discriminates" against some elderly but still-competent justices is a small price to pay for avoiding or at least reducing the threat.

competent is a disturbing one. Perhaps an extreme example will come to public attention sometime in the future and will galvanize public opinion, sweeping away all opposition to a compulsory-retirement amendment. Failing that, we will have to rely on family and friends to persuade or cajole a mentally decrepit justice into accepting the necessity of stepping down. That might seem like a counsel of despair, but informal processes of that kind have operated successfully with lower court judges on at least some occasions.[61]

Restoring Greater Democratic Accountability

Professors Calabresi and Lindgren marshal an impressive array of academics and other commentators who express concern that the system of life tenure for Supreme Court justices deprives "the public and political branches...of their one constitutionally provided method of ensuring that the Supreme Court accurately reflects the popular understanding of what the Constitution requires." They suggest that "the problem of democratic unaccountability is the primary reason cited by scholars for reconsidering life tenure."

I share the concerns about the "democratic unaccountability" of the Court today, but I doubt very much that the proposed reform would provide an effective cure. This is a large subject; I will explain briefly why I do not find the argument persuasive.

A key element of the argument is this: "The mechanism of the appointment process with the President nominating candidates and the Senate confirming them is the main and really the only guarantee that the Supreme Court will reflect public norms."[62] In my view, reliance on the Senate confirmation process to "guarantee that the Supreme Court will reflect public norms" is misplaced. For one thing, as recent history demonstrates, Senate rules and traditions give the minority enormous powers of delay and obstruction. We cannot assume that a nominee who wins confirmation by the Senate will come to the Court "instill[ed with] popular values of constitutional interpretation"[63]— much less that he or she will advance those values as a member of the Court.

More broadly, if divorcement from democratic accountability is reflected in the decisions of the current Court (as I believe it is), the phenomenon is

---

61. *See* H. R. Jud. Comm., *The Operations of Federal Judicial Misconduct and Recusal Statutes: Hearing Before the Subcommittee on Courts, the Internet and Intellectual Property,* 107th Cong. 91–92 (Nov. 29, 2001) (testimony of Arthur D. Hellman and Michael J. Remington).

62. *See supra* Calabresi & Lindgren, pp. 15–98 [ms. p. 27].

63. *Id.* at [ms. p. 28].

sustained and fed by forces that are largely impervious to correction by Senate confirmation processes. Here it is necessary to delve briefly into the question: What are the "public norms" that a more democratically accountable Court would embrace? On that point, I agree with Calabresi and Lindgren that "the American public is now more committed than are lawyerly elites to the notion that constitutional cases should be decided based on text and history."[64] I take this position, not on the basis of opinion polls or other surveys, but because it is hard to imagine how the public could be *less* committed to text and history in constitutional interpretation than the "lawyerly elites," particularly those in academia.

But it is a commitment to "text and history"—and to giving text and history priority over particular precedents that support new claims of liberty or equality—that gets nominees (at least Republican nominees) in trouble in the Senate. This is partly a consequence of pressure from interest groups, as discussed earlier in this essay, but it also reflects the zealously argued preferences of the dominant organs of the mainstream media and the "lawyerly elites" whose influence the Calabresi-Lindgren proposal seeks to circumvent.

Today, the mainstream media and the lawyerly elites applaud courts when they implement favored policy choices through the medium of constitutional interpretation. And they exhort Senators to reject nominees who do not share a commitment to an "evolving sense of the meaning of constitutional clauses."[65] These voices are likely to carry more weight in the confirmation process than the vaguely felt concerns of the general public, to whom the issues are remote and arcane.

Of course the media and the elites do not always prevail, but in the environment I have described, it is doubtful whether the confirmation process will foster democratic accountability of the kind that Professors Calabresi and Lindgren seek. In all likelihood, the Supreme Court will continue on its present course whether with the same membership or with new justices—and whether new justices join the Court at regular or irregular intervals. "No more Souters" may be an exhilarating rallying cry for those who are disappointed by the direction the current Court has taken, but I would not put money on it as a description of the Court in the foreseeable future, even if Republican Presidents are making all the appointments.

Is there, then, any hope for bringing greater democratic accountability to the Court? Ironically, today one of the greatest obstacles to pursuing even

---

64. *See supra* Calabresi & Lindgren, pp. 15–98 [ms. p. 79].
65. *That Scalia Charm*, N.Y. Times A16 (Mar. 21, 2005) (editorial).

modest measures is the rhetoric of some of the Court's critics.[66] Tom Delay calls for "hearings on the definition of good behavior" to help Congress "hold the judiciary accountable." Pat Robertson suggests that an out-of-control judiciary is a more serious threat to the nation than Al-Qaeda terrorists.[67] Senator John Cornyn appears to say that courthouse violence, although "without justification," can be attributed in part to "judges [who] are making political decisions yet are unaccountable to the public."[68]

Now recall the comments by Dean Kramer:

> The Constitution leaves room for countless political responses to an overly assertive Court: Justices can be impeached, the Court's budget can be slashed, the President can ignore its mandates, Congress can strip it of jurisdiction or shrink its size or pack it with new members or give it burdensome new responsibilities or revise its procedures.

But anyone who proposed any of these measures today would be condemned by the mainstream media, bar associations, and law professors as an ally of Tom DeLay and Pat Robertson seeking to destroy judicial independence. (As far as I have been able to determine, Dean Kramer did not defend DeLay when DeLay was attacked for his comments on an "unaccountable judiciary.")

For my own part, I am reluctant to embrace any of the rather drastic responses that Dean Kramer appears to suggest.[69] There may be some more modest measures that could bring a small degree of "democratic accountability" to the Court, but that is a topic for another day.

---

66. I recognize that the statements quoted here do not specifically target the Supreme Court, but that is a distinction that will matter little to those who are disturbed by the rhetoric.

67. *This Week With George Stephanopoulos* (ABC television broadcast, May 1, 2005), LEXIS, Nexis Library, ABC File.

68. 151 Cong. Rec. S 3126 (daily ed. Apr. 4, 2005). Senator Cornyn later clarified his remarks, saying, "I am aware of no evidence whatsoever linking recent acts of courthouse violence to the various controversial rulings that have captured the nation's attention in recent years." Sen. John Cornyn, *Letters; Senator Responds to Editorial on Judges*, Los Angeles Times B14 (Apr. 16, 2005).

69. In September 2004, a subcommittee of the House Judiciary Committee held a hearing on a bill that included two of the "political responses" proposed by Dean Kramer: impeachment and withdrawal of jurisdiction. I testified in opposition to these provisions and to the bill as a whole. See H.R. Jud Comm. *Constitution Restoration Act of 2004: Hearing Before the Subcommittee on Courts, the Internet and Intellectual Property of the House Judiciary Committee on H.R. 3799*, 108th Cong. 17–31 (Sept. 13, 2004).

An Interdisciplinary Perspective on the Tenure of Supreme Court Justices

Stephen B. Burbank[*]

Introduction

A great deal has been written about proposals to change the tenure of Supreme Court justices. Those proposals differ in numerous respects. Some rely on fixed terms, renewable or nonrenewable; others would mandate retirement at a certain age. Some proposed terms are long, others short. Some of the proposals would meld service on the Court with service on the lower federal courts, whether as an attempt to avoid the need for a constitutional amendment or a means to implement the proposer's vision of what is wrong with the system of life tenure crafted by those who wrote the Constitution.

Steven Calabresi and James Lindgren have made by far the most elaborate case for moving from life tenure to non-renewable eighteen-year terms. They present a variety of data showing that in the period since 1970: (1) justices have served far longer than the mean in the period prior to 1970 (25+ years vs. 14+ years), (2) they have served to a much older mean age (78+ vs. 68+), and (3) we have experienced both an increase in the mean interval between appointments (1.91 vs. 3.27 years) and a disproportionate share of the longest intervals between appointments. As a result, the authors argue, the Court, for which the appointment process is (in their view) the only plausibly effective check ensuring democratic accountability, does not receive regular refresh-

[*] David Berger Professor for the Administration of Justice, University of Pennsylvania.

ment drawing it closer to popular understandings of the Constitution; the incentive of presidents to appoint younger people to the bench is enhanced (depriving the nation of older, perhaps smarter and wiser people); the appointment process has become contentious and politicized to the detriment of the institution, and the problem of justices overstaying their time has increased in frequency, as has strategic partisan behavior of justices in timing their retirements.[1]

I will concentrate on the case that these and other authors have made to replace life tenure for Supreme Court justices with non-renewable eighteen-year terms. I do not intend to discuss the question whether, if our lawmakers deemed such a change desirable, they could implement it by statute as opposed to constitutional amendment. That question is neither uninteresting nor without difficulty. In the absence of unambiguous text or precedent in the form of court decisions, and mindful that "constitutional law" is not confined to court decisions, the answer to the constitutional question would turn on an (explicit or implicit) assessment of the policy implications of changing the status quo, which in turn would (or should) depend on a comparative assessment of the benefits and costs of the proposed alternative in light of the roles that the Supreme Court plays in our society.

It is easy to see how, so framed, and whether or not garbed in the language of constitutional law, a scholarly debate about judicial tenure could be dominated by the kind of "epistemic shallowness" for which law professors are infamous (the term is Richard Posner's describing doctrinal scholarship).[2] Indeed, the work of many engaged in the debate is quite relentlessly normative and replete with unsupported causal assertions. For that reason I have chosen to explore the question whether proponents' assertions and predictions about political phenomena are supported by the theories or empirical evidence produced by those whose business it is to study political phenomena. More broadly, my goal is to begin to fill what I perceive to be both theoretical and evidentiary gaps. Examining the literatures of other disciplines, particularly political science, I seek therein understanding whether there are serious problems warranting attention and whether non-renewable eighteen-year terms would solve those problems (without creating other problems).

Approaching the question from that perspective, I find that there is little evidence that life tenure on the Supreme Court as it operates today is responsi-

---

1. *See supra* Steven G. Calabresi & James Lindgren, *Term Limits for the Supreme Court: Life Tenure Reconsidered*, pp. 15–98; *see also infra* Paul D. Carrington & Roger C. Cramton, *The Supreme Court Renewal Act: A Return to Basic Principles*, pp. 467–471.

2. Richard A. Posner, *Overcoming Law* 88 (1995).

ble for some of the costs attributed to it, or that the costs themselves are serious enough to warrant changing a basic structural arrangement at this time. These include the costs proponents of change associate with presidential incentives in making nominations, the behavior of the justices in connection with retirement, and the contentiousness of the appointment process. The evidence also suggests to me that, in historical perspective, the problem of justices remaining beyond the time they are up to the job is less serious than it was in prior periods, before Congress enacted adequate provisions for retirement.

I then turn to arguments that the current system of life tenure for Supreme Court justices renders them insufficiently accountable to the public, threatening democratic legitimacy by distancing the justices from popular understandings of constitutional meaning. I argue that the accountability critique is impoverished because it focuses exclusively on the appointment process and treats judicial independence and judicial accountability as both dichotomous and monolithic. The focus on the appointment process obscures from view other executive and legislative powers that can render the Court accountable, together with norms, customs and dialogic processes that have developed in their shadow, as it does normative and empirical scholarship suggesting that the Court in fact never strays very far or for very long from majority preferences. The isolation of judicial independence from judicial accountability enables proponents to invoke comparative data that in fact tell us very little, and it may also cause them to treat less seriously than they should the potential costs of the frequent and predictable appointments that their system might entail. One of those costs may be a quantum and quality of democratic accountability, shaped by the incentives and concerns of interest groups aligned with political parties, that could swamp the putative independence augured by non-renewable eighteen-year terms viewed in isolation.

In examining proponents' claims concerning democratic legitimacy, I review the political science literature about the public's knowledge of the Court and its decisions and how that knowledge translates into support (or lack of it). I find little basis to believe that the public at large has understandings of constitutional meaning, as opposed to awareness of results in controversial cases or cases that are for some reason highly salient, let alone understandings of competing interpretive approaches. I also find no credible evidence that the Court today lacks public support to an extent that should concern us; indeed, it enjoys greater support than Congress.

Finally, I seek in the interest group literature clues to the sort of environment in which frequent and predictable appointments would likely play out. The evidence suggests that, far from reducing the contentiousness of the process, a system of frequent and predictable appointments might reinforce the worst tendencies of modern politics, causing a crisis in democratic legitimacy by shining more light, more frequently on the Court, and by draping the Court's work in the garb of the ordinary politics of which it would be seen as a part.

The Putative Costs of Life Tenure: Presidential Incentives, Mental Decrepitude, and Strategic Partisan Retirement

Calabresi and Lindgren are to be applauded for gathering and manipulating empirical data in order to quantify the perceived problems to which they respond. Like many other proponents of change, however, they seem fixated on the current institution—at the end of its existence as a "natural Court"[3]—and on incentives that may seem irresistible given the current political climate. Lacking historical and institutional perspective, the enterprise has the air of a self-fulfilling prophecy.

What, for instance, should we make of the claims that their proposal "will eliminate the incentive Presidents currently have to find candidates who are even younger,"[4] or that the "problem with the current nomination system is that youth has been elevated from one factor among many to one of the most important considerations"?[5] The average age at appointment has remained remarkably uniform (at circa fifty-three) over time. The basic incentive to appoint younger people is life tenure. As Ward Farnsworth suggests, logically, one would expect greater attention to age at appointment when life expectancies are short,[6] and empirical data support that logical supposition.[7] Given numerous long tenures prior to 1970 and the age of recent nominees,

---

3. "The period during which a court's membership remains unchanged is known to political scientists as a natural court." Linda Greenhouse, *Under the Microscope Longer than Most*, N.Y. Times § 4, 3 (July 10, 2005).

4. *See supra* Calabresi & Lindgren, p. 62.

5. James E. DiTullio & John B. Schochet, Student Authors, *Saving this Honorable Court, A Proposal to Replace Life Tenure on the Supreme Court with Staggered, Nonrenewable Eighteen-Year Terms*, 90 Va. L. Rev. 1093, 1113 (2004). *See id.* at 1110–16, 1122.

6. *See* Ward Farnsworth, *The Regulation of Turnover on the Supreme Court*, 2005 U. Ill. L. Rev. 407 (forthcoming 2005).

7. *See* John Gruhl, *The Impact of Term Limits for Supreme Court Justices*, 81 Judicature 66, 66 (Sept.–Oct. 1997) ("In the 18th and 19th centuries, the average age at appointment was 51.1 years").

it is implausible that the perceived lengthening tenure since then has had a significant impact on appointments, when compared for instance to a particular president's agenda in making appointments.[8] But we need not speculate; the question should be amenable to empirical investigation.

Before doing such work, however, one should perhaps seek perspective on the phenomenon of "lengthening tenure." Working with medians rather than means,[9] Kevin McGuire finds that "the tenure of the justices has been quite stable over time;" that the median age of the current justices (sixty-nine) is not substantially higher than the historical median (sixty-three; sixty-four from 1900); and that, although the median service of the justices today (eighteen years) is higher than the median amount of service since the Civil War, which has rarely exceeded fifteen years, the impending retirement of Justice O'Connor combined with the retirement of one of the Court's oldest members "would return the Court to its historical norm."[10]

The treatment of "mental decrepitude"[11] and strategic partisan retirement by most proponents of change also strikes me as historically tone deaf. Artemus Ward makes clear the importance of retirement arrangements in the historic progression from leaving the Court in a coffin to leaving when a justice chooses. Mental decrepitude is not a new problem; indeed, it is less of a problem today than it once was. Before adequate provisions were made for retirement, some justices had no choice but to hang on, often for many years, until the bitter end (unless Congress could be persuaded to

---

8. David Yalof's study of appointments from Truman through Reagan does not support the claim that age has become a more important criterion than it was in the (recent) past. *See* David Alistair Yalof, *Pursuit of Justices: Presidential Politics and the Selection of Supreme Court Nominees* 43, 104, 127 (1999). Perhaps most telling in that regard is Yalof's evaluation of age as a criterion in the Reagan administration. "Age was a concern, but unlike with Eisenhower and Nixon, the administration did not impose on his subordinates any fixed minimum or maximum at the outset that might preclude the consideration of especially worthy candidates." *Id.* at 134. *See id.* ("the most important criteria were ideological").

9. The use of means rather than medians for the relatively short period of 1971–present may distort comparison with means in the preceding period (1789–1970), particularly given the relatively small number of justices and the long interval since the last departure in the former period. Note also the potential effects of making the cut in 1970, since both Justices Black and Harlan retired in 1971.

10. Kevin T. McGuire, *An Assessment of Tenure on the U.S. Supreme Court*, 89 Judicature 8, 8, 10, 12 (2005). Chief Justice Rehnquist died shortly after this article was published, fulfilling the second condition.

11. *See* David J. Garrow, *Mental Decrepitude on the U.S. Supreme Court: The Historical Case for a 28th Amendment*, 67 U. Chi. L. Rev. 995 (2000).

enact a private bill).[12] Once adequate retirement provisions were in place, and given a discretionary docket and resources to hire (multiple) clerks, it is hard to explain mental decrepitude, to the extent that it has been a problem in recent decades, without considering ego and partisan strategic behavior.

Those who rely on anecdotal evidence in contending that strategic partisan retirement has become, not just more frequent, but a problem worthy of attention in recent decades, confront a number of difficulties.[13] Many of their examples involve justices whose supposed preference to retire strategically yielded to declining health and/or other personal considerations, while the evidence is lacking that partisan motivation strongly influenced, let alone dominated, the retirement decisions of many others.[14] The former instances in fact

---

12. *See* Artemus Ward, *Deciding to Leave: the Politics of Retirement from the United States Supreme Court passim* (2003). Of the forty justices departing between 1801 and 1896, ten did so by resignation or retirement, while thirty died in office. *See id.* at 47, 70. Because the 1869 legislation authorizing retirement (formally resignation on salary) applied only to those at least seventy years old and with ten years of service, special legislation was required to permit Justice Hunt, who became disabled before reaching ten years of service, to retire. *See id.* at 86–87. Similar legislation also proved necessary to permit the retirement of Justice Moody in 1910, *see id.* at 106, and of Justice Pitney in 1922. *See id.* at 116.

13. Robert Nagel correctly points out that "while somewhat unseemly from some perspectives, timed retirement decisions are not obviously different from any number of strategic decisions that justices routinely make in an effort to prolong and maximize their influence." *See supra* Robert F. Nagel, *Limiting the Court by Limiting Life Tenure*, p. 128. He also observes that, "even on the assumption that timed retirements are different from and more regrettable than other efforts at prolonged influence, it is not clear why they are suddenly such a serious problem as to warrant changing the long-standing practice of life tenure." *Id.*

14. This leads some proponents of change to rather odd conclusions. *See* DiTullio & Schochet, *supra* n. 5, at 1109 ("Though both men [Warren and Douglas] were ultimately prevented from strategically retiring, the very fact that they attempted and thought they could succeed in strategically departing demonstrates the weaknesses of the current system of appointments to the Court.").

> Based on the timing, their relative good health, or both, Justices Harlan, Stewart, Burger, White, and Blackmun can be classified as being motivated by partisanship in their departure decisions. While there is little direct evidence to substantiate such a conclusion for any of them, circumstances suggest as much. There is, on the other hand, direct evidence that Earl Warren was clearly partisan in his departure attempt, and that William O. Douglas and Lewis Powell had at least some partisan concerns. Though Justices Brennan and Marshall ultimately did not depart for partisan reasons, they were initially partisan in their departure considerations. Overall, these cases suggest a new level of partisanship in the departure decision-making of the justices.

provide anecdotal support for studies showing that, over time, partisan considerations have paled in comparison with other factors, including personal considerations and the availability of pension benefits, in motivating retirement.[15] The most recent of these studies found "no consistent support for justices taking partisan factors into account, either in their retirement decisions or in their decisions to remain on the bench."[16] As explained by Albert Yoon in a forthcoming study of judicial turnover on the federal courts as a whole:

> [W]hile judges may hold preferences regarding the political environment in which they vacate their seat, they do not appear to optimize solely over them. Much of this can be explained by judges' lack of control over the political environment. Judges, while they may desire a favorable political environment to emerge, cannot compel it…. Moreover, even when the political environment is favorable, the judge, when considering other factors—e.g., job satisfaction, institutional norms, a sense of civic duty—may choose to remain on the bench.[17]

There is, thus, reason to doubt whether some of the supposed costs of the current system constitute serious problems today, and it is clear that some of them are less serious than they once were. If any cost properly attributable to the current system of life tenure *is* deemed serious enough to warrant a change, those responsible for our institutions should consider more finely tailored solutions. In that regard, McGuire has sketched how pension incentives

---

Ward, *supra* n. 12, at 209. Note further that any partisanship attributed to Justice Blackmun's and Chief Justice Warren's retirement decisions/thinking involved presidents of the other party than that to which their appointing presidents belonged.

15. *See* Christopher J. W. Zorn & Steven R. Van Winkle, *A Competing Risks Model of Supreme Court Vacancies, 1789–1992*, 22 Pol. Behav. 145 (2000); Peverill Squire, *Politics and Personal Factors in Retirement from the United States Supreme Court*, 10 Pol. Behav. 180 (1988). *But cf.* Timothy M. Hagle, *Strategic Retirements: A Political Model of Turnover on the United States Supreme Court*, 15 Pol. Behav. 25 (1993). For other work disputing the importance of this phenomenon, see Saul Brenner, *The Myth that Justices Strategically Retire*, 36 Soc. Sci. J. 431 (1999).

16. Zorn & Van Winkle, *supra* n. 15, at 160.

17. Albert Yoon, *The End of the Rainbow: Understanding Turnover among Federal Judges*, ___ Am. L. & Econ. Rev. ___ (forthcoming 2005). Although Yoon finds that district court and court of appeals judges "are increasingly synchronizing their tenure of active service with their pension qualification [i.e., taking senior status as soon as eligible to do so]," *id.* at ___, he finds that phenomenon operating "essentially not at all among Supreme Court justices." *Id.* The point he makes in the passage quoted in the text is, however, equally applicable to the justices.

could be structured to encourage retirement at a given age, thereby addressing both mental decrepitude and strategic partisan retirement (to the extent they are currently problems worthy of legislative attention).[18]

More Putative Costs: Accountability and Legitimacy

Proponents of changing the tenure of Supreme Court justices claim that life tenure today, by reason of longer life expectancies and whatever other phenomena contribute to supposedly "lengthening tenure," results in the Court being too far removed from the will of the people, so that it is insufficiently democratically accountable and legitimate. An associated claim made in support of non-renewable eighteen-year terms is that, as a result of frequent and predictable appointments, the Court will better reflect popular understandings of the Constitution's meaning. Calabresi and Lindgren make an additional, analytically distinct, claim that the people favor textualism or originalism and thus that their proposal will not only bring the Court's decisions, but also its methods, into closer accord with majority preferences. Finally, because proponents in general tend to regard the appointment process as the only means of ensuring the Court's accountability and legitimacy, they regard the current Court as exercising power that is not only "great" but "totally unchecked."[19] I take up these claims regarding accountability and legitimacy separately below.

Accountability

Both the political science literature and interdisciplinary work on judicial independence and accountability suggest that, although the Supreme Court does exercise "great power," it is *not* "totally unchecked" in doing so. That is not surprising when one considers that "the Constitution would provide very little protection against an executive and legislature intent on controlling the

---

18. *See* McGuire, *supra* n. 10, at 15.

19. *See supra* Calabresi & Lindgren, p. 17. *See id.* at pp. 35–37. *Compare id.* at 36, n. 64 (acknowledging but disparaging the effectiveness of other "indirect means" of instilling "the public's political values") *with id.* at 72 (relying on existing "political checks" in answering argument that proposal would unduly impinge upon judicial independence). *See also infra* Carrington & Cramton, pp. 468–469 (discussing traits associated with "unchecked power").

decisional independence of the federal courts."[20] Proponents of changing the tenure of Supreme Court justices should thus treat more seriously (and consistently) a variety of means, in addition to the appointment process and the impeachment process, by which Congress and the executive branch have in the past exercised influence, even in matters of constitutional law, and can do so again in the future.[21]

Numerous political scientists, from Robert Dahl, to Robert McCloskey, to Gerald Rosenberg, have disputed, and provided empirical evidence controverting, the proposition that the Court is unaccountable to the other institutions of government when deciding cases.[22] Their work, together with more recent work by Lee Epstein, Jack Knight and Andrew Martin, and others who take a strategic perspective,[23] suggests that the Court does not often have the last word even on matters of constitutional interpretation, and that as a result it does not stray very far or for very long from what the majority wants. Moreover, as Barry Friedman has observed, "there is general agreement among political scientists, and increasing recognition among legal academics, that more often than not the outcomes of Supreme Court decisions are consistent with public opinion."[24]

An argument about accountability solely from the perspective of the appointment process is not necessarily inconsistent with Dahl, insofar as he stressed the regularity of appointments and hence, in his view, a likely congruence of the policy preferences of a Court majority and the policy aims of the dominant political coalition.[25] Yet, again, the appointment process is not

---

20. Stephen B. Burbank & Barry Friedman, *Reconsidering Judicial Independence*, in *Judicial Independence at the Crossroads: an Interdisciplinary Approach* 9, 14 (Stephen B. Burbank & Barry Friedman eds., 2002).

21. *See* Burbank & Friedman, *supra* n. 20, at 12–14 (court-stripping, jurisdictional regulation, court-packing, budgetary control, executive enforcement of judgments). *See also* Charles Gardner Geyh, *Customary Independence*, in *Judicial Independence at the Crossroads, supra* n. 20, at 160.

22. *See, e.g.,* Robert G. McCloskey, *The American Supreme Court* (3d ed., 2000); Gerald N. Rosenberg, *Judicial Independence and the Reality of Political Power*, 54 Rev. Pol. 369 (1992); Robert A. Dahl, *Decision-Making in a Democracy: The Supreme Court as a National Policy-Maker*, 6 J. Pub. L. 279 (1957).

23. *See* Lee Epstein, Jack Knight & Andrew D. Martin, *Constitutional Interpretation from a Strategic Perspective*, in *Making Policy, Making Law* 170 (Mark C. Miller & Jeb Barnes eds., 2004); Louis Fisher, *Judicial Finality or an Ongoing Colloquy?*, in *id.* at 153; Neal Devins, *Is Judicial Policymaking Countermajoritarian?*, in *id.* at 189.

24. Barry Friedman, *History, Politics and Judicial Independence*, in *Judicial Integrity* 99, 114 (Andras Sajo ed., 2004). *But see supra* Calabresi & Lindgren, p. 48 ("the post-1970 Supreme Court is, if anything, too insulated from public opinion").

25. *See* Dahl, *supra* n. 22, at 284–85.

the only means of making the Court accountable, a historical fact of institutional life that, it seems to me, renders even more attractive the argument of Epstein and her colleagues that the resolution of the countermajoritarian difficulty "rests not on a coincidence of preferences, as Dahl suggests, but on an important effect of the separation of powers system: a strategic incentive to anticipate and then react to the desires of elected officials."[26] Even if one does not accept this strategic account, it remains true, as Friedman has pointed out, that "the law itself provides a mechanism for achieving majoritarian results" through a built-in "set of standards deferential to government, if not public, will."[27]

From the perspective both of history and of neo-institutionalism, then, a view of accountability that begins and ends with the appointment process is impoverished because it focuses on one formal means of exercising power, excluding from view other such means, together with norms, customs and dialogic processes that have developed in their shadow and that may constitute the most important vehicles of "accountability" in a complex system of separated but interdependent powers. Among the norms and customs so neglected are the many ways in which, over time, the Court has exercised self-restraint, and which, John Ferejohn and Larry Kramer argue, are critical to its continuing ability to use independent judgment when such judgment is required.[28]

There is another and more basic problem with the view of accountability animating many proposals for change, however. The sponsors tend to treat judicial independence and judicial accountability as both dichotomous and monolithic. This problem might *not* have been avoided by reading the political science literature.[29] But recent interdisciplinary scholarship has revealed that, to the contrary, independence and accountability are different sides of the same coin. It has also made evident the fact that there is no one ideal mix of independence and accountability, but rather that the appropriate mix for a given court system, and indeed for a given court, depends upon what a polity

---

26. Epstein et al., *supra* n 23, at 186.

27. Friedman, *supra* n. 24, at 116.

28. *See* John A. Ferejohn & Larry D. Kramer, *Independent Judges, Dependent Judiciary: Institutionalizing Judicial Restraint*, 77 N.Y.U. L. Rev. 962 (2002). The fact that the Court has not always exercised such restraint, including in the recent past, should not lead us to lose perspective. *See infra* text accompanying notes 87–89.

29. *See* Stephen B. Burbank, *The Architecture of Judicial Independence*, 72 S. Cal. L. Rev. 315, 327 (1999) (arguing that common political science definition of judicial independence, "requiring virtual immunity from the influence of the other branches, or at least only minimal influence," is "theoretically and practically...too unforgiving").

seeks from that system or court.[30] We may agree that a non-renewable eight-een-year term (which is, after all, consistent with the historical mean and the current median) does not represent a plausible threat to judicial independ-ence when viewed in isolation. One cannot, however, determine whether the quantum or quality of judicial independence that non-renewable eighteen-year terms would afford the Supreme Court of the United States is sufficient without at the same time considering the quantum and quality of accounta-bility that such a proposal—and in particular the frequent and predictable va-cancies it would entail—portends, given what we seek from the Court today.

In this light, data about the terms of tenure of the judges on high or con-stitutional courts of other countries, or on the high courts of the states of the United States, although useful in stimulating thought about alternatives, are potentially misleading. It is not just that such data by themselves tell us very little about judicial independence and accountability in those polities. It is dif-ficult to draw reliable conclusions about the suitability for transplant of the arrangements made in different political systems without understanding those systems and the roles that courts are expected to play in them.[31]

Legitimacy

Gerald Rosenberg has noted the tension between, on the one hand, Dahl's claim that such power as the Court has derives from the "unique legitimacy attributed to its interpretations of the Constitution"[32] and, on the other hand, his "primary claim that the Court is a political institution, part of the domi-nant political alliance."[33] Rosenberg also argued that the evidence did not sup-port Dahl's (admittedly speculative) claims about legitimacy. I find no such tension in the work of proponents for change, and I believe that their notions about legitimacy are equally suspect.

As previously discussed, the dominant vision of democratic accountability among those advocating change apparently includes, and includes only, such accountability as the appointment process provides, leaving out of account other powers and processes, formal and informal, by which the Court, acting

---

30. *See* Burbank & Friedman, *supra* n. 20, at 14–22.

31. *See, e.g.*, Robert A. Kagan, *American Courts and the Policy Dialogue: The Role of Ad-versarial Legalism*, in *Making Policy, Making Law, supra* n. 23, at 13; Stephen B. Burbank, *The Roles of Litigation*, 80 Wash. U. L. Q. 705 (2002).

32. Dahl, *supra* n. 22, at 293.

33. Gerald N. Rosenberg, *The Road Taken: Robert A. Dahl's Decision-Making in a Democracy: The Supreme Court as a National Policy-Maker*, 50 Emory L. J. 613, 627 (2001).

strategically, may be influenced. This leads to the untenable claim that the Court today exercises not only great power, but that it is "totally unchecked" in doing so. It also helps to understand the assertions that, without more regular and frequent turnover, the justices are not accountable to current "popular understandings of constitutional meaning"[34] and that irregular and infrequent vacancies "can prevent the American people from being regularly able to check the Court when it has strayed from following text and original meaning."[35]

Calabresi and Lindgren assert that life tenure today fosters a gap between the Court's jurisprudence and popular understandings of the Constitution's meaning that is itself normatively undesirable and that threatens the Court's democratic legitimacy. Other proponents assert that "there should be some relationship between the voters' choice of a president and the relative influence that president has on the Court."[36] If the appointment process were the only check on the Court's power, and if popular understandings of constitutional meaning could faithfully be translated through that process, perhaps regular appointments would solve both alleged problems and an additional problem that proponents of change lay at the door of infrequent and irregular vacancies on the Court, to wit, the increasing contentiousness of the confirmation process, leading to the politicization of the Court.

Even those attracted by the view that the Court's jurisprudence should faithfully and currently reflect popular understandings of the Constitution's meaning or the country's political values, should presumably be interested in what the nature of those understandings is, how they are formed, and how faithfully they are represented by elected officials. Moreover, to the extent proposals for a fundamental change in the Court rely on a threat to democratic legitimacy, it is presumably relevant to ask how the public views that institution and, in particular, whether there is any evidence of such a threat today.

There is an extensive literature on what the public knows about the Court, how it comes by that knowledge, and how the knowledge members of the public have about the Court and its decisions translates into support for the institution. Not surprisingly, the controversy over the 2000 presidential election and the Court's role in that election through its decision in *Bush* v. *Gore*[37] has stimulated a great deal of recent scholarly research on these subjects, re-

---

34. *See supra* Calabresi & Lindgren, p. 60.
35. *Id.* at 38.
36. DiTullio & Schochet, *supra* n. 5, at 1117. *See also supra* Calabresi & Lindgren, pp. 35–39, 58–59.
37. 531 U.S. 98 (2000).

fining theoretical questions and furnishing quite current data on public attitudes towards the Court.

Study after study has shown that the public knows very little about the Court or its decisions, but that levels of awareness differ as between the attentive public, who tend to be better educated and more interested in politics and public affairs, and the non-attentive public. In addition, numerous studies demonstrate that most members of the public acquire the knowledge they have about the Court and its decisions from the mass media. Although this is not surprising, it may explain a frequent counsel of caution about invoking the public's ignorance, since research has also found that the public's knowledge of the Court's decisions varies depending upon a number of factors, including the extent and duration of media coverage and the perceived salience of the contested issue, e.g. its perceived relevance to a person's personal circumstances (race, religion) or to his or her circumstances as a member of a (geographic) community.

Gerald Rosenberg has noted that "[t]he positive relationship often asserted between Court decisions and legitimacy depends on a level of public knowledge about the Court that may be missing."[38] Although I believe his account of the relevant literature neglects an important distinction—between specific and diffuse support—which I shall discuss, one who has read that literature has difficulty understanding appeals to popular understandings of the Constitution's meaning. Indeed, (1) the distinction emerging in the literature between the attentive and non-attentive public and (2) the evidence that only high salience cases (issues) are likely to prompt knowledge among the inattentive public and that such knowledge relates less to constitutional meaning than it does to results—neither of which is surprising when one considers the sources of the public's information—suggest that what we have here is an appeal to the understandings of the portion of the public with which the person making it identifies. Certainly, the inferential evidence offered for the proposition that the people prefer constitutional interpretation that focuses on "text and history,"[39] pales in comparison with direct evidence of profound general

---

38. Rosenberg, *supra* n. 33, at 628.

39. We think the public has consistently voted since 1968 for presidential candidates who have promised to appoint Supreme Court justices who would interpret the law rather than making it up. Even the Democrats who have won since 1968, Jimmy Carter and Bill Clinton, were from the moderate wings of the Democratic party, and the two Democrats appointed to the Court since 1968 are well to the right of Earl Warren or William Brennan.

See *supra* Calabresi & Lindgren, p. 76.

ignorance of the institution, its methods, and the great bulk of its work product among most members of the public.

There is, in fact, some evidence that, when specifically offered choices, the public favors, in general, an approach to the interpretation of the Constitution that gives weight to "the intentions of the people who wrote the Constitution" and to the "Court's past decisions on similar matters," far more than they do one that reflects "whether the judges are liberals or conservatives."[40] In the same study, however, more than two thirds of the respondents believed that "what the majority of the public favors" should have either some impact or a large impact on Supreme Court decisions, while close to three quarters of them were of the same opinion as to "the judges' views of what is good for the public, even if it's not addressed in the Constitution." How does one fashion a coherent approach to interpretation from that, and how useful is it with respect to the great constitutional issues of the day? Moreover, what interpretive significance would the average member of the public accord to the intentions of those who *ratified* the Constitution? Would that person agree with James Madison that original intentions must at some point yield to precedent and to the "constitutional law" of practice?[41] Finally in this aspect, is originalism itself a "political value," and is it in any event well calculated to yield results that accord with "the country's political values?"

In the same group of respondents favoring an interpretive approach that privileges original intent and precedent over ideology, more believed that, in actual practice, ideology has a larger impact on Supreme Court decisions than either precedent or the intentions of the framers. This might suggest evidence of a problem of democratic legitimacy. For, as the authors of this study observe, "[i]f over time the public (and, especially, the political class) perceives the Court as 'just another political institution,' there may be grave consequences for the Court's legitimacy."[42] The authors did find that the discrepancies between respondents' normative preferences and their beliefs about the factors actually influencing the Court's decisions "detract[ed] from the Court's overall image."[43] But, while the strongest negative effect was associated with the intentions of the framers, the weakest was associated with ideology, sug-

---

40. *See* John M. Scheb II & William Lyons, *Judicial Behavior and Public Opinion: Popular Expectations Regarding the Factors that Influence Supreme Court Decisions*, 23 Pol. Behav. 181, 185 (2001) (Table 1).

41. *See* Richard S. Arnold, *How James Madison Interpreted the Constitution*, 72 N.Y.U. L. Rev. 267 (1997).

42. Scheb & Lyons, *supra* n. 40, at 181–82.

43. *Id.* at 187.

gesting that "the public appears to have by and large resigned itself to this influence."[44] Moreover, the respondents rated the performance of the Court higher than they did that of either the federal government in general or the Congress, and both their evaluation of the federal government and of the Court's performance in the criminal justice area were better predictors of their evaluation of the Court overall than was the "legal factor" (intent and precedent).[45]

Putting to the side questions about the kind of support that a question focused on the Court's "performance" measures,[46] these studies are hardly evidence of a serious problem of legitimacy, and I am aware of no such evidence elsewhere. To be sure, "legitimacy" is a slippery term in the literature of constitutional law, so much so that Richard Fallon was recently moved to write an article devoted to unpacking that concept.[47] It has the same elusive potential in political science, but far more work, theoretical and empirical, has been done to bring it to ground. That work is more important to the current inquiry than are discussions of "legitimacy" in constitutional law if only because, in seeking to test theory with evidence, it provides a basis for evaluating the claim that infrequent and irregular vacancies damage the Court's democratic legitimacy.

That which Fallon refers to as "sociological legitimacy" is akin to what political scientists call "diffuse support," that is, support for the institution whether or not one agrees with particular products (decisions). Political scientists distinguish diffuse support from "specific support," that is, support based on particular products (decisions). It is diffuse support, I believe, to which the late Judge Richard Arnold was referring when he stressed, as he often did, the need for the federal courts to have the "continuing consent of the governed,"[48] if they were to preserve the independence necessary for them

---

44. *Id.*

45. *See* John M. Scheb II & William Lyons, *The Myth of Legality and Public Evaluation of the Supreme Court,* 81 Soc. Sci. Q. 928, 936 (2000).

46. I am inclined to believe that a question asking whether the Court's "performance is generally poor, fair, good, or excellent," Scheb & Lyons, *supra* n. 40, at 190 (Appendix), measures specific support. *See* Benjamin I. Page, *Comment: The Rejection of Bork Preserved the Court's Limited Popular Constituencies,* 84 NW. U. L. Rev. 1024, 1024 (1990) ("performance...really taps specific support"); *infra* text accompanying note 55.

47. *See* Richard H. Fallon, Jr., *Legitimacy and the Constitution,* 118 Harv. L. Rev. 1787 (2005).

48. *See, e.g.,* Richard S. Arnold, *Judges and the Public,* 9 Litig. 4, at 5 (1983). *See also* Stephen B. Burbank, *Judicial Accountability to the Past, Present, and Future: Precedent, Politics and Power,* 27 U. Ark. Little Rock L.J. ___, ___ (forthcoming 2005).

to make unpopular decisions required by law. Some political scientists do not believe that it is possible to disaggregate specific and diffuse support. Most believe, however, that the distinction is theoretically valuable, and there appears to have been progress in designing instruments that permit one to make the separation.

Although the precise nature of the concern about democratic legitimacy is not clear, and even if (pace Judge Arnold) diffuse support is not a good measure of accountability to the public, those scholars who have been most insistent on the distinction between diffuse and specific support acknowledge that there is a dynamic process at work, such that repeated decisions eroding specific support might adversely affect diffuse support.[49] Moreover, polls regarding confidence in leadership seem to measure a combination of specific and diffuse support.[50] Where, then, is the empirical evidence that the Court's standing has suffered to an extent that should concern us because it is currently not accountable to the public or is so regarded by the public? Recent studies show that, to the contrary, the Court enjoys a deep reservoir of goodwill (diffuse support), notwithstanding *Bush v. Gore*.[51] Indeed, it enjoys greater diffuse support than Congress.[52] Moreover, "[t]he American people...consistently have expressed greater confidence in the Supreme Court and the federal judiciary than in Congress."[53]

It is possible, of course, to make an argument that Congress itself does not represent public values. Indeed, Jeffrey Rosen recently opined that the Court's moderate majority better represents the views of average Americans than either the president or the (highly polarized, bitterly partisan, entrenched by gerrymandering) Congress.[54] Perhaps both the Court's current power and its ability to draw on a deep reservoir of diffuse support reflect the instability of the dominant coalition and the extent to which that coalition is out of touch

---

49. *See* James L. Gibson, Gregory A. Caldeira & Lester Kenyatta Spence, *Measuring Attitudes toward the United States Supreme Court*, 47 Am. J. Pol. Sci. 354, 356 (2003).

50. *See id.* at 357; James L. Gibson, Gregory A. Caldeira & Lester Kenyatta Spence, *The Supreme Court and the Presidential Election of 2000: Wounds, Self-Inflicted or Otherwise?*, 33 Brit. J. Pol. Sci. 535, 555 (2003).

51. *See* Gibson, Caldeira & Spence, *supra* n. 49, at 358–59; Herbert M. Kritzer, *The American Public's Assessment of the Rehnquist Court*, 89 Judicature ___, ___ (forthcoming 2005).

52. *See* James L. Gibson, Gregory A. Caldeira & Lester Kenyatta Spence, *Why do People Accept Public Policies They Oppose? Testing Legitimacy Theory with a Survey-Based Experiment*, 58 Pol. Res. Q. 187 (2005). "[B]ut the difference is not great." *Id.* at 195.

53. Editorial, *Listening to Judge Lefkow*, 88 Judicature 240, 241 (2005).

54. *See* Jeffrey Rosen, *Center Court*, N.Y. Times Magazine §6, 17 (June 12, 2005).

with the country's political values. If so, however, that is hardly an advertisement for a proposed change a central premise of which is the ability of the appointment process faithfully to translate such values to the Court.

In that regard and ironically, the political science literature on legitimacy suggests the great difficulty that proponents of this change might encounter in bringing it about. For, whether in the form of a statute (if constitutional) or constitutional amendment, these proposals might be thought to involve a major change of the sort that research indicates is broadly opposed by the American people, whatever their partisan or ideological affiliations. It is questions about just such changes—as opposed to questions about confidence in the job the Court is doing, its performance, or confidence in its leaders—that those scholars who have written the most probing work on diffuse support deem best calculated to tease out differences between diffuse and specific support.[55]

The public might not, however, regard non-renewable eighteen-year terms as sufficiently fundamental to tap diffuse support, a possibility suggested by research on opposition to FDR's court-packing plan, research that reveals different views about court-packing and mandatory retirement.[56] In all likelihood, it seems to me, that would depend upon how the proposal was framed, and in particular, on whether equal time was given to possible costs and possible benefits. And it is the question of possible costs, as illuminated by the political science literature, that leads me to doubt the claim that the frequent and predictable appointments that would occur under the proposed system of non-renewable eighteen-year terms, once fully operational, would result in a less contentious nomination/confirmation process and in less politicization of the Court.

Possible Costs of Frequent and Predictable Appointments

At the outset, I question the premise that lengthening tenures have much to do with, let alone are a primary cause of, the increased politicization of the confirmation process, as I do the claim that Supreme Court confirmation con-

---

55. *See* Gregory A. Caldeira & James L. Gibson, *The Etiology of Public Support for the Supreme Court*, 36 Am. J. Pol. Sci. 635, 636–41 (1992); *supra* n. 46.

56. *See* Barry Cushman, *Mr. Dooley and Mr. Gallup: Public Opinion and Constitutional Change in the 1930s*, 50 Buff. L. Rev. 7, 71–73 (2002).

troversies have infected the process for making appointments to the lower federal courts. Both the relatively non-controversial confirmations of Justices Ginsburg and Breyer and a comparison of lower court nominations that generated controversy with those that did not suggest a much more likely causal influence: the increasingly common practice of presidents to pursue what Sheldon Goldman calls a policy agenda in making nominations to all federal appellate courts.[57] Doubtless, what Benjamin Page calls "the context of the times" also matters,[58] as, I argue below, does the interest group environment in which appointments are made. In any event, lumping Supreme Court and lower court nominations is hazardous from the perspective of the Senate,[59] and those who are inclined to see the treatment of Judge Bork as the root of all evil should recall President Reagan's judicial appointment agenda.[60]

Just as proponents of change tend to concentrate on formal powers and processes to the exclusion of informal processes and strategic interaction, so do they leave largely out of account (or make unsupported assertions about) the role of interest groups in shaping the environment in which Supreme Court nominations and confirmations take place. Moreover, they give insufficient attention to the potential effect of interest groups and the environment they can create on public support for the Court. I seek to fill that gap, first,

---

57. *See* Sheldon Goldman, *Picking Federal Judges: Lower Court Selection from Roosevelt Through Reagan* (1997); Yalof, *supra* n. 8, at 180–81, 185 (Attorney General Meese's "insistence [in 1987] on the pursuit of policy goals at all costs ultimately dealt a serious blow to the administration's partisan interests"); Mark Silverstein, *Judicious Choices: The New Politics of Supreme Court Confirmations* 166–71 (1994); Sheldon Goldman, Eliot Slotnick, Gerard Gyski & Sara Schiavoni, *W. Bush's Judiciary: The First Term Record*, 88 Judicature 244 (2005).

58. Page, *supra* n. 46, at 1028.

59. *See* Stephen B. Burbank, *Politics, Privilege & Power: The Senate's Role in the Appointment of Federal Judges*, 86 Judicature 24 (2002).

60. *See* Yalof, *supra* n. 8, at 133–67; Silverstein, *supra* n. 57, at 118–23. Dawn E. Johnsen, *Ronald Reagan and the Rehnquist Court on Congressional Power: Presidential Influences on Constitutional Change*, 78 Ind. L. J. 363, 366–67, 396–99 (2003).

As convenient as it may be to trace present-day ideological conflict in the judicial appointment process to particular high profile episodes, however, Senate rejection of Supreme Court nominees was hardly a new phenomenon in 1987. Indeed, statistical analysis suggests that Bork's rejection fits historical trends in the confirmation of Supreme Court justices. Rather, it is conflict over the appointment of circuit and perhaps even district judges that appears to have escalated. Moreover, this escalation was underway before the defeat of the Bork nomination.

David S. Law, *Appointing Federal Judges: The President, the Senate, and the Prisoner's Dilemma*, 26 Cardozo L. Rev. 479, 490 (2005) (footnotes omitted).

by reviewing what empirical research suggests about the incentives and tactics of interest groups in federal judicial appointments, and second, by considering the possible effects of frequent and predictable appointment controversies framed by interest groups in light of the theoretical and empirical literature on legitimacy. That literature suggests to me that, far from being a remedy for an existing or impending problem of legitimacy, the frequent and predictable vacancies occurring under plans for non-renewable, long-term appointments might create a crisis of legitimacy, cementing the worst tendencies of modern politics.

The work of Jack Walker and his colleagues suggests that interest groups are here to stay, and it also suggests that neither the incentives shaping their behavior nor their tactics bode well for the claim that frequent and predictable appointments at two-year intervals would generate less controversy and reduce the politicization of the Court.[61] Walker's work divides interest groups into a number of types: profit, non-profit, mixed and citizen. Citizen groups enjoyed the greatest growth in the period he studied. Walker found that "most citizen groups that emerged from social movements in the past have simply faded away once the intense enthusiasms of their followers began to cool, or when a string of policy defeats or compromises caused marginal supporters to lose hope."[62] He also found, however, that in the 1980s "many of the citizen groups born during the 1960s and 1970s were still in business, with help from their individual and institutional patrons, even though public interest in their causes had declined. These groups now promote concern for their issues and stand ready to exercise leadership whenever there is a new burst of public enthusiasm."[63]

Walker tested the extent to which various types of interest groups follow "inside" strategies (e.g., lobbying in Congress) or "outside" strategies (e.g., appeals to the public), and the reasons why they do so. His findings indicated that, in contrast to most occupational associations (e.g., the ABA), which concentrated on lobbying, most citizen groups followed "outside" strategies to appeal to the public through the mass media, telephone (and after his work was published, electronic mail and mobile text messages).[64] Perhaps most important for present purposes, Walker found that citizen groups "seeking to fur-

---

61. *See* Jack L. Walker, Jr., *Mobilizing Interest Groups in America: Patrons, Professions, and Social Movements* 34–35, 63 (1991).

62. *Id.* at 194.

63. *Id.* at 195.

64. *See id.* at 9, 113–14, 132. Moreover, "[o]nce either an inside or outside strategy becomes the association's dominant approach, it is very difficult to move in a new direction." *Id.* at 119.

ther a cause thrive on controversy and must gain the attention of the mass media in order to convince their patrons of the organization's potency, and also to communicate effectively with their far-flung constituents. The structure and operation of these citizen groups is determined by the requirements of an 'outside' strategy of influence."[65]

More recent work by Caldeira, Hojnacki and Wright in the specific context of federal nominations confirms a number of Walker's findings, while suggesting modifications in others. This research confirms that the groups studied tended not to vary the mixture and proportional use of tactics, although the intensity of use may have differed, in relation to the salience of particular nominations.[66] At the same time, however, the authors did not find any dichotomy between "inside" and "outside" tactics: "Groups generally engage in a wide range of activities on all types of federal judicial nominations."[67] They concluded that "organizations are not participating in nomination campaigns simply to maintain their organizations—that is, to give members or patrons the impression that their dues or contributions are being well spent," but rather that "they are seriously attempting to provide any and all information that might affect the outcome."[68] It is therefore no surprise that these authors believe that interest groups are also here to stay in the politics of federal judicial nominations.

As previously noted, if there is a dynamic relationship between specific and diffuse support, it appears that, although diffuse support can insulate the Court from serious damage as the result of an unpopular decision, an accumulation of such decisions may erode diffuse support. Some of the more theoretically sophisticated work in this area attributes the insulating capacity of diffuse support to a "framing effect" whereby unpopular decisions are cush-

---

65. *Id.* at 12.

> There is a theatrical quality to such fights in Washington that makes short-term national celebrities out of certain activists, such as Neas, who normally spend their time slogging in the C-SPAN trenches. Like a cicada, Neas surfaces once every few years to sing his liberal fight songs for a national audience. And the irony of his life is that the bigger the threat to his ideological worldview, the more enjoyable his job becomes.

Michael Crowley, *Secret Passion*, The New Republic 14 (Aug. 1, 2005).

66. *See* Gregory A. Caldeira, Marie Hojnacki & John R. Wright, *The Lobbying Activities of Organized Interests in Federal Judicial Nominations,* 62 J. Pol. 51, 52, 62 (2000).

67. *Id.* at 59. The latter finding led the authors to question "the conventional wisdom about the importance of resources in organizational choice of tactics." *Id.* at 67.

68. *Id.* Put otherwise, "[l]obbying [by which they mean all of the tactics used by interest groups]...is not merely about taking positions or engaging in limited action to maintain the organization or gain publicity; instead, lobbying is about winning politically and doing whatever is necessary to do so." *Id.* at 52.

ioned (the "bias of positivity frames") by general views about the Court and the rule of law.[69] Other research suggests that framing of a different sort can adversely affect diffuse support, namely framing of questions in terms of specific results (i.e., *Bush v. Gore* ended the election controversy) rather than general or abstract notions (i.e., partisanship, as to which, however, framing does influence specific support).[70]

Putting these two strands of legitimacy research together suggests reason for concern about frequent and predictable Supreme Court appointments in the interest group environment that Walker and subsequent researchers describe. For the study of federal nominations discussed above, which included five recent Supreme Court nominations (Bork through Kennedy), shows that, in each, citizen groups participated far more than did other types of interest groups and that, more generally, "citizen groups, professional associations, and institutional advocates [i.e., the Alliance for Justice] dominate the politics of federal judicial nominations."[71] It is, of course, an empirical question what information and messages such groups try to convey, and it seems likely that will vary depending on both the nominee and the audience (which is to say, on whether the particular tactic is "inside" or "outside"). In communicating with the public, directly and through the media, such groups may couch their concerns (pro or con) in terms of general issues such as ideology. Just as frequently, one imagines, they are likely to be concerned, or to project concern, about results (i.e., this appointment will determine the future of *Roe* v. *Wade*).

Regular exposure of the public to messages, whether received directly or through the mass media, that frame the Court's work in terms of results simpliciter could alter the frame through which the public reacts to specific decisions and, at the same time, affect diffuse support. That is, diffuse support among the general public might come to behave as if it were specific support, as research has found that it does among elites (the attentive public). This seems particularly likely if the results in question relate to issues salient to the public at large, such as race, religion and the like. Moreover, recalling that research has also found greater diffuse support for the Court among those who are less dogmatic, perhaps the ideologically committed should be regarded as a "community" in the same way, and with the same implications for awareness of the Court's decisions and support for the institution, as the geographical communities that have been subject to public opinion research.

---

69. *See* Gibson, Caldeira & Spence, *supra* n. 50, at 553–56.

70. *See* Stephen P. Nicholson & Robert M. Howard, *Framing Support for the Supreme Court in the Aftermath of* Bush v. Gore, 65 J. Pol. 676 (2003).

71. Caldeira, Hojnacki & Wright, *supra* n. 66, at 56. *See id.* at 58 (Table 2).

We know that the mass media play an important role in setting the national agenda, and we should question whether the Court is different from the presidency in the effect that greater media exposure has on the amount or variety of public criticism. Indeed, scholars have suggested that "the stability of the Court's evaluations over time may be a function of insufficient knowledge rather than an enduring level of trust," leading the authors to "wonder if greater awareness of the Court would result in more volatile evaluations and more problems of enforcement and compliance for an institution whose major currency is legitimacy."[72] That suggestion may seem inconsistent with research finding a correlation between greater awareness of the Court and its work and greater levels of diffuse support. Those findings concern the attentive public, however, those who are most likely to espouse "the belief that judicial decisions are based on autonomous legal principles."[73] I have suggested that some distinctions between the attentive and non-attentive public might disappear (or that the definition of the "attentive public" might change) with greater attention to the Court promoted and framed by interest groups. In that regard, the explanation other scholars have offered for the correlation between awareness and diffuse support involves exposure to "legitimizing messages."[74] If, on the other hand, greater awareness of the Court were brought about by delegitimizing messages (i.e., those framed in terms of results), would there not be less diffuse support? Indeed, whatever the dynamic between diffuse and specific support, if the frame were altered, might there not be less of both?

An assessment of the baneful effects that the incentives of, and tactics pursued by, interest groups could have on an appointment process that was put in play not just frequently but predictably should not assume, however, that such groups would be successful in creating the sort of conflictual environment in which they thrive. Again, the appointments of Justices Ginsburg and Breyer are instructive. Moreover, it is possible that the existence of predictable appointments would permit politics to play a more constructive role through log-rolling, as, according to Kim Scheppele, it does in other countries with high courts whose judges serve fixed terms.[75] The question requires one to

---

72. Charles H. Franklin & Liane C. Kosaki, *Media, Knowledge, and Public Evaluations of the Supreme Court*, in *Contemplating Courts* 352, 373 (Lee Epstein ed., 1995).

73. Scheb & Lyons, *supra* n. 45, at 929. *See id.* at 930–31.

74. *See* James L. Gibson, Gregory A. Caldeira & Vanessa A. Baird, *On the Legitimacy of National High Courts*, 92 Am. Pol. Sci. Rev. 343, 345 (1998). *Cf.* Scheb & Lyons, *supra* n. 40, at 190 ("reason to fear that popular demystification of judicial decision making may further erode popular esteem for the Court").

75. Kim Lane Scheppele, *Liberals Should Want Rehnquist to Retire Too*, <http://balkin.blogspot.com/> (July 1, 2005).

consider the tendencies of modern politics and to predict in which direction they are likely to lead. Here again, Jack Walker's work is helpful.

Walker, who welcomed the broader participation in government afforded by interest groups, was alert to their impact on parties. He reasoned that, "[w]hen interest groups begin to attract resources and attention to their causes, the parties are forced to alter their programs and reformulate their supporting coalitions to accommodate to shifts in the public's principal concerns"[76] and that "[t]he leaders of both political parties and interest groups are discovering that ideological commitment, under some circumstances, can serve as a sound basis for long-term organizational membership."[77] Moreover, he noted research finding "that most of the associations with formal and enduring access to the White House are citizen groups—the type that [...] enjoyed the greatest growth in the 1960s and 1970s."[78] Finally for present purposes, Walker concluded that "[a]s the circle of participants in the dialogue over public policy grows and the political system becomes increasingly polarized along ideological lines, each individual interest group will be under pressure to encourage the fortunes of the political party that affords it best access to government."[79]

Empirical evidence cannot tell us, of course, whether, in making nominations to the Court under the proposed system of non-renewable eighteen-year terms, the presidents of the future would be able to resist the demands of "ideological commitment" and react to interest group pressures as did President Clinton and, perhaps, President George W. Bush in his nomination of John Roberts, or whether they would react as have some other recent Republican presidents. Of course, the same is true of the reaction to nominations by the opposition party in Congress.[80] Even if log-rolling is plausible when there are two concurrent vacancies, it may be wishful thinking to imagine it for successive vacancies "in a two-party system with diverse coalitions of the left and right organized into single parties."[81] It is hard to believe, in any event, that

---

76. Walker, *supra* n. 61, at 14. *See id.* at 39.

77. *Id.* at 35.

78. *Id.* at 139 (citation omitted).

79. *Id.* at 156.

80. *See* Silverstein, *supra* n. 57, at 158 ("The current reality is that the confirmation process now demands a calculation of political variables so complex that even the most experienced and electorally secure senators are often unable to predict the course and outcome of the proceedings.").

81. Scheppele, *supra* n. 75.

There are reasons to think that today's levels of ideological conflict and gridlock have more to do with presidential efforts to push ideologically unpalatable nominees past unwilling senators, than with the inability of repeat play to sustain co-

frequent and predictable appointments would not become a fixture of partisan, if not of ideological, politics.

Notwithstanding research results tending to negate the influence of partisanship on diffuse support, one has to wonder whether the same would hold true if the Court became a frequent and predictable issue in, and if its work were framed to suit the needs of, partisan election campaigns. If it did, a system resulting in two vacancies in each presidential term could cement a process—treating courts as part, not just of a political system, but of ordinary politics—that should concern not just law professors and political scientists, but the general public. For in such a system, law could be seen as nothing more than ordinary politics, and judicial independence could become a junior partner to judicial accountability. As recently put by the *Washington Post*:

> The war [over Justice O'Connor's successor] is about money and fundraising as much as it is about jurisprudence and the judicial function. It elevates partisanship and political rhetoric over any serious discussion of law. In the long run, the war over the courts—which teaches both judges and the public at large to view the courts simply as political institutions—threatens judicial independence and the integrity of American justice.[82]

A major theme of Ward Farnsworth's defense of life tenure is that the presidential incentives that are a foundation of some proposals for change—such as to try to capture the Court for generations by appointing young justices—are subject to the braking force of the Senate.[83] Of course, in political circumstances like those obtaining today, that may be thought to depend on the survival of the filibuster as a tool of pivotal nomination politics.[84] Even with the filibuster at risk, the recent nomination of John Roberts may reflect precisely the sort of strategic dynamic that Farnsworth emphasizes.[85] If the fili-

---

operation among fellow senators.

Law, *supra* n. 60, at 506. *See id.* at 510 ("For senators, logrolling goes unremarked as collegiality or business as usual. Such behavior does not, however, characterize the presidency.") (footnote omitted).

82. Editorial, *Not a Campaign*, Wash. Post B6 (July 3, 2005).

83. *See supra* n. 6; *see also supra* the discussion in Ward Farnsworth, *The Case for Life Tenure*, pp. 251–269.

84. *See* Keith Krehbiel, *Pivotal Politics: a Theory of U.S. Lawmaking* 23–24 (1998); Law, *supra* n. 60, at 513.

85. Republicans warn Democrats that their obstructionism will cost them at the polls. Perhaps. But it also appears to have forced Bush into choosing a more conciliatory nominee. Bush seems to have calculated that, with the Iraq war, his

buster did not survive for judicial nominations, the concern about presidential incentives would be more serious, but again, the primary source of concern is not long tenures but rather the president's appointment agenda;[86] the appointment process is not the only means by which the Court can be held accountable, and, in light of the evidence from political science I have reviewed, frequent and predictable vacancies under a system of non-renewable eighteen-year terms seem more likely to feed the disease of power politics than to cure it.

Conclusion

In recent years there has been substantial progress in bridging the gaps, which once approached chasms, between the legal and political science literatures on courts. Today many scholars in both disciplines are seriously grappling with the traditional wisdom about judges and the judicial process they inherited, and they are thus trying to figure out the roles that law, individual preferences and strategic behavior play in judicial decisions, as they are also exploring the relationship between judicial independence and judicial accountability. These scholars understand that the traditional wisdom in both

---

> failed domestic agenda, and even the Karl Rove scandal, he cannot afford a contentious confirmation battle. He seems to have been geniunely spooked by the Democrats' threat of a filibuster.

Ryan Lizza, *Legal Theory*, The New Republic 15, 16 (Aug. 1, 2005).

86. In a very interesting paper my colleague Ted Ruger explores "judicial preference change," using Justice Blackmun as an exemplar but adducing recent studies suggesting that the phenomenon of justices "drifting" from the preferences they held at the time of appointment is common. He adumbrates some of the implications of this phenomenon, particularly with respect to the assumption of stable preferences underlying theories of "partisan entrenchment." *See* Theodore W. Ruger, *Justice Harry Blackmun and the Phenomenon of Judicial Preference Change* (unpublished manuscript) (copy on file with author). This perspective thus also calls in question assumptions underlying concern about "locking-up" the Court through the appointment of young justices, and it illuminates the attempt by presidents to appoint strong ideologues to the bench.

> A judge's political beliefs, his or her policy preferences, should not cause concern unless they hold sway with such power as to be impervious to adjudicative facts, competing policies, or the governing law as it is generally understood. When an individual's belief system about social needs or aspirations is that powerful, it seems fair to speak of ideology. And on this understanding, ideology is revealed as the enemy of judicial independence.

Stephen B. Burbank, *The Courtroom as Classroom: Independence, Imagination and Ideology in the Work of Jack Weinstein*, 97 Colum. L. Rev. 1971, 1999 (1997) (footnotes omitted).

disciplines is simplistic, that there is a place for both normative and empirical scholarship in seeking a more nuanced account that captures what is actually going on in courts, and similarly that there are limits to what either can accomplish, particularly if they proceed in isolation.

In a forthcoming article that considers the politics of the federal courts and the federal judiciary, I lament the tendency toward "posterity worship" and institutional self-aggrandizement of the current Court.[87] I am aware, however, that these are not unprecedented phenomena for that body,[88] as I am that the "current Court" will not remain such for very much longer. Mark Silverstein reminds us that

> [e]ven Frankfurter succumbed to the reformer's frustration with hyperactive judicial review. So great was his disaffection with the Supreme Court's use of the Fourteenth Amendment to strike down innovative state legislation that in 1922 he announced in the pages of the *New Republic* his support of the drastic step of repealing that amendment's due process clause.[89]

As I share the momentary frustration evident in the writings of some proponents of changing Supreme Court tenure, I invite them to share the perspective that a consideration of history and of the lessons of political science can provide. Whether or not scholars should be interested in affecting the course of public policy, when they make proposals that are designed to do that there is a duty, in my view, to escape disciplinary shackles, to discipline theory with evidence, to view contemporary phenomena in historical context, and to resist the natural human inclination to confuse personal preferences with social good.

---

87. *See* Burbank, *supra* n. 48, at ___.

88. *See, e.g.,* William G. Ross, *A Muted Fury: Populists, Progressives, and Labor Unions Confront the Courts, 1890–1937* (1994).

89. Silverstein, *supra* n. 57, at 40 (footnotes omitted). *See also id.* at 49 ("The crisis of the old order had been set in motion by a judicial arrogance founded on the mistaken belief that the resolute exercise of judicial review could withstand the political impulses of the times.").

Constitutionality of Legislation Limiting the Tenure of Justices

Constitutionality of Reforming the Supreme Court by Statute

*Roger C. Cramton**

Other contributors to this symposium amply demonstrate that life tenure for Supreme Court justices has had harmful consequences the Founders could not or did not foresee. As indicated in the Introduction, Paul Carrington and I are convinced that these harms are so serious that it is necessary and proper to use the hindsight we enjoy today to correct problems that arose over the years and that have become especially troublesome since 1970. After a brief summary of the relevant constitutional provisions, this paper examines the constitutionality of a legislative remedy, concluding that the Constitution's text, its history and its purposes support the conclusion that Congress has legislative authority to enact the needed statutory reform.

The History and Purposes of the Good Behavior and Compensation Clauses

Section 1 of Article III of the Constitution provides:

The judicial Power of the United States, shall be vested in one supreme Court, and in such inferior Courts as the Congress may from time to time ordain and establish. The Judges, both of the supreme and inferior Courts, shall hold their Offices during good Behaviour, and shall, at stated times, receive for their Services, a Com-

---

* Robert S. Stevens Professor of Law, Emeritus, Cornell Law School.

pensation, which shall not be diminished during their continuance in Office.

The Founders were aware of their English ancestors' long struggle to obtain a judiciary which, although appointed by the crown, was not subservient to either the executive or legislative branch of government. As Blackstone put it, "the life, liberty, and property [of citizens] would be in the hands of arbitrary judges" if judges were subservient to the ministers of the government.[1] One of the grounds for independence proclaimed in 1776 was that King George III had "made [colonial] Judges dependent on his Will alone, for the tenure of their offices, and the amount and payment of their salaries." The Constitution of at least three colonies—Virginia (1776), Maryland (1776) and Massachusetts (1780)—provided that judges hold office "during good behaviour." Other colonial constitutions provided for a limited term of office (eight years in New York) or for life tenure with removal by action of the legislature. (Today, all state constitutions reject life tenure for their high court judges, providing instead for limited tenure age-limits, term limits, or removal by address of the legislature.)

Records of the Federal Convention of 1787 and the state ratifying conventions indicate the Founders intended the Good Behavior Clause and the Compensation Clause to provide a federal judiciary that would exercise independent judgment in deciding cases, free from influence or control of the political branches of the federal government—the President and Congress. As James Wilson stated to the Pennsylvania ratifying convention, "the servile dependence of the judges [who are appointed and perhaps reappointed after five or seven years, as in some colonies] endangers the liberty and property of the citizen."[2] Opponents of the Constitution, such as Brutus, recognized that federal judges would be "independent, in the fullest sense of the word," but thought this unwise:

> [There is] no authority that can remove them, and they can not be controuled by the laws of the legislature. In short, they are independent of the people, of the legislature, and of every power under heaven. Men placed in this situation will generally soon feel themselves independent of heaven itself.[3]

Hamilton, in defending the Good Behavior Clause in Federalist No. 78, replied that "the permanent tenure of judicial offices" would provide the "in-

---

1. William Blackstone, 1 *Commentaries* 259–60 (1768), *quoted in* Philip B. Kurland & Ralph Lerner, 4 *The Founders' Constitution* 132 (1987) [hereinafter *Founders' Constitution*].

2. *See id.* at 139 (quoting from Elliot's Debate in Pennsylvania, Dec. 1987).

3. *Id.* at 141 (quoting from Brutus, No. 15, Mar. 20, 1788).

dependent spirit" that was essential to the faithful performance" of federal judges in carrying out their constitutional duty to keep the legislative branch of a limited government "within the limits assigned to their authority."[4] In Federalist No. 79, Hamilton argued that the Compensation Clause was also vital to judicial independence because "a power over a man's subsistence amounts to power over his will."[5] Salaries, however, should be subject to increase because a stipend sufficient at the beginning may prove inadequate because "judges, who, if they behave properly, will be secured in their places for life," may serve a long time.

Reflecting the circumstances of the time, Hamilton stated reasons why the Good Behavior Clause would not result in extremely long service or "in the imaginary danger of a superannuated bench." Most men did not survive that long: "few there are who outlive the season of intellectual vigor." Of those who did, the "deliberating and comparing faculties generally preserve their strength...."

The Founders acted at a time when experience with constitution-making was limited to the recent experience of the colonies. They accepted judicial review of legislative and executive action as an abstract idea but did not and could not know how its practice would evolve. They also had little experience with life tenure for judges in 1789 (the colonies had provided for life-tenured judges only after the Declaration of Independence). And judicial review of legislative action was not within the authority of British judges, who had been given life tenure earlier in the eighteenth century to increase their independence from the king and his ministers in adjudicating cases.

Moreover, the Founders had no conception of government service as a lifetime job. Only a century later did the concept of lifetime public office become possible with the establishment of the civil service. The Founders believed that public service was the duty of intelligent and propertied individuals, who would serve in government office for a period before returning to home, family, and original employment, just as George Washington would return to his plantation at Mount Vernon and John Adams to his farm in Brookline. In the earliest years this expectation was sometimes realized: three of the first ten justices resigned to take other offices or to return home.

Furthermore, the principle of rotation in public office governed all other branches of the federal government: representatives were elected for two-year terms; senators for six years; and the President for four, with continuance in office dependent upon re-election.

---

4. *Id.* at 142–43 (May 28, 1788).
5. *Id.* at 144 (May 28, 1788).

The Founders anticipated that many of those appointed to the Court would resign to engage in other activities, that others would die after relatively short periods of service, and, as a result, that new appointments would occur with some frequency. Throughout most of the nation's history this expectation was fulfilled.[6] During all this time the average age of appointment to the Court has been fifty-three, with most appointees falling between age fifty and fifty-five. Until 1970, justices served an average tenure of about fifteen years, and they resigned or died at an average age of sixty-eight. A new justice was appointed to the Court about every two years. Rotation in office as contemplated by the Founders has been the general rule, sometimes speeded by an expansion in the size of the Court or by the threat of such expansion.

Since 1970, however, the average tenure in office has increased to almost twenty-six years (an increase of eleven years), although the average age at appointment has not changed, and will increase further if no changes are made. The average age in leaving office has also risen eleven years, from sixty-eight to seventy-nine. Immediately prior to Justice O'Connor's 2005 resignation, the Court had served together without change for eleven years, the longest period in our history since 1824. The lengthening tenure of justices has nearly doubled the time between appointments from 1.7 years prior to 1970 to 3.3 years since then. Prior to 1970, almost every president serving a four-year term received at least one appointment to the Court. Since 1970, three of the last seven four-year presidential terms have had no appointments to the Court.

The language and history of the Good Behavior Clause, viewed in the light of the circumstances of the time, establish two propositions: (1) the Clause was intended to establish a judicial branch that would be independent from executive or legislative control, and (2) the Founders expected that vacancies on the Supreme Court would arise with a frequency that would prevent "superannuation" and result in fairly frequent appointment of new justices.

The Current Situation

The political prominence of the Court and its justices has steadily grown in recent decades. In each of the last six presidential elections, the identity of persons or types of person the rival candidates might appoint to the Court has

---

6. The source of the data in this and the following paragraph is a previous essay in this volume, Steven G. Calabresi & James Lindgren, *Term Limits for the Supreme Court: Life Tenure Reconsidered, supra* pp. 15–98 [hereinafter Calabresi & Lindgren].

been an important issue. In the 2000 election, the Court decided who would be the person to appoint its own members.[7] Supreme Court appointments have become politically contentious not only because justices exercise great power but because they exercise that power for so long.

The Founders, in providing for tenure during "good behavior," did not contemplate that life tenure would accentuate the tendency of justices to consider themselves "Platonic Guardians" for American society.[8] In Federalist No. 78 Hamilton expressed views about the Court that are quixotic in the light of contemporary reality.[9] The Court, he stated, would be "the least dangerous" branch of the federal government because it had neither the sword of the executive nor the purse and lawmaking powers of the legislature. The federal judiciary, Hamilton famously said, has "neither Force nor Will but merely judgment; and must ultimately depend upon the aid of the executive arm even for the efficacy of its judgments."[10] Hamilton described a Court that would parse judicial precedent and resolve narrow legal questions with rare legal skill; he stated that the major qualification for appointment would be the knowledge acquired by "laborious study" of existing precedents.[11]

No one today believes, as Hamilton said, that justices are "bound down by strict rules and precedents which serve to define and point out their duty in every particular case that comes before them."[12] That narrow view of the judicial function, especially as descriptive of the policy-oriented decisionmaking of the highest court of the land, is quaint but totally unreal.

The Constitutionality of a Statutory Solution

Congress has broad authority to, among other things, create and abolish federal courts (other than the Supreme Court), determine the jurisdiction of

---

7. Bush v. Gore, 531 U.S. 98 (2000).

8. Judge Learned Hand, who raised doubts about the legitimacy of judicial review in 1958, applied this term to the justices of the Court, which in his view had become a third legislative chamber: "For myself it would be most irksome to be ruled by a bevy of Platonic Guardians, even if I knew how to choose them, which I assuredly do not." *See* Learned Hand, *The Bill of Rights* (1958) at 73.

9. *The Federalist No.* 78 (Hamilton), reprinted in *Founders' Constitution, supra* n. 1, at 141–44. *See also* L. H. Larue, *Neither Force Nor Will*, 12 Constitutional Commentary 179–82 (1995).

10. *Id.* at 142.

11. *Id.* at 143.

12. *Id.*

federal courts (providing an uncertain minimum jurisdiction is left to the Supreme Court),[13] establish rules regulating federal courts, provide the terms of employment of judges subject to the Compensation Clause, and prescribe procedures by which the federal judiciary may discipline itself. The Supreme Court's appellate (as distinct from original) jurisdiction is exercised "with such Exceptions, and under such Regulations, as the Congress shall make."[14] The constitutional limitations on this legislative authority are that the regulation must not violate the prescribed methods for appointment and removal of Article III judges and must be consistent with the judicial independence protected by the Good Behavior and Compensation Clauses of Article III, section 1.

The constitutionality of the Carrington-Cramton proposal rests on a purposive reading of the Good Behavior and Appointments Clauses viewed in the light of the broad legislative authority of Congress to establish, regulate, abolish, and structure federal courts, their jurisdiction, and their procedure. Its consideration requires a review of some neglected history that sheds light on the power of Congress to redefine (within limits) the "office" of a Supreme Court justice.[15]

"Circuit Riding"

The legislative requirement that Supreme Court justices hear and decide cases in inferior federal courts began with the Judiciary Act of 1789 and lasted for more than a century; the final steps in the demise of circuit riding were taken by the Judiciary Act of 1911.[16] The practice imposed extreme hardship

---

13. *See* Richard H. Fallon, Jr., Daniel J. Meltzer, & David L. Shapiro, *Hart & Wechsler's The Federal Courts and the Federal System* (5th ed. 2003) at 28–54 (brief summary), 268–318 (original jurisdiction), 466–600 (review of state court decisions), 1552–1621 (review of federal decisions and certiorari policy).

14. U.S. Const., Art. III, §2.

15. Not considered here are the vexing questions of when and by whom the constitutionality of legislation enacting the Carrington-Cramton proposal (or similar legislation) could be considered. Although the "rule of necessity" might permit the Court to entertain a case even though the justices' own interests would be involved, the standing and ripeness doctrines present serious problems: (1) Does anyone other than the first justice rotated off the Court have standing to challenge its constitutionality? And (2) would that challenge be ripe until shortly before that justice would be rotated off? *See supra* the discussion in Alan Morrison, *Opting for Change in Supreme Court Selection, and for the Chief Justice, Too,* pp. 203–223.

16. *See* Joshua Glick, *On the Road: The Supreme Court and the History of Circuit Riding,* 24 Cardozo L. Rev. 1753 (2003) [hereinafter Glick].

on justices, especially in the first half of the nineteenth century, when long-distance travel by horse or early rail was difficult and onerous.[17] From the very beginning the justices complained about the circuit riding requirement and sought legislative relief from Congress. These pleas, rejected until late in the nineteenth century, became more compelling only when burgeoning caseloads threatened to overwhelm the Court. Members of Congress had good reasons to require circuit riding: it brought federal justice into contact with citizens throughout the nation, it gave the justices valuable experience in trying and deciding cases and appeals in lower courts, and it familiarized them with the practice and problems of the entire federal judicial system.

In the initial years of circuit riding, several justices (e.g., Jay and Marshall) wrote private letters stating or suggesting that the practice was unconstitutional.[18] But when a case questioning the constitutionality of circuit riding came before the Court in 1803, a unanimous Court rejected the arguments that the practice was unconstitutional,[19] and circuit riding continued to be required for most of the remainder of the century.

Circuit riding had another consequence. A vacancy on the Court was associated with a particular circuit, and the person appointed would "ride circuit" in that part of the country. This statutory requirement provided a practical limitation on the President's Article II power of appointment: usually, the President had to appoint a lawyer or judge from that circuit rather than make a selection from a nationwide pool, as is now the case.

Vestiges of circuit riding remain, even now. Each justice is assigned by the Court to a circuit and hears applications for temporary relief from that circuit. A retired justice "may be designated to perform such judicial duties in any circuit, including those of a circuit justice, as he is willing to undertake."

---

17. For letters from Supreme Court justices complaining about the burdensome nature of the long travel by carriage throughout the breadth of the country, see *Founders' Constitution, supra* n. 1, at 163 (letters of Chief Justice Jay on behalf of the Court and of Justice James Iredell).

18. *See id.* at 161–62 (undelivered letter, dated Sept. 15, 1790, from Chief Justice Jay to President Washington).

19. Stuart v. Laird, 5 U.S. (1 Cranch) 299 (1803). The case considered two arguments that a justice sitting on circuit lacked authority to render a valid judgment: (1) cases decided by the justices on circuit were not within either the original or the appellate jurisdiction of the Court, and the duties were incompatible because the Supreme Court was required to review appeals from the circuit courts; and (2) circuit riding required the justice to hold two offices at one time, and they had not been appointed by the President to the circuit court as required by Article II, section 2. *See also infra* text accompanying notes 21–24.

At least eight retired justices have utilized this provision since 1950; Justice Clark, for example, spent the last ten years of his life as a circuit court judge.[20]

Stuart v. Laird (1803)

In 1802, a Republican Congress and President Jefferson abolished the circuit courts created by a Federalist Congress and President Adams via the Judiciary Act of 1801.[21] New circuit courts and judgeships were substituted in their stead. None of the circuit court judges appointed by the Federalists was reappointed to the new courts, leaving sixteen Article III judges with no cases to decide. Although none of the judges who lost his office attacked the constitutionality of the 1802 legislation, those questions were raised in *Stuart v. Laird*.[22] A foreign creditor had obtained a judgment against a Virginia debtor in a circuit court created in 1801. When the creditor sought to enforce the judgment in the circuit court established by the 1802 legislation, Chief Justice Marshall, sitting as a circuit judge, upheld the judgment. In the appeal to the Court, the judgment debtor asserted several constitutional questions concerning the power of Chief Justice Marshall, acting as a circuit justice, to enforce a judgment that, it was argued, should have been enforced by the life tenured judges appointed for the Virginia circuit under the 1801 legislation. The questions briefed and argued were as follows:

First, could judges entitled to "hold their Offices during good Behaviour" be deprived of that office without an impeachment proceeding? The judgment enforced by Chief Justice Marshall while "riding circuit" was invalid, the judgment debtor contended, because the displaced circuit court judges were deprived of their offices without being removed by impeachment, in violation of the Good Behavior Clause. This argument was countered by reliance on other language in the same Article III section that authorized Congress to vest the judicial power "in such inferior Courts as the Congress may from time to time ordain and establish." Although this constitutional question was raised, argued, and rejected by the Court's decision affirming the judgment below, Justice Paterson's opinion dealt only with the power of the court enforcing the

---

20. *See* Glick, *supra* n. 16, at 1830–31 (listing justices who have served in lower federal courts after retiring from the Supreme Court).

21. 2 Stat. 132 (Mar. 8, 1802).

22. 5 U.S. (1 Cranch) 299 (1803). *Stuart* is discussed in David P. Currie, *The Constitution in the Supreme Court: The Powers of the Federal Courts, 1801–1835*, 49 U. Chi. L. Rev. 646, 662–63 (1982); and Glick, *supra* n. 16, at 1794–1829.

judgment and not explicitly with the abolition of a court and its previously created judgeships. The Court held, 5–0, with Chief Justice Marshall not participating, that Congress had constitutional authority to replace a previously existing court with another one and "to transfer a cause from one such tribunal to another." The opinion contains strong language of congressional authority to create, modify or abolish federal courts and their jurisdiction: "[T]here are no words in the constitution to prohibit or restrain the exercise of legislative power."[23]

Second, could a statute authorize Supreme Court justices to hear and decide cases in a lower federal court? This argument took two forms: (1) the statute assigning circuit duties to justices in effect appointed them as circuit judges in contravention of Article II's provision that appointments were to be made by the President with Senate consent. And (2) justices could not sit on circuit because the cases they would try there were outside the Supreme Court's original jurisdiction as defined by Article III. These are two aspects of the same question: Does Congress have legislative authority to mix the duties of one judicial office with that of another? Or, put another way, is the "office" of federal judges, including that of Supreme Court justices, subject to legislative modification or redefinition? Justice Paterson's opinion in *Stuart* upheld the power of Congress to require justices to ride circuit but did so without replying to the opposing arguments. He wrote, "[the] practice [of circuit riding], and acquiescence under it [by members of the Court], for a period of several years, commencing with the organization of the judicial system, affords an irresistible answer, and has indeed fixed the construction.... Of course, the question is at rest, and ought not now to be disturbed."[24]

In this symposium, Professors Calabresi and Lindgren discuss the constitutionality of statutory proposals.[25] An earlier version of their article took the position that their own statutory proposal, similar to the Carrington-Cramton proposal, was constitutional. The final version reaches the contrary conclusion, arguing that the text of the Good Behavior Clause, read together with the clause of Article I, section 3, that "the Chief Justice shall preside" over a presidential impeachment proceeding make the office of a Supreme Court justice unique and distinctive. Therefore, they conclude, historic judicial practices (i.e., circuit riding by the justices) and more recent practices of judicial administration (e.g., designation of justices for service on lower courts) are

---

23. 5 U.S. (1 Cranch) at 308.
24. *Id.* at 309.
25. *See supra* Calabresi & Lindgren, pp. 78–92.

all unconstitutional as applied to Supreme Court justices, who cannot be required to simultaneously or successively serve on a lower federal court. They argue that the true "originalist" position is that the First Congress, the Marshall Court (with Marshall recusing himself because of his involvement in the case), *Stuart v. Laird*, and the unquestioned continuance of the practice for 121 years are all wrong. Circuit riding, they conclude, was an unconstitutional practice and should not be relied upon today.

My view is that a practice certified as constitutional by the members of the First Congress, some of whom had been members of the Constitutional Convention and all of whom were familiar with the debates concerning its adoption, carries great weight. The additional fact that circuit riding was unanimously upheld as constitutional by the Marshall Court and practiced without question for more than a century make it an established part of the constitutional firmament. If "originalism" has force, it surely applies here.

Abolition by Statute of Existing Federal Courts and Judgeships

On four occasions during the first seventy-five years of U.S. history (1802, 1812, and twice in 1863), Congress abolished federal courts, leaving duly appointed Article III judges without any cases to decide. The first instance was the repeal by the Jeffersonian Congress in 1802 of the Federalists' Judiciary Act of 1801, depriving sixteen judges of their offices. The judges' challenge to the 1802 Act's constitutionality, raised before Congress but not in the courts, went unresolved until rejected in *Stuart v. Laird*.[26]

The second instance, in 1812, occurred when Congress passed the act admitting Louisiana as a state in the union and created a district judgeship for the state. The 1804 legislation that established the Territory of Orleans in what became Louisiana had provided for a district judge who would have the same jurisdiction and authority as district judges in a state. When the territorial government ended, the judgeship was abolished. This time, however, the same person who had held the office for the territory was appointed to the judgeship created by the statehood act.

In the third instance, in 1863, Congress abolished the circuit court and the criminal court for the District of Columbia and replaced them with the Supreme Court for the District of Columbia. The three judges of the circuit

---

26. *See supra* text accompanying notes 21–24.

court for the District of Columbia served with life tenure, and the legislation abolished the three judgeships. In effect, the three judges were removed from office by legislation abolishing their court and creating a new one. Nor were any of them appointed to the new court. Here, the background was the Civil War and the concern of President Lincoln and the Congress that one or more of the judges were Confederate sympathizers.

Fourth, also in 1863, Congress abolished the judgeship for the U.S. Circuit Court for the Circuit of California, although there was no incumbent judge at the time.

The four instances, including the Court's holding in *Stuart*, support the view that Congress may essentially remove lifetime tenure judges by abolishing the court on which they serve and recreating a successor court with newly appointed judges.

Subsequent Judicial Precedent

No decisions subsequent to *Stuart* directly address the constitutionality of a statute requiring an Article III judge to exercise responsibilities on more than one constitutional court or on the Supreme Court and an inferior Article III court. Three fairly recent decisions, however, discuss the constitutionality of statutes that mix the duties of an office subject to the president's Article II appointment authority.

Weiss v. United States[27] involved the question whether a military officer, commissioned as such, could serve as a judge of a court of military review. The Court held that serving in this capacity did not involve a different office than that of any commissioned officer because all military officers had always exercised judicial responsibilities as part of their military responsibilities.

Morrison v. Olson[28] rejected a separation-of-powers attack on the constitutionality of legislation authorizing the appointment of independent prosecutors not subject to the control of the President. The Court stated that the validity of the legislation turned on "whether the Act, taken as a whole, violates the separation of powers by unduly interfering with the role of the Executive Branch"[29] and concluded that impermissible interference was not involved. Both *Weiss* and *Morrison* support the proposition that if a justice is appointed

---

27. 510 U.S. 163 (1994).
28. 487 U.S. 654 (1988).
29. *Id.* at 693.

to an office that also includes service on another constitutional court, either simultaneously or in succession, the movement from one level of court to another does not require a second appointment and is consistent with the Good Behavior Clause.

The conclusion that legislative authority can enlarge an office to include duties of the same character as those of another office seems even more self-evident when a President is appointing an officer (an Article III judge) who is required by statute to exercise judicial duties on more than one constitutional court. The duties are known in advance to the President and the Senate, all duties are judicial in character, and the required duties do not unduly interfere with the president's appointment authority.

In *Mistretta v. United States*,[30] another highly relevant precedent, the Court held that the legislation creating the United States Sentencing Commission did not violate the separation-of-powers principle either by requiring federal judges to serve on the Commission, thus sharing their authority with non-judges, or by empowering the President to appoint Commission members or to remove them for cause. The conclusion that the Constitution does not prohibit Article III judges from undertaking extrajudicial duties was supported by "the historical practice of the Founders after ratification."[31] The Court cited a number of instances in which justices (including Jay, Ellsworth and Marshall) had served in other capacities as a result of a presidential appointment with the "advice and consent" of the Senate, followed by numerous other examples throughout the years, including Justice Jackson's service on the Nuremberg Tribunal in the aftermath of World War II and Chief Justice Warren's leadership of the national commission investigating the assassination of President Kennedy.

If the "office" of a Supreme Court justice permits service pursuant to legislation or executive appointment, why can it not also be combined with service on other constitutional courts? In language particularly pertinent to the mixing of judicial duties involved in circuit riding and to the Carrington-Cramton proposal, the Court said, "This contemporaneous practice by the Founders themselves is significant evidence that the constitutional principle of separation of powers does not absolutely prohibit extrajudicial service. *See Bowshar v. Synar*, 478 U.S., at 723–724...(actions by Members of the First Congress provide contemporaneous and weighty evidence about the meaning of the Constitution)."[32]

---

30. 488 U.S. 361, 397–412 (1989).
31. *Id*. at 398.
32. *Id*. at 399 (1989).

Judicial Designation and Discipline

A half-dozen sentences in the Constitution deal with the creation, jurisdiction, and regulation of federal courts. For many years Congress and the federal judiciary have struggled to apply this constitutional language to a federal judicial system that has currently grown to 853 authorized Article III judges and that carries on its judicial business with a total judicial complement that far outnumbers the authorized Article III judges and their senior status colleagues.[33] A large portion of federal judicial business is handled by nearly 3,000 judicial officers who do not have life tenure: 1,328 statutory judges (magistrates and bankruptcy court judges), 29 judges and senior judges of the Federal Court of Claims, and 1,370 administrative law judges.[34] Efficient utilization of the services of the minority who are Article III judges and who therefore select and supervise many of the non-tenured judicial officers is a major endeavor.

One longstanding practice authorized by statute, and always assumed to be consistent with the Constitution, involves the designation of Article III judges to provide judicial services in a court other than that of initial appointment.[35] These practices are designed to further the efficiency of the system and encourage the continuing involvement of Article III judges. By designation, a judge appointed by one federal court may handle the judicial business of another: (1) retired Supreme Court Justices and retired lower federal court judges may sit on other federal courts,[36] (2) the Chief Judge of a Circuit Court of Appeals may designate district judges to serve on appellate panels of the circuit court,[37] and (3) the Chief Justice and the Chief Judge of a circuit may designate a lower court judge of one judicial circuit to serve in another circuit.[38]

Problems of misconduct in office by Article III judges or physical or mental decrepitude interfering with the proper administration of justice have led to statutory procedures by which complaints against judges of U.S. district and circuit courts may be considered and remedied by action through the respective circuit councils.[39] On rare occasions the cases assigned to a judge have

---

33. *See* Judith Resnik, *Judicial Selection and Democratic Theory: Demand, Supply, and Life Tenure*, 26 Cardozo L. Rev. 579, 601–02 (2005).

34. *Id.* at 602–11.

35. 28 U.S.C. §§ 291–294.

36. 28 U.S.C. § 291(a).

37. 28 U.S.C. § 292(a).

38. 28 U.S.C. §§ 291(a), 292(d).

39. 42 U.S.C. §§ 351–364.

been reassigned and no new cases assigned, leaving an Article III judge without any cases to decide. These methods of judicial discipline, which are authorized by statute and implemented by the federal judiciary, have withstood challenges to their constitutionality.

In *Chandler v. Judicial Council of the Tenth Circuit*,[40] a district judge sought relief by mandamus of an order of the judicial council of the Tenth Circuit. The order permitted the judge to complete cases filed before a specified date but deprived him of all future cases. The judge had twice expressed agreement with this order and a prior one, but, changing his mind, he sought mandamus. The Court, 7–2, denied the application for mandamus on the ground that the case for extraordinary relief had not been made. In doing so, Chief Justice Burger stated in dictum: "[There is] no disagreement among us as to the imperative need for total and absolute independence of judges in deciding cases.... [But] the question is whether Congress can vest in the Judicial Council the power to enforce reasonable standards as to when and where court shall be held, how long a case may be delayed in decision, whether a given case is to be tried, and many other routine [administrative] matters.").[41] This power, on the facts of *Chandler*, includes denying new case assignments to a duly appointed Article III judge.

Justice Harlan, in a lengthy concurrence, stated that the Court had jurisdiction to entertain the proceeding and that, considering the case on its merits, the circuit council order removing cases from the district judge did not impair judicial independence and was a valid exercise of valid authority.[42] Justices Black and Douglas, dissenting, agreed with Harlan that the case was ripe for decision. Reaching the merits, they argued the order depriving the judge of any new cases effectively removed the judge from office without an impeachment proceeding and violated the Good Behavior Clause. In their view, the order impaired judicial independence and could not be justified on grounds of efficient administrative supervision.[43]

Although these internal disciplinary mechanisms do not apply to the Supreme Court, in at least one instance in the twentieth century the Court determined that the vote of an impaired Justice would not be taken into account if that vote would decide the case.[44]

---

40. 398 U.S. 74 (1970).
41. *Id.* at 84.
42. *Id.* at 89–129 (concurring).
43. *Id.* at 129–42 (dissenting).
44. *See* David J. Garrow, *Mental Decrepitude on the U.S. Supreme Court: The Historical Case for a 28th Amendment,* 67 U. Chi. L. Rev. 995, at 1054.

Conclusion:
Applying the History and Purposes of the Good Behavior and Compensation Clauses to the Carrington-Cramton Proposal

The Carrington-Cramton proposal was designed in the light of historic practices that have become part of current law. A senior justice would continue to participate in the work of the Supreme Court in two ways: (1) full participation in the rulemaking authority of the Court until retirement or death; and (2) the recall of a senior justice to fill a temporary vacancy or to provide a full Court in situations of recusal or temporary disability in the term or terms immediately following becoming a senior justice. The proposal is supported by a highly plausible reading of the constitutional text, by longstanding and consistent historical practices that began with the First Congress, and by modern legislation that provides a judicial mechanism by which judges themselves may police judicial behavior and reassign cases to maintain the efficiency of the federal judicial system.

The circuit riding required of Supreme Court justices in the nineteenth century (leading some Justices to retire early) and upheld by the Court in *Stuart v. Laird* establishes that today's justices could be required, for example, to spend three months per year handling cases as a circuit or district court judge. The question, then, is whether spreading alternative constitutional court service over time is somehow different from contemporaneous service.

Article III, Section 1 of the Constitution provides that "The Judges, both of the supreme and inferior Courts, shall hold their Offices during good Behaviour...." This language can be read as drawing a distinction between "Judges" of the Supreme Court and "Judges" of the inferior courts, even though both are entitled to life tenure. But this construction, reaching the conclusion that tenure as a Supreme Court justice must continue in that capacity for life, is not a necessary reading. An equally plausible and straightforward interpretation would read it as requiring that "Judges" at both levels must enjoy life tenure but that the office of each may include not only contemporaneous service, as held in *Stuart v. Laird*, but successive service that started in the Supreme Court and moved to a lower court or vice versa. The text of the Good Behavior Clause does not separate the "Judges" of the "supreme Court" from those of the "inferior courts." Instead, it lumps them together in the following language: "The judges, *both of the supreme and inferior Courts,* shall hold their Offices during good Behaviour...." Congress may define a judicial "Office" as including service in both the Supreme Court and an inferior Article III court.

Because the text of the Constitution is ambiguous, the choice between two plausible interpretations should be influenced or controlled by a purposive or functionalist reading of the Good Behavior Clause in conjunction with the Necessary and Proper Clause. The function and purpose of the Good Behavior Clause is apparent from the uniformity of statements both supporting and opposing the Constitution: its purpose was to ensure that federal judges acted in a judicial capacity that was not subject to the influence or control of the political branches of the federal government.[45] "Judicial independence" has become the rubric for an essential requirement: decisions of federal judges must be protected from improper executive or congressional influence, approval, or retaliation. This purpose is served by a definition of judicial office that guarantees life tenure and includes a lengthy and fixed term of service in the judicial work of the Supreme Court.

The proposed statute is constitutional because (1) it provides for life tenure on one or more constitutional courts and (2) the term of full service on the Supreme Court is lengthy, fixed in time, non-renewable, and cannot be affected by the political branches of government. The Carrington-Cramton proposal protects judicial independence just as well as do current arrangements.

---

45. *See supra* text accompanying notes 5–8 (discussing the statements of the founding generation (both those supporting and opposing ratification of the Constitution), as evidence that judicial independence was the purpose of the Good Behavior and Compensation Clauses).

THE POWER OF CONGRESS OVER THE TERMS OF JUSTICES OF THE SUPREME COURT

*John Harrison**

Sometimes "What we all 'know' is wrong."[1] When that happens, there is much to be learned.

Sometimes what we all know is right. When that happens, there may be less to learn, but still something. Everyone knows that the President, with the advice and consent of the Senate, appoints to the Supreme Court judges whose principal function will be to serve on that Court by participating in pretty much all the Court's decisions. They will do so until they die, resign, or are removed on conviction by the Senate after impeachment by the House of Representatives.

That bit of what we all know is right, and it poses insurmountable obstacles to any attempt so far devised to provide by statute that judges of the Supreme Court will, in effect, serve for fixed terms short of life.

This particular commonplace follows from a small number of features of the Constitution. Some are fundamental, like the status of the Supreme Court as a separate institution. Others are less basic, but still important, like the status of judge of the Supreme Court as a distinct office. All follow straightforwardly from the text and, like most straightforward implications of the text, they reflect design choices of the Federal Convention. Function follows form here.

The Federal Convention debated whether the federal judiciary should consist of a single supreme court or of a supreme court and inferior tribunals.

---

* D. Lurton Massee Professor and Horace W. Goldsmith Research Professor, University of Virginia School of Law. Thanks to other participants in this symposium for comments and discussion on this topic.

1. Robert H. Bork, *The Antitrust Paradox: A Policy At War With Itself* 15 (1978).

Eventually it adopted the approach sometimes known as the Madisonian Compromise,[2] in which the Constitution itself creates the Supreme Court of the United States and leaves to Congress the decision whether there shall be any other federal courts: "The judicial power of the United States shall be vested in one supreme Court, and in such inferior courts as Congress may from time to time ordain and establish."[3] The Supreme Court is thus a single distinct institution, separate from and superior to any other courts Congress may create.

Within the lines drawn by the Constitution itself, Congress has some room to make important choices through its power to pass laws necessary and proper to carry the Court's judicial power into execution. Congress thus may decide on the size of the Court, which has varied over time.[4] Exactly how much is left to Congress is of course to some extent unclear.[5]

Closely related to the institutional separateness of the Supreme Court is the principle that it has its own judges. Article II authorizes the President to nominate, and with the advice and consent of the Senate to appoint, "Ambassadors, other public Ministers and Consuls, Judges of the supreme Court, and all other Officers of the United States whose Appointments are not herein otherwise provided for, and which shall be established by law." Article II thus contemplates, and in conjunction with Article III creates, the office of judge of the Supreme Court. Article III, consistent with this feature of the Constitution, refers to "the Judges, both of the supreme and inferior Courts," and provides that they "shall hold their Offices during good Behaviour."

Article III taken alone is, strictly speaking, ambiguous as to whether it contemplates federal judges in general or two distinct categories of supreme court judges and inferior court judges.[6] By itself, it might mean "the judges of the supreme court and the judges of the inferior courts," referring to two distinct constitutional offices; or it might mean "the judges, who may serve on the

---

2. 1 Max Farrand, *The Records of the Federal Convention* 125 (1937). *See also* Michael G. Collins, *Article III Cases, State Court Duties, and the Madisonian Compromise*, 1995 Wisc. L. Rev. 39 (questioning the belief that the inferior courts are fully optional).

3. U.S. Const., Art. III, sec. 1.

4. The Court today consists of nine judges, 28 U.S.C. 1, as it has for more than a century. The Judiciary Act of 1789 provided for a Court of six. Act of September 24, 1789, Section 1, 1 Stat.73.

5. For example, the question has never been resolved whether and to what extent Congress may provide that the Court shall sit in panels or divisions while still acting consistently with the principle that the Court is one.

6. John O. McGinnis, *Justice Without Justices*, 16 Const. Comm. 541, 545 (1999). McGinnis does not appear to think that this possibility, although grammatically available, will bear much weight. He introduces the point with a disclaimer: "The most natural read-

supreme or inferior courts or both," referring to a single office of Article III judge as it would be put today. Article III may be ambiguous in isolation, but the Constitution as a whole conveys a clearer message. Article II, by referring to judges of the Supreme Court, disambiguates Article III, and shows that the first of the two possible readings is correct.[7] Just as there are Senators, who alone are Senators, so there are judges specifically of the Supreme Court.[8] And just as the Senate is made up of Senators, so the Supreme Court is made up of its members, the justices.

It is easy to see why the Federal Convention would have intended or assumed that the justices would be distinct from any other federal judges. As members of the federal government's highest court, the justices would have to be selected with considerable care, care that a busy President and Senate might not be able to lavish on all judicial nominees, especially as the country and the federal judiciary expanded. That care might involve difficult political compromise, given the Court's nationwide power, the kind of compromise that could be unnecessary for nominations to other, less final and less nationwide tribunals.[9]

Together these basic features of the constitutional structure rule out congressional adoption of proposals, like that put forward by Professor John McGinnis, under which the Supreme Court would be staffed by generic federal judges with life tenure in that generic role, judges whose actual time of service on the Court itself would be selected by Congress.[10] But only judges appointed to the Court as such may serve on it. "Supreme Court riding" by inferior court judges is not consistent with the Constitution's text and structure or the purpose underlying them.

---

ing may require (and the Framers certainly expected) judges to be appointed to a distinct Supreme Court, but the language is ambiguous." *Id.*

7. The reference elsewhere in the Constitution to the chief justice confirms this point. U.S. Const., Art. I, sec. 3, para. 6 (when the President is tried before the Senate, the Chief Justice presides).

8. Article III leaves open whether there is or may be an *office* of judge of the inferior courts, such that a judge may serve generally on any of the inferior courts. When read with Article II, however, it does not leave open whether there are judges "of the Supreme Court."

9. *See* Henry J. Abraham, *Justices and Presidents: A Political History of Appointments to the Supreme Court* 144–146 (3d ed. 1992) (noting the importance—because the Court is a nationwide institution—of regional balance and of political appeal in selecting Justices). *See also* 28 U.S.C. 1295 (creating the substantively specialized United States Court of Appeals for the Federal Circuit).

10. Professor McGinnis suggests that his system of "Supreme Court riding" might be adopted by Congress, but has doubts as to whether it is within Congress's power and prefers a constitutional amendment as the vehicle. McGinnis, *supra* n. 6, at 545.

As the phrase "Supreme Court riding" suggests, the main argument to the contrary comes from the longstanding practice of "circuit riding," under which justices routinely served, and still serve now and then, on lower federal courts.[11] If Supreme Court Justices may serve on the inferior courts, the argument goes, there must be some interchangeability of federal judges. Maybe, for constitutional purposes, there really is just a single category of Article III judge, or at least maybe historical practice requires that the Constitution be so read, whatever the text otherwise would indicate.

Circuit riding was controversial from its beginnings, however, and John Marshall himself had serious reservations about it.[12] Marshall apparently was prepared to accept it simply because of acquiescence over the course of several years, without endorsing the practice on its merits.[13] The Court seems to have taken that position in *Stuart* v. *Laird*.[14] Those who think the Constitution requires strict separation of personnel between the supreme and inferior courts may accept circuit riding on grounds of precedent and practice without believing they therefore must accept any further deviation from what they regard as the constitutional design.

It is also possible to accept circuit riding by justices as actually consistent with the Constitution while rejecting the possibility of Supreme Court riding by inferior court judges. To do so, one needs to believe that the relationship between the tiers of the federal judiciary is not symmetrical in this respect. That it is otherwise not symmetrical is clear. Only the Supreme Court is

---

11. The Judiciary Act of 1789 provided for the appointment of justices of the Supreme Court and judges of the District Courts. Act of Sept. 24, 1789, sec. 1, sec. 3. It provided for Circuit Courts staffed by one district judge and two justices, *id.* at sec. 4, and so began the system of circuit riding. Today justices are allotted to circuits as circuit justices, 28 U.S.C. 42, and as circuit justices may sit as judges of the courts of appeals to which they are allotted, 28 U.S.C. 43(b).

12. David P. Currie, *The Constitution in the Supreme Court: The First Hundred Years, 1789–1888* 77–78 n.102 (1985) (noting Marshall expressed "strong constitutional scruples" about circuit riding in a letter to fellow Justice William Paterson in 1802).

13. *Id.*

14. 5 U.S. (1 Cranch) 299 (1803). Marshall recused himself because he had addressed the issue on circuit. In *Stuart* the losing party in a circuit court objected to the presence on that court of the Chief Justice, riding circuit, arguing that "the judges of the supreme court have no right to sit as circuit judges, not being appointed as such, or in other words, that they ought to have distinct commissions to that purpose." *Id.* at 309. In response, the Court found it "sufficient to observe, that practice and acquiescence under it for a period of several years, commencing with the organization of the judicial system, affords an irresistible answer, and has indeed fixed the construction." *Id.*

supreme.[15] An inferior court may not reverse the Supreme Court of the United States. To extend that asymmetry to personnel is to say that the justices may participate in the work of the inferior courts, just as they may review that work, but the judges of the inferior courts may not participate in the Supreme Court's work, just as they may not review the Court's decisions.[16] Uniform practice supports this asymmetrical structure. Many justices have sat on many inferior courts, but no judge not specifically confirmed to the Supreme Court has ever participated in deciding one of its cases. Supreme Court riding for a limited time is not an option.

Professors Carrington and Cramton propose accepting the distinction between justices and other Article III judges, but propose to rely on congressional power to define the precise duties and authority of justices in order to produce, in effect, a system of fixed and non-renewable terms for justices. Under their proposal each justice would begin the term with eighteen years of full participation in the Court's decisions, exercising the powers that justices have exercised since the founding. After that, each justice would remain in office, but with dramatically different powers and duties—powers and duties that would include the full-time exercise of Article III judicial power but little or no participation in the Court's decisions.

Like the McGinnis proposal, Carrington and Cramton's suggestion draws on the experience of circuit riding, but in a different way. Rather than assume Article III judges are fungible, it assumes that justices are distinct but that they can have functions other than sitting on the Supreme Court. And the Carrington-Cramton proposal assumes Congress can divide Supreme Court and non-Supreme Court functions by assigning them to sequential parts of each justice's term of office. Rather than sit on the Supreme Court for six months and on the lower courts for six months of every year, each justice would sit on the Court for eighteen years and then on the lower courts for the remainder of the justice's term.

For this proposal to be constitutional, there must be some space between holding the office of Supreme Court Justice and participating in the Court's decisions, because the proposal provides that justices may spend many years during which they participate little or not at all in the Court's work. Carrington and

---

15. Defending the structure set up by Article III, Hamilton as Publius wrote: "That there ought to be one court of supreme and final jurisdiction, is a proposition which has not been, and is not likely to be contested." *The Federalist* No. 81 at 542 (J. Cooke ed. 1961).

16. Indeed, one justification for circuit riding is that it is a means by which the justices in effect oversee the decisions of the inferior courts by participating in those decisions; it is, in effect, an aspect of their court's appellate jurisdiction. That argument works only in one direction.

Cramton do not, of course, propose literal statutory term limits for justices: the Constitution provides for good behavior, and good behavior it must be. Rather, they argue it is permissible for someone to be a justice of the Court while no longer having much or anything to do with the Court's business.

To say there is a particular office of Supreme Court Justice, as opposed to federal judge in general, is to say that the Constitution contemplates some connection between the justices and the work of the Court. Otherwise, there would be no point in distinguishing the justices from other judges. The crucial question, then, is the nature of that connection—in particular, the extent to which membership on the Court, which comes with being a justice, entails participation in the Court's decisions. The closer the connection between membership and participation, the more difficult it will be to sustain a proposal like Carrington's and Cramton's, which loosens that connection by providing a justice may spend many years having little to do with the Court's decisions. I think that the Constitution assumes, instead, a quite close connection between membership on the Court and participation in its decisions; but even if the required connection were somewhat weaker than I believe it to be, it would still be closer than would be consistent with Carrington's and Cramton's idea.

The closer version of the connection, which I believe to be the better interpretation, is that membership in a collegial body entails participation in substantially all the body's final decisions, unless the rule creating the body indicates specifically to the contrary; a requirement of participation in substantially all, but not all, of the body's decisions permits, for example, temporary absence and recusal. That is certainly the Constitution's assumption with respect to the other collegial bodies it creates, the Senate and House of Representatives. Indeed, the principle is so obvious and the assumption so natural that it explains an otherwise strange omission: the Constitution does not explicitly provide that each Representative shall have one vote in the House's decisions, and in all of them.[17]

To see the strength of this principle, consider a statute providing that on even-numbered days the senior senator from every state would vote, while on odd-numbered days the junior senator from every state would vote. (Or even-numbered bills and resolutions and odd-numbered bills and resolutions.) All

---

17. It does provide for one vote with respect to Senators, U.S. Const., Art I., sec. 3, para. 1, and does so because the States are equal in representation in the Senate but widely unequal in population, and because representation of the people is a basic principle of American politics. See U.S. Const., Amend. 14, sec. 2 (apportioning representatives among States according to population). It is natural to wonder whether the votes of Senators are weighted by the population of their States. To make clear they are not, the Constitution reaffirms that the upper house is indeed badly malapportioned, giving each Senator one vote.

senators would be equal under that rule, but no senator would vote on every decision made by the Senate. It is hard to imagine that such a rule would be consistent with each senator's membership in the Senate.

A similar default assumption with respect to the courts of appeals helps explain the development of the en banc mechanism. Faced with a statute that granted power to courts of appeals while apparently authorizing them to sit in panels composed of only some of their members, the Supreme Court concluded that the full court had implicit power to revise the decision of its panels.[18] All the judges together were entitled to make the final decision for their court if they thought that necessary. The Court's strong assumption in interpreting the statute seems to have been that when power is vested in an institution that can operate through some of its members, final power is in the whole institution, which meant that all the component members of the institution were empowered to participate at the last stage of decision.

The Carrington-Cramton proposal rejects this idea of what it means to be a judge of a court. It assumes that the key is substantial and equal participation in the court's decisions, not full or nearly full participation. This is a weaker connection than I think the Constitution provides, but even if it is enough the proposal is not consistent with the Constitution's idea of a term. Under their scheme each justice would participate in substantially all of the Court's decisions for the first eighteen years of that justice's term. After eighteen years, justices would participate little or perhaps not at all. Over the course of a term on the Court, each justice would participate in a significant portion of the Court's decisions, but that portion could in the aggregate be far from 100 percent. A justice who served for thirty years, for example, would be involved in a little over half of the Court's decisions over the course of that time, including cases in which the justice was called to participate after the first eighteen years because of vacancies or recusals.

To make this extent of involvement in a body's decisions a plausible understanding of membership in that body requires two steps. The first, and easier, step draws on a structure that is familiar because it closely resembles the organization of the larger federal district courts. On district courts that have a substantial number of judges, each case is allocated to one judge, cases are evenly distributed among judges, and the court never or hardly ever sits en banc.[19] Each

---

18. *See* United States v. American-Foreign S.S. Corp, 363 U.S. 685, 689 (1960) (noting a 1948 amendment to the Judicial Code ratified the Court's earlier construction of statutes endorsing the practice of sitting en banc).

19. For example, the District Court for the District of Columbia has fifteen judges. 28 U.S.C. 133(a). Its local rules provide that each case is to be assigned to one judge, D.C. L.

judge thus handles a caseload that is roughly the same as that of every judge and that constitutes a significant fraction of the court's total docket, but that does not come close to being the whole caseload.[20]

It is not enough, however, for proponents of the Carrington-Cramton proposal to say that this idea of membership on a court is the Constitution's idea of membership on the Supreme Court. The next step that must be taken is to say that substantiality of participation is to be calculated over each justice's entire term as a justice, not at every point in time. If that step is sound, only dramatic breakthroughs in life expectancy would threaten the proposal's constitutionality; under the current mortality tables, eighteen years is a substantial fraction of the time anyone would spend as a justice.[21]

That second step encounters a severe difficulty: the idea of a term. However membership in a decisionmaking body is understood—be it full, nearly full, or substantial involvement in the body's decisions—the point at which membership so defined permanently ceases is the end of a term. Imagine being told, first, that membership on the Supreme Court entails participating in a substantial fraction of the Court's decisions, and second, that after eighteen years each justice no longer performs that function and is succeeded in it by someone else who has been appointed a justice.[22] If then asked what the term of a justice on the Court is, the natural answer would be eighteen years.

Cv. R. 40.1(a), that cases be randomly assigned in order to assure an even distribution of case-load among judges, *id.* R. 40.2(a), and that cases be classified and random assignment made within classifications, *id.* R. 40.3(a), in order to account for the different workload associated with different types of cases. The rules are thus designed to distribute the court's workload evenly among its judges.

20. A similar result would obtain on the courts of appeals that have significantly more than three judges if they had no en banc mechanism.

21. The Carrington-Cramton proposal draws less support from the tradition of circuit riding than it may appear. It may seem plausible to liken a justice who spends eighteen years on the Court and eighteen more years on the lower courts to a circuit-rider who spent six months of each year in Washington and six months on circuit. Circuit riding, however, did not keep the justices from participating in substantially all the Court's decisions while they were justices. The Court was not sitting while they were away on circuit. Spending half their time on the Court therefore did not mean spending half of their terms of office on the Court in the sense in which that would be true under the Carrington-Cramton system. Circuit riding was in addition to service on the Court; the Carrington-Cramton idea would make service on the lower courts a substitute for service on the Court, which it never was. Accepting the tradition thus entails accepting only that justices may be given duties besides their primary duties, not that additional responsibilities may replace work on the Court itself.

22. Under the Carrington-Cramton proposal, it is true, justices would continue to participate to some extent in the Court's work after eighteen years, but that participation would not be substantial and would not satisfy any reasonable idea of the connection between the

The Vice President of the United States, for example, has, as such, two functions under the Constitution. One is to preside over the Senate with a casting vote, the other is to participate in the mechanism governing temporary presidential disability set up by Article II and the Twenty-Fifth Amendment. Every four years an individual's empowerment to perform those functions ends and is transferred to someone whose empowerment derives from a temporally distinct source; that is, every four years the Vice President's term ends and the office must be filled anew. Because justices serve on good behavior, and not for a renewable term, when their term comes to an end someone else begins to exercise the function that they previously exercised. If that function is to participate substantially in the Court's decisions, justices cease to do so and are replaced at the end of their terms; the point at which they cease to do so and are replaced is the end of their terms.

Terms of office perform an extremely important function in a system like ours. They determine the temporal allocation of government power among individuals. That allocation is a major matter: the point at which one person replaces another in the exercise of power, and in particular in the exercise of power on the Supreme Court, is of immense importance because when that point arrives, whoever controls the presidency and can muster a majority of the Senate decides who will next take part in the Court's decisions. The whole point of the Carrington-Cramton proposal is to bring regularity to precisely those moments, making their arrival predictable and not manipulable. Were that proposal to be adopted, those moments of turnover on the Court would be far more important for practical purposes than the moment at which an individual justice ceased permanently to exercise all judicial power through resignation, death, or removal. There is no getting around it: Those moments are the points at which terms on the Court end.

To see their importance, consider two possible courts. Each court has ten members, and the judges serve for ten years. On Court A, each judge individually decides one-tenth of the court's cases every year, and there is no en banc mechanism. On Court B, each judge spends the first year in office deciding all the court's cases that year, and then decides no cases for the next nine years. The terms of all of the judges on Court A begin and end on the same day, so that every ten years whoever is in a position to make appointments is able to appoint all the court's judges. The terms of the judges on

---

office of justice and the work of the Court. Congress could not by statute provide for a tenth justice who would sit on cases only when another justice was recused or otherwise unavailable or another seat was vacant. Being a member of the Court must mean more than that.

Court B are staggered so that every year the term of one of them ends and a replacement is appointed.

Suppose that both courts decide 100 cases every year. In the course of a term of office, judges on Court A will decide 100 cases, ten cases every year for ten years. In the course of a term of office, judges on Court B likewise will decide 100 cases, 100 in the first year and none thereafter. In terms of the total number of cases decided during a term of office, the judges of those courts will participate to the same extent in the work of their courts. Yet the timing of that participation would make the two arrangements very different from the standpoint of someone who wanted to exercise the power to make appointments. For Court A, it would be very important to be in control of the appointing power once every ten years. For Court B, one year in control of the appointing power would be like another. From the standpoint of someone who cared about the power to make appointments, it would be natural to say that the judges on Court A serve for ten years, whereas the judges on Court B serve for one. From that standpoint, the additional nine years in office of the judges on Court B would be irrelevant, a mere formality.[23]

Under the Constitution, the function of a term of office is to identify the point at which crucial personnel decisions are to be made and thereby to determine who makes those decisions, which is whoever has the relevant power at the relevant time. Candidates for office want their supporters to be in a majority at the crucial time, the election, and are interested in what happens at other times mainly insofar as it bears on what will happen come the election. That is why a Senator elected in 2008 would much rather have some bad publicity in 2009 than in 2014, and why first-term Presidents would rather an economic recession be early in the term than late. For the Supreme Court, the point at which crucial personnel decisions are to be made is the point at which there is substantial change in the identity of the people who will be making the Court's decisions. That is why a term on the Court is measured as to service on the Court, not service in some other capacity that may also attach to the office of justice. Justices are judges of the Supreme Court, and the function of the concept of a term demands that their term be defined by their connection to the Court. As to terms, at least, there is not enough room between

---

23. The difference between the staggered terms for Court B and the all-at-once replacement of judges for Court A resembles, and is an extreme form of, the difference between a system with fixed terms, like Carrington's and Cramton's, and one in which vacancies arise randomly and are therefore likely to be substantially more bunched than they would be with fixed terms. Randomness is not evenness, and when vacancies arise randomly, control of the appointing power when they happen to arise is very important.

the office of judge and the judge's court to accommodate the Carrington-Cramton proposal.

The Constitution means that judges of the Supreme Court serve on that court during good behavior.

It may seem that in delving into details of the text and the concepts it uses, like the idea of a term on the Court, I have missed the big picture. For Carrington and Cramton, a crucial feature of the big picture is that their proposal is consistent with, and maybe even advances, the primary purpose of the Constitution's rule of life tenure.

The purpose of life tenure is to ensure judicial independence, to make certain that Article III judges are not trying to please anyone on whom they depend for continuation in office. A central attraction of a move from life tenure to fixed, non-renewable terms is that the latter also preserve judicial independence. A judge with a non-renewable term, like a judge with life tenure, has no thought of reappointment and no incentives derived from that possibility. Moreover, because their proposal is not strictly speaking one for non-renewable fixed terms, Carrington and Cramton can claim the further independence-enhancing feature of having provided justices with a respectable and remunerative job for life, a status that in practice likely would turn into a form of distinguished semi-retirement. Carrington and Cramton can thus claim to have changed merely the form, while keeping the substance—judicial independence—intact. To a non-formalist, that is an important consideration.

This is not the whole story, however, even for non-formalists, because it deals with only one of the purposes—albeit a central one—of Article III's rules for judicial terms: judicial independence. Another aspect of the story, another important purpose of Article III, would be defeated if the Carrington-Cramton proposal were constitutional. For a non-formalist, the departure from that purpose should count heavily against the idea. That purpose is so basic it is easy to lose sight of: constitutionalization itself is often a good thing. Just as it is sometimes more important to have a rule than any particular rule, so it is sometimes more important that a rule be fixed by the constitution than that it have any particular content. (And even when the content matters a good deal, the fixity likely matters too.)

An example close to the present context is the fixity of congressional and presidential terms. It may not matter much that representatives serve for two years and not three. It does matter, though, that neither the leadership of Congress nor the President nor both together may dissolve Congress and call elections: they cannot choose a propitious time to go to the country and thereby enhance their chances of being reelected. The term of every Congress is set by the Constitution, as is that of the President; every four years, no sooner and no later, the American Olympiad brings the presidency before the voters. Fixed terms are an important feature of the system, one that sharply distinguishes it from other, similar constitutional structures in which parliaments can be dissolved.

A congressional power to adopt a proposal like Carrington and Cramton's would have perverse effects, effects constitutionalizing the issue of terms on the Court prevents. For one thing, proponents of statutorily fixed terms do not suggest that their proposal is mandatory; part of their argument is that Congress may choose. That means Congress may change its choice over time. Suppose that the Carrington-Cramton system were in effect, and one political party came to control the House, the Senate, and the presidency. That party would be sorely tempted to revert to life tenure for its appointee or appointees, perhaps afterwards shifting back to limited terms just in case the next appointee was not one of theirs. This is the sort of gamesmanship that proponents of fixed terms (of which I am one) deplore. If the Constitution permits it, one of the purposes of having a constitution fails, which suggests that the Constitution does not permit it.

For another, because the status of senior justice under the Carrington-Cramton proposal is a statutory product, Congress could eliminate it. Congress could enact a statute recalling justices with eighteen-year track records to full active service and in effect pack the Court in an especially predictable way. Once again, it is easy to produce such a scenario. One party appoints several justices, then has a bad run electorally. When fortune shifts in its favor, the party controls Congress and the presidency. It faces a hostile majority of active justices on the Court, but waiting to return are several now-senior justices appointed during the previous fat years. Congress eliminates the restrictions that come with senior justice status, the Court in effect expands through the return of several justices who, formally speaking, never left it but just took on new duties, and it has been packed without a single appointment.

There are good reasons the Constitution, not Congress, sets the period during which justices substantially participate in the Supreme Court's decisions.

The means of giving justices fixed, non-renewable terms by statute proposed in this symposium and discussed here are not consistent with the Constitution, although the goal of those proposals is desirable as a matter of policy. Life tenure produces random vacancies and the bunching that comes with randomness; or it produces vacancies that are not random because the incumbent has chosen the moment of resignation for political reasons, often staying on the Court despite infirmity in order to do so. Bunching, strategically timed resignations, and decrepit justices are all undesirable. The other systematically predictable effect of life tenure under current conditions is very long service on the Court.[24] That too will be undesirable as long as the Court makes important political decisions. Because justices are not and should not be subject to reappointment, popular political control over the Court, which is appropriate for a political body, comes only at the appointment stage. But the issues the justices will confront, and their responses to those issues, can be predicted for the short and medium term at best, which means that the coalition that appoints a justice can, through that appointment, exercise its own choices only through the short and medium term; after that the choices of the appointers become irrelevant and the accidents of the justices' views become dominant. That is not democracy. An institution that makes the kind of decisions the Supreme Court makes should have fixed, non-renewable terms that are much shorter than thirty years, and in my view a constitutional amendment to that end would be wise.

---

24. *See supra* Steven G. Calabresi & James Lindgren, *Term Limits for the Supreme Court: Life Tenure Reconsidered,* pp. 15–98.

LIFE TENURE AND THE SUPREME COURT: WHAT IS TO BE DONE?

Sanford Levinson[*]

Many contributors to this volume are united in the belief that life tenure for Supreme Court justices is in fact a dysfunctional part of the American political system. The major dissenter to this proposition is Ward Farnsworth, but even he concedes[1] he would not in fact advise anybody drafting a constitution today to emulate the American practice. His argument therefore boils down to a version of, "It isn't (very) broken, so it doesn't need fixing." Interestingly enough, he presents evidence as to the "broken" (or at least dysfunctional) aspects of life tenure in noting the possibility that presidents could in effect "lock-up" the Supreme Court for many presidential terms by making several appointments of young justices, thus effectively denying at least their immediate successors—who may, of course, be members of a different political party—the opportunity to make any appointments at all.

Such opportunities to reshape the Court may also be forestalled by a justice's timing his or her eventual resignation to fit political imperatives. In this regard, Potter Stewart, a Republican, remained on the Court throughout Jimmy Carter's presidency and resigned almost immediately after Ronald Reagan's inauguration in 1981. Among other things, this meant that Carter became the first President since Andrew Johnson not to appoint a single member to the Supreme Court.

---

* W. St. John Garwood and W. St. John Garwood Jr. Centennial Chair in Law, University of Texas Law School; Professor, Department of Government, University of Texas at Austin.
    1. *See supra* Ward Farnsworth, *The Case for Life Tenure*, pp. 251–269.

Although George H. W. Bush got to name two justices in his four-year term, one can be confident that both Byron White and Harry Blackmun took some pleasure in their ability to hang on long enough to give the choice of their own successors to the Democrat Bill Clinton. And Thurgood Marshall and William J. Brennan literally almost died trying to hang on to their seats. Brennan would probably take genuine pleasure in his successor, David Souter, though Clarence Thomas in effect vindicates Marshall's effort to do whatever he could to deprive Bush of the opportunity. Needless to say, all these examples give the lie to any notion that the Supreme Court, and its justices, are "above" or "beyond" politics. As any political scientist would testify, the Supreme Court is intimately connected, in every conceivable way, with the national political process.

Life tenure for members of the Supreme Court is an idea whose time has passed. Life tenure for other members of the federal judiciary is not, practically speaking, a significant problem. Serving as a judge on an "inferior court" is in fact far more onerous than being a member of the Supreme Court. The workload is far harder and the cases often far less interesting, not to mention the practical fact that the power, influence, and status of lowly district or even appellate judges is far less than that of Supreme Court justices. District and appellate judges are far more likely to retire as soon as they can and enjoy their full-salary pensions (and, of course, for some, "of counsel" status in law firms). Supreme Court justices, on the other hand, seem to treat "life tenure" as a literal boon of the office, so that only serious illness or death will remove them from the bench. And, as David Garrow demonstrates, even serious illness, especially if it affects "only" mental capacities, seems unavailing in all too many instances.[2]

So the question is that asked by Lenin over a century ago: "What Is to Be Done?" More precisely, since none of this symposium's contributors finds the abuses of life tenure to be *so* serious as to generate revolutionary impulses, the question resolves, at least for constitutional lawyers, into whether desired changes can be accomplished by statute rather than by constitutional amendment. Although this essay focuses primarily on this basically legal question, I do in fact warmly support the notion that members of the Supreme Court be appointed for non-renewable eighteen-year terms, with full-salary pensions (including any increases that active justices might receive presumably in reflection of cost-of-living exigencies) at the end of the eighteen years. But I have no objection to the Carrington-Cramton proposal, which takes into account the unfortunate fact that current members have been appointed under the pre-

---

2. *See* David J. Garrow, *Mental Decrepitude on the U.S. Supreme Court: The Historical Case for a 28th Amendment*, 67 U. Chi. L. Rev. 995 (2000). *See also* David N. Atkinson, *Leaving the Bench: Supreme Court Justices at the End* (1999).

sumption of life tenure and which therefore tries to accommodate this reality by what is in effect a "court-packing plan" that would work to deprive long-term justices of their practical ability to hear cases except when one of the nine more recently appointed justices was unable to participate. The retired justices could, of course, "ride circuit," as did their predecessors until 1891, when the current system of appellate courts was adopted. My own view is that such "circuit riding duties" would in fact be beneficial for the judicial system, as Supreme Court justices would have the opportunity to observe law "closer to the ground," as it were, and provide a valuable mechanism for feedback both to and from the different levels of the federal judiciary. One thinks, for example, of Tom Clark's genuine contributions along these lines following his own retirement from the Supreme Court in 1966. In any event, the ensuing discussion focuses concerns only whether any such proposals, regardless of the details, would necessarily require a constitutional amendment or could instead, as I believe is the case, be accomplished through statutory means.

Professors Calabresi and Lindgren make the definitive case for the unwisdom of life tenure and the need to do something about it.[3] However, they also argue that the only way to do this is through the vehicle of an Article V constitutional amendment. Although, all things considered, an amendment would be *preferable*, given the concrete, practical realities posed by ratification, such a proposal might well doom the project in which they are such important contributors. It is as if Paul Revere, after announcing that the British were coming, followed up by saying that Concord and Lexington had to convene their town meetings in order to engage in a legally mandated three-day long debate before acting to resist the Redcoats.

Why be so pessimistic about this aspect of their proposal? The reason is quite simple. As Donald Lutz amply demonstrates,[4] the United States Constitution is literally the most difficult to amend of all currently operating national constitutions in the world. That honor used to be held by Yugoslavia, but, presumably, its constitution is now a thing of the past, and America now holds this altogether dubious, number one position.[5] Whether Article V is, as Pro-

---

3. *See supra* Steven G. Calabresi & James Lindgren, *Term Limits for the Supreme Court: Life Tenure Reconsidered*, pp. 15–98.

4. Donald S. Lutz, *Toward a Theory of Constitutional Amendment*, in *Responding to Imperfection: The Theory and Practice of Constitutional Amendment* 237 (Sanford Levinson ed., 1995).

5. I also put to one side that certain constitutions—Germany's and India's are certainly the most prominent—contain "unamendable" provisions dealing with human rights or, as in Germany, maintaining a federal system of governance.

fessor Griffin has suggested, the "stupidest" single provision of the Constitution,[6] it certainly ranks very high in competition and, as a practical matter, is unquestionably detrimental to our own political system.[7]

What I have elsewhere labeled "the amendment game"[8] is stacked remarkably in favor of what might be termed the "defense" against those who propose a remedial constitutional amendment. First, proponents would have to capture control of two-thirds of each house of Congress—or, as a matter of theoretical possibility, two-thirds of the state legislatures which could, under Article V, mandate the calling of a constitutional convention. But, thereafter, proponents would have to gain control of a minimum of seventy-five legislative houses in thirty-eight states (assuming that Nebraska is one of those states). Those opposing an amendment need gain only the support of one-third plus one of either house of Congress or, failing that, a maximum of thirteen legislative houses in separate states. On top of difficulties posed by these sheer numbers is the lamentable attitude fostered by Kathleen Sullivan and others, under the label "amendmentitis,"[9] suggesting a very heavy, almost unsustainable, burden of justification rests on anyone who would disturb a single letter of our presumptively near-perfect Constitution. One sees an unfortunate display of such an attitude in the otherwise fine essay by Professor Farnsworth,[10] which adopts an ostensibly "Burkean" perspective cautioning against change in the absence of overwhelming urgency.

Whatever might be the admitted desirability of formal constitutional amendment, therefore, anyone who is truly serious about responding to the problems caused by life tenure on the Supreme Court *must* seek a statutory solution, such as that suggested by Professors Cramton and Carrington. And, of course, they must present reasons why that solution is not only wise as a matter of policy, but also constitutional.

---

6. *See* Stephen Griffin, *"The Nominee is…Article V,"* in *Constitutional Stupidities, Constitutional Tragedies* 51–53 (William Eskridge & Sanford Levinson eds., 1998). *See also* Sanford Levinson, *Designing an Amendment Process,* in *Constitutional Culture and Democratic Rule* 271 (John Ferejohn, Jack N. Rakove, & Jonathan Riley eds, 2001).

7. *See* Sanford Levinson, *Presidential Elections and Constitutional Stupidities,* in *Constitutional Stupidities,* at 61–66 (stating my own first choice as "stupidest" provision, the one-state/one-vote rule in the House of Representatives for breaking deadlocks in the Electoral College).

8. *See* Levinson, *supra* n. 6, at 283.

9. Kathleen Sullivan, *Constitutional Amendmentitis, The American Prospect,* <http://www.prospect.org/ print/V6/23/sullivan-k.html> (September 21, 1995).

10. *See supra* Farnsworth, pp. 251–269.

This task can be approached in two ways. The first involves creating what might be termed a "lawyer's argument," one faithful to the modalities of constitutional argumentation, that the statute would in fact be constitutional. The second involves a more "Holmesian" task of predicting the likely response of courts—including the Supreme Court itself (assuming it would not feel compelled to recuse itself from deciding any such case)—to something like the Carrington-Cramton statute.

As to the "lawyer's argument," the central difficulty is thought to be Article III, section 1: "The judges, both of the supreme and inferior courts, shall hold their offices during good behaviour...." The first thing to note, of course, is that this clause does not explicitly say "hold their offices for life." Most lawyers believe—and law professors have taught—that "during good behaviour" just *is* the same thing as "for life." But neither the text nor the presumed purpose of the clause rules out the following argument: The "good behaviour" clause guarantees that judges, *whatever their term of service,* cannot be removed from office for partisan political reasons that would, by definition, threaten the very idea of judicial independence. "Legislative judges" such as magistrates and bankruptcy judges—whose offices are the product of the congressional power "to constitute tribunals inferior to the Supreme Court" under Article I, §8, do not have life tenure. But, presumably, they cannot be removed—"fired," as it were—because Congress concludes the magistrate or judge in question is too "liberal" or too "conservative." That is, so long as their "behaviour" is within the range viewed as "good," which most certainly includes issuing controversial opinions that might antagonize part of the public, then they are protected against losing their positions.

As this example of Article I judges demonstrates, judicial independence can be protected without granting life tenure. As for Article III judges, one could argue that the "good behaviour" clause is a protection against partisan impeachment, but most definitely not an assignment of the office literally for life. To this argument one might respond that the difference between Article I and Article III judges has now been collapsed inasmuch as the only significant difference is thought to be "life tenure." To some extent, that may be true, but the distinction can be retained by requiring that federal judges be guaranteed a sufficiently long term (unlike, most dramatically, magistrates) that one would have no fear for their independence. One possibility is an age limit, such as service until seventy or seventy-five. The only thing wrong with age limits is that, like life tenure, they do nothing to ameliorate the incentive for agenda-driven Presidents (joined, presumably, by a sympathetic Senate) to appoint young justices who can "lock-up" the Court for years to come.

This is why I strongly prefer eighteen-year terms, which, as Lindgren and Calabresi demonstrate, is even a bit longer than the historical average of length of service, at least prior to 1970. I think it is unreasonable to believe that such a term of office, especially when coupled with a full-salary pension upon leaving the bench, would not provide all the independence one could reasonably want. Indeed, eighteen years is considerably longer than most nations allow members of their constitutional courts to serve. For example, judges on the highly respected constitutional court of South Africa are limited to twelve years of service or to seventy years of age, whichever comes first.[11] Even if one were to share the current American parochialism presuming that we have nothing to learn from those outside our borders, then one might look at state supreme courts, most of which have rejected life tenure. Roger Traynor, for example, lost none of his luster—or rigorous independence—because he sat on a court without life tenure. To believe that life-long tenure is necessary for judicial independence—or otherwise contributes to the public welfare—is supported by neither logic nor experience.

To be sure, it would be somewhat awkward for an American constitutional lawyer to argue that the 200-year-long identification of "good behaviour" with "life tenure" is mistaken, but why should it be viewed as fatal to the enterprise? After all, American lawyers often argue that venerable readings of the Constitution are wrong. The fact is that Congress has never seriously challenged this identification. The multitude of cases repeating it are doing so in a basically thoughtless manner, reiterating an initial assumption that has never been subjected to the kind of statutory attack suggested by Professors Cramton and Carrington.

Is it not relevant, for example, that "life" almost undoubtedly meant something different to people in 1787 than it does to us today with respect to *life expectancies*? Even in 1900, the average forty-year-old male could look forward to only 27.7 years of life; a male who made it to sixty might expect to live 14.4 years.[12] If one assumes an average age at appointment of fifty, actually three years younger than Calabresi and Lindgren tell us is the case, and if one simply splits the difference between 27.7 and 14.4, one would expect the typical

---

11. *See* S. Afr. Const., Art. 176. "(1) A Constitutional Court judge is appointed for a non-renewable term of 12 years, but must retire at the age of 70," <http://www.polity.org.za/html/govdocs/constitution/saconst08.html? rebookmark=1#167>.

12. *See Historical Statistics of the United States*, Vital Statistics and Health and Medical Care, Series B-116-125, Expectation of Life at Specified Ages, by Sex and Race, 1900–1970, p. 56.

appointee in 1900 to serve until seventy-one (i.e., twenty-one years), even though the average length of service was in fact considerably less. There appear to be no readily available national statistics for an earlier period that do not begin with birth, which skews expectancy figures because of high infant mortality rates. Massachusetts figures indicate, though, that in 1850 white males of sixty could expect to live another 15.6 years.[13] One suspects, but I cannot document, that Massachusetts had considerably better medical care than did, say, North Carolina or Vermont. In any event, inasmuch as most justices did not die in office because they had the good grace to retire, the expected length of service was in fact less than the expected life rate. Death-rate figures do not, of course, provide vitally important information about physical decline and debility. Surely not every sixty-year-old, even one "expecting" to live another fifteen years, was in the pink of health. As Lindgren and Calabresi demonstrate, the average age of a justice departing the Supreme Court prior to 1970 was 68.3.

Whatever "life" meant to Americans in 1787, I am relatively confident that its meaning was much closer to the proverbial "three score and ten years" than our sense today, when we regularly refer to someone who dies at seventy—or even seventy-five—as "young." It has become a staple of contemporary news articles, of course, that the life expectancies of Americans—both male and female—are increasing impressively,[14] especially for well-off persons with access to the best medical care (which, of course, describes members of the United States Supreme Court). Just as the notion of "cruel or unusual punishment" is inevitably "dynamic," requiring that one look to contemporary expectations rather than to practices acceptable in 1791, so one should realize that notions of "life" and "death" are equally dynamic. Even if the Framers in 1787 did believe "good behaviour" was synonymous with "life tenure," there is good reason to assume their conception of the length of that tenure was considerably less than our own today. It would thus be foolish for Congress (or reviewing courts) to be bound by the expectations of 220 years ago. The "good behaviour" clause should be liberated from its tether to "life tenure," es-

---

13. *See id.* Series B 126–135, Expectation of Life at Specified Ages, by Sex, for Massachusetts, 1850 to 1949–51.

14. *See, e.g.,* Center for Disease Control, National Vital Statistics Reports Table 7 ("Life Expectancy at selected ages by race and sex: United States, 2002"), <http://www.cdc.gov/nchs/data/nvsr/nvsr53 /nvsr53_05acc.pdf> (Oct. 12, 2004). White women have the longest life expectancies: a fifty-five-year-old white woman can expect to live another 27.9 years, whereas her white male counterpart can expect to live only 24.3 years. The rates for black men and women are 21.0 and 25.4 years, respectively.

pecially because the "good behaviour" clause still has an important role to play—keeping partisan politics out of the judicial office. Or so I would argue, in what I hope is a perfectly respectable legal argument.[15]

That there *is* a respectable legal argument available is no small point—it is, I believe the dispositive point—when moving to the second stage of the analysis: the probability of a court's (including, of course, the Supreme Court's) *accepting* it in any litigation following the passage of the statute (which would itself, presumably, follow consideration by the Congress of various constitutional arguments). For *if* a proposal like Cramton's and Carrington's were to pass, it would do so, obviously, only as the result of an energized—and bipartisan—political movement. Indeed, one of the most encouraging aspects of the Duke conference is that it brought together people from all sides of the political spectrum. Steve Calabresi, a principal founder of the Federalist Society, and I differ on all sorts of political issues, including many issues of constitutional interpretation. But we are in complete agreement that life tenure is bad and that something should be done about it. Although Calabresi unfortunately seems to disagree that a statute would be constitutional, it is surely the case that a successful statute would require the support from others identified with the Federalist Society and similar organizations, as well as denizens of the American Constitutional Society or the American Civil Liberties Union. The lack of bi-partisan support would surely doom the prospects for passage of such a statute, either because it would provoke a filibuster in the Senate or face a veto from an unsympathetic President. Indeed, inasmuch as the move toward term-limits could be viewed as a limitation on the political ability of an incumbent President to appoint young judges who would promote the President's political or judicial agenda into the indefinite future, one might predict a propensity toward a presidential veto, which would by definition require at least two-thirds support in each House to overcome.

---

15. I also note Professor Cramton's own constitutional argument, built in substantial measure on *Stuart v. Laird*, 5 U.S. (1 Cranch) 299 (1803): I relish that *Stuart* is finally getting the attention it deserves, instead of being completely effaced by the shadow of the far less important (at the time) case of *Marbury v. Madison*, 5 U.S. (1 Cranch) 137 (1803). A brilliant delineation of the importance of *Stuart*, relative to *Marbury*, can be found in Bruce Ackerman, *The Failure of the Founding Fathers: Jefferson, Marshall, and the Rise of Presidential Democracy* 163–198 (2005). Some argue to the contrary, as Professor Harrison does in his contribution to this Symposium, *see supra* John Harrison, *The Power of Congress over the Terms of Justices of the Supreme Court*, pp. 361–373. For reasons to be sketched out presently, I believe that the central question is not which set of arguments, in the abstract and out of political context, most appeals to the legal academic, but, rather, whether there *are*, indeed, respectable arguments upholding the legislation.

So imagine that a statute *does* clear these various hurdles and is now presented to a court for judicial review. The Supreme Court itself might be estopped from considering the case, unless, of course, as may be likely on political grounds, current members are "grandparented" from any of the new limitations imposed by the statute. If, as with the *Alcoa* case during World War II, the Court did feel a duty to recuse itself, then the issue would presumably be decided by a specially appointed court consisting of judges of "inferior courts." Those judges might in fact have an incentive to uphold the statute inasmuch as it would likely provide more opportunities for vacancies in Supreme Court positions, which they themselves might be tapped to fill.

In any event, whoever is ultimately presented with the burden of decision would be presented not only with the "lawyer's arguments" outlined above, but also, and perhaps more importantly, with the knowledge that a strong bipartisan consensus favors the proposition that the present system of life tenure must be eliminated. One need not be a complete Realist to believe that courts pay at least some attention to the election returns and that they would realize a decision striking down the proposed statute would (rightly) be perceived as monumental, basically narcissistic, judicial hubris.

Thus I am inclined to say of the prospects for judicial success of the Carrington-Cramton proposal what pundits often say about a John McCain presidency. The problem lies in his getting the Republican nomination, not in his winning the general election. Similarly, the problem for the Carrington-Cramton proposal is not its ultimate judicial ratification, but, rather, the creation of a national constituency that first accepts the underlying arguments, so ably spelled out by Calabresi and Lindgren, that something really must be done to cure the disease of life tenure and, second, organizes to put sufficient political pressure on Congress to pass relevant legislation.

Whether such a constituency can in fact be created, of course, is open to question. Ironically, the very bi-partisanship of the group supporting change means that it is not likely to be taken up as a cause by either of the ever-more-partisan political parties. Nor do even most proponents of change believe that the cost of life tenure approaches, for example, those of global warming or of innocent lives lost by abortion, to name only two "hot-button," "single issues" that have proved successful in mobilizing mass political movements. Still, academics should do what they can to encourage such a political movement, and the first steps are demonstrating there is a real problem, which Calabresi and Lindgren do superbly, and then posing a plausible political solution to the problem, which is, I believe, legislation.

Constitutional Futility of Statutory Term Limits for Supreme Court Justices

*William Van Alstyne**

Introduction

The Carrington-Cramton proposal for rotating judges on and off the Supreme Court is the most ingenious of the many to have appeared virtually from the founding era itself. Their particular proposal contemplates a secure eighteen years of regular Supreme Court service for each judge confirmed as a member of that Court, and it evenly spaces the occasion for new appointees, one every two years, providing a more uniform rhythm in the continuity of Supreme Court service than the country has previously enjoyed. Once the transition period has been traversed, and once the next generation will have become accustomed to the normalcy of the new process, it could, as they claim, bode well as a better way of balancing and of reconciling stability, accountability, continuity, independence, responsiveness, and gradualism in the judicial exposition of our constitutional law, than anything we have had in the past or currently possess.

Moreover, precisely because it is proposed as an experiment by statute, rather than by amendment, the Carrington-Cramton proposal intelligently takes into account a recognition that even the best laid plans may be upset by time and events, counseling modifications that may be well warranted:

---

* Lee Professor of Law, Marshall-Wythe School of Law, College of William & Mary.

modifications more readily capable of accommodation when the experiment is offered, as this one has been offered, in statutory form rather than as an amendment pursuant to Article V. And last, though assuredly not least, it is a special tribute to the Carrington-Cramton proposal that the endorsements it has already received by major scholars in constitutional law are not merely impressive in sheer number, but impressive also in their sheer diversity and array.

Despite these virtues, however, and despite the list of endorsements from so many major constitutional law professors,[1] I do not think it is within the discretion of Congress to do this by mere enactment. I mean to say why. It will contribute to that demonstration, however, if we begin with a very clear statement of just what the Carrington-Cramton proposal means to do and of just how far-reaching it is in fact. Its intention is effectively to remove a sitting justice *de jure* (i.e., unequivocally as a matter of law) from all regular service on the Supreme Court after a fixed term of years, and to do so according to what Congress presumes to declare is "enough." Once we understand what it means, and how it would operate, I mean at once to turn to the relevant constitutional provisions as they have always been commonly understood even by Congress itself (an understanding that is as I shall argue itself entirely correct). The Constitution vests in Congress no such power to limit one's term of service on the Supreme Court as the Carrington-Cramton proposal would presume to do. The conclusion we shall reach then swiftly follows at the end. If term limits for service on the Supreme Court *are* now to be prescribed, an amendment will be required either itself to prescribe them or empower Congress to prescribe them. In the meantime, however, while Congress may—as we shall see—doubtless do *many* things to make retirement or resignation an attractive alternative to continuing service on the Supreme Court, it may not by mere legislative fiat presume to contradict what the Constitution now provides, namely, that these judges, once appointed, hold their office during "good behavior," and not just for such seasonable, shorter tenure as Congress in its (alleged) wisdom might somehow prefer.

I

It is the frank objective of the proposal to put an end to a sitting justice's regular participation in the core constitutional responsibilities of the Supreme

---

1. That both Richard Epstein and Frank Michelman would put their names on the same petition, for example, is remarkable.

Court, not later than at the conclusion of the eighteenth year of such participation. That is, to take him or her from the circle of nine, and to terminate any power to be counted equally (and instead to be counted *not at all*) in the following respects of what it means to *be* a judge on the Supreme Court:

(a) to decide what cases to hear or not to hear;

(b) to determine what issues and questions are to be resolved—or not resolved—by the Court;

(c) to pass on such preliminary motions as may be submitted in respect to any pending case;

(d) to participate as a visible, equal judge, when the case is called;

(e) to propound questions and to offer observations from the bench;

(f) to attend, speak, and vote in the conference wherein the case itself is provisionally decided;

(g) to be fully eligible to draft the Court's Opinion or author a separate Opinion of one's own.

In short, to do *anything* one can *sensibly* list or suitably identify as to why it matters whether one is a justice or not a justice and whether, therefore, one is in practical effect actually no longer "on" as distinct from "off" the Court. (As much, as one might say, colloquially, as in being "on or off the bus.")

Now, it strikes me, as it surely must strike some others as well, that an Act of Congress just bluntly providing that "no person appointed to the Supreme Court shall participate in the regular business of the Supreme Court after eighteen years of consecutive service on that Court," would be very unlikely to muster the support or endorsement of nearly so many as have apparently endorsed the Carrington-Cramton proposal. And it strikes me also that the obvious reason that that would be so would be not just their doubts but, rather, their near certainty that, whether it would be desirable or otherwise that Congress would be able to disqualify any Justice's effective tenure on the Court in just this way, it currently has no such authority so to provide. If it were enacted simply and forthrightly *as* a statutory "term limit" on Supreme Court tenure of office, without any additional filigree, I believe nearly all, including the academic notables who have endorsed the Carrington-Cramton proposal, would subscribe to the view that the Constitution simply does not now sanction any power in Congress to enact such a law.

With but trivial distinctions, however, this is exactly—and clearly by design—what the proposal does. The first trivial distinction is merely this, namely, that on its face the proposed enactment does not use any fatal words. The proposal says nothing about "eighteen years and out" *as such*. Still, that is precisely what it means to do. It treats the Supreme Court bench as a kind of fixed tray, open at each end and capable of holding exactly nine dominoes, neither more nor less. It then goes on to provide that as this tray capable of containing nine dominoes is continuously replenished at one end (as it will be by pushing a new domino into that end of the tray every two years), it must also follow that each domino will inch one-ninth of the distance toward the other end so that, every two years, *a domino falls out of the tray*.

To be sure, there is an effort to say otherwise (i.e., to deny that anyone "falls from the tray") because one does not relinquish the formal title of Supreme Court justice, and one is not stripped of the usual emoluments of the office. Rather, one is simply assigned to "different" tasks including such things as standby status for possible recall, a role filled, however, even in any ordinary Broadway production by a mere understudy when the principal actor (the "real" actor) may suffer strep throat and the production require a stand-in for the night. But granted all its nice distinctions (and they amount to very little in point of practical effect), it is still difficult for me to see how anyone, least of all those in academic life, could be deceived into thinking these distinctions of sufficient significance even in their aggregate to render the scheme constitutional, as I think it plainly fails to be.

The plainest comparison one might offer is simply to what academics themselves understand to be involved in "tenure" in their *own* case, and compare with that the status of equivalent tenure on the Supreme Court. Universities that subscribe to the famous 1940 Joint Statement of Principles on Academic Freedom and Tenure operate under tenure systems, with tenured faculty members having a "tenure" in respect to their respective responsibilities not unlike that which judges appointed to the Supreme Court now have respecting their own. The principal distinction is merely that, typically, tenure-track academic appointees are subject to a kind of probationary service for up to seven years before the security of tenure, whereas appointees to the Supreme Court get "instant tenure" (i.e., tenure without a term of probationary service). Beyond that difference, however, each is thereafter entitled to be sustained in their respective positions during "good behavior." Which means, essentially, acquitting one's professional responsibilities (as a judge on the one hand and as an academic on the other hand) without impeachable abuse respecting those responsibilities—in teaching, in research, and otherwise within the usual mix of university services one is reasonably called upon to perform as a member of the sustaining faculty. Those either appointed with tenure (or "indefinite tenure" as is sometimes the usage), or who are awarded tenure after suitably rigorous assessment by the university so to qualify, are removable thereafter—but only for "cause." And that status—tenure—is critical for them, surely, not because (or at least not *just* because) it enables each to count on carrying a certain title and to enjoy certain emoluments from year to year until retirement or death. Rather, it is critical because it guarantees that one will continue to be an equal, participating, full faculty member, in contemplation of the core cluster of responsibilities and prerogatives one identifies as central to that position and role, until cause can be shown in a fair hearing why one should be stripped of those responsibilities, such as they are. Moreover, universities with tenure systems do not operate with some sort of "Catch-22" making one's professional standing to share in those core faculty functions contingent on what the university otherwise may do—or not do—by way of adding others to the faculty, whether in a given year or over the course of several years.

So, for example, the university might provide that "one new faculty person may be appointed every two years." That it would so provide would of course be unusual, if only because the rigidity of such an appointment schedule would not make a great deal of sense. Assuming it chose so to provide, however, and for whatever good reasons it might have, that it *may* do so does not and cannot affect the "tenure" (and its meaning) of those *already there*, i.e., they cannot thereby be "pushed out" the other end of some (limited) tray. Nor, to complete the analogy, would anyone in academic life seriously suggest that even if stripped of all the usual core participating rights of what it *is* to be tenured in a given department (to teach one's courses, to conduct research, to attend and vote on department standards, etc.), one still has "tenure" as the profession itself understands that term, even if nonetheless allowed still to carry a professorial title—and even idly also to draw one's pay.

Which is not to say, of course, that universities may not have their own version of "term limits" even for the tenured faculty. As a drily legal prerogative, they may, and, indeed, even now, some do. The most commonplace example, quite widely shared among universities until two decades ago, was a "term limit" in the sense of a mandatory, uniform, retirement age (now no longer permitted them under federal law). The point remains, however, that each such "limit" was—and is—recognized and treated as such. And if, for a useful comparative example, a university were by its bylaws even now to provide that "after eighteen years of consecutive, full time service, tenured members of the faculty shall rotate from full time classroom service to mere standby classroom service, albeit with no reduction in salary," it would at once be recognized as a major forfeiture of one of the *essential* attributes of *being* a "professor" at the university, namely, the continuing responsibility for teaching others, face-to-face, in classrooms, with materials of their professional selection and with ideas of their inspiration, ideas they desire to share.[2]

Treated squarely, as a proposal quite deliberately to place an eighteen-year ("enough is enough") term limit on one's service on the Supreme Court *as* a United States Supreme Court Associate Justice (or *as* Chief Justice of the United States), I have no doubt that the Act is simply doomed and precluded by the express provisions in Article III, most notably those providing that "The judicial Power of the United States, shall be vested in one supreme Court, and in such inferior Courts as the Congress may from time to time ordain and establish," and the accompanying provision that "The Judges, both of the supreme and inferior Courts, shall hold their Offices during good Behavior..."[3] All understood these provisions when they were adopted in lieu of alternative proposals, to be in exclusion of any power in Congress to prescribe some limited term of years, whether eight, eighteen, or twenty-eight. Nor has Congress itself ever presumed to suggest otherwise. And by now it must be very plain to any good faith reader of those provisions, with a good faith understanding of the context in which they were proposed and adopted, that what it was that was thus to be furnished protection from any congressionally-selected term limit were not the mere trappings of office without its substance, but the share of the "judicial power" one holds as a Supreme Court justice in the undiminished, full and equal sense with all others confirmed by the Senate and commissioned to that office, however few or many they may be.

That Congress may add new Supreme Court justices, even as it has sometimes done (including sometimes in the hopes of diluting the effect of current justices) may assuredly be true.[4] That Congress may also prospectively reduce

---

2. For an excellent example, *see* Levin v. Harleston, 770 F. Supp. 895 (S.D. N.Y. 1991), *aff'd in part and vacated in part*, 960 F.2d 85 (2d Cir. 1992) (university president's deliberate ad hoc creation of a "shadow course" so students offended by tenured philosophy professor's First Amendment-protected political views could disenroll his classes, *held* to undercut plaintiff's tenure by undermining his ability to teach in the classroom, and injunctive relief granted).

3. Relevant, also, are the respective clauses in Art. II, §2 ("He [the President] shall nominate, and by and with Advice and Consent of the Senate, shall appoint...Judges of the supreme Court....") and Art. II, §3 ("He shall...Commission all the officers of the United States."). (Once one's "commission" as a "Judge of the supreme Court" has been signed by the President and sealed, the office irrevocably "vests"). (*See* Marbury v. Madison, 5 U.S. (1 Cranch) 137 (1803).

4. *See*, e.g., Act of March 3, 1863, 12 Stat. 794, Sec. 1 (increasing Supreme Court from nine to ten members, to enable President Lincoln to add a tenth judge). (Again, some fair comparison with tenured faculty members may be appropriately noticed: i.e., an administration may bring in new tenured faculty to a department, sometimes even over the ob-

the Court (to forestall new appointments), as it has likewise sometimes presumed to do[5] is true as well, for no minimum or maximum number of judges is constitutionally specified for the Supreme Court. Moreover, Congress substantially controls the Court's budget and may use that control to reduce the number of clerks (even perhaps to discontinue them completely), or affect its equipment, reduce its secretarial help, require it to convene in less grand quarters, even to the end of making life onerous (and, by making life on the Court onerous, perhaps also thereby "encouraging" early retirements at full pay). No doubt it may likewise authorize many more entitlements of appeal to the Court than it does currently, as distinct from the current ninety-nine percent discretionary certiorari jurisdiction of the Court. This may be so if only because the Court's appellate jurisdiction (the great bulk of all its jurisdiction) is itself very much subject to "such Regulations as the Congress shall make," even as the Court itself concedes.[6]

But whether one may regard one or more of these powers in Congress as at least as significant a means of influencing the Court, disciplining its members, or putting them under greater pressure to retire as anything the mere proposal of a reasonable (eighteen-year) term limit may do, is, for now, constitutionally speaking, neither here nor there. Whatever their potential for good or bad, these were powers granted to Congress. Imposing a term limit was not. The provision, to "hold their Offices *during good Behavior*," was a conscious choice in rejection of alternative proposals, both moderate and extreme. And it ought not require lengthy citations to agree that "to *hold* their Offices," means, indeed, to hold the *substance* of the office. It was surely not meant merely to have a name on the door, a good retirement pension, and a filigree of minor tasks (e.g., sitting on lower federal courts, being available "on call," and the like), while effectively being shoved out the end of a nine-domino tray.

---

jection of its existing faculty, and do so, in part, because dissatisfied with the work of those tenured and currently in the majority).

5. *See* An Act to provide for the more convenient organization of the Courts of the United States, 2 Stat. 89 (1801); *see also* Act of July 23, 1866, 14 Stat. 209, Sec. 1 (prospectively reducing the number of judges on the Supreme Court to seven, to forestall any nominations by Andrew Johnson), and Act of April 10, 1869, 16 Stat. 44 (raising the authorized number of Supreme Court judges once again to nine, following election of President Grant).

6. *See*, e.g., Ex Parte McCardle, 74 U.S. 509 (1869).

II

To be sure, it is said that the proposal may find support in the Supreme Court's own decisions, perhaps most notably that in *Stuart v. Laird*,[7] pursuant to which the Court, in 1803: (a) sustained an Act of Congress adopted in 1802 that eliminated several lower federal courts, all of which had just been created by the lame duck Federalist Congress a year earlier in order to staff them with Federalist judges; and (b) also sustained that part of the same Act that re-imposed circuit court obligations required of the chief justice and the associate justices of the Supreme Court itself, as they had previously existed for the first twelve years prior to their recent repeal by the same act of 1801. Without doubt, *Stuart v. Laird* is an interesting and significant case, such as it was. It is, however, no authority at all for the notion that Congress may effectively strip a justice of the Supreme Court of the powers that are part-and-parcel of holding that office, and relegate him or her to some other tasks and mere "standby" status which, effectively and by design, the Carrington-Cramton proposal means to do.

Stuart v. Laird simply stands for the proposition that insofar as the creation of federal courts inferior to the Supreme Court is expressly given to the discretion of Congress, Congress may reduce the number of such courts, even while providing for the transfer to other federal courts of such cases as might require further orders to effectuate the judgments of those newly discontinued courts.[8] This narrow holding did not even address the extent to which Congress may eliminate such lower federal courts and whether, by doing so, thereby also eliminate the judgeships of those appointed to those particular courts. Rather, the sole issue actually examined in this part of the very spare opinion for the Court (a mere two paragraphs) by Justice Paterson (Marshall recused himself), was whether Congress has "constitutional authority…to transfer a cause [a case] from one" inferior federal court "to another." Paterson then merely observed: "In this last particular [i.e., respecting power in Congress to provide for such transfers], there are no words in the Constitution to prohibit or restrain the exercise of legislative power" (i.e., "no words" forbidding Congress from adopting legislation providing for such venue transfers), thus the objection raised by the party objecting to such a transfer was properly disallowed by the transferee court.

At the very most, and then only by negative implication, *Stuart v. Laird*, in this dimension may roughly also stand for the proposition that, despite the provision in Article III that judges appointed to courts inferior to the Supreme

---

7. 5 U.S. 308 (1803).

8. *See* the very able review of this matter, in David Currie, *The Constitution in Congress: The Jeffersonians 1801–1829* at pp. 12–22 (2001).

Court also hold *their* offices "during good behavior," if, notwithstanding that guarantee, the legislation that originally established such an optional court to which a judge was appointed is itself simply repealed, the judge's service may itself come to an end along with the court. But even such a rationale of the case in this dimension is not helpful here. Congress is given no power to abolish the Court as such, nor is anyone suggesting that it try.

And as to the second question reviewed in *Stuart v. Laird*, the Court's response was dispositive, but equally perfunctory. It was: given the fact that judges of the Supreme Court, though commissioned merely as judges of that court,[9] had nonetheless also been directed to sit as circuit judges when the Supreme Court was not in session, albeit without "distinct commissions for that purpose,"[10] and given also that they had done so without previous objection, the Court would simply accept the fact of such "practice and acquiescence under it for a period of several years," as being a "practical exposition" of its constitutionality, "too strong and obstinate to be shaken or controlled."

---

9. *See*, e.g., the Commission issued to John Marshall himself, dated January 31, 1801 in VI *The Papers of John Marshall* 61–62 (Charles Hobson ed., 1990).

10. This was one—of several—constitutional bases for the objection raised in this part of the case. And, in fact, while not acknowledged in Paterson's opinion, the objection could claim strong support from no less a figure than John Marshall himself. When the 1802 Act was under consideration in Congress, Marshall noted in correspondence with the other judges that one of its features was to re-impose circuit riding obligations on the several justices, albeit to a "less burthensome" extent than those imposed in the comparable section of the Judiciary Act of 1789, prior to its repeal in the Act of 1801. And he took up the specific question as to whether his fellow judges would be of the same view as he represented to be his own (namely, that "I more than doubt the constitutionality of this measure & of performing circuit duty without a commission as a circuit Judge," and that "I am not of the opinion that we can under our present appointments hold circuit courts"). He went on to say (by letter of April 19, 1802 to Justice Cushing) that he was endeavoring to "collect the opinion of the Judges," after which he would "communicate the result." Assuming only that they held a "contrary opinion" (i.e., an opinion different from his own), he added, he would yield his objection and "conform" to theirs.

In a lengthy reply to Marshall's inquiry, by letter of April 24, 1802, Justice Chase emphatically agreed with Marshall's conclusion, albeit on even broader grounds than Marshall suggested ("I am inclined to believe, that a Judge of the Supreme Court cannot act as a Judge of a Circuit Court, *without* or *with* a commission"). Paterson, Cushing, and Washington evidently thought the issue to be unwise to pursue, however, and Marshall then decided to let sleeping dogs lie. Thus, when the critical time came, having found no consensus with his colleagues to test Congress by declining to resume circuit duties, Marshall went back on circuit. (Indeed, it was he who granted enforcement to the judgment in *Stuart v. Laird* itself, which had been transferred to that particular circuit court pursuant to the 1802 Act.) *See generally*, VI The Papers of John Marshall 108–118, *supra* n. 9.

The solitary paragraph reviewing the question concluded rather drily that, on that account alone, "the question is at rest, and ought not now to be disturbed."

Assuming the Court's brief perfunctory treatment of this part of *Stuart v. Laird* was correct,[11] however, nothing about the case suggests that should Con-

---

11. There is good reason to think that it is not. The single paragraph in *Stuart v. Laird* to address the question does not in fact actually hold "on the merits" that there *is* any such a power given to Congress so to authorize or to require persons appointed and commissioned as judges of the Supreme Court also to hold office on such "inferior courts" as Congress may establish, and indeed to do so even without any separate commission authorizing them so to serve. Justice Paterson's statements decline even to identify clearly what the constitutional objections might have been, much less does his opinion then go forward to elaborate why each, in turn, lacks merit. Rather, as noted in the text, he but invokes "practice and acquiescence," and then pronounces it to be a "practical exposition...too strong and obstinate to be...controlled." Left to dangle as a possibility, of course, is that perhaps the imposition of circuit service even without separate commission may well be unconstitutional; but that the Court was simply not prepared so to declare, perhaps from fear of retaliatory actions by Congress, including the possibility of impeachment (an ordeal soon to be brought against Justice Chase, and feared by Marshall himself). See George Lee Haskins & Herbert A. Johnson, 2 *History of The Supreme Court of The United States: Foundations of Power: John Marshall*, 209 (1981) ("[I]mpeachment was certainly being considered by the President and his lieutenants as a method of controlling and removing Federalist judges and for appointing sound Republicans in their stead.")

In support of that view, moreover, as others have noted, the reason given by the Court for declining to give any serious attention to the issue was not a whit different from what had been argued, *unavailingly*, in *Marbury v. Madison*, by Charles Lee. And in that respect, these two seminal cases are exceedingly at odds. After observing that the provision in the Judiciary Act of 1789 at issue in *Marbury* had itself come from the very first Congress, Lee then went on to observe: "Hence it appears there has been a legislative construction of the constitution upon this point, and a judicial practice under it, for the whole time since the formation of the government." 5 U.S. (1 Cranch) at 149. The parallelism of the argument *rejected* in *Marbury*, to that *accepted* in *Stuart v. Laird*, is striking. *See also* Susan Low Bloch & Maeva Marcus, *John Marshall's Selective Use of History in* Marbury v. Madison, 1986 Wisconsin L. Rev. 301, 322–332 (1986) (elaborating and noting the inconsistency of this aspect of *Marbury* with *Stuart v. Laird*.)

The real difference between the two cases, as others have also noted, may simply be that whereas, in *Marbury*, by reaching the constitutional question and resolving it *against* the act, the Court permitted itself a means to dismiss a case and thereby *avoid* any further action that could trigger strong executive or congressional measures against the Court. (*See* Haskins & Johnson, *supra* at 185 ("There were open threats by the Republicans to impeach Marshall himself if he were to decide in favor of Marbury")). In *Stuart v. Laird*, the peril was from the opposite direction. Had the judges refused to resume any appearance in the circuit courts (under claim that the act of Congress requiring them so to do was without

gress so desire, it might also impose some fixed limit to a Supreme Court justice's full and equal participation in the business of that Court, excluding them thereafter from all essential powers to be exercised by that Court, and switch them to some part time (or, for that matter, full time) duties on some circuit or some district court or courts, until such time as they might thereafter resign, retire, die, or be impeached. Obviously no such issue was then before the Court. Nor for that matter, has it—or anything like it—ever been suggested in any other case, or in any other act of Congress, before or since. And I think it unimaginable that the Court's response even in 1803 would have been so yielding, much less in equivalent circumstances would it now be,[12] had anything of that far more invasive sort been involved in the enactments of the Jefferson Republican Congress that displaced the Federalist Party in the election of 1800.

That early on, that some tolerable degree of circuit court duties might reasonably be expected of the several judges on the Supreme Court when not occupied with their service on the Supreme Court, would be fairly unsurprising. The business of the Court was light at the time and the practice, originating with the Federalists, might well have then seemed reasonable, as well as plausibly within the discretion of Congress so to provide.[13] The busi-

---

constitutional basis), that refusal to serve could itself trigger impeachment proceedings against the recalcitrant judges.

Yet another example of Supreme Court practice under Marshall equally at odds with its casual treatment of the constitutional issue raised in *Stuart v. Laird*, is furnished in a Marshall Court response to government reliance on established practice when it came to a critical question of federal criminal prosecutions. Prior to 1812, lower federal courts (including several presided over by Supreme Court judges on circuit) had quite regularly conducted federal criminal trials based not on an act of Congress but simply on some (supposed) federal criminal *common* law. Even so, that established practice, such as it was, did not persuade the Court when, in United States v. Hudson & Goodwin (11 U.S. (7 Cranch) 32 (1812)), the question was finally raised in serious fashion in the Supreme Court itself, respecting the constitutional basis for such jurisdiction; and it was—notwithstanding prior (unquestioned) practice—held to be without constitutional basis. (*See* the discussion and review in Edward A. Hartnett, *Not The King's Bench*, 20 Constitutional Commentary 283, 303–305 (2003).)

12. It is a commonplace (but nonetheless true) observation that the overall "standing" of the Supreme Court is today far, far greater, and so, too, is its confidence, than it was in Marshall's day. Its judgments, controversial as they sometimes surely are, are complied with to a degree that in some respects is quite astonishing—as in Bush v. Gore, 531 U.S. 98 (2000), or Nixon v. United States, 506 U.S. 224 (1993), or Powell v. McCormack, 395 U.S. 486 (1969).

13. Although, as early as the Washington administration, the first Chief Justice (John Jay) drafted a letter suggesting that no one person could be appointed as two (different)

ness of the Court, sitting *as* the Supreme Court, was nothing in the nature of what it was later to become.[14] Doubtless the imposition of such duties and the associated burdens of travel could render the post of Supreme Court justice significantly less attractive, still it is very clear that nothing in the arrangement in any respect or any degree presumed to reduce or to lessen the full and equal participating powers of any judge once commissioned as a judge on the Supreme Court. Neither then nor, indeed, since has Congress regarded itself as possessed of any such "dilutional" authority sufficient to impair or otherwise to set some kind of "term limit" on a justice's participating responsibilities in full service on the Supreme Court. Framed in terms of Congress's power to declare "enough is enough," as a term limit for regular service on the Supreme Court, in brief, there is no constitutional basis for the Carrington-Cramton proposal. It is inconsistent with the "good behavior" provision in Article III, and so totally lacking in historical pedigree or support that, despite its numerous endorsements, I would forecast that Congress itself will not accept its invitation to try thus to undercut those confirmed as judges on the Supreme Court.[15]

III

It is necessarily a guess on my own part (and perhaps an unfair one at that), but I think it likely that the impressive number of eminent endorsements the

---

judges (i.e., to the Supreme Court and also to the district or circuit court), under the provisions of Article III. (*See* 1 Griffith J. McRee, *The Life and Correspondence of James Iredell* 293–296 (1858) (letter from Jay to Washington). Circuit service as (re-)imposed by the 1802 Act was finally ended by Act of March 3, 1891, 26 Stat. 826.

14. Indeed, John Jay, the first Chief Justice, thought so little of it that after a mere half-dozen years on the Court (1789–1795), he resigned in favor of running for Governor of New York. Nor, when his successor (Oliver Ellsworth who served as Chief Justice from 1796 to 1800) resigned in failing health, could Jay be persuaded (by President Adams) to return to serve again.

15. Even if I may be wrong in that forecast, so direct an attack on the Article III "life tenure" provision for service on the Court—which, with all respect, despite all of its alleged good intentions is how the measure must straightforwardly be seen (in terms of *whom* it is meant to affect and *how* it is meant to affect them)—could hardly be expected to pass into accepted practice without serious challenge. If and when the proposed act would come, the draft of a per curiam opinion by the Court itself, holding it in excess of any power granted to Congress (and, moreover, precluded by the provisions of Article III) would, in my view, virtually "write itself."

Carrington-Cramton statutory proposal has received is due at least as much to the seemingly persuasive reasonableness of the proposed term it would enact as to the frankly very thin veneer (and to me, quite unconvincing) of constitutional arguments offered in its defense. Eighteen years, followed by automatic and utterly impersonal de jure[16] rotation off the Court, one such rotation every two years, appears to be quite generously calculated, even as the authors say it is. It is allegedly more than adequate to insure the independence of the justices during their active tenure, as well as to provide very fair opportunities to develop their own jurisprudence and to make their own mark (so to speak) in the ebb and flow of both constitutional and statutory applications and interpretations. As an original proposition,[17] it is thus very arguably (and I think they make this argument quite well) an active term limit proposal neither too long nor too short. Certainly the authors' own well-researched observations with respect to other courts (including all of the more recently established constitutional courts in other nations[18]), respecting the terms of assured service on such courts, help to reinforce their argument that the present tenure-of-office ("good behavior" *endless* tenure) of our own Supreme Court justices has evidently inspired few, *if any*, nations. By the contemporary standards of other nations, and of comparable constitutional courts, a fixed, nonrenewable term of eighteen years seems generous and reassuring, indeed.

On the other hand, it is plausible, too, that the evident generosity of the proposed term of eighteen years rather than, say, twelve, or ten, or eight, was tendered also on a merely prudent basis, that is, by *being* generous, indeed by being *so* generous (as it is made to appear to be), it would, by that same token, stand a better chance not merely of gathering professional support and some real measure of popular and congressional support as well, but also establish far better odds of being upheld. Indeed this generosity seems aimed at influ-

---

16. "De jure" (and not merely "de facto") because, as already explained, roughly ninety-nine percent of what one properly identifies as the participating powers of a Supreme Court justice, as a member of *that* Court, will be taken away at the end of his or her eighteenth year on the Court as a matter of law (as well as a matter of fact).

17. Perhaps as a proposition for which one might want to venture some support if offered simply as a Twenty-Eighth Amendment even as, or just as, the Twenty-Second Amendment addresses a reasonable limit on Presidential service of two consecutive four-year terms.

18. Including, for example, the highly independent and highly influential Constitutional Court of Germany, where the judges serve by constitutional provision for a single, fixed, twelve-year term.

encing the Supreme Court sufficiently to "accept" it—meaning, of course, somehow to rule it constitutional—when otherwise (i.e., if it provided some shorter term), the act might well be deemed unauthorized (indeed, in fact, just flatly forbidden under the terms of Article III).

The task of persuading the Court itself that Congress may prescribe some "not unreasonable" limit for continuous, full time participation by judges appointed to the Supreme Court,[19] however, will still require that the Court "reread" Article III, *not* to have enacted life tenure subject only to some determination of behavior less than "good." It will require that the Court be persuaded to read the relevant constitutional provisions in Article III as though they declared the following proposition (which in fact they do not), namely that "the conditions and terms of tenure of those appointed to the Supreme Court[20] are subject to the power of Congress to prescribe such reasonable limitations as are not inconsistent with maintaining the independence of the Court and of its several judges who sit and serve on that Court."[21]

This approach would of course seek to substitute a spirit of "functionalism" for that of mere "formalism" or mere "textualism." The extended conceit on which it must be built, however, must necessarily come by way of a "translation," of Article III, together with other relevant clauses, in the following all-embracing, syllogistic way.

A. In its several provisions respecting Article III courts, the Constitution means to provide an ample security for those appointed to those courts, including the Supreme Court,[22] even while otherwise vesting in Congress a reasonable latitude of legislative discretion respecting how best to structure and to provide for those courts;[23]

---

19. This is what the proposal will require if it is to be sustained. It *will* so require of the Court, moreover, even though the proposal still would permit each affected judge to retain title (as "active" rather than "retired" or "emeritus" judge); would leave intact their full continuing compensation; and would provide for service elsewhere within the federal court system and even an opportunity for possible recall to the Supreme Court itself.

20. And presumably also of those appointed to any other Article III courts (though we need not now cross that bridge.) (Since no proposal currently goes this far, I see no need to enmesh the "inferior" federal courts in this discussion even though it might be additionally illuminating to do so, even here.)

21. This formulation would necessarily become the new "test" against which alterations in the statutory term(s) of service would be judged, as, indeed, it is the touchstone test proposed by the authors and endorsers pretty much as such.

22. We shall call this "the prime principle."

23. We shall call this "the second principle." (We make it the "second" principle because, while we value it greatly, we regard it as subordinate to the prime principle.)

B. If, and only if, an act of Congress directed to those holding office as judges of Article III Courts satisfies *both* conditions as articulated in A. *supra*, it is constitutional. If it fails in respect to *either* condition, it is not;

C. The Carrington-Cramton proposal plainly satisfies both conditions set forth in A. *supra*.

Q.E.D: The Carrington-Cramton proposal, enacted, would be constitutional.

The obvious key here is in the explication of the text of A. If it is a correct and complete representation of what the Constitution provides in reference to those appointed to Article III courts, and most of all in respect to all those appointed to the Supreme Court, the balance of the syllogism works out even as suggested. But, for reasons we have largely already canvassed, however, I think the syllogism is quite plainly incomplete. In fact, proposition A, albeit not in any obvious way incorrect, is nevertheless incomplete; and in that incompleteness it is also, ultimately, incorrect. This is what is wrong.

The proposition in A, correct as one may regard it to be in a large, generic sense, is nonetheless merely derivative, that is, it represents a kind of review of the various provisions in Article III (and elsewhere) in the Constitution, and then seeks compactly to sum them up in some quick and useful shorthand way. It is derivative simply in the plain sense that it "derives" its own content by searching out some unifying thought or general principle from the more particular provisions. Then, and most notably without actually repeating *any* of those particular provisions, it offers itself as the synecdoche or generic substitute for the provisions themselves. The derivative (or "derived principle") is substituted. By looking at this substitute, the particular provisions thus recede into the background. A particular law[24] is then framed against the backdrop of "the principle" and only then is the question asked, whether the law as thus framed is, or is not, within the principle. If it is, or at least if it seems to be, then the admitted fact of its congruence supports and directs a holding that the law, not being inconsistent with "the principle" but in full congruence with it, is valid (i.e., constitutional).

We may—and many understandably do—call this general approach to constitutional issues a form of "functional" analysis. In a large sense, moreover, in some substantial fashion we are *all* functionalists, in some degree, in the vineyards of constitutional law.

---

24. In this instance, it is a "law" that is to be framed and considered (namely, the Carrington-Cramton proposal enacted into law and then applied in respect to service on the Supreme Court).

The relevant point to be made here is not that there is anything objectionable in the content of ("functional") proposition A. It is, rather, in the first instance, strongly to *agree* with it as a general sentiment, but then also to insist that we press on to show *more exactly*, and *in what measure*, the Constitution went about that task. Perhaps the relevant provisions, whether or not in Article III, were *meant* to—and also even widely thought to—provide "an ample security" for all Article III judges, but in certain respects one may find, on closer inspection, that in one's own view, at least in some respects, they seriously missed the mark.[25] Perhaps the Constitution requires some repair by amendment to fill those gaps. Perhaps it is also the case that the Constitution enacted some provisions that reasonable people may well conclude overshot the mark, providing more security than we think appropriate, and now seem increasingly objectionable in the manner in which they appear to work. If we think they did the latter, do we then presume to ignore these provisions or "interpret" them out of view? If not, just what shall we do?

The provision that "The Judges, both of the supreme and inferior Courts, shall hold their Office during Good Behaviour," neither more nor less, may be such a clause, i.e., perhaps it is "excessive." I do not now agree, not because I regard the provision as ideal (it is surely not) but, rather, because I think the alternatives, even including the idea of a constitutional amendment for eighteen-year fixed terms not subject to congressional manipulation, would have its own problems and that nothing in our current circumstances warrants a

---

25. For example, perhaps it was a mistake to provide that the judges shall "hold their Offices during good Behaviour," and not to specify whether that is meant to be synonymous with the more stringent words of the impeachment clause ("treason, bribery, or other high crimes and misdemeanors") or whether, instead, it permits removal of an Article III judge for lack of "good behaviour" in some more general sense, absent a claim that the offending judge committed anything plausibly describable as a "crime" at all? Or, for another example, whether, bolstered by some "suitable" act of Congress directing their authority so to proceed, some federal judges may be empowered to sit in judgment of other federal judges and proceed to subject them to expensive, formal proceedings, with powers to disable them from presiding over their own courts. *See*, e.g., Chandler v. Judicial Council of the Tenth Circuit of the United States, 398 U.S. 74 (1970) (presenting that question which, however, the Court evaded by declining to consider it as suitably presented on the facts). *See also* United States v. Will, 449 U.S. 200 (1980) (holding that there is no constitutional obligation on Congress to increase judicial salaries even to the extent the increase would merely offset inflation and thereby avoid a state of de facto "diminished" compensation.) The proper resolution of quarrels in these matters (as well as some others) is left quite uncertain by constitutional text, and unsurprisingly, therefore, each in turn has necessarily generated a great deal of heat and of disagreement, arguably due in part simply to the Constitution's lack of more specific text.

change of this sort.[26] Others strongly disagree, however, and "incentives" for timely retirement having failed to do the job they think needs doing, they

---

26. In fact, the prospect that those appointed as judges on the Supreme Court might well serve quite substantially longer than eighteen years or even more than twenty-four years, was perfectly well understood. It was in fact quite quickly demonstrated in actual experience: first by John Marshall (appointed at age forty-five by President Adams in 1801and serving until 1835, thus thirty-four years in all) and again with Joseph Storey (appointed by Madison at age thirty-two in 1811 and serving until 1845, just short of thirty-four years).

That it was perfectly well understood that judges appointed to the Supreme Court might also far outlast not merely the elected administration of the particular President who appointed them, but also outlast an indefinite number of succeeding administrations as well, moreover, is strongly confirmed in an instructive passage from Federalist No. 79. The very issue is expressly examined in Federalist No. 79 where Hamilton compares the constitutional provision affecting "the compensation of the President" with that "of the judges." So first, Hamilton notes: "It will be observed that a difference has been made by the convention between the compensation of the President and of the judges." What is that difference? "That [i.e., the compensation] of the former can neither be increased nor diminished; that of the latter can only not be diminished."

A glance at the Constitution confirms what Hamilton has just declared. So, the pertinent provision in Article II regarding the President is that he shall receive "a Compensation, which shall neither be encreased nor diminished during the Period for which he shall have been elected." Whereas the equivalent provision, regarding Article III judges, merely provides that for their service during good behaviour, they shall receive "a Compensation, which shall not be diminished during their Continuance in Office." Why this difference in treatment? It is because, Hamilton declares, the term set for the President, within which he has tenure (before facing a new election) is fixed for four years and that being so, such compensation as is unalterably fixed by Congress for that term is likely to remain adequate even assuming a fair amount of inflation. But, he then goes on to observe, "with regard to the judges, who, if they behave properly, will be secured in their places for life, it may well happen…that a stipend, which would be very sufficient at their first appointment, would become too small in the progress of their service." And just how long might that "service" be contemplated to be? Quite long, indeed. Here is what Hamilton says: "What might be extravagant today, might in half a century become penurious and inadequate. It was therefore necessary to leave it to the discretion of the legislature to [be able to provide occasional *increases* in the judges' stipend, during *their* terms of service, though not equivalently so, in the case of the President, whose term, before a new election, is a mere four years]."

In brief, Hamilton himself underscores this: under the provisions of Article III one might be in service on the Supreme Court not merely periods of eighteen or twenty-four years, or even thirty-four years (as nearly at once proved true for two of the Court's most distinguished justices, Marshall and Story), but indeed such service might extend even to "half a century." An extravagant suggestion, perhaps, but useful nonetheless to underscore that extended years of service on the Supreme Court—fifty years—were clearly contemplated by those who drafted and ratified the Constitution in 1789.

earnestly desire some additional way to insure a more regular turnover within the Court. They obviously cannot find a suitable pressure point in the "during Good Behaviour" part of the crucial clause in Article III. They must and do, therefore, try instead to gain sufficient purchase for their task by latching onto the word "hold" (as in the phrase "hold their Office during good Behavour"). Their translation of it is that to "hold" an office is to possess the trappings (title, salary, etc.) albeit not necessarily its authority, for as to that, one may be instructed to give it up, after eighteen years, they say, just as Congress declares. Their's is the story of The Emperor's New Clothes revisited and revised, with justices of the Supreme Court playing the role of the (nearly) naked king. They are to be persuaded that if they get to wear real robes, though they have no real authority, they are still real Supreme Court judges (i.e., they "hold" that office in the manner contemplated by Article III). It is a most interesting, even if it is also, for me, a most risible idea. If, indeed, this is acceptable to the Court, or even to Congress, I will be most surprised, won't you?

OTHER LEGISLATIVE AND CONSTITUTIONAL ALTERNATIVES

Increasing the Size of the Court as a Partial but Clearly Constitutional Alternative

Philip D. Oliver[*]

Introduction and Background

The problem of life tenure for justices of the Supreme Court of the United States is vexing in the sense that it is difficult of resolution, but of such importance that a proper resolution would be highly desirable. I considered the matter at length nearly twenty years ago and put forth a proposal to amend the Constitution to provide staggered eighteen-year terms.[1] I largely put the matter out of my mind for two decades, unsurprised at the folly of Congress in not promptly submitting my proposal to the States.

My interest in the topic was revived earlier this year by two related events. The first of these was learning of the proposal from Professors Paul Carring-

---

* Byron M. Eiseman Distinguished Professor of Tax Law, University of Arkansas at Little Rock.

1. Philip D. Oliver, *Systematic Justice: A Proposed Constitutional Amendment to Establish Fixed, Staggered Terms for Members of the United States Supreme Court*, 47 Ohio St. L. Rev. 799 (1986).

ton and Roger Cramton for a statutory resolution of the problem.[2] The Carrington-Cramton proposal would finesse the constitutional objection to ending life tenure by statute, utilizing the technique of granting Supreme Court
justices life tenure in the federal judiciary, but not on the Supreme Court. The
proposal allows justices who are to be effectively term-limited off the Court
to remain technically members of the Court for life, performing some limited
duties of current justices. But their full power as justices—and what a full
power it is!—would be limited to a shorter period, usually eighteen years. The
central element is that a new justice would be appointed every two years, and
the full power of justices would be limited to the nine most recently appointed.
Assuming that no justice died or for other reasons left the Court prematurely,
this would effectively limit justices to eighteen years, but the maximum effective term would be extended by premature death or departure of more junior
justices.

I was impressed by the ingenuity of the proposal, never having even considered a statutory approach myself, and supported and still support it in substance. I was equally impressed by the fact that the proponents actually meant
to see something happen. Unlike the case with my earlier academic offering,
they actually hoped to see Congress enact their proposal.

The second thing that piqued my interest in the topic anew was an excellent symposium held at Duke University Law School on April 9, 2005, to consider the problem of life tenure on the Supreme Court in general as well as the
Carrington-Cramton proposal and other proposals for change. If nothing else
came from the conference, there was the realization that among an informed
group who had been thinking deeply about the issue, few defended life tenure
for Supreme Court justices.

It was not that everyone was in general agreement about what to do, or
even whether to do anything at all. There was, for example, considerable disagreement over exactly what form of tenure would be preferable, and about
what problems and abuses would flow from whatever new structure were selected to replace life tenure. At least one person opined that some of the reformers' arguments for ostensibly nonpolitical change of structure were actually politically-charged arguments directed at the substance of the Court's
decisions. Certainly the view that the justices' life tenure should be continued—at least in preference to any proposal on the table—found support. But
what I found striking was that no one defended life tenure on the merits and

---

2. *See infra* Paul D. Carrington & Roger C. Cramton, *The Supreme Court Renewal Act:
A Return to Basic Principles*, pp. 467–471.

in the strongest sense: If we were drafting a new Constitution today, either for the United States or, more realistically, as advisors to one of the many representative governments around the globe that are considering a new constitution, would we include the curious notion of life tenure for the judiciary? I say "curious" because we live in the world's most respected democratic republic, and life tenure is a concept most often associated today with the title "President-for-Life" that Third World dictators sometimes confer on themselves.

Let me make clear my preference for a resolution by constitutional amendment. The best approach, I remain convinced, is something along the lines I suggested in my proposal of two decades past. The Carrington-Cramton proposal, which I support even as a statute, would be much improved, in my view, if it took the form of a constitutional amendment. The Constitution, however, is notoriously difficult to amend.

Professors Carrington and Cramton, therefore, propose to end life tenure by statute. A major problem with any proposal to end life tenure by statute is that it is subject to challenge on the grounds that it unconstitutionally violates Article III, section 1 of the Constitution. This provision assures that "[t]he Judges, both of the supreme and inferior Courts, shall hold their Offices during good Behaviour." While the phrase "during good Behaviour" can, no doubt, be interpreted so as not to require life tenure, it has been understood to require life tenure since 1789, and even more certainly since President Jefferson's failure to reconstitute the federal courts through impeachment at the start of the nineteenth century.

I do not understand Carrington and Cramton to argue that the Constitution does not require life tenure; instead, as noted above, they attempt to avoid the problem by assuring life tenure as federal judges to those appointed to the Supreme Court, though not life tenure as Supreme Court justices, or at least not with the full power of justices. It is an open question whether this approach is constitutional. Given that the Supreme Court would itself ultimately be called upon to decide the question, and that the Court will not issue an advisory opinion, the uncertainty probably cannot be resolved without enacting the statute, then waiting until a justice resisted being forced off the Court. This entails a long period of uncertainty.

Thus, while continuing to support a constitutional amendment as the preferred route, and continuing to support the Carrington-Cramton statutory proposal as a clear improvement over the status quo, I consider here another route: whether it is possible to achieve most of the goals sought by those who would end life tenure, while utilizing a statutory approach that is not subject to constitutional challenge. I propose a statute that is not subject to serious constitutional challenge, and which at the same time removes, or at least significantly mitigates, many of the negatives of life tenure on the Supreme Court. (The question of life tenure on the inferior federal courts is of considerably less importance, and raises quite different issues.)

A Proposal Involving Fluctuation in the Size of the Court

The proposal advanced here is based on the power of Congress to change the size of the Court. Congress has exercised this power a number of times in the past, first to increase the original size of the Court, which started with six justices and ultimately had as many as ten, then was cut to eight, and finally settled at nine in 1869. Despite congressional inaction for the past 136 years, this early history of repeated statutory changes in the Court's size would seem to insulate the proposal from serious constitutional challenge. The important question of whether such an approach would be seen as politically legitimate is discussed below.

My proposal is this: Life tenure would continue, thus avoiding serious constitutional challenge. Congress, by statute, would provide that the size of the Court be increased by one justice at the start of each new Congress, which is to say by two justices in each presidential term. However, the same statute would provide that the Court be diminished in size upon the death, retirement, resignation, or removal by impeachment of any justice. The net effect would be to allow every President exactly two appointments per four-year term. The size of the Court would expand or shrink as necessary to maintain this balanced presidential power. Moreover, the appointments due the President would be the first order of business in each odd-numbered year, reducing the likelihood that the President would be denied an appointment by delays in the confirmation process engineered by an opposition hoping for victory in the next election. Indeed, the first of the President's two appointments would come during the "honeymoon" of the just-elected (or just-reelected) President.

Given the recent tendency of justices to serve considerably more than eighteen years, it is likely that the Court would generally have more than nine members under this proposal. In theory, however, the Court could reduce in size. No doubt the statute implementing the proposal should specify some minimum number of justices, perhaps seven. The most likely reason for such a reduction in size would be a terrorist attack directed at the Court. In a similar vein, since September 11, 2001, the House of Representatives has begun to consider what should happen if a majority, or large minority, of its seats suddenly became vacant.

Benefits of the Proposal

The proposal would secure significant advantages over the status quo, and, in some respects, over the Carrington-Cramton proposal as well. First, each presidential election would carry equal importance in shaping the Court. This would be an improvement over the "crap-shoot" arrangement that allowed President Taft six appointments in a four-year presidency, while allowing President Carter none (and the current President none in his first term).

Second, and in my view more importantly, it would end the wholly pernicious practice of justices timing their retirements to assure that like-minded Presidents name their replacements. Justice Douglas provided perhaps the most blatant example, his actions lending credence to the accuracy of reports of his remark, "I won't resign while there's a breath in my body—until we get a Democratic President."[3] It is quite enough for unelected justices to wield their unaccountable power for life, without continuing to influence the Court indirectly for decades after leaving. While life tenure can be defended (or not) as necessary to ensure judicial independence, I submit that no principled defense can be stated for unnecessarily giving justices this additional power.

Third, I believe that the proposal would spur earlier retirement. Given that this proposal is put forward as an alternative designed to duplicate many of the benefits of proposed constitutional amendments or statutes that would directly end life tenure, the question of whether these earlier retirements would in fact materialize is significant. I assert that adoption of this proposal would speed retirements for a number of interrelated reasons.

---

3. *See Douglas Finally Leaves the Bench*, Time 69 (Nov. 24, 1975). Ironies abound in this case. Notwithstanding his determination to hold on until the next election, Douglas ultimately resigned under President Ford, who had attempted to impeach Douglas, only a year before Ford's defeat by President Carter. Yet, if Douglas could have read the future, probably not even a justice appointed by George McGovern would have proved more to Douglas's liking than Ford's choice, John Paul Stevens.

Why Justices Would Retire Earlier
under the Proposal

First, the proposal removes an incentive for staying on. Because a justice could not affect his replacement by the timing of his retirement, there would be no tendency to hang on in the hope that a like-minded President would be elected. In theory, of course, this effect might be offset by removing the incentive to retire earlier than a justice would otherwise have wished before the end of the term of a like-minded President. The example of Earl Warren attempting to leave the Court in time to allow President Lyndon Johnson to name his replacement, while unsuccessful, tells us that this eventuality is not wholly fanciful. Nonetheless, my experience with life tells me that people seldom leave a job for such a reason much before they want to, and are far likelier to be looking for an excuse to hold on.

In addition to removing an incentive to staying on, the proposal would offer affirmative inducements to retire. The equivalent of an early-retirement package will not work, because finances do not explain even in part why justices have chosen to remain on the Court for many years after they could have retired at full salary. The key to justices staying on is *power*. Although justices have been able to retire at full pay since FDR's failed attempt at "Court packing," they cannot retire and retain full power. The power of an individual justice is considerable. In one knowledgeable observer's view, "the individual Supreme Court Justice probably has more actual power than any other individual in American public life except the President."[4] In the history of the world, the overwhelming practice of men—history offers less experience concerning women, though I believe the same observation holds—is not to relinquish voluntarily positions of great power. Under the proposal, each justice would become less powerful, because, for reasons explained above, the Court can be expected to grow. If the Court grew to a dozen justices, or fifteen, each justice would find his position substantially less powerful.

Closely related, each justice would be a bit less exalted. At least in the legal world, where most justices have lived their entire professional lives, justices are feted as the holders of ultimate power and prestige. If a justice wishes, any summer can include an all-expenses-paid trip to a pleasant European setting for some light-duty speaking to fawning law students and professors. As the number of justices increased, and the power of each individual justice corre-

---

4. Jerome Frank, *Marble Palace: The Supreme Court in American Life* 8–9 (1958).

spondingly decreased, some of the luster would be lost. Consider that most lawyers and many law students can name every member of the Court. Who can name every member of the Senate? As the Court increased in size, with new justices regularly entering the Court to take some attention from older members, retirement might seem more attractive. And this exaltation of justices is only increasing. It was once suggested that justices should live like monks. A more apt career comparison for the modern justice might be "rock star." Increased size of the Court, and a steady supply of new justices, could reduce this effect.

An increase in the Court's workload would be a further incentive for voluntary retirement. It is not necessary to go back to the days when justices rode circuit on horseback to find a time when they worked harder than at present. At least on the surface, the job of justice seems much easier than in the recent past. In the 2002 term, the Court disposed of seventy-eight cases with full opinion. No justice wrote more than nine opinions of the Court. Twenty years earlier, the case load was approximately double, as the Court decided 192 cases with full opinion and no justice wrote fewer than fifteen opinions of the Court.[5] If Congress were to decide that we were not getting our money's worth from the Court—as might be more likely if the number of justices expanded and the Court's total workload did not—it could address the problem by statute. For example, Congress might require that the Court decide with hearing and opinion a specified minimum number of cases each term or even require that some body other than the Court itself decide which cases, and how many, the Court heard. It seems doubtful that any serious objection to either approach on constitutional grounds could be lodged, at least if the Court had discretion to decide other and additional cases. After all, the Court's control of its docket is based on legislation that can be repealed or changed.

Finally, there is the intangible fact that a justice could no longer so easily think of his position as "his" seat on the Court, in the sense that it belonged to him and not to any other. New justices would come, regardless of whether he stayed or left. While I concede that this factor would significantly affect few justices, and I cannot state with certainty that it would affect any, I suspect that it would have some marginal effect. Even if the proposal did not cause justices to retire earlier, it might prove beneficial by reminding them that the Court is not theirs, but the Republic's.

---

5. The data comes from *The Supreme Court, 2002 Term*, 117 Harv. L. Rev. 1, 480 (2003) and *The Supreme Court, 1982 Term*, 97 Harv. L. Rev. 1, 295 (1983).

Drawbacks Specific to This Proposal

First, there is the obvious fact that, far from encouraging earlier retirement, the proposal could instead work to postpone retirement. If the Court's reduced caseload and the stable of talented clerks available to each justice have already made the job cushy, at least as compared to the Court of the past, an increase in the Court's size would reduce the workload even more. Each justice, or his clerks, would have to produce an average of perhaps one majority opinion for each dozen cases, instead of one for each nine. I do not see this as a major factor, because I doubt that this slight change in workload would prove a significant factor in retirement decisions. Moreover, the Court already decides for itself how hard it wishes to work by deciding how many cases it will hear.

Second, under the proposal it would be as likely as not that at any given time the Court would have an even number of justices, which would increase the likelihood of tie votes. This might be addressed by the Court establishing a tradition of the chief justice voting only to break ties. Such a tradition could lead to odd effects on a President's selection of a chief justice. Might the President "kick upstairs" an associate justice with whom he disagreed, in order to reduce the likelihood of that justice voting in a close case? While possible, I doubt it. Alternatively, the Court could establish a practice of setting tie-vote cases for rehearing in the next term following the appointment of a new justice.

Third, some would argue that the Court could not effectively operate if its size were much greater than nine. Some courts, of course, do. The International Court of Justice—which, like the Supreme Court, decides a small number of high-profile cases—has fifteen members, and it is hard to see the Supreme Court surpassing that size under the proposal. (The proposal calls for one justice to be named every two years, so a Court of fifteen members implies an average term of thirty years.) Or, especially if the Court were again to decide the number of cases it did twenty years ago, the Court could hear some cases in panels. For example, if the Court grew to more than thirteen justices, it could split into two panels of equal size, each of which would have at least seven members. The membership of the panels could vary at random, as in the courts of appeal. Alternatively, panels could be set for an entire term of Court, perhaps one panel hearing constitutional cases and the other federal question cases. Under this latter approach, the panels should be reconstituted each term, with some arrangement to assure that all justices would switch panels regularly, perhaps each term.

My own preference would be for the Court to continue to hear cases en banc, even if the Court grew to a size of fifteen or sixteen justices. The use of panels, while efficient, would make decisions of the Court less definitive. Moreover, if the suggestion of year-long panels of distinct subject matter jurisdiction were adopted and known in advance, litigants might manipulate the timing of cases in order to get a favorable panel.

Drawbacks Inherent to Any Statutory Approach to Abolition of Life Tenure

Far more serious are the problems inherent in any statutory proposal to abolish life tenure. First is the question of political legitimacy, which could prove problematic for both the Court and Congress. Even when making politically charged and unpopular decisions, the Court enjoys great prestige. Consider the response to FDR's Court-packing plan, at a time when Congress was overwhelmingly Democratic, and the legislation that was being struck down surely enjoyed majority popular support. More recently, consider the response to *Bush v. Gore*, when Democrats griped but accepted the decision without real question. If the Court begins to resemble just one more federal agency, which regularly changes with each election, will the Court's prestige decline? (Of course, one should consider the related question of whether it would be bad for the Court to be, if not removed from its pedestal, at least made conscious that the pedestal had been lowered a notch.) Meanwhile, the public would have yet another reason to view Congress as a group of power brokers unconcerned about principle or the Constitution.

Even more serious, in my view, is that any statutory modification of life tenure, or of the size of the Court, would tend to encourage or legitimize further change. For at least the past twenty years—I date the bad blood in Congress, at least concerning the judiciary, to the poisonous Senate consideration of Robert Bork's nomination to the Court, though others may choose different milestones—the guide to Congressional action has been less and less traditional understandings, and more and more "what my party can get away with." At present, the makeup of the Supreme Court is "off the table." There are nine justices, not more or less, and they serve for life if they choose. Once one Congress changes the rules, what assurance have we that a future Congress will not again change the rules—for example, by using adoption of this proposal as a precedent to create a new seat every year instead of every two years, thereby allowing a favored President additional appointments?

While this danger is quite real, and members of Congress from both parties have given us much reason for concern in recent years, traditional and legally unenforceable understandings continue to have considerable force.

While I was writing this essay, the Senate reached compromise on the issue of filibustering judicial nominees in an agreement that could be viewed as protecting traditional understandings: of generally deferring to the President's appointments and of protecting the power of the Senate minority to filibuster.

Serious problems are presented by any statutory proposal. The necessary, and hopefully sufficient, antidote would be overwhelming bipartisan support coupled with the strongest possible assurances from Congress that no further change would be made without similarly overwhelming bipartisan support. Such support in Congress would probably require an effective date for the statute some years in the future—so that neither party could confidently predict whose ox was to be gored—but if such support could be found it might provide legitimacy in terms of public acceptance and a measure of insurance against frequent modifications in the future.

Conclusion:
A Constitutional Amendment after All?

The foregoing thoughts lead to a final observation: If overwhelming bipartisan support is available for the statutory approach, perhaps we might almost as easily enshrine the bargain in a constitutional amendment, which would assure that it could not be easily changed in the future. Perhaps a constitutional amendment ending life tenure would not prove significantly more difficult to enact than a statute. For either, the primary stumbling block is likely to be Congress. A constitutional amendment would require a two-thirds majority of each house of Congress before submission to the states, but, as discussed above, political realities dictate that a successful statutory approach would require broad bipartisan support likely amounting to two thirds of each house. Once a proposed constitutional amendment were submitted to the states, it is not obvious that a significant block of states, or indeed any single state, or either political party, would find its interests particularly affected. If the proposal were simply considered on the merits by state legislators, whose own state courts seem to function satisfactorily without life tenure, I believe that ratification would be attainable.

Mandatory Retirement for Supreme Court Justices

Richard A. Epstein[*]

Introduction:
Term Limits and Good Behavior

During this past year Professors Paul Carrington of the Duke Law School and Roger Cramton of the Cornell Law School have mounted an impressive campaign to introduce a sensible term limit of eighteen years for appointment to the Supreme Court. Their candid and long overdue proposal comes in the midst of a change of guard on the Court. The confirmation of John Roberts to replace the late William Rehnquist is over. The effort to fill the seat of Sandra Day O'Connor with Samuel Alito has just begun. The current politics of confirmation are sure to stifle any serious consideration of major institutional reforms, especially ones that challenge the conventional wisdom on judicial service. But they are right to pursue this matter on the ground that serious issues of constitutional design should always be a fair topic for public discussion and debate. I heartily applaud their willingness to speak candidly about issues that have for too long been swept under the rug for fear that they would offend sitting justices or public sensibilities.

That said, their admirable proposal for term limits runs into two major sets of objections from the outset. The first is that the proposed statute, while highly desirable on policy grounds is, I believe, inconsistent with the Constitution of the United States, the relevant provision of which states that "The judges, both of the supreme and inferior Courts, shall hold their Offices dur-

---

[*] James Parker Hall Distinguished Service Professor of Law at the University of Chicago and Peter and Kirsten Bedford Senior Fellow at the Hoover Institution.

ing good Behaviour,...."[1] That provision has widely been understood to require that judges serve for life unless their dismissal can be justified on grounds of cause, narrowly construed. The obvious advantage of this provision is that it insulates all judges from the political pressures that might call for their removal.[2] As such, it works to insure the independence of the judiciary, universally regarded as an essential element in any sound and durable constitutional scheme.

In my view, the ingenious arguments that Carrington and Cramton have advanced to insist that term limits for Supreme Court justices do not require a constitutional amendment fall short of the mark, especially in light of the unbroken historical practice to the contrary. The gist of their proposal is to appoint new justices to the Court, at regular two-year intervals. Of these, the nine most junior in seniority would constitute the "active" justices; the more senior justices would remain, as it were, "in the bullpen" to hear cases when one of the active justices is unable to hear cases. In order to avoid political intrigue, they are to be called back into service, in reverse order of seniority, the most recent first.

Carrington and Cramton defend their proposal on the ground that "[t]he office to which these justices are appointed will still result in judicial service as a constitutional court judge 'during good behavior,' and they will continue to exercise Article III judicial power until they die, elect to retire, or are removed from office."[3] The authors are no doubt correct that the mechanical fashion in which this proposal works is a strong protection of the independence of the judiciary, which of course was one of the primary reasons for the original constitutional design. Nonetheless, that desirable feature does not guarantee that their proposal can be squared with the constitutional text.

It is hard to see how justices subjected to such a substantial reduction in judicial powers could still be thought to be holding judicial "office." The term office, for example, is also used in Article II, section 1, which provides that

---

1. U.S. Const. Art. I, §1.

2. For a careful exposition of the problem, *see* Robert Kramer & Jerome A. Barron, *The Constitutionality of Removal and Mandatory Retirement Procedures for the Federal Judiciary: The Meaning of "During Good Behavior,"* 52 Geo. Wash. L. Rev. 455 (1970). Kramer and Barron argue that Congress can soften the meaning of "good behaviour" about the edges, so as to include, for example, cases of mental disability within the definition. But they do not argue, nor do they present any historical evidence that suggests, that term limits are a viable option without a constitutional amendment. The basic understanding is that life terms were a norm defeasible only for certain reasons.

3. *See infra* Paul D. Carrington & Roger C. Cramton, *The Supreme Court Renewal Act: A Return to Basic Principles,* pp. 467–471.

"the executive Power shall be vested in a President of the United States. He shall hold his Office during a Term of four Years...." The "term" in this context clearly refers to continuous service to the position created, and the same seems true of Supreme Court justices as well. There may well be situations in which gaps that are created at one level can be temporarily filled by taking judges from another level, as happens when district court judges sit by designation on the various circuit courts. In addition, judges on the various courts of appeals often serve as trial judges. And the Supreme Court justices are all circuit judges. But none of this remotely suggests that forcible displacement from active participation is consistent with the constitutional guarantee of continued service to the relevant office. A demotion from starting pitcher to permanent benchwarmer looks very like removal from office. Carrington and Cramton intend their new rules to transform the operation of the Supreme Court, a goal achievable only by changing the nature of the offices that the justices hold.

In sum, the brief constitutional text quoted above may contain many loose ends, but it does make tolerably clear that the appointment for each judge is to a particular office, and that service in that office is what is guaranteed for the length of good behavior. The Constitution's reference to judges on both the Supreme and inferior courts suggests that judges are appointed to a single position, and not to the bench, and that this requirement not only describes the appointments process for sitting judges, but also the appointments process that is presently required for future judges at all levels as well. It looks therefore to me that a constitutional amendment is needed to make the changes for term limits that Carrington and Cramton suggest. My response is let's do it, and now.

Our Imperfect Constitution

Let us start from one simple premise. The Constitution of 1789 and the Ten Amendments from 1791 that compose the Bill of Rights together constitute the greatest achievement of political statecraft in the history of the world. When one looks at the kinds of governmental structures that were available for imitation and instruction before its adoption, and the difficulties inherent in organizing a system that contains strong features of separation of powers, of federalism, and of the protection of individual rights, it is clear that the Constitution was light years ahead of anything that preceded it, and vastly superior to most of the more modern constitutions, many of which now lie useless in the dustbin of history.

That said, the Constitution is replete with major mistakes in design, structure, and purpose. Some of these should have been apparent at the time of its adoption; the unsoundness of other provisions became clear only with the passage of time. To give but one example of initial mistakes, there seems little doubt that the Electoral College was intended, as its name suggests, to be a deliberative body whose work was the last stage in an elaborate process designed to secure the indirect election of the President. That effort to place layers of deciders between the popular electorate and the choice of president was consistent with the general view of the time that ordinary democracy was, as understood in classical political philosophy, a degenerate form of a republican institution.[4] The Founders, therefore, opted for complex structures that blunted the enormous perils of majority will.

Indeed, in ways that have since been forgotten, that objective was enshrined in the (misunderstood) provision that states that "The United States shall guarantee to every State in this Union a *Republican* Form of Government."[5] But it took little time to realize that secret electoral college debates could deprive the new government of its legitimacy whenever the choice of President was less clear than that of George Washington. The electoral college thus quickly became a counting device, in all but some extreme cases, by the convenient fiction of allowing electors to pledge themselves to a particular candidate before the vote.

Consider, in similar fashion, the unwise provisions for the selection of the Vice President, which guaranteed that the chief opponent of the President would become his Vice President. In a short period of time the arcane provisions of the Twelfth Amendment changed the procedures to their modern form, where President and Vice President are of the same party. In so doing, they laid bare the oddity that the Vice President, unlike any vice chancellor, held an office of little power, and was chiefly there as a president in waiting. Indeed, there is an eerie similarity between the senior justices in the Carrington-Cramton proposal and the Vice President under our current arrangements.

There is, I think, little reason to go on with the list of possible infirmities in the Constitution, save the one in question here. The provision of lifetime appointment for judges is a mistake; and, while not a boneheaded one, it is a mistake that should have been apparent at the time the Constitution was drafted. That judges must be independent is not in dispute, but judicial in-

---

4. Paul Carrington also suggests that the College may have had an adjudicative function, which was to keep the courts out of Presidential disputes of the sort that arose in Bush v. Gore, 531 U.S. 98 (2000).

5. U.S. Const., Art. IV, §4. The emphasis is obviously added.

dependence is not inconsistent with term limits. The terms here do not have to be as short as those for political offices (which vary), but should be long enough to allow continuity in office and to prevent an endless succession of nominees before the Senate. A period of eighteen years for service on the Supreme Court, such as Carrington and Cramton propose, seems to achieve that end quite well. I put aside the question of similar term limits on lower court judges, where the stakes are much lower.

At the Supreme Court, some justices make the admirable decision to step down while still healthy, as Justice Sandra Day O'Connor recently has tried to do, but in other cases, as occurred still more recently at the end of Chief Justice Rehnquist's year-long bout with cancer, they die in office. Carrington and Cramton are right to insist that voluntary behavior by Supreme Court justices, even under the gentle suasion of family, friends, colleagues, and physicians does not close the gap. Term limits are the appropriate response because they avoid all the ugliness and potential partisan abuse associated with complex deliberations to determine whether a sitting justice, or judge, should be dismissed for cause. Their case seems to me to be impeccable as a matter of first principle.

Age Discrimination

In my view, the Carrington-Cramton proposal does not go far enough. It would be most welcome to introduce an additional provision into the Constitution that imposes maximum age limits on sitting Supreme Court justices. I might suggest seventy years of age, which matches limitations that have been imposed as a matter of state law with respect to state judges, and which is in fact older than the retirement ages for senior executives and partners in many firms today.[6] The effect of this provision would be to limit the term of any person appointed to the Supreme Court after his or her fifty-second birthday to less than the full eighteen-year term. As such, it would incline presidents to appoint younger persons to the Court, which again is welcome in my view because it increases the odds that the Court will be populated with jurists who are in the prime of their intellectual careers. After all, even young justices appointed today will grow old in time. And if term limits are thought to be too tough, then by all means adopt this provision alone, so that justices appointed in their forties could serve more than eighteen years, but come to a full stop at

---

6. For a comprehensive review of these statutes, which indicates their declining popularity, *see* Christopher McFadden, *Judicial Independence, Age-Based BFOQs, and the Perils of Mandatory Retirement Policies for Appointed State Judges*, 52 S. C. L. Rev. 81 (2000).

their seventieth birthday. Note too that this proposal shares one feature of the Carrington-Cramton proposal, which is that its mechanical nature cuts down the risk of ugly deliberations on the performance of sitting justices, which could happen if one softened the current tough standards on impeachment and instituted a regime that would allow justices to be removed for "cause" or for "mental or physical incapacity." So loose a standard could easily be infected, especially in modern times, with partisan rancor and intrigue.

I have no doubt in the current climate of opinion this proposal will run into the same objections that fueled the passage of the Age Discrimination in Employment Act of 1967 (ADEA).[7] Much of the political momentum behind the statute came from an exhaustive study on age discrimination prepared by the Department of Labor.[8] Justice Brennan summarized the results of that study in *EEOC v. Wyoming*:[9]

> The report of the Secretary of Labor, whose findings were confirmed throughout the extensive factfinding undertaken by the Executive Branch and Congress, came to the following basic conclusions: (1) Many employers adopted specific age limitations in those States that had not prohibited them by their own antidiscrimination laws, although many other employers were able to operate successfully without them. (2) In the aggregate, these age limitations had a marked effect upon the employment of older workers. (3) Although age discrimination rarely was based on the sort of animus motivating some other forms of discrimination, it was based in large part on stereotypes unsupported by objective fact, and was often defended on grounds different from its actual causes. (4) Moreover, the available empirical evidence demonstrated that arbitrary age lines were in fact generally unfounded and that, as an overall matter, the performance of older workers was at least as good as that of younger workers. (5) Finally, arbitrary age discrimination was profoundly harmful in at least two ways. First, it deprived the national economy of the pro-

---

7. 29 U.S.C. §§ 621–633a.

8. *See,* Age Discrimination in Employment: Hearings on S. 830 and S. 788 before the Subcommittee on Labor of the Senate Committee on Labor and Public Welfare, 90th Cong., 1st Sess. (1967); Age Discrimination in Employment: Hearings on H. R. 3651 et al. before the General Subcommittee on Labor of the House Committee on Education and Labor, 90th Cong., 1st Sess. (1967); *see also* Retirement and the Individual: Hearings before the Subcommittee on Retirement and the Individual of the Senate Special Committee on Aging, 90th Cong., 1st Sess. (1967).

9. 460 U.S. 226 (1983).

ductive labor of millions of individuals and imposed on the governmental treasury substantially increased costs in unemployment insurance and federal Social Security benefits. Second, it inflicted on individual workers the economic and psychological injury accompanying the loss of the opportunity to engage in productive and satisfying occupations.[10]

These findings were in turn the foundation of the Age Discrimination and Employment Act (ADEA), whose findings stressed the raw deal that older employees in the job market are often given. These findings note that these workers are "disadvantaged in their efforts to retain employment, and especially to regain employment when displaced from jobs." The findings then state that the high levels of unemployment lead to "deterioration of skill, morale, and employer acceptability," and that the problem is "great and growing," just as the unemployment problems of senior workers are grave. At this point the statutory findings give the obligatory nod to the bloated reading of the Commerce Clause by concluding that "arbitrary discrimination in employment because of age, burdens commerce and the free flow of goods in commerce." The purpose of the ADEA was to remove these fetters in order "to promote the employment of older persons based on their ability rather than age; [and] to prohibit arbitrary age discrimination in employment."[11]

There is one fundamental objection to these findings: properly qualified, *every* so-called stereotype about older individuals is true—an admission that comes with some pain to a writer who has turned sixty-two.[12] One major difficulty lies in the meaning of the central term: "stereotype." One standard definition of the term refers to "an oversimplified standardized image or idea held by one group or group of another."[13] Any oversimplified view of the world must, by definition, be wrong. What makes for an oversimplified account? We need a reliable assessment of how a person's productive abilities vary with age. It seems quite sufficient to look at the matter as people approach retirement age, for in earlier years it is sensible to argue that overall productivity in many occupations increases with age as a result of experience and judgment. But which occupations? If anyone said that athletes on average performed better

---

10. *Id.* at 230–231.

11. 29 U.S.C. §621.

12. On this point, I do not recant the full-throated attack I made against the age discrimination laws in Richard A. Epstein, *Forbidden Grounds: The Case Against Employment Discrimination Laws* 441–479 (1992).

13. Microsoft Word dictionary.

at age fifty than at age twenty-five, he or she should be sentenced to watch Olympic Game reruns for some extended period of time.[14]

But what about the converse proposition, which says that all athletes at age twenty-five are better than all athletes at age fifty? Here one obvious stereotypical assessment is that the first generalization just has matters backwards. The converse proposition, too, should be judged a stereotype because it ignores the *variance* in performance. People who are at the top of their game at age fifty can often trounce couch potatoes, or even athletes of average skill, who are twenty-five. But that defect in analysis is easily cured by the observation that *on average* individuals are better athletes at age twenty-five than at age fifty. The analysis can be made more precise still by identifying the means and variances in a normal distribution for both populations, yielding a curve for younger athletes clearly to the right of that for older ones. To call an accurate distribution of the performance level of a population a stereotype is to invite falsehoods at every turn in the analysis. The trends found in sports can be found for all occupations. Look at the means and the variances of given populations in all occupations, and it becomes painfully clear to this sixty-two-year-old scholar that these curves are not invariant with age.

This point is not entirely responsive to the concerns with age discrimination because it does not necessarily quantify the decline in performance that takes place with age. But the declines that are so obvious in professional athletes also occur on average in other disciplines as well. Thus one exhaustive review of the literature reaches, with qualifications that are unimportant here, the basic conclusion that: "One empirical generalization appears to be fairly secure: If one plots creative output as a function of age, productivity tends to rise fairly rapidly to a definite peak and thereafter decline gradually until output is about half the rate at the peak."[15] And this general finding does not take into account any additional loss of performance that is attributable to fatigue or other demands of the job: looking only at those few who remain productive in later years could bias the account to ignore those who have dropped out of the system.

---

14. Here is one illustration. Eligibility for the senior men's tour in golf starts at age fifty. Virtually all wins in major events on the tour are by golfers who are close to fifty in age. The decline in strength, concentration, acuity, and the like sets in well before the retirement age, which is of course true in all sports.

15. Dean Keith Simonton, *Age and Outstanding Achievement: What Do we Know after a Century of Research*, 104 Psychological Bulletin 251, 252 (1988). The study continues to note that the location of the peak and the rate of decline are sensitive to disciplines. Law was not specifically included, but appears on average to fit with writing, history and general scholarship where the peak comes in the late forties or early fifties.

In the face of this general evidence, that most redoubtable of judges, Richard Posner (an exception to any rule) argues that the high level of productivity of older judges is an instructive exception to the general rule of declining productivity, which he attributes to the importance of such elusive intangibles as "wisdom" and "experience," augmented by two other happy circumstances.[16] First, judges often reach their career late in life, and thus retain a zest for the job that others might not have. And second, their shorter time horizon means that they are less likely to have some long-term political agenda.[17] Many of these points are true for judges in general, but they do not deflect from the overall conclusion, especially with respect to Supreme Court justices.

Experience and knowledge of the game did not make Michael Jordan a better athlete at thirty-five than at twenty-five, and so too for judges, these plusses wear out with time, as other factors dominate. The only hard question is when does the turn take place for Supreme Court justices. Age seventy provides a useful stopping point. After seventy the traits of wisdom and experience are likely to be overshadowed by a general decline in fitness, energy and innovative ability. By the same token the enormous influence of the job makes it highly unlikely that justices will be dispassionate with their legacies. Quite the opposite, they may be induced to write more sweeping opinions in an effort to preserve their influence into the next generation. Why gamble on the decline being slow, when the risk can be easily avoided?

The basic biological points then seem too strong to be denied, but we must still address the obvious objection that as the gaps get narrower, the differences between the two distributions, accurately described, become smaller—even if they never quite disappear. After all, it is perfectly plain that many individuals at the age of seventy-one are far more fit for judicial (or any other) service than some who are sixty-nine. The question is whether any hard-edged rule that calls for retirement at age seventy can be dismissed as a ham-handed proposal to be rejected for the very reasons that prompted the adoption of the statute in the first place. But on this question, too, the answer is an emphatic "no."

The use of hard-edged lines based on age is commonplace in multiple social settings. We have minimum ages for drinking, driving, driving rental-cars, driving as chauffeurs, marrying and the like. It is perfectly plain to just about everyone that some individuals who are younger than the minimum age limits are more competent than those who are over them. But the complexities in-

16. Richard A. Posner, *Aging and Old Age*, 193–194 (1995).
17. *Id.* at 194–195.

herent in generalized case-by-case determinations (a true oxymoron) make them both politically and practically infeasible. The use of the hard age cut resolves ninety-nine percent or more of the individual cases. The few exceptional cases are better dealt with by principled exceptions to the rule. We routinely recognize hardship exceptions to minimum age requirements, and block individuals of full age from engaging in certain activities based on their mental capacity, criminal records, and the like. Similar rules are used at the opposite end of the spectrum, including those for eligibility for various programs such as social security, Medicare and Medicaid. Here too a hard number sets the basic norm, with some exceptions for disability made on a case-by-case basis.

The case for using hard-edged rules in the retirement age context is even stronger. The first point here is that these rules, where they are currently in place, unlike the minimum age requirements, are not imposed by the state. They are imposed by individual firms acting in their own best interests. The use of the practice by one firm does not bar hiring of an able worker by another. The findings of the Department of Labor noted that some firms use these restrictions while other firms do quite well without them. The Department's report drew the wrong inference from this observation and assumed that *every* firm should adopt the successful strategies of hiring that *some* firms in an unregulated market adopt. But there is a good reason for the diversity of strategies.

Many firms adopt a mandatory retirement age because they cannot tolerate the administrative cost, hard feelings, and political intrigue that come with case-by-case decisions regarding worker termination and retention. Once this strategy is adopted by many firms, other firms will do quite well by deciding to *hire*, on a case-by-case basis, workers who have been terminated from their previous jobs due to their age. The per se rule on termination is a strong signal that some of the discharged workers are still fit for service. As such, age-discriminating firms can avoid the internal strife of terminating employees, and those older employees who would not otherwise have been terminated can move laterally to a non-age-discriminating firm. Indeed the firm that has a fixed retirement age for its long-term workers could well go into the market to hire older workers to fill specialized niches. It is a great fallacy to assume that every firm in the land (or every department in every firm) has to be open to hiring workers above a certain age for the market to be efficient. The mixed strategies that were condemned by the report were a sign of the strength of the overall marketplace, even in 1967 (when somewhat shorter life expectancies reduced the anticipated utility of hiring retired workers).

A similar argument applies to the observation that, on average, older workers in the workplace do about as well as their younger peers. That of course is exactly the result that should be expected in an efficient and unregulated market. There is little reason for any given employer to prefer a young but inefficient worker to an old but efficient one, particularly in the modern world where workers frequently shift jobs before retiring. Yet rough parity of performance in the marketplace is observed precisely because the level of labor force participation declines to some extent by age through either voluntary retirements or forced terminations.

The proper inference to draw therefore is that this conclusion should no longer hold once the state anti-discrimination law prevents the turnover found in voluntary markets. Inferior workers given job protection will remain in their current positions long after they have passed their productivity peak. Since the employment continues apace, the sensible substitution of newer for older workers becomes heavily disrupted. There is no reason to expect that the rough parity of performance will continue after the ADEA changes the composition of the workforce from what it was before. A finding that supports the efficiency of the current markets is wrongly turned into a condemnation of the operation of an unregulated and competitive labor market. Nor can that result be justified on any ostensible protective grounds. Private pensions are intended to provide for income in the retirement age; and those who want to work can supplement their income elsewhere.

The errors in particular understandings feed into a large point about the unsoundness of this entire regulatory adventure. At no point do the so-called findings of the ADEA explain why it is that Congress acting from afar has a better understanding of employment relations than the thousands of individual firms whose economic survival depends on their sound employment decisions. The firms have better knowledge of their local circumstances, stronger incentives to get matters right, and far superior feedback loops that allow them to make adjustments over time. There is no doubt that individual firms will make mistakes in particular cases—they could for example hold unproductive workers for too long, or let productive workers go too soon—but any individual mistake can be rectified by decisions of market actors. The ironclad state rule is impervious to modification and correction owing to the enormous obstacles that stand in the way of legislative reform. The case of Supreme Court justices is somewhat different because the government is the employer, not the regulator, of the justices, but here it should follow the lead of other organizations that use retirement rules to foster the orderly transition of power between the generations.

There are, moreover, several ways to verify the disruptive effect of the ADEA on labor market efficiency. The 1986 Amendments to the ADEA expanded the act's basic protection to all workers over forty, without any mandatory retirement age. One exception to this lasted for seven years for tenured professors at universities and other institutions of higher education.[18] At the end of that period, this restriction was lifted on the strength of a report from the National Academy of Science that concluded that universities, even research universities, could continue to function without any mandatory retirement age. To mirror the language of the ADEA itself, the lifting of mandatory retirement should force people to correct their stereotypes about older faculty members.

The situation never quite worked out that way, in a manner that is most instructive for the position of Supreme Court justices. The major research universities (which were afraid, alas, to oppose the removal of mandatory retirement publicly) immediately developed programs that allowed them to buy out faculty members who were protected under the current law. Contractual arrangements of this kind would not be expected had the shift in the rule not resulted in such massive inefficiencies that universities (not known for being the earliest of adaptors) were spurred to energetic efforts to contract back to the prior position by offering buyouts unambiguously tied to age. The procedures of these contractual waivers of the statutory protection are today heavily regulated under the ADEA,[19] and there is little likelihood that senior workers who prefer the cash to the job would tolerate any effort to block their use.

These buyouts bring up several points. First, even their adoption does not get us back to the efficient market solution. The only way that these programs work is by making take-it-or-leave-it offers to all faculty of a given age, for otherwise individual bargaining would doom the programs. The upshot is that the most able faculty members are the ones most likely to take these offers because they are the ones who are most likely to attract job offers from other institutions. The weakest faculty members are therefore, on average, the ones most likely to hang on. Second, the transaction costs in these cases are by no means trivial, but they are hardly prohibitive. In good Coasean fashion we see that the market here seeks to correct a massive inefficiency attributable to the ADEA.[20] Finally, the ADEA should be seen for what it is: a wealth transfer program in favor of a powerful interest group bloc, a function having nothing to do with the stated legislative purposes of the Act.

---

18. ADEA at § 12(d).

19. *See* Age Discrimination in Employment Act, 104 Stat. 983, 29 U.S.C. §§ 621–633a, § 626(f), often listed as section 7(f), introduced in the Older Workers Benefit Protection Act. These procedural safeguards for workers are treated as strict conditions precedent for the settlement in Oubre v. Entergy Operations, Inc., 522 U.S. 422 (1998).

20. Ronald H. Coase, *The Problem of Social Cost*, 3 J. Law & Econ. 1 (1960).

Another instructive feature of the ADEA is the explicit provision in the statute that permits firms to demand at age sixty-five the compulsory retirement of their highly-compensated employees.[21] If the ADEA's odd view of market transactions were correct, then the greatest social losses from age discrimination in employment should come from the elimination of the high-priced talent that is at the core of any modern business. Yet these workers are not cut out from the market, and in many cases are able to recontract for new jobs elsewhere. But reality within any particular firm works in exactly in the opposite direction. It is absolutely critical to have an orderly turnover in key leadership in all firms. To wait until a high executive has shown the demonstrated incompetence that would justify a for cause dismissal is to wait until the firm has suffered serious business losses that could easily jeopardize the welfare of all its employees, young or old. The ADEA would not have passed if this exemption had not been included. Yet there is no explanation as to why the findings of the Department of Labor Report do not apply with full force to this most critical portion of the workforce. The only sensible conclusion in this area is that the overall decline of performance with age takes its greatest toll on senior employees. And these are the people who are most difficult to dislodge from their positions when protected by statutory rules.

Mandatory Retirement for Judges

This overall discussion has obvious implications of vital importance for the mandatory retirement rules for judges. Especially at the Supreme Court level, it is critical that the persons selected be at the peak of their power. And it is better to err on the side of keeping some weak individuals off the court, even at the cost of keeping able individuals off as well. Our ablest individuals would still have many opportunities for useful careers on lower courts, the practice or teaching of law, movement into political or public life if forced to leave the high Court at seventy. The arguments in this direction have had their force in the states, which in their appointment rules are not bound by the "good behavior" clause of the federal constitution. One such provision, Article V, §26, of the Missouri Constitution, provides that "all judges other than municipal judges shall retire at the age of seventy years." There is little reason to go over the usual arguments in favor of this provision, save to say that many states fear

---

21. *See* ADEA §12(c).

the declining performance of aging judges, which in some instances has risen to the level of scandal.[22]

This provision nonetheless was challenged under the ADEA in *Gregory v. Ashcroft*.[23] The state judges caught by this provision sued then Missouri governor John Ashcroft in a case that raised three interrelated issues. The first was whether the ADEA's applicability to state judges under the broad reading of the commerce clause could withstand the reservation of state rights found in the Tenth amendment.[24] The second question was, if the ADEA did reach state judges, whether they fell into an exception from the ADEA that applied to "an appointee on the policymaking level."[25] The third question was whether, if the

---

22. The one performance that immediately comes to mind is that of Marshall McComb of the California Supreme Court who was totally inert for many years before he was removed. The California law seeks to finesse the problem by providing that judges cannot be paid if they work after seventy, a provision that counts as a facial violation of the ADEA. Unfortunately, many judges are independently wealthy, and McComb was one of them, so he soldiered on until a bloody proceeding resulted in his long overdue removal. For samples of the truly horrendous litigation need to pry him out of his seat, see McComb v. Commission on Judicial Performance, 564 P.2d 1 (Cal.1977), which dealt with an endless array of procedural, statutory and constitutional objections to the special removal procedure in California only to conclude as follows:

> The record establishes specific instances of bizarre behavior by Justice Mc-Comb which, if viewed in isolation, would support discipline for conduct prejudicial to the administration of justice which brings the judicial office into disrepute. That conduct must be considered as symptomatic of the condition of chronic brain syndrome (senile dementia) which we find to exist. Balancing the gravity of the conduct against the reason for it and the public interest in an effective judiciary, we conclude that discipline in the form of removal from office or reprimand is not appropriate. The public interest is sufficiently served by the retirement of Justice McComb.

Id. at 8.

For the earlier contempt proceedings against McComb for his refusal to be deposed, see McComb v. Superior Court, 137 Cal. Rptr. 233 (1977).

23. 501 U.S. 452 (1991).

24. The Commerce Clause provides: "Congress shall have the power to regulate...commerce with foreign nations, among the several states and with the Indian tribes." U.S. Const. Art. 1, §8, cl. 3, which has been read so broadly to allow it to reach all forms of productive activities within the state, including the activities of state governments. *See* EEOC v. Wyoming, 460 U.S. 226 (1983). The Tenth Amendment reads: "The powers not delegated to the United States by the Constitution, nor prohibited by it to the States, are reserved to the States respectively, or to the people."

25. The full provision reads: "The term 'employee' means an individual employed by any employer except that the term 'employee' shall not include any person elected to public office in any State or political subdivision of any State by the qualified voters thereof, or

state court judges fell within that exception, whether the statute was sustainable against a rational basis challenge—that of the lowest sort—mounted under the Equal Protection Clause. In the end the majority of the Supreme Court held that the commerce clause reached this case but that the statutory exemption both applied and met the requirements of rational basis review. The Court's reasoning, especially on the last two issues, offers a revealing glimpse as to the Supreme Court's view of its own role.

On the first question, the Court took the basic view that the Congress had the power under the Commerce Clause to impose the ADEA on state court judges notwithstanding the reservation of powers given to the states under the Tenth Amendment. In dealing with this issue, Justice O'Connor, writing for a five-member majority, took seriously the advantages that federalism offered in a decentralized system. The issue, however, showed the usual schizophrenia that comes into play whenever a conscientious judge is forced to defend the intellectually indefensible. Justice O'Connor, of course, felt obliged to take for granted the broad reading of the Commerce Clause that was endorsed in *EEOC v. Wyoming,* which followed such key New Deal cases such as *Wickard v. Filburn,*[26] which had removed any meaningful limitations on federal power.[27] Thus, O'Connor's analysis notes the advantages that decentralized government has in controlling the abuse of power by setting state against state, and all states against the federal government. She duly quotes from Madison's famous remarks in Federalist Number 45 regarding the powers of the national government.[28] To this she adds a number of quotations from pre-1937 cases that stress the many virtues of equal and independent sovereigns in the federal sys-

---

any person chosen by such officer to be on such officer's personal staff, or an appointee on the policymaking level or an immediate adviser with respect to the exercise of the constitutional or legal powers of the office." 29 U.S.C. §630(f).

26. 317 U.S. 111 (1942). I have spoken my piece against this case, and the entire New Deal structure so often, that I shall not raise my voice above the storm yet another time. For one statement of those views, see Richard A. Epstein, *The Proper Scope of the Commerce Power,* 73 Va. L. Rev. 1357 (1987).

27. Note that this decision was before the boomlet in Commerce Clause jurisprudence initiated by United States v. Lopez, 514 U.S. 549 (1995), which for these purposes is most important for its affirmation of *Wickard* insofar as it applies to general economic matters. The analysis of this problem, accordingly, does not change at all.

28. *See* Gregory v. Ashcroft, 501 U.S. 452 (1991) at 458. "The powers delegated by the proposed Constitution to the federal government are few and defined. Those which are to remain in the State governments are numerous and indefinite.... The powers reserved to the several States will extend to all the objects which, in the ordinary course of affairs, concern the lives, liberties, and properties of the people, and the internal order, improvement, and prosperity of the State." The Federalist No. 45, pp. 292–293 (C. Rossiter ed., 1961).

tem.[29] These quotations, properly understood, are all apposite for the proposition that *Wickard* and its progeny are dead wrong—a conclusion that could not be voiced in polite company, especially in 1983.

But Justice O'Connor, in line with modern authority, only uses them for the more modest purpose of saying that the legitimate justifications for federalism in the post-New Deal period require (and only require) a clear statement from Congress of its intention to run roughshod over the internal operations of state governments. In her view the ADEA's statutory definition of employer did not compel the view that judges were included in the group of persons who worked at the policy level. Hence she relied on the clear rule to salvage the exemption in the face of the apparent ambiguity.

The two dissenting opinions attacked her use of this saving presumption, but reached diametrically opposite conclusions on the underlying question of statutory interpretation. Justice White, writing for himself and Justice Stevens, insisted that the statutory exception did apply, and then agreed with the equal protection analysis of Justice O'Connor. Justice Blackmun, writing for himself and Justice Marshall, insisted that the statutory exception did not cover judges, as opposed to ordinary appointed officials, and then took a discreet pass on the equal protection question, since he thought that there was no age-based distinction to defend.

The ins and outs of this statutory interpretation are instructive to the problem considered in this article. The simplest way to dispose of the case stresses

---

29. *Gregory*, 501 U.S. at 457.

'The people of each State compose a State, having its own government, and endowed with all the functions essential to separate and independent existence,'...'Without the States in union, there could be no such political body as the United States.' Not only, therefore, can there be no loss of separate and independent autonomy to the States, through their union under the Constitution, but it may be not unreasonably said that the preservation of the States, and the maintenance of their governments, are as much within the design and care of the Constitution as the preservation of the Union and the maintenance of the National government. The Constitution, in all its provisions, looks to an indestructible Union, composed of indestructible States.

Texas v. White, 74 U.S. 700 (1869), quoting Lane County v. Oregon, 74 U.S. 71 (1869). Note that *Lane County* held that "an 1862 statute," which authorized the issuance of United States notes to be used as legal tender to pay debts, imposed no restriction upon the states in the collection of taxes." *Texas v. White* held that all the acts of the Texas legislature during the recent rebellion were null and void, including bond sales to third persons, because they were not signed by the governor of Texas. It is clear why the nature of the federal union was so much in issue in these post-civil war cases that have nothing to do with the commerce clause.

the importance of the word "appointive office" in the statutory framework. Although these judges were initially appointed, their subsequent service on the bench depended on winning an uncontested election, which seems to move them into a different category, namely that of "any person elected to public office in any State or political subdivision of any State by the qualified voters thereof," who are explicitly exempt from the ADEA.[30] But even if we pass that point by, the phrase "any person chosen by such officer to be on such officer's personal staff, or an appointee on the policymaking level or an immediate adviser with respect to the exercise of the constitutional or legal powers of the office" seems to refer to persons who work for some executive or legislative official in a high-ranking position. But that point was ignored in favor of a learned disquisition of whether judges in fact exercise policymaking or work at the policy level.

This discussion is one that tracks the statutory exemption found for high-ranking employees within the firm, and thus raises the question of how much discretion these judges really have. In dealing with these state court judges, Justice O'Connor is content to adopt the Holmesian position that judges are persons who necessarily have to make legislative decisions of a sort, but only on an "interstitial" basis insofar as they act in their common law role.[31] Yet the odd point about this analysis is that nowhere is it mentioned that state law judges have powers to construe their own states' constitutions as well as that of the United States. At this point she thinks that there is enough to allow the state law to survive under the clear statement rule. Justice White is more emphatic in that conclusion, and the dissent of Justice Blackmun stressed, rightly in my view, that judges were not the kind of policymakers to whom the ADEA exception was meant to apply, and much more dubiously, that the Court

---

30. 29 U.S.C. §630(f). *See also* Kimel v. Florida Bd. of Regents, 528 U.S. 62 (2000), which holds that states retain sovereign immunity from suits based in the ADEA.

31. *Gregory*, 501 U.S. at 465–466:

> The Governor argues that state judges, in fashioning and applying the common law, make policy. Missouri is a common law state. See Mo. Rev. Stat. §1.010 (1986) (adopting "the common law of England" consistent with federal and state law). The common law, unlike a constitution or statute, provides no definitive text; it is to be derived from the interstices of prior opinions and a well-considered judgment of what is best for the community.

Thereafter she quotes from Justice Holmes on judicial lawmaking in *The Common Law*, traceable to views of public policy in the last analysis. Oliver Wendell Holmes, *The Common Law* 35–36 (1881). Not to be outdone, Justice White adds quotations to similar effect from Justice Cardozo. Benjamin N. Cardozo, *The Nature of the Judicial Process* 113–115 (1921), cited in *Gregory*, 501 U.S. at 482.

should defer to the EEOC in its interpretation of a doubtful position, even before the Court's decision in *Chevron U.S.A., Inc. v. Natural Resources Defense Council, Inc.*[32]

For our purposes, however, it seems clear that any limited view of judicial power as policy does not ring true with a Supreme Court that has struck down segregation, ordered redistricting, invalidated state abortion laws, struck down prohibitions against sodomy, and countermanded innumerable other federal and state laws. The Court's discretionary power is manifest, even for those who do not buy into the common view of the legal realists that the justices make law. If the arguments raised above are correct, it is better in the long term that this discretionary power be turned over to justices who are under age seventy.

The Supreme Court weighed in on this question in connection with the rational basis challenge to the statute. In my view, the right answer is one that many justices of the Supreme Court are simply unable to give but would meet the highest standards of judicial scrutiny under the equal protection clause in light of the manifest improvements it promises to the overall level of adjudication with the states. But instead here is what was said by a court that contained five judges over seventy (Warren Burger, seventy-six; William Brennan, seventy-seven; Thurgood Marshall, seventy-five; Harry Blackmun, seventy-five; Louis Powell, seventy-seven).

Justice O'Connor cites a decision by the Missouri Supreme Court which stressed the desire to avoid case-by-case determinations on fitness, and to open up new opportunities for younger judges within the ranks.[33] She also notes, rightly, that voluntary retirement will not always be sufficient, judicial elections are usually perfunctory affairs, and that impeachment is an unrealistic alternative in most cases, all surely correct. The opinion does not offer a single reason to oppose the mandatory retirement position, but concludes with this revealing observation:

> The Missouri mandatory retirement provision, like all legal classifications, is founded on a generalization. It is far from true that all judges suffer significant deterioration in performance at age 70. It is probably not true that most do.... But a State "'does not violate the Equal Protection Clause merely because the classifications made by its laws are imperfect.'" "In an equal protection case of this type... those challenging the...judgment [of the people] must convince the

---

32. 467 U.S. 837 (1984).
33. O'Neil v. Baine, 568 S.W.2d 761, 766–67 (Mo. 1978) (en banc).

court that the…facts on which the classification is apparently based could not reasonably be conceived to be true by the…decisionmaker." The people of Missouri rationally could conclude that the threat of deterioration at age 70 is sufficiently great, and the alternatives for removal sufficiently inadequate, that they will require all judges to step aside at age 70. This classification does not violate the Equal Protection Clause.[34]

The use of the rational basis test by Justice O'Connor invites the oblique sort of discourse here in which she casts doubt on a proposition that she knows has at least some truth. At no point does she enter into any analysis of the error costs associated with removing judges who are still able, relative to those who are not. And she does not revert back to the other systemic justifications that Missouri put forward for the law, namely, keeping a constant flow of new talent within the system. Nor at any point does she ask the question of whether the well-nigh uniform practices on mandatory retirement in the private marketplace prior to the ADEA, and even under it for senior executives, give some real evidence as to the risks associated with these processes. Nor is there any recognition in this statement of the far greater risks of old age in the Supreme Court as distinct from any private body. There are lots of private businesses; if one falters, its competitors can pick up the slack.

The Supreme Court is the quintessential monopolist, not subject to competition of any sort from any quarter. The responsible social response to monopoly power ordinarily is some form of regulation lest too much power be concentrated in the hands of too few. The only sensible response to the Court's monopoly of constitutional interpretation is some restriction on the length of service. As a practical matter any movement in that direction is welcome, such as the sensible and courageous decision by Justice O'Connor to walk out under her own steam once her replacement is confirmed. But social reform cannot depend on isolated acts of self-abnegation and common sense. Limiting terms is one strong movement in the right direction. A seventy-year age maximum for Supreme Court justices is another. Both together are ideal. It is time to get started.

---

34. *Gregory*, 501 U.S. at 473 (citations omitted). Justice White accepted the equal protection analysis of the Court, *id.* at 474, while Justice Blackmun did not reach the question, *id.* at 495, after a spirited endorsement of the overall principles of the ADEA.

PROMOTING EQUITY IN THE DISTRIBUTION OF SUPREME COURT APPOINTMENTS

Terri L. Peretti*

Proposals for changing the tenure of Supreme Court justices are growing in number and support. This essay adds to both. Most reformers seek to address the "pathologies associated with life tenure" such as judicial decrepitude, strategic retirement, and the aggrandizement of political power, making the Court "an imperial (and imperious) presence in [our] national life."[1] I share the reformers' desire for change but not their motivation, rejecting the notion that life tenure inevitably tempts a justice to become "the law's master rather than its servant."[2]

My goal, in contrast, is to improve the performance of the appointment process as a democratic engine of constitutional policy change. I wish to direct our attention to a periodic (and recent) problem in American politics: ineffective democratic control over the Supreme Court's membership and policy direction. Its causes are two-fold. First, presidential elections too often fail as opportunities for a national dialogue over the Court's future. Limiting the fruits of such a dialogue, in any case, is the second and more potent and proximate cause—the uneven distribution of Supreme Court appointment opportunities. I consider several reforms, including a mandatory retirement age and staggered, nonrenewable judicial terms of eighteen years. Because of the obstacle posed by Article III, these efforts to regulate turnover are rejected in

---

* Associate Professor and Chair of Political Science, Santa Clara University. Special thanks to Brad Joondeph, Melinda Hall, and Robert Bradley for their helpful comments.

1. John O. McGinnis, *Justice Without Justices*, 16 Constitutional L. Qtrly. 541, 543 (1999).

2. *Id.* at 544.

favor of a more modest approach that creates new appointment opportunities. More specifically, I advocate a guaranteed Supreme Court appointment
in each presidential term.

The Appointment Process
As a Tool of Democratic Control:
Promise and Performance

In *The Least Dangerous Branch*, Alexander Bickel offered his classic statement regarding the "countermajoritarian difficulty": because the Supreme
Court "exercises control, not in behalf of the prevailing majority, but against
it," judicial review is "a countermajoritarian force in our system" and is accordingly "undemocratic."[3] Although a number of scholars have revealed serious flaws in this account,[4] it remains true that the Supreme Court is not a
traditionally democratic institution. Its members are unelected, life-tenured,
and nearly impossible to remove from office. Furthermore, the Court's constitutional decisions can be reversed only through the exceptionally difficult
and rarely-used amendment process.

Ameliorating our concern with the Court's undemocratic character is the
fact that it is subject to a variety of effective political checks. The primary
check is the appointment process. Supreme Court justices are chosen by a recently elected President and Senate, with ideology and partisanship serving as
the dominant selection criteria for both.[5] With regular turnover—a vacancy
has on average occurred every 2.1 years—the ideological views prevailing on
the Court at any point in time are, or might reasonably be expected to be, representative of the current or recent electorate. Furthermore, we know that justices' ideological views strongly influence their decisions[6] and that most justices most of the time fulfill the expectations of the president who appointed
them, particularly in the modern era and for presidents carefully selecting
their appointees.[7] This completes the democratic chain: the values guiding the

---

3. Alexander M. Bickel, *The Least Dangerous Branch* 16–17 (1962).

4. Mark A. Graber, *The Nonmajoritarian Difficulty: Legislative Deference to the Judiciary*, 7 Studies in American Political Development 35 (1993); Terri Peretti, *In Defense of
a Political Court* (1999).

5. Jeffrey A. Segal & Harold J. Spaeth, *The Supreme Court and the Attitudinal Model
Revisited* 178–222 (2002).

6. *Id.*

7. Peretti, *supra* n. 4.

justices' decisions have been deliberately planted on the Court by recently elected officials.

For most of our history, the appointment process has worked rather well in creating a democratic anchor for the Court's constitutional policy path. After all, the Court's decisions—including its rulings of unconstitutionality— comport with public opinion a majority of the time and at about the same rate as Congressional decisions.[8] Empirical evidence also demonstrates that, consistent with this model, the primary cause of policy change on the Court is membership change. New appointees with different policy preferences can and do change the content and direction of the Court's policies,[9] with Democratic presidents shifting the Court to the left and Republican presidents tilting it to the right. For example, the Kennedy and Johnson appointments greatly increased the Court's support for civil liberties, while the appointments of Richard Nixon and George H. W. Bush substantially decreased the proportion of decisions favoring civil liberties.[10]

Nonetheless, the appointment process has not worked as well or as consistently as it could have. Weaknesses can occur at several points in the democratic chain. For example, the electoral process may not produce a president and Senate who truly represent the people's views. Presidential campaign discussions regarding Supreme Court appointments and constitutional issues may have been limited and weak. A further potential defect is that the president and Senate may not always employ ideological criteria in the selection of justices. The linkage might also be broken by a justice not deciding in accordance with the ideological premises of her appointment.

Dashed presidential expectations are, however, the exception and not the rule, with presidents enjoying a success rate in the seventy-five to eighty percent range historically and even higher in the modern era.[11] Segal and Spaeth provide further support with their findings of "fairly strong correlations between presidential preferences and the justices' behavior: 0.45 in civil liberties cases and 0.58 in economic cases."[12] However, this congruence between presidential ideology and the decisions of his appointees declines over time, falling

---

8. Thomas R. Marshall, *Public Opinion and the Supreme Court* (1989); Thomas R. Marshall & Joseph Ignagni, *Supreme Court and Public Support for Rights Claims*, 78 Judicature 146 (1994).

9. Lawrence Baum, *Membership Change and Collective Voting Change in the United States Supreme Court*," 54 Journal of Politics 3 (1992).

10. Lawrence Baum, *The Supreme Court* (8th ed. 2004).

11. Peretti, *supra* n. 4.

12. Segal & Spaeth, *supra* n. 5, at 219.

in civil liberties cases from 0.55 in the first four years of a justice's tenure to 0.10 in years 11 to 20.[13] This suggests a final area of concern, and the primary focus of this essay: if justices serve unusually long terms, the rate of membership turnover may be inadequate to insure that the Court remains sufficiently representative. Two periods of low turnover stand out in the twentieth century—the 1930s and 1990s—with each potentially presenting problems of democratic accountability for the Court's decision making.

Failures in the democratic chain can produce a Court that is significantly out of step with the people's views and at odds with the other branches. Such a Court may then illegitimately set (or keep) the nation on a constitutional path that is opposed by the people. The conservative Court of the early New Deal period is typically offered as a perfect example of this phenomenon. After all, by the start of 1937, FDR had served a full term and been elected twice by overwhelming margins, yet had not made a single appointment to the Court. Dozens of his popular New Deal programs were being scuttled by a hostile Court majority, including the Four Horsemen (VanDevanter, McReynolds, Sutherland, and Butler) who averaged seventy-four years of age and whose tenure mean was 18.5 years, with VanDevanter having served twenty-five years and McReynolds twenty-two years. Not only had there been no appointments in the previous four years, there had been only three appointments in the previous ten years, instead of the five (4.76 to be exact) that normally would have been expected. Even one appointment opportunity in FDR's first term would have averted the political crisis and Court-packing episode that ensued, since many of the Court's anti-New Deal rulings were 5–4 decisions. The unsurprising result of FDR failing to receive a single appointment in his first term was that the Court was out of step with the New Deal ideology that suddenly and dramatically came to dominate our national elections and government in 1932. Considerable popular criticism and inter-branch hostility resulted, culminating in the Court-expansion proposal offered by a president impatient with waiting for an appointment opportunity. According to the conventional wisdom, the constitutional crisis ended as the Court was brought to heel and properly abdicated the field of economic policy. Although this folk history has justly received a second look from many scholars,[14] important lessons remain, first, regarding the clear potential of the appointment process to update the

---

13. *Id.*; Jeffrey A. Segal et al., *Buyer Beware: Presidential Success in Supreme Court Appointments,* 53 Pol. Res. Qtrly 557 (2000).

14. Martin M. Shapiro, *The Constitution and Economic Rights,* in *Essays on the Constitution of the United States* (M. Hudd Harmon ed., 1978); Barry Cushman, *Rethinking the New Deal Court* (1998).

Court and maintain its representational quality and, second, regarding the important goal of regularizing turnover due to its erratic performance.

Although the democratic model of judicial accountability did not perform as well as it could have in the New Deal period, neither did it perform as poorly as most assume. A more appropriate target of criticism for the model's ineffectiveness might be the recent era, characterized by low turnover on the Court, an impoverished national debate over judicial appointments and constitutional policy, and extraordinary conflict in the judicial selection process. Low turnover is the primary culprit.

Many scholars have observed the recent trend of justices retiring at a later age and serving for longer terms, enabled by a reduced workload and improvements in health care and longevity.[15] As Calabresi and Lindgren report,[16] the average term of office for Supreme Court justices has increased from 15.2 years historically to 25.5 years since 1971, with the average retirement age increasing nearly ten years in the same time period—from 68.5 to 78.8 years of age. The current Court reflects this trend, though not starkly, with the average age at 70.2 years (seventy-two if Thomas is excluded), only one justice under sixty-five years of age, and the average tenure in office at 18.4 years. Most striking about this era is the eleven-year span, from 1994 to 2005, in which a single vacancy did not occur, the longest in our history for a nine-member Court.

Since Supreme Court vacancies occur on average every 2.1 years, with presidents averaging close to two appointments per term, there should have been nearly five appointments from 1995 to 2005 instead of none, seven vacancies from 1990 to 2005 instead of the three that actually occurred, and nine or ten appointment opportunities from 1985 to 2005 instead of the six that were actually afforded presidents.[17] The Court should have been remade, but has not been, in the last two decades. With four instead of only two Clinton appointees and two first-term Bush appointees rather than none, we would today have a less Republican and more politically-balanced Court, one that properly reflected the results of recent presidential elections rather than electoral outcomes from two and even three decades ago. By 2008, the end of Bush's

---

15. Artemus Ward, *Deciding to Leave* (2003); David Atkinson, *Leaving the Bench* (1999).

16. *See supra* Steven G. Calabresi & James Lindgren, *Term Limits for the Supreme Court: Life Tenure Reconsidered*, pp. 15–98.

17. There was considerably more regularity in Court turnover prior to and during the New Deal period. For example, in the decade prior to 2005, there were no appointments to the Court compared to three in the decade preceding 1937. There were twice as many vacancies (six compared to three) in the fifteen-year period preceding 1937 compared to the same time span prior to 2005.

second term, turnover and replacement regularity should have produced a Court composed nearly equally of Clinton and Bush appointees. This would indeed be a divided Court, but this is as it should be given that we have been a divided nation.

The objective, of course, is not to produce a Court that is ideologically-balanced, but to guarantee that its membership and policy direction reflect and are tied to presidential election outcomes. A Republican president who ran and won on a conservative platform should be able to shift (or maintain) the Court in a conservative direction, and a victorious Democratic candidate should be empowered to shift (or maintain) the Court in a liberal direction. Their legitimacy to do so was earned electorally. It is the people's right and authority to influence the Court, exercised through the president and Senate. How profoundly the president or a political party can move the Court is dependent on important democratic factors such as control of the Senate and the number of successive electoral victories. This system enables a measure of democratic control over the Court that is considerable and consistent.

Distributing presidential appointment opportunities unevenly, if not randomly, undermines this ideal of democratic control characterized by significance, consistency, and proportionality. As a result of irregularity, presidential and partisan influence over the Court is not a function of popular and electoral support, depending instead on luck and happenstance. For example, President Taft made six appointments to the Court in his single term, and President Harding appointed four justices in his three years in office. In contrast, two full-term presidents failed to make a single appointment to the High Bench—Andrew Johnson, with Congress denying him two appointment opportunities by reducing the size of the Court as each vacancy occurred,[18] and Jimmy Carter, who was simply unlucky.[19] Ten presidents appointed only one Supreme Court justice, and eleven presidents appointed four or more, while George Washington and Franklin Roosevelt, assisted by obviously special circumstances, appointed ten and nine justices respectively. No vacancies occurred in FDR's first term of office, Bill Clinton's second term, or George W. Bush's first term. These unfortunate presidents were denied their right to influence the Court, while Taft and Harding were empowered to pack the Court beyond what they earned electorally. This uneven distribution of influence is clearly unfair to presidents and to the voters who elected them. No legitimate

---

18. Actually, Johnson made one nomination, but the Senate failed to act and Congress promptly enacted a law abolishing that particular vacancy and the next one to occur.

19. A total of four presidents did not appoint a single member to the Court. In addition to Johnson and Carter, Presidents Harrison and Taylor died soon after reaching office.

reason exists for granting no influence over the Court to some electoral majorities, while giving an enormous amount to others. For example, why should twelve years of Democratic rule under Presidents Carter and Clinton result in only two Democrats being added to the Court, while twelve years of Republican rule under Reagan and Bush produces six new appointments? The Republicans' recent good fortune in Supreme Court appointments extends further to the eight years of Nixon and Ford Administrations during which five vacancies occurred.

Solving the Problem of Irregular Turnover

The irregularity of turnover and replacement opportunities stands as an impediment to the exercise of democratic influence on the Supreme Court, an especially strong impediment in recent years. Several proposals for regularizing turnover have been offered to deal with this problem and others related to it. The two standards that will be used for evaluating these reform ideas are effectiveness and feasibility. An effective proposal will have a high likelihood of producing regularity in turnover and a more even distribution of presidential appointment opportunities. Additionally, effective proposals will have fewer harmful consequences, whether reducing judicial independence, losing judicial talent, or needlessly increasing conflict in the confirmation process. Political feasibility is the second, and an equally important, criterion. A perfectly effective solution has little value if it stands no chance of being adopted. Proposals that require a constitutional amendment will be less feasible and thus viewed less favorably than those requiring only statutory enactment.

Several proposals will be reviewed, including a mandatory retirement age and term limits. The proposals offered in this volume providing for eighteen-year terms that are staggered and nonrenewable will be given special attention. Statutory alternatives will also be examined, including a guaranteed appointment in the second year of each president's term.

Mandatory Retirement Age

From time to time, presidents have proposed, Congress has considered, and Supreme Court justices have favored replacing life tenure with a mandatory retirement age, typically seventy or seventy-five years of age. Compulsory retirement for judges is not uncommon. For example, Epstein, Knight, and Shvetsova found that almost half of the twenty-seven European countries they studied impose a compulsory retirement age for justices serving on their constitutional courts, with the mean retirement age at sixty-nine years.[20] Additionally, many states mandate retirement for their judges, most commonly at age seventy. Finally, a majority of Americans (sixty percent in a 2004 Associated Press poll)[21] favor a mandatory retirement age for Supreme Court justices.

The primary motivation for adopting this alternate tenure rule is the fear that elderly justices are choosing to "stay…too long at the fair," contributing less to and harming the quality of the Court's work.[22] Physical and mental disabilities increase with age, and mental infirmities in particular can affect a justice's ability to render sound legal judgments, add constructively to Court deliberations, and share fully in opinion-writing tasks. Additionally, there is to some the appeal of adding youth, energy, and fresh ideas to the bench.

A mandatory retirement rule, however, is a crude tool for addressing the problem of infirmity. Any fixed age limit is inevitably arbitrary, as some justices can perform at a very high level of competence in their eighth decade, while others suffer serious decline in their sixth. As Ward notes, even an age limit of "eighty-five would have been too low for Oliver Wendell Holmes, Jr., who stepped down at ninety-one. Conversely, seventy was too high for Ward Hunt, who became disabled at age sixty-seven."[23] Other eminent jurists who might have been lost at the peak of their careers, in addition to Holmes, include John Marshall, Joseph Story, the first John Harlan, Hugo Black, and William Brennan. Furthermore, some justices with distinguished careers might never have been nominated in the first place, including Cardozo who was appointed at age sixty-one, Earl Warren (appointed at sixty-two), Harry Blackmun (sixty-one), Lewis Powell (sixty-four), and Ruth Bader Ginsburg (sixty).

Beyond this difficulty, how would a mandatory retirement age affect turnover? Ward, too quickly I believe, assumes that a mandatory retirement age, such as would be required by his proposed constitutional amendment for compulsory retirement at age seventy-five, would shorten terms and increase turnover. A closer look reveals that, over the last sixty years, the average age of Supreme Court justices sitting on the bench has been sixty-four years.[24]

---

20. Lee Epstein, Jack Knight, & Olga Shvetsova, *Comparing Judicial Selection Systems*, 10 Wm. and Mary Bill of Rights Journal 7, 23 (2001).

21. See <http://www.msnbc.msn.com/id/6602068/print/1/dispolaymoe/1098/>.

22. Sanford Levinson, *Contempt of Court: The Most Important Contemporary Challenge to Judging*, 49 Wash. & Lee L. Rev. 339, 341 (1992); David J. Garrow, *Mental Decrepitude on the U.S. Supreme Court: The Historical Case for a 28th Amendment*, 67 U. Chi. L. Rev. 995 (2000).

23. Ward, *supra* n. 15, at 242.

24. Atkinson, *supra* n. 15, at 191–2.

Historically, the average age of justices when departing from the bench is 68.8 years. The average departure age in the modern era is significantly higher: 71.4 years of age since 1937 and 78.8 years of age since 1971. In light of these numbers, mandating retirement at age seventy-five would not seem to have that much effect. Surprisingly, though, nearly half of the justices leaving the bench since 1937 (fourteen out of thirty-two) were at least seventy-five years of age, although only four justices out of thirty-two would have lost five years or more of service under such a retirement provision. Overall, it seems reasonable to conclude that this mandatory retirement rule would have a modest impact.

A provision mandating retirement at seventy years of age would no doubt have a much stronger effect. After all, four of the nine justices on the Court in 2005—Stevens, Rehnquist, O'Connor, and Ginsburg—would have been forced into "early" retirement by such a provision, with Scalia and Kennedy only a couple of years away. Additionally, twenty of the thirty-two justices leaving the bench since 1937 (62.5%) were seventy years old or older. But would mandating retirement at age seventy effectively achieve the goal of increasing turnover and more evenly distributing presidential appointment opportunities? While the retirement of any individual justice could be predicted under this new regime, the timing of retirements could remain quite irregular, and turnover would continue to be unsystematic and dependent on the appointment proclivities of presidents. Especially significant, a mandatory retirement age might very well lead presidents to nominate more youthful candidates able to influence legal policy over a longer period of time. In this way, term lengths could remain quite long or even increase, and turnover could actually decrease.

Such a rule would have affected turnover and presidential appointments in the last twenty years. For example, the first President Bush would have enjoyed an additional (third) appointment opportunity, replacing Stevens upon his seventieth birthday in 1990. Both Bill Clinton and George W. Bush would have received the four appointments they "deserved" (given the average of roughly two appointments per term), with Clinton replacing Rehnquist in 1994 and O'Connor in 2000 and Bush replacing Ginsburg in his first term of office and Scalia, Kennedy, and Breyer in his second. This represents a far more equitable distribution of presidential appointment opportunities than actually occurred over the last two decades. Whether that pattern would continue, however, is difficult to determine.

For example, my assumption that presidents will appoint individuals who are fifty years of age (most appointees are fifty to fifty-five and the average is fifty-three) produces significant improvement in regularizing and equalizing presidential appointment opportunities: under a mandatory retirement age of seventy, two vacancies would arise in the presidential term occurring in the 2009–2012 term, one departure in the 2013–2016 term, and two vacancies in the 2017–2020 term. But these conclusions remain speculative for two reasons: deaths or early retirements may occur (increasing turnover) and presidents may seek to prolong their influence by nominating younger candidates (decreasing turnover).

A mandatory retirement age, if set at age seventy rather than seventy-five, does have considerable potential to increase turnover. However, it does not provide a direct and logical solution to the problem of low and irregular turnover. While it seems reasonable to expect significant improvement in turnover and a more equitable distribution of presidential appointment opportunities, there is no guarantee. On the other hand, inconsistent performance is a certainty. Furthermore, its unfortunate side effects include the potential loss of judicial talent and an increase in the incentives for presidents to nominate youthful candidates, in turn undermining the goal of regularizing turnover. Thus, the mandatory retirement age proposal must be regarded as, at best, modest in terms of effectiveness.

Given that this reform would require a constitutional amendment, it performs very poorly in terms of feasibility, with the chances of its successful passage being very slim unless highly publicized instances of mental decrepitude on the part of a justice or justices result in a climate of change. Although a majority of Americans currently favors a mandatory retirement age for Supreme Court justices, those views are not intensely held or expressed. Certainly, there is no groundswell of support as there was for congressional term limit proposals in the 1980s and 1990s, which were unsuccessful despite their popularity. A mandatory retirement age for Supreme Court justices simply lacks popular appeal and is unlikely to tap into or provoke the intensity of feeling necessary for passage. Even constitutional amendment proposals with great popular appeal and strong majority support, like the Equal Rights Amendment, are not guaranteed of passage, since an impassioned minority can easily defeat them. A mandatory retirement age is, in the end, a weak proposal.

Term Limits

An alternative tenure system is term limitation, which some states and many European countries employ. An amazing variety of judicial terms— non-renewable, renewable through various means, and lasting as short a time as two years and as long as twenty—exists in the states. Over three-quarters of the twenty-seven European countries studied by Epstein et al. have term limit provisions for their Supreme Court justices, with terms ranging from six to twelve years and a term length mean of 9.3 years, though two-thirds of these countries permit reappointment.[25]

A variety of term limitation proposals have been offered over the years. For example, Collier advocated a twelve-member Court with staggered, nonrenewable twelve-year terms; Fleming proposed a fixed, nonrenewable term of sixteen years; and Lazarus has urged a term limit of eighteen years.[26] What might be the impact of term limits of twelve to eighteen years on turnover and the distribution of appointment opportunities?

Historically, Supreme Court justices have served an average of 16.3 years.[27] This might initially lead us to conclude that limiting terms, particularly under the most popular eighteen-year term limit proposal, would have little impact. However, the length of service of Supreme Court justices has varied considerably, from the one year and two months served by Thomas Johnson to the astounding thirty-six years and seven months completed by William Douglas. Nonetheless, among the thirty-four justices appointed since 1937, nearly three quarters (twenty-five) served over ten years, seventy percent (twenty-four) completed at least twelve years, and fifty-nine percent (twenty) served over fifteen years. Thus, a majority of justices since 1937 would have been forced into retirement earlier than they desired had term limits of ten to fifteen years been in place. Gruhl observes that even an eighteen-year term limitation "would have…a major effect" with nearly forty percent of justices in the twentieth century being forced off the bench.[28] Although turnover would very likely increase, the timing of the forced departures could remain unpredictable and haphazard, thus failing to guarantee a more equitable distribution of presidential appointment opportunities.

Seeking to address that particular problem is the reform advanced by Oliver in 1986 and Calabresi and Lindgren in 2005—a constitutional amendment

25. Epstein et al, *supra* n. 20, at 30–1.

26. Charles S. Collier, *The Supreme Court and Principle of Rotation in Office*," 6 Geo. Wash. L. Rev. 401 (1938); Macklin Fleming, *Is Life Tenure on the Supreme Court Good for the Country?* 70 Judicature 322 (1987); Edward Lazarus, *Why We Should Consider Abolishing Life Tenure for Supreme Court Justices*, <http://writ.news.findlaw.com/lazarus/20010206.html> (Feb. 6, 2001); Paul D. Carrington, *Restoring Vitality to State and Local Politics by Correcting the Excessive Independence of the Supreme Court*, 50 Alab. L. Rev. 397 (1999).

27. Epstein et al., *supra* n. 20, at 368–70.

28. John Gruhl, *The Impact of Term Limits for Supreme Court Justices*, 81 Judicature 66 (1997).

providing for staggered, nonrenewable terms of eighteen years.[29] Under the Calabresi-Lindgren proposal, Supreme Court justices would be limited to eighteen-year, nonrenewable terms, with one term expiring every two years, ensuring that the Court's entire membership would be replaced over an eighteen-year span. Reappointment is not permitted, and "replacement" justices can only serve the remainder of the term of the departing justice rather than a full eighteen-year term. The chief justice is selected from among the associate justice ranks, although he may not serve beyond the eighteen-year limit that commenced when he was appointed as associate justice. Finally, justices forced to leave the Court at the end of their eighteen-year term can serve for life on the lower federal courts.

There is much to commend this proposal. First, it results in regular turnover and guarantees that presidents will make two appointments per presidential term, ensuring each president equal power to influence the Court. In addition to great effectiveness in achieving this key goal, it produces several additional benefits and suffers from few harmful collateral consequences. For example, keeping terms below the twenty-year mark will help prevent the problem of judicial decrepitude and "assure a relatively vigorous Court."[30] Gruhl, actually an opponent of judicial term limits, believes nonetheless that they will produce a more representative and "up-to-date" Court that would be less prone to gross miscalculations and "self-inflicted wounds." Calabresi and Lindgren point to additional benefits: preserving judicial independence since terms remain long and nonrenewable, inhibiting strategic retirement since a justice's replacement can only serve the remainder of her eighteen-year term, and reducing the incentives for presidents to select younger candidates since justices can only serve eighteen years regardless of age. Another proposed benefit is that partisan acrimony in the Senate confirmation process will be reduced because an eighteen-year term lowers the stakes compared to life tenure and because the process will be invoked more regularly and thus become routinized. (I am not strongly persuaded on this point. The process will continue to be contentious to the degree that the Court remains a partisan and ideological prize, as it has been throughout its history, and as long as strong partisan divisions continue to exist.)

---

29. *See also* Philip Oliver, *Systematic Justice: A Proposed Constitutional Amendment to Establish Fixed, Staggered Terms for Members of the United States Supreme Court*, 47 Ohio St. L. J. 799 (1986); L. A. Powe, Jr., *Old People and Good Behavior*, 12 Constitutional Commentary 195 (1995); James E. DiTullio & John B. Schochet, *Saving This Honorable Court: A Proposal to Replace Life Tenure on the Supreme Court with Staggered, Nonrenewable Eighteen-Year Terms*, 90 Va. L. Rev. 1093 (2004).

30. Oliver, *supra* n. 29, at 313.

Switching from life tenure to eighteen-year staggered, nonrenewable terms would indeed be highly effective in increasing and regularizing turnover and ensuring equality in presidential appointment opportunities. However, several weaknesses must be acknowledged. First, as Gruhl points out, term limits could very well result in a significant loss of judicial talent since the justices rated "great" tend to serve long terms; he estimates that, had term limits been in place, we would have lost more great justices than poor ones.[31] Others argue that the great justices have contributed their creative ideas in the first eighteen years and have operated on intellectual autopilot in later years. DiTullio and Schochet also have responded that the Twenty-Second Amendment embodies a policy establishing that Americans are willing to accept potential losses of talent and that more turnover "may actually allow more 'great men' (and great women) to serve on the Court."[32]

A second potential problem is that, as McGinnis puts it, "an office holder will perform less responsibly to make a name for himself in the short time available."[33] Particularly as the end of a justice's term approaches, she might become more impatient in pursuit of her own policy goals, striking out more boldly and seeking to leave a strong legacy. Justices being forced to retire early could very well become more ideological and less strategic in their decision-making behavior, acting more aggressively to make their mark on constitutional policy and legal doctrine. A change like this—more ideologues (like Douglas) and fewer strategists (like Brennan)—would not be welcome.

Finally, term limitation suffers from a near fatal defect: such a change would require a constitutional amendment, which is extremely unlikely. This proposal, although superior to a mandatory retirement age in terms of equalizing presidential influence over the Court, might be even less likely to be adopted, given its relatively greater complexity and thus its reduced popular appeal.

Statutory Alternatives

It is worthwhile to examine statutory alternatives since it is highly unlikely that a constitutional amendment on this topic would be successfully enacted. Such statutory options derive from Congress's power under the Constitution to regulate the Court's size. Historically the Court has varied in size from five

---

31. Gruhl, *supra* n. 28, at 68, 72.
32. DiTullio & Schochet, *supra* n. 29, at 1133.
33. McGinnis, *supra* n. 1, at 543.

to ten members, with Congress changing the number several times in the nineteenth century either to grant favored presidents (e.g., Jackson, Lincoln, Grant) additional seats or to deny appointment opportunities to opposition presidents (e.g., Jefferson, Andrew Johnson) by reducing the Court's size as vacancies occurred. This political tool fell into disuse and disrepute in the twentieth century. As evidence, we only need to observe that Congress has not altered the size of the Court since 1869 and that Franklin Roosevelt failed to convince a friendly Congress to expand the Court at a time when both were united in their antagonism toward the Court because of its hostility to New Deal legislation.

The Supreme Court Renewal Act advanced by Carrington and Cramton is an attempt to enact staggered, nonrenewable eighteen-year terms statutorily. Every president would be guaranteed two appointments to the Court—one for each two-year congressional term. The Court's membership would grow, but only the nine most recently appointed justices would be regarded as active, with the remainder being placed on senior status upon completing eighteen years of service.

Like its constitutional counterpart, this proposal for staggered, eighteen-year terms is highly effective, guaranteeing each president two appointments and thus equal influence in shaping the Court. In addition to great success on this measure, its authors claim another benefit: its enactment requires only a simple legislative act and is thus more feasible.

This is true, however, only if the Act is able to survive a constitutional challenge, an unlikely outcome in my view. Article III provides that "Judges, both of the supreme and inferior Courts, shall hold their Offices during good Behavior, and shall, at stated Times, receive for their Services, a Compensation, which shall not be diminished during their Continuance in Office." Life tenure and protection against salary diminution may not, in theory or practice, be a necessary condition for judicial independence, as has been effectively argued in this volume. However, it is the mechanism chosen by the Framers and written into the Constitution. Opponents of the Act would argue that removing a justice from active service on the Court and disallowing him or her to vote in its decisions amounts to a denial of Article III's guarantee of life tenure. The critical question would be whether life tenure attaches to the appointment to the federal bench generally, in which case active or senior status is irrelevant, or whether tenure protections attach to the specific appointment—a life-time seat on the Supreme Court. I regard the latter interpretation as more reasonable and would be surprised if Supreme Court justices, with so much at stake personally, would rule otherwise.

Proposals to rotate federal judges in and out of the Supreme Court at either six-month[34] or five-year intervals[35] suffer from the same constitutional defect. McGinnis argues, however, that "Supreme Court riding" (his "counterfactual label" for rotation) is permitted by the ambiguous language of Article III and supported by the historical practices of circuit-riding and retiring justices sitting on courts to which they were not appointed. While these are not unreasonable arguments, they are not so compelling that a self-interested Court would be required to accept them.

I too have searched for and strongly prefer a statutory rather than constitutional solution to the problem of irregular turnover and inequality in the distribution of Supreme Court appointments. My proposal is more modest, guaranteeing each president one appointment to the Supreme Court, with the nomination occurring in the first week in January in the president's second year in office.[36] Rather than forcing sitting justices into senior status and rotating them back to the lower federal bench, I would allow the size of the Court to vary, both above and below the current standard of nine justices. To prevent the Court from growing too large and some presidents from exercising disproportionate influence over it, I propose adding a regulatory provision mandating that a president can make no more than two appointments in a single term. Thus, if a vacancy occurs after a president has reached his maximum two appointments, it will go unfilled and the Court's size will be reduced accordingly. If the chief justice leaves the Court after the president has reached his limit of two appointments, the president will be required to nominate a replacement from among the ranks of associate justices, and the associate justice vacancy will then be left unfilled. Finally, Congress should stipulate that the reform will not go into effect until the next presidential election.

The single-appointment guarantee is a superior reform for several reasons: it is quite effective in equalizing presidential influence over the Court, is more feasible than other proposals, and suffers from fewer harmful side effects. First, with regard to effectiveness, it guarantees every president at least one appointment and some influence over the Court. Jimmy Carter and the party and voters supporting him deserved and under this proposal would have received at least one seat on the Court. The same goes for George W. Bush in his first term and Bill Clinton in his second. As a result of this reform, the val-

---

34. McGinnis, *supra* n. 1.

35. Laurence Silberman, *Keynote Address to the Federalist Society: Revisiting the Philadelphia Plan*, 1 Georgetown J. of Law & Public Policy 5 (2002).

36. *See also supra* Philip D. Oliver, *Increasing the Size of the Court as a Partial but Clearly Constitutional Alternative*, pp. 405–414.

ues winning electoral validation will be guaranteed a place on the Court, which will become more representative, reflecting current (in addition to recent) election outcomes. Of course, unlike with staggered eighteen-year terms, perfect equality in distributing Supreme Court appointments will not result, nor will turnover be increased or regularized. No statutory scheme yet devised can accomplish either goal without running afoul of Article III. Although some inequity in presidential appointment opportunities remains, it is minimized by limiting presidents to two appointments per term.

The beneficial effects of a single-appointment guarantee emerge from a review of what would have happened if it had been in place over the last three decades. For example, at least four new seats would have been created in the 1976–2005 period—in Carter's term, Reagan's first term, Clinton's second term, and Bush's first term—representing four opportunities for the people and their elected leaders to reinforce or reset the Court's constitutional path. Additionally, the distribution of appointment opportunities and presidential influence would have been greatly improved. Since all presidents would have received at least one but not more than two appointments per term, we would have seen a much smaller range of variation in presidential influence over the Court and a complete elimination of the problem of some presidents being unfairly denied a chance to shape the Court. Even when this system would have resulted in no change in the number of appointments a president received, their distribution would have been more even. For example, Reagan would still have received four appointments in his two terms in office. However, under the new scheme, Reagan would have appointed two justices in each term instead of one in his first and three in his second.

The regulation dictating no more than two appointments per term would likely have come into play several times. In Reagan's second term, the Rehnquist and Powell vacancies would have remained unfilled, reducing the Court's size from twelve seats to ten. This provision would also have been activated in the first Bush presidency and in Clinton's first term and would likely become relevant again in Bush's second term. Once Bush successfully replaced O'-Connor and Rehnquist, he would be prohibited from making any more appointments, even if one or more retirements were to occur. As intended, the two-appointment limit would thus substantially have reduced inequities in the distribution of Supreme Court appointment opportunities, while keeping the Court from growing too large and unwieldy.

The single-appointment guarantee also performs well on the feasibility criterion. It can be accomplished statutorily, avoiding the nearly impossible challenge of constitutional enactment. Additionally, under this new appointment system, life tenure remains and sitting justices do not lose their status or voting power on the Court. Thus, it lacks the constitutional infirmities of the Carrington-Cramton and other rotation proposals. While we must, of course, not assume that Congressional passage is a simple task, the one-seat guarantee does not inherently favor one party over another, thus eliminating partisan division as an obstacle to passage. This nonpartisan character would be reinforced by delaying the reform's implementation until after the next presidential election.

Nonetheless, altering the Supreme Court appointment process offers no obvious electoral benefits to members of Congress, winning them neither votes nor campaign contributions. A one-seat guarantee, while not involving the near impossibility facing proposals for a constitutional amendment, will still not be an easy sell politically, especially since Congress has not exercised its power to alter the Court's size in over a century. Because these reform ideas will excite few voters or groups, they are unlikely to excite Congress. A more likely outcome is that they will remain dormant in journals devoted to legal scholarship and reform and will be ignored like so many other good government proposals.

In addition to performing well on the effectiveness criterion and better on the feasibility criterion, a reform that promises at least one and no more than two Supreme Court appointments has more positive than negative collateral effects. For example, this appointment guarantee does not sacrifice judicial talent. Skilled justices can remain on the bench, while opportunities for new talent and fresh ideas are added. There are no perverse incentives to nominate youthful candidates, or at least no new incentives to do so, unlike a mandatory retirement age proposal. A third positive corollary impact might be an enhanced focus in presidential election campaigns on Supreme Court appointments. The certainty that a president will fill one seat on the Court a year after taking office could enhance voter and media interest and create pressure on candidates to discuss their selection criteria and potential nominees, a point on which I am hopeful but not optimistic.

On the negative side of the ledger are several weaknesses, some of which have already been mentioned. First, under the single-appointment guarantee, turnover remains erratic and often low (though by necessity, in order to protect it from constitutional challenge). Additionally, some inequity in presidential influence over the Court remains, though it is small. An additional weakness is that a one-seat guarantee lacks sufficient popular appeal to ensure its enactment in Congress. Yet another possible concern is the creation of a new opportunity for strategic retirement behavior: a justice might choose to retire after an opposite-party president had filled his maximum two seats, thus ensuring that the president could not provide an ideologically-unacceptable replacement. For example, liberal justices might have chosen the end of Bush's single term or the end of Reagan's second term to retire, after those presidents had already filled two seats, thus denying them the opportunity to appoint conservative replacements. While possible, this opportunity will often be ignored due to the powerful attraction of continued service on the Court.[37] Furthermore, even when it does occur, it will have a positive effect—reducing the Court's size.

An additional concern for some might be the possibility of a "feedback effect," in which guaranteeing the president the opportunity to make at least one appointment to the Court creates or reinforces the notion that the justices are mere ideological agents of the president. The Court's public legitimacy could accordingly be weakened, as could the constraints that the legal model currently exerts on judicial behavior. With regard to the former claim, public opinion data easily disprove the notion that the Court's legitimacy is dependent on the public's belief that it adheres to legal norms such as impartiality. Instead, public evaluations of the Court are realistic and political, based on substantive agreement with the Court's policies.[38] The latter claim that behavioral norms attached to the judicial role could be dangerously weakened relies on two faulty assumptions—first, that Supreme Court justices will readily abandon their sense of independence and willingly submit to presidential authority and, second, that such role constraints currently inhibit the justices from deciding in an ideological fashion, which social scientific studies have proven false.[39] Personally, I would welcome this small dose of realism and would regard as a positive development a new and widely-shared norm that, with his electoral victory, the president has earned the right to place an ideological ally on the Court. It might improve the quality of presidential campaign discussions of judicial appointments and contribute to the goal of enhancing the Court's representativeness.

A final consideration is the reform's potentially problematic impact on Court size. The Court's membership would likely grow, especially in light of the trend already noted of justices serving longer terms and into later age. For example, my application of the proposal to the period from 1976–2006 indicated that, had the one-appointment guarantee been in place in 1976, the Court would have indeed grown, to perhaps thirteen members by 2006. This could produce two harmful consequences. Tie votes would result during periods when the

---

37. Saul Brenner, *The Myth that Justices Strategically Retire*, 36 Social Science Journal 431 (1999).

38. Peretti, *supra* n. 4.

39. Segal & Spaeth, *supra* n. 5.

Court is both divided and even-numbered. Consensual decisionmaking and opinion writing, already a problem on the Court, could become even more difficult as the size of the minimum winning coalition increased from five to six or seven. This is a significant and inevitable drawback to the one-seat guarantee. I rejected a two-seat guarantee in large part because of its more severe impact on Court size and decisionmaking manageability.

Conclusion

The uneven distribution of Supreme Court appointment opportunities has reduced the effectiveness of the appointment process as a tool of democratic control. The one-appointment guarantee will serve as an excellent first step in correcting this flaw. It offers considerable improvement though not complete equality in the distribution of presidential influence, with each president being empowered to shape the Court on behalf of his party and his supporters by making at least one but not more than two appointments. The addition of new talent and viewpoints will also make the Court more vigorous and more representative. Furthermore, this modest reform may sharpen the focus and enhance the quality of presidential candidates' discussions of the Court's future membership and direction. The one-seat guarantee is a worthwhile experiment that promises to enhance democracy by making the Supreme Court more representative and more legitimate.

Restraining the Court by Curbing District Court Jurisdiction and Improving Litigation Procedure

George W. Liebmann[*]

Diverse proposals advanced in this symposium are directed at various perceived ill consequences of life tenure for Supreme Court justices, including the increasing divisiveness of the confirmation process derived from the high stakes involved when justices serve for many decades, and the arrogance, hubris, and abuse to which long tenure frequently gives rise. The proposals that follow are suggested as complements to, not substitutes for, the Carrington-Cramton or other reform proposals. They rest on the premise that the high stakes of each appointment to the Court derive at least in part from the assumption by the federal courts of legislative functions, including a policy veto akin to the executive veto, and that the arrogance, hubris, and abuse derive in part from the ability of courts to act with excessive haste, on inadequate records, with inadequate participation by affected parties,[1] in a manner that encourages judicial policy making and imperils some of the goals of ad-

---

[*] Principal in Liebmann and Shively, P.A. of Baltimore. Formerly Simon Industrial and Professional Fellow at the University of Manchester and a Visiting Fellow of Wolfson College, Cambridge.
  1. *See*, e.g. Martin v. Wilks, 490 U.S,755 (1989) (reversing denial of intervention), and, for similar behavior at the state level, Montgomery County v. Bradford, 345 Md. 175 (1997) (4–3 decision denying intervention).

judicative procedure: accuracy in the determination of facts and application of law; fairness to litigants and persons affected by the decision; and efficiency in the resolution of contested matters.

The proposals below do not at all affect the exercise of traditional judicial functions by either the Supreme Court or the lower federal courts. The central function of courts in all societies is the administration of what Aristotle and Aquinas called "corrective" justice or "restorative" justice:[2] cases involving individuals. These cases are designed to restore and enforce pre-existing social norms by punishing criminals who depart from them, or awarding tort or contract damages to persons injured by their breach. The power of United States district courts to adjudicate criminal and ordinary civil cases is unaffected by these proposals, as is the power of the courts of appeal to review such cases. The proposals also do not alter in any way the jurisdiction and power of the Supreme Court or implicate the so-called *McCardle*[3] issue: whether Congress may deprive the Supreme Court, as distinct from the lower federal courts, of jurisdiction to decide constitutional questions.

Instead, the proposals are addressed entirely to actions by the lower federal courts when they effectively exercise a suspensory veto over state and local legislation with inadequate deliberation, on inadequate records, with insufficient participation by affected parties, under rules that grossly disadvantage defendants. Some of the proposals, like the Norris-La Guardia Act, are designed to enhance the quality and care of deliberation in the lower federal courts. Others, like the Tax Injunction Act and the Johnson Act, are designed to channel limited classes of constitutional challenges into the state courts, which are sworn to the same oaths of office. Such channeling relieves congested federal dockets, allows focus on federal specialties, insulates the lower federal courts from especially volatile and controversial issues in which the premature announcement of national rules is undesirable, and protects states and localities from having to endure duplicative and consecutive challenges to new legislation.

The first set of proposals is largely inspired by the Norris-LaGuardia Act[4], one of the most beneficent pieces of legislation in American history. Prior to the Norris-La Guardia Act, federal judges habitually issued injunctions against

---

2. *See* Aristotle, *Nicomachean Ethics*, Book V; Aquinas, *Summa Theologica*, 1a,xxi,I.

3. Ex parte McCardle, 74 U.S. 506 (1868) (Wall.) (congressional repeal of federal court jurisdiction to issue writs of habeas corpus during the Reconstruction period deprived the circuit courts and the Supreme Court of appellate jurisdiction).

4. 29 U.S.C. §§ 101–115; *see* Felix Frankfurter & Nathan Greene, *The Labor Injunction* (1930).

labor unions, frequently on ex parte application, and in almost all instances through the use of procedures placing strikers and their unions at a heavy disadvantage. In the decades preceding enactment of the statute, signed by President Hoover in 1932, there were literally hundreds of instances in which federal troops were called out to enforce carelessly issued federal injunctions in labor disputes.[5] In the years following enactment of the statute, there were few such instances, and the burden of maintaining order in labor disputes was placed on state and local police and the state National Guards. While there was much labor violence in the 1930s and many deaths in labor controversies, the blame for these occurrences was widely dispersed. The United States Army did not enter World War II stigmatized as the perpetrator of bloodshed in labor disputes. Yet the restrictions in the Norris-LaGuardia Act were almost wholly procedural.

The evils that are addressed by the first proposal below—the Constitutional Litigation Improvement Act—require only short summary. Ex parte restraining orders, sought and obtained just before a statute or ordinance takes effect, are all too common. The claims are brought by advocacy groups with national resources who have prepared their cases over many months; they are defended by young and inexperienced state assistant attorneys general or assistant city solicitors who are given hours to master important and complex areas of public policy. Not infrequently, the nominal defendant is in sympathy with the plaintiff, and a conspiracy against the public fisc ensues in which the parties adversely affected do not receive notice of the litigation or are denied the right to intervene in it. Frequently there are adequate state remedies, and the resultant failure of the inchoate federal case is followed by renewed challenges in state courts under state constitutions. All too frequently, United States district courts deliver hortatory pronouncements of invalidity, without analysis of facts, and without appropriate limitation of injunctive relief. Frequently, relief is later given to plaintiffs who have not tried to participate at all in the political process, who have not availed themselves of administrative remedies,[6] and who indeed may even have defied the law. In some instances,

---

5. Robert W. Coakley, *The Role of the Federal Military Forces in Domestic Disorders, 1789–1878* (1988); Jerry M. Cooper, *Federal Military Intervention in Domestic Disorders,* in *The U.S. Military Under the Constitution of the United States, 1789–1999* (Richard H. Kohn ed., 2001).

6. Patsy v. Regents of Florida, 457 U.S. 496 (1982); Charles Alan Wright & Mary Kay Kane, *Law of Federal Courts* § 49 (6th ed., 2002); McKart v. United States, 395 U.S. 185 (1969); Eisen v. Eastman, 421 F.2d 560, 269 (2nd Cir. 1969) (Friendly, J.); Kenneth Culp Davis, *Administrative Law Treatise* § 20.01 (1970).

public officers sympathetic to the plaintiffs undertake to bind their successors, and insulate the positions of their political party against the danger of reversal at the polls.[7]

The second proposal—The Constitutional Litigation Expediting Act—is inspired by the practices of the French and German constitutional courts[8] and by the procedure applied when declarations that British legislation is inconsistent with European law are sought under the British Human Rights Act.[9] The Expediting Act reserves to the federal courts of appeal acting en banc the power to issue injunctions or declarations of invalidity. This limits forum-shopping for sympathetic district judges, limits the number of conflicts between lower court decisions, and creates a climate in which district judges will be chosen for their trial experience and skills, not their views on contested questions of national policy. A similar purpose inspires the provisions of the federal Administrative Procedure Act, which directs appeals from the federal administrative agencies to the courts of appeal[10] rather than to the district courts. A provision of this sort was suggested by Donald Richberg as an alternative to President Roosevelt's infamous "court packing" proposal.[11]

The third proposal—The Family Law Consolidation Act—is designed to channel especially controversial legislation over issues related to family and education to the state courts.[12] A long political and judicial tradition in the United States has left these matters largely to local and state governments with very little intrusion by the federal courts. The definition of these issues is the privacy definition employed by the Supreme Court in the *Roe*[13] and *Webster*[14] cases. Such issues are best determined by the courts closest to the people; to the extent that decisions rest on state grounds, their potential for national controversy is more limited, and the existence of differing rules as between states will leave a larger portion of the population satisfied than would be satisfied

---

7. *See* Ross Sandler & David Schoenbrod, *Democracy by Decree* (2002); and Jeremy Rabkin, *Judicial Compulsions: How Public Law Distorts Public Policy* (1989).

8. *See* Mary Ann Glendon, Michael Wallace Gordon, and Christopher Osakwe, *Comparative Legal Traditions* 65–119 (1985).

9. Human Rights Act, 1998.

10. 28 U.S.C. 2341; Wright & Kane, *supra* n. 6 at § 103.

11. George T. McJimsey, *Documentary History of the Franklin D. Roosevelt Presidency* vol. 1 (*Packing the Supreme Court and the Judicial Reorganization Bill, January–July 1937*) at 61–65 (2001), (memorandum of Donald Richberg to FDR, November 16, 1936).

12. Paul Bator, *Congressional Power over the Jurisdiction of the Federal Courts*, 27 Vill. L. Rev. 1030 (1982).

13. Roe v. Wade, 410 U.S. 113 (1973).

14. Webster v. Reproductive Health Services, 492 U.S. 490 (1989).

by a unitary national rule. Moreover, the legislation does not deprive the Supreme Court of power to intervene in egregious cases. Two highly successful enactments illustrate the benefits. The Johnson Act[15] and the Tax Injunction Act,[16] designed to channel cases involving state taxes and state utility regulations into the state courts, have been successful in advancing their objectives. Since their enactment, Supreme Court intervention in these areas has been rare and that by the lower federal courts rarer still. The restrictions on federal contempts by publication in the federal contempt statute of 1825[17] supply another example.

The fourth proposal—The Civil Rights Attorneys' Fees Act—is designed to ease the vulnerability of small local governments and school districts, who frequently succumb to threats of litigation by well-funded national advocacy groups because of fear of the large costs with which they would be saddled under the federal Civil Rights Attorneys' Fees Act[18] if those groups were even partially unsuccessful in the extensive litigation that otherwise would occur.

Here are the draft statutes in a conceptional and preliminary form.

Constitutional Litigation Improvement Act

Whereas, hundreds of actions are brought each year challenging the validity of state and local statutes and ordinances. These statutes and ordinances, the product of deliberation by elected officials after public debate which can be joined by any citizen, are entitled to practical as well as theoretical presumptions of constitutionality. There is need for greater care in decision of cases asserting rights under the United States Constitution, greater speed in their final decision, and greater uniformity in their decision. Present procedures preclude the preparation of adequate defenses, exclude persons and parties who should have a right to be heard, invite haste, carelessness and partiality in decisionmaking, and can give rise to collusive judgments. Whereas, it is enacted that:

No court of the United States, as defined in this chapter, shall have jurisdiction to issue any findings of fact, conclusions of law, declaratory judgments, temporary restraining orders, or temporary or permanent injunctions founded on any issue as to the constitutionality of any statute or ordinance of

---

15. 28 U.S.C. 1342.
16. 28 U.S.C. 1341.
17. 18 U.S.C. 401.
18. 42 U.S.C. 1988.

any state, territory, insular possession, or political subdivision, except in strict conformity with the provisions of this chapter and in accordance with the public policy declared in its preamble.

No court of the United States, in any such proceeding, shall issue any findings, conclusions, judgments, orders or injunctions unless each of the following requirements have been met:

(a) a complaint has been made under oath [29 U.S.C. 107];

(b) the court has heard the testimony of witnesses in open court (with opportunity for cross-examination) in support of the allegations of the complaint, and testimony in opposition thereto, if offered [29 U.S.C. 107];

(c) unless the action involves the incarceration or physical detention of the complainant, sixty days notice of the hearing of the action has been given to the Attorney General and Governor of a state, territory or insular possession whose statute has been challenged, or within which an ordinance of a political subdivision has been challenged, and to the chief executive officer(s) and chief law officer of each political subdivision whose ordinance has been challenged. In the case of newly enacted ordinances whose effectiveness is sought to be prevented, a lesser period of notice may be given, but such notice must be given before one-half the time between the enactment of the ordinance and its effective date has elapsed [28 U.S.C. 2284(b)(2)];

(d) the state, insular possession, or territory, through its Governor and/or Attorney General, and any political subdivision within such state, insular possession or territory, through its chief executive officer(s) and/or chief law officer, not limited to a political subdivision named as a defendant, shall have been given leave to intervene for presentation of evidence, if evidence is otherwise admissible in the case, and for argument on the question of constitutionality, provided that leave to intervene is sought within thirty days of the notice provided for by paragraph (c). [28 U.S.C. 2403; FRCP 24(c)];

(e) it has been shown, by clear and convincing evidence, that as to each item of relief granted, greater injury will be inflicted on plaintiff by denial of relief than will be inflicted on defendants by the granting of relief [29 U.S.C. 107(c)];

(f) it has been shown, by clear and convincing evidence, that complainants have no adequate remedy at law [29 U.S.C. 107(d)];

(g) it has been shown, by clear and convincing evidence, that complainants have no plain, speedy and efficient remedy in the courts of the state, territory, or insular possession [28 U.S.C. 1341, 28 U.S.C. 1342(4)];

(h) it has been shown, by clear and convincing evidence, that each person or entity against whom the order, judgment or injunction is being entered has threatened or committed an unlawful act or has actually authorized or ratified the same after actual knowledge thereof [29 U.S.C. 107(a)];

(I) the reasons for the issuance of the judgment, order, or injunction have been set forth [FRCP 65(d)];

(j) the persons subject to the judgment, order or injunction are limited to the parties to the action, their officers, agents, servants, employees and attorneys, and those persons in active concert or participation with them who receive actual notice of the judgment, order, or injunction [FRCP 65(d)];

(k) the facts have been specially found and conclusions of law have been separately stated prior to the issuance of the judgment, order, or injunction [29 U.S.C. 109, FRCP 52(a)];

(l) it has not been shown that the complainant failed to comply with obligations imposed by law involved in the dispute, or violated the challenged statute or ordinance in advance of the findings, judgment, order, or injunction [29 U.S.C. 108];

(m) it has not been shown that the complaint lacks equity because of complainant's failure to avail himself of political or administrative remedies, such as testimony at legislative and executive hearings and proceedings before administrative agencies [29 U.S.C. 108)]; and

(n) the order has not been entered upon consent, unless all parties and intervenors have consented thereto, and unless the duration of the judgment, order, or injunction is limited to the remaining terms of office of the public officials consenting [28 U.S.C. 2323)].

Constitutional Litigation Expediting Act

Whereas, the conduct of constitutional litigation in cases against state and local governments is protracted, expensive, and lacking in finality, and frequently results in conflicting judgments as between jurisdictions and in lengthy delays in the effectiveness of valid statutes and ordinances, as cases are appealed from United State District Courts, to Courts of Appeal, to Courts of Appeal sitting en banc, and then to the Supreme Court:

Section 1. No court of the United States except the Supreme Court shall have jurisdiction to determine any issue as to the validity under the United States Constitution of any statute or ordinance, or any portion thereof, of any state, territory, insular possession or political subdivision thereof, except as herein provided.

Section 2. If such an issue of constitutionality is raised in any proceeding now pending or hereafter removed to or instituted in any Court of the United States, other than the Supreme Court, then the Court shall proceed forthwith to take any evidence offered, which is relevant to a determination of such issue, to hear arguments upon the facts and the law and thereafter issue findings of fact and conclusions of law, including a finding either that:

(a) a constitutional issue has been properly raised and stated in the proceeding which, in the opinion of the Court, may be held decisive of the entire proceeding and which the Court will, therefore, certify to the Court of Appeals, en banc, for its decision, upon request of any party to the proceeding or intervenor therein; or

(b) a constitutional issue has been raised which has been decided by a previous ruling of the Supreme Court or Court of Appeals, en banc, on the same issue as to the same statute or ordinance or provision, in accordance with which ruling the Court is required to enter a final judgment disposing of the entire proceeding, in which case such a final judgment shall be forthwith entered; or

(c) there has not been raised any decisive constitutional issue and therefore the case shall proceed to final judgment on the merits, regardless of those constitutional issues which have been raised and which may be presented for the determination of the Court of Appeals, en banc, in the event that its appellate jurisdiction is successfully invoked as herein provided.

Section 3. The Courts of Appeal, en banc, shall have appellate jurisdiction to decide constitutional issues certified to them directly prior to final judgment, as hereinbefore provided, by the court of original jurisdiction, and shall have appellate jurisdiction to review any final judgment by any District Court presenting in the opinion of the Court of Appeals, en banc, a substantial constitutional question. In the exercise of the appellate jurisdiction hereby conferred upon the Courts of Appeal, en banc, expedited and preferential consideration shall be given to cases presenting constitutional issues as above defined over all other cases not presenting such issues.

Section 4. It shall constitute a breach of good behavior for any judge of a District Court, or of a Court of Appeals, not sitting en banc, to restrain any legislative or executive officer from performing any public duty, in accordance with any law of any state, territory, or insular possession, or in accordance with any local ordinance, unless such judicial action has been specifically required by a decision of the Supreme Court or of the Court of Appeals, en banc.

Section 5. All laws and parts of laws in conflict with or inconsistent with the limitations and requirements of this Act are hereby repealed; provided, that the jurisdiction conferred upon the various courts of the United States may be exercised by such courts as have been hitherto created and empowered without modification of practice and procedure, except so far as may be necessary to conform their jurisdiction, powers and procedure to the limitations and requirements of this Act.

Family Law Consolidation Act

Whereas the courts of the United States have traditionally abstained from granting relief and interpreting laws impinging on domestic and family relations, and the Congress, by reason of both prudential and constitutional limitations, has refrained from enacting statutes impinging on this subject, and these circumstances render it desirable that litigation concerning the federal constitutionality of state statutes impinging upon family relations, family privacy, and family education be determined, subject to Supreme Court review, by state trial courts experienced in the adjudication of such matters and by state appellate courts with the authority to apply at the same time the limitations of state constitutions and to construe state statutory and common law to avoid needless constitutional difficulties; and whereas withdrawal of these frequently unfamiliar and divisive issues from the jurisdiction of lower federal courts will allow them, and the persons appointing and confirming them, to focus on their central functions, it is enacted as follows:

No court of the United States other than the Supreme Court shall have jurisdiction to determine any issue as to the constitutionality of any statute or ordinance (or any provision thereof) of any state, territory, insular possession or political subdivision thereof concerning marriage, procreation, contraception, family relationships, child rearing, or education.

Civil Rights Attorneys' Fees Act Amendment

Whereas, experience under the Civil Rights Attorneys' Fees Act indicates that it has generated litigation, particularly but not limited to litigation against small school districts, that has deterred enactment of meritorious local ordinances and interfered with school discipline; and whereas application of the normal 'American Rule' relating to fee shifting to such cases will not deter the bringing of meritorious damage claims and claims for class injunctive relief enjoying the support of legal services offices and advocacy groups, and whereas the Act serves a meritorious purpose in its application to mental patients and prisoners not enjoying the ability to readily recruit counsel, it is therefore enacted as follows:

42 USCA 1988(b) is amended by adding after "In any action or proceeding" the words "based on unlawful detention or confinement."

APPENDIX:
THE EDITORS' INITIAL PROPOSAL

The Supreme Court Renewal Act: A Return to Basic Principles

Paul D. Carrington & Roger C. Cramton

As revised, January 2005, and abbreviated, July 2005

A. The Need for Legislative Action

Article III of the Constitution of the United States provides that judges of constitutional courts shall serve during "good behavior." The purpose of that provision was to secure the independence of the federal judiciary from any efforts of others with political power to influence judicial decisions improperly. The term has often been assumed to mean that Supreme Court justices may hold office until they resign, die or are removed for serious misfeasance. Our nation has greatly benefitted from the exceptional independence of the federal judiciary, but the independence principle does not require lifetime tenure for justices. The conventional assumption has become unsound because of increases in our longevity and other changes that have increased the tenure of justices.

The Founders, acting at a time when life expectancy at birth was less than forty years, could not foresee that lifetime tenure would result in persons holding so powerful an office for a generation or more. Today an American at age forty has a life expectancy of thirty-nine years and at age fifty-three (the average age of appointees to the Supreme Court) a life expectancy of about thirty years. These changes have at least three unwelcome secondary consequences that need to be addressed:

First, as Justices Serve Ever Longer Terms, Rotation in Office Occurs Infrequently and the Higher Stakes of Appointing a Justice for 25–40 Years Places Stress on the Confirmation Process.

The political prominence of the Supreme Court and its justices has been steadily enlarged in recent decades. In each of the last six presidential elections the identity of persons or types of persons the rival candidates might appoint to the Court has been an important issue. In the 2000 election, the Court decided who would be the person to nominate its own members. Supreme Court appointments have become politically contentious not only because the justices exercise great power but because they exercise it for so long.

This problem of persons holding very high political office for decades on end is unique to the Supreme Court of the United States. In the last century and a half, hundreds of constitutions have been written and ratified. Many of these became the law of American states, while many others have been adopted in nations that share our commitment to individual freedom and representative democracy. None of these hundreds of constitutions has provided for a court of last resort staffed by judges who are entitled to remain in service until they die or are found guilty of very serious misfeasance. Every group of constitution makers — forced to think responsibly about the issue under modern conditions — has concluded that there must be periodic movement of persons through offices in which so much power is vested, either through the imposition of term limits or age limits, by requiring reelection from time to time, or by allowing for removal by legislative action.

Applying any of these remedies to the Supreme Court would require a constitutional amendment. Our effort has been to craft a statutory provision falling within the broad authority of Congress to legislate concerning matters relevant to the definition of the "office" of being a judge of an Article III court such as the Supreme Court. Congress possesses and has long exercised broad legislative authority concerning the structure of the federal court system, the jurisdiction and procedure of federal courts, the number of judges or justices, the terms of their service and retirement, and their compensation.

Second, the Power and Status of Supreme Court Justices Carry Dangers of Arrogance, Hubris and Abuse that Can Only Increase as Terms Lengthen.

The Federalist Papers emphasized that representative government was dependent upon rotation in office on the part of those exercising political authority and that the exercise of political power had to be checked by the tripartite structure of the federal government and the role of the states as governments closer to the people. While Article III judges were exempt from rotation, eighteenth and nineteenth century circumstances made fairly frequent rotation in the chambers of the Supreme Court almost certain to occur.

And it did occur until recently. During the 215 years of the Court's history (1789–2004), 102 justices have been appointed to the Court—an average of a new appointment every 2.1 years. But justices in the past thirty years have been about ten years older at the time of retirement or death than their predecessors during the prior two hundred years. In the spring of 2005 the current nine justices had served together for more than ten years; the last previous appointment had been made in 1994.

Unchecked power, the Founders correctly believed, has a tendency to produce a degree of hubris and arrogance among those who exercise that power. Many thoughtful citizens are persuaded that even now the Supreme Court's conception and exercise of its power have manifested those traits. And more are likely to reach that conclusion if the trend toward longer periods of service continues.

The result is a situation needing correction. Liberals and conservatives will identify different decisions or lines of authority that they believe involve overreaching by the current Court and its recent predecessors, but both can agree that the extension of the Court's political role and its unchecked quality have created a serious problem that will only grow worse if left unattended.

Third, Increased Longevity Enables Supreme Court Justices, Unlike Lower Court Federal Judges, to Continue Serving Until Incapacitated Because the Conditions Under Which They Now Work Enable Them to Do So.

It has long been recognized that the life tenure of federal judges has created problems of sitting judges who have suffered loss in energy or mental capacity, become disabled or disturbed, or have served too long. During the twentieth century the Congress gradually devised a system of dealing with the aging of federal judges that works reasonably well with judges of United States district courts and circuit courts. These judges are provided with very generous retirement benefits, and those who take "senior status" can enjoy full paychecks with a reduced workload. Elderly judges of these courts generally subside with grace when their time comes. And Congress has devised a procedure, conducted by the judiciary itself through the circuit councils, of reducing or canceling the work assignments of those district and circuit judges who are physically or mentally unable to perform.

The rotation in office that results from the retirement of lower federal court judges is assisted by the fact that the workloads of these judges are not under their own control but are dependent on the caseloads created by litigants and their lawyers. Substantial and regular growth in the caseloads of trial and appellate federal courts often occurs faster than congressional willingness to create new judicial positions. The heavy case load and the burden of work that can not be delegated to others lead these judges to choose senior status and retirement as they age.

None of these forces apply to justices of the Supreme Court who may be disabled or superannuated or have been in service too long. Although justices are permitted by law to take senior status, none do so unless their personal condition has rendered further service on the Court virtually impossible or there is reason to believe that a timely surrender of a seat will assure the appointment of a successor who is like-minded on the issues that come before the Court.

Unlike the judges of lower federal courts, the Supreme Court controls its own workload. This control was conferred in 1925 and then broadened in 1988 by the virtual elimination of the right of a party to invoke the jurisdiction of the Court. Although the Court assured Congress in 1925 that it would continue to decide about 350 cases a year on the merits, the Court year after year has reduced the number of cases decided on the merits and now decides fewer than 100 cases a year on the merits. Meanwhile, conflicting decisions between lower federal courts on federal questions have continued to grow in number, creating disuniformity in the administration of the national law with resulting injustices.

The Court sits nine months a year and, during that time, a justice must write on average about one opinion of the Court a month; there were only seventy signed opinions of the Court in the 2003–2004 Term. Time spent hearing oral argument has been reduced to an average of six hours a week during term time. A comparable amount of time is required for conferences with other justices. Justices may and do choose to write concurrences and dissents. And time must be spent to decide which cases should be among the few the Court will decide.

To perform these duties, each justice is provided with four very able and energetic young law clerks and with ample secretarial and other help. Justices are, of course, deeply concerned with the quality of work done in their chambers, but much of the work of the justices can be delegated and each justice is provided with capable delegates. Justices do very little "scut work" and are thus liberated from the wear and tear associated with most jobs. A justice must be in very bad shape indeed to be unable to perform at a level that does not call attention to his or her disabilities. This is particularly the case when a justice has served a number of years on the Court and has well-developed positions on constitutional and other policy questions.

B. The Supreme Court Renewal Act of 2005

To address these concerns, Congress should enact the following as section 1 of Title 28 of the United States Code:

(a) The Supreme Court shall be a Court of nine Justices, one of whom shall be appointed as Chief Justice, and any six of whom shall constitute a quorum.

(b) One Justice or Chief Justice, and only one, shall be appointed during the first session of Congress after each federal election, unless during that Congress one or more appointments are required by Subsection (c). Each appointment shall become effective on August 1 of the year following the election. If an appointment under this Subsection results in the availability of more than nine Justices, the nine who are junior in commission shall sit regularly on the Court. Justices who are not among the nine junior in commission shall serve as Senior Justices to sit on the Court when needed to assure a full bench, participate in the Court's authority to adopt procedural rules, and perform other judicial duties in their respective circuits or as otherwise designated by the Chief Justice.

(c) If a vacancy occurs among the nine sitting Justices because of retirement, death or removal a new Justice or Chief Justice shall be appointed and considered as the Justice required to be appointed during that Congress, if that appointment has not already been made. If more than one such vacancy arises, any additional appointment will be considered as the Justice required to be appointed during the next Congress for which no appointment has yet been made.

(d) If recusal or temporary disability prevents a sitting Justice from participating in a case being heard on the merits, the Chief Justice shall recall Senior Justices in reverse order of seniority to provide a nine-member Court in any such case.

(e) Justices sitting on the Court at the time of this enactment shall be permitted to sit regularly on the Court until their retirement, death, removal or voluntary acceptance of status as a Senior Justice. No appointments shall be made under subsection (b) before the Congress that begins after the last of the current Justices so leaves the Court.

Index